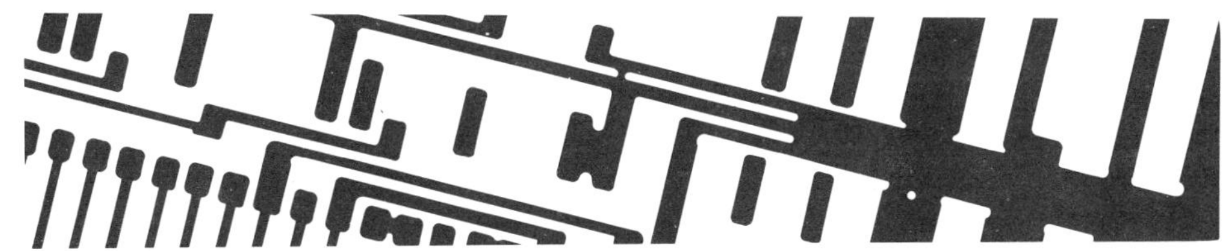

FORTRAN 77: A Practical Approach

Fourth Edition

Wilfred P. Rule
Northeastern University

PWS PUBLISHERS
Boston

PWS PUBLISHERS
Prindle, Weber & Schmidt · Willard Grant Press · Duxbury Press ·
Statler Office Building · 20 Providence Street · Boston, Massachusetts 02116

PWS is a division of Wadsworth, Inc.

ISBN 0-87150-390-5

Library of Congress Cataloging in Publication Data

Rule, Wilfred P.
FORTRAN 77.

Includes index.
1. FORTRAN (Computer program language) I. Title. II. Title: FORTRAN 77
QA76.73.F25R835 1983 001.64'24 82-22278
ISBN 0-87150-390-5

Cover photograph by Bud Strauss—Globe Photos, Inc. Cover and text design by Trisha Hanlon. Typeset by A & B Typesetters, Inc. Artwork by Julie Grecha. Covers printed by The Alpine Press, Inc. Text printed and bound by Hamilton Printing Company.

87 86 85 84 83 — 10 9 8 7 6 5 4 3 2 1

Printed in the United States of America

Preface to the Instructor

For over a decade, FORTRAN has developed a well-deserved reputation as an efficient language for accomplishing a wide variety of algebraic and scientific computing tasks. Today, however, FORTRAN is being seriously challenged. Highly structured languages such as PASCAL and ADA are being offered as alternatives for engineers, scientists, and other applications programmers. If FORTRAN is to maintain its competitive status, it must be taught and implemented in its most modern and advanced form.

The new structured languages place heavy emphasis on writing clear, easy-to-follow programs. Disruptive branches (such as the arithmetic IF) that produce what is called "spaghetti" logic are not allowed. Instead, the more advanced features of the IF-THEN-ELSE construct are used, to facilitate a single entry to and exit from each module of code. The implementation of the FORTRAN 77 standards permits the rules of structured programming to be maintained consistently. These are progressive steps, not the single prerogative of the new languages, and can be utilized quite readily in FORTRAN, as they are in this text.

Outstanding features of the text

***Balanced Approach**—A good FORTRAN text should: (1) teach the grammar of the language, (2) show how to apply the language, and (3) demonstrate how to write a program properly with structure. Often the balance in presenting these topics is incorrect. Too early an emphasis on structure, when the student does not have any grasp of the language, is a common mistake. This text tries to use a balanced approach. Structure and style are taught from the first chapter to the last, but are introduced gradually. As the student's ability develops, structure is emphasized more and more, and is accorded a comprehensive and explicit treatment in Chapter 8.

***Comprehensiveness**—This text takes students with no background in computers or computer programming through all the important topics in FORTRAN. All the elementary topics are covered and numerous applications given, both numeric and non-numeric. Where it may be necessary to cover advanced applications, an optional section is offered.

***Readability**—The fact that computer programming is a somewhat difficult skill required of students early in their careers presents the challenge of trying to explain sometimes advanced topics in simple and easy-to-understand terms. Every effort is made to accomplish just that. Having spent over a decade in teaching FORTRAN, the author has tried and rejected various methods. Because readability is a prime goal of the text, new methods are used where old ones have proven insufficient. The result is a book that is not difficult to read, yet one that does not overly compromise on the level and rigor of presentation.

***Numerous Examples**—Few books present as many applications and follow-up programs as does this. These programs are graded in difficulty from the most simple to the more complex, and are chosen to cover the broadest range of applications. There are business, mathematics, physics, engineering, and computer science problems, as well as games, drawings, graphics, and quizzes. By seeing such a wide range of problems, the student gets a feel for the many ways a computer can be used in his or her field of interest.

***Modernity**—This book uses the most advanced form of FORTRAN language, namely FORTRAN 77. The more modern list-directed input/output is used except in those circumstances where it is convenient to do otherwise. A large section on character manipulation is presented, including a number of programs that suggest how word processing is accomplished. The topic of generic library functions is used to make COMPLEX, DOUBLE PRECISION and LOGICAL variables easier to understand.

***Self-paced**—To retain the attention of the student and to provide maximum feedback, there are a large number of quizzes throughout the text. The student covers a topic and is then quizzed on his or her retention and mastery of the subject. The quiz may simply consist of questions, but typically involves both questions and the writing of a short program. Most chapters have a large number of ''Review Exercises'' that also pace the student through the chapters.

***Multiple Exposure**—Chapters 1 and 2 provide a quick overview of programming. The important foundation topics are explained in the simplest terms possible, with the understanding that a detailed explanation follows shortly. Chapters 3 to 7 cover topics mentioned in the *overview* in more complete detail. Those students who find it necessary can gain a third exposure to any topic by choosing an appropriate example problem from the many offered at the end of each chapter.

***Tested Material**—Each of the programs has been compiled and tested on a computer. The printouts are true computer printouts and represent a large effort on the part of the author and his supporting staff.

***Consistent Documentation**—Each of the programs has been prepared in a consistent, well-documented fashion. The purpose of the program is stated. Important variable names are listed and described briefly. Important modules within the program are separated by blank comment lines and given explanatory titles where necessary.

Differences between the third and fourth editions

The third edition was directed towards the more traditional FORTRAN market, where the major emphasis is on applications programming. The instructors are more interested in showing how the computer and the FORTRAN language can be used to support the student in the pursuit of his major, than in showing all the niceties of correct modular style and structure. It also used format-controlled input/output. This method is sometimes forced on the instructor in those installations where *batch* operations are the major method of computation. Lastly, the third edition was written when many of the new, structured features of the FORTRAN language were being introduced. An attempt was made to ''play it half way'' by including these topics, but not in the early chapters.

Installations using *terminals* find list-directed, or format free, input/output the best method of operations. Not having to cover FORMAT codes usually allows time for earlier coverage of algorithm development, with emphasis on modularity, structure and style. It was for these reasons that the fourth edition was written. Features such as CHARACTER variables, counting DO's with real index, block IF's, DO WHILE, and other FORTRAN 77 features are shown in considerable detail.

Finally, I would like to thank the following reviewers for their helpful suggestions: Robert H. Dourson, California Polytechnic State University; Joseph Matti, Saginaw Valley State College; Michael Murphy, University of Houston Downtown College; and Sanford H. Stone, San Diego State University.

Wilfred P. Rule

Preface to the Student

This text is specifically designed for students with no previous experience in computer programming, and this edition is the result of the experience gained from the publication of three previous editions. In each of these editions, the author has paid careful attention to the feedback from numerous students and instructors who have used the book.

One of the main objectives of this edition has been to make the text as readable as possible. This is not to imply that each and every topic presented will be easily mastered by a single reading. There is considerably more to computer programming than learning the grammar of the language. As a matter of fact, learning the statements that constitute the FORTRAN instruction set is not very difficult at all. What is difficult is learning how to combine the individual instructions into a logical sequence (into a program) that effectively and correctly solves the problem at hand. Furthermore, it is no longer acceptable to write a program and consider an assignment complete the minute a seemingly correct output is generated. The program must be written in a clear, well documented fashion. The individual statements must be written according to an established set of rules, called the rules of structured programming. The program must then meet certain performance standards and be tested with a wide range of input to assure the program works properly.

A key feature of this text is the number and variety of sample programs used to supplement the formal presentation of the text material. While these illustrations and case studies assist in the mastery of the mechanics of the language, they serve a much more important function. They develop a feel for the tremendous potential application of computers and show the versatility of computer programs. By versatility we mean the ability to take a problem such as a business problem, a mathematics problem, a physics problem, or an engineering problem and organize the relatively limited number of operations a computer is capable of performing into an effective solution to the problem. That is the responsibility of the programmer. It is a responsibility that requires intelligence, technical training, and very often a creative approach to problem solving. Because it takes time to develop the skills involved, many example problems are presented and analyzed to promote them.

The text sets a moderate pace, bringing key concepts in gradually so that students can build skills and confidence slowly before moving into more advanced topics. Repetition is resorted to where necessary to make sure a solid foundation is laid in the introductory material. Correct style and correct structure are observed in the example problems presented so that no poor programming habits are developed in learning the elementary concepts. Structured programming techniques are introduced as early as Chapter 2 where the concept of modularity is presented and the student is shown the various constructs (decision, loop and sequence) available. The level of rigor is kept purposely low. The student who is struggling with the language and other details is not burdened with rules of structure, but rather is asked to emulate the examples shown. In Chapter 8 the formal coverage of structured programming is presented. Numerous rules and recommendations are presented and explained. A comparison of structured and unstructured programs is made with emphasis on the advantages of structure.

The text has several features to build student interest and encourage participation in the learning process.

1. Frequent quizzes are provided. They give questions and short programming problems for students to check their progress. The answers to these quizzes are given so that the student can score his or her own exam.
2. Almost every chapter has review exercises to reinforce important points and to show how the FORTRAN language is applied to solving word problems.
3. "Additional Applications" sections follow most chapters to illustrate algorithm development in solving real-world problems in business, engineering, mathematics, the social sciences and many other fields.
4. The appendices provide a guide to programming statements in the full and subset FORTRAN language, a guide to system dependent statements and solutions to numerous programming assignments.

The inside back cover provides a quick reference chart of various FORTRAN rules and required statement layouts. This reference chart saves the student from being swamped by details in the early stages of learning.

A note on the author

Wilfred P. Rule is Chairman of the Graphic Science Department and Acting Chairman and Professor in the Department of Industrial Engineering and Information Systems of Northeastern University, where he has taught for twelve years. Coauthor (with Percy Hill) of *Mechanisms—Analysis and Design* (Allyn & Bacon), Professor Rule taught previously at Tufts University and, as Senior Staff Engineer at AVCO Corporation, worked on the advanced research and design of the LORV missile system. He holds degrees in Mechanical Engineering from Tufts University and the Massachusetts Institute of Technology.

Contents

1

Introduction to Digital Computers

It is important that you approach Chapters 1 and 2 of this text in the correct frame of mind. These are very special chapters in that they attempt to give you a quick exposure to what computers are all about, in the form of an **overview**. The amount of information in these chapters is considerable, but it is being presented for *background* information only! Each topic covered now is covered later in considerable detail. On the second time around, however, you will have a better idea of how any one topic relates to all the others. That is the purpose of an overview. Read these first two chapters somewhat casually and do not expect to master the subject at this time.

This overview takes a quick look at the various hardware components that constitute a digital computer. This is followed by a brief description of how these components contribute to the overall operation of the computer system. Finally, we touch upon the important parts of a set of instructional commands (computer language) that a programmer uses to coordinate and direct these computing activities. We want you to see how the whole system works before getting down to the sometimes drab details associated with any one of its parts.

Many students feel that the only important part of computer programming is learning the various elements of the computer language. As part of the overview, we show that this is just not true. As it turns out, learning the language is the easy part. Learning the various commands that constitute the FORTRAN language is not difficult. The challenge lies in combining these individual commands **(instructions)** into a logical sequence (a **program**) that efficiently and correctly solves the problem at hand.

> WARNING: *Learning the elements of a computer language is relatively easy. Learning how to combine these elements into an efficient program can be difficult.*

As part of the overview approach, we try to focus your attention on this hidden obstacle. Accordingly we emphasize the general strategy or game plan associated with writing complete programs, rather than the individual statements. This should give you some idea of how each instruction contributes to the functioning of the total program.

1.1 Basic Operations

The operations that a computer is capable of performing can be grouped into a surprisingly short list.

1. Input/output
2. Arithmetic
3. Logic/control
4. Specification

NOTE: *All programs, no matter how complicated they may appear, can be resolved into some combination of these basic operations.*

The list is presented to organize your dealings with the computer and it should be used in the following way. When writing a program, it is not uncommon to become confused as to what to do next. The organized approach we are promoting suggests that when this happens, you return to this list. Attempt to get things started again by classifying which basic operation should be accomplished next.

Each of the listed operations is implemented by a specific piece of computer hardware. For example, all computers have one or more input devices, such as a card reader, a terminal, or some other unit. There must also be some output device, possibly a printer, a typewriter, or a video screen. Other important hardware items include a unit that adds, subtracts, multiplies, and divides. Collectively these components are what make up the total computer system.

In writing a program, we are in effect lining up this equipment in a sequence appropriate to solving the problem. FORTRAN uses a list of key words or symbols, such as READ, PRINT, +, and −, to identify which piece of equipment is needed next. If we issue the READ instruction, in effect we are signaling that the input device is needed. (Actually the instruction involves more than the word READ, but those details will be covered shortly.) If the instruction that follows uses the symbol + or −, the appropriate arithmetic hardware will be activated.

In the next few pages we describe each of the four basic operations in more detail. Try to get a feel for what each operation accomplishes and the key words or commands associated with that operation. Note that the terms command, instruction, and statement are used interchangeably.

Input/Output

Basic Commands: READ / PRINT

At times during the execution of a program, the programmer will want to *give* new information to the computer—to provide a fresh set of data values, for example. On other occasions, the programmer might want to *receive* information (such as the results of a calculation just performed) from the computer. *Two-way dialogue* or communication is a part of every program and is accomplished by input/output instructions.

You will soon be dealing with a program that computes the volumes of a number of cylinders. The radius and height of each cylinder represent *input* to this program. The computed volume represents *output*. Issuing a READ instruction turns on whatever hardware device your system is using for providing input. If you are sitting at a terminal, a READ instruction in your program signals that the next hardware component needed in the solution of the problem is the terminal keyboard. Accordingly, the keyboard is activated and the computer waits for you to enter two numbers. (On some systems a question mark appears on the screen indicating that input is wanted, but this feature is not universal.) When you hit the RETURN key, you are signaling the completion of the input operation and the line you entered is received and stored.

On other systems, card input is used. Assume you have punched the radius and the height of each cylinder on a card and these cards are stacked in the card reader. Each time we want the computer to accept a new card (defining a new cylinder), we issue the READ instruction.†

Later, after all the calculations are completed, we issue the PRINT instruction to obtain output. Here again, the PRINT command activates whatever hardware your system uses as the normal output device. Systems that use card input usually use a line printer for output. Each PRINT command generates a line of output at the printer.

Most terminals use a video screen as the major output device. Each PRINT command causes the generation of a new line on the screen. Each line on the screen is the equivalent of a line physically printed on a sheet of output paper. When satisfied with the output that appears on the screen, the programmer usually can run the program again, using some hard copy device (a device that produces printed output on a sheet of paper) in place of the video screen.

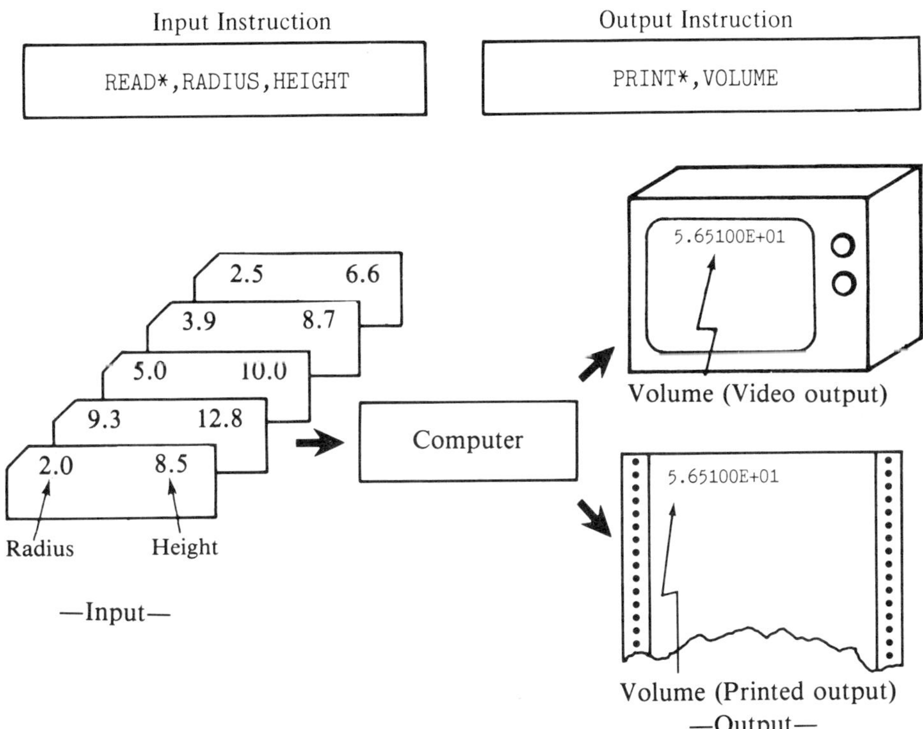

Arithmetic

Basic Commands: + − * /

Computers have electronic circuitry (hardware) that adds, subtracts, multiplies, and divides. These pieces of equipment are activated in FORTRAN by the symbols +, −, *, and /. These symbols are preferred to the words ADD, SUBTRACT, MULTIPLY, and DIVIDE so that FORTRAN will have an algebraic likeness or similarity. Each symbol identifies a specific operation (electronic component) available to accomplish the mathematics of the problem being solved.

The following set of instructions demonstrates that a computer program does *not* have to be complex and intimidating. You should have little difficulty under-

† This represents a substantial simplification of the actual process. Because many people will be using the computer at any given time, all your data cards are read when your program is submitted. They are used to build what is called an input file. Each time a READ command is executed, the information associated with one of your data cards is taken from this input file.

standing how the computer would respond. Three values are read from input. A sequence of add operations is specified, producing what appears to be answer 1. A second sequence of mathematics (multiplication of X by Y; then division by Z) is stipulated, producing a second answer. These answers are then displayed (sent to output).

Program

```
READ*, X, Y, Z
ANS1 = X + Y + Z
ANS2 = X * Y / Z
PRINT*, ANS1, ANS2
```

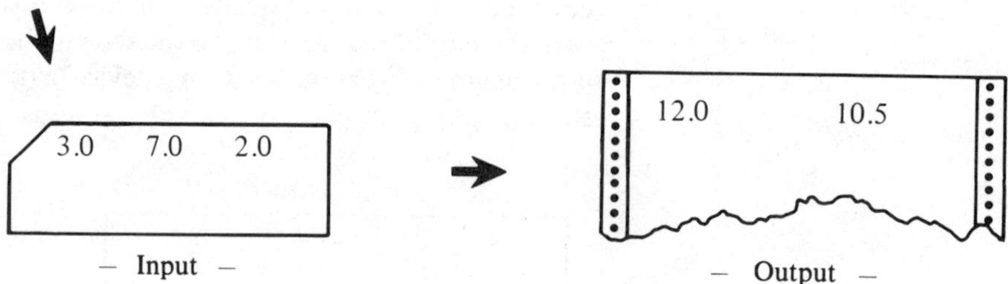

Logic/Control

Basic Commands: IF DO DO WHILE GO TO STOP

Statements in a program are usually executed in sequential order. That is, the first instruction you write will be the first executed. Upon completion of that instruction, the computer looks at line two of your program to see what should be done next. Let's set up some circumstances where this normal control sequence (one-after-another processing) is not appropriate to the task at hand. Two categories quickly come to mind. The first is when you wish several statements to be executed over and over again, (i.e., set up a loop). The other situation is when an internal decision must be made and, based on that decision, one group of statements is executed rather than an alternative group of statements.

Logic/control statements are used when normal processing of statements must be interrupted to establish some alternative pattern of processing.

Alternative Control Structures

Loop The key words DO and DO WHILE allow the programmer to cause the repeated execution of a series of statements.

Decision The key words IF, THEN, and ELSE allow the programmer to cause the execution of one group of statements in favor of an alternative group based on some test.

Assume a payroll program is running in the normal control mode (sequential processing of statements). A point is reached at which it is necessary to determine if a person has worked more than 40 hours, that is, to test for the condition of overtime. If the result of this test turns out to be true, the computation of the worker's pay will be performed one way. However, if the test evaluates as false, pay will be computed in a different way.

DECISION CONSTRUCT | **KEY WORDS** ⟶ IF-THEN-ELSE-ENDIF

Example

```
           ┌──────────────means "greater than"
           ▼
IF(HOURS.GT.40.0) THEN

    REGHRS = 40.0
    OVERHR = HOURS - 40.0
    PAY = REGHRS * RATE + OVERHR * 1.5 * RATE

ELSE

    PAY = HOURS * RATE

ENDIF
```

The key words IF, THEN, ELSE, and ENDIF identify the statement as belonging to the logic/control group, specifically the *decision* construct.

The IF-THEN-ELSE construct will now be used in one more example program segment. After reading information specifying that a package should be shipped from warehouse A to distribution point B, the program computes the distance between these two points. A test is made on this value to determine how the package should be shipped. If the distance is less than 500 miles, the package will be shipped by local trucking; otherwise air freight will be used.

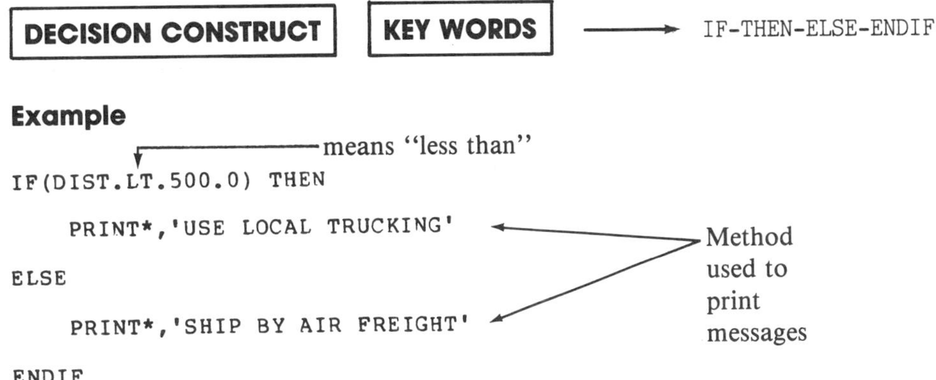

LOGICAL IF

A *simpler* IF version of the decision construct is available and is shown in the next two IF statement examples.

Example

```
IF(LINES.LE.100) PRINT*, A, B, C
```

Meaning: A programmer is told to periodically print the values of A, B, and C to monitor their behavior. However, the number of lines of output is not to exceed 100 lines. A memory location called LINES is created, and the contents of this memory location is advanced by 1 each time a line of output is printed. The IF test compares the contents of LINES with the specified upper limit of 100 to determine if another PRINT operation is appropriate.

Example

```
IF(BALNCE.LT.0.00) GO TO 8
```

Meaning: Banks use a program to examine a depositor's balance. If that balance goes negative, the account is overdrawn. Control is passed to an instruction with the label 8 in the program.

The simple IF statement is used when the decision process is directed at a *single* statement (the PRINT statement or the GO TO statement in the example shown). The technical name for this control statement is a LOGICAL IF.

Loop Structures

We will now take several of the last example's IF constructs and convert them to loop control constructs.

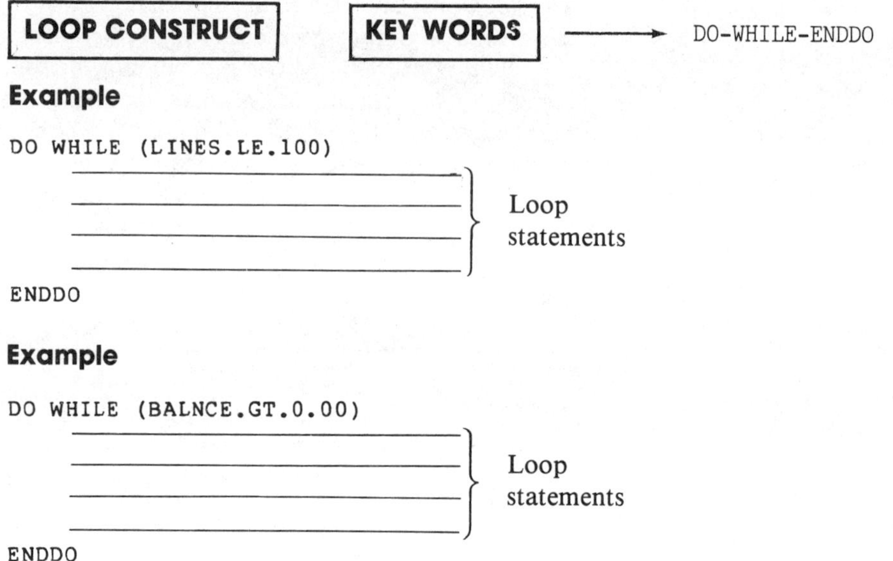

To set up a loop construct, the key word DO WHILE is used followed by a logical expression (just like the logical expression portion of the IF statement). When the DO WHILE statement is reached, the logical expression is evaluated. If the expression is true, the loop statements are executed (the statements between the DO WHILE and the ENDDO). Control passes back to the top of the loop and the logical expression is evaluated again. If the expression is still true, the loop statements are executed again. The process continues until the logical expression becomes false, which terminates the construct. Note how the ENDDO is used to show where the loop ends.

Another form of loop control statement is used when the programmer wants the loop statements to be executed a specific number of times. In the next example we want the loop statements to be executed 100 times.

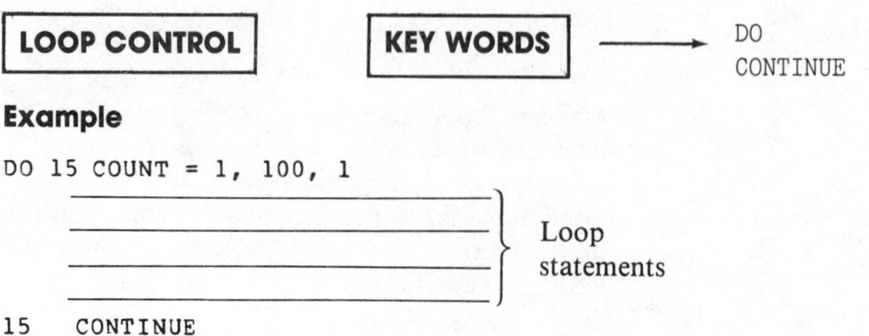

This loop control statement will require a good deal of explanation when it is formally presented later on. For the moment, however, note that the header statement contains the key word `DO` (to identify the statement) followed by a number. This number identifies the bottom of the loop (the last statement in the loop) which contains the key word `CONTINUE`. `CONTINUE` serves the same purpose as the `ENDDO` statement in the `DO WHILE` construct.

The remaining portion of the header statement allows the programmer to specify an integer variable (in this case, `COUNT`) to serve as a "loop counter." The programmer then specifies:

1. The value the loop counter should have on the first pass through the loop (in this case, the value 1)
2. The value the loop counter should have on the last permitted pass through the loop (in this case, the value 100)
3. The value the loop counter should be advanced each time a pass through the loop is completed (in this case, the value 1)

> If you leave this section being able to define what a control statement does and know that there are two major types of control constructs (decision constructs and loop constructs), the purpose of this introduction will be served.

Specification

Basic Commands: `INTEGER` `CHARACTER` `REAL`

Fortunately you will not be dealing with very many specification statements until much later in the text. The ones you are required to know are the ones that are easy to understand. We start with three specification statements identified by the key words `INTEGER`, `REAL`, and `CHARACTER`. These statements, like many of the other specification statements, must be located at a *specific* point in your program, namely, at the very beginning. Since the specification group assists/supports the implementation of the other (action†) statements, that assist/support information is needed before any of the action group can be implemented.

Consider this specific example. Before issuing a `READ` statement (or any other statement), a good programmer first identifies each variable name used in the program and declares the type of information stored in that variable. For each of these names, a memory location will be set aside and identified by that variable name. Each memory location can contain one of three types of information:

1. Integer number—a number with no fractional portion, such as a phone number or social security number.
2. Real number—a number containing a whole and a fractional portion, such as the volume of a cylinder or the balance in a bank account.
3. Character information—letters of the alphabet, digits, or other keyboard characters, such as a person's name or address.

† The word action will shortly be more formally defined as "executable." Executable statements cause some hardware to be activated. Nonexecutable statements (specification group) supply supporting information, but do not activate hardware.

The specification statements

```
REAL RADIUS, HEIGHT
INTEGER LINES, COUNT, AGE
CHARACTER NAME*10
```

might be located at the top of a program to indicate that the programmer is using the names RADIUS and HEIGHT to identify two memory locations in which real numbers are to be stored. LINES, COUNT, and AGE are names of memory locations where integers are stored. Finally, a storage facility called NAME is needed that is capable of storing 10 characters associated with a person's name.

Summary

Unless you use an organized, structured approach to programming, you may find it a chaotic, confusing activity. In the near future, you are going to get hung up in a program and not know what to do next. You do not have many options. You can read or print (input/output). You can do more calculations (arithmetic). You can set up one of the special (control) constructs, either a decision or a loop construct. If it is to be a loop construct, ask yourself if you want the statements to be executed a specific number of times or until a certain condition changes.

1.2 Combining Statements

It is important that you learn how to write complete programs as soon as possible. As the first step in that direction, the following examples suggest how individual statements can be combined to accomplish a specific task. You should be able to recognize most of these statements and may even be able to follow a good deal of the logic being used.

Programming Example
Which Number Is Larger?

Given two numbers as input information, determine and report which is the larger.

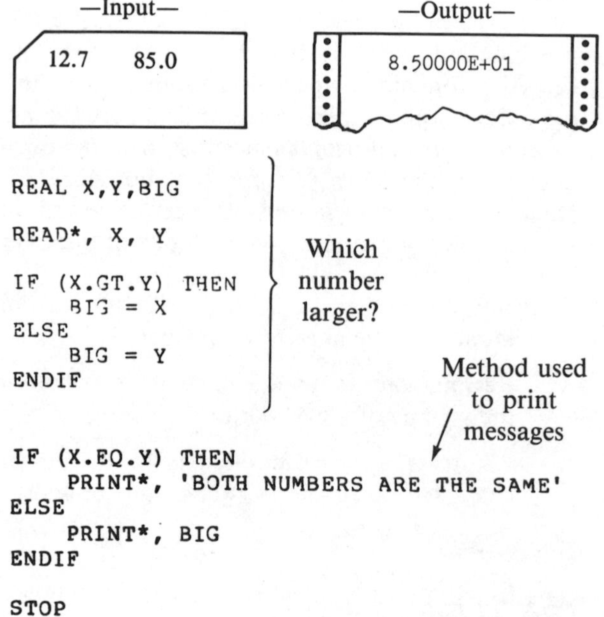


```
REAL X,Y,BIG

READ*, X, Y

IF (X.GT.Y) THEN
    BIG = X
ELSE
    BIG = Y
ENDIF

IF (X.EQ.Y) THEN
    PRINT*, 'BOTH NUMBERS ARE THE SAME'
ELSE
    PRINT*, BIG
ENDIF

STOP
```

Programming Example–Which Number Is Larger? continued

Discussion

X, Y, and BIG are declared as reals. An input record is then read defining X and Y. An IF test asks, "Is X greater than Y?" If the answer is yes, memory location BIG is assigned the value of X. If the answer is no, memory location BIG is assigned the value Y. Before printing the output, a final check is made to see if X and Y are possibly equal.

Programming Example
Honors List

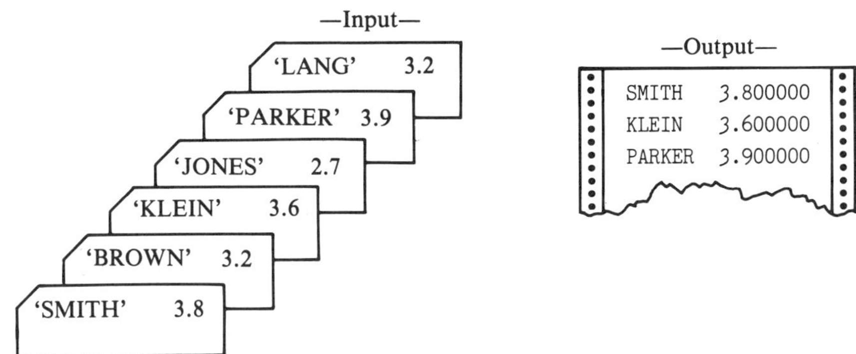

Each record of an input file gives the name (6 characters maximum) and the scholastic average of a high school student. Write a program to print the names of all students with a 3.5 average or better. Assume there are 512 students in the school.

```
      INTEGER COUNT
      REAL AVRAGE
      CHARACTER NAME*6

      DO 20 COUNT = 1, 512, 1
            READ*, NAME, AVRAGE
            IF(AVRAGE.GE.3.5)PRINT*,NAME, AVRAGE
20    CONTINUE

      STOP
```

Programming Example
Different Pay Rates

—Input—

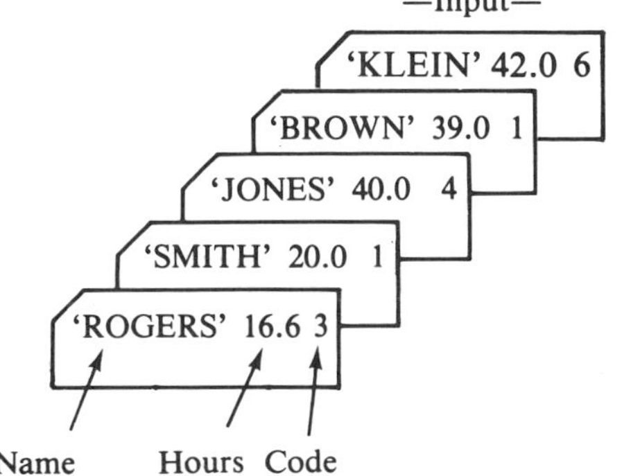

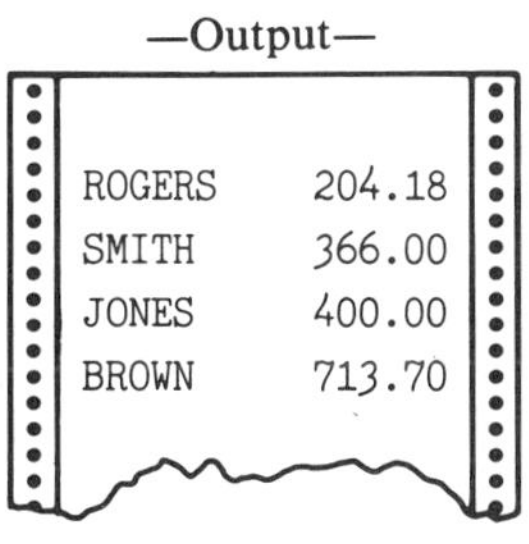

Programming Example–Different Pay Rates continued

Each record of an input file gives the name (6 characters maximum) of an employee and the number of hours worked this week. The next number indicates which of several hourly rates should be used in computing this individual's pay (see pay rate table). People in rate categories 1 through 4 are *not* allowed overtime and are positioned at the front of the input data file. People in category 5 or 6 are authorized overtime and are located at the end of the data file. Determine and report the amount due each worker in categories 1 through 4 only. The other workers will be processed later.

Rate Table

Rate	Amount
1	18.30
2	14.40
3	12.00
4	10.00
5	8.00
6	6.00

```
INTEGER CODE
REAL RATE,HOURS,PAY
CHARACTER NAME*6
    READ*,NAME,HOURS,CODE
DO WHILE (CODE.LE.4)
    IF (CODE.EQ.1) RATE=18.30
    IF (CODE.EQ.2) RATE=14.40
    IF (CODE.EQ.3) RATE=12.00
    IF (CODE.EQ.4) RATE=10.00
    PAY = RATE * HOURS
    PRINT*,NAME,PAY
    READ*,NAME,HOURS,CODE
ENDDO
STOP
END
```

Discussion

Since the program is to process people in categories 1 through 4 only, a loop construct is established, a `DO WHILE` construct. Once inside the construct, one of four `RATE` values must be selected. The individual's `PAY` is computed and reported. A `READ` is executed in preparation for making another pass through the loop. Control passes back to the `DO WHILE` and a test is made (is this a worker in one of the first four categories).

Common Student Error

Note the `READ` statement just before the `DO WHILE` statement. Why is it necessary? The answer is obvious enough; the value of `CODE` must be known when the `DO WHILE` is reached. Without the `READ`, the value of `CODE` would be undefined when the `DO WHILE` was executed the first time. As simple as this may sound, students frequently forget this initial `READ`, which causes loop control problems.

Another `READ` is needed at the bottom of the loop to pick up another record from the input file, namely the record that will be processed on the next pass through the loop (if there is one). If this `READ` is omitted, the loop keeps processing record number one in the input file and the program goes into an endless loop. The loop statements are processed over and over again.

Programming Example
Number Search

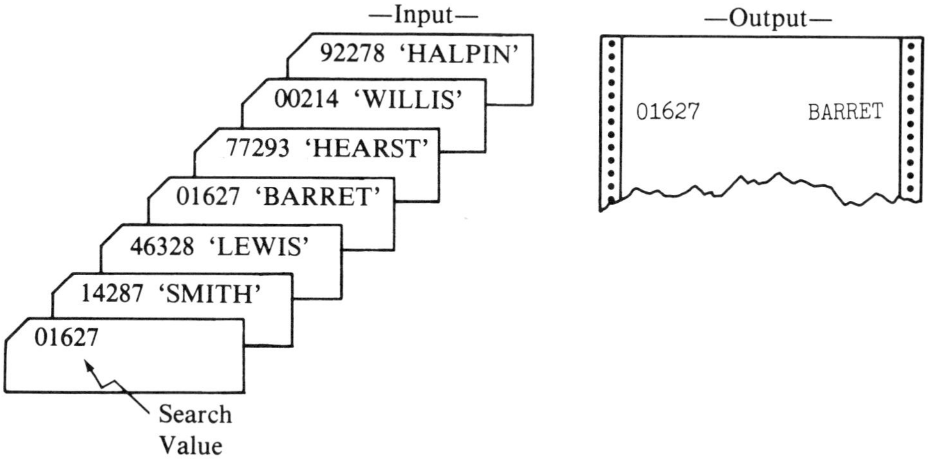

—Input—

92278 'HALPIN'
00214 'WILLIS'
77293 'HEARST'
01627 'BARRET'
46328 'LEWIS'
14287 'SMITH'
01627

Search Value

—Output—

01627 BARRET

The first record of a data file contains an identification number. We want to know the name of the student assigned this number. Read the remaining records, which tell the name associated with each ID number in active use. When the number is found, print the student's name. SEARCH is used to hold the identification number we are searching for, and IDNO holds the number on each of the main body data cards.

```
INTEGER SEARCH, IDNO
CHARACTER NAME*6

READ*, SEARCH
READ*, IDNO, NAME

DO WHILE (IDNO.NE.SEARCH)

    READ*, IDNO, NAME

ENDDO

PRINT*, NAME, IDNO
STOP
END
```

(NE means "not equal to")

Discussion

This is a typical search activity. Search information is read from the first record in the data file. The remaining records are now examined as follows. The next record is taken into memory. The DO WHILE is then reached. If the record in hand is not the correct record, a new record is read inside the loop. In all probability, record after record will be read by the loop READ statement. When the correct record is found, the loop terminates and control passes to the output statement. The program terminates.

Quiz 1
Review

Part 1: Answer the following review questions.

1. What are the four basic groups of statements (operations) in FORTRAN?
2. What words or symbols are used in FORTRAN to call out these operations?
3. Is it difficult to learn the details of any one of these statements? Is it the important part of FORTRAN?
4. Is there a fixed sequence in which FORTRAN statements should appear? For example, should a READ statement always be followed by an arithmetic statement?

Part 2: The following program segment is used to arrive at a student's grade based on homework and exam performance.

```
READ*,HW1,HW2,HW3,HW4,HW5,HW6
HWAVE=(HW1+HW2+HW3+HW4+HW5+HW6)/6.0
READ*,EXAM1,EXAM2,EXAM3,FINAL
EXAMS=(EXAM1+EXAM2+EXAM3)/3.0
GRADE=.20*HWAVE+.30*EXAMS+.50*FINAL
PRINT*,HWAVE,EXAMS,GRADE
```

Examine the program segment and answer the following questions.

5. Describe the input to this program.
6. In computing the grade, how much did the homework count?
7. In computing the grade, how much did the final exam count?
8. Could the second READ statement be moved up one line, that is placed before the computation of the homework average?
9. Could the PRINT statement be moved up one line, placed before the computation of GRADE?

1.3 Hardware Organization

We now take a closer look at the computer's hardware components and how they are interconnected (see Figure 1.1).

All computers have at least one input device. However, a large computer facility may have many input units. There could be two or three card readers, four or five magnetic tape drives, and the potential of linking up to virtually hundreds of terminals. As a beginning programmer, you will probably be involved with *one* input device only. For some, this will be the card reader; for others, input will be via a terminal. In either case, it will appear to you that there is only one input unit in active operation, namely, the one you are using. Whether dealing with cards or with the terminal, the basic input command is READ. As we progress, we will make a relatively easy transition to deal with all the other input devices, such as magnetic tapes and disks. We will still use the command READ, but in an expanded form to incorporate all other means of input.

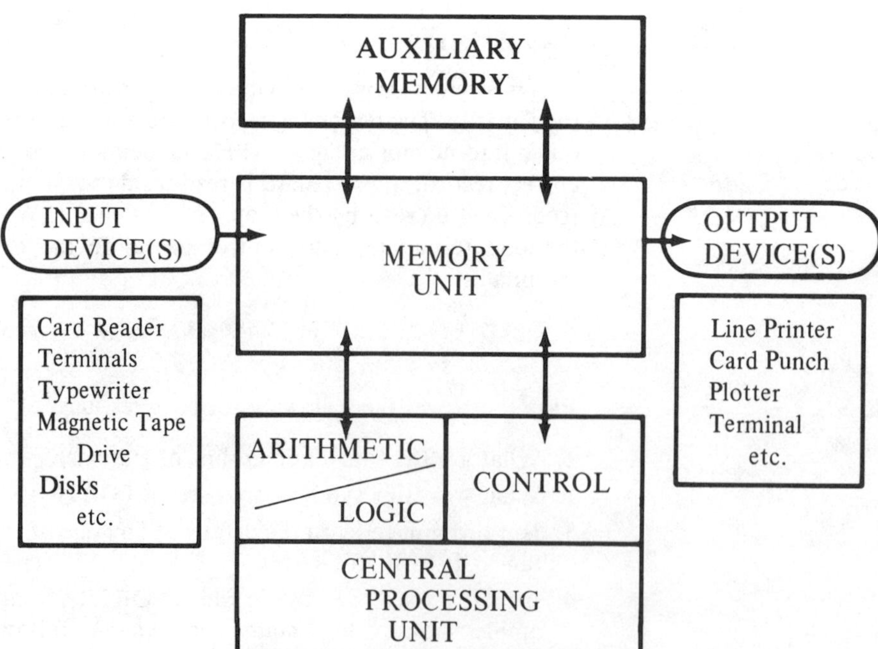

Figure 1.1 Organization of a digital computer

One final point needs clarification. Input is not just the presentation of a problem's data values. It also includes providing the logic to solve the problem (the FORTRAN instructions). Thus the input device is used to place in memory an *instruction* set and a *data* set in a form compatible with high-speed operations. We will discuss this form later, but for now consider it as an electronic image of what was on a card, if card input is used.

The **memory unit** is the name given to the device used for the internal storage of information. It is capable of storing massive amounts of information in a relatively small space. For example, it must hold all the information associated with your program as well as that of all the other programs that are running along with yours. This unit must not only have a large capacity to store information, it must also be able to retrieve any specific piece of information *directly*. This feature is called **random access.** Backing up main memory are usually one or more disk drives (description follows). These units have an exceptional capacity to store information, but do not have the same retrieval speed that main memory does.

The Central Processing Unit (CPU) is the most active of all the hardware components. It is subdivided into two major units: the **arithmetic/logic unit** and the **control unit**. The arithmetic unit is where all arithmetic operations (adding, subtracting, multiplying, and dividing) are performed. If you are wondering whether the arithmetic unit can perform high-order mathematics, such as computing trigonometric values, taking roots of equations, or evaluating logarithms, the answer is that it can, but not directly. Such high-order operations are accomplished by a clever combination of the basic operations of adding, subtracting, multiplying and dividing. We will get to that shortly.

Another feature of the arithmetic unit is its ability to determine if one number is larger than another or whether the result of a calculation is zero, negative, or positive. This feature is used by the logic/control group of operations to provide the decision-making instructions described earlier.

The control unit is the boss or supervisor of all activities. Its job is to sequentially fetch your instructions (the program) from memory and interpret the operation required. Depending on the instruction, the control unit activates the appropriate hardware and coordinates the movement of information involved. This could be the activating of an input device and the coordinating of the transfer of information into memory. It might involve transferring information from memory to the arithmetic unit for numeric processing and transferring the result back to memory. In any event, this is part of the internal processing in which the programmer is seldom directly involved.

Finally, output is achieved on any of several devices capable of conveying to the programmer the values stored in specific memory locations. A common output device is the **line printer. Terminals** are equally popular and have both an input and output capability. Terminals allow the programmer to interact with the computer more directly than when cards are used.

We have discussed the general layout of the hardware that constitutes a computer system. (Figure 1.2 shows the impressive layout of the total computer system.) Programming will be more meaningful to you if you are aware of the equipment you are controlling and understand (even superficially) how it works. Read the next few pages with this limited objective in mind.

1.4 The Input Unit

We have mentioned that all information presented to the computer falls into two categories: instructions, followed by data values. The instructions must be presented in a rather rigid, fussy form (otherwise they are undecipherable by the computer). If input is to be by cards, the programmer can obtain specially printed cards that display the required layout or form each instruction must have. The cards are taken to a typewriter-like machine called a **keypunch** (see Figure 1.3). As you type on this machine, a pattern of punched holes is imposed on the card, and typing appears across the top. The typing is for you to read; the holes are for the computer (card reader) to interpret. At the appropriate time we will reference operating instructions for this keypunch and go into more detail on preparing the instruction cards.

After the instruction cards are prepared, the data values are keypunched, forming what we call the **data deck.** These two groups of cards are presented (all in one batch) to a **card reader** (see Figure 1.4). The card reader uses some high-speed electronic device, such as a series of photoelectric cells, to detect the pattern of punched holes and convert them into an electronic image for transmittal to memory.

The alternative to this batch card operation is input via terminals (see Figure 1.5). The mechanics are very similar. To start with, the layout or form of each line (instruction) typed at the terminal is the same as the layout required for card input. For example, when key punching an instruction on a card, the instruction must not go beyond column 72 of the card. Accordingly, a vertical line is drawn on the card to remind the programmer not to go past this point. At the terminal, you may very well hear a beep or a bell any time you pass column 72.

Figure 1.2 A total computer system (Photo courtesy of IBM Corporation)

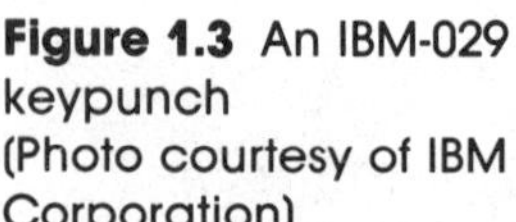

Figure 1.3 An IBM-029 keypunch (Photo courtesy of IBM Corporation)

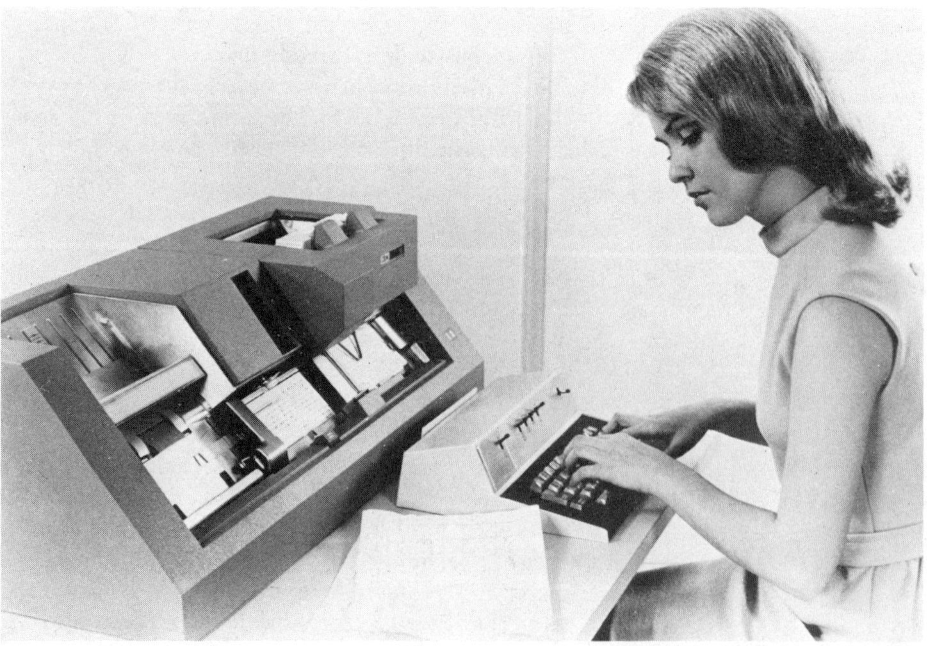

Figure 1.4 The card reader
(Photo courtesy of Control Data Corporation)

Figure 1.5 A typical CRT terminal
(Photo courtesy of Control Data Corporation)

As you type each line on the terminal keyboard, a pattern of electronic pulses is generated and either sent directly to the computer or transmitted over telephone lines. As each line of information (an instruction or a data record) is transmitted, the computer builds a file of information until all the instructions or all the input records are received. These files, the instruction file and the input data file, are now in a form almost identical to the files established when input was by cards.

The entry of data at a terminal may be accomplished as just described (by building a complete input file), or it may be entered interactively (as the program is running). The interactive input usually starts with a `PRINT` statement that issues a message, such as "PLEASE ENTER A VALUE OF RADIUS AND A VALUE OF HEIGHT." This "prompt" line appears on the screen. The next statement is then a

READ statement. When the READ statement is executed, some systems display a symbol to indicate a request for input (this symbol might be a question mark). The computer waits for you to type a line of input and hit the RETURN key. A programmer may now enter another line of input and wait and see what the results are before entering another line. We are able to get immediate "turn around" this way, giving rapid two-way communications with the computer that is not available in "batch" operations. The use of the prompt messages provides a *conversational* mode of operations that is again a feature of terminal operations.

Input can also be entered via magnetic tapes and disks. The tape is made of the same material as a home tape recorder except it is of higher quality. The long plastic tape is covered with a thin coat of brown or black iron oxide and wrapped on large reels. Information is recorded on the tape in the form of a pattern of magnetic spots that is retained by the iron oxide. Information can be "packed" much more tightly on the tape. One tape is the equivalent of over 100 boxes of cards. A box contains 2000 cards. Because the information is coded magnetically, it can be processed at much higher rates than information punched on cards. A reel of tape is mounted on a magnetic tape drive (Figure 1.6) which controls the movement of the tape during read/write operations.

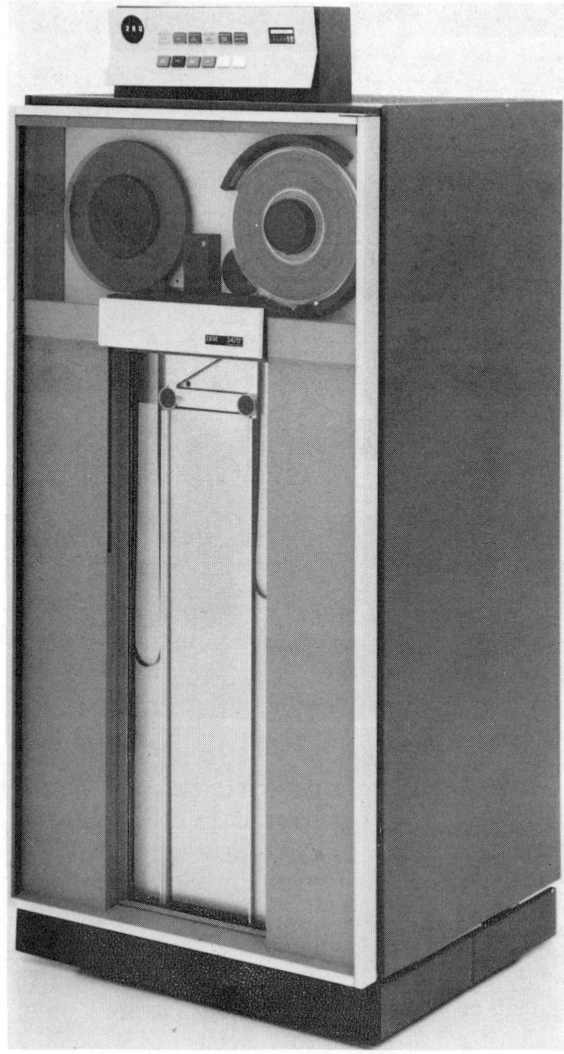

Figure 1.6 Magnetic tape drive
(Photo courtesy of IBM Corporation)

Figure 1.7 Magnetic disk drive
(Photo courtesy of IBM Corporation)

Magnetic disks use a similar technique for storing information. These units resemble a group of large phonograph records stacked as in a 1950-vintage juke box. The disks are covered with the same iron oxide (organized in concentric tracks) as used on tapes. Information is stored on each track in the form of a string of magnetic spots imposed on the iron oxide surface. Either side of any disk in the stack is available for almost instantaneous reading. This is because each side is equipped with its own movable "reading head" somewhat like the tone arm on a phonograph. The disks are continuously rotating at very high speed. Any portion of the disk can be reached directly by one of the reading heads, which gives what is called **direct access**. (Tapes, of course, must be read sequentially.) Magnetic disks are run on a drive similar to that shown in Figure 1.7.

1.5 The Output Device

As is the case with input, many different devices may serve as output units. Very often we see a computer writing answers on an electronic typewriter. Although electric typewriters are used by computers to print brief, coded, technical messages to the computer operator, they are far too slow to be used for general program output. Many students' programs can be completely run in the time it takes to type one character on an electric typewriter. For that reason high-speed **line printers** have been developed to handle printed output (see Figure 1.8).

A line printer will print a whole line of approximately 132 characters in less time than it takes to type one character. (Each output device may have a different line size, but consider the value 132 as typical.) A line printer will fill a 60-row page of computer output paper with answers in half the time it takes to type one line of output on the typewriter.

If output is needed on cards, a device called a **card punch** can punch answers on cards. Although faster than an electric typewriter, it is many times slower than any other output device discussed here. It is used only when absolutely necessary.

Magnetic tapes and disks are much more efficient input/output devices. The electromagnetic design of these units permits an exceptionally rapid transfer of information to and from internal memory. For this reason, information supplied by slower input/output units (card input, for example) is often transferred to a disk before being sent to internal memory.

Figure 1.8 The high speed line printer
(Photo courtesy of Control Data Corporation)

1.6 How Memory Is Organized

The computer stores instructions and data brought from the input unit in the **memory unit.** It is here that intermediate answers are stored pending their use in later computations. It is here that the final output is stored ready to be sent to the output unit for printing when requested by the programmer.

The memory unit is organized into tens of thousands of elements known as **memory locations.** It serves as a useful learning device if the student will think of each memory location as a post office box, one for each variable in the program. Each box has the following features.

1. It can store a number (input value, output value, or intermediate calculation) or it can store character information.
2. It can be assigned a name (as in algebra) to be used each time the contents of the box are needed.

Thus the instruction

```
X = 4.5
```

in fact says, "Store the value 4.5 in a memory location." It further says, "Allow the programmer to reference that memory location by a label or name of his or her choosing (by the name X)." The instruction

```
Y = X + 2.0
```

says, "Add 2.0 and the value stored in memory location X together; store the result in a new memory location and label that location Y."

Some operations change the contents of a memory location, whereas others do not. Take the READ and PRINT operations, for example.

```
READ*,X,Y       (Contents of X and Y change)
PRINT*,X,Y      (Contents do not change)
```

The READ instruction is specifically designed to bring in fresh data from input, replacing the old values. The PRINT statement merely asks for a display of the contents of memory locations X and Y, not for a change in their value. Actually a copy of the contents of locations X and Y is made and sent to output. Similarly, the instruction

```
Z = X + Y
```

does not change the contents of X or Y. It merely requires a copy of the contents of locations X and Y to be made and sent to the arithmetic unit. Only the contents of memory location Z is changed by the preceding operations.

It will be useful to adopt the practice of portraying each memory location as a labeled box with its present value written inside, such as

X	Y
8.3	2.1

As each instruction is encountered, you update the contents of each box. Keep track of the contents of memory location X and Y as the following typical instruction is issued.

```
Y = 3.6
```

Result:

Note that by storing a new value in location Y the former value has been destroyed.

Consider the effect of the instruction

```
X = Y
```

Result:

The instruction says, "Get a copy of the contents of memory location Y and store the copy in memory location X." A new value is stored in memory location X, displacing or destroying the original value. The contents of memory location Y are unchanged.

Any one of the memory locations just discussed consists of a connected series of small elements each capable of storing a 0 or a 1. Figure 1.9(a) shows one of the original designs that uses small donut-shaped cores (about the size of a pinhead) made of soft iron. The iron cores are connected by thin wires and each core can be magnetized either clockwise (CW) or counterclockwise (CCW), thereby storing a 0 or a 1.

Magnetization	**Value Represented**
CW	0
CCW	1

Any individual string of cores can be accessed directly, thereby providing the random-access feature mentioned previously. This explains why numbers are stored in binary form (0s and 1s) and not in decimal form.

Figure 1.9(b) shows a design innovation called **bubble memory**. The small chip in Figure 1.9(b) is divided into *one million* domains that may or may not contain a bubble. An individual bubble can be moved into or out of a specific domain by the action of a magnetic field. The presence of a bubble corresponds to the value 1. The absence corresponds to the value 0.

Figure 1.9(a) Magnetic cores

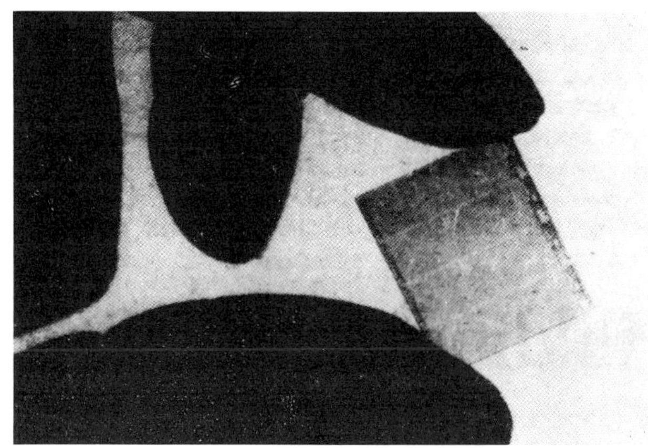

Figure 1.9(b) Bubble memory

We are seldom interested in dealing with a single bubble or single core of memory. For this reason, several of these binary elements are usually grouped together for the purpose of storing a single decimal digit or alphabetic character. An even more practical arrangement is to group many of these binary elements to form a unit called a **word** which can hold a number of decimal digits or alphabetic characters. The next section describes how the binary number system is used to represent both decimal quantities and alphabetic information.

1.7 Number Systems

The conversion of numeric values from decimal to binary for internal storage takes place almost automatically. Most programmers are not and need not be aware of what is going on. However, a programmer should be at least familiar with the binary system of number representation.

Reading a decimal string of numbers and reading any other string is really quite similar. Consider the string of digits in Figure 1.10 as might appear on an old-fashioned desk calculator, i.e., as a decimal string. It is immediately interpreted as six *thousand*, four *hundred*, thirty-seven. Through years of drilling, it has become second nature to recognize the six as being in the thousands position, the four in the hundreds position, and so on.

Realize that each digit is contributing something to the final answer. To determine each digit's contribution, you multiply the digit by some power of 10 (which is the base of the system). The power depends on where the digit appears in the string. Then add up all the individual contributions. This will be easier to understand if we move out of a base 10 system into some other, let us say a base 8 system.

If the wheels of our desk calculator had only eight possible positions, we would number them 0 through 7 and be forced into the octal number system. The number 6437 in octal has the following meaning.

$$\begin{aligned} 6437_8 &= \boxed{6} \times 8^3 + \boxed{4} \times 8^2 + \boxed{3} \times 8^1 + \boxed{7} \times 8^0 \\ &= \boxed{6} \times 512 + \boxed{4} \times 64 + \boxed{3} \times 8 + \boxed{7} \times 1 \\ &= 3072 + 256 + 24 + 7 \\ &= 3359_{10} \end{aligned}$$

Again each digit contributes something to the final answer; only this time you multiply by some power of 8 (the new system base).

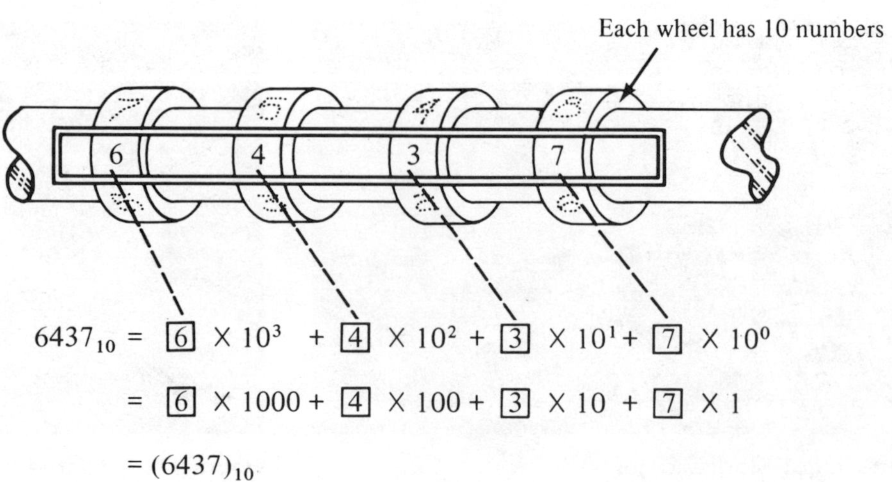

Figure 1.10 Decimal number representation

NOTE: *In a discussion involving various number systems, it is necessary to show what system a number is being written in. Here the subscript 8 reminds us that the system is to be interpreted according to the octal system.*

Having reached this point, we are now ready to handle binary numbers. If, for some reason, our wheels had only two positions, we would label them 0 and 1. Consider the pattern (binary string) shown in Figure 1.11. It represents the decimal number 19.

Figure 1.11 Binary representation

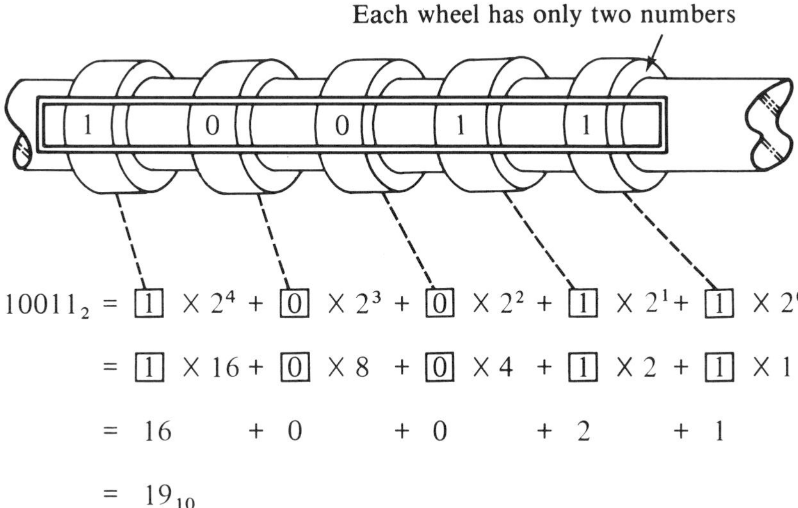

Confining the storage of all information to a form using the numeric digits 0 and 1 does not restrict the computer in any way. It can store all kinds of information, such as letters of the alphabet, as well as special characters, such as periods, commas, and dollar signs. This is done by simply coding all such nonnumeric characters into two or three digit numbers. For example, an A can be represented by a 41, and B by 42, and C by 43, and so on. The numbers are then converted to binary and stored as a string of 0s and 1s.

As a quick exercise, determine the decimal value of the following binary numbers:

Exercise	a. 1000	b. 1010	c. 1011	d. 1111
Answer	a. 8	b. 10	c. 11	d. 15

1.8 Machine Language versus FORTRAN

The discussion of the design of the memory unit pointed out that all information stored in memory must be in binary form. This means that instructions as well as data values must ultimately be transformed into binary form before they can be stored in memory.

Don't panic. Just as data values are expressed in decimal form and somehow internally converted to binary, instructions will be handled in a similar way. A student's first FORTRAN program will contain instructions such as:

```
X = Y + Z
```

These instructions will be read and converted to a form acceptable to the computer by a special program called the **compiler**. It is like a translator. It converts instructions written in FORTRAN into instructions that the machine can understand called

machine language instructions. A single FORTRAN statement may require a whole series of basic operations to be performed. For each basic operation, a machine language instruction will be generated by the compiler. Each of these instructions is converted to a string of binary digits automatically.

All of this is not your problem; it is the compiler's. However, add two new terms to your expanding computer vocabulary: *source* program and *object* program. A computer program written in a higher level language, such as FORTRAN, is referred to as the **source program**. Its translated or machine language equivalent is called the **object program**.

All FORTRAN programs must be translated (compiled) before they can be executed. During compilation, the computer is under the control of the compiler. Your FORTRAN statements will be read one after another. If you have issued a `READ` instruction, that instruction will be converted to the appropriate machine language code. If you have issued a `STOP` instruction, that instruction will be translated into machine language. When *all* statements in your program have been properly translated into machine language, the compiler is released and control passes to the first statement in your program (now in machine language). This marks the beginning of an entirely different phase of operations. Your instructions take over control of the computer, that is, they are executed.

When a `READ` instruction is reached, information associated with one of your data records is transferred to internal storage. When a `STOP` instruction is encountered, the computer terminates the execution of statements in your program. As you can see, compilation and execution are two distinctly different operations.

All computer programming languages that require compilation before being usable by the computer are referred to as **compiler languages**. FORTRAN, the language presented by this book, is by no means the only compiler language. It is the most widely used language in the field of mathematics, science, engineering, statistics, and probability. Its name is derived from the words *FOR*mula *TRAN*slation. COBOL, the *CO*mmon *B*usiness *O*riented *L*anguage, is another very popular compiler language. It is designed for use in bookkeeping and accounting applications. Nothing would be gained by attempting to list all other compiler languages in use today. There are many different languages, each designed with some specific application in mind.

1.9 Hardware versus Software

A brief word about two frequently used terms. The computer itself is composed physically of nuts, bolts, cabinets, wires, resistors, transistors, cores, and so on. Just as you might suspect, these items are referred to as its **hardware**. The arithmetic unit is able to obey an `ADD` instruction because there are electronic circuits physically wired into it that enable it to add. The computer's ability to add is "a part of its hardware capability."

The basic philosophy of computer design is, however, to provide no more hardware than is absolutely necessary. This places a large responsibility on the programmer. We are constantly taking a minimal configuration of hardware and somehow combining these basic operations into a sequence of instructions that accomplishes any and all tasks assigned. This is where the concept of software comes in.

Each computer is equipped with a large group of prerecorded programs that extend its capabilities above and beyond those provided by the hardware. These capabilities include its ability to raise to a power, to take sines and cosines, to find roots, to take logarithms, and to compile source programs into object programs, naming just a few. These prerecorded programs are what is referred to by the term **software**.

The idea of accomplishing some high-order mathematics by combining a sequence of basic operations can be shown by the application of the following relatively obscure formula

$$\text{Sin}(X) = X - \frac{X^3}{3 \cdot 2 \cdot 1} + \frac{X^5}{5 \cdot 4 \cdot 3 \cdot 2 \cdot 1} - \frac{X^7}{7 \cdot 6 \cdot 5 \cdot 4 \cdot 3 \cdot 2 \cdot 1} + \frac{X^9}{9 \cdot 8 \cdot 7 \cdot 6 \cdot 5 \cdot 4 \cdot 3 \cdot 2 \cdot 1}$$

(*Note: X* must be in radians.)

This formula would have exceptionally limited application except for one thing. Look at the operations needed to evaluate the equation. Addition, subtraction, multiplication, and division are needed. Raising to a power can be accomplished by repetitive multiplication. Do you see what this means? We can obtain the sine value by writing a small block of code that calls the basic operations (hardware capabilities) we already have! The ability to compute the sine becomes a software feature. This block of code (software routine) is but one of many that are organized into a software library and supplied by the computer manufacturer. Each of these library functions is as available to the programmer as readily as any of the hardware components. We use names like SIN or COS to evoke a particular software routine in the same way we use + and − to evoke a particular hardware component. For the moment, however, it is only important to recognize the term software and know how it relates to the term hardware.

Review Exercises

(The answers to starred questions can be found in Appendix C.)

★ 1. A digital computer is superior to a desk top calculator because it has a large memory unit. What type of information is stored in memory? (a) Numbers (b) Instructions (c) Both of these (d) None of these

2. The first information read by the computer is a list of instructions on how to solve the problem. What is this list of instructions called?

★ 3. What does the term CPU mean and what is its function?

4. Name the two most common means of input.

★ 5. Name four basic arithmetic operations that are performed by hardware components in the arithmetic unit.

6. Can the computer make logical decisions? If so, describe how this is accomplished.

7. Give an example of when the computer would have to make a logical decision.

★ 8. How is information recorded on cards?

9. The information punched on a card may also appear typed at the top of the card. Does the computer look at this typed line?

10. How is information stored on magnetic tape or disks?

★ 11. Which is faster, card input or magnetic tape input?

12. The line printer has an approximate capacity of 132 characters. What does this mean?

13. Why does memory use binary numbers? Why not decimal?

14. Describe what happens inside the computer as a result of the statement

    Z = A + 6.0

★ 15. Are the contents of memory location A modified as a result of the preceding statement?

★ 16. Are the contents of memory location Z affected by the statement?

17. What are "cores" used for and why are they associated with the binary number system?

★ 18. Express the number 5 in binary.

19. What is an octal number?

20. Describe the difference between a FORTRAN program and a machine language program.

★ 21. Why must each FORTRAN statement be processed by the compiler?

22. What is the source program?

23. What is the object program?

24. Why does FORTRAN use the symbols +, −, *, and / instead of the words ADD, SUBTRACT, MULTIPLY and DIVIDE?

★ 25. During the compiling of your program, describe what happens when a READ instruction is reached.

26. Why is the typewriter seldom used as an output device?

27. What is the function of a specification statement? Where should they be located?

★ 28. Where does the name FORTRAN come from?

29. Why is software preferred over hardware? What does the term minimal hardware configuration mean?

30. The text indicates that learning the various commands of a computer language is not the important part of programming. What is the important part?

31. What does the term compiler language mean?

2 Programming: A General Description

The purpose of Chapter 1 was to provide general background material relative to the concept of digital computation and to describe some of the internal design and organization of a digital computer. In that chapter we classified the basic operations that the computer is capable of performing, examined some of the individual FORTRAN instructions, and partially explained what a complete program looks like. Chapter 2 amplifies these latter topics. We will look at several other programs to see how they are constructed and how they are physically presented to the computer. It is still too early to expect that all the parts to this puzzle will fit together right before your eyes. You should continue to read for *general understanding only*. Most of the material presented at this time will be formally discussed in subsequent chapters.

More specifically, the purposes of this chapter are:

1. To reinforce your understanding of the terms *compilation* and *execution*.
2. To continue an introductory presentation of the components of a complete computer program.
3. To describe the difference between integer and real numbers used by the computer.

2.1 Compilation versus Execution of a Program

It is important to realize that the computer must be given a *full* set of instructions, which must be translated and stored before any single instruction can be executed. A computer receives instructions in the same way a tourist receives directions from a policeman. The policeman might say, "Walk to the end of this block. Turn right. Walk another two blocks, and the bus station will be directly in front of you." The tourist must first receive a full set of instructions, then understand each instruction, and finally memorize the sequence in which they were given. Then and only then can an attempt be made to obey (execute) the first instruction. A similar set of conditions prevails when a program is presented to the computer.

> STORED PROGRAM CONCEPT: All instructions of a program are stored in the computer's memory before any of them are executed.

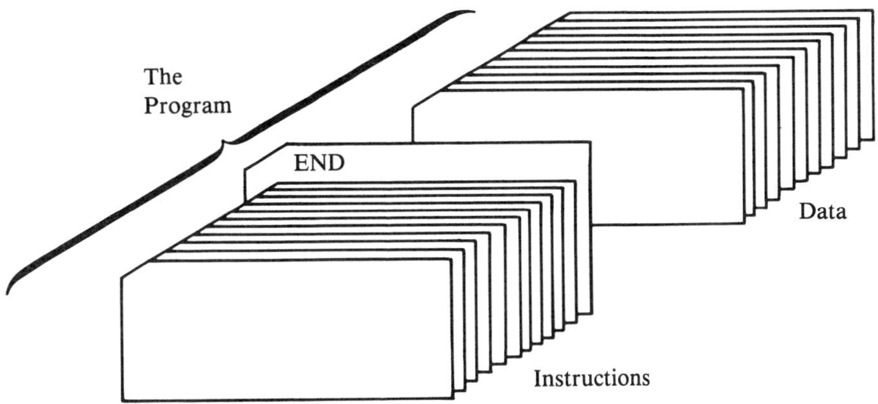

Figure 2.1 The program

A program that is presented to the computer in the form of punched cards has the appearance of a single deck called the **program deck**. This program deck has two subdivisions: the *instructions* followed by the *data*. The instruction part contains a sequence of instructions to be followed in the solution of the problems, and the data part contains those variable quantities (usually numbers) that are to be used in the computations. If the program deck is fed to the computer through the card reader, the first action the computer takes is to cause the contents of the entire instruction deck to be read. At this time the computer is being controlled by the compiler, which is serving as a translator. Each FORTRAN instruction is being translated into machine-language instructions.

We must somehow mark the end of the instruction deck. Otherwise the compiler will start processing data cards as though they contained FORTRAN instructions. (See Figure 2.1.) Thus, at the end of the instruction deck, we place a card that contains the one word END. When the END card is detected, the compiling process is terminated and the computer releases the compiler. Control passes back to the first instruction of your program (now in machine-language form) commencing the *execution* of the program.

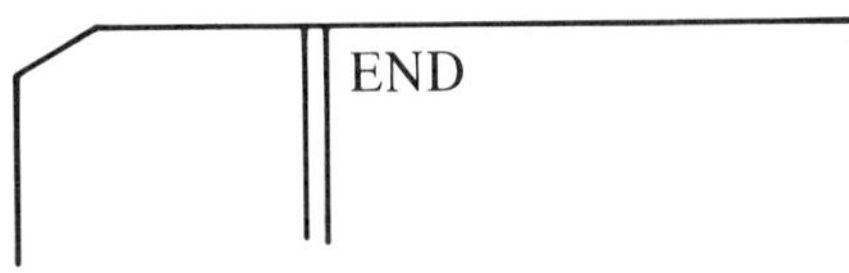

If you are using a terminal, you will type line after line at the keyboard. Each line represents one of your FORTRAN instructions, which will be displayed on your screen for possible correction. When you have typed all the instructions, you enter one additional line containing the word END. This is the way you signal the end of the instruction set.

From this discussion, you should conclude that processing a computer program in fact occurs in two distinct phases: **compilation** followed by **execution**. Compilation describes the reading, translating, and storing of instructions in the computer's memory. By the way, if you write any of your FORTRAN statements incorrectly (make a grammatical error), the compiler indicates the nature of the error. If the error is not serious, the compiler attempts to fix it and go on. If there are no errors, compilation continues until the END statement is detected. The program then goes into execution. The computer goes back to your first instruction (now in memory and now in machine language) and starts *obeying it*.

2.2 A Sample Program

The following programming example is used to provide additional information concerning:

1. Deck configuration.
2. Sequential processing of statements.
3. Use of statement numbers.
4. Branching using the GO TO statement.

Programming Example

Write a program to compute the volume of a cylinder, given its radius and height.

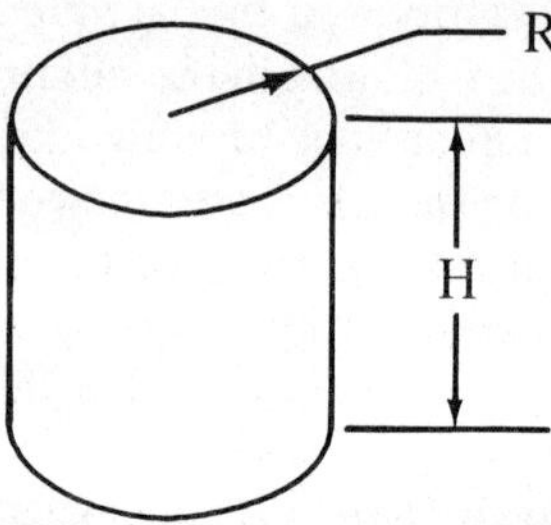

Suggested Variables:

RADIUS = Radius of cylinder
HEIGHT = Height of cylinder
AREA = Area of cylinder
VOLUME = Volume of cylinder

$$\text{Volume} = \text{Area} \times \text{Height}$$
$$= \pi R^2 \times H$$

The program for this is as follows:

```
      REAL RADIUS,HEIGHT,VOLUME,AREA
      READ*,RADIUS,HEIGHT
      AREA=3.14*RADIUS**2
      VOLUME=AREA*HEIGHT
      PRINT*,VOLUME
      STOP
      END
```

After the program's variables are declared, the value of the radius and height of the clyinder are read from data. The programmer has elected to compute the area of the cylinder's base as a separate calculation defining the quantity called AREA. The statement

```
AREA=3.14*RADIUS**2
```

Programming Example continued

needs a little explanation, since it introduces a new symbol. The single asterisk means to multiply. A double asterisk means to raise to a power. The statement says, "Evaluate the expression on the right of the equal sign, which involves raising the contents of memory location RADIUS to the power 2 and multiplying the result by 3.14. Store the value thus obtained in a memory location and label it AREA." The volume is then computed by multiplying AREA by HEIGHT, and a PRINT statement displays the value obtained.

To run this program, six statements must be entered as separate lines on the terminal or punched on statement cards. These six statements plus the END statement are then assembled into the instruction deck. (See Figure 2.2.) A single typed line of input or a single data card form the data deck. (A card in the data deck is called a *data card*.) This record contains the value of the radius and the height of the cylinder whose volume is to be computed. After the instruction deck is read and compiled, the computer begins execution.

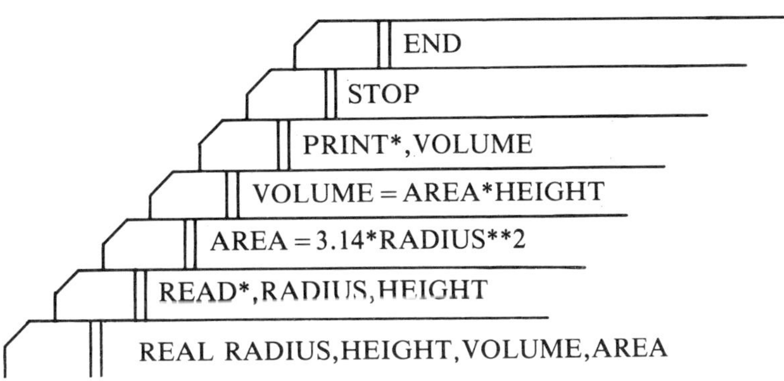

Figure 2.2 Typical instruction deck

The first statement executed is the READ statement. Often a student will want to put a data card immediately after the READ statement. "After all," the student asks, "doesn't the computer need that data record as soon as it is told to read it?" The answer is no, because all instructions are stored in the computer's memory before the READ statement (or any other statement) is executed. By the time the READ statement is executed, all instruction cards have been processed during the compilation of the instruction deck. Any remaining records should be data records waiting to be processed by the execution of a READ command. *The instruction deck is consumed during compilation. Records in the data deck are processed during the execution phase.*

In what order are instructions executed? Without hesitation you would respond, "Why, they are executed in the same order they appear in the instruction deck! First one first, second one second, last one last!" And you are correct. By now you are aware of the normal mode of processing instructions. You know that, except when obeying a CONTROL instruction, the computer executes instructions sequentially.

Suppose the problem was to compute the volume of three different cylinders. One not-too-clever approach to that problem would be to rewrite the program as follows.

Instruction	Meaning
READ*,RADIUS,HEIGHT	Read the 1st data record.
AREA=3.14*RADIUS**2	Compute the 1st area.
VOLUME=AREA*HEIGHT	Compute the 1st volume.
PRINT*,VOLUME	Print the 1st volume.
READ*,RADIUS,HEIGHT	Read the 2nd data record.
AREA=3.14*RADIUS**2	Compute the 2nd area.
VOLUME=AREA*HEIGHT	Compute the 2nd volume.
PRINT*,VOLUME	Print the 2nd volume.
READ*,RADIUS,HEIGHT	Read the 3rd data record.
AREA=3.14*RADIUS**2	Compute the 3rd area.
VOLUME=AREA*HEIGHT	Compute the 3rd volume.
PRINT*,VOLUME	Print the 3rd volume.
STOP	Stop execution.
END	

Three input records would be required in the input file, one for each cylinder, and three answers would be printed. The program involves essentially three repetitions of the same four instructions. Although it is only a mild annoyance to be required to enter three duplicates of each instruction, the situation would be intolerable if the volume of 250 cylinders were to be calculated. As a possible alternative solution, consider the idea of establishing a loop by using a GO TO statement. This may appear to be a clever approach, but the improvement is only modest.

```
      REAL RADIUS,HEIGHT,VOLUME,AREA
    5 READ*,RADIUS,HEIGHT
      AREA=3.14*RADIUS**2
      VOLUME=AREA*HEIGHT
      PRINT*,VOLUME
      GO TO 5
      END
```

The original program has been modified by labeling the READ instruction with an identifying number, in this case the number 5, and by inserting the GO TO 5 statement after the PRINT instruction. The number 5, called a statement number, is a label and nothing more. It has no numerical significance and is never used in the mathematics of calculating the volume. In programs where many statements must be numbered, their numbers do not have to be in numerical order. Statement numbers are used whenever there is a need to mark the intended destination of a branching instruction, such as the GO TO.

The use of statement numbers has two major restrictions, both logical and easy to remember:

1. A statement number cannot be greater than 99999. (This is because they must be able to fit into the five spaces allowed for them on the instruction card).
2. Statement numbers cannot be duplicated within one program. (This is for the same reason that two rooms cannot be numbered alike in the same building. A

person told to "Go to Room 5" would not know where to go if more than one room were numbered 5. A computer told to "GO TO 5" would likewise be "confused" if more than one statement were labeled 5 in the program.)

The following list summarizes the points to remember about statement numbers.

1. They are not required on all statements.
2. Order is unimportant.
3. No duplicates are allowed.
4. None can be greater than 99999.
5. None can be less than 1.
6. They must *be integer numbers.*

Inserting the GO TO 5 statement in our cylinder program modifies the execution of statements as follows. The statements

```
5  READ*,RADIUS,HEIGHT
   AREA=3.14*RADIUS**2
   VOLUME=AREA*HEIGHT
   PRINT*,VOLUME
```

are executed sequentially as before. The next statement is GO TO 5. This branching statement stops sequential execution of instructions and sends the computer back to the statement labeled 5.

```
5  READ*,RADIUS,HEIGHT
```

The computer executes this instruction, causing the reading of another data record. Because this instruction is not a branching instruction, the computer resumes sequential execution of the following statements.

```
AREA=3.14*RADIUS**2
VOLUME=AREA*HEIGHT
PRINT*,VOLUME
```

Again the GO TO 5 statement is reached, and the program branches back to the READ statement. This process is repeated over and over until the data file is depleted.†

Sequential Execution Without Branching

```
REAL RADIUS,HEIGHT,VOLUME,AREA
READ*, RADIUS, HEIGHT
AREA = 3.14 * RADIUS ** 2
VOLUME = AREA * HEIGHT
PRINT *, VOLUME
STOP
```

Result: Only one pass through program.

Sequential Execution With Branching

```
  REAL RADIUS,HEIGHT,VOLUME,AREA
5 READ*, RADIUS, HEIGHT
  AREA = 3.14 * RADIUS ** 2
  VOLUME = AREA * HEIGHT
  PRINT *, VOLUME
  GO TO 5
```

Result: As many passes through program as there are data records.

† Stopping a program by allowing it to run out of data is considered to be about as clever as stopping a car by allowing it to run out of gas.

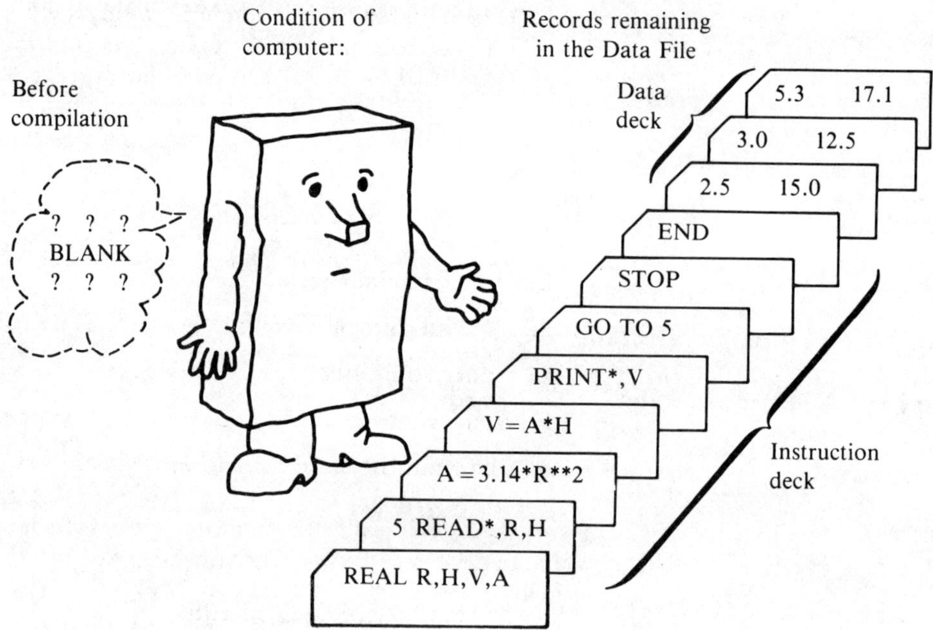

Figure 2.3 Before compilation

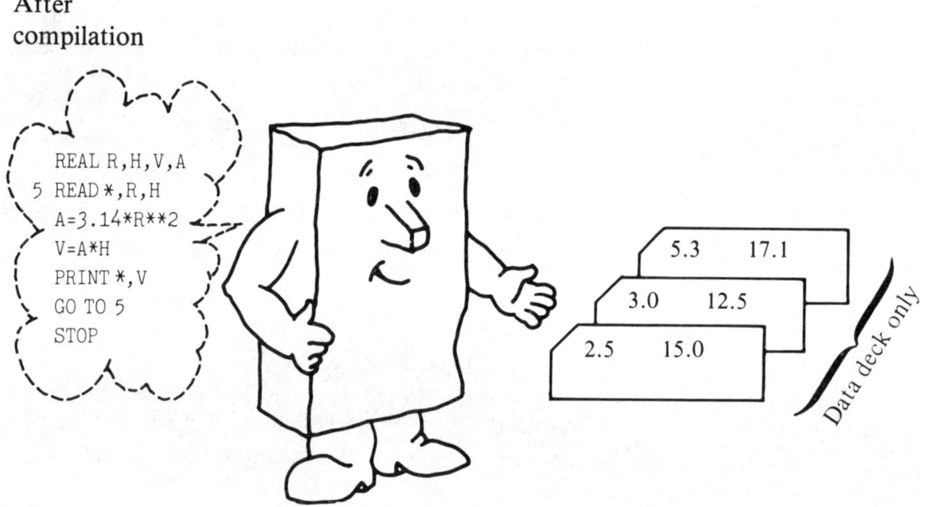

Figure 2.4 After compilation

Try to envision the actions taking place inside the computer as your program is being processed. Figures 2.3 and 2.4 depict the compilation of the program (when the computer is being told how to solve the problem). This is when the instruction deck (file) is consumed.

To understand what is going on during the execution phase, consider the following table. It shows the state of various memory locations as each instruction is being executed. The number of records in the input file and the status of the output device (output file) are also shown at each step in the program. Because of space limitations, the various variable names have been abbreviated to a single letter.

Instruction Just Executed	Condition of Memory Locations	Records in the Input File	Results Appearing on Line Printer
5 READ*, R,H	R 2.5 A H 15.0 V	5.3 17.1 3.0 12.5	
A=3.14*R**2	R 2.5 A 19.6 H 15.0 V	5.3 17.1 3.0 12.5	
V=A*H	R 2.5 A 19.6 H 15.0 V 294.0	5.3 17.1 3.0 12.5	
PRINT*,V	R 2.5 A 19.6 H 15.0 V 294.0	5.3 17.1 3.0 12.5	2.940000E+02
GO TO 5	R 2.5 A 19.6 H 15.0 V 294.0	5.3 17.1 3.0 12.5	2.94000E+02
5 READ*,R,H	R 3.0 A 19.6 H 12.5 V 294.0	5.3 17.1	2.940000E+02
A=3.14*R**2	R 3.0 A 37.5 H 12.5 V 294.0	5.3 17.1	2.940000E+02
V=A*H	R 3.0 A 37.5 H 12.5 V 468.8	5.3 17.1	2.900000E+02
PRINT*,V	R 3.0 A 37.5 H 12.5 V 468.8	5.3 17.1	2.9000000E+02 4.6880000E+02
GO TO 5	R 3.0 A 37.5 H 12.5 V 468.8	5.3 17.1	2.9000000E+02 4.6880000E+02
5 READ*,V,H	R 5.3 A 37.5 H 17.1 V 468.8		2.9000000E+02 4.6880000E+02

The problems with this solution are:

1. Eventually a READ instruction will be executed and the input file will be empty (this causes an abnormal termination).
2. A loop has been established, but that fact is not known until the bottom of the loop is reached.

As your programming ability develops, demands will be placed on you to write not just a program that works, but one that works well. Is it easy to follow? Consider this last alternative solution to this problem and evaluate its merits for yourself.

To avoid running out of input records, an extra record is added to the file. The values of RADIUS and HEIGHT are listed as zero. This input record will serve the purpose of terminating a WHILE loop when this input record is reached.

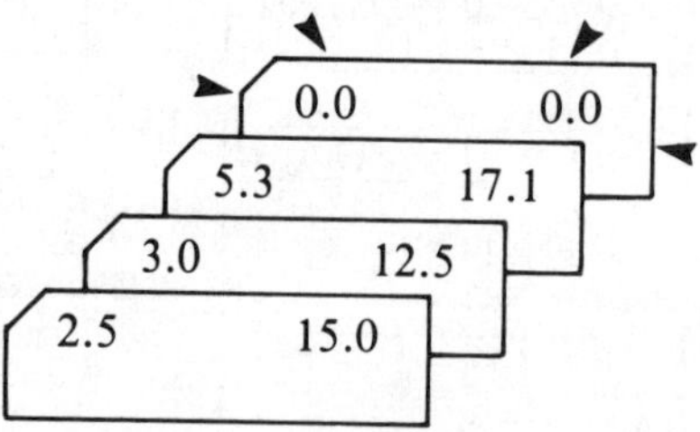


```
REAL RADIUS, HEIGHT, VOLUME, AREA
READ*, RADIUS, HEIGHT

DO WHILE (RADIUS .NE. 0.0)
     AREA = 3.14*RADIUS**2
     VOLUME = AREA * HEIGHT
     PRINT*, VOLUME
     READ*, RADIUS, HEIGHT
ENDDO

STOP
END
```

2.3 FORTRAN Instruction Cards and Coding Forms

Although the most common input device is a terminal, it is easier to explain input via cards. Since the "layout" of information for both devices is the same, it really does not make much difference which device is used. A card consists of 80 vertical columns, each of which may contain a letter, a number, or one of the other characters used in FORTRAN.

The card in Figure 2.5 shows the keypunched appearance of the digits 0 through 9, the 26 letters A through Z, and the other special characters. Collectively, these are referred to as the **FORTRAN character set**. A keypunch machine is used to impose the desired pattern of punched holes in response to entries made at its typewriter-like keyboard. Note that digits are represented by a single punched hole in the column, letters by a double hole punch, and only selected special characters involve a triple punch. At the top of each column, the keypunch types the character represented in the column so that the programmer can verify that the card has been punched correctly.

Figure 2.5 Character representation on an 80-column card

These cards will be used to prepare both statement cards and data cards. If a card is to contain a FORTRAN statement, however, specific columns on the card are reserved for each part of the FORTRAN statement. For example, the statement number (if any) must appear in the first five columns of the card. To help the programmer meet these location requirements, most computer facilities make available what is called a **FORTRAN statement card.** These cards are overprinted with lines that divide the 80 columns into zones. Each zone has a title or label to remind the programmer what information belongs in this zone. (See Figure 2.6.)

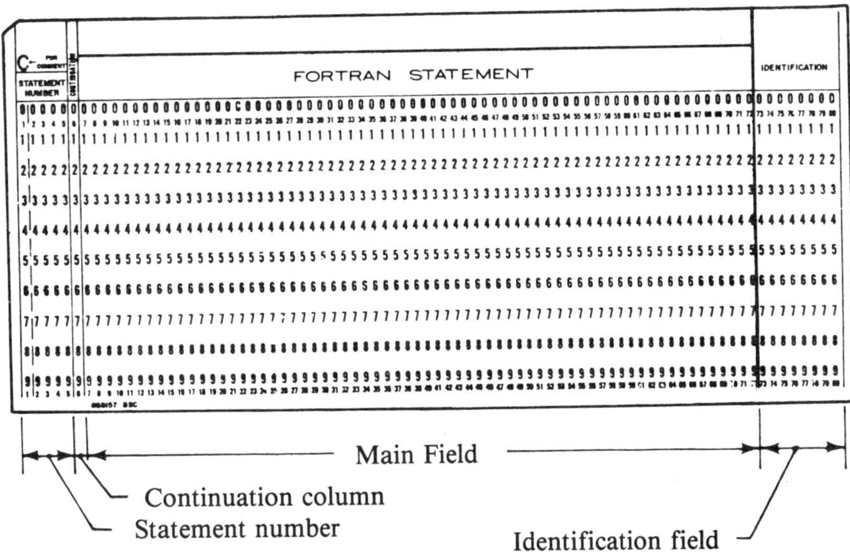

Figure 2.6 The FORTRAN statement card

As we said, columns 1–5 are used for statement numbers. If a statement needs to be numbered, the number should appear in this zone, otherwise leave the zone blank. If you are entering the instruction at a terminal, you can use a TAB button on the keyboard to jump across these columns quickly. Columns 7–72 on the card are used to contain the actual FORTRAN statement. The computer looks here for the instruction you are issuing. Columns 73–80 are ignored by the compiler. This zone provides room on the card for any special (identifying) information the programmer might want on each card. One possibility is your initials and a three-digit identification number. These characters would prove useful if the cards got out of order or got mixed up with someone else's cards.

Column 6 is known as the continuation column. It is used whenever it is necessary to continue a long statement onto one or more (continuation) cards. All statement information *must* be confined to columns 7–72. If you need more than one card to express a long statement, you must punch a character other than a blank or zero in column 6 of each additional card used. (The latest FORTRAN standards require the compiler to accommodate at least nine continuation cards.) If, for example, a statement is so long that it requires three continuation cards, one possibility is to put a 1 in column 6 of the first continuation card, a 2 in column 6 of the second continuation card, and so on. Another appealing technique is to put a plus sign, +, in column 6 of each continuation card. This tends to suggest that the information on this card is needed in addition to that on the previous card to complete the statement. Note that no character is punched in column 6 of the first card of a long statement.

The same holds true for terminal input. If your FORTRAN statement won't fit between columns 7–72 you must go on to another line. Put a nonblank character in column 6 of this next (continuation) line to indicate that the line you are now typing is an extension of the previous line.

In a program deck, it is desirable to insert statements containing English-language comments that make the program easier to read and understand. We might precede each segment of FORTRAN code with a brief description of what the code is trying to accomplish. Such carefully chosen and properly placed comments can greatly ease the job of understanding a program written by someone else or one that has been on the shelf for several months. The computer would try to interpret such English-language comments as FORTRAN statements if it was not told otherwise. A letter `C` in column 1 signals that the card contains one of these comments and the computer is thereby advised to ignore this card during compilation. The card is then called a **comment card**. Figure 2.7 shows some typical comment statements.

Figure 2.7 Typical comment statements

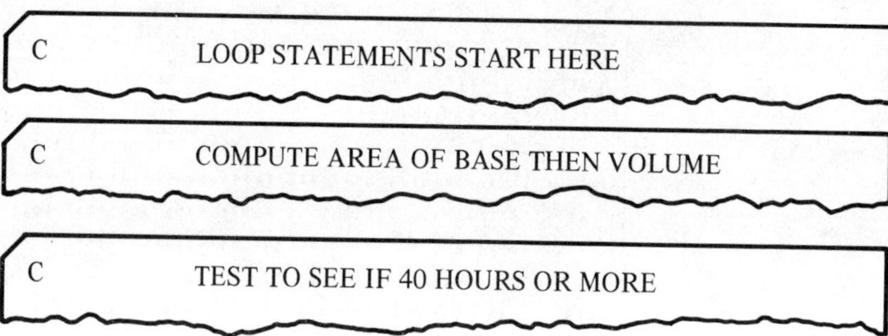

Spacing Is Not Critical

Spaces typed in the process of giving an instruction are permissible and have no effect on the compilation of that statement. From the compiler's point of view the statement

```
AREA  =  3.14  *  RADIUS  **  2
```

Many embedded blanks

is equivalent to the statement

```
AREA=3.14*RADIUS**2
```

as long as neither statement begins before column 7 nor extends beyond column 72. From the programmer's point of view, it is desirable to place spaces in statements wherever it makes the statement more legible.

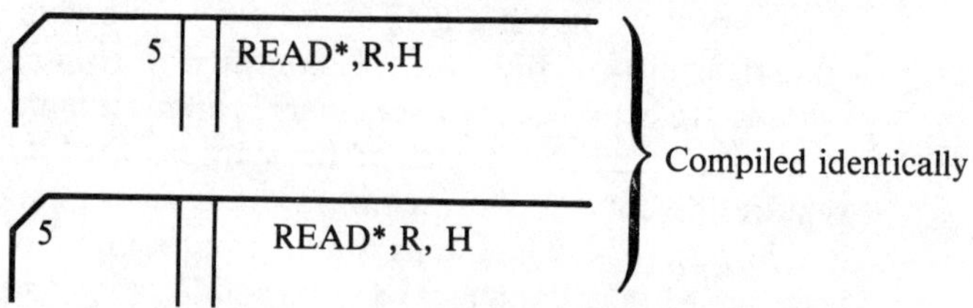

When writing a FORTRAN program out in long hand, FORTRAN coding forms are available to assist in proper spacing (see Figure 2.8). Each line on the coding form corresponds to a single instruction. These forms show, for example, which statements are too long to fit on one line. However, their greatest usefulness comes when it is time to type the program.

Note that the column restrictions discussed here pertain to *statement* cards only, that is, records that make up the instruction deck. These restrictions do *not* apply to the data deck.

FORTRAN CODING FORM

Program ______ Coded By ______ Checked By ______

Identification 73 80

Date ______ Page ______ of ______

C FOR COMMENT | STATEMENT NUMBER | Cont | FORTRAN STATEMENT

Figure 2.8 The FORTRAN coding form

Data Cards (Records)

The 80 columns of a data card can be divided into whatever zones the programmer finds appropriate to hold the input values. The compiler allows data to be presented in two basic forms. One form, called "free format," only requires that one data value be separated from another by at least one blank column. The other form requires the programmer to tell exactly where each piece of data is located on the card by providing a `FORMAT` statement.

When the `FORMAT` statement is not supplied, the input record must be scanned to determine where each piece of information is located (this explains why each element of data must be separated by one or more blanks). A comma or a slash may also be used to separate data values. To read any one item, a process is initiated to take in one character at a time until another delimiter (space, comma, or slash) is detected. When a `FORMAT` statement is used, this information (the field width) is supplied directly.

```
   READ 10, NUM 1, NUM 2, NUM 3
10 FORMAT (I5, I5, I7)
```

codes to describe card layout

The `FORMAT` statement uses three codes (inside the parentheses) which convey the information that the input record contains three data items. The letter `I` in each code reveals that each item is an integer number. Finally, the number portion of the code indicates that five columns have been reserved for the first and second integer value and seven columns for the last integer. Figure 2.9 shows a typical data card.

Figure 2.9 A typical data card

3.0 6.0 19.765

Quiz 2 Program Preparation

1. The END statement should appear just once in your program. True or false?
2. What is the purpose of the END statement?
3. Why is it necessary to number a FORTRAN statement? Must these numbers be in order?
4. What is the normal order of executing statements in your program? How can this order be interrupted?
5. In what columns should your FORTRAN statement be written?
6. What is the purpose of column 6 when entering a FORTRAN statement?
7. Describe the function of a comment statement.
8. How do you inform the computer that you are using a comment statement?
9. When a program is being compiled, what happens when the statement

```
READ*, A, B, C,
```

is reached?

10. When a program is being executed, what happens when the statement

```
READ*, A, B, C
```

is reached?

2.4 Integer versus Real Constants

It is now necessary to become embroiled in a sticky and sometimes confusing aspect of computers, namely, that they can do arithmetic in *two* different ways. One method, called **integer arithmetic**, is used only when whole numbers are involved (numbers that have no fractional or decimal part). Integer mathematical operations have the feature of being exceptionally fast. This speed is achieved by the special way in which integer numbers are stored and by the fact that all integer calculations (like a division operation) are terminated as soon as the decimal point in the answer is reached. (There is not supposed to be anything after the decimal point, so why keep on calculating?) You will soon see that this represents a considerable saving of time.

The alternate and more common form of arithmetic is called **real arithmetic**, which is long and time consuming. Let us see why. Assume you are computing the average number of cars passing a dangerous intersection. You observe 40 cars in a three-minute period of time. The average rate is:

$$\frac{40}{3} = 13.33333333333333333333333333333333 \ldots \text{ cars/minute}$$

This answer is clearly a number with a fractional part. it is called a **real number.**

Even if every core or bubble in memory is committed to storing this unfortunate (but not uncommon) value, some inaccuracy is inevitable. Therefore, each memory location that is to hold a real number must be relatively large to keep the inaccuracy (the part of the number that gets chopped off) as small as possible. The more digits we retain in memory, the smaller the inaccuracy. Some computers store real numbers to an accuracy as high as 15 to 20 decimal digits.

$$\underbrace{13.3333333333333}_{\substack{\text{15 digits}\\ \text{retained}}}\ \underbrace{33333333333333\ldots}_{\substack{\text{Remainder lost}\\ \text{(truncated)}}}$$

If real numbers are stored to this accuracy, consider what effect this has on a typical arithmetic operation such as multiplication. Fifteen (or more) digits of the first number must be multiplied by each of the 15 digits of the second number. That is a relatively long process, and even then some inaccuracy is still present. This is a typical feature of real numbers and real calculation.

Constants versus Variables

Recall one of the arithmetic statements used in the last programming example:

```
AREA = 3.14 * RADIUS ** 2
```

The quantities RADIUS and AREA may take on several different values during the execution of the program and are, therefore, called **variables**. On the other hand, 3.14 and 2 are obviously **constants**. However, the computer recognizes two distinctly different forms of constants (integer constants and real constants) and two different forms of variables (integer and real). The remainder of this section demonstrates when the integer form is used and when the real form is necessary.

An account number at a bank, a telephone area code, a student ID number, the ZIP code in a mailing address are all typical examples of integer numbers. These numbers *never* get involved in complicated arithmetic. We might sort mail by ZIP code number or count the number of students who have better than a 3.5 scholastic average, but we would never divide one of these numbers by another producing an answer with a fractional component. *Integer calculations have an important but somewhat specialized use in computer programming.*

By way of contrast, consider the problem of computing the interest earned in a savings account or the price-to-earnings ratio of a stock. Clearly, you would not want to perform these calculations in the *integer* mode. These calculations should be performed in the *real* mode using *real* numbers (those with a fractional component.)

Real calculations are easy to recognize because they are typical of the arithmetic you deal with on a day-to-day basis. These calculations are more frequently associated with involved or complicated arithmetic operations compared to integer quantities.

If a real number was stored as an integer, the fractional or decimal part would be lost. For example, storing the real value 5.75 as an integer (in an integer memory location) would result in losing its decimal portion. It would be stored as 5. On the other hand, the integer value 5 *could* be stored as a real value without any loss of accuracy. It would be stored as

$$\underbrace{5.00000000000000}_{\text{15 decimal digits}}$$

For that reason, the novice programmer is tempted to conclude that for the sake of simplicity he should use real numbers only. This would be an unfortunate mistake. As you get deeper into programming, the need for high speed integer mathematics becomes more obvious. Integers will be used for "loop control" (counting how many times you have gone around a given loop in the program); for "deck control" (counting how many data cards have been read); and for "subscript control" (providing a subscript for a subscripted variable). In each case, the need for integer arithmetic is very important.

When writing arithmetic expressions, the way in which we distinguish a real from an integer constant is by the presence or absence of the decimal point.

No Decimal Point	Decimal Point Present
| 1 | 5 | |	| 1 | 5 | . |
Constant is *integer.*	Constant is *real.*

Other examples are as follows:

Integer Numbers	Real Numbers
+28374	3.14159
−19	−29.003176
0	0.0
−87132	+6431000.

As you can see, a plus or minus sign may be attached to any constant. If there is no sign, the value is considered as positive. Note that commas are not allowed:

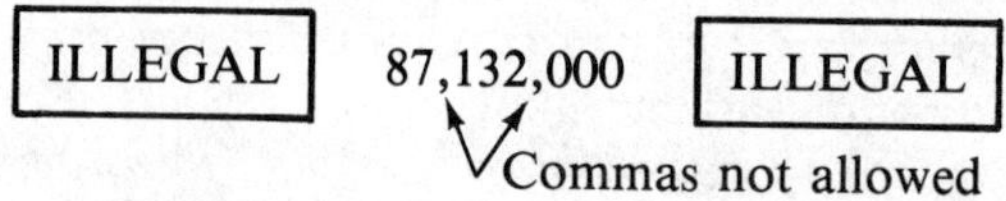

The following table outlines the rules governing the writing of integer and real constants.

	Constants	
	Integer	**Real**
Rules	1. No decimal point 2. No commas 3. No letters 4. + − allowed but no other special characters 5. For size limitations see computer manual.	1. Must have decimal point 2. No commas 3. No letters except E† (to express a constant in scientific notation) 4. + − allowed but no other special characters 5. For size limitations see computer manual.
Valid Examples	−1 2164 +13 0 9 108	−1.000004 2164.798 +13.2 0.0 9.0 E + 06† 108.54
Invalid Examples	−1. (decimal point) 31,000 (comma) 71E (letter)	1 (no decimal point) $108.54 (special character $) 7B. (letter)

† The letter E is used to express a real constant in scientific notation. This topic will be covered shortly.

Rule 5 speaks of a size limitation. This gets back to the internal design of memory. Each computer uses a different number of binary elements for the storing of a real or integer number. The more elements used, the larger a number may be held by that memory location. Remember, this was called the computer's **word size**. Computers having a relatively small word size must limit the number of digits (and maximum value) a constant may have. The limits are different for each model and make of computer.

When a constant is more than 7 or 8 digits in length, you could be in trouble. Check with your instructor or see Appendix A of this text entitled "System Characteristics." All systems impose a limit to the magnitude of a real number. On some machines a real value may be as large as 10^{75} or as small as 10^{-75}. On other systems the limit is 10^{32} to 10^{-32}. Realize that you should not normally be generating numbers outside this range, unless, of course, you do something wrong (such as divide by zero.) It is by no means imperative that you know the exact value of the size and magnitude limitation of your computer. You should, however, be aware that these limitations do exist.

2.5 Developing a Program's Algorithm

When setting up a problem for solution on the computer, it is important that you go about the task in a methodical and orderly fashion. You should develop a very fixed, very controlled approach to the solution of each and every problem you are assigned. If you rely on a *random* method, your chances of success will be diminished substantially.

Ultimately the solution of any problem will take the form of a computer program. However, writing the program (FORTRAN code) is one of the relatively trivial aspects of breaking the problem down into a well-defined connected series of easy-to-understand steps. This series of steps is called an **algorithm**. An algorithm defines in outline or schematic form how the problem is to be solved. It frequently takes the form of a block diagram where each step is expressed in simple English (not FORTRAN). Developing correct and efficient algorithms is a very important and sometimes difficult aspect of programming.

While solving a problem, you may easily become overwhelmed for several reasons. You may not understand the original statement of the problem sufficiently well. You may not have spent enough time analyzing the problem and breaking it down into more manageable (simpler) parts. You may not be sure of the data values involved or have used uninformative variable names to represent them. If you are like most beginning students, you will be trying to solve the problem all at once (proper code, correct logic, deck construction, equations, and so on).

All these difficulties can be avoided if you learn to tackle the problem one step at a time. Strategy comes first, details later. At various points in this text, we will identify a methodical and structured procedure for solving a problem. Later on we will tabulate these various recommendations, providing a precise and efficient approach to developing a program's algorithm. This is such an important part of your learning that we will use the following technique each time one of these special topics or recommendations is presented. The specific recommendation is stated below the heading "Programming Style." An explanation of the recommendation follows immediately.

Programming Style

Resist the temptation to start writing FORTRAN code immediately

Many steps are needed to properly analyze a computer problem. Writing FORTRAN code is the last step, not the first.

Unless a problem is very short, many steps are needed to properly construct an algorithm to solve the problem. Jumping in and starting to write FORTRAN code immediately (with the idea of straightening things out later) is a bad mistake. The time it takes to track down faulty logic and make several rounds of corrections far exceeds the time to develop the program algorithm correctly the first time.

The proper way to start a problem is to:

1. Spend a reasonable amount of time to get a clear understanding of the definition of the problem.
2. Familiarize yourself with the input to the problem and make sure it is compatible with the problem definition.
3. Attempt a hand calculation of the problem to define the logic and equations involved.

In the next programming examples, we introduce a number of recommendations, each concerned with getting a proper start in the development of a reasonably complex algorithm. Here are the first two recommendations.

Programming Style

Problem statement—don't start until you're sure

The first step in developing a program's algorithm is to make sure you understand what problem you are solving. Read the problem statement carefully—two or three times, if necessary. Do you understand all aspects of the problem? Has the problem been defined clearly enough? A problem that is clearly understood is well on the way to being solved.

Programming Style

Get a firm grasp on the problem's input

Part of a problem's definition is its input. The input and problem statement must be compatible. Organize your input as to name, type, and meaning (by table or comment statements) so that these details will not distract you when developing the problem's logic.

The next programming example shows the importance of these suggestions.

Programming Example
Blood Donor

Each record of an input data file gives information on possible blood donors. It gives:

1. Donor's name (15 characters maximum)
2. Blood type (a number code is used)
3. Donor's telephone number
4. Distance the donor lives from the hospital

Programming Example–Blood Donor continued

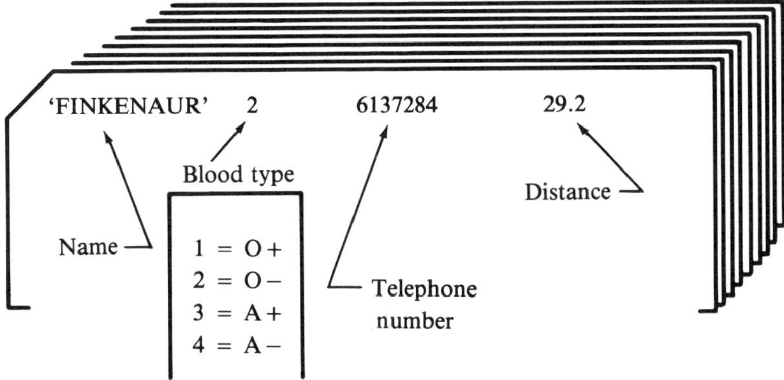

First Request: Write a program to search the data file for all people with O-blood who live within 50 miles of the hospital. Report the name and telephone number of all donors who meet these requirements.

Second Request: This program would be more general if it could be used to search for any type blood and if the distance limitation was allowed to be variable. To permit these improvements, assume that on each run of the program a record is placed at the front of the existing data file. It contains two values telling what type of blood to search for this time and at what maximum distance.

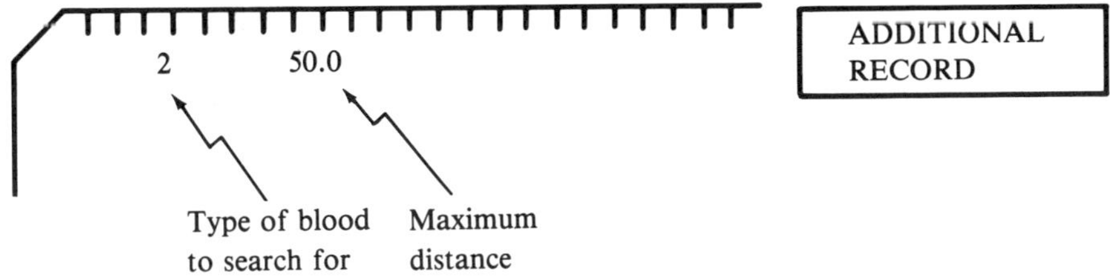

The complete input file now appears as follows

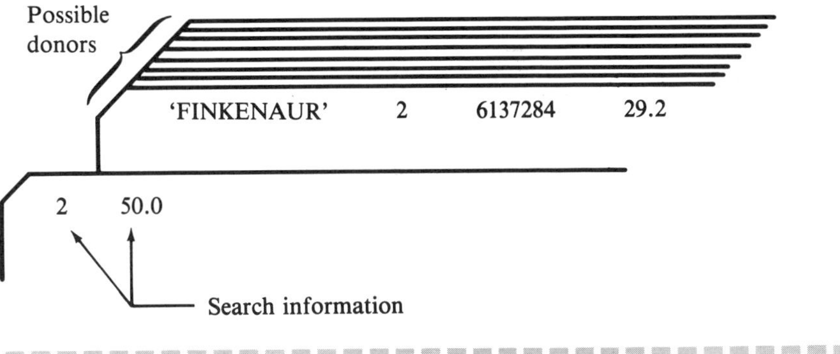

This is obviously not a trivial problem. It is not intended to be. Go back and read the problem statement (several times, if necessary). As you read, concentrate on understanding the problem and not on how to solve it (that comes later). Until you gain a degree of proficiency, limit yourself to a one-step-at-a-time approach and proceed in a relatively fixed pattern or sequence. Do not try to do everything at once.

If you find the Second Request difficult to handle, try the simpler version of the problem first. Think about searching just for O– blood at a distance of 50 miles from the hospital. Now try to generalize your understanding to handle the improvements that were suggested. Does the extra record at the front of the input file (containing the search information) bother you? If the answer is no, you are ready to move on to the next step.

Get a firm grip on the input data. Make sure the input is consistent with the problem definition. If there is no conflict, spend some time to come up with descriptive variable names for storing the data. Read these names over a couple of times so that you will not be distracted by having to look up a name while writing the general logic. Record all names in one place for easy reference. Any one of three techniques is recommended. These are shown in Figure 2.10.

Figure 2.10 Documenting input value

(a) Method 1 Table

FIRST RECORD
1 WANT desired blood type
2 MAXDST maximum distance
REMAINING RECORDS
1 NAME donor's name
2 TYPE donor's blood type
3 NUMBER telephone number
4 DIST travel distance

(b) Method 2 Sketch

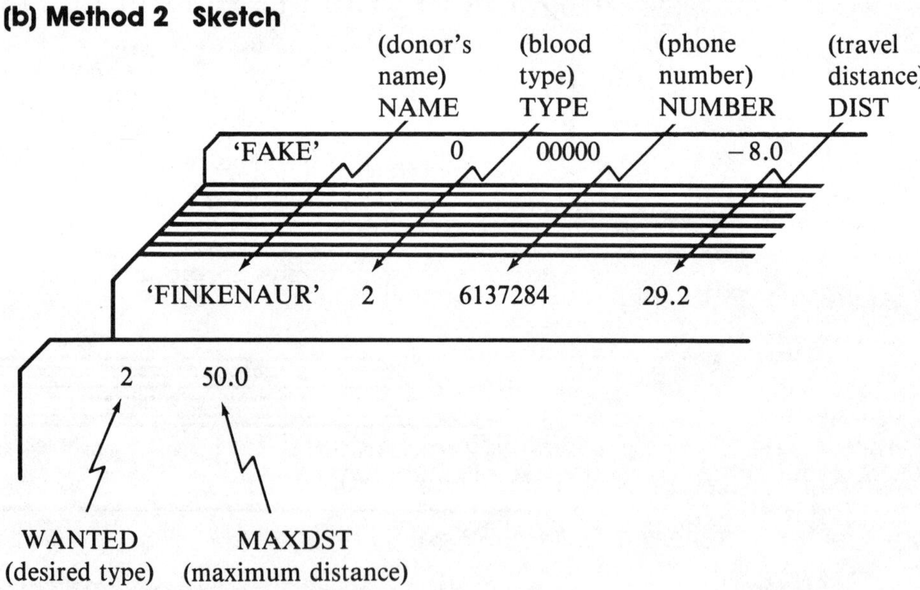

(c) Method 3 Comment Statements

```
C-----------------IMPORTANT VARIABLES------------------
C----WANTED  DESIRED BLOOD TYPE------------------
C----MAXDST  MAXIMUM DISTANCE SET-------------
C----NAME    DONOR'S NAME---------------------------
C----TYPE    DONOR'S BLOOD TYPE------------------
C----NUMBER  DONOR'S TELEPHONE NUMBER-----
C----DIST    DISTANCE DONOR MUST TRAVEL--
```

Some programmers like to set up a *table* that lists all the variables and gives a brief explanation of what each one means. An equivalent procedure is to make a *sketch* of the data deck displaying the same information appearing in the table. A final alternative is to use a series of *comment statements* at the beginning of the program describing each variable. This is the most popular method because it is an integral part of the program and does not involve an extra (external) item. Look at these methods and adopt whichever one appeals to you the most.

Now it is time to start thinking about how to solve the problem, but only in the most general terms. We want to identify those steps needed in the solution of the problem. This technique forces the programmer to subdivide the problem into smaller and therefore more manageable parts.

Programming Style

Pseudocode first:

- **Identify the steps**
- **Subdivide problem**

Attempt to break the problem down into simpler (more manageable) parts. Express these parts or modules in English, not FORTRAN. Think of the logic that would be used if the problem was to be solved by hand. Express each step clearly and in detail. (You don't have to be brief and to the point at this stage.) Number the steps and show how each can be reached. We call all this **pseudocode**.

An example of pseudocode is seen in Figure 2.11.

Figure 2.11 Pseudocode

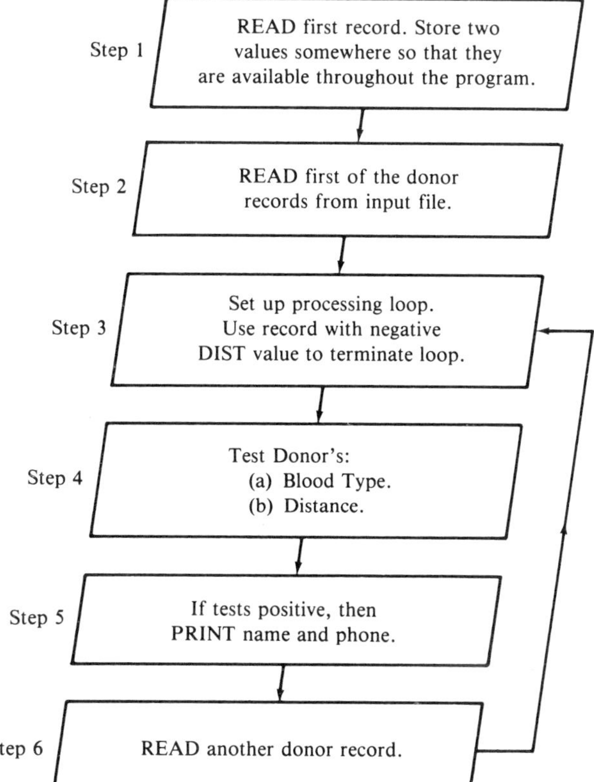

About this time the more advanced students are saying, "I could have the program written, keypunched and run in the time it takes to do all this." That is probably true, but what happens when the problems really get hard? We are trying to establish good habits and a style of programming that will stand up when the going gets rough.

Note that statement numbers in the following program correspond to steps in the pseudocode. Note also that comment statements with blank lines are used to clearly separate various blocks of code. Any technique that makes a program easier to follow is of value.

```
C.............................................................
C..    PURPOSE - SEARCH A DATA FILE FOR THE POSSIBLE BLOOD     ..
C..              DONORS WHOSE BLOOD TYPE AND PROXIMITY TO      ..
C..              THE HOSPITAL ARE AS SPECIFIED ON A LEADING    ..
C..              DATA RECORD.                                  ..
C.............................................................
C
C                 ---IMPORTANT VARIABLES---
C
C      --WANTED   BLOOD TYPE BEING SEARCHED FOR                     --
C      --MAXDST   MAXIMUM DISTANCE FROM HOSPITAL                    --
C      --NAME     NAME OF BLOOD DONOR                               --
C      --NUMBER   TELEPHONE NUMBER OF BLOOD DONOR                   --
C      --TYPE     DONOR BLOOD TYPE                                  --
C      --DIST     DISTANCE DONOR LIVES FROM HOSPITAL                --
C
       CHARACTER NAME*15
       INTEGER   NUMBER,TYPE,WANTED
       REAL      DIST,MAXDST
C
C      .....READ HEADER RECORD....SET SEARCH VALUES.....
C
   1   READ*,WANTED,MAXDST
C
C      .....SET UP LOOP STRUCTURE.....
C
   2   READ*,NAME,TYPE,NUMBER,DIST
   3   DO WHILE (DIST.GE.0.0)
C
   4      IF(TYPE.EQ.WANTED)THEN
C
   5         IF(DIST.LE.MAXDST)PRINT*,NAME,NUMBER
          ENDIF
C
          READ*,NAME,TYPE,NUMBER,DIST
C
       ENDDO
C
       STOP
       END
```

The following programming example shows how to deal with a table.

Programming Example
Car Insurance

Rate Table (cost per thousand)

Age	Good Driving Record	Poor Driving Record
Under 25	27.50	42.86
25 or older	20.80	30.00

Programming Example–Car Insurance continued

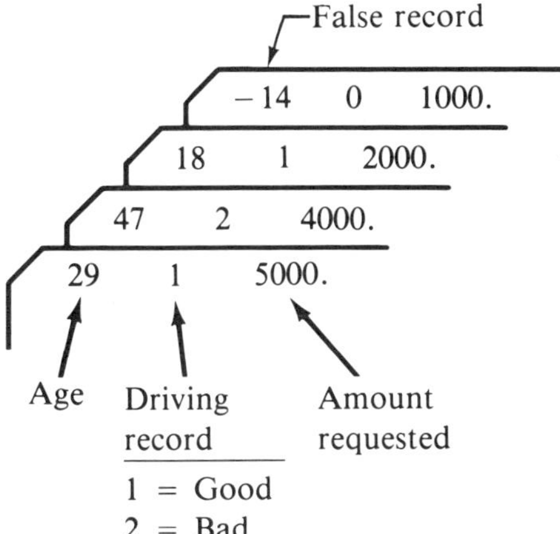

The cost of automobile insurance is based on two factors: age and driving record. The rates for drivers under 25 are shown in the top line of the rate table. The figures given are the cost for $1,000.00 of insurance coverage. Drivers with good driving records pay substantially less than those with poor records. Each record gives the age and past driving record of an applicant. The last value on the record is the amount of insurance coverage requested. Write a program to compute the charges to be made for the coverage requested.

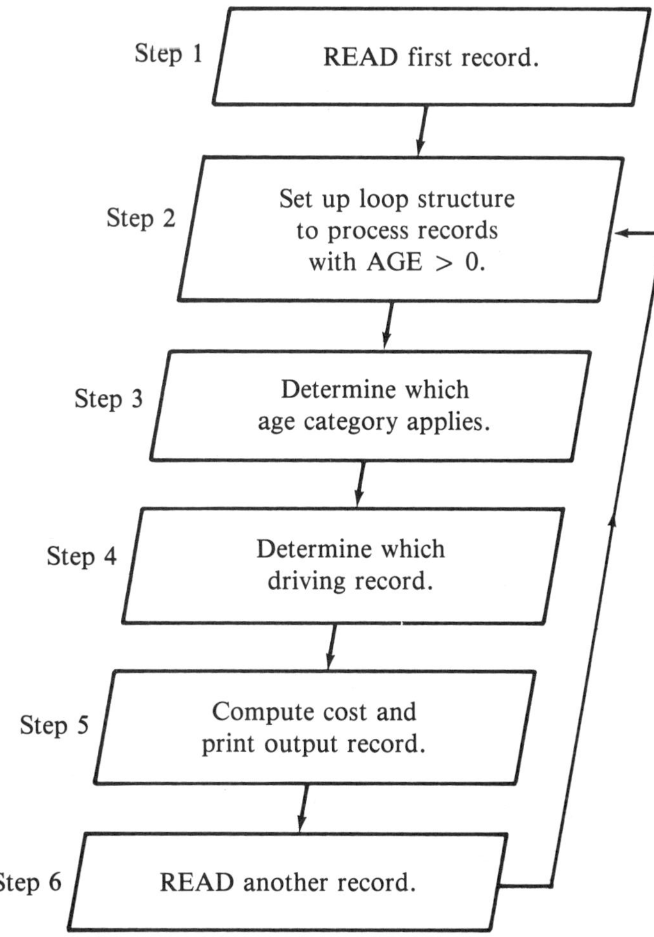

Programming Example–Car Insurance continued

```
C...........................................................
C..    PURPOSE - COMPUTE INSURANCE CHARGES USING A DOUBLE    ..
C..              ENTRY TABLE OF VALUES (AGE VS. DRIVING      ..
C..              RECORD).                                    ..
C...........................................................
C
C                 ---IMPORTANT VARIABLES---
C
C      --AGE      AGE OF DRIVER                                --
C      --RECORD   NUMBER OF PAST DRIVING RECORD                --
C                   CODE      1 = GOOD
C                             2 = BAD
C      --AMOUNT   DOLLAR AMOUNT OF THE COVERAGE REQUESTED      --
C      --COST     COST OF THE COVERAGE                         --
C
       INTEGER AGE, RECORD
       REAL    AMOUNT, COST
C
   1   READ*, AGE, RECORD, AMOUNT
C
   2   DO WHILE (AGE.GT.0)
C
   3       IF(AGE.LT.25)THEN
C
C              .....THIS SECTION APPLIES TO YOUNG DRIVERS.....
C
   4           IF(RECORD.EQ.1)RATE=27.50
               IF(RECORD.EQ.2)RATE=42.86
C              ..........................................
           ELSE
C
C              .....THIS SECTION APPLIES TO OLDER DRIVERS.....
C
               IF(RECORD.EQ.1)RATE=20.80
               IF(RECORD.EQ.2)RATE=30.00
C              ..........................................
           ENDIF
C
   5       COST=AMOUNT/1000.*RATE
           PRINT*, AGE, RECORD, AMOUNT, COST
           READ*, AGE, RECORD, AMOUNT
C
       ENDDO
C
       STOP
       END
```

Quiz 3 Programming Details

1. The computer does mathematics two ways, integer mathematics and real mathematics. Which is faster?
2. Some real numbers cannot be stored accurately. There is a truncation error. Why?
3. Does this mean that some computer-generated results will be inaccurate? How large will the error be?
4. Circle the integer constants that are improperly written.
   −19 18,200 $14.50 14.50
5. What does the term algorithm mean?
6. Describe one method to avoid confusion regarding the names you have assigned to the variables in your program.
7. What does the term pseudocode mean? What is its purpose?

8. Students want to start the solution to a program by immediately writing several lines of FORTRAN code and giving it a try on the computer. What is wrong with this approach?
9. An input record can contain numbers (like the radius and height of a cylinder). Can the record contain alphabetic information (like the name of a person)?
10. How observant have you been? When alphabetic information appears on an input record along with several numbers, how can we tell where the alphabetic information starts and ends?

Review Exercises

1. Describe the difference between compilation and execution.

★ 2. Does the computer execute each instruction immediately upon receipt or does it wait until all instructions have been received before executing any one of them?

3. How is your program ultimately stored in memory?

★ 4. What is the last card in the instruction deck?

5. Which type of records follow the instruction deck?

6. Describe what happens if the following instructions are given to the computer:
   a. `READ*,X`
   b. `Z = X * X`
   c. `PRINT*, Z`
   d. `STOP`

★ 7. Is it true that the computer normally executes instructions in the order in which they are given, i.e., sequentially?

8. What is the purpose of a branching instruction?

★ 9. Must all statements be numbered?

10. Why should any statement be numbered?

★ 11. Can two statements have the same number?

12. On a FORTRAN statement, what are the following zones used for:
    a. Columns 7–72
    b. Columns 73–80
    c. Columns 1–5
    d. Column 6

    Do these zones apply for terminal input?

13. What is a comment card?

★ 14. Do the zones described in question 12 apply to data records or can data appear in any column (1 through 80)?

15. Describe the difference between integer and real numbers. Which would more likely be used to store the velocity and acceleration of a particle in free fall?

16. Give two examples of an invalid integer constant.

17. Are constants restricted in their size? Why?

★ 18. What type of memory location would be used to store the flight number of an aircraft?

19. Is it true that the computer performs its arithmetic to an infinite degree of accuracy and, therefore, there is never any error in its answers?

20. Which of the following are valid real constants:
    a. \$108.54 b. 16 c. 1,167.2 d. 1.06×10^5

★ 21. The program deck consists of two parts. Name these two parts.

22. Give your understanding of what each of the following programming style recommendations means.
    a. Problem statement—Don't start until you're sure.
    b. Get a firm grasp on the problem's input.
    c. Pseudocode first:
       • Identify the steps
       • Subdivide problem

23. What is pseudocode and why is it used?

24. In writing a program you can sometimes make the mistake of writing the same variable name in several slightly different ways. How can this be avoided?

★ 25. What does the term word size mean? Do all computers have the same word sizes?

26. There is an upper limit on the magnitude of a real variable (10^{32} or 10^{75}, for example.) Under what circumstances could a number this large be generated?

27. What is the purpose of a coding form?

28. Are blanks allowed within a statement field?

29. What does the term algorithm mean?

30. For what reasons might a student sometimes become overwhelmed while attempting to solve a problem?

31. When writing pseudocode, why are the steps written in English and not FORTRAN?

★ 32. What is wrong with the way in which this instruction, the last line of an instruction deck, is presented?

33. You have written a FORTRAN program in which several statements have been written incorrectly. Describe how the compiler will handle this situation.

★ 34. A program is said to contain a loop. What does the term loop mean?

35. A program is being compiled and the END statement is reached. Describe what happens next.

★ 36. A statement is very long and will not fit on one line. Describe how to handle this situation.

37. What are some of the steps to be followed when initially formulating the algorithm to solve a problem?

Additional Applications

Note that the numerous programming examples at the end of each chapter are purely supplemental. They are intended to show the many ways in which the information learned in that particular chapter can be applied. Many areas of interest are covered. Select for study *only* those problems that parallel your area of interest. By all means, do *not* expect to follow each and every program presented.

Programming Example
Unit Cost

When purchasing an item sold by weight at the supermarket, it is sometimes difficult to know which item is the best buy:

Item	Price
18 oz.	$1.15
2 lbs.	$2.18
1 lb - 6 oz.	$1.80

To help the consumer, the government requires that all items sold by weight be labeled with a *unit cost* figure (price per pound).

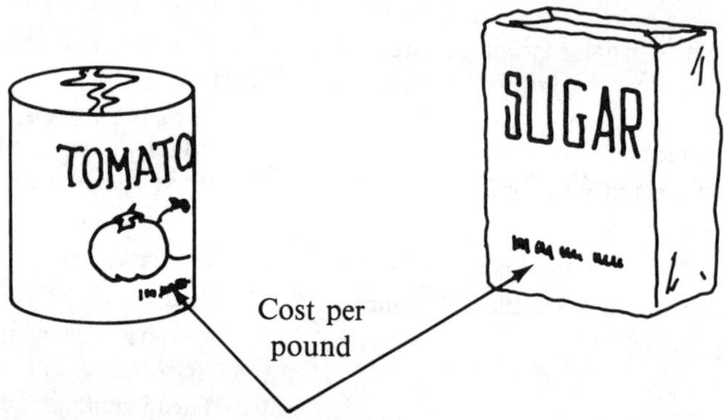

Each record of the input file gives the name (15 characters) and weight of an item (pounds followed by ounces.) The last two values give the total cost and inventory control number of the product.

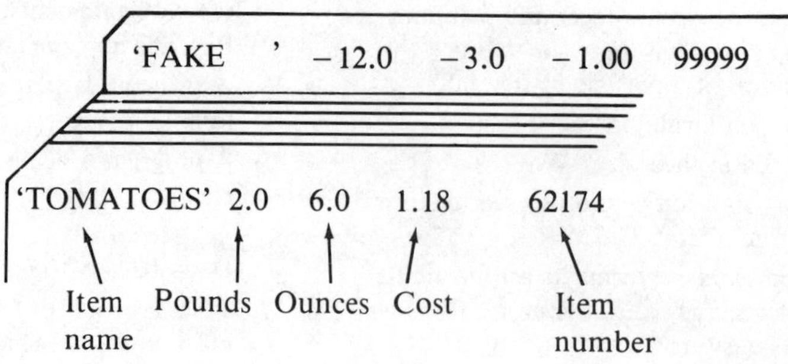

Programming Example–Unit Cost continued

Write a program to:

1. Convert the weight to pounds
2. Compute the unit cost (cost/pound)
3. Generate (as closely as possible) the output suggested

Item number	Item name	Weight (pounds)	Unit cost (pennies per pound)
62174	TOMATOES	2.375	49.68
62175	SUGAR	5.000	24.50
62176	FLOUR	10.000	13.33
62177	SALT	0.162	96.00
62178	CEREAL	0.500	84.00

```
C.......................................................
C..   PURPOSE - COMPUTE ...PRICE PER POUND... VALUE FOR   ..
C..             STANDARDIZED LABELING OF PRODUCTS.        ..
C.......................................................
C
C                ---IMPORTANT VARIABLES---
C
C     --NAME      NAME OF FOOD PRODUCT (15 CHARACTERS)     --
C     --ITEMNO    ITEM NUMBER                              --
C     --POUNDS    FIRST WEIGHT FIGURE (LBS)                --
C     --OUNCES    SECOND WEIGHT FIGURE (OZS)               --
C     --COST      COST OF ITEM (DOLLARS)                   --
C
C                 COMPUTED QUANTITIES
C
C     --WEIGHT    WEIGHT IN POUNDS                         --
C     --UNIT      UNIT COST OF ITEM                        --
C
      CHARACTER NAME*15
      INTEGER   ITEMNO
      REAL      COST,OUNCES,WEIGHT,UNIT,POUNDS
C
      READ*, NAME, POUNDS, OUNCES, COST, ITEMNO
      DO WHILE (COST.GT.0.0)
C
C         .....CONVERT WEIGHT TO TOTAL POUNDS.....
C
          WEIGHT=POUNDS+(OUNCES/16.0)
C
C         .....COMPUTE UNIT COST IN CENTS PER POUND.....
C
          UNIT=COST*100./WEIGHT
C
          PRINT*, ITEMNO, NAME, WEIGHT, UNIT
          READ*, NAME, POUNDS, OUNCES, COST, ITEMNO
C
      ENDDO
C
      STOP
      END
```

Programming Example
Credit Request

A bank allows customers to borrow money automatically up to a certain limit, and that limit depends on the individual's credit rating. The first record in an input file gives the account number of the person asking for credit. The remaining records identify all active accounts at this bank. Each record gives:

1. The number of an active account
2. Who that number belongs to (15 characters)
3. Any loans already made to that person
4. That individual's credit rating

Rating	Maximum Loan
1	$10,000.00
2	5,000.00
3	2,500.00
4	1,000.00

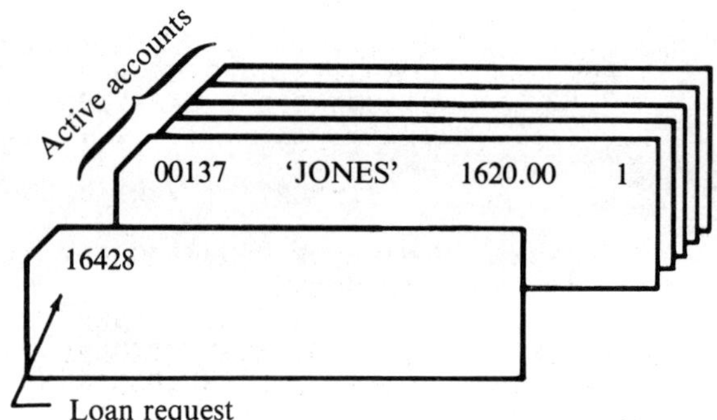

Search the data file for that particular account number. Determine how much credit already has been extended. Determine how much additional credit can be extended based on this individual's credit rating. The following sketch shows what variable names will be used.

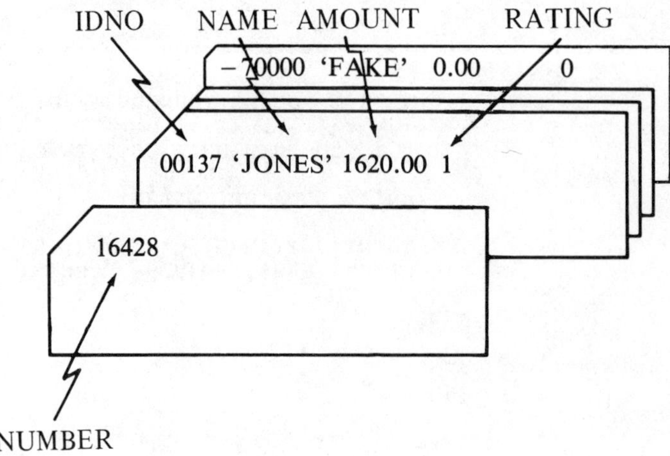

Programming Example–Credit Request continued

Make provisions for an *unsuccessful* search. Have a printout of the message:

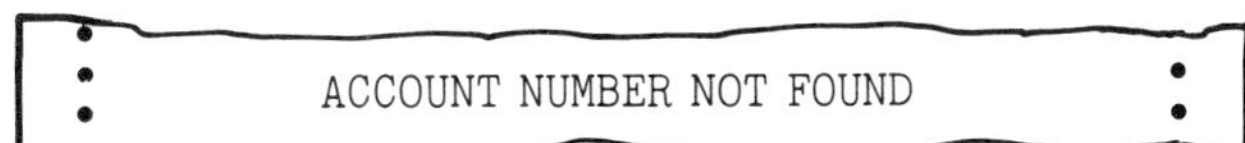

if the end of the data file is reached without a match in the two account numbers.

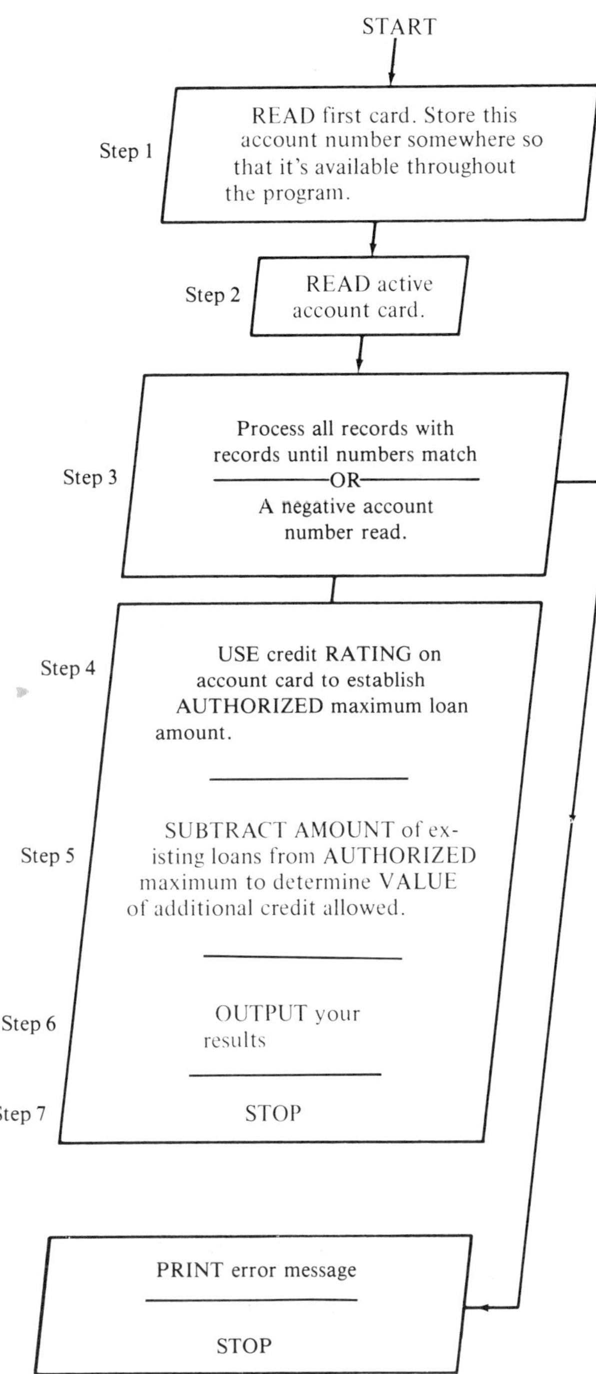

Programming Example–Credit Request continued

```
C.................................................................
C..    PURPOSE - SEARCH FOR A SPECIFIC ACCOUNT NUMBER AND       ..
C..              DETERMINE HOW MUCH ADDITIONAL CREDIT CAN       ..
C..              BE EXTENDED TO THAT PERSON.                    ..
C.................................................................
C
C                 ---IMPORTANT VARIABLES---
C
C      --NAME     NAME OF APPLICANT (15 CHARACTERS)             --
C      --NUMBER   ACCOUNT NUMBER OF APPLICANT                   --
C      --IDNO     INDIVIDUAL ACTIVE ACCOUNT NUMBERS             --
C      --AMOUNT   AMOUNT OF CREDIT ALREADY EXTENDED             --
C      --RATING   NUMBER OF CODE OF CREDIT RATING               --
C      --AUTHOR   MAXIMUM TOTAL CREDIT AUTHORIZED               --
C      --VALUE    AMOUNT OF ADDITIONAL CREDIT                   --
C
      CHARACTER NAME*15
      INTEGER   IDNO,NUMBER,RATING
      REAL      AMOUNT,AUTHOR,VALUE
C
  1   READ*, NUMBER
C
  2   READ*, IDNO, NAME, AMOUNT, RATING
  3   DO WHILE (IDNO.NE.NUMBER)
C
          IF(IDNO.LT.0)THEN
              PRINT*,'ACCOUNT NUMBER NOT FOUND'
              STOP
          ELSE
              READ*,IDNO,NAME,AMOUNT,RATING
          ENDIF
C
      ENDDO
C
C         STATEMENTS ABOVE CAUSE LOOPING UNTIL
C         CORRECT NUMBER IS LOCATED IF PRESENT
C
  4   IF(RATING.EQ.1)AUTHOR=10000.00
      IF(RATING.EQ.2)AUTHOR= 5000.00
      IF(RATING.EQ.3)AUTHOR= 2500.00
      IF(RATING.EQ.4)AUTHOR= 1000.00
C
  5   VALUE=AUTHOR-AMOUNT
      IF(VALUE.GT.0.0)THEN
  6       PRINT*,'AMOUNT OF ADDITIONAL CREDIT: $',VALUE
      ELSE
          PRINT*,'NO ADDITIONAL CREDIT ALLOWED'
      ENDIF
C
  7   STOP
      END
```

Programming Example Number Game

One of the nice features of using terminal input/output is that interactive (two-way conversation) is possible. We will use this feature to allow two players to participate in a number guessing game. In the program that follows, special print statements are used to instruct the first player to enter a four-digit secret number. These four digits are stored as N1, N2, N3, and N4.

Programming Example–Number Game continued

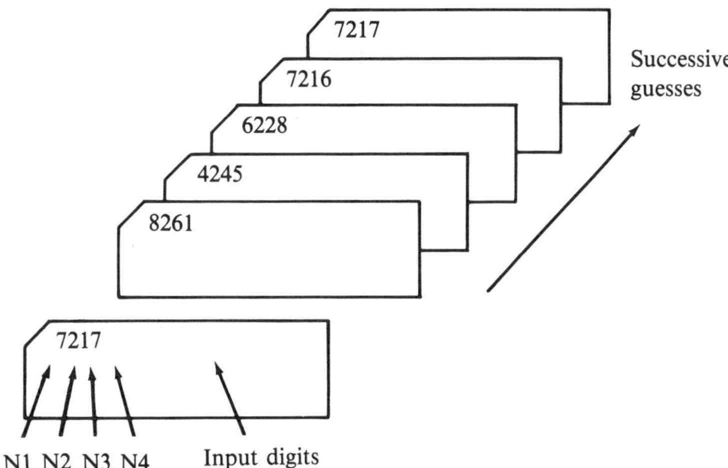

Instructions are then given to let the second player take over and attempt to guess the four-digit sequence. This player enters a guess which is stored as GUESS1, GUESS2, GUESS3, and GUESS4. A message will then be given for each digit:

```
YOUR FIRST DIGIT TOO HIGH-TRY AGAIN
YOUR SECOND DIGIT IS CORRECT
YOUR THIRD DIGIT TOO HIGH-TRY AGAIN
YOUR FOURTH DIGIT TOO LOW-TRY AGAIN
```

Play continues until all four digits have been guessed correctly. At that point a CONGRATULATIONS message is issued and the program stops.

```
C.............................................................
C..   PURPOSE - NUMBER GAME...GUESS THE FOUR DIGIT NUMBER      ...
C..             ON THE FIRST RECORD (UNKNOWN TO YOU )IN THE    ...
C..             LEAST NUMBER OF TRIES.                         ...
C.............................................................
C
C           ---IMPORTANT VARIABLES---
C
C     --N1,N2,N3,N4      FOUR DIGITS TAKEN FROM LEADER RECORD  --
C     --GUESS1,GUESS2    FOUR DIGITS REPRESENTING A GUESS      --
C     --GUESS3,GUESS4         OF THE ORIGINAL NUMBER           --
C
      CHARACTER PLAYER1*15,PLAYER2*15
      INTEGER   N1,N2,N3,N4,GUESS1,GUESS2,GUESS3,GUESS4
C
      PRINT*,'PLEASE TYPE THE NAME OF FIRST PLAYER'
      READ*,PLAYER1
      PRINT*,'PLEASE TYPE THE NAME OF SECOND PLAYER'
      READ*,PLAYER2
C
      PRINT*,PLAYER1,'TYPE IN YOUR SECRET NUMBER, BUT'
      PRINT*,'LEAVE A SPACE BETWEEN EACH DIGIT'
      READ*,N1,N2,N3,N4
C
C............................................................
C
      PRINT*,PLAYER2,'ENTER YOUR FIRST GUESS OF THE SECRET NUMBER,'
      PRINT*,'BUT LEAVE A SPACE BETWEEN EACH DIGIT'
      READ*,GUESS1,GUESS2,GUESS3,GUESS4
      DO WHILE(N1.NE.GUESS1  .OR.  N2.NE.GUESS2  .OR.  N3.NE.GUESS3
     1                    .OR.    N4.NE.GUESS4)
```

Programming Example–Number Game continued

```
C       .....LOOP STARTS HERE.....
C
C       .....CHECK FIRST DIGIT.....
C
          IF(GUESS1.GT.N1)PRINT*,'YOUR FIRST DIGIT IS TOO HIGH'
          IF(GUESS1.EQ.N1)PRINT*,'YOUR FIRST DIGIT IS CORRECT'
          IF(GUESS1.LT.N1)PRINT*,'YOUR FIRST DIGIT IS TOO LOW'
C
C       .....CHECK SECOND DIGIT.....
C
          IF(GUESS2.GT.N2)PRINT*,'YOUR SECOND DIGIT IS TOO HIGH'
          IF(GUESS2.EQ.N2)PRINT*,'YOUR SECOND DIGIT IS CORRECT'
          IF(GUESS2.LT.N2)PRINT*,'YOUR SECOND DIGIT IS TOO LOW'
C
C       .....CHECK THIRD DIGIT.....
C
          IF(GUESS3.GT.N3)PRINT*,'YOUR THIRD DIGIT IS TOO HIGH'
          IF(GUESS3.EQ.N3)PRINT*,'YOUR THIRD DIGIT IS CORRECT'
          IF(GUESS3.LT.N3)PRINT*,'YOUR THIRD DIGIT IS TOO LOW'
C
C       .....CHECK FOURTH DIGIT.....
C
          IF(GUESS4.GT.N4)PRINT*,'YOUR FOURTH DIGIT IS TOO HIGH'
          IF(GUESS4.EQ.N4)PRINT*,'YOUR FOURTH DIGIT IS CORRECT'
          IF(GUESS4.LT.N4)PRINT*,'YOUR FOURTH DIGIT IS TOO LOW'
C
          PRINT*,' '
          IF(N1.EQ.GUESS1  .AND.  N2.EQ.GUESS2  .AND.  N3.EQ.GUESS3
     1       .AND.  N4.EQ.GUESS4) THEN
             PRINT*,'CONGRADULATIONS....YOU WON'
             STOP
          ELSE
             PRINT*, 'PLAYER2,MAKE ANOTHER GUESS'
             PRINT*,PLAYER2,'ENTER YOUR NEXT GUESS'
          ENDIF
C
        READ*,GUESS1,GUESS2,GUESS3,GUESS4
C
        ENDDO
C
        END
```

This book is written for students who are *not* heavily involved in mathematics as well as for those who are. To that end, examples that require a degree of mathematical sophistication will be presented, but usually at the end of each chapter, and will be labeled with double asterisks. Each student should decide if that problem is appropriate to his or her career objectives.

Programming Example Quadratic Equation**

Write a program to find the two roots of the quadratic equation, assuming only equations with real roots are to be solved:

$$3x^2 + 6x + 1 = 0$$

After reading the statement of the problem, the programmer should recall the following equation that will yield the desired roots.

$$x = \frac{-b \pm \sqrt{b^2 - 4ac}}{2a}$$

Programming Example–Quadratic Equation continued

where: $a = 3$
$b = 6$
$c = 1$

This equation will in effect direct the writing of the FORTRAN code.

```
C.............................................................
C..   PURPOSE - DETERMINE ROOTS TO A SPECIFIC QUADRATIC      ..
C..             EQUATION.                                    ..
C.............................................................
C
      REAL A,B,C,XONE,XTWO,Z
C
C     .....ESTABLISH INITIAL VALUES.....
C
      A = 3.0
      B = 6.0
      C = 1.0
C
C     .....COMPUTE VALUE UNDER RADICAL.....
C
      Z=(B**2-4.0*A*C)
C
C     .....CHECK FOR REAL ROOT.....
C
      IF(Z.GT.0)THEN
C
          XONE=(-B+Z**0.5)/(2.*A)
          XTWO=(B+Z**0.5)/(2.*A)
          PRINT*,'XONE=',XONE,'XTWO=',XTWO
C
      ELSE
C
          PRINT*,'ROOTS ARE IMAGINARY'
C
      ENDIF
C
      STOP
      END
```

Common Errors

The use of the constants 3.0, 6.0, and 1.0 in the instruction portion of the previous program is highly undesirable. Using these values now limits the program to being able to solve only one specific quadratic equation. If you decide to solve a different equation, you must change several statements; the program must be recompiled and then reexecuted. Simply stated, your program would not be considered a *general* program to say the least.

Before writing any constant in statements that are part of your instruction deck (FORTRAN statements), make sure you are dealing with a true constant. By that we mean, does this value apply to each and every running of the program? If the answer is no, you are not dealing with a constant; you are dealing with a variable. Variables belong in the data deck. This means that the three assignment statements (defining A, B, and C) should be replaced by a READ statement. In this way, we define A, B, and C but in a way that allows the program logic to be reapplied to any number of quadratic equations, not just one. (See the next program.)

```
C.......................................................................
C..   PURPOSE - MORE GENERAL SOLUTION OF QUADRATIC EQUATION ..
C.......................................................................
C
      REAL A,B,C,XONE,XTWO,Z
C
C     .....READ INITIAL VALUES.....
C
      READ*, A, B, C
C
C     .....COMPUTE VALUE UNDER RADICAL.....
C
      Z=(B**2-4.0*A*C)
C
C     .....CHECK FOR REAL ROOT.....
C
      IF(Z.GT.0.0)THEN
C
          XONE=(-B+Z**0.5)/(2.*A)
          XTWO=(B+Z**0.5)/(2.*A)
          PRINT*, 'XONE=', XONE, 'XTWO=', XTWO
C
      ELSE
C
         PRINT*,'ROOTS ARE IMAGINARY'
C
      ENDIF
C
      STOP
      END
```

Common Errors

Beginning programmers sometimes use a sequence of assignment statements to define a series of variables and then execute a READ command that redefines these variables.

$$\left.\begin{aligned} A &= 3.0 \\ B &= 6.0 \\ C &= 1.0 \end{aligned}\right\} \quad \text{First assignment}$$

READ*, A, B, C   Second assignment

The READ statement overrides the effect of the three assignment statements. You should either use the first method (the assignment statements) or the second method (the READ statement), but it does not make any sense to use both. In all probability, you should use the READ only.

Programming Example
Linear Interpolation**

A sometimes troublesome calculation is to enter a table with a value that lies between the table listings. Finding the sine of 39.67 degrees from the accompanying table would be a typical example. Since the need to interpolate applies to trigonometry tables, log tables, tax tables, and the like, it might be appropriate to computerize the procedure. Write a program to accomplish linear interpolation between two tabular entries.

Before you start this problem, make sure you really understand the concept of **linear interpolation**. Values in the table represent known points on a curve—in this

Programming Example–Linear Interpolation continued

case the sine curve. Interpolation involves approximating the curve between the two closest known points with a straight line. Computing Y on this straight line for the input X value is accomplished by proportions and approximates the Y value on the curve.

Degrees	Sine
0°	.0000
1°	.0175
2°	.0349
3°	.0523
4°	.0698
5°	.0872
6°	.1045
7°	.1219
39°	.6293
40°	.6428
41°	.6561
42°	.6691
43°	.6820
44°	.6947
45°	.7071

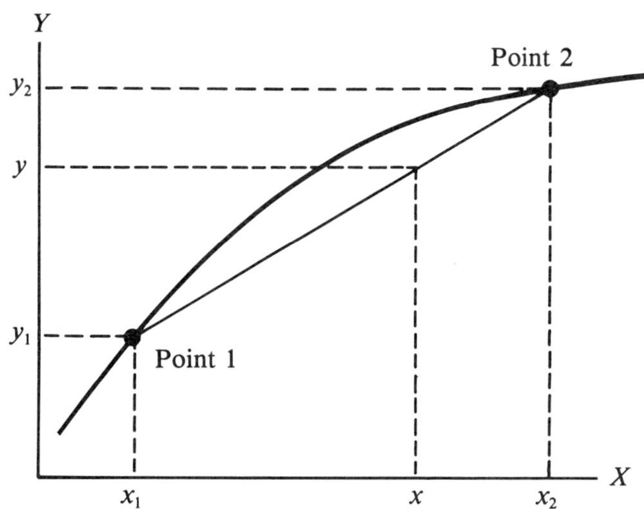

The next sequential step in the solution is to *clearly define the data values* with which you will be dealing. Having a weak or marginal understanding of these values will complicate matters later on when you attempt to set up your equations.

X	Input to the table
X1 Y1	Table values immediately above input value
X2 Y2	Table values immediately below input value

Select a sample set of input data values and show how they will be presented to the computer. Do not start with complicated input. Use the simplest values possible.

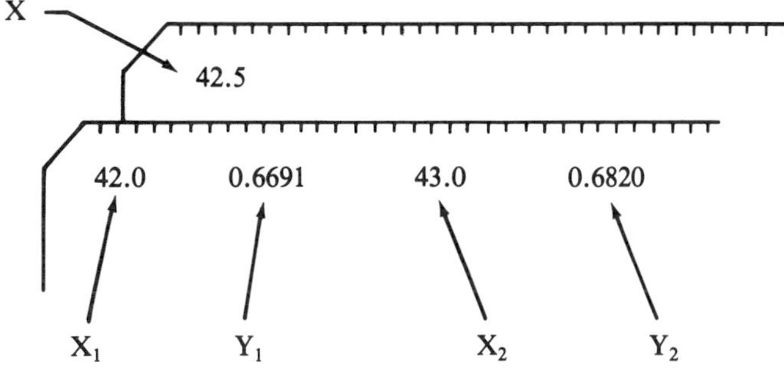

Sample test data

Programming Example–Linear Interpolation continued

After completing these initial two steps in the problem solution, if the logic is still not clear, try a hand calculation.

> **Programming Style**
>
> **If you are having difficulties, deal with a specific example—generalize later**
>
> Don't handle too many abstractions at once. Most students find it easier to define the logic of a problem if they deal with a specific example first. When this is completed, the algorithm can be made more general.

As you do the calculation, mentally talk out the steps you are taking. To demonstrate this, determine the sine of the angle 42.5° from the following input.

$$\begin{array}{ll} X1 = 42.0 & Y1 = 0.6691 \\ X\ = 42.5 & Y\ = ? \\ X2 = 43.0 & Y2 = 0.6820 \end{array}$$

1. I must first determine the change in X and the change in Y of the value listed in the table:

$$\begin{array}{ll} \Delta X = X2 - X1 & \Delta Y = Y2 - Y1 \\ \quad = 43.0 - 42.0 & \quad = 0.6820 - 0.6691 \\ \quad = 1.0 & \quad = 0.0129 \end{array}$$

2. The input value 42.5 lies what fraction of the distance between the table values:

$$\text{fraction} = \frac{42.5 - 42.0}{43.0 - 42.0} = \frac{1}{2}$$

3. I must now add ½ the change in Y to the initial table entry.

$$Y = Y1 + \tfrac{1}{2}\Delta Y$$
$$= 0.6691 + \frac{0.0129}{2} = 0.67555$$

Note that each step in the solution is a little easier to see when a specific example is being worked. Steps taken in this solution will suggest factors that must be accounted for in the general solution. There will be a close parallel between this solution and the pseudocode solution.

The final FORTRAN code can now be written as the last step in this slow but methodically developed algorithm.

Programming Example–Linear Interpolation continued

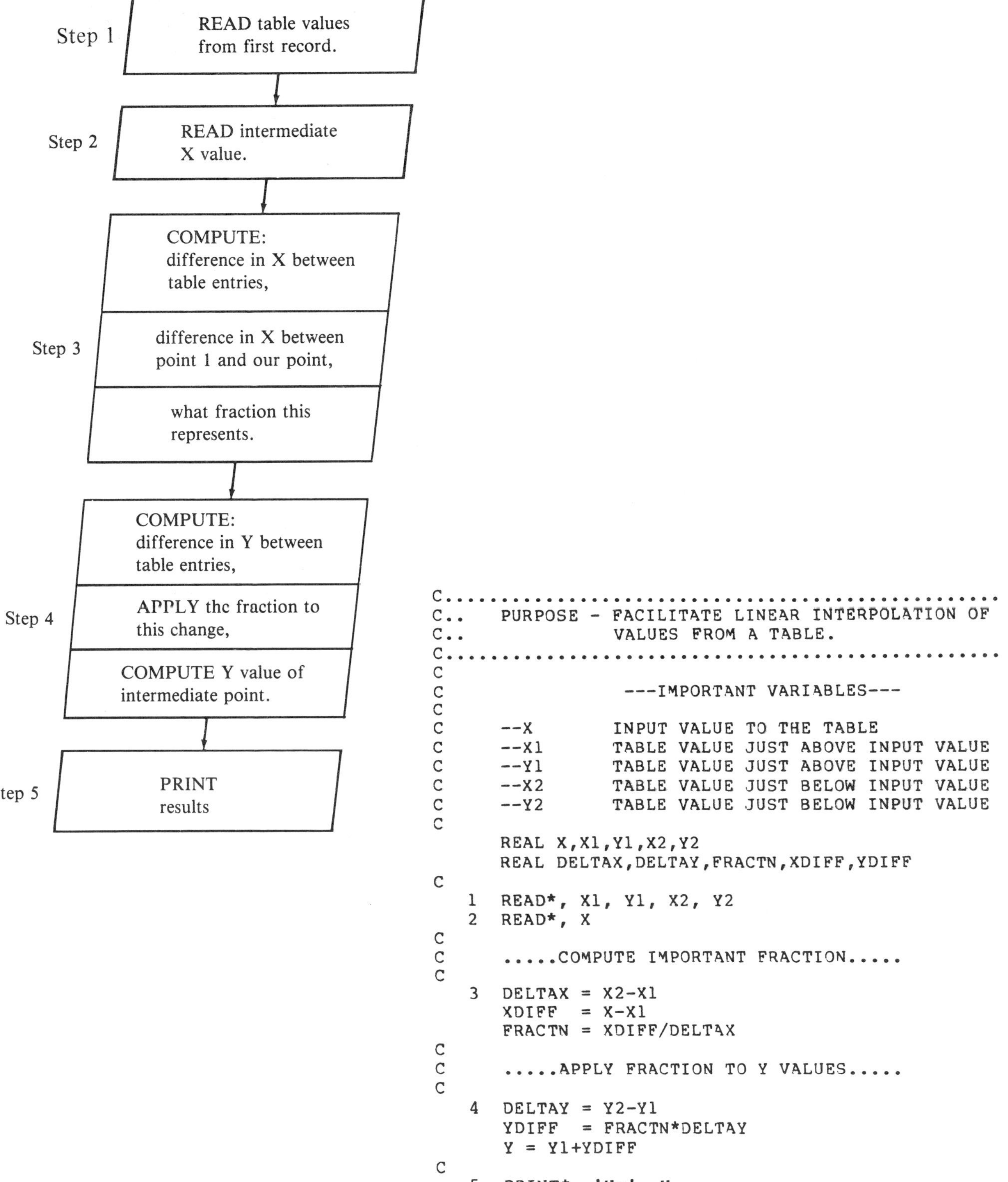


```
C.....................................................
C..    PURPOSE - FACILITATE LINEAR INTERPOLATION OF
C..              VALUES FROM A TABLE.
C.....................................................
C
C                  ---IMPORTANT VARIABLES---
C
C      --X       INPUT VALUE TO THE TABLE
C      --X1      TABLE VALUE JUST ABOVE INPUT VALUE
C      --Y1      TABLE VALUE JUST ABOVE INPUT VALUE
C      --X2      TABLE VALUE JUST BELOW INPUT VALUE
C      --Y2      TABLE VALUE JUST BELOW INPUT VALUE
C
       REAL X,X1,Y1,X2,Y2
       REAL DELTAX,DELTAY,FRACTN,XDIFF,YDIFF
C
    1  READ*, X1, Y1, X2, Y2
    2  READ*, X
C
C      .....COMPUTE IMPORTANT FRACTION.....
C
    3  DELTAX = X2-X1
       XDIFF  = X-X1
       FRACTN = XDIFF/DELTAX
C
C      .....APPLY FRACTION TO Y VALUES.....
C
    4  DELTAY = Y2-Y1
       YDIFF  = FRACTN*DELTAY
       Y = Y1+YDIFF
C
    5  PRINT*, 'Y=', Y
C
       STOP
       END
```

3 Arithmetic Assignment Statements

The next three chapters cover some of the details of the FORTRAN instructions used thus far. We delay the presentation of broad *program development* concepts until these details are out of the way. Your reading should become more deliberate and you should strive to gain a complete understanding of the topics presented. The overview phase has been completed. Adjust your approach to these chapters appropriately.

3.1 General Form and Operational Symbols

Take a look at the following equations:

$$\underbrace{Y = 2X - 12}_{\text{Explicit}} \qquad \underbrace{2X - Y = 12}_{\text{Implicit}}$$

Both express the same relationship between X and Y, but the equation on the left is more direct in showing how to compute Y for any given value of X. It is called the *explicit* form of the equation. FORTRAN arithmetic assignment statements must have this same "explicit" form. (If an arithmetic statement is to be generated from a mathematical equation, the equation must be in the explicit form, or converted thereto, prior to constructing the FORTRAN statement.)

The right-hand portion of the statement must explicitly define how the basic arithmetic capabilities of the computer are to be combined to determine a desired value. A single variable name must appear to the left of the equal sign (replacement symbol). It tells where in memory the single numerical value thus obtained should be stored.

$$\underbrace{\text{Y}}_{\substack{\text{Single}\\ \text{Variable}\\ \text{Name}}} \quad \underbrace{=}_{\substack{\text{Replace-}\\ \text{ment}\\ \text{Symbol}}} \quad \underbrace{\text{2.0 * X - 12.0}}_{\text{Expression}}$$

Arithmetic Assignment Statement

General Form	Variable Name = Expression
Example	Z = 3. * X ** 2. + 6. * X − Y − 12.
Invalid Example	X − 3.4 = Y Improper Form

Note that the expression is a sequence of constants, previously defined variables, operational symbols, and other parameters that define what operations are to be performed. In interpreting an expression, the compiler first looks at the operational symbols to determine what hardware component to use. It then looks to the left and to the right of each symbol to determine which constants or variables are to be involved in that particular operation. As you will soon see, however, the computer does *not* perform operations in the order of their appearance (left to right) in the arithmetic statement.

The following table shows a complete list of operational symbols allowed in FORTRAN. Each of these symbols has been used in previous programs.

Symbol	**Operation**
+	ADDITION
-	SUBTRACTION
*	MULTIPLICATION
/	DIVISION
**	EXPONENTIATION

Parentheses may also appear in arithmetic statements, but observe that they are not included in the list of operational symbols. The parentheses symbols, ( ), convey the operation of multiplication in mathematics, but not so in FORTRAN. Parentheses have a special clarifying function, the details of which we describe now.

3.2 Rules of Interpreting Expressions: Hierarchy of Operations

The purpose of any arithmetic statement is to express an equation in a proper and correct form to the computer. The FORTRAN standards demand specific rules for translating (evaluating) expressions, but allow each compiler to implement these rules in whatever way is most efficient for that particular computer. Accordingly, each compiler uses a different (and rather complex) *algorithm* for expression evaluation. The description that follows represents an oversimplification of that process. It is intended to make the interpretation process more meaningful from a programmer's point of view.

Sometimes the arithmetic statement and the equation it represents are almost identical in appearance.

Equation	Arithmetic Statement
$y = 6x^2 - 4x + 1$	`Y = 6. *X**2 - 4. *X + 1.`

At other times, the FORTRAN statement will be different. There are two reasons for this. One obvious reason is that the arithmetic statement must appear on *one continuous line*, whereas the equation does not. As a result, parentheses sometimes will be needed in the arithmetic statement that were not needed in the equation. The second reason is that the compiler gives preference to some operations (they will be accomplished first) while ignoring all other operations. Let us take a specific example.

Equation	Arithmetic Statement
$y = \dfrac{x + 6}{b - c}$	`Y = (X + 6.)/(B - C)`

To solve this equation, the computer must at some time perform the operations of addition, subtraction, and division, but *the order in which these operations are performed is important*. That is, in this equation addition and subtraction must take place first. Then and only then can division be initiated. Parentheses are needed to convey to the computer this desired sequence of operations.

This example calls attention to two things:

1. The order in which mathematical operations are accomplished is important.
2. Parentheses can be used to force certain operations to be performed before others.

All that remains is to learn in what sequence the computer normally performs mathematical operations and then to learn how to use parentheses to force an alternate sequence should it be necessary.

As we said before, the computer does *not* perform mathematical operations in the order in which they appear in an equation. Certain arithmetic operations take precedence over others. (There is a hierarchy of operations.) Stated briefly, all exponentiation (raising to a power) is accomplished first. Next, any multiplication or division will be handled. Finally, addition and subtraction are undertaken.

Order	Operation	Symbol
1st	EXPONENTIATION	**
2nd	MULTIPLICATION and DIVISION	* and /
3rd	ADDITION and SUBTRACTION	+ and –

The statement is scanned by the computer from left to right at least three times before processing is complete. Unless directed otherwise (by using parentheses), the operation of exponentiation is accomplished on the first pass. All other operations are ignored. On the second pass, multiplication and division are performed in the order of their appearance (from left to right). Finally, addition and subtraction are accomplished on the third pass.

Consider the following arithmetic statement:

```
Y = X + 6./B - C
```

Look familiar? It is the same arithmetic statement discussed earlier, but formed without parentheses! On the first scan, the compiler is looking for any exponentiation to be performed. None is required. On the second scan, it looks for any multiplication or division. When the / symbol is reached, the constant 6 will be divided by B. On the final or third sweep, addition and subtraction are accomplished. This means that the normal sequence of operations will interpret this statement to represent the equation:

$$y = x + \frac{6}{b} - c$$

Because this is clearly not the intended equation, parentheses are needed.

```
        Evaluated first
Y = (X + 6.)/(B - C)
        Evaluated next
```

Parentheses force the compiler to handle the equation in parts. Expressions inside parentheses are handled first. If there are several levels of nested parentheses, the expression in the *innermost* set of parentheses is evaluated first (inside out sequence). An expression inside parentheses is treated as a separate entity. It is "cleared out" as if it were the only expression present. In the preceding example statement, it will take three scans to clear the expression inside the left pair of parentheses. Another three scans are needed to clear the expression inside the right pair of parentheses. Finally, three more scans are required to process the expression as a whole.

In clearing the first expression, addition becomes the first operation to be performed. In clearing the second expression, subtraction takes place. In processing the expression as a whole, division takes place. This is a sequence that correctly expresses the equation we had in mind as shown in Figure 3.1. Omission of either or both sets of parentheses will result in an incorrect equation.

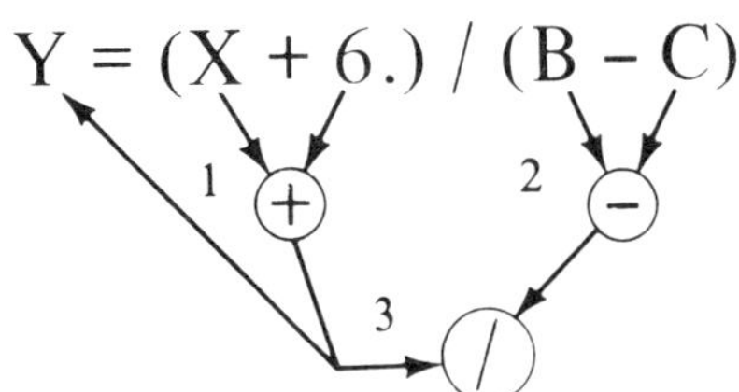

Figure 3.1 Forced sequence of operations

FORTRAN Arithmetic Statement	**Equivalent Algebraic Equation**
`Y = (X + 6.)/B - C`	$y = \frac{x + 6}{b} - c$
`Y = X + 6./(B - C)`	$y = x + \frac{6}{b - c}$
`Y = X + 6./B - C`	$y = x + \frac{6}{b} - c$

To express an equation, the following procedure is recommended:

1. Write the equation on *one continuous line*.
2. Include any parentheses that were part of the original equation.
3. Simulate the scanning (translating) process performed by the compiler as the statement is presently written.

Each time the normal hierarchy of operations is contrary to what is needed by your equation, add extra parentheses to force the proper sequence.

Are parentheses needed to make the arithmetic statement on the right properly express the equation on the left?

Equation	Statement
$y = x^{1/3} + 4.6$	`Y = X ** 1.0/3.0 + 4.6`

Remember, the answer is best found by "playing computer." As the statement now stands, the first operation to be performed is exponentiation (raising to a power). The compiler looks to the left and to the right of the double asterisk to see what numbers are involved: `X` and `1.0`. Hold it! That is not the correct power; it should be one-third. This suggests that parentheses are needed, namely to get the computer to divide one by three prior to raising to a power.

```
Y = X ** (1.0/3.0) + 4.6
```

Are parentheses needed in this example?

Equation	Statement
$y = \frac{6}{x^2 - 1}$	`Y = 6.0/X ** 2.0 - 1.0`

Without parentheses the first operation will be raising to a power and the value of x is squared (no trouble as yet). On the second sweep, the divide symbol is recognized and 6 will be divided by X square. That is not what we want, so parentheses are needed.

```
Y = 6.0/(X ** 2.0 - 1.0)
```

When In Doubt

Since parethneses are used for clarifying an expression, a good rule to follow is: *If there is any doubt as to how an expression will be read, use parentheses*! The presence of redundant parentheses does not affect the final result. The arithmetic statements:

`Y = A/B * X` and `Y = (A/B) * X`

both result in the equation

$$y = \frac{a}{b} \cdot x$$

> **Programming Style**
>
> **Parenthesize if it makes it clearer**
>
> When writing complex arithmetic expressions, some programmers will only use those parentheses demanded by hierarchy considerations. That is a mistake. If additional parentheses will make the expression clearer and easier to read, those parentheses should be used.

Test Data

The compiler can tell if you have a missing left or right parenthesis (unpaired set). It cannot, however, tell how many pairs of parentheses are needed by your particular equation. You are on your own. For this reason, it is important to test each statement with sample data values. Look at the equation and come up with a combination of input values that allows you to solve the problem in your head. For the statement:

```
Y = (X - 6.)/(B - C)
```

the test data might be:

```
X = 7   B = 1   C = 0
```

These values should give the result, Y equals 1.

Later, a more exhaustive range of input values should be used to make sure your equations will work under all sets of circumstances.

A program that is run without at least *three* sets of test data should be viewed with suspicion. Note, however, it is not the number of data sets that make for a good test but the *variation* of the data and the way it covers the range of the program variables.

> **Programming Style**
> **Test data are essential to every program**
>
> Just because a program has been compiled successfully and has given output values in no way guarantees the output to be correct. It must be verified using test data.

Two Operational Symbols

When evaluating any portion of an expression, the compiler looks to the left and to the right of any operational symbol to see what numerical values are involved. These values are called the **operands**. It expects to see a constant or a variable on either side—not another operational symbol.

Permitted	Not Permitted
`6. * B`	`A * - B`

Two operational symbols may not appear together. As shown below, parentheses are used to separate adjacent operational symbols.

Permitted	**Not Permitted**
`A * (-B)`	`A * - B`
`C/(-D)`	`C/-D`
`10. ** (+X)`	`10. ** + X`

Note that the operational symbol for raising to a power, **, is considered a single symbol, even though two characters are used to denote it.

3.3 Programming Examples

Not all programmers are required to deal with long, complicated equations resulting in wild arithmetic statements. For these people, the simple examples in the following table should be studied to firm up their understanding of the very important material just presented. More complex examples will be presented later, but are intended for math/science majors only.

Arithmetic Statement Examples

Statement	Meaning
`Y=A*B/C`	$y = \frac{ab}{c}$
`Y=A/B*C`	$y = \frac{ac}{b}$
`Y=A/(B*C)`	$y = \frac{a}{bc}$
`Y=A·B`	Not allowed—the • is an improper operational symbol
`Y=A(B+C)`	Not allowed—missing operational symbol
`Y=A*-B`	Not allowed—two operational symbols appearing together
`Y=(X-6.)**0.5`	$y = \sqrt{x - 6}$
`Y=X**2.-6*X+1.`	$y = x^2 - 6x + 1$
`H=X*Y*Z/A*B*C` `H=(X*Y*Z)/A*B*C`	$h = \frac{xyzbc}{a}$

Quiz 4 Understanding Arithmetic Statements

Part 1: Indicate which arithmetic statement is correct for each of the following algebraic equations:

1. $y = \frac{x^2 - 10}{\sqrt{x}} - 6$
2. $y = x^2 - \frac{10}{\sqrt{x} - 6}$
3. $y = \frac{x^2 - 10}{\sqrt{x} - 6}$
4. $y = x^2 - \frac{10}{\sqrt{x}} - 6$

(a) `Y=X**2-10./X**0.5-6.`
(b) `Y=(X**2-10.)/X**0.5-6.`
(c) `Y=X**2-10./(X**0.5-6.)`
(d) `Y=X**2-10./(X-6)**0.5`
(e) `Y=(X**2-10.)/(X**0.5-6.)`

Part 2: Examine the following arithmetic statements and indicate any errors they may contain:

5. `A=(B**3+4.)/-3.`
6. `Y=5.(X**2.5-1.)-4.`
7. `X-Y=3.*(X**2./3.)`
8. `Y=A/(B+C)**4+D)`

(a) Unpaired parentheses
(b) Missing operational symbol
(c) General form incorrect
(d) Two consecutive operational symbols
(e) Valid statement

Part 3: Indicate the *minimum* number of parentheses needed to express the following equations:

9. $y = x^2 - \frac{6}{x}$
10. $y = \frac{1}{x} + \frac{1}{a}$
11. $y = (x - 1)^{2/3} + \frac{1}{x}2 + 1$
12. $y = x^{3-z} + \frac{11}{a^2 + b^2} - 2$

(a) None
(b) One pair
(c) Two pairs
(d) Three pairs
(e) Four pairs

Part 4: For each of the following arithmetic statements, show the algebraic equation it represents:

13. `X=H**2-70./H+5.`
14. `X=H**2-70./(H+5.)`
15. `X=(H**2-70.)/(H+5.)`
16. `X=(H**2-70.)/H+5.`

The following table represents more difficult arithmetic statements and is intended for math/science majors.

Arithmetic Statement Examples for Math/Science Majors Only

Statement	Meaning
`H=X*Y*Z/(A*B*C)` `H=(X*Y*Z)/(A*B*C)`	$h = \frac{xyz}{abc}$
`X=(Y*(Z-6.2)/(Y+1))**2.`	$x = \left(\frac{y(z - 6.2)}{(y + 1)}\right)^2$
`Z=A**X/Y**2-B*C+1.`	$z = \frac{a^x}{y^2} - bc + 1$
`Z=A**X/Y**(2.-B)*C+1.`	$z = \frac{a^x c}{y^{(2 - b)}} + 1$
`Z=A**X/(Y**2.-B)*(C+1.)`	$z = \frac{a^x}{y^2 - b}(c + 1)$
`Y=((C**2+B)/(T/C-6.))**2-1.`	$y = \left[\frac{c^2 + b}{\frac{t}{c} - 6}\right]^2 - 1$
`Y=(X**(-2.)/(C+1.))/(X**2-C)-6.`	$y = \frac{\frac{x^{-2}}{c + 1}}{x^2 - c} - 6$
`Y=((C**(A+B)-1.)/(X**2-6.)**2)**1.4`	$y = \left[\frac{c^{a+b} - 1}{(x^2 - 6)^2}\right]^{1.4}$

One of the examples in this table is the statement

```
X=(Y*(Z-6.2)/(Y+1.))**2.
```

As can be seen there are two inner pairs of parentheses and one outer pair. In processing this statement, the inner parentheses will be cleared first. That is, `6.2` is subtracted from `Z` and `1` is added to `Y`. In clearing these inner parentheses, each expression is treated as a separate entity and is scanned three times looking first for exponentiation, then multiplication or division, and so on. At this point, the following values have been determined

$$Z - 6.2 \qquad \text{and} \qquad Y + 1$$

Next, the outer parentheses are cleared (again three sweeps). "Y" is multiplied by "Z − 6.2" and then division by "Y + 1" takes place. We now have

$$\frac{y(z - 6.2)}{y + 1}$$

Finally, with all the parentheses cleared, the remainder of the statement is scanned three times in the usual left-to-right fashion.† The only activity is on the first sweep where exponentiation is accomplished.

$$x = \left(\frac{y(z - 6.2)}{y + 1}\right)^2$$

† There is one exception to the "left-to-right" processing of operations at the same hierarchy level. Consecutive exponentiation operators are evaluated from right to left. `Y=X**4**2` is equivalent to `Y=X**(4**2)`.

Figure 3.2 illustrates the processing of this statement.

Figure 3.2 Sequence of Operations for X=(Y*(Z−6.2)/(Y+1.)**2

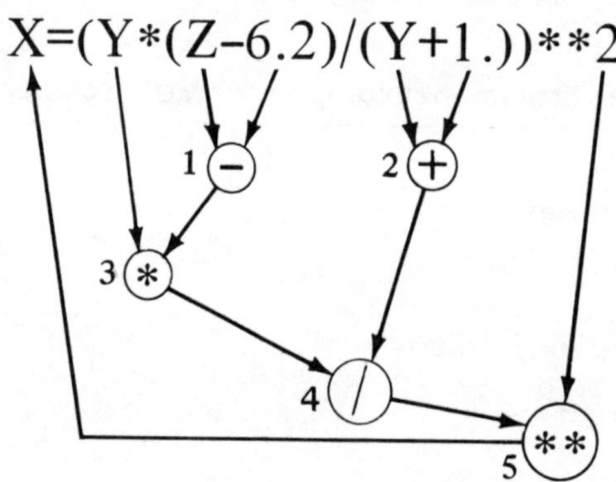

3.4 Naming Variables

In this chapter, the majority of equations have been written using single-letter variable names. When dealing with one equation having no more than two or three variables, single-letter variable names are possible. As soon as a problem takes on any level of complexity, an improved method of naming variables is needed. It is absolutely essential that the programmer be able to quickly recognize each variable in a program. The following table gives two possible representations of each of several equations. One uses highly descriptive variable naming, the other uses single-letter descriptions. Obviously, descriptive variable naming is preferred.

Descriptive Variable Naming

Equation	Single-Letter Naming (Discouraged)	Descriptive Naming (Preferred)
$a = \frac{1}{4}\pi d^2$	`A=1./4.*P*D**2.`	`AREA=1./4.*PI*DIAM**2.`
$v = \frac{4}{3}\pi r^3$	`V=4./3.*P*R**3.`	`VOL=4./3.*PI*RAD**3.`
$s = \frac{1}{2}at^2$	`S=1./2.*A*T**2.`	`SP=1./2.*ACC*TIME**2.`

In the following list of rules for naming a variable, note that there are two methods to distinguish *real* from *integer* variable names.

1. Names must not exceed *six* characters in length.
2. All characters must be *letters* or *digits*.
3. The *first* character must be a *letter:*
   a. If the variable type has been explicitly declared as `INTEGER`, `REAL`, or `CHARACTER` (by using an appropriate specification statement) no additional restrictions are placed on the first character.
   b. If the variable is not declared explicitly by using an appropriate type statement, an implicit definition is assumed. If the first character is I, J, K, L, M, or N, the variable is assumed to be an integer.
   c. Otherwise, the variable is assumed to be real.

A simple way to remember the I, J, K, L, M, or N group is to observe that they are bounded by I and N, which are the first two letters of the word INteger.

A variable name is used not only to identify where in memory a value has been stored, but also to convey *how* the value is stored. Because real and integer numbers are stored differently, the variable name must identify the mode of storage. *Integer* numbers are stored as you might expect, as a simple string of digits. *Real* numbers are stored in a more complex form: a string of digits representing a mantissa and a second string representing an exponent. The variable name identifies

1. An address
2. A mode of storage

The compiler uses variable names when processing arithmetic statements in the following way. The statement

```
A = 6.5
```

means, for example, "Store the value 6.5 in a memory location. Store the value in the real mode.† Identify the address of this memory location by the name A." The statement

```
A = B + C
```

means, "Obtain copies of the memory locations B and C. Interpret the contents of these memory locations as real numbers.† Add these numbers and store the results in a memory location to be called A."

This somewhat elaborate explanation has been given to help in the interpretation of the following statement

```
N = N + 1
```

It means, "Fetch a copy of the integer value stored at the address associated with the name N. Add 1 to this value and store the results of that calculation back in the memory location identified by the name N."

This example clearly shows that the symbol = does not have the traditional meaning of "is equal to." In FORTRAN, the symbol = is called the **replacement operator** and is understood to mean "is to be replaced by." For that reason, the statement N = N + 1 is interpreted to mean, "Replace the value stored in N with its former value plus 1."

The following table illustrates some correct and incorrect implicit naming of variables. It should be studied to reinforce the rules just presented.

Correct Variable Names	**Incorrect Variable Names**	
Integer Variables		Integer Variables
ITEM	K-5	(illegal character used)
MONEY	NUMBERS	(too many characters)
JOB	L(6)A	(illegal characters used)
LINE	6N	(first character not a letter)
N6	VALUE	(incorrect first letter)
Real Variables		Real Variables
DIA4	VELOCITY	(too many characters)
TIME	ASUM$	(illegal character used)
B1	NUMBER	(incorrect first letter)
ACC	4B	(first character not a letter)
	A60.	(illegal character used)
	X-RAY	(illegal character used)
	LENGTH	(incorrect first letter)

† In the next paragraphs you can assume A, B, and C have been declared as reals and N declared as integer (or you can assume implicit naming).

When groups of variables are related to one another, they may be given similar names. For example, the value of the velocity of a projectile may be computed at ten-second intervals for one minute. These values may be given the names

```
VEL0   VEL10   VEL20   VEL30   VEL40   VEL50   VEL60
```

Here the names are similar but not identical.

3.5 Explicit Type Statements

The previous section shows that FORTRAN permits the type of a variable to be defined in two ways: implicit definition or explicit definition. Implicit definition is sometimes considered the more convenient form of type declaration in that the programmer is freed from having to start each program with a series of specification statements, such as

		INTEGER CASES,BOXNO,X,Y
		REAL ITEM,MONEY,COST
		CHARACTER NAME*20,TOWN*15

On the other hand, explicit definition is gaining in popularity. By using a group of specification statements known as *type statements*, the programmer is free to use whatever variable name is most appropriate for the quantity at hand. There is no need to reject a name like MONEY because it starts with the wrong letter for the type of information it represents. More importantly, the use of type statements establishes a consistency of documentation in a program that is valuable. Anyone reading the program knows ahead of time where to look for a listing of the variables used by the program and a declaration of their data type.

Character variables *cannot* be declared implicitly. A type statement must be used. The general form of the CHARACTER statement is

		CHARACTER NAME1*LENGTH1,NAME2*LENGTH2, . . .

The reason that the length of a character variable must be specified warrants some explanation. Each computer manufacturer establishes the number of binary elements that are to be grouped together to store a single instruction. This is referred to as the *word size* of the machine. Once this size is set, the usual practice is to store a real or an integer number in this same modular space. For this reason it is not necessary to give a length size to real or integer quantities. When storing character information the situation is not the same. The number of elements needed to store the character string is dependent on how long the string is (number of characters in the string). It is therefore necessary to follow a variable name with the length of the string that name is to represent. In the CHARACTER statement

```
CHARACTER NAME*20, TOWN*15, WORD*8
```

the compiler will reserve sufficient space to store 20 characters of information and identify the space reserved as NAME. Two other strings of character information, TOWN and WORD, are set aside having lengths of 15 and 8 characters, respectively.

A variable can be declared in only one type statement. The name X, for example, could not be declared as both a real and a character variable. When you choose a variable name, do so with care. Use descriptive, meaningful names.

> **Programming Style**
>
> **Use highly descriptive names, and display them clearly**
>
> Highly descriptive variable names are one of the trademarks of a well-written program. They have been shown to reduce the error count in programs as well as the time required to track down errors. Once variable names have been selected, list them in a table or sketch for easy reference to ensure their proper use. (See Figure 2.10 for the suggested methods of documentation of variable names.)

3.6 Real and Integer Mode Calculations

Chapter 2 described the difference between integer and real numbers and the effect this difference has on the way in which these numbers are stored. This difference appears again in attempting to manipulate numbers in an arithmetic assignment statement.

The expressions shown in the following table result in typical real calculations. These calculations are performed to a high degree of accuracy because of the possibility of a fractional component. The result is a real number, which must be stored in a real (floating point) memory location to preserve the fractional component. This mode of calculation is more common than the alternate: integer mode calculation.

Real Mode Calculations

Expression	Result
4.08*2.2	8.976
3.69/3.	1.23
4.08*2.2+3.69/3.	10.206
10.9-2.*.45	10.0

An **integer calculation** is a simpler truncated version of real mode calculation in that digits to the right of the decimal point are dropped irrespective of their value. The result of this mode of calculation is an integer value. Because the digits to the right of the decimal point are truncated, some strange results occur when integers are divided. Even if the result of a division operation was supposed to be 8.99999, the value would be truncated to 8. Furthermore, this truncation can occur more than once in the evaluation of an integer expression. Several examples of integer mode calculations are shown in the following table.

Integer Mode Calculations

Expression		Result
5+3		8
2*6		12
33/5		6
3/2		1
4/3+5/4	=1+1=	2
16/3*(6/4+1/2)	=5*(1+0)=	5

Expressions in an arithmetic assignment statement should be written in a consistent mode. The expression should be real or it should be integer. Avoid mixing modes in an expression.

Quiz 5 Understanding Arithmetic Statements

1. In the following statement, two expressions would be described as "inner expressions" and one expression as an "outer expression." Identify these expressions

```
Y=6.0*((X-3.1)**2.+(X**1.4/3.0))**0.5
```

2. In the statement shown in question 1, which operation will be performed first? Second? Third?
3. Are the expressions identified in question 1 all written in a consistent *mode*? What is that mode?
4. Are real and integer values stored in the same way?
5. Describe the way in which the contents of memory locations X and C are affected by the statement

```
C=X+5.0
```

6. The statement

```
A=B+C
```

causes the computer to "Obtain a copy of memory locations B and C. The contents of these memory locations are interpreted as real numbers." What does this mean?
7. The statement

```
N=N-2
```

shows that the symbol = does not have the traditional meaning "is equal to." Describe what it does mean.
8. If N has the value 16 when the statement in question 7 is executed, describe in detail how the statement is interpreted.
9. The following variable names are identical except for one character.

```
TIME10  TIME20  TIME 30  TIME40
```

Does that mean each variable will still be assigned a different location in memory?
10. When defining the mode of a variable, which definition overrides, the implicit or explicit definition?

3.7 Keeping Topics in Perspective

This chapter has covered some of the finer details of constructing arithmetic assignment statements. Unfortunately these details are an unavoidable aspect of any computer language. Don't let these details divert your attention from the more important task you face, namely the task of developing the master strategy for solving problems on a digital computer. With this in mind, we conclude this chapter with an example program.

Programming Example
Temperature Conversion

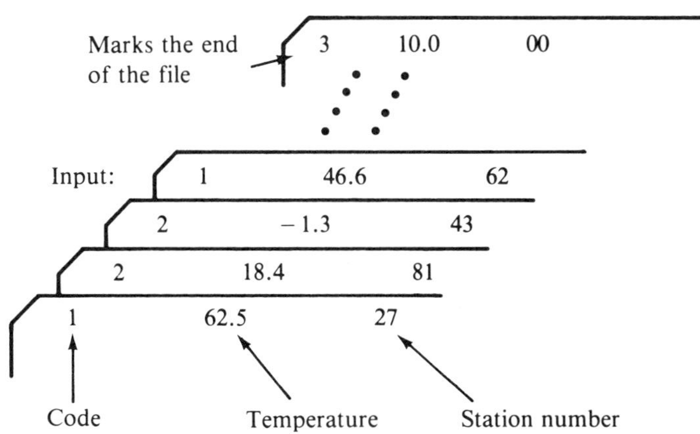

The temperatures at various weather stations are recorded by the data records shown. Unfortunately, some of the temperatures are reported in degrees Fahrenheit and others are reported in degrees Celsius. The first digit on each record tells which value is being reported (1 = Fahrenheit, 2 = Celsius). A record has been placed at the end of the data file using a digit 3 to signal the end of the file. Write a program to report all the temperatures in both degrees Fahrenheit and degrees Celsius. Make the output of the program look as close as possible to the output shown.

As part of this problem, identify several "test" temperatures to be used in determining if the arithmetic assignment statements used in the program are functioning correctly. The governing equations are

$$F = 1.8C + 32.0 \quad \text{and} \quad C = \frac{5}{9}(F - 32.0)$$

Output

```
STATION 27  FAHRENHEIT = 62.5  CELSIUS = 17.5
STATION 81  FAHRENHEIT = 65.1  CELSIUS = 18.4
STATION 43  FAHRENHEIT = 29.7  CELSIUS = -1.3
STATION 62  FAHRENHEIT = 46.6  CELSIUS =  8.0
```

```
C..............................................................
C..   PURPOSE - READ TEMPERATURES IN DEGREES FAHRENHEIT OR    ..
C..             DEGREES CELSIUS. REPORT TEMPERATURES IN       ..
C..             BOTH FORMS.                                   ..
C..............................................................
C
C                 ---IMPORTANT VARIABLES---
C
C     --CODE      A CODE TELLING WHICH TEMPERATURE IS GIVEN    --
C                      1 = FAHRENHEIT      2 = CELSIUS
C     --VALUE     TEMPERATURE AS PROVIDED ON INPUT RECORD      --
C     --CELSUS    COMPUTED TEMPERATURE (DEGREES CELSIUS)       --
C     --FARNHT    COMPUTED TEMPERATURE (DEGREES FAHRENHEIT)    --
C     --STATION   STATION NUMBER                               --
C
      INTEGER CODE,STATION
      REAL    VALUE,CELSUS,FARNHT
C
      READ*, CODE, VALUE, STATION
      DO WHILE (CODE.NE.3)
C
C        .....WHICH TEMPERATURE IS BEING REPORTED.....
C
```

Programming Example–Temperature Conversion continued

```
         IF(CODE.EQ.1)THEN
C
C           *****VALUE IN DEGREES FHARENHEIT*****
C
            CELSUS=5.0/9.0*(VALUE-32.0)
            FARNHT=VALUE
C
         ELSE
C
C           *****VALUE IN DEGREES CELSIUS*****
C
            FARNHT=1.8*VALUE+32.0
            CELSUS=VALUE
C
         ENDIF
C
         PRINT*,'STATION',STATION,'FAHRENHEIT=',FARNHT,'CELSIUS=',CELSUS
C
         READ*, CODE, VALUE, STATION
C
      ENDDO
C
      STOP
      END
```

Common Error

A student who has had difficulty compiling a program and has had to make numerous corrections goes into orbit when some output finally appears on the output sheet. While it is true that the end of the program is in sight, there is one more important step to take. Send some test data through your program.

In the program just written, two arithmetic statements were written. The equation for CELSUS requires one set of parentheses. What would happen if the parentheses were omitted? The compiler could not detect that error; you have to. Using 32° F and 212° F as sample test data should generate 0.0° C and 100° C as output. Using 0.0° C and 100° C should generate 32° F and 212° F. It all looks so simple, yet it is extremely important.

Quiz 6 Writing a Program

Write a program that will determine which way a beam will rotate when two weights are placed on the beam as shown.

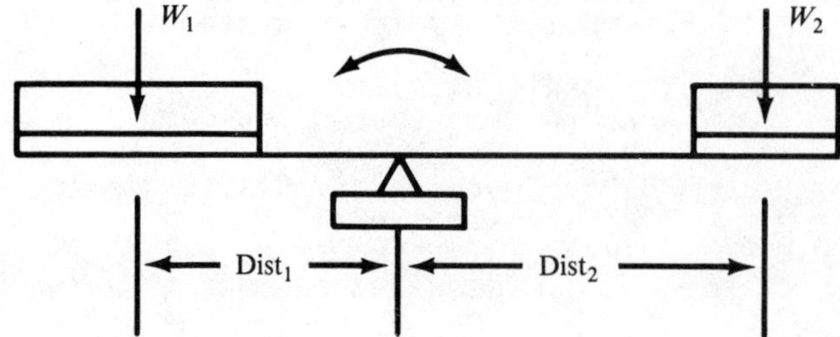

The program should print one of the following three messages:

```
BEAM WILL ROTATE CLOCKWISE
BEAM WILL ROTATE COUNTERCLOCKWISE
BEAM WILL BALANCE
```

INPUT FILE

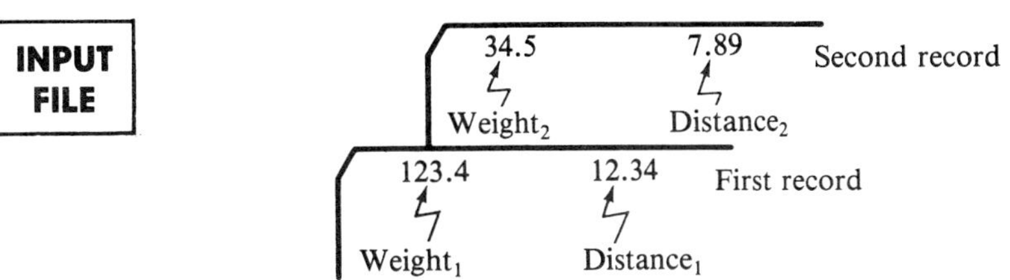


```
C       PURPOSE - DETERMINE WHICH WAY BEAM WILL ROTATE.
C
C
C                ----IMPORTANT VARIABLES----
C
C     -WT1      MAGNITUDE OF WEIGHT 1
C     -DIST1    DISTANCE FROM FULCRUM
C     -MOMNT1   MOMENT CAUSED BY WEIGHT 1
C
C     -WT2      MAGNITUDE OF WEIGHT 2
C     -DIST2    DISTANCE FROM FULCRUM
C     -MOMNT2   MOMENT CAUSED BY WEIGHT 2
C
        REAL WT1, DIST1, MOMNT1, WT2, DIST2, MOMNT2
C
        READ*, WT1, DIST1
        READ*, WT2, DIST2
C
        MOMNT1 = WT1 * DIST1
        MOMNT2 = WT2 * DIST2
C
C       .....WHICH MOMENT IS LARGER?.....
C
        IF(MOMNT1.GT.MOMNT2)PRINT*,'BEAM ROTATES COUNTERCLOCKWISE'
        IF(MOMNT1.EQ.MOMNT2)PRINT*,'BEAM WILL BALANCE'
        IF(MOMNT1.LT.MOMNT2)PRINT*,'BEAM ROTATES CLOCKWISE'
C
        STOP
        END
```

Test Data

WT1 = 100 WT2 = 120
DIST 1 = 10 DIST2 = 10

Review Exercises

The left-hand column contains numbered questions or examples. The right-hand column contains lettered answers or comments. One or two items in the right-hand column can apply to any given item in the left-hand column. Read the numbered question and choose the correctly lettered answer(s).

Part A: Identify the following FORTRAN quantities assuming implicit naming of variables:

★ 1. `0.`
2. `0.6`
3. `A3`
★ 4. `13`
5. `A1.`
6. `23`
★ 7. `23.`
8. `NUM`
9. `VALUE`
★ 10. `3,582.`

(a) Real constant
(b) Real variable
(c) Integer constant
(d) Integer variable
(e) Unacceptable

Part B: Most of the following integer names are unacceptable. Indicate in each case the error(s), if any.

★ 11. `1-6`
12. `6I`
★ 13. `I6`
14. `VALUE`
★ 15. `MVALUES`
16. `LOGF`
★ 17. `(X)`

(a) Valid name—acceptable
(b) Invalid—too many characters
(c) Invalid—illegal character
(d) Invalid—incorrect first character
(e) None of these

Part C: Most of the following real names are unacceptable. Indicate in each case the error(s), if any.

18. `ZTWO`
★ 19. `Z2`
20. `2Z`
★ 21. `2/Z`
22. `Z2,3`

(a) Valid name—acceptable
(b) Invalid—too many characters
(c) Invalid—illegal character
(d) Invalid—incorrect first character
(e) None of these

Part D: Each of the following FORTRAN statements contains at least one error. Indicate the error(s).

23. `Y=(A+3.)/X**-2`
24. `Y=X**2/3.+M`
★ 25. `I=(X-Y)(B+7.)`
26. `Y=(A3,7-B2)/(B67)`
27. `P=π*R**2`
★ 28. `Y=((W+X)/(Y2+Z-1)`
29. `Y-1.=C`
★ 30. `2.=A+B**2/3.`

(a) Mixed mode
(b) Missing operational symbol
(c) Invalid variable name
(d) Unpaired parenthesis
(e) None of these

Part E: Given J = 10; K = 2; X = 10.; Z = 2. Indicate the result of the following FORTRAN calculation:

31. `I=J/K+2/3`
★ 32. `B=J/K+2/3`
33. `I=X/Z+2./3.`
34. `Y=X/Z+2./3.`
★ 35. `I=J/Z+2./3`
36. `I=J/K*(5/3*6/4)`
37. `Y=J/K*(B/3*6/4)`
★ 38. `Y=X/Z*(3./10.)*3.`

(a) 5
(b) 5.0000
(c) 4.5
(d) 5.6666
(e) Not allowed

Part F: What is the minimum number of parentheses needed to express the following equations in a FORTRAN arithmetic statement?

39. $y = \dfrac{x^2 - 6}{x + 1} - 1$

★ 40. $y = \dfrac{1}{2}(x - 6) + \dfrac{x}{2}$

41. $y = x^2 - \dfrac{6}{x} + 1$

42. $y = x^{-3} - 6x^{-2} + 3$

43. $y = 10 - \dfrac{a}{b}\sin(90° - c)$

★ 44. $y = \sqrt{b^2 - 4ac}$

(a) None
(b) One pair
(c) Two pairs
(d) Three pairs
(e) Four pairs

Part G: Provide brief responses to the following questions:

45. Describe the normal hierarchy of performing arithmetic operations.

★ 46. Parentheses are not included in the table of arithmetic operators. Why?

47. What are the two reasons an equation and its arithmetic assignment statement are different?

★ 48. If an arithmetic statement has several nested expressions (one expression contained within another), which expression is evaluated first?

49. If several pairs of redundant parentheses are used in a statement, will this have a detrimental effect?

50. What is to be gained by using test data on a program?

★ 51. Two operational symbols cannot appear together. How do you avoid this?

52. In the statement

```
Z=A**X/(Y**2.-B)*(C+1.)
```

describe the sequence in which arithmetic operations are performed. How many scans are needed to completely process the statement?

Additional Applications

Programming Example
Computing Interest

A bank is offering 5% interest rates on all deposits. The following illustrates the increase in value a $1,000.00 account would experience over a four-year period.

YEAR	PRINCIPAL	(1 + RATE)$^{\text{No. of Years}}$	=	TOTAL
1	$1000.00	$(1 + 0.05)^1$	=	$1050.00
2	$1000.00	$(1 + 0.05)^2$	=	$1102.50
3	$1000.00	$(1 + 0.05)^3$	=	$1157.63
4	$1000.00	$(1 + 0.05)^4$	=	$1215.51

The first six records of an input file give the rates offered by different banks in our local area. Read these values and for each, produce a table similar to the one shown.

Input:

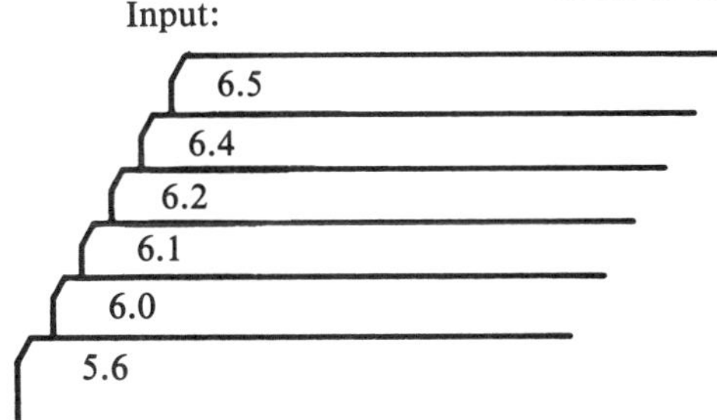

Output:

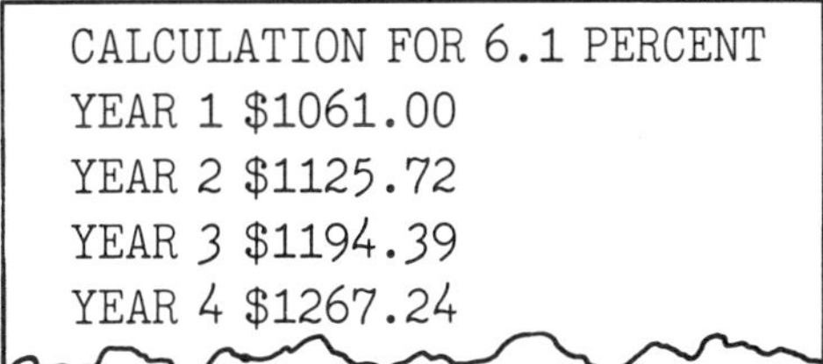

Programming Example–Computing Interest continued

Money market funds give substantially higher interest, but are not insured. The next six records list the rates being offered by this type of investment. Read these values and produce the appropriate tables. Put a heading at the top of this group of tables indicating these are MONEY MARKET RATES.

Input:

```
14.0
13.5
13.0
12.3
11.5
10.0
```

Output:

```
CALCULATION FOR 10.0 PERCENT
YEAR 1 $1100.00
YEAR 2 $1210.00
YEAR 3 $1331.00
YEAR 4 $1464.10
```

```
C.............................................................
C..   PURPOSE - COMPUTE GROWTH OF $1,000.00 OVER FOUR YEAR   ..
C..             PERIOD AT VARIOUS INTEREST RATES.            ..
C.............................................................
C
C                   ---IMPORTANT VARIABLES---
C
C     --TABLE     INTEGER TELLING WHICH TABLE IS BEING
C                 GENERATED                                  --
C     --RATE      INTEREST RATE READ FROM DATA               --
C     --VALUE1    VALUE OF PRINCIPAL AT END YEAR ONE         --
C     --VALUE2    VALUE OF PRINCIPAL AT END YEAR TWO         --
C     --VALUE3    VALUE OF PRINCIPAL AT END YEAR THREE       --
C     --VALUE4    VALUE OF PRINCIPAL AT END YEAR FOUR        --
C
      INTEGER TABLE
      REAL    RATE,VALUE1,VALUE2,VALUE3,VALUE4
C
      DO 40 TABLE=1,12,1
          READ*, RATE
C
C         .....TEST FOR SPECIAL HEADING.....
C
          IF(TABLE.EQ.7)THEN
              PRINT*,' '
              PRINT*,'        MONEY MARKET RATES'
              PRINT*,' '
          ENDIF
C
C         .....PRINT HEADING SHOWING RATE.....
C
          PRINT*,'CALCULATION FOR',RATE,'PERCENT'
C
C         .....APPLY INTEREST EQUATION.....
C
          VALUE1=1000.00*(1.0+RATE/100.)**1
          VALUE2=1000.00*(1.0+RATE/100.)**2
          VALUE3=1000.00*(1.0+RATE/100.)**3
          VALUE4=1000.00*(1.0+RATE/100.)**4
C
C         .....OUTPUT ALL VALUES.....
C
          PRINT*,'YEAR 1 $',VALUE1
          PRINT*,'YEAR 2 $',VALUE2
          PRINT*,'YEAR 3 $',VALUE3
          PRINT*,'YEAR 4 $',VALUE4
C
40    CONTINUE
C
      STOP
      END
```

Programming Example
Volume of Tray

A baking pan is to be made from a piece of sheet metal that measures 17″ by 22″. A square cut is to be made at all four corners and the piece folded as shown. The resulting dimensions of the pan are as shown. Two possible values of x (the square cutouts) are being considered. Read these values from data.

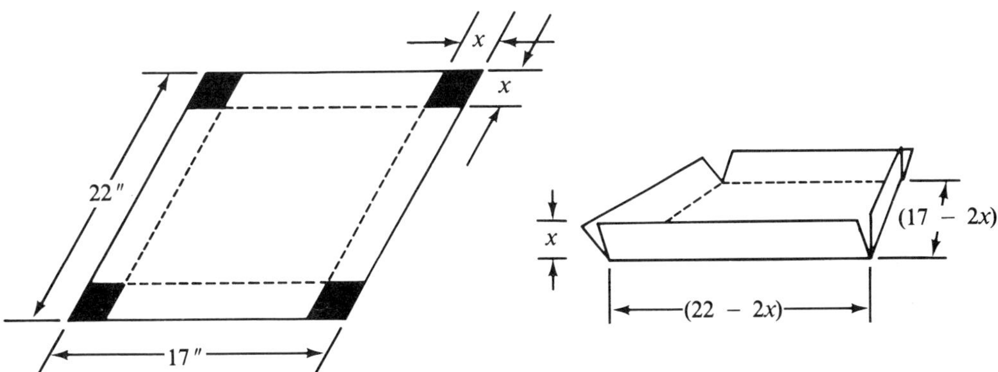

Determine and report which value of x produces the larger volume baking pan.

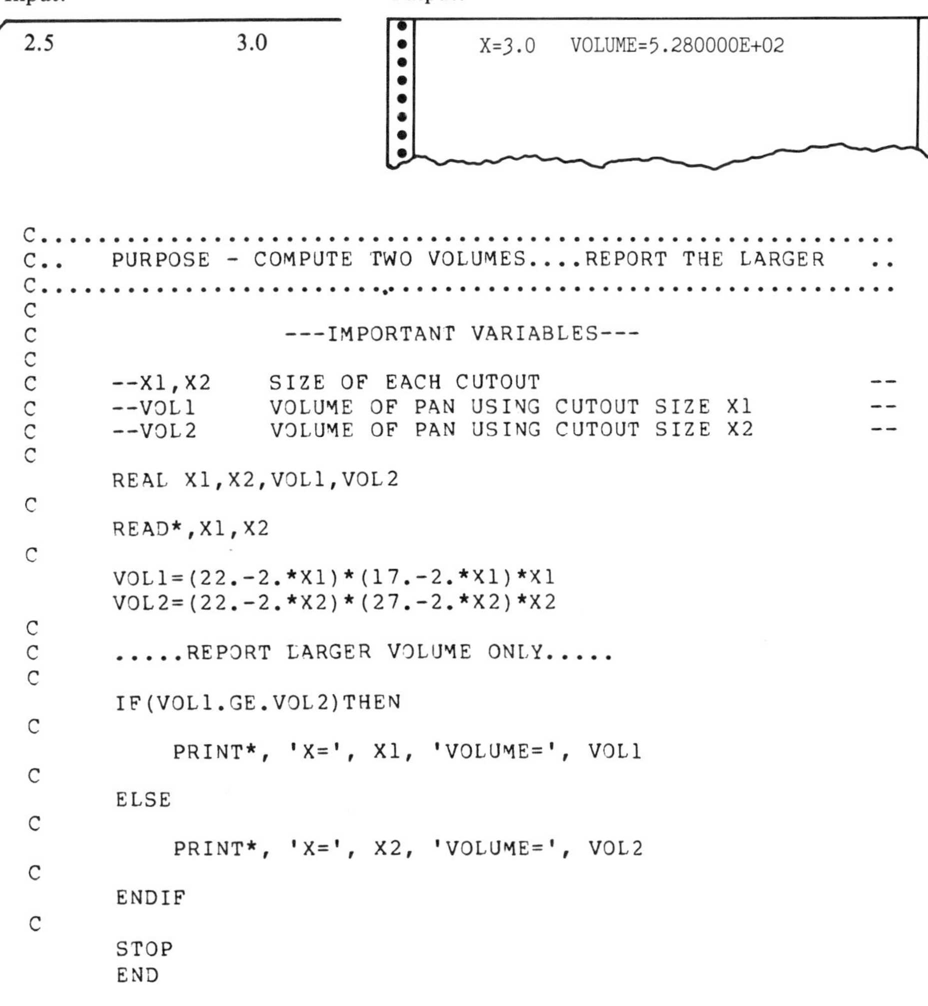

Input:

```
2.5                3.0
```

Output:

```
X=3.0   VOLUME=5.280000E+02
```

```
C.............................................................
C..   PURPOSE - COMPUTE TWO VOLUMES....REPORT THE LARGER    ..
C.............................................................
C
C                   ---IMPORTANT VARIABLES---
C
C     --X1,X2     SIZE OF EACH CUTOUT                         --
C     --VOL1      VOLUME OF PAN USING CUTOUT SIZE X1          --
C     --VOL2      VOLUME OF PAN USING CUTOUT SIZE X2          --
C
      REAL X1,X2,VOL1,VOL2
C
      READ*,X1,X2
C
      VOL1=(22.-2.*X1)*(17.-2.*X1)*X1
      VOL2=(22.-2.*X2)*(27.-2.*X2)*X2
C
C     .....REPORT LARGER VOLUME ONLY.....
C
      IF(VOL1.GE.VOL2)THEN
C
          PRINT*, 'X=', X1, 'VOLUME=', VOL1
C
      ELSE
C
          PRINT*, 'X=', X2, 'VOLUME=', VOL2
C
      ENDIF
C
      STOP
      END
```

Programming Example
Stock Report

Computers provide an important management tool by their report generating activity. Assume a company has some of its assets invested in the stock market. Each stock owned is represented by a record in the input file. The first record indicates 200 shares of Chrysler purchased at $15.75 per share and now selling for $18.25.

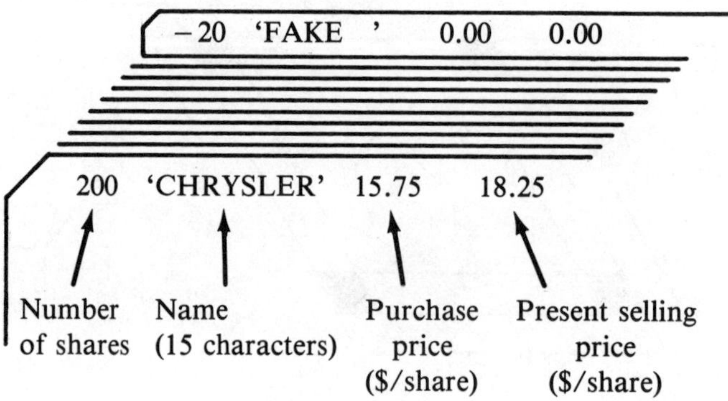

Management needs up-to-date reports to evaluate the performance of their stocks. In a subsequent example, we will generate this whole report including the headings and printing the real numbers in the layout (format) shown. For the moment, consider the problem of generating the lines in the middle of the report. There are seven pieces of information on each of these lines. Four of these values are read from data. This means we must compute the missing values (TOTAL COST, TOTAL VALUE, and PROFIT).

STOCK REPORT

NAME OF SECURITY	NO. OF SHARES	PURCHASE PRICE	TOTAL COST	TODAY'S PRICE	TOTAL VALUE	PROFIT (LOSS)
ALCOA	40	130.00	5200.00	138.75	5550.00	350.00
DISNEY	20	75.00	1500.00	125.00	2500.00	1000.00
DOW CHEM	100	38.65	3865.00	48.65	4865.00	1000.00
IBM	80	43.41	3472.00	42.45	3396.00	-76.80
MONSANTO	45	83.75	3768.75	38.70	1741.50	-2027.25
⋮	⋮	⋮	⋮	⋮	⋮	⋮
TEXACO	60	62.50	3750.45	93.47	5608.20	-2562.40
TOTALS			54521.90		53751.05	-770.85

```
C.............................................................
C..    PURPOSE - GENERATE DETAIL LINE FOR STOCK REPORT SHOW-  ..
C..              ING HOLDINGS, PROFIT OR LOSS INFORMATION     ..
C..              FOR EACH STOCK.                              ..
C.............................................................
C
C                   ---IMPORTANT VARIABLES---
C
C      --NAME      NAME OF STOCK                              --
C      --NUMBER    NUMBER OF SHARES HELD                      --
C      --PRICE     PURCHASE PRICE ($/SHARE)                   --
C      --VALUE     PRESENT VALUE OF EACH STOCK ($/SHARE)      --
```

Programming Example–Stock Report continued

```
C      ----------------COMPUTED VALUES------------------
C      --TCOST    TOTAL COST OF EACH BLOCK OF STOCK              --
C      --TVALUE   TOTAL VALUE OF EACH BLOCK OF STOCK             --
C      --PROFIT   PROFIT OR LOSS FOR EACH BLOCK OF STOCK         --
C
      CHARACTER NAME*15
      INTEGER   NUMBER
      REAL      PRICE,VALUE,TCOST,TVALUE,PROFIT
C
      PRINT*, '                    STOCK REPORT'
      PRINT*, 'NAME OF SECURITY  SHARES   PRICE  COST'
     *,'PRICE    VALUE'
      PRINT*,'-------------------------------------------------'
     *,'--------------'
C
      READ*,NUMBER,NAME,PRICE,VALUE
      DO WHILE (NUMBER.GT.0.0)
C
            TCOST=NUMBER*PRICE
            TVALUE=NUMBER*VALUE
C
            PROFIT=TVALUE-TCOST
C
            PRINT*,NAME,NUMBER,PRICE,TCOST,VALUE,TVALUE,PROFIT
            READ*,NUMBER,NAME,PRICE,VALUE
C
      ENDDO
C
      STOP
      END
```

Programming Example
Series Expansion**

The simple mathematics described in this chapter can be used to obtain higher order operations without an additional hardware commitment. Write a program that will read the value of an angle (expressed in degrees) from data. Convert the angle to radians and then use the equations shown to compute the sine, cosine, and tangent of the angle.

Input:

Angle	*X*
26.3 →	$\frac{26.3}{57.3}$
Angle in degrees	Convert to radians

Equation 1
$$\sin(X) = \underbrace{X}_{\text{Term 1}} - \underbrace{\frac{X^3}{3\cdot2\cdot1}}_{\text{Term 2}} + \underbrace{\frac{X^5}{5\cdot4\cdot3\cdot2\cdot1}}_{\text{Term 3}} - \underbrace{\frac{X^7}{7\cdot6\cdot5\cdot4\cdot3\cdot2\cdot1}}_{\text{Term 4}} + \underbrace{\frac{X^9}{9\cdot8\cdot7\cdot6\cdot5\cdot4\cdot3\cdot2\cdot1}}_{\text{Term 5}}$$

Equation 2
$$\sin^2(X) + \cos^2(X) = 1 \text{ or } \cos(X) = \sqrt{1 - \sin^2(X)}$$

Equation3
$$\tan(X) = \frac{\sin(X)}{\cos(X)}$$

The most substantial part of this program is evaluating the various terms in the series expansion of Equation 1.

Programming Example–Series Expansion continued

```
C.................................................................
C..   PURPOSE - DEMONSTRATE SOFTWARE TECHNIQUES BY COMPUT-      ..
C..             ING TRIGONOMETRIC VALUES USING A SERIES         ..
C..             EXPANSION.                                      ..
C.................................................................
C
C             ---IMPORTANT VARIABLES---
C
C     --ANGLE   VALUE OF ANGLE READ FROM DATA (DEGREES)         --
C     --X       VALUE OF ANGLE CONVERTED TO RADIANS             --
C     --SINVAL  OUTPUT SINE VALUE                               --
C     --COSVAL  OUTPUT COSINE VALUE                             --
C     --TANVAL  OUTPUT TANGENT VALUE                            --
C
      REAL ANGLE,X,SINVAL,COSVAL,TANVAL
      REAL TERM1,TERM2,TERM3,TERM4,TERM5
C
      READ*,ANGLE
      X=ANGLE*3.14/180.
C
C     .....FORM TERMS IN SERIES EXPANSION.....
C
      TERM1=X
      TERM2=-X**3/(3.*2.*1.)
      TERM3=X**5/(5.*4.*3.*2.*1.)
      TERM4=-X**7/(7.*6.*5.*4.*3.*2.*1.)
      TERM5=X**9/(9.*8.*7.*6.*5.*4.*3.*2.*1.)
C
C     .....COMPUTE OUTPUT VALUES.....
C
      SINVAL=TERM1+TERM2+TERM3+TERM5
      COSVAL=(1.0-SINVAL**2)**0.5
      TANVAL=SINVAL/COSVAL
C
      PRINT*,ANGLE,SINVAL,COSVAL,TANVAL
C
      STOP
      END
```

This program is not very efficiently written. Several improvements might be considered. The first would be to express the factorial values as a single constant.

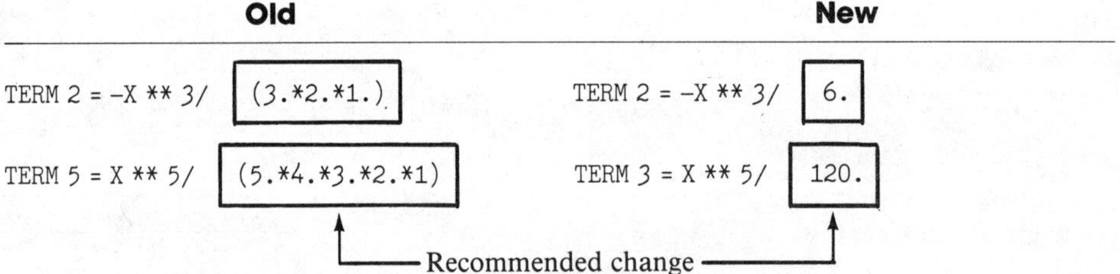

This change does eliminate a substantial amount of repeated calculations without obscuring the method of solution. Such a change is recommended.

Let us consider another possible change. Each term in the numerator, X**9 for example, is obtained by repeated multiplication (*X* is multiplied by itself nine times). This involves a lot of multiplication:

X**5 (X is multiplied by itself 5 times)
X**7 (X is multiplied by itself 7 times)
X**9 (X is multiplied by itself 9 times)

Programming Example–Series Expansion continued

A small savings could be had by recognizing that the numerator for any new term could be obtained by multiplying the numerator of the old term by -X**2:

```
TERM5 = TERM4*(-X**2)/120.
```

A change such as this is highly questionable in that the basic method of solution is being obscured.

Programming Style

Avoid tricks: keep it simple

A clever programmer can devise numerous diabolical techniques to save one or two memory locations a program needs or make the program run a few thousandths of a second faster. If, in the process, the ability to easily follow the program logic is forfeited, the price is too high.

4 Elementary Input/Output/Format Statements

We have not been telling the whole story with regard to input statements. The READ statement used thus far is called a *list directed* READ in that the sequence of variable names following the READ* command (this sequence of names is called the *list*) is used to provide direction for the overall read activity. There are several other list directed READs, for example

```
READ(5,*)list
READ (5,*,END=40)list
```

and an entirely different set of READ operations called *FORMAT controlled* READs, such as

```
READ 10, list
READ (5, 10) list
READ (5, 10, END = 40) list
```

We will continue to emphasize the READ you are most familiar with, but you at least should be able to recognize the other forms of READ statements.

4.1 List Directed READ

To get some idea of how a list directed READ is accomplished, consider the following statement that reads two integers COUNT1, MAX and a single real value X.

```
READ*, COUNT1, MAX, X
```

The most common scheme is to read column after column of the input record until the first nonblank character is detected (this signals the beginning of COUNT1). The column-by-column process continues, but now, as each column is read, the character taken in is checked to see if it is a legal character for an integer variable. (If the first nonblank character is a +, −, or digit, the character is legal.) As each character is read, it is used to build the quantity COUNT1. When a blank, a slash, or a comma is detected, this building process terminates. The value COUNT1 has been established. A similar procedure is initiated for the next variable in the list.

As a final remark about this procedure, you should be aware of what happens if an illegal character is detected (for example, a decimal point in what is declared as an integer field). A diagnostic error will be generated indicating that there is a conflict in type or a format discrepancy has been detected.

```
ERROR ON INPUT - CONFLICT IN TYPE
```

If one of the variables in the list of the READ statement has been declared a CHARACTER variable, the character-by-character building of this variable starts as soon as a quote (quotation mark) is detected on the input record and terminates when a second quote is read (the quotes serve as delimiters). In past examples the characters between quotes have been alphabetic, but any keyboard character is permitted (letters, digits, and special characters). This set of characters is given the name *alphanumerics*.

Alternative Forms

The alternative forms of *list* directed READ statements deserve attention because they provide two extremely useful features. Because computer facilities often have more than one input device available the programmer must identify (for each READ statement issued) which input device should be used for this particular READ operation. The statement

```
READ (5,*) NAME, NUMBER, ITEM
```

Device code (5) — List (NAME, NUMBER, ITEM)

provides this feature. This READ permits the specification of a number, called a *device code*, following the word READ. (Note the requirement of parentheses to enclose this device code and the asterisk.) This number identifies which input device to use for this READ. The manager of the computation center assigns each input device a unique number. A list is usually available at the center. To activate any particular input device you merely use the device code for that unit in the expanded read statement (the one that allows *device specification*).

The second special feature available is called an *end-of-file-check*. This is really useful. The programs you have seen so far have used some special mechanism to make sure the READ command is executed just the correct number of times. (One technique is placing a special record at the end of the file to signal its end—a sentinel record.) Remember, executing the READ command more often than there are records to support each read causes a termination of your program and an error message such as:

```
ERROR ON INPUT - END OF FILE DETECTED
```

This error message suggests that one of your READ instructions attempted to pull a record from the input file, but instead retrieved the mark (end of file mark) used to signal the end of the input file.

What happens when you are assigned a problem where the number of records in the input file is not specified. We cannot go out of business just because the size of the input file is not known. As just described, one solution is to add a record to the end of the file and assign to some item on the record (age, for example) some impossible value (a negative number). Statements are then used to test for this record and terminate processing when the record is detected. This "bogus" record is called a *sentinel record* because it signals the end of input. A program at the end of this chapter simulates the betting at a roulette table. A record at the end of the file seems to suggest a person wants to place a bet on the number −140. This is either a terribly uninformed gambler or it is a sentinel record.

An even easier method of avoiding the end-of-file error is to use the following read statement:

```
READ(5,*,END=120) NAME, NUMBER, COUNT
```

Tells where to pass control when end-of-file is detected (pointing to END=120)

This READ provides for the inclusion of an additional quantity, END= statement number, which directs the transfer of control to the statement specified (statement 120, in the example give) whenever this READ is executed and the end-of-file is detected. If you use this form of READ statement, you do not have to construct a sentinel record. All you have to do is establish where in the program you want control transferred when the input file is depleted. You assign that statement a number and reference the number in the END= part of the READ statement.

Quiz 7 Input/Output Statements

1. Is the statement

   ```
   READ *, END= 70, A, B, C
   ```

   one of the permitted forms of input commands?
2. What is meant by the term "list" when discussing input statements?
3. How are elements of the list separated from one another?
4. What does the error diagnostic CONFLICT IN TYPE mean?
5. What is a device code and how are these codes assigned?
6. What is an end-of-file mark?
7. What happens when a READ statement picks up the end-of-file mark?
8. What is meant by a sentinel record? Why is it used?
9. Blanks are used to separate items in an input record. Is this the only symbol to delimit these items?
10. When character information appears on an input record, is a blank or a slash a sufficient delimiter?

4.2 Input with FORMAT Control

The alternative to a list directed READ operation is called a FORMAT controlled READ. The following table shows the FORMAT directed version of the list directed read statements already discussed.

List Directed	FORMAT Directed
READ*, NAME, I, X	READ 20, NAME, I, X
READ(5,*) NAME, I, X	READ (5, 20) NAME, I, X
READ (5,*,END=100)NAME,I,X	READ(5,20,END=100)NAME,I,X

The major difference between the two types of statements is the use of a statement number (in these examples, the statement number 20) in place of the *. The asterisk is understood to mean list directed input or output. Using a number in place of the asterisk indicates FORMAT controlled input. As you might expect, statement 20 is a FORMAT statement that will supply information to assist the READ operation

```
20 FORMAT (A15, I6, F10.2)
```

The FORMAT statement contains a series of codes which give detailed information of the layout of the input record. By layout we mean:

1. Defining the number of columns reserved for each data item (the field width).
2. Defining the type of information contained within each field specified.

The following codes are relatively easy to read and understand.

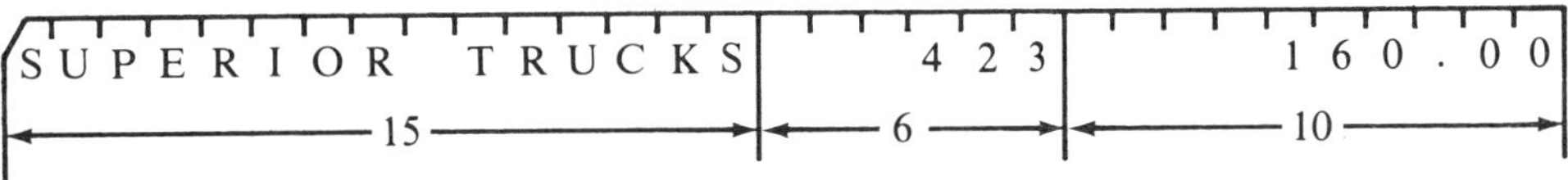

Code	Meaning
A15	Information is alphanumeric (letters of the alphabet or numbers—actually any keyboard character is allowed) contained within the first 15 columns of the record.
I6	Information is an integer number and is positioned in the next 6 character positions of the input record.
F10.2	Information is a real (sometimes called a floating point) number. The field width for this value is 10 columns. If no decimal point is specified, the point is considered to be located just in front of the last 2 columns of the field (before column 9 of the 10-column field). If a point is specified, this last specification is overridden.

FORMAT controlled input can sometimes be bothersome. If the information is not precisely located within its designated field an error will result. On the other hand, FORMAT controlled output can sometimes have advantages over list directed output. We will, for the most part, stick with list directed input/output. When it suits our purpose, however, we will use FORMAT control taking care to give a complete explanation of the meaning of the format codes used.

Common Errors

Example 1

Until students fully understand the concept of general programming, they feel an urge to specify values in the instruction deck that should be specified as part of the data file. In other words, do not specify a value as a constant when the value is a variable. Follow this rule. Before you write in the instruction deck any FORTRAN statement that includes reference to a quantity by specific value (by a constant) ask yourself, "Is this value appropriate for each and every execution of the program?" If the answer is no, specifying the value as a constant will limit the application of the program. *It will not be a general program.*

The correct procedure is to place the value as an element of the input data file and use an appropriate variable name to represent the quantity in the instruction deck. (You were warned about this before in the solution of the quadratic equation program.)

Example 2

Each record in the data file should contain those numbers or characters that change for each execution of the instruction deck. *That is all that should appear.* Students sometimes place the variable names of each quantity before the actual value as shown here.

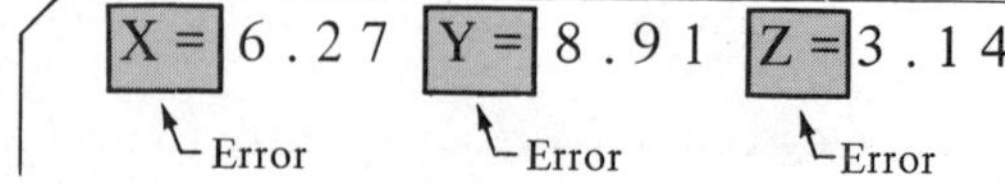

The preceding record is in error. The names X, Y, and Z do not belong as part of the record. These names are assigned by the READ statement in the instruction deck. This is done on a one-to-one correspondence basis. Successive values in the input file are identified as belonging to variable names specified in the instruction deck by a matching process. Names following a READ command are matched on a one-to-one basis with the sequential data values appearing on each input record. A corresponding sequence of format codes (if they are used) supports this activity, otherwise the elements in the input file are separated by a blank, a comma, or a slash.

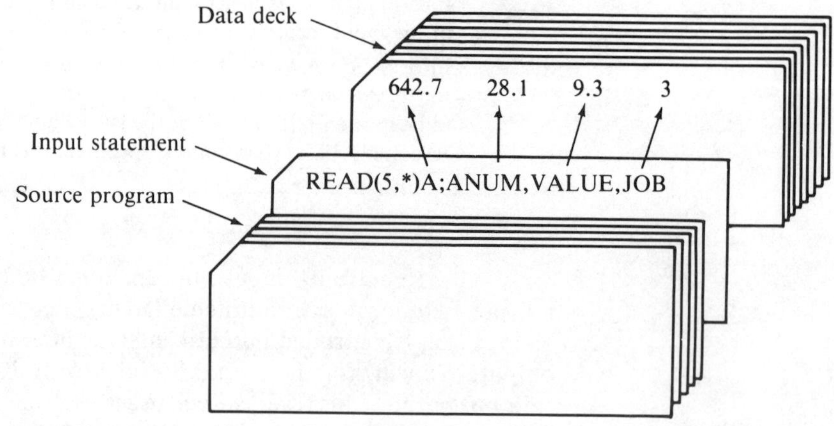

Figure 4.1 One-to-one correspondence

4.3 Output Statements

To show the various alternative forms of output statements available in FORTRAN, consider the following

List Directed	FORMAT Controlled
`PRINT*,NAME,I,J`	`PRINT 40, NAME, I,J`
`WRITE (2,*) NAME,I,J`	`WRITE (2,40) NAME,I,J`

A `PRINT` statement can be used that references a `FORMAT` statement (in this example, statement 40) to direct exactly how the output should appear on the line printer or on the terminal screen. We will use this feature in the next example problem to circumvent a difficulty we have faced several times already, namely, to print real numbers representing dollar amounts so that the number is not printed in scientific notation, but rather printed as a two-place decimal (like on a paycheck).

The next higher form of output statement is the one to direct which output device to use. This command uses the key word `WRITE` rather than the familiar `PRINT` command. There are historical reasons for this, but it may be easier for you to remember the `WRITE` command if you realize that in advanced applications, output may be sent to a variety of devices (to magnetic tapes or to one or more magnetic disk drives). While the word `PRINT` is appropriate for sending output to a video screen or a printer, the `WRITE` command is more appropriate for sending output to these other devices. `WRITE` has a more inclusive connotation.

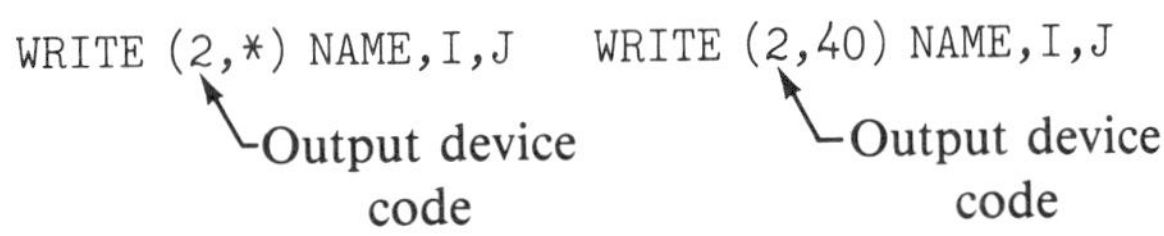

As before, an identifying number (an output device code) is used to specify which of several possible output devices is to be used for this particular output operation. This text uses the number 2 for the student output device code. Your instructor will tell you the device codes of equipment available for students at your installation.

Note that both list directed and `FORMAT` controlled output statements are available. When list directed output is used, each data item is printed according to a predetermined form. If a programmer wants to control the exact location and form of each element printed, the `FORMAT` controlled output statements must be used. Without getting too deeply involved, let's see how this process works. Figure 4.2 shows a layout sheet being used to gauge the appropriate column locations of various fields of an output record so that the output is pleasant to look at and easy to read. This layout sheet is like the coding forms used for preparing a FORTRAN statement layout; it has just been made larger.

Figure 4.2 Output layout sheet

```
1 2 3 4 5 6 7 8 9 10 11 12 13 14 15 16 17 18 19 20 21 22 23 24 25 26 27 28 29 30 31 32 33 34 35 36 37 38 39

                 THE  ANSWERS  ARE
     I       |      X      |       Y       |      Z
    21       |    5.230    |   62.3000     |   0.2847
   182       |    9.263    |   13.4819     |  12.9470
     8       |   52.953    |    0.2847     |  81.8623
   142       |    0.036    |   16.3859     |  54.3905
    56      8|   26.395    |    5.3793     |   7.1192

|<---6--->|<-----10----->|<-----10----->|<-----10----->|
```

From the layout sheet we see that the top line should have the first 12 columns blank followed by the title THE ANSWERS ARE. This could be obtained by a list directed PRINT statement such as

```
PRINT*, 'ƀ ƀ ƀ ƀ ƀ ƀ ƀ ƀ ƀ ƀ ƀ ƀ THE ANSWERS ARE'
```

The equivalent FORMAT controlled output statement might be

```
   PRINT 10
10 FORMAT ('ƀ ƀ ƀ ƀ ƀ ƀ ƀ ƀ ƀ ƀ ƀ ƀ THE ANSWERS ARE')
```

We are using the symbol ƀ to indicate a blank or space.

The next feature to consider is the blank line appearing between the top or title line and the column headings. This blank line could be generated by either of the following output statements.

List Directed	**FORMAT Controlled**
`PRINT*, 'ƀ'`	`PRINT 20` `20 FORMAT ('ƀ')`

Generating the column headings is not much different than producing the top or page title line. The output statement of real importance is the statement controlling the main body lines of output, namely printing one integer and three real numbers. This line is sometimes called the detail line. The sequence of numbers suggests we will be using one I-code and three F-codes. The lower portion of Figure 4.2 indicates the field width wanted to make the numbers line up under the column headings. Finally, X is to be published to three-digit accuracy, whereas the other real (floating point) numbers are to be printed to four-place accuracy. By accuracy we mean number of digits after the decimal point.

```
   PRINT 30, I,X,Y,Z
30 FORMAT (I6,F10.3,F10.4,F10.4)
```

Each of these numbers will be positioned in their respective fields *right justified*. Further, by specifying a larger than required field width, the numbers are nicely separated from each other by several blank columns.

An alternative example of output is shown in Figure 4.3.

Figure 4.3 Elegant output

```
                    THE ANSWERS ARE

I= 21          X=  5.230          Y=62.7330          Z=   .6486
I= 82          X=  9.273          Y=12.9476          Z=  1.1684
I=  8          X= 52.532          Y=  .6488          Z= 86.8372
I=124          X=  8.035          Y= 7.3857          Z=167.7940
I= 56          X=537.938          Y=46.5667          Z= 20.0375
I=  5                                                Z=  7.3950
```

The typing (fixed character string) of column headings has been moved into the detail line.

```
    PRINT 30,I,X,Y,Z
30  FORMAT('bbI=',I3,'bbbbX=',F8.4,
           'bbbbY=',F7.4,'bbbbZ=,'F8.4)
```

The FORMAT statement now specifies eight fields: four fixed character string fields and four number fields.

4.4 Words of Caution—Another Example

There are many additional aspects of FORMAT control. There are format codes to cause a page eject (go to the top of a new page), to cause double or triple spacing of output, to tab across to a specified column in a line before printing a value. These features are more useful to the experienced programmer and are therefore covered later in the text.

You are advised to use list directed input/output unless there is a compelling reason not to. When FORMAT controlled output is used, a word of caution is necessary. Many of the special control features (such as a page eject) are implemented by putting a special character in column 1 of the output line.

```
40 FORMAT ('1',F8.2, . . .
```

↑ Control character

For example, placing a 1 in the first column causes a page advance to the top of a new page. The recommendation is that you place a blank in this column 1 position which will cause normal (single line advance) printout. This can be accomplished as follows:

```
50 FORMAT ('b', F8.2, . . .
```

↑ Blank in column 1

As a final word about FORMAT statements, they are nonexecutable statements. They provide the "assisting information" needed in a READ or WRITE operation. For this reason the placement of the statement is not critical. It can be positioned immediately after the READ or WRITE statement, but it does not have to be there.

Programming Example
Addressing Payroll Checks

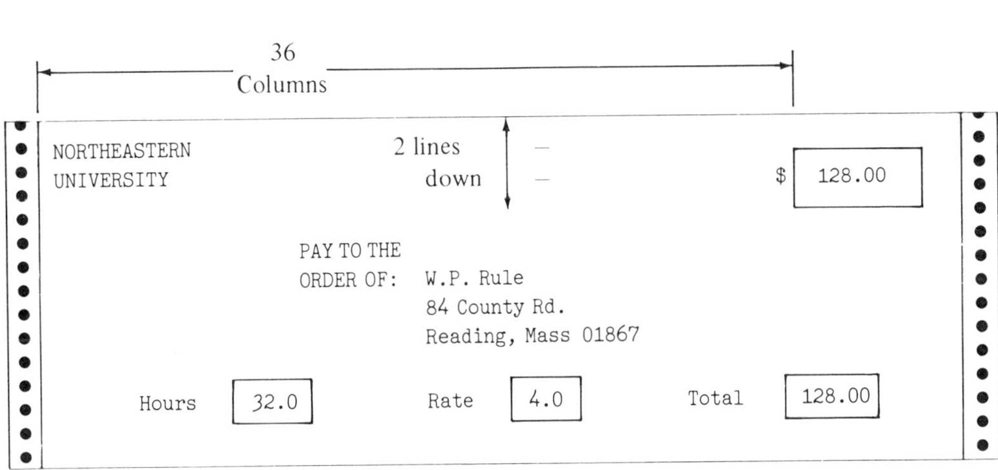

Programming Example–Addressing Payroll Checks continued

To put an address on an employee's check, each record in an input data file contains the following information:

Column	Meaning
1–20	Employee's name
21–40	Employee's street address
41–60	Employee's town address
61–65	Employee's zip code

To make this problem a little more interesting, we are going to try to print two checks at one time instead of the single check just shown. This means we will have to read two input records at a time (two names and two addresses). We must then generate output statements to produce the two checks as suggested in the next illustration.

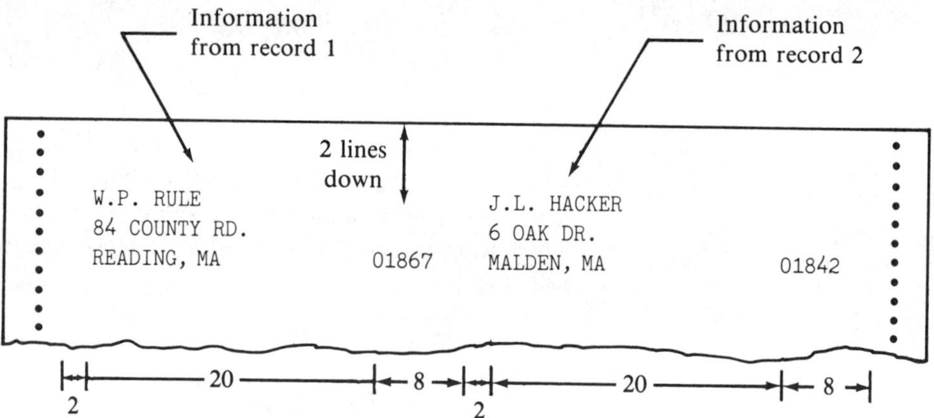

Note that several blank records have been added to the input file so that you do not have to worry about an odd number of records in the input file.

```
C.......................................................
C..   PURPOSE - PRINT NAME AND ADDRESS OF EMPLOYEES,   ..
C..             TWO PER LINE.                          ..
C.......................................................
C
C                  ---IMPORTANT VARIABLES---
C
C     --NAME1,NAME2      NAME PORTION OF ADDRESS LINE       --
C     --STRT1,STRT2      STREET PORTION OF ADDRESS LINE     --
C     --TOWN1,TOWN2      TOWN PORTION OF ADDRESS LINE       --
C     --ZIP1,ZIP2        ZIP CODE PORTION OF ADDRESS LINE --
C
      CHARACTER NAME1*20,NAME2*20,STRT1*20,STRT2*20
      CHARACTER TOWN1*20,TOWN2*20
      INTEGER   ZIP1,ZIP2
C
C     .....READ A PAIR OF CARDS.....
C
   10 READ (5,20,END=100) NAME1, STRT1, TOWN1, ZIP1
   20 FORMAT(A20,A20,A20,I5)
      READ (5,20,END=100) NAME2, STRT2, TOWN2, ZIP2
C
C     .....SKIP DOWN TWO LINES.....
C
      PRINT 30
   30 FORMAT(' ')
      PRINT 30
```

Programming Example–Addressing Payroll Checks continued

```
C      .....PRINT ADDRESSES.....
C
       PRINT 40, NAME1, NAME2
   40  FORMAT('  ',A20,'          ',A20)
       PRINT 50, TOWN1, ZIP1, TOWN2, ZIP2
   50  FORMAT('  ',A20,I8,'  ',A20,I8)
C
       GO TO 10
C
  100  STOP
       END
```

4.5 The Output List

The "list" of an output statement has been defined as the sequence of variable names used in a PRINT or WRITE statement to identify those memory locations whose contents are to be transferred to an output device.

```
                Variable
                names
WRITE (2,*) A,B,C
            List
```

Elements of the list for the most part have been specified by giving a variable name. Although this is by far the most common means of identifying the desired output, it is not the only means.

```
                Expressions
                permitted
WRITE (2,*) A+6.,B/2.,C+D
```

Almost all compilers allow *expressions* as elements of the output list.

Quiz 8
READ/WRITE Operations

1. What are the advantages of list directed READs over FORMAT controlled one?
2. A student has prepared the following input record. What is wrong with this record?

```
RADIUS=1.2 HEIGHT=2.7
```

3. Must a FORMAT statement be numbered?
4. May a FORMAT statement be used by more than one READ or WRITE statement?
5. What does the term "right justified" mean?
6. Why is it necessary in FORMAT controlled output to put a blank in Column 1 of the output record?
7. The output list of a PRINT statement may include expressions as well as variable names. True or False.
8. How are items in the data file matched to variable names in a READ/WRITE operation?
9. Each time a READ instruction is executed a new record from the input file is processed. Each time a WRITE instruction is executed a new record is sent to the output file. True or False.
10. A memory location holds a real number representing a monetary transaction. The transaction is a deposit or a withdrawal less than a thousand dollars. How can the value be printed in its natural (not scientific) form?

Programming Example
Roulette Wheel

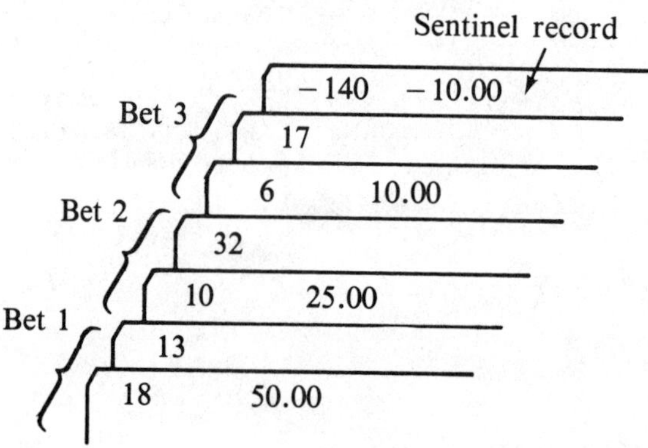

Each pair of records in the input file represents the betting action at a roulette table. The first record of a pair indicates the number being played and the amount of the wager. The second record of the pair indicates the winning number.

Write a program to process each bet. If it is a winning bet, issue a message indicating a winner and the amount of the payoff (35 to 1 are the betting odds).

```
YOU ARE A WINNER - AMOUNT WON IS $ 120.00
```

otherwise print the message:

```
YOU LOSE - DO YOU WISH TO PLAY AGAIN?
```

This program terminates when the number bet on is a negative number. You may assume that fewer than 100 bets are represented in the input file.

```
C.......................................................
C..   PURPOSE - PROCESS RECORDS REPRESENTING BETS AT A  ..
C..             ROULETTE TABLE.                         ..
C.......................................................
C
C              ---IMPORTANT VARIABLES---
C
C     --NUMBER  NUMBER BEING PLAYED                     --
C     --AMOUNT  AMOUNT OF WAGER                         --
C     --WINNER  WINNING NUMBER                          --
C     --PAYOFF  AMOUNT TO BE PAID TO WINNER             --
C     --COUNTR  LOOP CONTROL VARIABLE                   --
C
      INTEGER NUMBER, WINNER, COUNTR
      REAL    AMOUNT, PAYOFF
C
      DO 40 COUNTR = 1, 100, 1
C
          READ *, NUMBER, AMOUNT
          IF(NUMBER .LT. 0) STOP
C
          READ *, WINNER
C
          IF (NUMBER .EQ. WINNER) THEN
              PAYOFF = 35. * AMOUNT
```

Programming Example–Roulette Wheel continued

```
                 PRINT 20, PAYOFF
 20              FORMAT('  YOU ARE A WINNER - AMOUNT WON =',F10.2)
            ELSE
                 PRINT 30
 30              FORMAT('  YOU LOSE - DO YOU WISH TO PLAY AGAIN?')
            ENDIF
C
 40   CONTINUE
      END
```

Review Exercises

1. What two important features do the new READ statements (presented in this chapter) provide to the programmer?
2. Define the term "field width" and how it is specified.
3. What is used in place of a specified field width in list directed READ operations?
4. If the number of records in the input file is not declared in the problem statements, what two techniques can be used to avoid an end-of-file error?
5. When numbers were printed under FORMAT control, why was an extra large field width used when constructing the output line?
6. What is so special about column 1 of any line of FORMAT controlled output?
7. How does one make sure the first column of any line of FORMAT controlled output is blank?
8. Describe the data items being specified by the following format codes:

   a. I7 b. F8.2 c. A10
9. What is the largest negative number that can be printed using an I4 code?
10. How would the following value appear on output if controlled by the codes shown?

    3.14159265358979

    a. F16.4 |_|_|_|_|_|_|_|_|_|_|_|_|_|_|_|_|

    b. F16.2 |_|_|_|_|_|_|_|_|_|_|_|_|_|_|_|_|

    c. F16.8 |_|_|_|_|_|_|_|_|_|_|_|_|_|_|_|_|

    d. F8.7 |_|_|_|_|_|_|_|_|
11. What is the purpose of the "input device code"?
12. How could you cause output to be printed at your console and on magnetic tape during the execution of your program?
13. How is it possible to get the error message CONFLICT IN TYPE?
14. When preparing a FORTRAN statement, it is necessary to put information in specific fields (main statement in columns 7 to 72.) What restrictions are placed on the placement of information or on input (data) record?
15. If a real number is specified with an F8.1 code and no decimal point is present, where can you assume the point to be located?
16. Before specifying a constant in the instruction deck, what question should you ask yourself to make sure the program will be a general program?
17. Write a series of statements that will print the letter H 15 units high and 15 units wide centered on the output device you use, as shown.

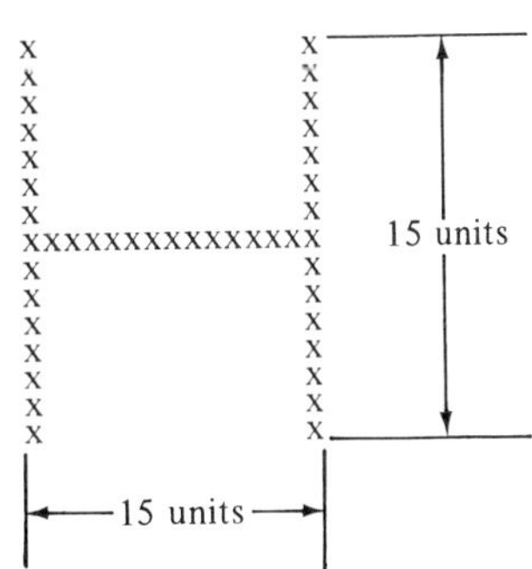

18. A data file consists of records containing a single real value. This value may be positive or negative and represents DEPOSITS or WITHDRAWALS to a bank account.

DEPOSITS	WITHDRAWALS
200.00	-16.50
10.00	-25.00

    Post these transactions as shown.

    a. Provide statements to produce the column headings shown at the top of an output page.

    b. Post the individual transaction amount on the left or the right of the page as appropriate.

19. A fraternity wants a banner made of letters 30 lines tall and 20 characters wide. This is a tedious job of writing 30 pairs of WRITE/FORMAT combinations to obtain the desired output. Write the statements necessary to obtain the top two lines of the output wanted.

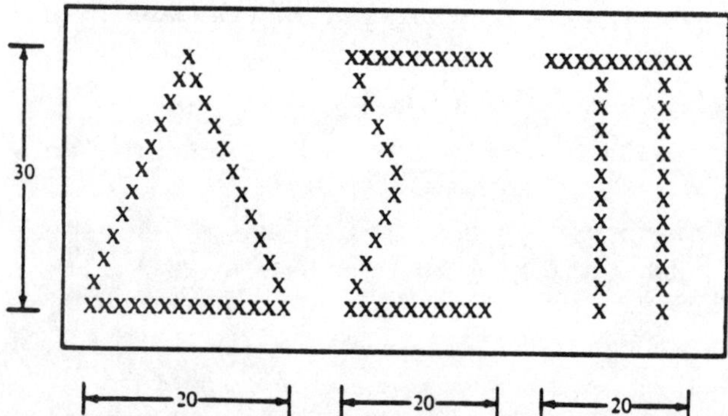

20. Write a program to produce the *X* and *Y* axis of the graph as shown.

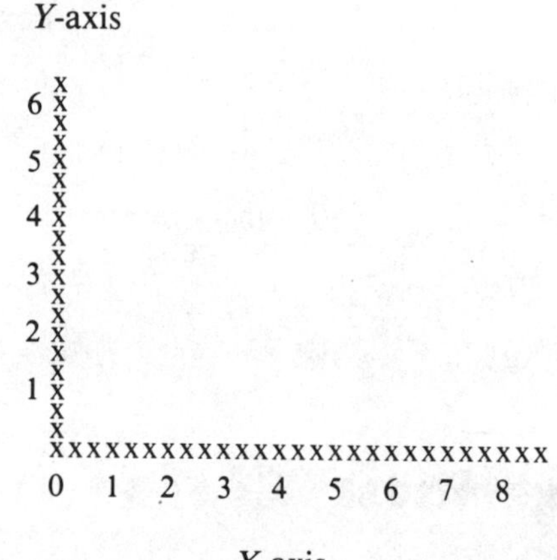

Additional Applications

Programming Example
Hit-and-Run Driver

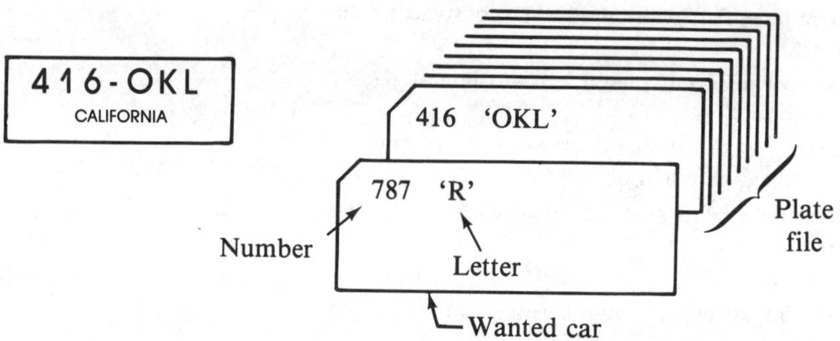

Assume the license plates in your state have a three-digit number followed by three letters of the alphabet. Assume further that the victim of a hit-and-run accident was able to get the first three numbers and the first letter of the runaway car (see first record in the input file). Write a program to search the remainder of the file for all registered cars and print all those that fit the description of the runaway car.

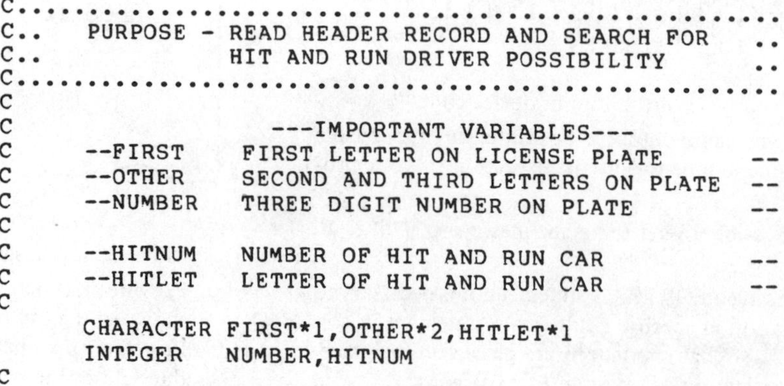

```
C.......................................................
C..     PURPOSE - READ HEADER RECORD AND SEARCH FOR      ..
C..               HIT AND RUN DRIVER POSSIBILITY         ..
C.......................................................
C
C                   ---IMPORTANT VARIABLES---
C       --FIRST     FIRST LETTER ON LICENSE PLATE        --
C       --OTHER     SECOND AND THIRD LETTERS ON PLATE    --
C       --NUMBER    THREE DIGIT NUMBER ON PLATE          --
C
C       --HITNUM    NUMBER OF HIT AND RUN CAR            --
C       --HITLET    LETTER OF HIT AND RUN CAR            --
C
        CHARACTER FIRST*1,OTHER*2,HITLET*1
        INTEGER   NUMBER,HITNUM
C
```

Programming Example–Hit-and-Run Driver continued

```
C      .....PROCESS HEADER CARD.....
C
       READ (5,*) HITNUM, HITLET
C
C      .....ECHO CHECK.....
C
       PRINT *, 'FIRST LETTER = ', HITLET
       PRINT *, 'THREE DIGITS = ', HITNUM
C
C
   10  READ (5,20,END=100) NUMBER, FIRST, OTHER
   20  FORMAT(I3,A1,A2)
C
C         ......SEARCH LOOP STARTS HERE.......
C
          DO WHILE (NUMBER.NE.HITNUM .OR. FIRST.NE.HITLET)
C
C                   .....THIS IS NOT.....
C                 ...THE WANTED VEHICLE...
C               ... LOOK AT THE NEXT RECORD...
C
               READ(5,20,END=100) NUMBER, FIRST, OTHER
C
          ENDDO
C
C                     ..WE GOT OUR SUSPECT..
C
          PRINT *, NUMBER, FIRST, OTHER
C
          STOP
C         - - - - - - - - - - - - - - - - - - - - - - - - -
C
C         ....SEARCH COMPLETE....SUSPECT NOT FOUND...
C
  100     PRINT*, 'END OF FILE REACHED..NO LUCK'
C
         STOP
         END
```

Programming Example Restock—Different Method

It is the responsibility of a store manager to monitor the stock level of the various items in his or her store. The following table shows the reorder point of various items. If the stock on hand falls below the reorder point, a replacement order for the amount shown in the table should be made.

Reorder Points

Item Number	Reorder Point	Quantity To Order
0125	100	200
0136	1200	5000
⋮	⋮	⋮
6273	50	100
6281	120	180
6294	4000	7000

Programming Example-Restock—Different Method continued

The first record in a data file contains the item number and present stock level of a product that appears to be running low. Each of the remaining records in the data file represents a line in the table of reorder points.

Assume that exactly 1000 lines are in the reorder table. Search the table for the item on the header record. Determine if we should reorder this item and, if so, in what quantity. If the item is not found in the table, issue the message:

```
ITEM NOT FOUND
```

```
C.......................................................................
C..    PURPOSE - SEARCH TABLE OF REORDER POINTS - INDICATE            ..
C..              IF STOCK LEVEL IS SUFFICIENT                         ..
C.......................................................................
C
C                    ---IMPORTANT VARIABLES---
C      --CHECK    ITEM NUMBER OF STOCK BEING CHECKED                   --
C      --PRESNT   PRESENT STOCK LEVEL OF THIS ITEM                     --
C
C      --ITEM     ITEM NUMBER OF VARIOUS TABLE ENTRIES                 --
C      --LOWEST   REORDER POINT OF THIS ITEM                           --
C      --MORE     QUANTITY TO ORDER WHEN REORDERING                    --
C
      INTEGER CHECK,PRESNT,ITEM,LOWEST,MORE,COUNTR
C
C      .....READ HEADER---DEFINE SEARCH VALUES.....
C
      READ (5,*) CHECK, PRESNT
      PRINT *, 'CHECK ITEM NO.', CHECK
      PRINT *, 'PRESENT STOCK LEVEL =', PRESNT
C
      DO 50 COUNTR = 1, 1000
C
          READ (5,*,END=60) ITEM, LOWEST, MORE
          IF(CHECK.EQ.ITEM) THEN
              IF(PRESNT.LE.LOWEST) THEN
                  PRINT *, 'STOCK TOO LOW, ORDER', MORE, 'MORE'
              ELSE
                  PRINT *, 'STOCK SUFFICIENT'
              ENDIF
          STOP
          ENDIF
   50 CONTINUE
C
   60 PRINT *, 'END OF FILE DETECTED'
      PRINT *, 'ITEM NOT FOUND IN TABLE'
      PRINT *, 'CHECK SEARCH INFORMATION'
C
      STOP
      END
```

Programming Example Computerized Letters

A company specializes in "Computer Correspondence." It offers up to 90 different letters containing various business messages. Three typical letters appear in the next illustration. These letters are triggered from a data card that starts with a two-digit number code telling which message to generate. The next 60 columns give the name

Programming Example–Computerized Letters continued

and address of the recipient. Two real values contain variables that must appear in the main body letter.

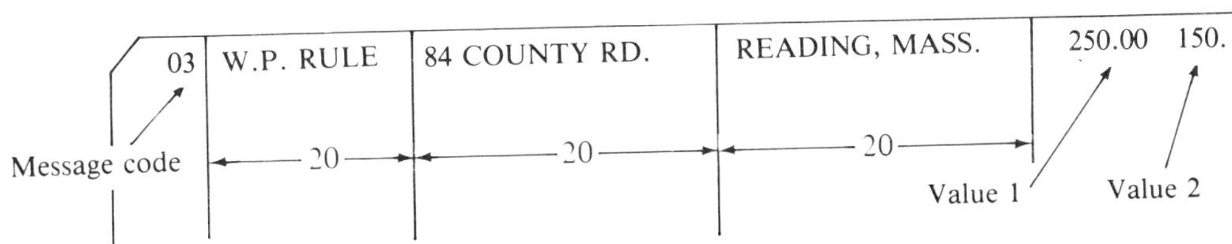

Write statements that would generate the following three messages.

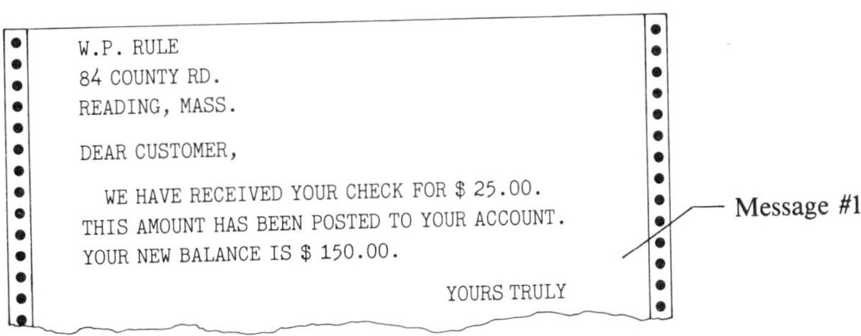

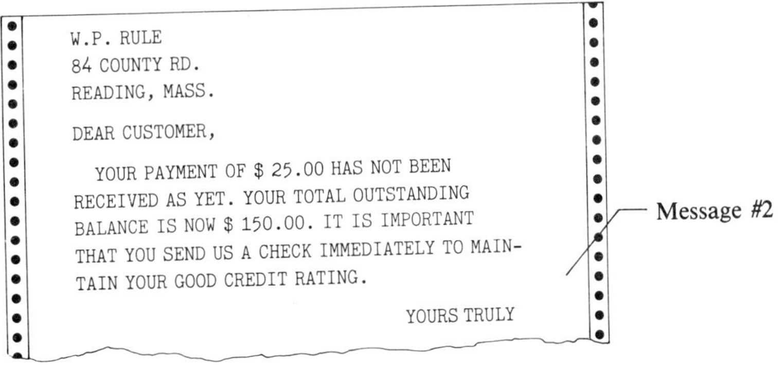

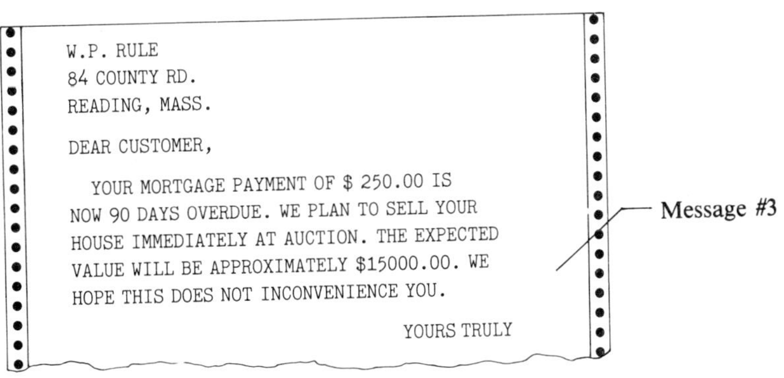

Programming Example–Computerized Letters continued

```
C......................................................
C..   PURPOSE - GENERATE VARIOUS BUSINESS LETTERS    ..
C......................................................
C
C           ---IMPORTANT VARIABLES---
C
C     --CODE     NUMBER TELLING WHICH LETTER IS WANTED  --
C     --NAME     NAME PORTION OF ADDRESS                --
C     --ST       STREET PORTION OF ADDRESS              --
C     --TOWN     TOWN PORTION OF ADDRESS                --
C     --VALUE1   FIRST VARIABLE NUMBER IN MESSAGE       --
C     --VALUE2   SECOND VARIABLE NUMBER IN MESSAGE      --
C
      CHARACTER NAME*20,ST*20,TOWN*20
      INTEGER   CODE
      REAL      VALUE1,VALUE2
C
      READ (5,100) CODE, NAME, ST, TOWN, VALUE1, VALUE2
  100 FORMAT(I2,A20,A20,A20,F8.2,F8.2)
C
C     .....PRODUCE ADDRESS AND OPENING SALUTATION.....
C
      WRITE (2,200) NAME
  200 FORMAT(' ',A20)
      WRITE (2,200) ST
      WRITE (2,200) TOWN
      WRITE (2,300)
  300 FORMAT(' ')
      WRITE (2,400)
  400 FORMAT(' DEAR CUSTUMER,')
C
C     .....TEST FOR MESSAGE NO. 1.....
C
      IF(CODE.EQ.1) THEN
C
C         .....SECTION FOR MESSAGE NO. 1.....
C
          WRITE (2,500) VALUE1
  500     FORMAT('     WE HAVE RECEIVED YOUR CHECK FOR $',F8.2)
          WRITE (2,501)
  501     FORMAT(' THIS AMOUNT HAS BEEN POSTED TO YOUR ACCOUNT.')
          WRITE (2,502) VALUE2
  502     FORMAT(' YOUR NEW BALANCE IS $',F8.2)
      ENDIF
C
C     .....TEST FOR MESSAGE NO. 2.....
C
      IF(CODE.EQ.2) THEN
C
C         .....SECTION FOR MESSAGE NO. 2.....
C
          WRITE (2,503) VALUE1
  503     FORMAT('     YOUR PAYMENT OF $',F8.2,' HAS NOT BEEN')
          WRITE (2,504)
  504     FORMAT(' RECEIVED AS YET.  YOUR TOTAL OUTSTANDING')
          WRITE (2,505) VALUE2
  505     FORMAT(' BALANCE IS NOW $'F8.2,'.  IT IS IMPORTANT')
          WRITE (2,506)
  506     FORMAT(' THAT YOU SEND US A CHECK IMMEDIATELY TO MAIN-')
          WRITE (2,507)
  507     FORMAT(' TAIN YOUR GOOD CREDIT RATING.')
      ENDIF
C
C     .....TEST FOR MESSAGE NO. 3.....
C
      IF(CODE.EQ.3) THEN
C
C         .....SECTION FOR MESSAGE NO. 3.....
C
```

Programming Example–Computerized Letters continued

```
          WRITE (2,508) VALUE1
 508      FORMAT('      YOUR MORTGAGE PAYMENT OF $',F8.2,' IS')
          WRITE (2,509)
 509      FORMAT(' NOW 90 DAYS OVER DUE.  WE PLAN TO SELL YOUR')
          WRITE (2,510)
 510      FORMAT(' HOUSE IMMEDIATELY AT AUCTION.  THE EXPECTED')
          WRITE (2,511) VALUE2
 511      FORMAT(' VALUE WILL BE APPROXIMATELY $',F8.2,'.  WE')
          WRITE (2,512)
 512      FORMAT(' HOPE THIS DOES NOT INCONVENIENCE YOU.')
      ENDIF
C
C     .....PRODUCE END OF LETTER.....
C
      WRITE (2,300)
      WRITE (2,513)
 513  FORMAT('                          YOURS TRULY')
      STOP
      END
```

Programming Example Computing Resistance**

A data card gives the values of three resistors used in an electric circuit.

120. 300. 50. 2

R_1 R_2 R_3 Which circuit

The total resistance of the circuit depends on the way in which the resistors are joined together (series, parallel, or series-parallel).

Equation 1 $R_{TOTAL} = R_1 + R_2 + R_3$

Equation 2 $R_{TOTAL} = \dfrac{R_1 \cdot R_2 \cdot R_3}{(R_1 + R_2) + (R_1 + R_3) + (R_2 + R_3)}$

Equation 3 $R_{TOTAL} = \dfrac{R_2 \cdot R_3}{R_2 + R_3} + R_1$

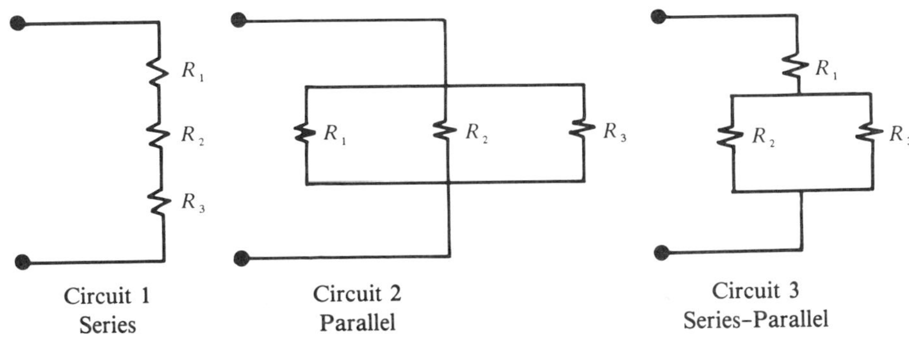

Circuit 1 Series

Circuit 2 Parallel

Circuit 3 Series–Parallel

The last value on the data card is the number 1, 2, or 3 and tells which of the three circuits is being used. Compute and report the appropriate total resistance.

Programming Example–Computing Resistance continued

```
C.......................................................................
C..     PURPOSE - COMPUTE RESISTANCE IN ONE OF THREE POSSIBLE         ..
C..               CIRCUITS.                                           ..
C.......................................................................
C
C                  ---IMPORTANT VARIABLES---
C
C     --R1,
C       R2,R3     RESISTANCE VALUES                                   --
C     --CODE      INTEGER TELLING WHICH TYPE CIRCUIT
C                     1 = SERIES
C                     2 = PARALLEL
C                     3 = SERIES-PARALLEL                             --
C     --TOTAL     TOTAL RESISTANCE OF CIRCUIT                         --
C
      INTEGER CODE
      REAL    R1,R2,R3,TOTAL
C
      READ *, R1, R2, R3, CODE
C
      PRINT *, 'R1=',R1
      PRINT *, 'R2=',R2
      PRINT *, 'R3=',R3
C
C         .....SELECT CORRECT EQUATION.....
C
      IF(CODE.EQ.1) TOTAL=R1+R2+R3
      IF(CODE.EQ.2) TOTAL=(R1*R2*R3)/((R1+R2)+(R1+R3)+(R2+R3))
      IF(CODE.EQ.3) TOTAL=(R2*R3)/(R2+R3)+R1
C
      PRINT *, 'TOTAL RESISTANCE =',TOTAL
C
      STOP
      END
```

5 Elementary Control Statements

By numerous examples we have shown that the computer processes statements in the order of their appearance. This means that the programmer first exercises control over the sequence in which statements are executed by the order in which the statements appear in the instruction deck. If this "one-after-another" sequence were the only control available, programs would be highly inflexible. Only one straight path of solution would be possible.

5.1 Control Statements (GO TO)

Control statements allow the programmer to interrupt this one-after-another processing for the purpose of making the program more dynamic and, therefore, more useful. One of the simplest control statements is the GO TO statement:

```
GO TO n
```

It contains the command GO TO followed by a statement number that serves as a label.

Example	Meaning
GO TO 25 (GO TO: Command; 25: Statement number)	The next statement to be executed is statement number 25

This statement number identifies where in a program control is to be passed when this control statement is reached.

A GO TO statement produces what is called an *unconditional* transfer of control because no testing or decision is involved in the process. This unconditional transfer has a tendency to interrupt the smooth logical flow of a program. For this reason, you should use the statement very sparingly.

Common Errors

A GO TO statement is sometimes used at the bottom of a block of FORTRAN code for the purpose of passing control back to the top of the block thereby establishing a loop in the program.

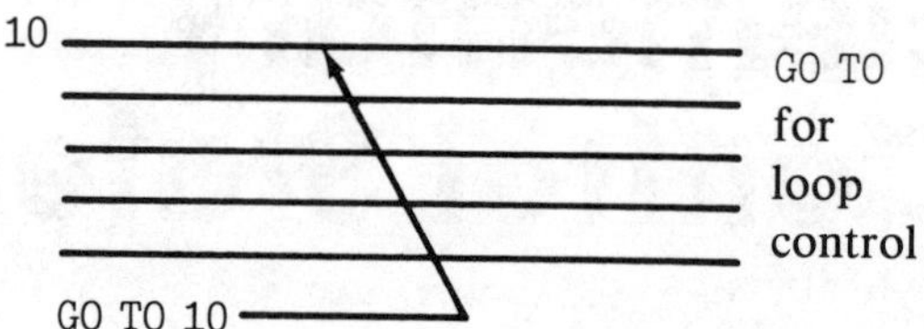

This loop can be more clearly established by a DO statement or by a WHILE statement. Take a look at the following example.

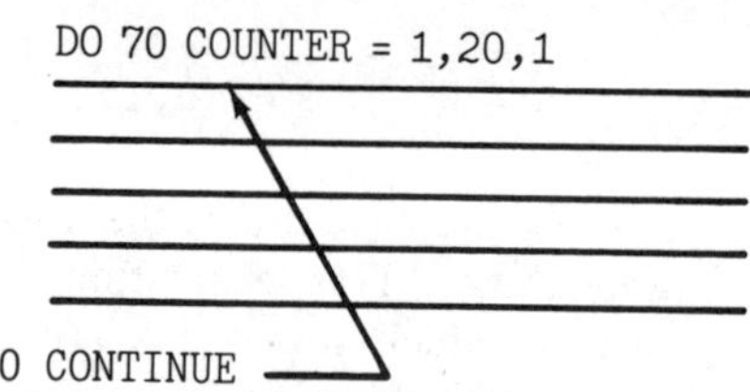

Note the improvement. The DO statement immediately reveals the control structure you are establishing. The bottom of your control loop is clearly and definitively identified by the CONTINUE statement. None of this is provided by the GO TO statement. As a matter of fact, you can be at the bottom of a loop established by a GO TO and never be aware that you ever entered a loop.

5.2 Logical IF

The GO TO statement produces what is called an *unconditional* transfer of control. More often than not, the transfer of control needs to be *conditional*, that is, based on some decision or test:

Has hours worked exceeded 40?

Has the balance dropped below zero?

Is X greater than 10?

While most programs have a normal path of logic, a *general program* must accommodate all possible variations and alternatives. Conditional control statements, such as the logical IF, allow us to test for these special conditions and account for that condition. A typical example is as follows:

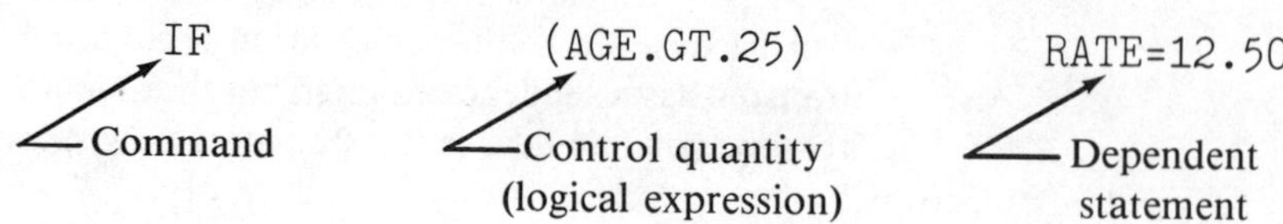

There are three parts to this statement. The IF command identifies the statement and signals a possible interrupt. What follows next is a "logical expression" contained within parentheses. This expression has two possible values: true or false. If the expression is evaluated as true, the dependent statement is recognized (executed); otherwise, it is ignored. If the dependent statement is ignored, no interruption takes place and normal processing resumes.

The "true/false" value of the logical expression serves as a control quantity for a two-way branch, that is, to determine which of two statements will be executed next:

True	False
Execute the statement to the right of the logical IF.	Execute the statement below the logical IF.

General Form

The general form of the logical IF is

IF (logical expression) Dependent Statement

Some examples are:

```
IF(X.EQ.3.5)STOP
IF(HOURS.LT.40.)PAY=HOURS*RATE
IF(AVRAGE.GT.90.)WRITE(2,8)NAME
```

Observe that the statement appearing to the right of the logical IF is not restricted severely. It can be a READ or a WRITE statement. It can be an arithmetic assignment statement. It cannot, however, be another IF, a DO, or a WHILE statement.

It may be helpful to think of the logical expression as a switch, a logical switch, placed in front of the dependent statement. If the logical expression is true, the switch is on and the dependent statement becomes part of your program. If the expression is false, the switch is off and the statement is ignored.

The logical IF is a "junior" version of the IF-THEN-ELSE construct. The logical IF is used when a decision must be made as to whether a *single statement* should or should not be executed. How does the compiler distinguish between the logical IF and its big brother, the IF-THEN-ELSE statement? If the word THEN appears after the logical expression, the statement is recognized as the header of an IF-THEN-ELSE construct. Otherwise it is a logical IF.

5.3 Constructing Logical Expressions

The symbols used in mathematics to describe the relationship of one quantity to another are shown in the left-hand column of the following table.

Symbol	Relational Operators	
$=$	.EQ.	equal
$\neq$	.NE.	not equal
$>$	.GT.	greater than
$<$	.LT.	less than
$\geq$	.GE.	greater than or equal to
$\leq$	.LE.	less than or equal to

In mathematics, we say that one quantity is "greater than" or "less than" or "not equal to" another. For each of these mathematical symbols, the equivalent FORTRAN symbol (relational operator) consists of two letters preceded and followed by a period. You have used symbols such as +, −, *, and / to construct arithmetic expressions. The symbols .EQ., .GT., .LT., and so on are used to construct logical expressions. These symbols are easy to remember and are included in the summary charts on the back cover for easy reference.

It is important to realize the full potential of the logical IF. It is used in banking problems, calculus problems, aircraft loading problems, medical problems, and so on. The following table shows some sample uses to suggest just how versatile the statement is.

Sample IF Statements and Their Uses

Problem Type	Statement	Meaning
Aircraft Loading	IF(WEIGHT.GT.9000.)STOP	Is the aircraft overloaded (cargo weight greater than 9000 lbs)?
Water Treatment	IF(TEMP.LT.32.0)Y=1.68*H	Has the temperature of water dropped below freezing?
Trig Problem	IF(ANGLE.EQ.90.)GO TO 5	Are we dealing with a right triangle?
Missile Control	IF(ALT.LE.0.0)PRINT*,'CRASH'	Is the missile still airborne or has it crashed?
Slope of a Line	IF(Y2.GT.Y1)WRITE(2,*)Y1	Is the slope of a line positive?
Banking Problem	IF(DEBIT.GT.CREDIT)STOP	Is the account overspent?
Medical Problem	IF(PRES.GT.134.)WRITE(2,*)NAME	Is the patient's blood pressure greater than normal?

5.4 Compound IF Statements

The majority of IF tests are as simple as those suggested thus far. However, on occasion, more complex testing is required. These more complicated tests are merely a sequence of simple tests joined together by the .AND. operator or the .OR. operator.

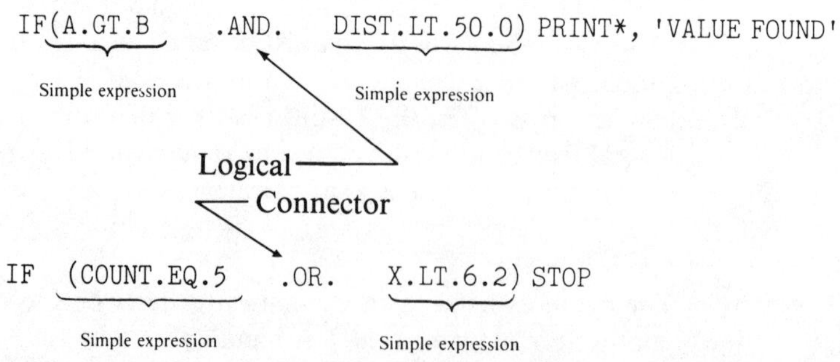

The two most common connectors are the .AND. and .OR. operators. When the .AND. operator is used, the two expressions it connects must *both* be true for the compound expression to be true.

```
IF(TYPE.EQ.3..AND.DIST.LT.50.0)PRINT*,'DONOR LOCATED'
```

In this example, TYPE must be equal to 3, and the value of DIST must be less than 50 for the expression to be evaluated as true.

When the `.OR.` operator is used, the complex expression is true if *either* (or both) of the simple expressions is true.

```
IF(COUNT.EQ.5.OR.X.LT.0.0)STOP
```

The `STOP` statement will be executed when:

1. `COUNT` equals 5, or
2. `X` is less than zero, or
3. `COUNT` equals 5 and `X` is less than zero.

It is possible to construct even more complex logical expressions. We will cover this later. For the moment, keep your logical expressions as simple as possible.

5.5 Flowcharts

As the number and complexity of control statements in a program increases, there is a corresponding increase in the number of alternate paths through the program's logic. Attempting to trace each loop and each branch can be an overpowering task for the programmer and for anyone attempting to use the program. We need some sort of "road map" to assure the correct passage of control for each branch in the logic.

Pseudocode diagrams provide a little "path" information, but not in the right form. They are verbose, awkward, and difficult to read. A more abbreviated and direct means of symbolically representing the program's algorithm is through the **flowchart**.

Flowchart Symbols

Symbol	Meaning	Explanation
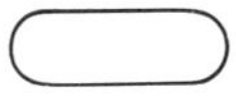 (oval)	Program Start/Stop	The oval shows the beginning and end of a program.
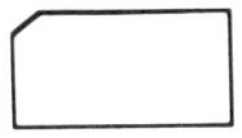  (card) / (printed sheet)	Punched Card Input/Output Line Printer Output	Input by cards and output on the line printer are represented by these easily remembered symbols (a card and a sheet of output paper).
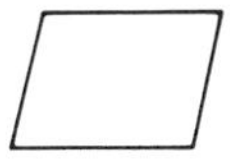 (parallelogram)	General Input/Output	The parallelogram is the generalized input/output symbol. It represents input/output in any form—tapes, cards, disk, or terminals.
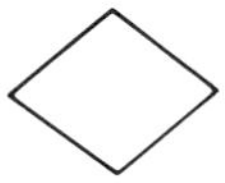 (diamond)	Decision Statement	The diamond represents a decision-making statement, a logical `IF`, for example.
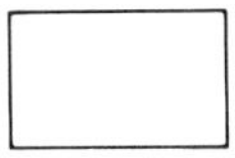 (rectangle)	Processing Step	The rectangle represents a processing step, usually an arithmetic assignment statement.
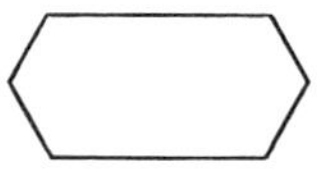 (hexagon)	Loop Construct	This symbol represents the top of a loop construct. Either a `DO` or a `DO WHILE` construct.
(small circle)	Continuation Point	The small circle is used to connect two points on a diagram that, for some reason, cannot conveniently be connected by lines; for example, when the diagram carries over onto another page.

Flowcharts are schematic diagrams that use a set of symbols to display in a highly graphical form the executable statements of a program. Each symbol suggests the type of statement being used and shows how control can be passed to and from that statement by one or more arrows connected to the symbol. The flowchart is in effect a short hand representation of the logic originated in the pseudocode. You will soon find it to be an indispensable tool for planning, designing, and checking complex programs.

A well-constructed flowchart shows much more than just the possible paths through the program. A flowchart displays each variable name chosen to represent input, output, and intermediate values. It indicates each important equation and all decision-making factors. This diagram along with a well-documented program is usually all that is needed to describe even the most complex problem. Read the next programming example and see if you do not agree.

Programming Example
Volume Discount

To encourage sales, a wholesale distributor offers its customers a discount if they buy in volume (six items or more). The larger the order, the larger the discount.

Discount Policy

Number Purchased	Discount
1–5	no discount
6–10	10%
11–20	16%
21 or more	20%

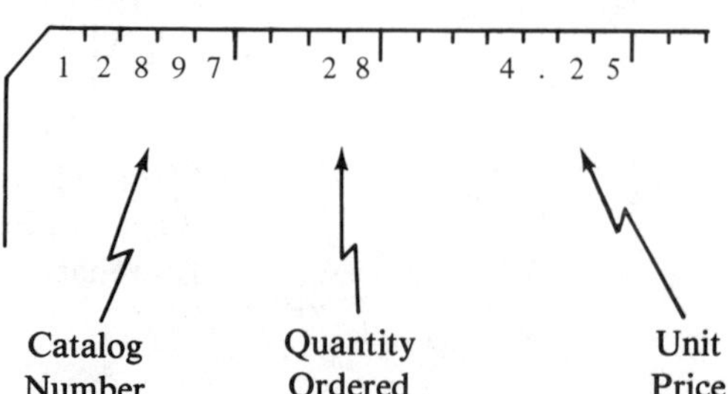

Each order received is represented by a record in the input file. The record gives the catalog number of the item ordered, number of units ordered, and the unit price (cost before discount). Write a program to determine what discount is allowed for the size order, and provide the information needed for a packing slip that will be shipped with the order.

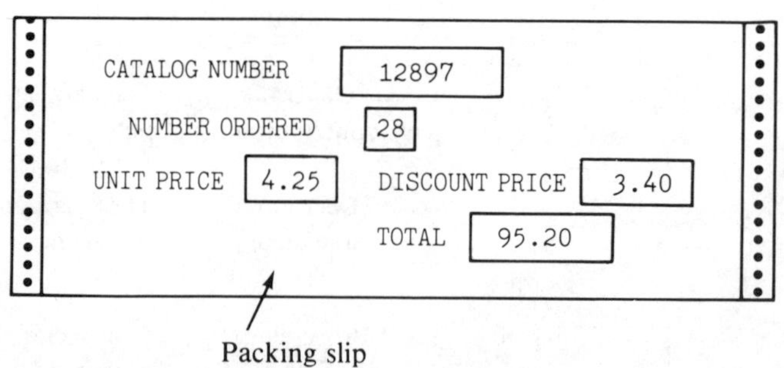

Packing slip

The following flowchart suggests that the program starts with a READ statement followed by a series of IF tests that determine which discount level to use. Control passes to one of four statements that sets the appropriate discount rate. After the discount is established, control is transferred to a series of closing statements that compute the total bill, print the output and terminate the program. The numbers placed near a flowchart symbol correspond to a statement number that will be used in writing the program. These tie the program and the chart closer together.

Take a moment and look at the numerous comment statements used in this program. They make the logic easy to follow.

Programming Example–Volume Discount continued

Programming Style

Use comment statements: make them meaningful

Comment statements are an important tool to:

1. Provide assistance in reading the program.
2. Isolate and identify important segments of modules of the program.
3. Show the program's structure.

Comment statements should be used frequently, but should *not* be direct copies of the FORTRAN code:

```
C  READ X FROM DATA
   READ (5,*) X
```

Such comment statements are not very meaningful.

Another feature of this program, a *bad* one, is the number of GO TO statements used. Count them up, there are nine in total. The program can easily be written with *no* GO TOs.

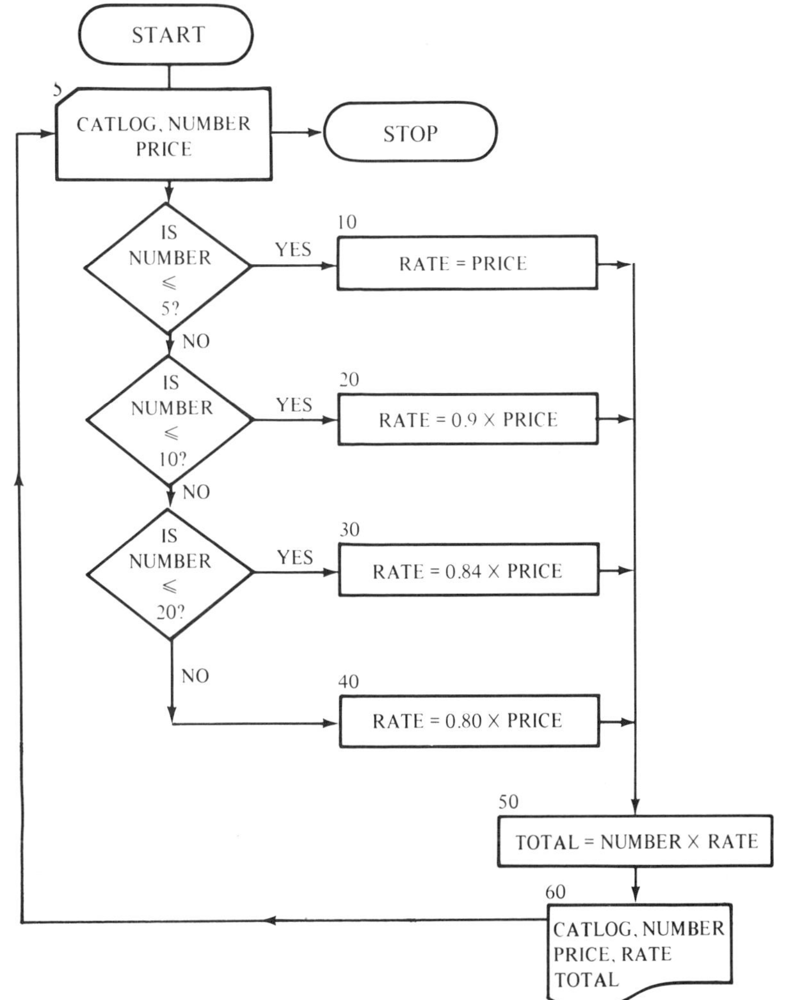

Programming Example–Volume Discount continued

```
C.................................................................
C..    PURPOSE - TO DETERMINE THE APPROPRIATE DISCOUNT     ..
C..              WHEN ITEMS ARE PURCHASED IN VOLUME.       ..
C.................................................................
C
C            ---IMPORTANT VARIABLES---
C
C      --CATLOG  CATALOG NUMBER OF ITEM                       --
C      --NUMBER  QUANTITY OF ITEMS ORDERED                    --
C      --PRICE   UNIT PRICE PRIOR TO DISCOUNT                 --
C      --RATE    UNIT PRICE AFTER DISCOUNT                    --
C      --TOTAL   TOTAL COST OF UNITS ORDERED                  --
C
      INTEGER CATLOG,NUMBER
      REAL    PRICE,RATE,TOTAL
C
    5 READ(5,*,END=100)CATLOG,NUMBER,PRICE
C
C     .....SELECT CORRECT CATEGORY.....
C
      IF(NUMBER.LE.5) GO TO 10
      IF(NUMBER.LE.10) GO TO 20
      IF(NUMBER.LE.20) GO TO 30
      IF(NUMBER.GT.20) GO TO 40
C
C     .....LEVEL 1 DISCOUNT CATEGORY.....
C
   10 RATE=PRICE
      GO TO 50
C
C     .....LEVEL 2 DISCOUNT CATEGORY.....
C
   20 RATE=0.90*PRICE
      GO TO 50
C
C     .....LEVEL 3 DISCOUNT CATEGORY.....
C
   30 RATE=0.84*PRICE
      GO TO 50
C
C     .....LEVEL 4 DISCOUNT CATEGORY.....
C
   40 RATE=0.80*PRICE
      GO TO 50
C
C     .....TERMINATION SECTION.....
C
   50 TOTAL=NUMBER*RATE
C
      PRINT*,CATLOG,NUMBER,PRICE,RATE,TOTAL
C
      GO TO 5
C
  100 STOP
      END
```

Whenever a program uses a large number of GO TOs, it's a signal that the program logic is weak and could be improved.

Programming Style

Don't patch bad code: rewrite it

There are many signals that show that a program's logic is not working out well (excessive GO TOs is one). Making superficial changes to "patch things up" is a mistake. Reexamine the logic. Rewrite the code.

With this recommendation in mind, let's go back and rewrite the program with fewer GO TO statements. Our goal will be to make the flow of logic more linear in fashion (less disruptive). Anyone attempting to follow the program will start at the top and progress straight down through the program without any wild detours. We will eliminate all but one of the GO TOs. It will be your job to eliminate the last one.

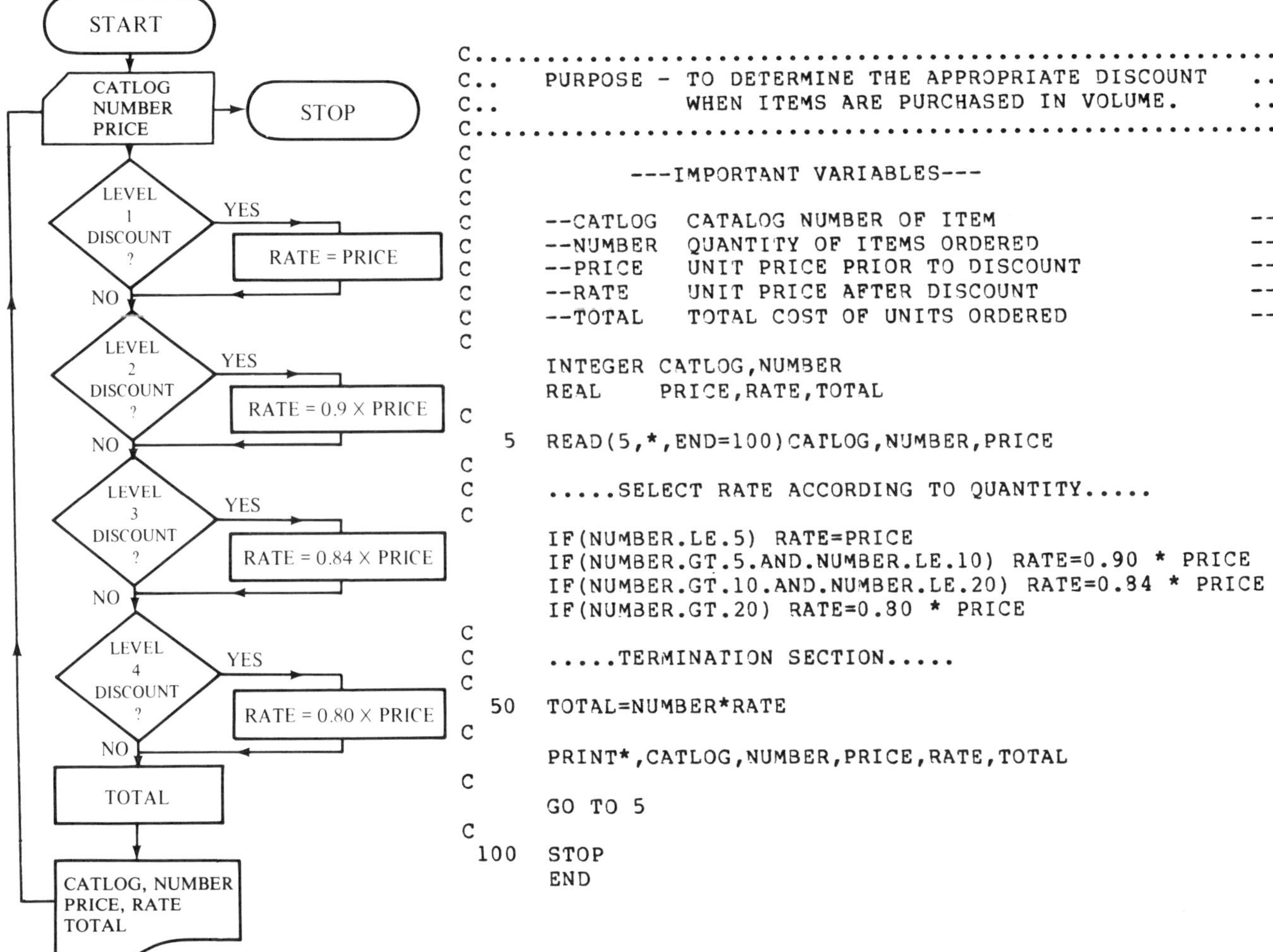


```
C.......................................................
C..    PURPOSE - TO DETERMINE THE APPROPRIATE DISCOUNT    ..
C..              WHEN ITEMS ARE PURCHASED IN VOLUME.      ..
C.......................................................
C
C            ---IMPORTANT VARIABLES---
C
C      --CATLOG  CATALOG NUMBER OF ITEM                    --
C      --NUMBER  QUANTITY OF ITEMS ORDERED                 --
C      --PRICE   UNIT PRICE PRIOR TO DISCOUNT              --
C      --RATE    UNIT PRICE AFTER DISCOUNT                 --
C      --TOTAL   TOTAL COST OF UNITS ORDERED               --
C
       INTEGER CATLOG,NUMBER
       REAL    PRICE,RATE,TOTAL
C
    5  READ(5,*,END=100)CATLOG,NUMBER,PRICE
C
C      .....SELECT RATE ACCORDING TO QUANTITY.....
C
       IF(NUMBER.LE.5) RATE=PRICE
       IF(NUMBER.GT.5.AND.NUMBER.LE.10) RATE=0.90 * PRICE
       IF(NUMBER.GT.10.AND.NUMBER.LE.20) RATE=0.84 * PRICE
       IF(NUMBER.GT.20) RATE=0.80 * PRICE
C
C      .....TERMINATION SECTION.....
C
   50  TOTAL=NUMBER*RATE
C
       PRINT*,CATLOG,NUMBER,PRICE,RATE,TOTAL
C
       GO TO 5
C
  100  STOP
       END
```

This problem represents a special class of problem in programming. While it is clearly a *decision* type of problem, it is not the usual true/false type of decision. One of four possible RATEs must be established. Keep this example problem in mind because we will come back to it later in the chapter to demonstrate what is called a first-case construct.

5.6 IF-THEN-ELSE Construct—Block IF

When a decision must be made as to whether a *group* or *block* of statements (as opposed to a single statement) should be executed, we employ the IF-THEN-ELSE construct. Unlike the logical IF, this control statement (known as the "block IF") is not written on one continuous line. The statement has three parts, each written on a separate line:

Part	General Form	Definition
1	IF *(logical expression)* THEN	The *header* portion used to identify the top of the construct and the type of construct.
2	ELSE	A separator used to separate the "true" statement group from the "false" statement group.
3	ENDIF	The terminator that identifies where the construct ends.

As shown in Figure 5.1, the logical expression is used to determine whether a "true" group or a "false" group of statements should be executed. The right portion of Figure 5.1 shows that the true statements are positioned (as a block) immediately below the header statement. The end of this group of statements is signaled by the ELSE statement, which also serves as the header statement to show where the false group or block of statements starts. Finally, the ENDIF statement signals the termination of the IF construct and directs the resumption of normal (sequential) processing.

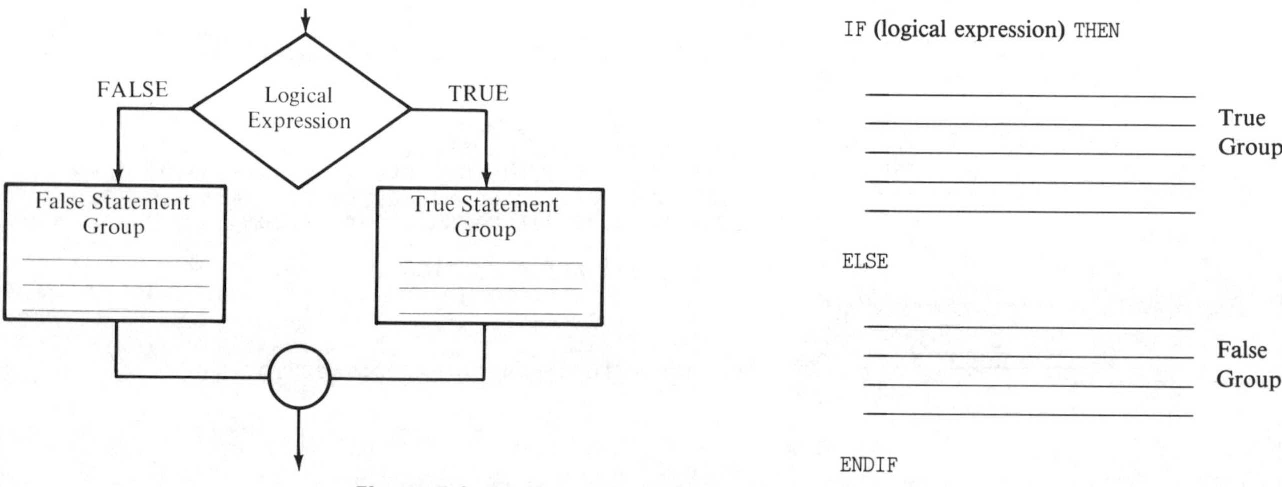

Figure 5.1 IF-THEN-ELSE construct

To further emphasize the structure of this construct, good programming style dictates that statements in both the true group and the false group be **indented** from the IF, ELSE, and ENDIF statements. This shows the subordination of the true and false groups to assist in the clear understanding of how the program works. Make note of this important feature in the examples that follow.

Programming Example #1

Determine which of two values, A and B, is the larger.

```
C.....................................................
C..   PURPOSE - DEMONSTATE IF-THEN-ELSE STATEMENT    ..
C.....................................................
C
      REAL A,B,BIG,SMALL
C
      READ*,A,B
C
      IF(A.GT.B) THEN
C
          BIG=A
          SMALL=B
C
      ELSE
C
          BIG=B
          SMALL=A
C
      ENDIF
C
```

Programming Example #2

Determine the absolute value of a quantity.

```
C
        READ*, X
C
        IF(X.GE.0.0) THEN
            VALUE = X
        ELSE
            VALUE = -X
        ENDIF
C
```

Programming Example #3

Write an IF-THEN-ELSE construct to determine how many points must be added to each student's grade to have a class average of at least 65.

```
        IF(AVE.GT.65.0) THEN
            ADD = 0.0
        ELSE
            ADD = 65.0 - AVE
        ENDIF
C
```

5.7 Single Alternative IF (Abbreviated Form)

Figure 5.2 shows an abbreviated form of the IF-THEN-ELSE construct. In the situation shown, there is a group of statements to be executed if the logical IF is evaluated as true, *but there is no false group* to be executed. This is called the **single alternative IF** in which the ELSE clause (or qualifying portion) is omitted from the construct.

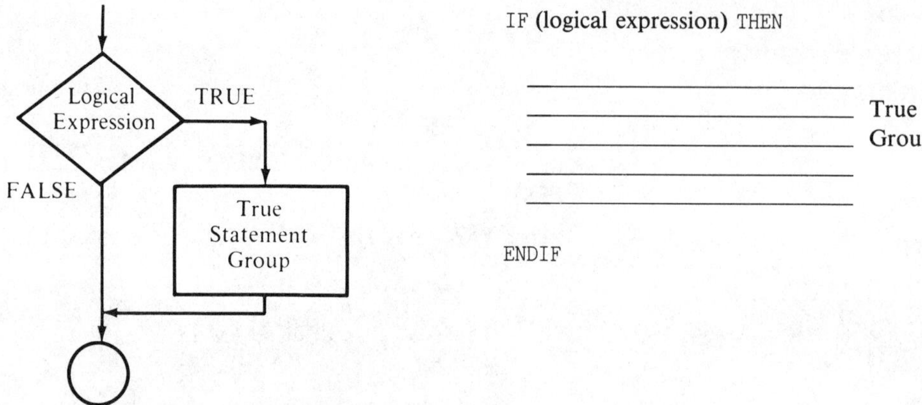

Figure 5.2 Single alternative IF

Programming Example
Sufficient Output?

Test the contents of a memory location called LINES. If the value of LINES is greater than 100 print the message "SUFFICIENT OUTPUT GENERATED," and terminate the program.

```
C
      IF(LINES.GT.100) THEN
C
         PRINT*, 'SUFFICIENT OUTPUT GENERATED'
C
         STOP
C
      ENDIF
```

5.8 Case Construct (Multiple Alternatives)

There is one more application of the IF statement that is extremely important. It is called the multiple alternative or case construct. A typical example of this class of problem is deciding if a person should be given an A, B, C, D, or F as a letter grade on an exam. The distinguishing feature of this problem is that more than a two-way decision is involved. We must select one of many choices (five different alternatives in this example). To see how this new construct works, you must recognize the pattern in which each IF test is written.

Portion	Usage
True	To identify one of the possible cases.
False	To examine the remaining cases (possibilities).

Figure 5.3 addresses the problem of awarding a letter grade to a student. The first IF statement tests to see if the student should get an A. If the answer is yes, an A is printed. Because this print completes the true portion of the IF construct, the construct terminates. No further testing takes place.

Assume the student did not get an A on the exam. We must now consider the statements following the word ELSE. These statements represent a simpler subset of the originally stated problem. One of the cases has been removed. (The possibility of an A has already been eliminated.) Following the word ELSE we set up a second IF

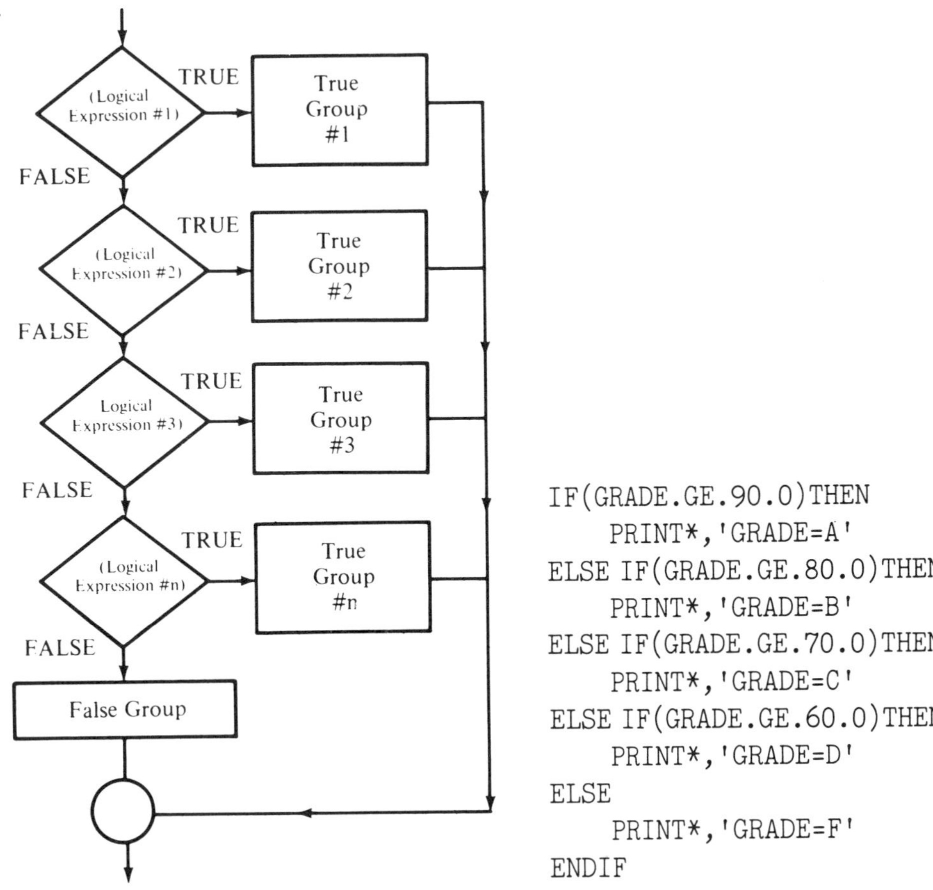

Figure 5.3 First case construct

test. We test for the awarding of a B. Again, this IF statement has two parts: the true part followed by a false part. The true part causes the printing of a B grade. The false part causes examination of the remaining possibilities. Each of the remaining alternatives are tested in sequence by a second, third, and fourth IF test. These latter IF statements are considered nested because they are placed after the ELSE portion of a previous IF statement. Let's test this construct using a specific value of GRADE.

Assume a student scored an 85 on the exam. The logical expression of the first IF test will be evaluated as false and the first alternative (awarding an A) will be rejected. The statements following the word ELSE are chosen for execution. These statements are the ones that test for the remaining alternatives. This second IF test has two parts. Because our student got an 85, the true portion of this IF test is executed. The student is awarded the grade of B and the construct terminates.

The flowchart of Figure 5.3 shows the most important feature of the case construct. Only *one group* of statements (one of multiple alternatives) will be executed, namely those statements associated with the first true expressions encountered as the nested IF tests are made. For this reason, the construct is sometimes called the first-case construct.

When this construct is encountered, a test will be made of the first case, then the second, then the third, and so on. If *none* of the cases (logical expressions) is evaluated as true, the final ELSE (followed by a corresponding false set of statements) will be executed if they are present. A single ENDIF statement shows the end of the construct.

This construct should be viewed as an extension of the basic IF-THEN-ELSE construct. It merely allows the ELSE clause to be followed by another IF test. This IF is considered nested or subordinate to the IF test above it. Any subordinate IF will never be reached if a test above it is evaluated as true. Additional subordinate IFs are written to cover each possible alternative (case) present. The general form would be

```
ELSE IF  (logical expression)  THEN
```

Figure 5.4 General form of multiple alternatives

Header (Test for 1st case)	IF (logical expression #1) THEN ________ ________ ________ ________	True Group #1
ELSE IF (Test for 2nd case)	ELSE IF (logical expression #2) THEN ________ ________ ________ ________	True Group #2
ELSE IF (Test for 3rd case)	ELSE IF (logical expression #3) THEN ________ ________ ________ ________	True Group #3
	⋮ ⋮ ⋮ ⋮ ⋮	
ELSE IF (Test for *n*th case)	ELSE IF (logical expression #n) THEN ________ ________ ________ ________	True Group #n
ELSE (When none of above)	ELSE ________ ________ ________ ________	False Group
ENDIF (Terminator)	ENDIF	

Programming Example
Volume Discount

A problem at the beginning of this chapter involved determining which of four discount policies should be used when filling an order by a wholesale distributor. The larger the quantity ordered, the larger the discount. This first-case construct is tailor-made for this type of problem.

Programming Example–Volume Discount continued

Discount Policy

Number Purchased	Discount
1-5	no discount
6-10	10%
11-20	16%
21 or more	20%

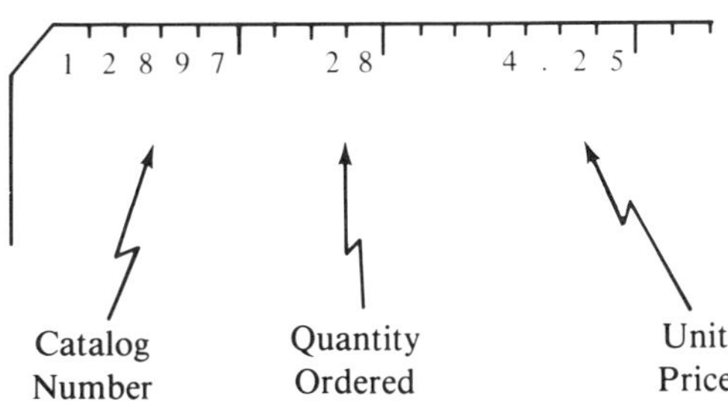

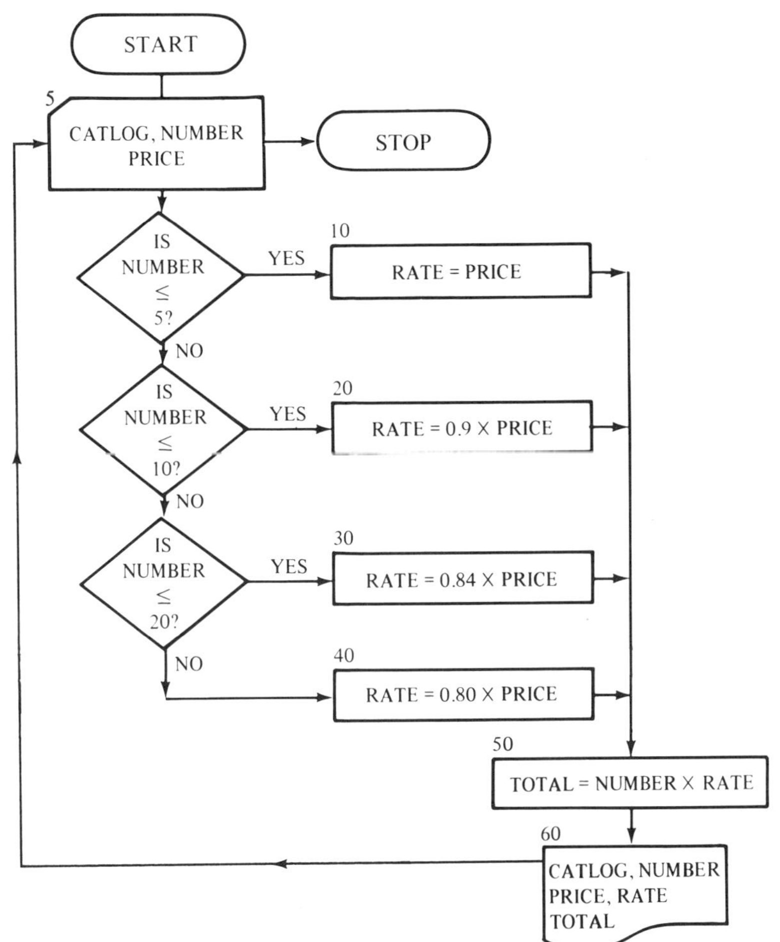

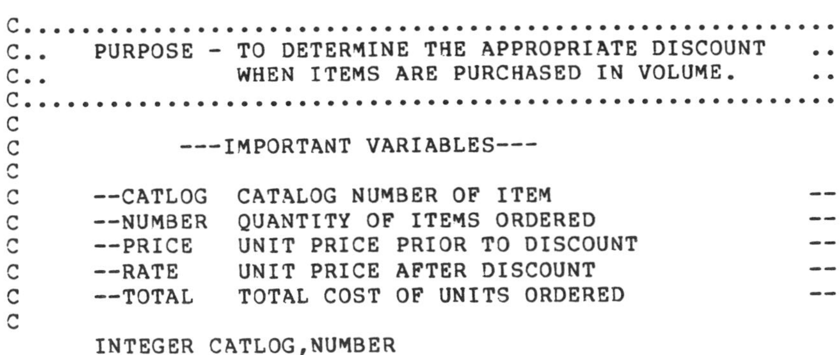

```
C.........................................................
C..   PURPOSE - TO DETERMINE THE APPROPRIATE DISCOUNT    ..
C..             WHEN ITEMS ARE PURCHASED IN VOLUME.      ..
C.........................................................
C
C            ---IMPORTANT VARIABLES---
C
C     --CATLOG  CATALOG NUMBER OF ITEM                   --
C     --NUMBER  QUANTITY OF ITEMS ORDERED                --
C     --PRICE   UNIT PRICE PRIOR TO DISCOUNT             --
C     --RATE    UNIT PRICE AFTER DISCOUNT                --
C     --TOTAL   TOTAL COST OF UNITS ORDERED              --
C
      INTEGER CATLOG,NUMBER
      REAL    PRICE,RATE,TOTAL
```

Programming Example–Volume Discount continued

```
    5 READ(5,*,END=100)CATLOG,NUMBER,PRICE
C
C       .....SELECT RATE ACCORDING TO QUANTITY.....
C
      IF(NUMBER.LE.5) THEN
         RATE=PRICE
      ELSEIF(NUMBER.LE.10) THEN
         RATE=0.90 * PRICE
      ELSEIF(NUMBER.LE.20) THEN
         RATE=0.84 * PRICE
      ELSE
         RATE=0.80 * PRICE
      ENDIF
C
C       .....TERMINATION SECTION.....
C
   50 TOTAL=NUMBER*RATE
C
      PRINT*,CATLOG,NUMBER,PRICE,RATE,TOTAL
C
      GO TO 5
C
  100 STOP
      END
```

Quiz 9
IF Statements

1. Why is the `GO TO` statement generally avoided when writing a program?
2. Distinguish between an unconditional control statement and a conditional control statement.
3. Name the six relational operators used when setting up a logical expression.
4. What symbol in a flowchart represents:
   a. An `IF` test?
   b. Generalized input/output operator?
5. How does the compiler distinguish the logical `IF` from the block `IF` (the `IF-THEN-ELSE`)?
6. Must the `ELSE` statement appear as a part of all block `IF`s?
7. Under what circumstances is the first-case construct used in a program?
8. What is wrong with the `IF` statement

```
IF(X.GT.10.0)BIG=X,GOTO 6
```

Programming Example
Throw Out Lowest Grade

An instructor plans to give four quizzes before the final exam, but with the understanding that the lowest quiz grade will be dropped (quiz average based on best three scores). Write a program to compute the quiz average based on this agreement.

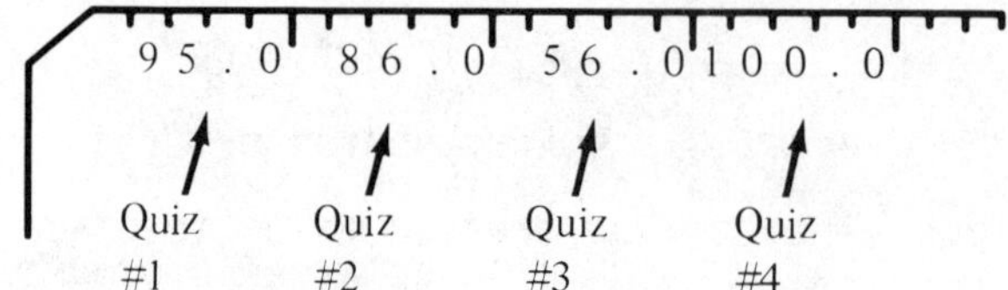

This problem is being presented to show a method of solution that occurs quite frequently in data processing. It is a method used when conducting what is called a

Programming Example–Throw Out Lowest Grade continued

"minimum/maximum" search. In this problem we are searching for the minimum value of the four values given on an input record. The approach is as follows:

1. Assume the first value (`QUIZ1`) is the lowest value

   ```
   SMALL=QUIZ1
   ```

2. Compare the remaining values (`QUIZ2` through `QUIZ4`) with this established value of `SMALL`

   ```
   IF(QUIZ2.LT.SMALL)
   ```

3. Any time one of these tests detects a value that is smaller than `SMALL`, redefine `SMALL` as equal to that value

   ```
   SMALL=QUIZ2
   ```

These words are somewhat abstract. The use of a flowchart should help you understand this methodology.

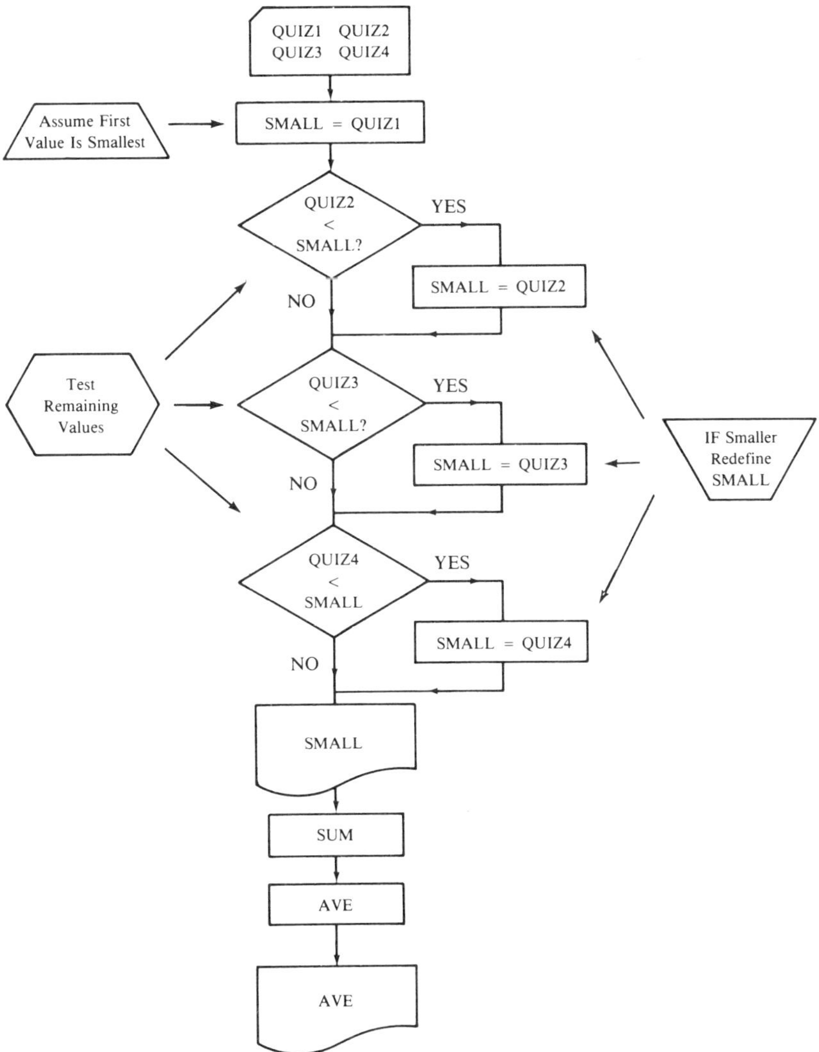

The bottom portion of the flowchart shows that once the value of `SMALL` is known, we add all the quizzes together and then subtract `SMALL` from this sum. It is then a simple matter to compute the desired average.

Programming Example–Throw Out Lowest Grade continued

```
C.............................................................
C..    PURPOSE - DROP SMALLEST OF FOUR GRADES. COMPUTE       ..
C..              QUIZ AVERAGE BASED ON REMAINING THREE       ..
C..              QUIZZES.                                    ..
C.............................................................
C
C                   ---IMPORTANT VARIABLES---
C
C      --SMALL   LOWEST GRADE OF FOUR QUIZZES                --
C      --SUM     TOTAL OF THREE BEST QUIZ GRADES             --
C      --AVE     AVERAGE GRADE                               --
C
      REAL SMALL,SUM,AVE
      REAL QUIZ1,QUIZ2,QUIZ3,QUIZ4
C
      READ*,QUIZ1,QUIZ2,QUIZ3,QUIZ4
C
      SMALL=QUIZ1
C
      IF(QUIZ2.LT.SMALL) SMALL=QUIZ2
      IF(QUIZ3.LT.SMALL) SMALL=QUIZ3
      IF(QUIZ4.LT.SMALL) SMALL=QUIZ4
C
      PRINT*,'LOWEST GRADE=',SMALL
C
      SUM=QUIZ1+QUIZ2+QUIZ3+QUIZ4-SMALL
C
      AVE=SUM/3.0
C
      PRINT*,'AVERAGE=',AVE
C
      STOP
      END
```

This search procedure is an important topic. To strengthen your understanding of just how it works, a slightly more advanced application will be presented.

Programming Example
Calibrate a Scale

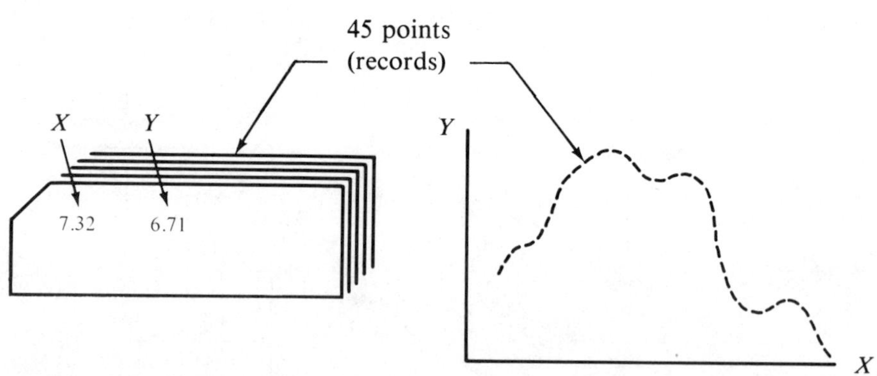

We have been asked to plot a series of 45 data points. Each record of an input file describes a single data point by giving a value of X followed by a value of Y. Before actually plotting all these points, we want to know what is the largest Y value we will encounter and what is the smallest Y value. This information will be needed when calibrating the Y scale.

The program starts as before by reading the first value of Y and setting a memory location called `YBIG` and a memory location `YSMALL` equal to this first value.

Programming Example–Calibrate a Scale continued

A DO construct will then examine all the remaining records in the input file. Any time one of these values of Y is larger than any seen thus far YBIG will be redefined. At the same time, each Y value will be compared with YSMALL to see if that variable needs redefinition.

Clearly this is not a trivial problem. Accordingly we will elect to display a considerable amount of intermediate output to see if the program functions properly. As in other programs, the output is a little more elegant than you are capable of producing at this time, but that is not important—it is the monitoring process.

NUMBER OF DATA POINTS IS 45

POINT	X	Y	YBIG	YSMALL
1	1.62	3.87	3.87	3.87
2	1.74	4.02	4.02	3.87
3	1.79	4.48	4.48	3.87
4	1.92	4.90	4.90	3.87
47	82.61	-19.71	189.71	-19.71
48	83.05	-21.14	189.71	-21.14
49	84.12	-20.03	189.71	-21.14
45	86.72	-18.61	189.71	-21.14

RUN COMPLETE: YBIG = 189.71 YSMALL = -21.14

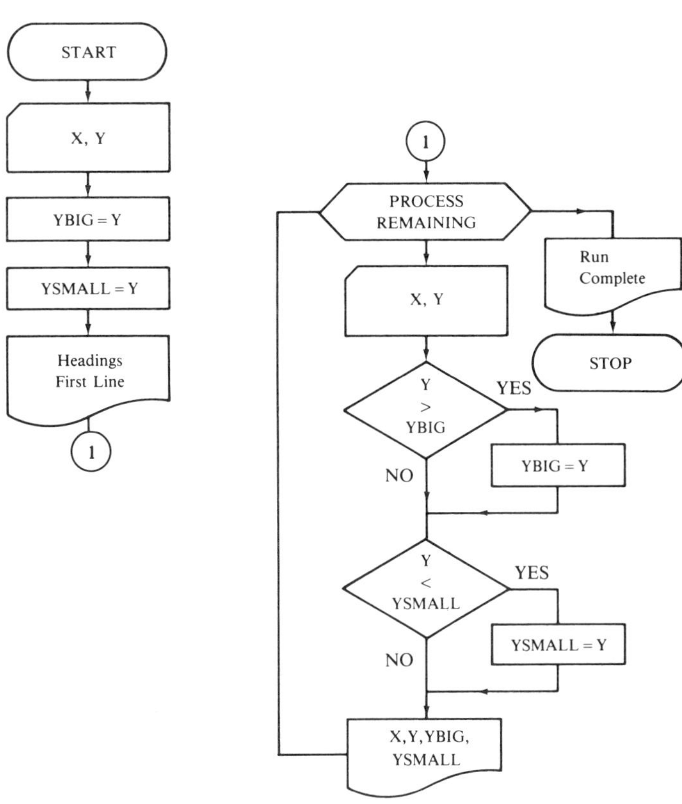

Programming Example–Calibrate a Scale continued

```
C.......................................................
C..   PURPOSE - DEMONSTRATE SEARCH METHOD FOR FINDING    ..
C..             MINIMUM AND MAXIMUM VALUE A VARIABLE.    ..
C.......................................................
C
C                  ---IMPORTANT VARIABLES---
C
C      --NPOINT   NUMBER OF DATA POINTS                     --
C      --COUNT    CARD COUNTER                              --
C      --X,Y      VALUE OF INDIVIDUAL DATA POINT            --
C      --YBIG     MAXIMUM VALUE OF Y                        --
C      --YSMALL   MINIMUM VALUE OF Y                        --
C
       INTEGER NPOINT, COUNT
       REAL    X,Y,YBIG,YSMALL
C
C      .....DEFINE INITIAL VALUE OF YBIG AND YSMALL.....
C
       READ*,X,Y
C
       YBIG=Y
       YSMALL=Y
C
       PRINT*, 'NUMBER OF POINTS IS 45'
       PRINT*,'  '
C
       PRINT*,'POINT        X         Y       YBIG          YSMALL'
       PRINT*,' 1 ', X, Y, YBIG, YSMALL
C
       DO 30 NPOINT=2,45,1
C
          READ*, X, Y
C
          IF(Y.GT.YBIG) YBIG=Y
C
          IF(Y.LT.YSMALL) YSMALL=Y
C
          PRINT*, NPOINT, X, Y, YBIG, YSMALL
C
   30  CONTINUE
C
C      .....LOOP EXIT POINT.....
C
C      .....FINAL MESSAGE TO OUTPUT.....
C
       PRINT*,'RUN COMPLETE   YBIG=', YBIG, 'YSMALL=', YSMALL
C
       STOP
       END
```

Review Exercises

1. A logical expression is used as a control quantity in both the logical and block IF statement. What values may the expression have?
2. If you choose to join (compound) two simple logical expressions to form a complex logical expression, what logical connectors are allowed?
3. Answer the following questions as true or false.
   a. The statements at the right of a logical IF statement can only be another control statement.
   b. The statement at the right of a logical IF can be any statement allowed in FORTRAN.
   c. Only one statement is allowed to the right of a logical IF.
4. Under what conditions would you use a block IF?
5. When do you use the "multiple case" construct?
6. How is the "multiple case" construct formed?
7. Extra print statements are often added to a program during the initial testing of the program's algorithm. Why?
8. What information does a well-constructed flowchart provide?
9. Describe the method of determining the maximum value of a variable in an input file.
10. You have been told to program defensively. What does this mean?

11. A data record contains two real values that are the X and Y coordinates of a point. Write a program to read this record and determine the distance the point lies from the origin.
12. A record similar to that in exercise 11 gives the X and Y coordinates of a point and the radius R of a circle. Write a program that makes use of a block `IF` to print a message indicating that the point lies inside the circle or outside the circle. Do not worry about the point lying on the circle.

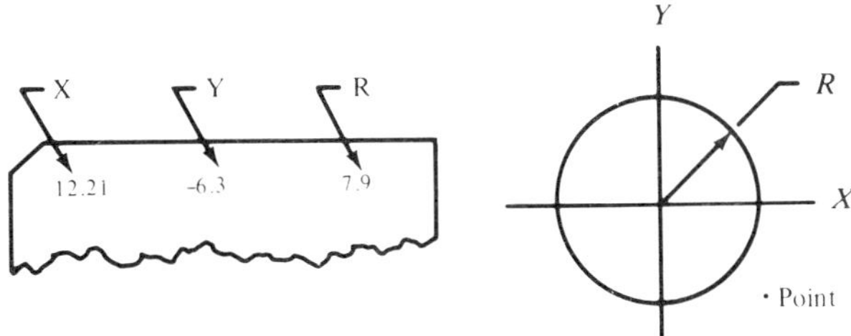

13. Repeat exercise 12 except include the possibility that the point lies on the circle. Use a first-case construct.
14. A data file consists of 100 records. Each record gives the dollar amount of a deposit or a withdrawal to a checking account. Negative values are withdrawals. Positive values are deposits. Print the record number and transaction amount of all withdrawals.
15. Repeat exercise 14 except report the record number of all transactions over $200.00. Put withdrawals on the left of the output sheet and deposits on the right. Label both.

★ 16. A data card contains four real values which are the X and Y coordinates of point 1 and point 4 as shown.

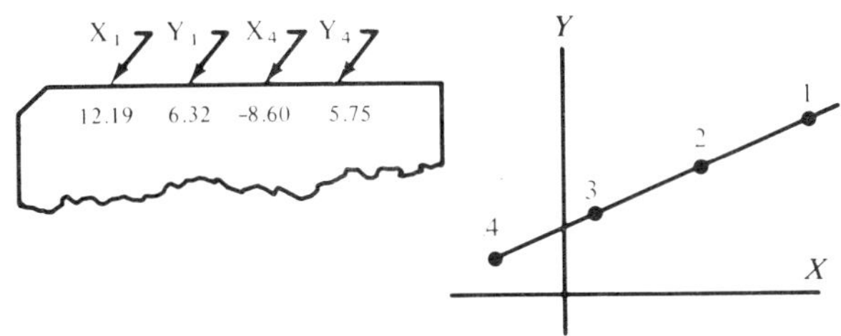

These points form the line 1–4. Write a program to determine and report the X and Y coordinates of points 2 and 3 which divide the line into three equal parts. Check your answer by comparing distances 1–2, 2–3, and 3–4 which should, of course, be equal.

17. The gas company uses the following rate schedule in billing its customers based on the number of cubic feet of gas used.

First 1000 cubic feet	2.5¢/ft.^{3}
Next 1000 cubic feet	2.0¢/ft.^{3}
Remaining 1000 cubic feet	1.8¢/ft.^{3}

Write a program to read the amount of gas used by a customer and calculate the charge appropriately.

18. A programming course involves six large projects, each of which is graded on a scale of 0 to 10.

9 9 7 0 5 9

Write a program to read these six grades and determine the lowest of the six grades listed. Drop this lowest grade and compute the average score based on the remaining five grades.

19. We want to predict the price of gasoline in 1990. The first record of a data file gives five sample prices of gasoline in 1970. The next record gives five sample prices in 1980. Determine the average price in 1970 and 1980. Compute the price in 1990 if the same rate of increase prevails. Print a message `''PRICE IS OVER $2.00 PER GALLON''` or the message `''PRICE IS UNDER $2.00 PER GALLON.''`

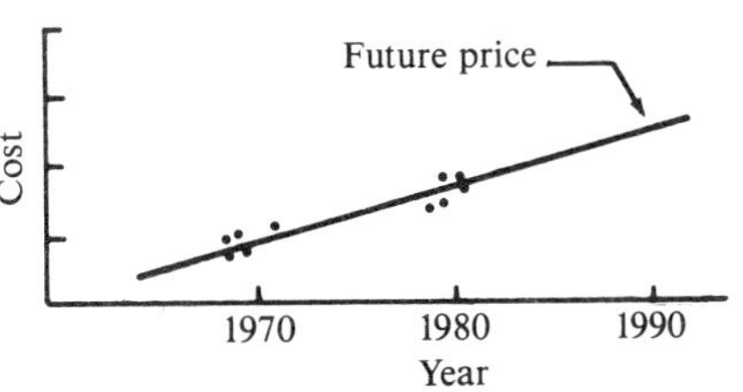

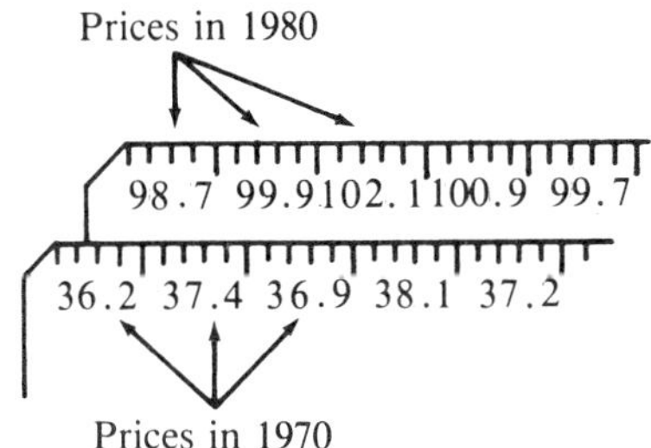

20. The first record in a data file tells the weight of a piece of cargo to be shipped. This is followed by two integers telling the zone number of where the cargo is to be shipped from followed by the zone number of the destination point. Determine and report the cost to ship this article using the following table.

Weight (lbs)	**Number of Zone Changes Rate-per-thousand lb**		
	1	**2**	**3**
0–199	$ 7.63	$ 9.29	$12.86
200–299	$12.26	$18.87	$21.03
300–399	$20.53	$28.43	$37.51
400–499	$42.67	$54.00	$62.04
500–over	$79.81	$84.15	$96.82

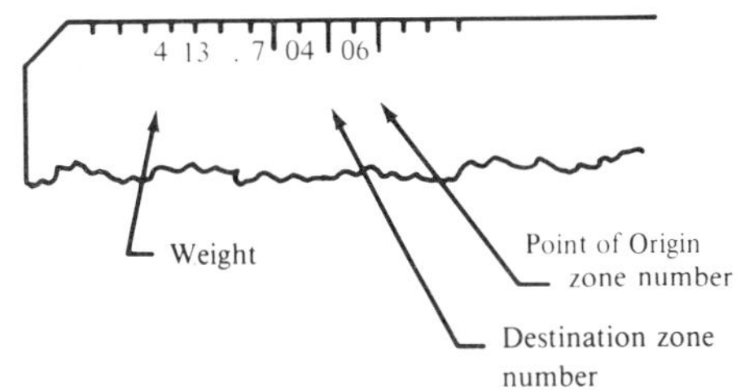

21. Consider the following series of numbers:

    1/2, 1/3, 1/4, 1/5, · · ·

    Write a program to produce the first twenty terms in this series listing each term on a separate line of output. Include statements in your program, however, that will print the message "TERM TOO SMALL" (and stop the program) if a term less than 10^{-10} is generated.

22. A file consists of 100 records each containing a single value of X. These X values have been sorted (smallest X is first, largest X is last.) Collectively, this file is called a "table." A record is placed at the front of this file and it represents a new value of X that is to be added to those already in the file. Write a program to print one of the following messages:

    ```
    NEW X VALUE BELONGS IN FRONT HALF OF TABLE
    ```

    ```
    NEW X VALUE BELONGS IN BACK HALF OF TABLE
    ```

Additional Applications

Programming Example
Qualifying Events

In order to qualify at a swimming meet, you must participate in three preliminary events. Each of these events involves six swimmers. Your time in *each* event must be better than the average time for that event or you are disqualified.

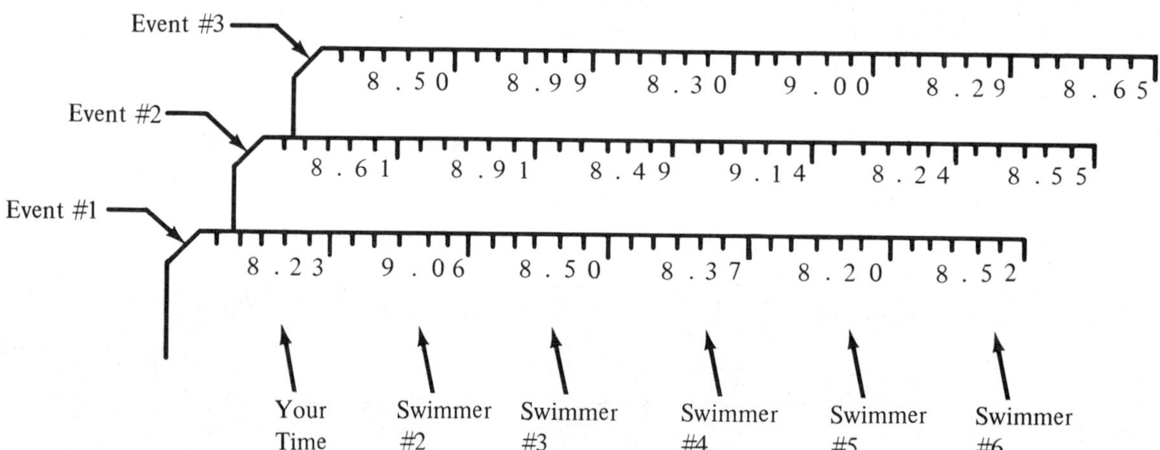

Write a program to see if your time is better than the average time in each of the three events. (Award a point for each successful event. Three points are needed to qualify.) Output of this program should be one of the following messages:

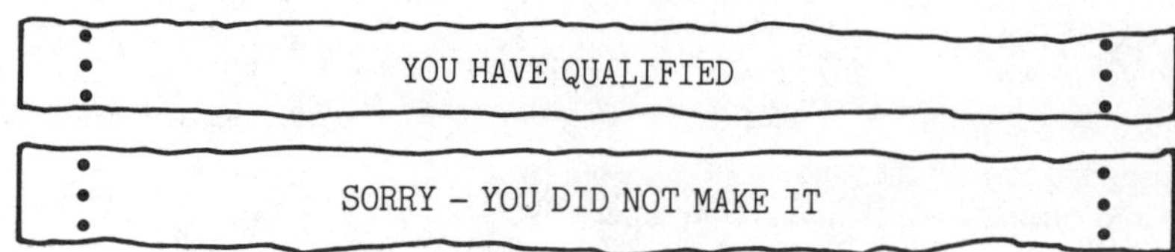

Programming Example–Qualifying Events continued

Variable Names	Meaning
T1 to T6	Time of each swimmer
AVE	Average time of an event
PT1, PT2, PT3	Points for events 1, 2, and 3
TOTAL	Total number of points

Read first record.
Compute average time.
Award point if appropriate.

Read second record.
Compute average time.
Award point if appropriate.

Read third record.
Compute average time.
Award point if appropriate.

Total up points.
Print appropriate message.

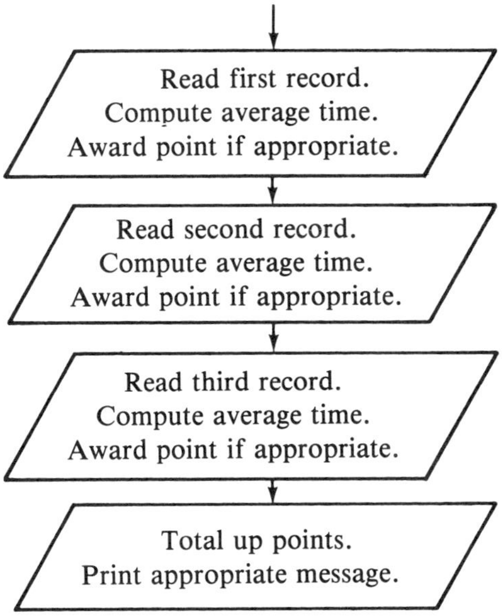

```
C...........................................................
C..   PURPOSE - DETERMINE IF SWIMMER QUALIFIES            ..
C...........................................................
C
C                 ---IMPORTANT VARIABLES---
C
C     --T1...T6     TIME FOR EACH SWIMMER                 --
C     --AVE         AVERAGE TIME FOR THAT EVENT           --
C     --PT1..PT3    ONE POINT GIVEN FOR EACH EVENT        --
C     --TOTAL       TOTAL NUMBER OF POINTS AWARDED        --
C
      INTEGER PT1,PT2,PT3,TOTAL
      REAL    T1,T2,T3,T4,T5,T6
C
      READ*,T1,T2,T3,T4,T5,T6
      AVE=(T1+T2+T3+T4+T5+T6)/6.0
C
      IF(T1.LE.AVE)THEN
          PT1=1
      ELSE
          PT1=0
      ENDIF
C
      READ*,T1,T2,T3,T4,T5,T6
      AVE=(T1+T2+T3+T4+T5+T6)/6.0
C
      IF(T1.LE.AVE)THEN
          PT2=1
      ELSE
          PT2=0
      ENDIF
C
      READ*,T1,T2,T3,T4,T5,T6
      AVE=(T1+T2+T3+T4+T5+T6)/6.0
```

Programming Example–Qualifying Events continued

```
C
      IF(T1.LE.AVE)THEN
          PT3=1
       ELSE
          PT3=0
       ENDIF
C
       TOTAL=PT1+PT2+PT3
C
       IF(TOTAL.EQ.3)THEN
          PRINT*,' YOU HAVE QUALIFIED'
       ELSE
          PRINT*,' SORRY YOU DID NOT MAKE IT'
       ENDIF
C
       STOP
       END
```

Programming Example
Simple Curve Fit

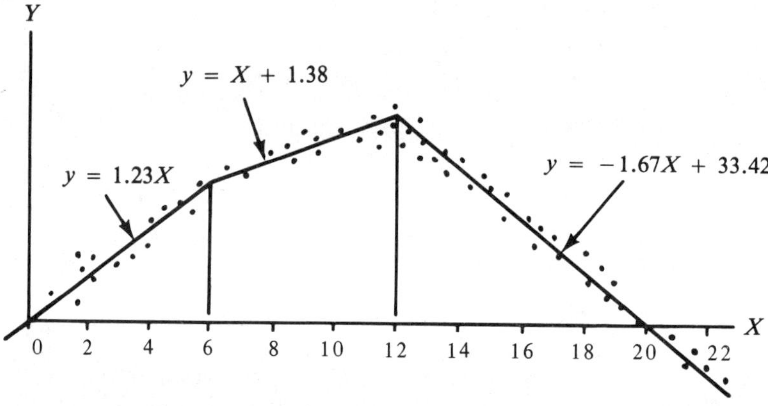

A series of data points have been plotted and between X = 0 and X = 6 they seem to be approximated by the equation

```
EQ.1 Y=1.23*X
```

Between X = 6 and X = 12, the slope of the curve changes and is better approximated by the equation

```
EQ.2 Y=X+1.38
```

Finally, for values of X greater than 12, the slope turns negative and should be approximated by the equation

```
EQ.3 Y=-1.67*X+33.42
```

Part A: Write a program to read a series of X values from input and determine which equation should be used to evaluate Y. Use a series of logical IF tests to make this decision. If X is less than 0.0 or greater than 22.0, do not attempt a calculation.

Programming Example–Single Curve Fit continued

```
C.............................................................
C..   PURPOSE - READ RANDOM VALUES OF X...SELECT CORRECT    ..
C..             EQUATION.                                   ..
C.............................................................
C
C
      REAL X,Y
C
 10   READ(5,*,END=60)X
C
C     ......DETERMINE IF X IN DEFINED RANGE.....
C
      IF(X.LT.0.0) STOP
      IF(X.GT.22.0) STOP
C
C     .....TEST TO SEE WHICH EQUATION TO USE.....
C
      IF(X.LT.6.0) Y=1.23*X
      IF(X.GE.6.0.AND.X.LE.12.0) Y=X+1.38
      IF(X.GE.12.0) Y=-1.67*X+33.42
C
C     .....REPORT BOTH VALUES.....
C
      PRINT*,'Y=',Y,'X=',X
C
      GO TO 10
C
 60   STOP
      END
```

Part B: Solve the same problem using a first-case construct.

```
C.............................................................
C..   PURPOSE - READ RANDOM VALUES OF X                     ..
C.............................................................
C
C
      REAL X,Y
C
   10 READ(5,*,END=60)X
C
      IF(X.LT.0.0) THEN
          STOP
      ELSEIF(X.LT.6.0) THEN
          Y=1.23*X
      ELSEIF(X.LE.12.0) THEN
          Y=X+1.38
      ELSEIF(X.GE.12.0) THEN
          Y=-1.67*X+33.42
      ELSE
          STOP
      ENDIF
C
      PRINT*,'Y=',Y,'X=',X
C
      GO TO 10
C
   60 STOP
      END
```

Programming Example
IF-THEN-ELSE (Car Insurance Repeated)

Rate Table (cost per thousand)

Age	Good Driving Record	Poor Driving Record
Under 25	27.50	42.86
25 or Older	20.80	30.00

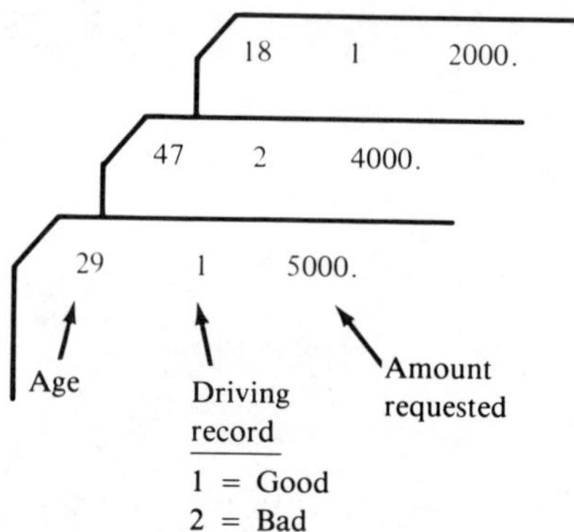

The automobile insurance problem presented in Chapter 2 is repeated here. Write a program to solve the problem, but this time use an `IF-THEN-ELSE` construct. Include a flowchart to show the program logic.

The cost of automobile insurance is based on two factors: age and driving record. The rates for drivers under 25 are shown in the top line of the rate table. The figures given are the cost for $1,000.00 of insurance coverage. Drivers with good driving records pay substantially less than those with poor records.

Each data card gives the age and past driving record of an applicant. The last value is the amount of insurance coverage requested. Write a program to compute the charge to be made for the coverage requested.

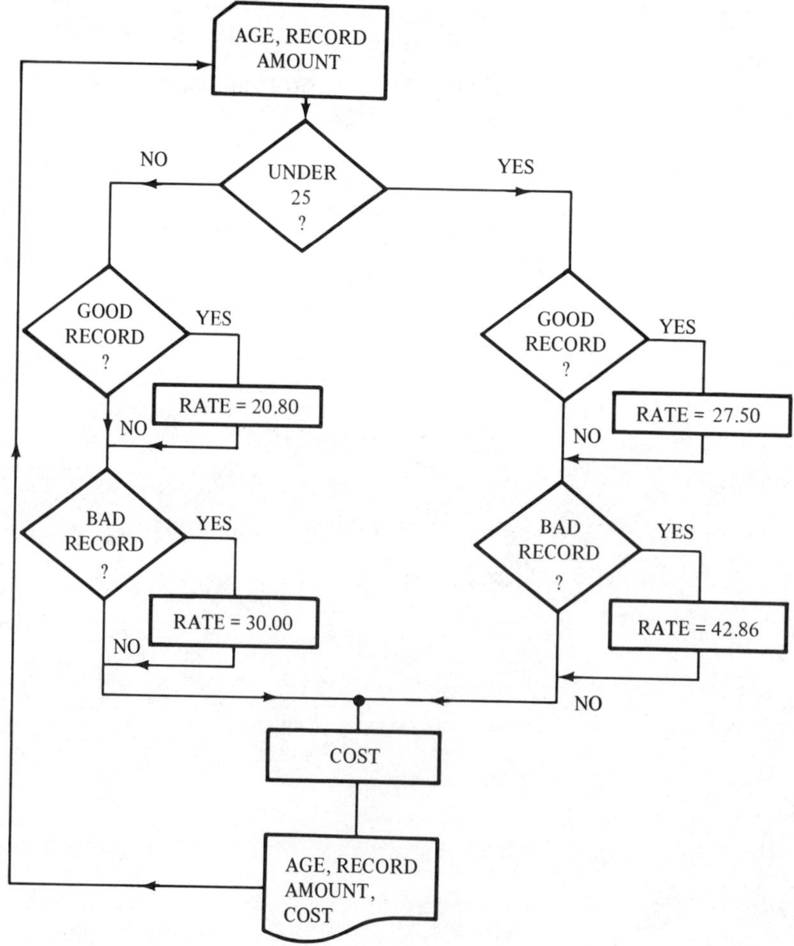

Programming Example–IF-THEN-ELSE (Car Insurance Repeated) continued

```
C.........................................................
C..   PURPOSE - DEMONSTRATE USE OF IF-THEN-ELSE CONSTRUCT   ..
C.........................................................
C
C             ---IMPORTANT VARIABLES---
C
C     --AGE       AGE OF DRIVER                                    --
C     --RECORD    NUMBER OF PAST DRIVING RECORD                    --
C                   CODE      1 = GOOD
C                             2 = BAD
C     --AMOUNT    DOLLAR AMOUNT OF THE COVERAGE REQUESTED          --
C     --COST      COST OF THE COVERAGE                             --
C
      INTEGER AGE,RECORD
      REAL    AMOUNT,COST
C
   10 READ(5,*,END=20)AGE,RECORD,AMOUNT
C
C     .....TEST FOR AGE CATEGORY.....
C
      IF(AGE.LT.25)THEN
C
           IF(RECORD.EQ.1)RATE=27.50
           IF(RECORD.EQ.2)RATE=42.86
C
      ELSE
C
           IF(RECORD.EQ.1)RATE=20.80
           IF(RECORD.EQ.2)RATE=30.00
C
      ENDIF
C
C     .....COMPUTE AND REPORT COST.....
C
         COST=AMOUNT/1000.*RATE
C
         PRINT*,'AGE=',AGE,'RECORD=',RECORD
         PRINT*,'AMOUNT=',AMOUNT,'COST=',COST
C
      GO TO 10
C
   20 STOP
      END
```

Data Checking

An often-neglected aspect of writing effective FORTRAN programs is the topic of *internal data checking*. The programmer is so involved with attempting to develop the correct logic that other important aspects are sometimes overlooked. The last program is a typical example.

As written, the program logic depends on the value of RECORD being either 1 or 2. If this value is keypunched incorrectly, nothing very dramatic happens. An incorrect answer will probably be generated and may well slip through undetected. Assume RECORD is keypunched as equal to 3 on the last data card. For this card, none of the IF tests will be evaluated as true and the quantity RATE is never redefined. *It maintains the value it had from the previous card.* Obviously, the value COST is computed and reported incorrectly. Including the value of RECORD in the output line may cause the error to be detected, but it would be much better to include a "data check" in the program logic as follows:

```
IF (RECORD.NE.1.OR.RECORD.NE.2)
```

Programming Example
Shortest Tie-In

A community is serviced by a network of underground natural gas pipe lines. Points 1 through 6 represent possible points to tie into this system.

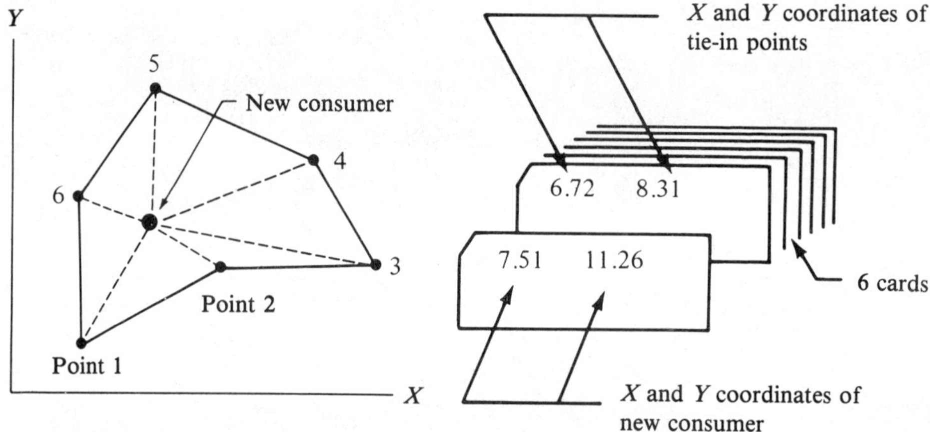

The first record of a data file gives the X and Y coordinates of a new customer. The remaining records describe the X and Y locations of possible tie-in points. Determine the distance to each tie-in point. Produce output similar to that shown.

```
          LOCATION OF NEW CUSTOMER

          X=7.51           Y=11.26

POINT          LOCATION              DISTANCE

  1        X= 6.72  Y= 5.09             7.43
  2        X=18.91  Y=12.26            14.47
  3        X=25.37  Y=27.37            24.53
  4        X= 4.22  Y=21.80            12.89
  5        X= 1.04  Y=10.14             7.12
  6        X=11.16  Y=10.01             4.21
```

Print as a final message the shortest tie-in distance and the number of that tie-in point. This is a special request in that you must not only determine the shortest distance, but also identify that tie-in point. This will be accomplished as follows. Any time we redefine the value SHORT (it holds the shortest distance), we will immediately redefine a value called BESTPT (best point) defining the point that gives this shorter tie-in point.

Programming Example–Shortest Tie-In continued

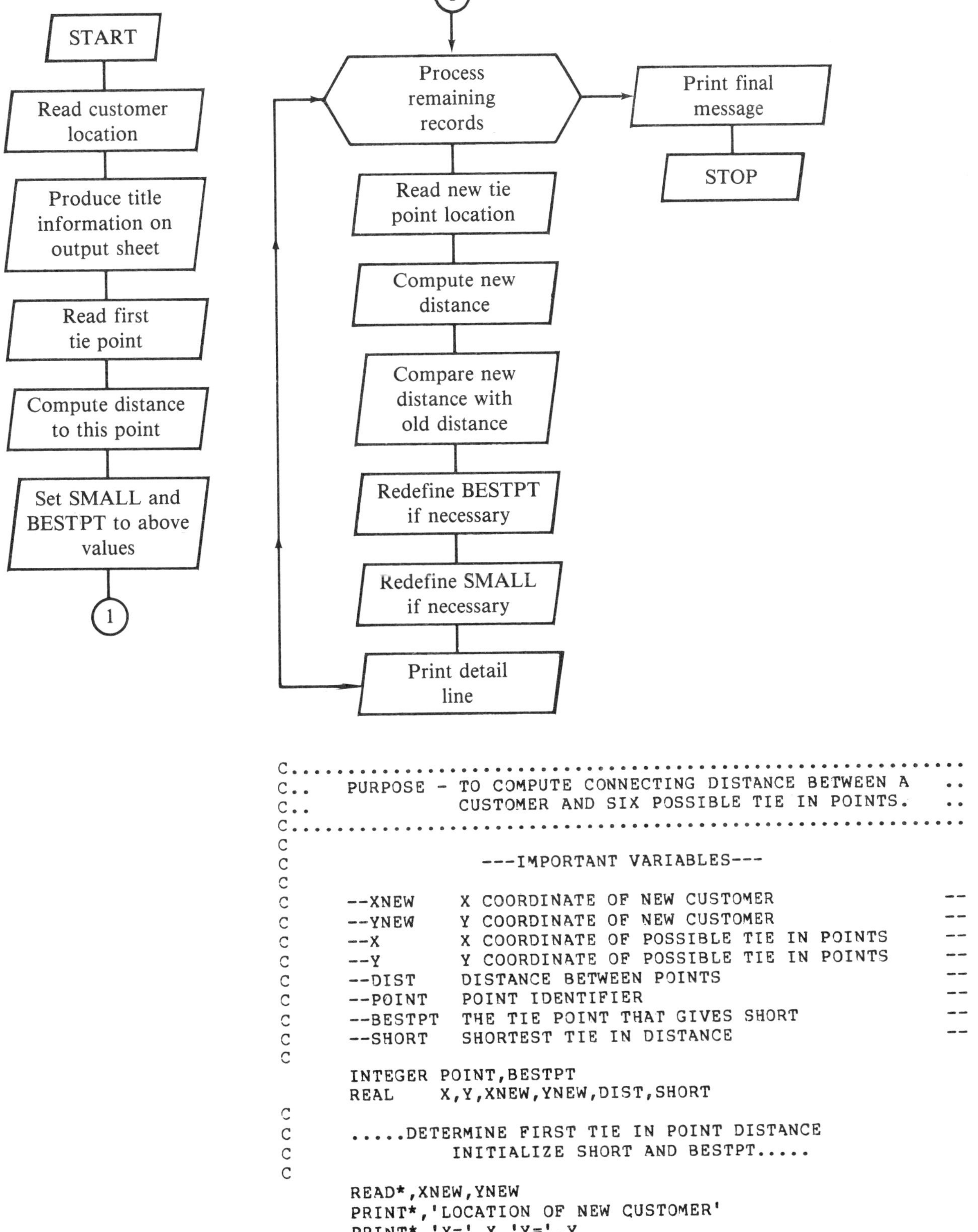


```
C.............................................................
C..   PURPOSE - TO COMPUTE CONNECTING DISTANCE BETWEEN A     ..
C..             CUSTOMER AND SIX POSSIBLE TIE IN POINTS.     ..
C.............................................................
C
C                  ---IMPORTANT VARIABLES---
C
C     --XNEW    X COORDINATE OF NEW CUSTOMER                    --
C     --YNEW    Y COORDINATE OF NEW CUSTOMER                    --
C     --X       X COORDINATE OF POSSIBLE TIE IN POINTS          --
C     --Y       Y COORDINATE OF POSSIBLE TIE IN POINTS          --
C     --DIST    DISTANCE BETWEEN POINTS                         --
C     --POINT   POINT IDENTIFIER                                --
C     --BESTPT  THE TIE POINT THAT GIVES SHORT                  --
C     --SHORT   SHORTEST TIE IN DISTANCE                        --
C
      INTEGER POINT,BESTPT
      REAL    X,Y,XNEW,YNEW,DIST,SHORT
C
C     .....DETERMINE FIRST TIE IN POINT DISTANCE
C             INITIALIZE SHORT AND BESTPT.....
C
      READ*,XNEW,YNEW
      PRINT*,'LOCATION OF NEW CUSTOMER'
      PRINT*,'X=',X,'Y=',Y
      PRINT*,'POINT     LOCATION     DISTANCE'
C
```

Programming Example–Shortest Tie-In continued

```
      READ*,X,Y
      DIST=((XNEW-X)**2+(YNEW-Y)**2)**0.5
C
      SHORT=DIST
      BESTPT=1
C
      PRINT*,1,'X=',X,'Y=',Y,DIST
C
C     .....PROCESS REMAINING POINTS.....
C
      DO 80 POINT=2,6,1
C
          READ*,X,Y
          DIST=((XNEW-X)**2+(YNEW-Y)**2)**0.5
C
          IF(DIST.LT.SHORT) THEN
C
              SHORT=DIST
              BESTPT=POINT
C
          ENDIF
C
          PRINT*,POINT,'X=',X,'Y=',Y,DIST
C
   80 CONTINUE
C
C     .....PRINT FINAL MESSAGE.....
C
      PRINT*,'SHORTEST DISTANCE=',SHORT
      PRINT*,'BEST TIE POINT=',BESTPT
C
      STOP
      END
```

6 Loop Control Statements

6.1 Loop Constructs

One of the more important features of the computer is its ability to accomplish *iterative* operations, that is, to repeat a series of operations or calculations again and again. By now you know that this simply means establishing a loop. When the number of iterations (passes through the loop) is known, the loop is established one way: by a DO statement. If the number of iterations is not known, the DO WHILE statement is used. Both of these statements are extremely important. We will examine the DO statement first.

Each part of the DO statement is given a special name. These parts are shown in Figure 6.1. The first part is the command DO which identifies the type of control statement being used (loop control with automatic counting facilities). Next is a number (in this case, statement number 10) which defines the range of the statements to be included as part of the loop structure. The remaining items (called parameters of the DO) are features needed to establish the automatic counting.

Figure 6.1 Parts of the DO statement

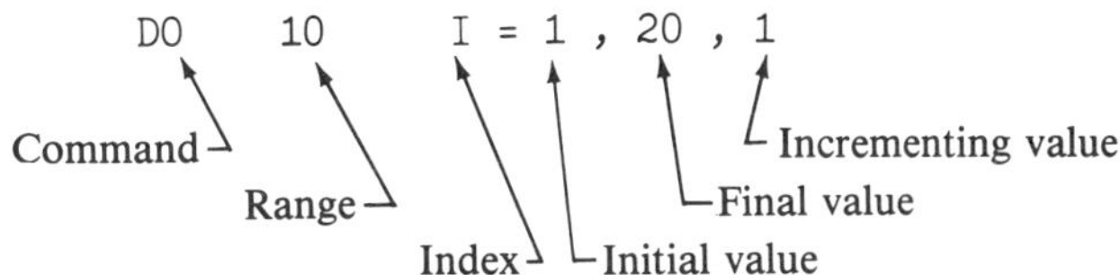

The INDEX is usually an integer variable the name of which is selected to fit the application appropriate to the function of the loop. This name could be COUNT, IDNUMB, LINE, or any other name the programmer chooses. The programmer next exercises control over the behavior of the index by stipulating its first value, its last value, and its incrementing value. The incrementing value is the value by which the index is to change each time the last statement in the range of the loop is executed. *If the incrementing value is not specified, its value is assumed to be 1.*

Consider the DO statement of the general form

```
DO 35 K=4,104,2
```

The parts of this statement are explained in the following table.

General DO Statements

Part	Meaning	Explanation
DO	Command	The command DO calls out iteration. Read as: SET UP A LOOP STRUCTURE THAT INCLUDES ALL STATEMENTS THAT FOLLOW UP TO AND INCLUDING STATEMENT NUMBER ______.
35	Range	The range of the DO includes the statements that are to be executed repeatedly. The last statement must be identified by number, and this statement number follows the command DO.
K	Index	Each DO statement has associated with it an INDEX. Frequently this INDEX is an integer variable used by the programmer to keep track of the number of times the statements within the RANGE have been executed.
4	Initial Value	The programmer may exercise considerable control over the indexing variable and may dictate its INITIAL VALUE, that is, its value on the first execution of the statements in the range of the DO.
104	Final Value	This is the last value the INDEX should have, that is, the value of the index on the last iteration of the loop.
2	Indexing Increment	A final control over the INDEX is obtained by an ability to specify how much the INDEX is to increase upon each execution of the statements in the range of the DO—in this case, by 2. *If no value is specified, the indexing increment is understood to be 1.*

The preceding DO statement is in its most elementary form. Many variations are permitted. First, any of the parameters of the DO may be variables (provided they are defined prior to the execution of the DO statement. Next, almost all compilers allow any of the parameters to be expressions. The index can be made to go backwards (start at a high number and move toward a lower number) by using a negative incrementing value. Finally, the index can be a *real* value with real parameters (initial, final, and incrementing quantities). Consider the following examples.

Statement	Explanation	Variation
DO 20,KING=1,40	Statements up to and including statement 20 are to be executed 40 times—first with KING=1, then with KING=2, etc.	The ommission of the indexing increment causes the increment to be one. There is an optional comma after the RANGE parameter.
DO 8 JOB=2,N,3	The index JOB has an initial value of 2, then 5, then 8, etc. The upper limit of index JOB is N.	The final value is specified as a variable.
DO 12 M=I,LOVE,K	Index M has an initial value of I, then I + K, then I + 2K, etc. The upper limit of index M is LOVE.	The initial, final, and incrementing values are variables.
DO 106 JOB=40,2,-2	Statements up to and including statement 106 are to be executed 21 times, first with JOB = 40, then with JOB = 38, then 36, then 34, etc.	Index JOB is being controlled to have only even values beginning with 40 and ending with 2.
DO 8 X=-10.,B-3.,0.1	Index X has an initial value of -10.0, then -9.9, then -9.8, etc. The lower limit of the index is to be B - 3.	The index is real, the initial value is negative, the final value is an expression.

Trip Counter

Each time a DO statement is executed, the computer sets up its own independent *trip counter*. It then examines the parameters of the DO to find out how many excursions through the loop are needed to advance the index from its initial value to its final value using the incrementing rate specified. When this value is known (the trip count) the loop is entered and iteration takes place. Once inside the loop, the programmer has no control over the trip counter. The programmer, for example, may redefine the index or change the incrementing value, but this does not affect the trip counter.

6.2 The CONTINUE Statement

When reading a block of FORTRAN code, it is very important to be able to distinguish those statements that are inside a loop and those that are not. The DO statement very clearly defines the top of a loop. It is important to show the bottom of the loop with equal clarity. This can be accomplished by the CONTINUE statement.

The CONTINUE statement is used for one purpose only, namely to end a DO loop. It is a "null" or "do nothing" statement in the sense that no hardware is called into play when this statement is executed. It does have the important feature of focusing attention on where the DO loop ends. Actually there is another reason for making the last statement in the range of a DO the CONTINUE statement. Without going into detail at this time, the last statement in the range of a DO loop can be a READ or WRITE or arithmetic statement. The last statement may *not* be an IF or GO TO or other control statement. By using the CONTINUE statement, you automatically avoid any such difficulties.

6.3 The DO WHILE Statement

Loop structures that do not involve counting are best handled by the DO WHILE construct. This type of looping is one that should continue as long as a particular condition exists. As suggested in Figure 6.2, the logical expression (following the command DO WHILE) is the control quantity that determines if another iteration of the loop statements should take place. Upon completion of any pass through the loop,

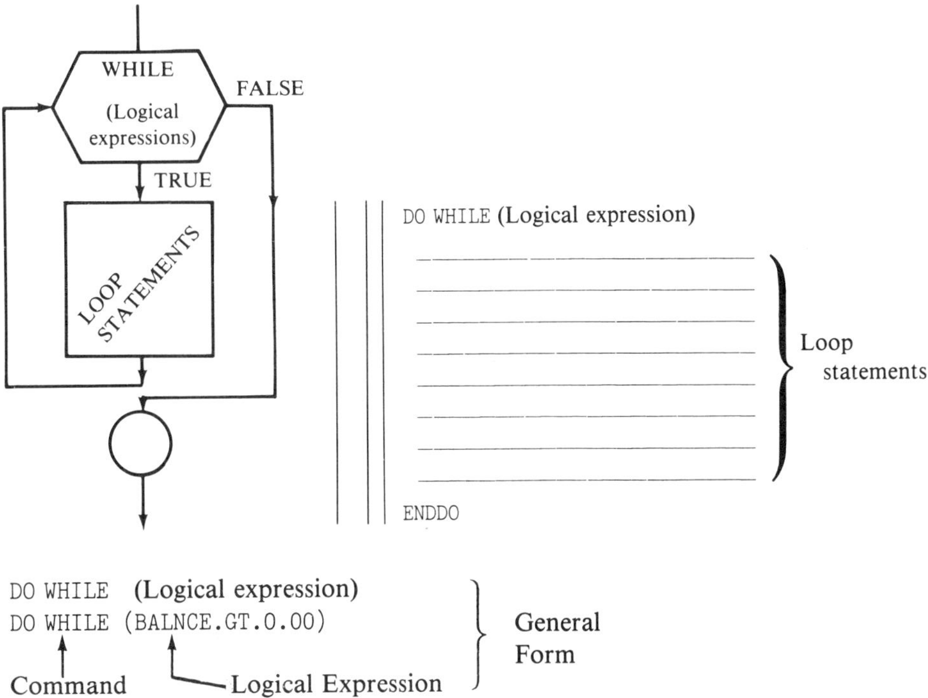

Figure 6.2 The DO WHILE construct

the ENDDO statement causes control to pass back to the top of the loop to the header statement. The logical expression in the header is reevaluated. If the expression is still true, another iteration of the loop statements takes place. If the expression is false, iteration ceases and control passes to the bottom of the construct, that is, to the statement following the ENDDO statement. If the logical expression is false when the DO WHILE statement is first encountered, the loop structure terminates before it ever gets started. Control passes directly to the statement following the ENDDO without any of the loop statements being executed.

As simple as the DO WHILE statement is to implement, a number of precautions must be observed if the statement is to function properly. Let us examine a specific example. Assume a program has a series of statements that are used to make payment of a household bill, for example, the electric bill or the phone bill. We wish to execute these statements (the loop) until there are no more bills or until the balance in our checking account is less than $200.00. (We want to keep a little money in reserve.) The statement

```
DO WHILE (BALNCE.GE.200.00.AND.BILLS.GT.0)
```

will be used to control the loop. Two variables are serving as control quantities: BALNCE and BILLS. Observe the following:

1. Statements inside the loop must change BALNCE or BILLS so that eventually the loop structure terminates.
2. The control quantities BALNCE and BILLS must be defined before the DO WHILE statement is executed.

If either of these conditions is violated, the loop will not behave properly. Not only will the loop not behave properly, but the programmer will not even realize why the program is generating faulty output.

When setting up a loop structure, it is important to know if the loop statements executed the correct number of times, if they executed at all, or if they executed too many times. All these questions are answered by the inclusion of a PRINT statement immediately after the header statement:

```
DO WHILE (BALNCE.GE.200.00.AND.BILLS.GT.0)
    PRINT*,'INSIDE PAY-BILL LOOP'
    PRINT*,'BALANCE=$',BALNCE,'BILLS=,'BILLS
```

Quiz 10
Loop Structures

1. Name the "parameters" of a DO.
2. How can the index of a DO be made to go backwards (from a high value to a low value)?
3. Write a DO statement that will make the index take on the following values: (40, 38, 36, . . ., 4, 2, 0.)
4. May the index of a DO be real? May it be an expression?
5. When the incrementing value of a DO is not specified, what value is assumed?
6. What is the purpose of the trip counter?
7. Once inside the loop, how can the value of the trip counter be changed?
8. Why is it recommended that a PRINT statement be positioned at the top of a loop construct?
9. When is the DO WHILE construct used?
10. Should the statements inside a DO WHILE be indented as we did for statements inside the counting DO structure?

6.4 Common Control Activities: Counting/Deck Control

As you write more and more programs, you will soon detect a recurring pattern of events. Take, for example, the way in which a data file is organized. There are three basic methods of organization. Knowing which method of file organization is being used and supplying the appropriate control structure (`DO` or `WHILE`) to handle the situation is known as *deck or file control.*

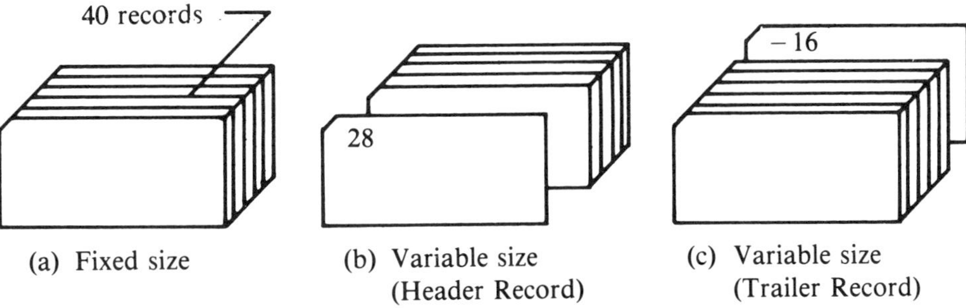

Figure 6.3 File organization

If you are told there are 40 records in a data file (see Figure 6.3a) this is known as a fixed size file that is easily handled by a `DO` construct. The data file may be variable in size with the number of records specified on the first record in the file, called a header record or a leader record. See Figure 6.3b. Finally, the number of records in a file may not be known, but rather a special record has been placed at the end of the file, called a sentinel record or a trailer record. When this special record is reached (as detected by a `WHILE` construct), normal processing is terminated.

Another recurring event in programming is *counting*. You may be asked to determine how many students passed an exam or how many zip codes start with the digits 24. In covering deck control and counting in detail, we are expanding your repertoire of commonly occurring activities in programming which should make future programming easier for you.

> **Programming Style**
>
> **Separate the familiar from the unfamiliar**
>
> In establishing a program's algorithm, there are bound to be a number of steps with which you are familiar. They are part of almost any problem. Being quick to recognize these steps will help break down the problem and make it more manageable.

Counting algorithms involves a small amount of cleverness in the use of an integer memory location. Assume we must process a data file containing 4000 records. Each record contains a value of X and a value of Y. We are asked to print any record with a value of X greater than 10.0. There may be just a few such records, but there may also be a large number of the records described. Accordingly you are instructed to limit the lines of output (number of records printed) to 20. The following three statements will manipulate an integer memory location called `COUNT` in a way that causes `COUNT` to behave like a counter.

Statement	Classification	Meaning
COUNT = 0	Initialization statement	Zero counter
COUNT = COUNT + 1	Indexing statement	Advance counter
IF(COUNT.EQ.20)STOP	Test statement	IF 20 lines, STOP

These statements will be used now to solve the problem at hand (see Figure 6.4).

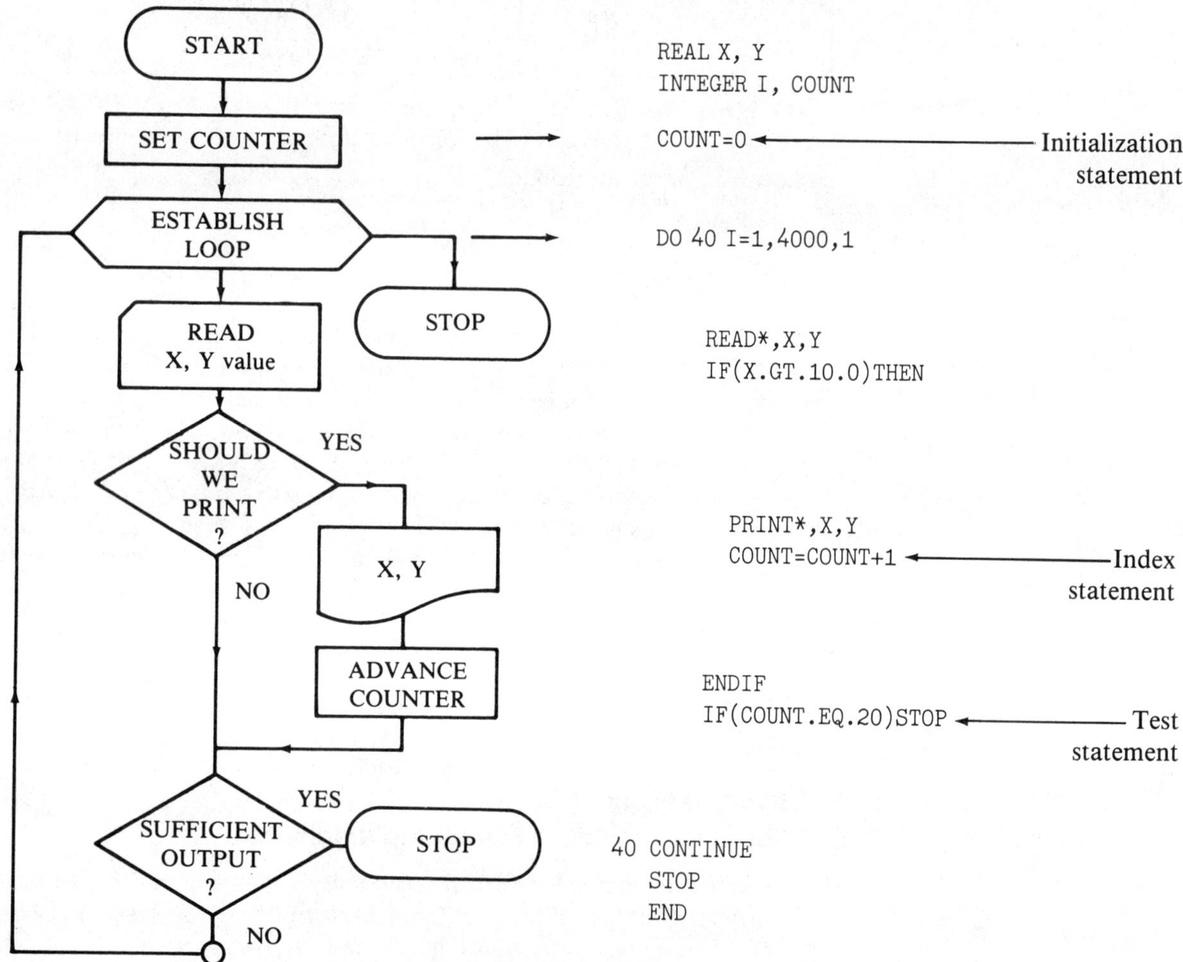

Figure 6.4 Typical counting application

The statement COUNT = 0 is made early in the program and sets the initial value of the counter at zero. The statement

```
COUNT = COUNT+1
```

is the key to the counting process. It is called an indexing statement because each time it is executed the contents of memory location COUNT increases by one. To understand how this statement works recall the way in which the replacement symbol (equal sign) is interpreted in an assignment statement.

Symbol	Meaning
=	"is replaced by"

Recall also that the compiler causes the expression to the right of the replacement symbol to be examined first. When the result of that expression has been determined, that value will be sent to the memory location identified to the left of the replacement symbol.

Example	Meaning
`N=N+1`	N is to be replaced by its current value plus 1
`COUNT= COUNT+5`	COUNT is to be replaced by its current value plus 5 (counting by 5s)
`N=N-1`	N is to be replaced by its current value *minus* 1

The statement `COUNT=COUNT+1` says, "Fetch a copy of the contents of memory location `COUNT`. Add one to this value completing the evaluation of the expression (right side of statement.) Store the results thus obtained back in memory location `COUNT`."

Common Errors

1. Note that the initialization statement `COUNT = 0` is positioned above the `DO` loop in Figure 6.4. In this position it is executed once and only once. For some unexplainable reason, students will frequently position this statement *inside the* `DO` *loop*, for example, just before the `READ` statement. In this position the initialization statement will be executed over and over again (4000 times in this case.) Every time the counter is advanced because of a large X value, the count value will be lost because of the incorrect placement of the initialization statement.
2. Frequently students will use no initialization statement at all. "After all," they say, "I didn't have to initialize other variables. What's special about this one?" Any quantity appearing in the expression portion of an arithmetic assignment statement should be defined when that statement is reached. For example, X and Y must be defined when the statement `ANS = X/Y` is reached, possibly by a `READ` operation. Since the variable `COUNT` appears in the expression portion of an assignment statement `COUNT = COUNT + 1`, it must be defined when this statement is first executed.

6.5 Deck Control (Variable Size)

When the size of a data file is different for each run of a program, one technique is to place at the front of the data file a record giving size information, that is, a record containing a single integer number declaring how big (how many records) the file is for this particular run of the program. This extra record is called a header record or a leader record.

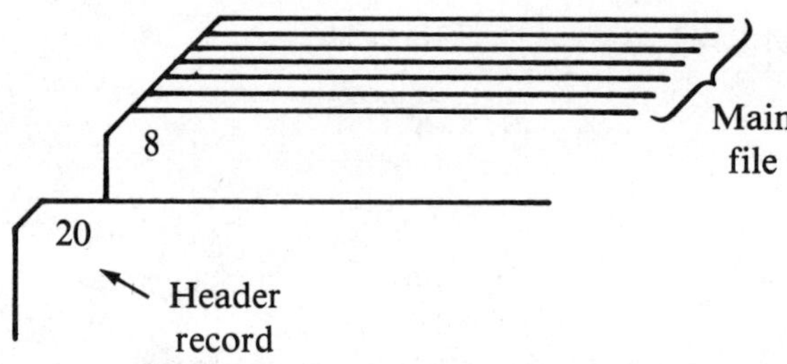

The problem that follows asks you to determine how many times the number 5 appears in a data file. The size of the data file is variable. This sets up a special class of problem. It represents a problem where the entire data file must be examined before a meaningful answer can be given (how many 5s are in the file).

The first record of a data file contains an integer that tells how many records follow (gives size information). Each remaining record contains a single integer value. These integers are supposedly chosen at random, which would suggest that the number 1 appears as often as the number 2 and as often as the number 3, etc. Write a program to determine and report how many times the number 5 appears.

Two counting activities are associated with this program. One counter called `CARDS` is needed to keep track of how many records have been read from the data file. Another counter, `FIVES`, counts the number of appearances of the digit 5 in that data file. A `DO` construct is used to automatically provide control over the counter `CARDS`. We will have to control the counter `FIVES` ourselves.

As a final feature of this program, we are again going to discuss the importance of using extra print statements in your program. For some reason, beginning programmers are usually optimistic that everything will go well. Experienced programmers, on the other hand, continually anticipate disaster. They expect things to go wrong and build into a program certain safeguards that will let them know when and why their programs malfunctioned. One way to do this is with extra printouts. While this program calls for only one output value, look at all the output a cautious programmer would generate.

```
RECORD BEING                      CONDITION
  PROCESSED      VALUE READ      OF COUNTER
      1               8               0
      2               1               0
      3               5               1
      4               2               1

     17               4               2
     18               7               2
     19               5               3
     20               3               3

RUN COMPLETE: FINAL RESULT 3
```

This output displays the state of the card counter (left-hand column) to verify that it is working properly. The center column displays each number read from data to show if the fives counter (right-hand column) is detecting the number 5 properly. We encourage you to take the same precautions when writing a program.

> **Programming Style**
>
> **Program defensively: print—print—print**
>
> Of all the recommendations given thus far, this is the most important one. Use extra print statements at every opportunity to monitor the correct behavior of your program. They will help to detect and isolate incorrect code.

We continue to develop the problem solution in a series of gradual steps: pseudocode first, followed by variable name table, flowchart, and finally FORTRAN code.

Variable Names

NUMBER	Value read from data
CARDS	Card counter
FIVES	Number of 5s counter
SIZE	Deck Size

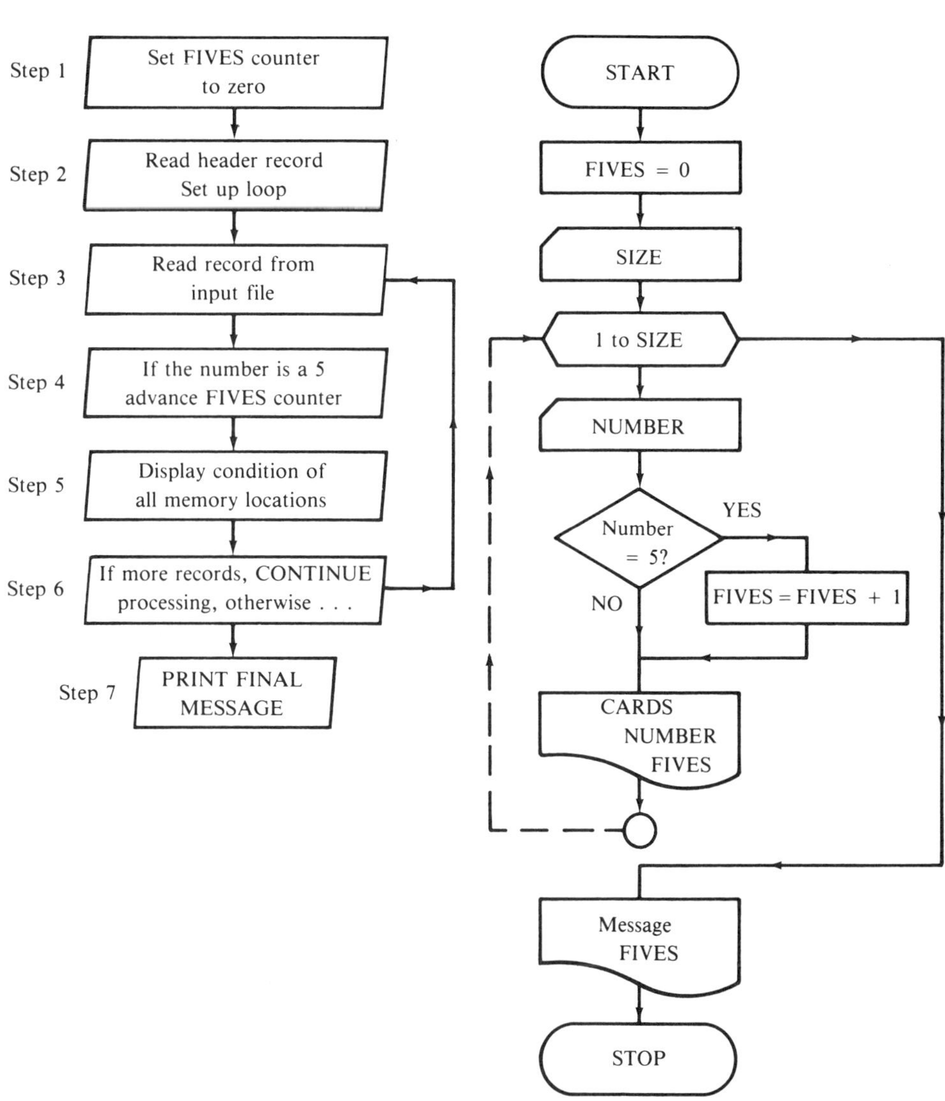

```
C.......................................................
C..    PURPOSE - DEMONSTRATE DECK CONTROL USING HEADER  ..
C..              RECORD.                                ..
C..                  ------------------------          ..
C..              COUNT NUMBER OF TIMES A 5 APPEARS      ..
C.......................................................
C
C            ---IMPORTANT VARIABLES---
C      --CARDS    THE CARD (RECORD) COUNTER                --
C      --NUMBER   VALUE READ FROM THE INPUT RECORD         --
C      --FIVES    COUNTER RECORDING NUMBER OF 5'S          --
C      --SIZE     SIZE OF INPUT FILE - HEADER CARD         --
C
      INTEGER CARDS, SIZE, NUMBER, FIVES
C
C     .....INITIALIZE FIVES COUNTER.....
C
      FIVES = 0
C
C     .....PROCESS HEADER RECORD......
C
      READ *, SIZE
C
C     .....SET UP PROCESSING LOOP.....
C
      DO 60 CARDS = 1, SIZE, 1
C
          READ *, NUMBER
C
C         .....TEST FOR A 5 ON THIS RECORD.....
C
          IF (NUMBER .EQ. 5) FIVES = FIVES + 1
C
C         .....DISPLAY CONDITION OF ALL MEMORY LOCATIONS.....
C
          PRINT *, CARDS, NUMBER, FIVES
C
   60 CONTINUE
C
C         .....LOOP ENDS HERE.....
C
      PRINT *,'RUN COMPLETE...THE NUMBER 5 OCCURS ',FIVES,' TIMES'
C
      STOP
      END
```

The method of deck control used by this problem and the previous one is not the most reliable. A safer and therefore more popular technique is covered in the next section. It does not involve counting, but instead uses a trailer or sentinel record.

Programming Style

Deck control by counting: use with caution

Deck control that involves counting requires special precautions. If the deck is one record short or one record over, problems occur. If the deck size changes, the leader record must be changed.

Quiz 11
Deck Control

1. What does the term "deck or file control" mean?
2. What are three typical ways in which an input file is organized?
3. Describe a header (leader) record and why one might be used.
4. When setting up your own counter, describe three statements that are used in the process.
5. Why is it advisable to use extra print statements when writing a program?
6. A flowchart should begin and end with what symbol?
7. Why is it necessary to initialize a counter?
8. What happens when a programmer inadvertently places the initializing statement inside a processing loop?

6.6 Deck Control (Trailer Record)

The last method of file control you have seen several times before. It consists of placing an extra record at the end of the file instead of the front. This record must have the same general format as all the other records, but has at least one field containing ridiculous information used to terminate the processing loop. This method of file control is the most popular because it does not involve counting and is safer to use than the others.

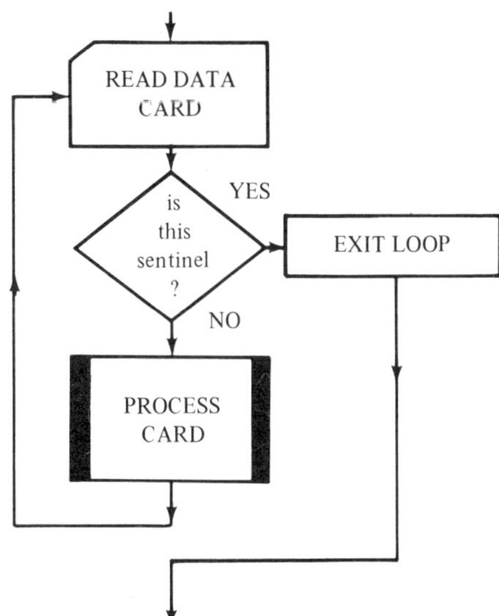

A student might well ask, "Why must we learn these alternative methods of file control? Can't we use the automatic end-of-file option in our READ statements?" To understand the answer to this question you must realize that the data files you have seen so far are extremely simple files consisting of records of basically all the same type. In actual practice an input file may contain several parts. The first portion of an inventory file might list the stock on hand at the start of a report period. The next part of the file might list any shipments we received from our supplier. The last portion of the file lists shipments we made to our customers. The file has three parts. Each part must be identified by one of the techniques we have been studying.

Programming Example
Small Lot Trading

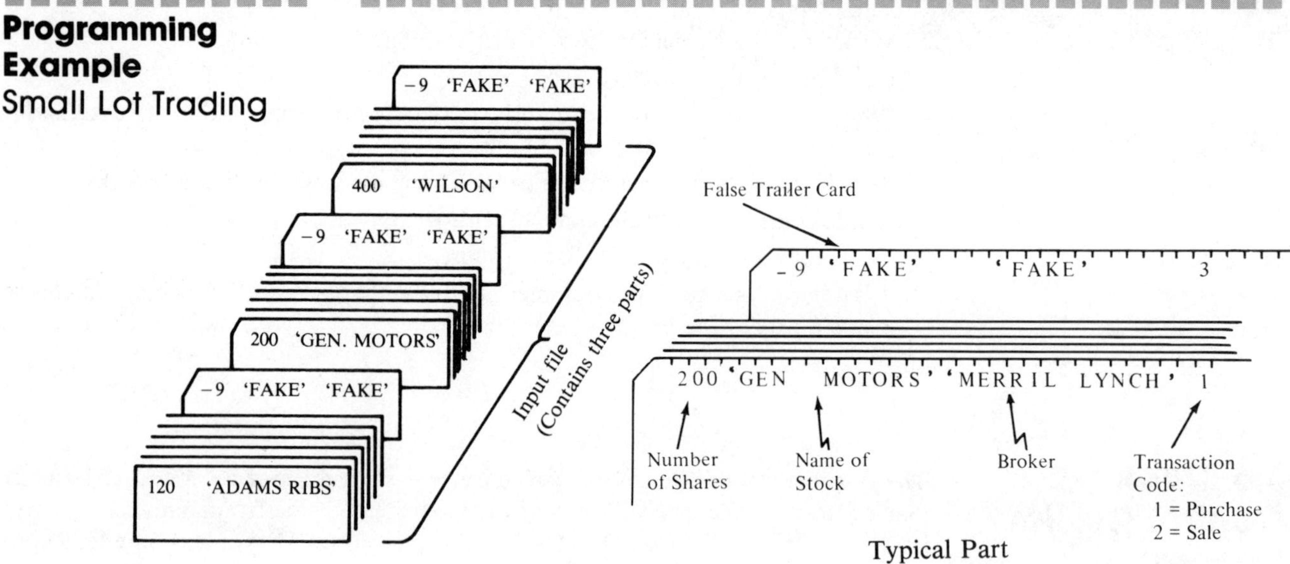

A large data file records a series of stock transactions. Each record lists the number of shares traded, the name of the stock (12 characters), the broker (12 characters), and a code telling if it was a buy or sell order. The file, however, is divided into three parts. The first part represents transactions on the American stock exchange. This portion of the file ends with a sentinel record that lists a negative number in the zone telling the number of stocks traded. The second portion of the file represents transactions on the New York exchange and uses the same type of sentinel record. The third group of records lists transactions on the over-the-counter market. For this program, we want information for *each* of these three groups of records.

People in finance are interested in what is called, "small or odd lot trading," which means transactions of under 100 shares. It is felt that small investors make this type of purchase or sell order, whereas large institutions tend to deal in larger blocks of stock. For each of the three stock exchanges:

1. Determine how many transactions are represented in the data file (use a counter called CARDS).
2. Determine how many transactions were "small lot transactions" (use a counter called NSMALL).
3. Determine what percent of the trading the small lots accounted for.
4. Print the condition of all counters for the first ten stocks processed.

We have talked about stepwise refinement of a program. It is now time to implement this valuable technique. There is just too much going on in this program to use other than a very controlled approach.

Two distinctly different activities or strategies are needed to solve the problem. You can call it a master or outer strategy followed by a minor or inner strategy. The inner or minor strategy is basically the details of processing any one record in the input file: what tests to make; what counters advanced? The outer strategy involves setting up the proper loop control structures and file control techniques to properly process the various records. It is best to leave the minor strategy go for the moment and concentrate on the master plan of attack: what outer loop is needed; what inner loop; what *number* and *position* of READ statements is required to handle this type of input file?

Programming Example–Small Lot Trading continued

The outer loop is one that will iterate the main body statements three times:

```
      DO 100 LOOP = 1, 3, 1
        Main Body Statements
100   CONTINUE
```

We show this loop in heavy outline in the diagram.

With this aspect out of the way, we are free to process the file as if there were only one stock exchange represented. We will use a DO WHILE construct that terminates when a record with a negative number of shares is reached. This means a READ will be necessary prior to entering the DO WHILE loop.

Note how the details of processing an individual record is handled at this stage of the refinement process. A box that says, ''PROCESS STOCK TRANSACTION'' appears in the diagram. That's all. We are not concerned with those statements yet. We are more interested in deck or file control and making sure another READ statement appears inside the DO WHILE loop.

We now move to the next level of refinement. The strategy for processing one record is to advance a counter called CARDS to indicate that another transaction card is being processed. If the transaction involves fewer than 100 shares, a second

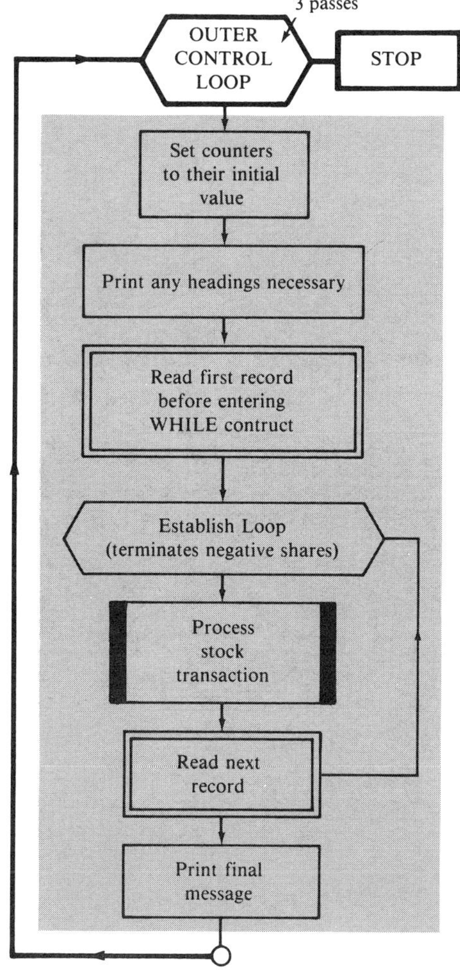

First Level Refinement

Programming Example–Small Lot Trading continued

counter called NSHARES is advanced. Finally, if CARDS is less than or equal to 10, a PRINT statement that monitors the correct behavior of major memory locations is executed.

An *intentional* error has been built into this program. The reason for doing this is to show that without the extra printouts it would be almost impossible to find the error. We now combine the algorithm developed thus far in the following flowchart.

Important Variables

Name	Meaning
LOOP	Outer loop counter
CARDS	Card counter
NSHARE	Number of shares
NSMALL	No. of small transactions
NAME1	Name of stock
NAME2	Name of broker
PERCNT	Percent small transactions

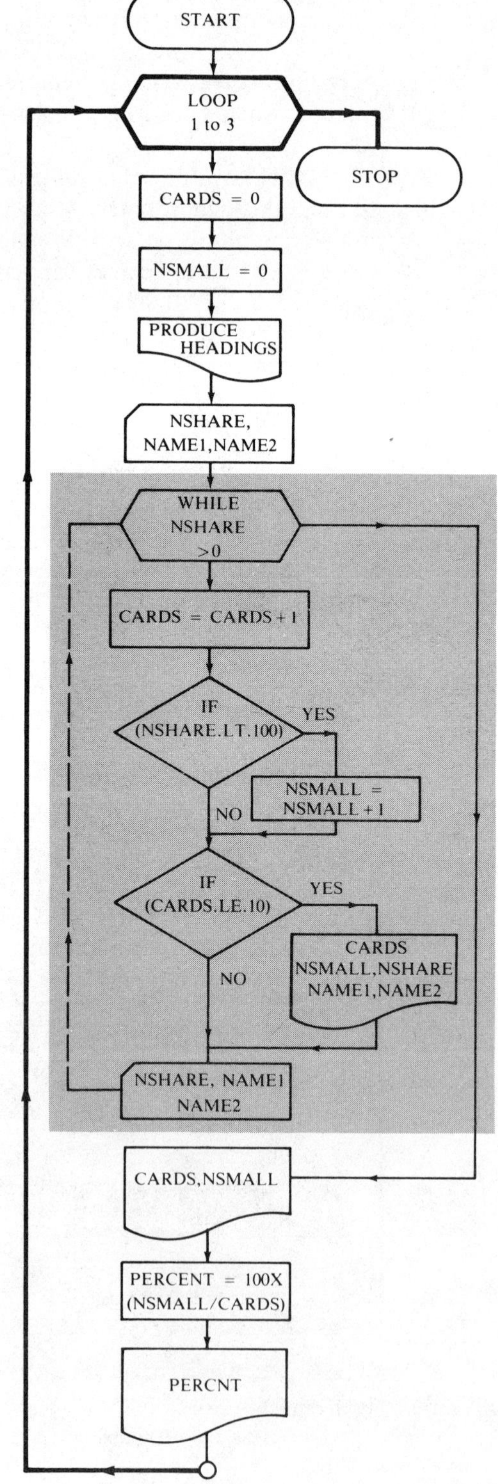

Programming Example–Small Lot Trading continued

```
C.............................................................
C..   PURPOSE - DEMONSTRATE DECK CONTROL BY TRAILER RECORD   ..
C..             -----------------------                      ..
C..             COMPUTE PERCENT OF SMALL LOT TRADING         ..
C.............................................................
C
C             ---IMPORTANT VARIABLES---
C     --LOOP      OUTER LOOP COUNTER                          --
C     --NSHARE    NUMBER OF SHARES TRADED                     --
C     --NSMALL    NUMBER OF SMALL LOT TRANSACTIONS            --
C     --NCARDS    NUMBER OF CARDS (STOCK RECORDS)             --
C     --NAME1     NAME OF STOCK                               --
C     --NAME2     NAME OF BROKER                              --
C
      CHARACTER NAME1*12, NAME2*12
      INTEGER  CARDS, NSHARE, NSMALL, LOOP
      REAL     PERCNT
C
C     -------------SET UP OUTER LOOP-----------------------
C
      DO 100 LOOP = 1, 3, 1
C
C
C         .....INITIALIZATION SECTION.....
C
          NCARDS = 0
          NSMALL = 0
C
          PRINT *, '   CARD     SHARES     NAME     SMALL LOT'
C
          READ *,NSHARE, NAME1, NAME2,
C
C         .....ENTER INNER LOOP HERE.....
C
          DO WHILE (NSHARE .GT. 0)
C
              CARDS = CARDS + 1
C
              IF (NSHARE .LT. 100) NSMALL = NSMALL + 1
C
              IF (CARDS .LE. 10) PRINT*,CARDS,NSHARE,NAME1,NSMALL
C
C             .....LOOP READ STATEMENT.....
C
              READ *,NSHARE, NAME1, NAME2,
C
          ENDDO
C
C         .....TERMINATION SECTION.....
C
          PRINT *,'    TOTAL NO. STOCKS    ', CARDS
          PRINT *,'    NO. SMALL LOT       ', NSMALL
C
C         .....COMPUTE PERCENT SMALL LOT TRADING.....
C
          PERCNT = (NSMALL/CARDS) * 100
C
          PRINT *, ' AVERAGE = ', PERCNT
C
  100 CONTINUE
C
C     .....OUTER LOOP STOPS HERE.....
C
      STOP
      END
```

Examination of the output shows that everything is going well until the final average is printed out. The reported value is 0.0%.

```
                                              SMALL LOT
   CARD    SHARES          NAME                COUNTER

    1        200      GEN. MOTORS                 0
    2         75      I.B.M.                      1
    3         60      U.S. STEEL                  2
    4        500      SQUIBB                      2
    5       1000      BAXTER                      2
    6

    8        400      CHRYSLER                    4
    9         20      HONDA                       5
   10        500      MELVILLE                    5

     TOTAL NO. STOCKS     673
     NO. SMALL LOT        206
                              AVERAGE = 0.0%
```

The counters are working correctly but the computed value of average small-lot trading is coming out as zero. The error must be somewhere between the printing out of the final counter values and the printout of PERCNT. The trouble is with the statement:

```
PERCNT = NSMALL/CARDS*100
```

The first operation performed is the division of NSMALL by CARDS. Notice that both are integer values. The result will be a number less than one, which in integer arithmetic comes out to zero. Avoiding this type of difficulty is covered in the next chapter.

6.7 Computed GO TO Statement

IF constructs allow one-way and two-way branches in a program. When multiple branches are necessary, the first-case construct is used. This construct is very efficient provided the number of branches lies within reason. A problem, however, that has a 26-way branch (see the example to follow) is perhaps better handled using the "computed GO TO" statement, which allows transfer of control to almost an unlimited number of points in your program.

```
GO TO ( 12, 108, 9, 15, 56 ) , J
```

Command — GO TO; Statement Numbers — 12, 108, 9, 15, 56; Selector — J

The statement consists of the GO TO command followed by a series of statement numbers separated by commas and enclosed in parentheses. All this is followed by a comma and an integer variable or an integer expression called the selector quantity.

The statement shown in this example allows transfer to any one of five statements, depending on the value of the integer variable J, which is used as follows:

1. If J has the value 1, control is passed to the first statement number in the series, that is, to statement 12.
2. If J has the value 2, control is passed to the second statement number in the series, that is, statement 108.
3. If J has the value 3, control is passed to the third statement number in the series, that is, statement 9, etc.

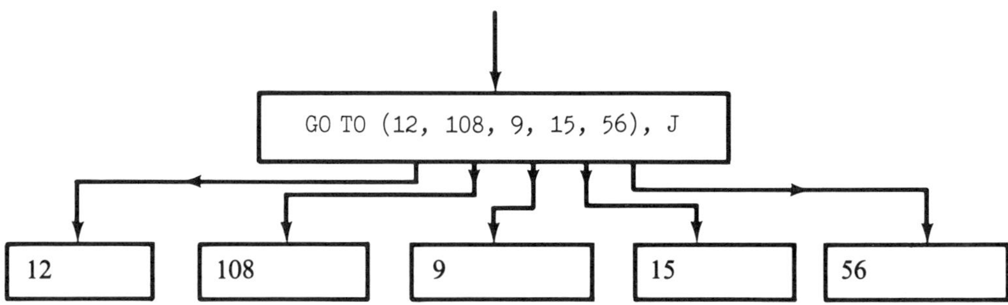

This particular computed GO TO is the equivalent of the following five statements:

```
IF (J.EG.1) GO TO 12
IF (J.EQ.2) GO TO 108
IF (J.EG.3) GO TO 9
IF (J.EQ.4) GO TO 15
IF (J.EQ.5) GO TO 56
```

Additional examples:

```
GO TO (103,5,13,4),NUM
GO TO (3,2),JOB
GO TO (4,41,18,32,75,108,109,11,302,5),KING
```

A problem that would require a large number of branches is now presented. A popular student pastime is to get together as a group and write a program that prints each student's name in large letters as suggested by the following "name banner."

```
RRRRRRRRRRR   UU        UU  LL            EEEEEEEEEEEE
RRRRRRRRRRRR  UU        UU  LL            EEEEEEEEEEEE
RR        RR  UU        UU  LL            EE
RR        RR  UU        UU  LL            EE
RR        RR  UU        UU  LL            EE
RR        RR  UU        UU  LL            EE
RR        RR  UU        UU  LL            EE
RRRRRRRRRRRR  UU        UU  LL            EEEEEEEE
RRRRRRRRRRR   UU        UU  LL            EEEEEEEE
RR        RR  UU        UU  LL            EE
RR        RR  UU        UU  LL            EE
RR        RR  UU        UU  LL            EE
RR        RR  UU        UU  LL            EE
RR        RR  UU        UU  LL            EE
RR        RR  UUUUUUUUUUUU  LLLLLLLLLLL   EEEEEEEEEEEE
RR        RR  UUUUUUUUUUUU  LLLLLLLLLLL   EEEEEEEEEEEE
```

The students divide up the responsibility for writing 26 different blocks of code. Block 1 produces a large letter A, block 2 produces a large letter B, etc. The first statement in each block is numbered as suggested in the next illustration. These blocks are nothing more than a series of WRITE statements.

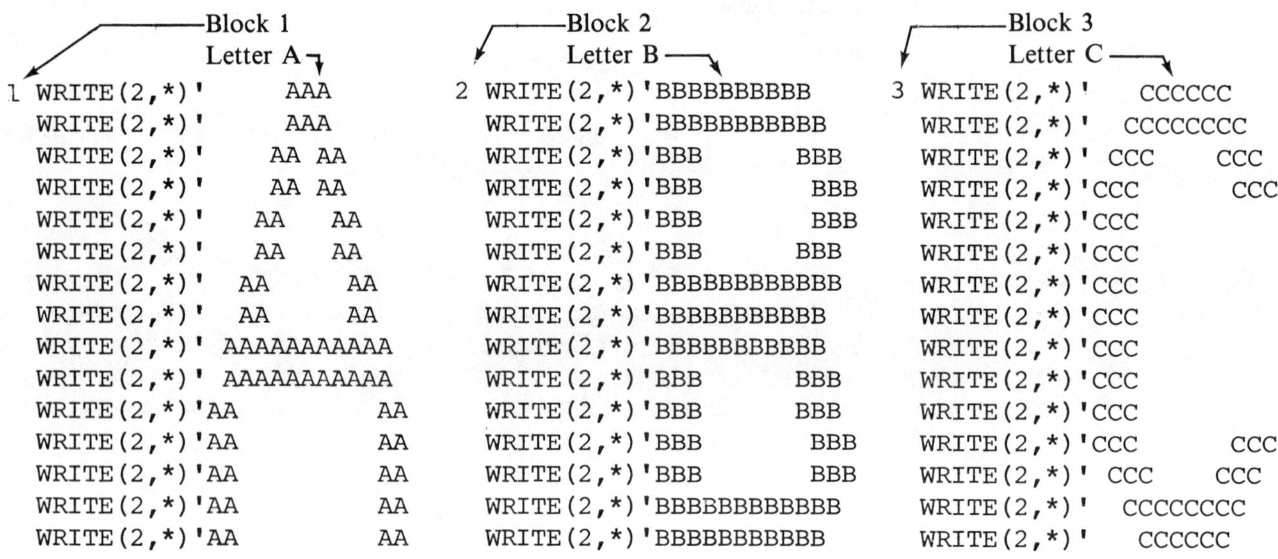


```
1 WRITE(2,*)'     AAA
  WRITE(2,*)'     AAA
  WRITE(2,*)'    AA AA
  WRITE(2,*)'    AA AA
  WRITE(2,*)'   AA   AA
  WRITE(2,*)'   AA   AA
  WRITE(2,*)'  AA     AA
  WRITE(2,*)'  AA     AA
  WRITE(2,*)' AAAAAAAAAAA
  WRITE(2,*)' AAAAAAAAAAA
  WRITE(2,*)'AA         AA
  WRITE(2,*)'AA         AA
  WRITE(2,*)'AA         AA
  WRITE(2,*)'AA         AA
  WRITE(2,*)'AA         AA
```

```
2 WRITE(2,*)'BBBBBBBBBB
  WRITE(2,*)'BBBBBBBBBBB
  WRITE(2,*)'BBB       BBB
  WRITE(2,*)'BBB        BBB
  WRITE(2,*)'BBB        BBB
  WRITE(2,*)'BBB       BBB
  WRITE(2,*)'BBBBBBBBBBBB
  WRITE(2,*)'BBBBBBBBBBB
  WRITE(2,*)'BBBBBBBBBBB
  WRITE(2,*)'BBB       BBB
  WRITE(2,*)'BBB       BBB
  WRITE(2,*)'BBB        BBB
  WRITE(2,*)'BBB        BBB
  WRITE(2,*)'BBBBBBBBBBBB
  WRITE(2,*)'BBBBBBBBBBB
```

```
3 WRITE(2,*)'    CCCCCC
  WRITE(2,*)'   CCCCCCCC
  WRITE(2,*)' CCC      CCC
  WRITE(2,*)'CCC         CCC
  WRITE(2,*)'CCC
  WRITE(2,*)'CCC
  WRITE(2,*)'CCC
  WRITE(2,*)'CCC
  WRITE(2,*)'CCC
  WRITE(2,*)'CCC
  WRITE(2,*)'CCC
  WRITE(2,*)'CCC         CCC
  WRITE(2,*)' CCC      CCC
  WRITE(2,*)'   CCCCCCCC
  WRITE(2,*)'    CCCCCC
```

For each letter in a person's name, control is passed to the computed GO TO at the top of the program. This GO TO then causes a transfer to one of 26 different blocks of code (like those just shown) to produce the desired large letter.

Like the conventional GO TO statement, the computed GO TO is considered somewhat disruptive. Although it gets you to a particular block of statements rather easily, it usually needs another GO TO at the end of each block to avoid the blocks that follow. This awkwardness will be demonstrated in the next example problem and then corrected by a first-case construct method of solution.

Programming Example
GO TO**

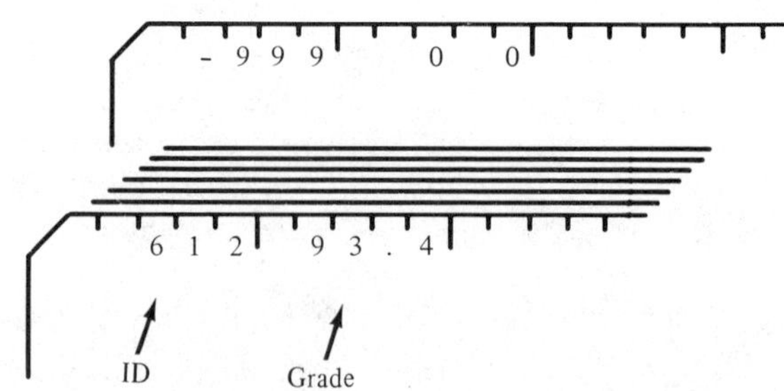

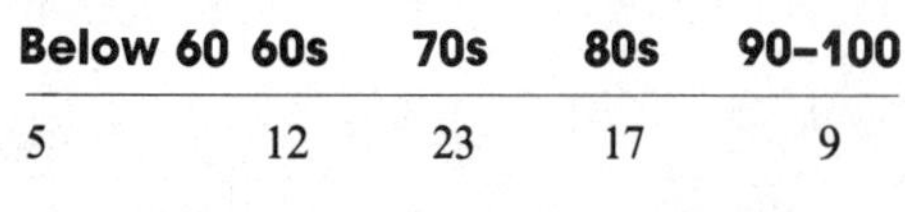

Below 60	60s	70s	80s	90–100
5	12	23	17	9

An input file lists the examination grades of a large class of students. Each record contains a student's identification number and an examination grade. The end of this file contains a record with a negative value where the ID number belongs. Write a program to determine:

1. Number of students represented in the data file.
2. Highest and lowest score in the file.
3. Distribution of grades: number of As, Bs, Cs, Ds, and failures.

Programming Example–GO TO continued

The first-case method of solution is presented first. Memory locations `HIGH` and `LOW` store the highest and lowest grade. Memory location `COUNT` counts the number of students taking the exam. Finally, five counters are used:

Counter	Meaning
NOAS	Number of students getting an A
NOBS	Number of students getting a B
NOCS	Number of students getting a C
NODS	Number of students getting a D
NOFS	Number of students getting an F

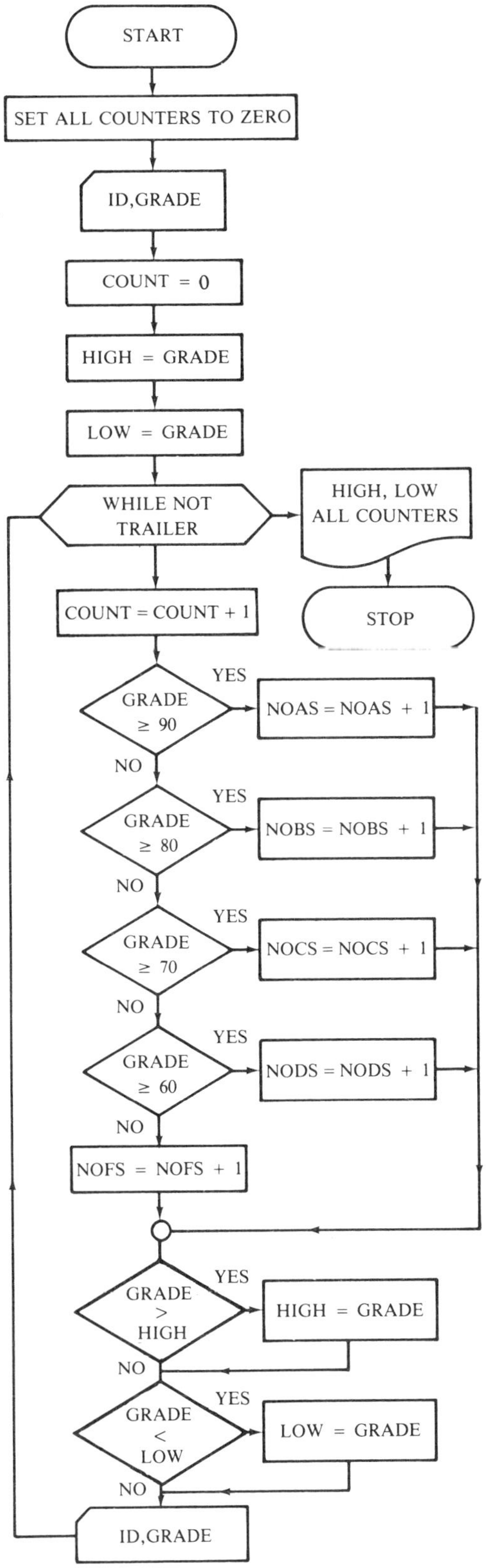

START
SET ALL COUNTERS TO ZERO
ID,GRADE
COUNT = 0
HIGH = GRADE
LOW = GRADE
WHILE NOT TRAILER
HIGH, LOW ALL COUNTERS
STOP
COUNT = COUNT + 1
GRADE ≥ 90 YES NOAS = NOAS + 1
NO
GRADE ≥ 80 YES NOBS = NOBS + 1
NO
GRADE ≥ 70 YES NOCS = NOCS + 1
NO
GRADE ≥ 60 YES NODS = NODS + 1
NO
NOFS = NOFS + 1
GRADE > HIGH YES HIGH = GRADE
NO
GRADE < LOW YES LOW = GRADE
NO
ID,GRADE

Programming Example–GO TO continued

```
C.....................................................................
C..   PURPOSE - ANALYZE GRADE DISTRIBUTION                          ..
C..           - SHOW USE OF TRAILER RECORD                          ..
C..           - SHOW FIRST CASE CONSTRUCT                           ..
C.....................................................................
C
C                 ---IMPORTANT VARIABLES---
C
C     --GRADE    STUDENT'S GRADE                                    --
C     --ID       STUDENT'S IDENTIFICATION NUMBER                    --
C     --COUNT    NUMBER OF STUDENTS TAKING EXAM                     --
C     --HIGH     HIGHEST EXAM SCORE                                 --
C     --LOW      LOWEST EXAM SCORE                                  --
C     --NOAS     NUMBER A GRADES                                    --
C     --NOBS     NUMBER B GRADES                                    --
C     --NOCS     NUMBER C GRADES                                    --
C     --NODS     NUMBER D GRADES                                    --
C     --NOFS     NUMBER F GRADES                                    --
C
      INTEGER ID,COUNT,NOAS,NOBS,NOCS,NODS,NOFS
      REAL    GRADE,HIGH,LOW
C
      NOAS=0
      NOBS=0
      NOCS=0
      NODS=0
      NOFS=0
C
      READ*,ID,GRADE
      COUNT=0
C
      HIGH=GRADE
      LOW=GRADE
C
      DO WHILE (ID.GT.0)
C
          COUNT=COUNT+1
C
          IF(GRADE.GE.90) THEN
              NOAS=NOAS+1
          ELSEIF(GRADE.GE.80) THEN
              NOBS=NOBS+1
          ELSEIF(GRADE.GE.70) THEN
              NOCS=NOCS+1
          ELSEIF(GRADE.GE.60) THEN
              NODS=NODS+1
          ELSE
              NOFS=NOFS+1
          ENDIF
C
          IF(GRADE.GT.HIGH) HIGH=GRADE
          IF(GRADE.LT.LOW) LOW=GRADE
C
          READ*,ID,GRADE
C
      ENDDO
C
C     .....LOOP EXIT POINT.....
C
      PRINT*,'NUMBER TAKING EXAM =',COUNT
      PRINT*,'HIGHEST SCORE =',HIGH
      PRINT*,'LOWEST SCORE =',LOW
      PRINT*,'NO. OF As  NO. OF Bs  NO. Cs  NO. OF Ds  NO. OF Fs'
      PRINT*,NOAS,NOBS,NOCS,NODS,NOFS
C
      STOP
      END
```

Programming Example–GO TO continued

To make use of a computed GO TO statement in this problem, it is necessary to take a student's grade and somehow convert it into a selector value. One possibility is to divide the grade by 10 and store the result in an integer memory location called J. J can then be used as a selector to pass control to one of our five counters.

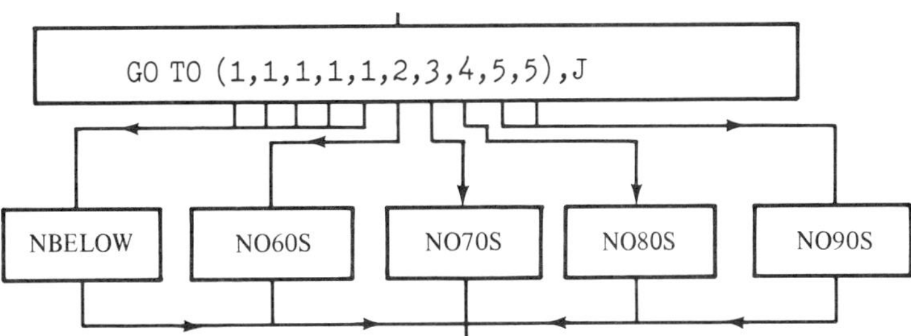

If a student scored in the 90's or scored a 100, J will be 9 or 10. The ninth and tenth choices in the GO TO alternatives pass control to a block of statements such as:

```
C. . . .MODULE 5. . . .''A'' GRADE. . .
5  NOAS = NOAS + 1
   GO TO 10
```

If a student scored in the 30's or 40's or 50's, J will be a 3 or 4 or 5. Control will pass to a block of statements such as:

```
C. . . .MODULE 1. . . .''F'' GRADE. . .

1  NBELOW = NBELOW + 1
   GO TO 10
```

Let us look at the complete program and then analyze some of the difficulties encountered.

```
C.........................................................
C..   PURPOSE - ANALYZE GRADE DISTRIBUTION              ..
C..           - SHOW USE OF COMPUTED GO TO              ..
C.........................................................
C
C           ---IMPORTANT VARIABLES---
C
C     --GRADE   STUDENT'S GRADE                          --
C     --ID      STUDENT'S IDENTIFICATION NUMBER          --
C     --COUNT   NUMBER OF STUDENTS TAKING EXAM           --
C     --HIGH    HIGHEST EXAM SCORE                       --
C     --LOW     LOWEST EXAM SCORE                        --
C     --NOAS    NUMBER A GRADES                          --
C     --NOBS    NUMBER B GRADES                          --
C     --NOCS    NUMBER C GRADES                          --
C     --NODS    NUMBER D GRADES                          --
C     --NOFS    NUMBER F GRADES                          --
C     --J       SELECTOR VALUE                           --
C
      INTEGER ID,COUNT,NOAS,NOBS,NOCS,NODS,NOFS,J
      REAL    GRADE,HIGH,LOW
C
      NOAS=0
      NOBS=0
      NOCS=0
      NODS=0
      NOFS=0
```

Programming Example–GO TO continued

```
C
      READ*,ID,GRADE
      COUNT=1
C
      HIGH=GRADE
      LOW=GRADE
C
      DO WHILE (ID.GT.0)
C
          COUNT=COUNT+1
C
C         .....FORM SELECTOR VALUE.....
C
          J=GRADE/10
C
          GO TO (1,1,1,1,1,1,2,3,4,5,5),J
C
C         .....MODULE 1.....FAILING GRADES.....
C
   1      NOFS=NOFS+1
          GO TO 100
C
C         .....MODULE 2.....LOW GRADES.....
C
   2      NODS=NODS+1
          GO TO 100
C
C         .....MODULE 3.....'C' GRADES.....
C
   3      NOCS=NOCS+1
          GO TO 100
C
C         .....MODULE 4.....'B' GRADES.....
C
   4      NOBS=NOBS+1
          GO TO 100
C
C         .....MODULE 5.....'A' GRADES.....
C
   5      NOAS=NOAS+1
C
 100      IF(GRADE.GT.HIGH) HIGH=GRADE
          IF(GRADE.LT.LOW) LOW=GRADE
C
          READ*,ID,GRADE
C
      ENDDO
C
C     .....LOOP EXIT POINT.....
C
      PRINT*,'NUMBER TAKING EXAM =',COUNT
      PRINT*,'HIGHEST SCORE =',HIGH
      PRINT*,'LOWEST SCORE =',LOW
      PRINT*,'NO. OF As  NO. OF Bs  NO. Cs  NO. OF Ds  NO. OF Fs'
      PRINT*,NOAS,NOBS,NOCS,NODS,NOFS
C
      STOP
      END
```

The first difficulty is a rather minor one. It has to do with the statement:

```
IF(J.EQ.0)J=1
```

This statement is needed to cover the possibility of a student scoring very low in the exam, possibly getting less than 10 points. Such a low value would make the selector value J equal to 0 and that is not a reasonable value for a selector. It is therefore changed to a value of 1.

Programming Example–GO TO continued

The next difficulty is the one mentioned previously. Although the computed GO TO does a reasonable job in passing control to the desired module of code, a statement must be placed at the end of each module (the GO TO 100 statement) to avoid the execution of the various modules that follow the one you want executed.

Review Exercises

1. What does the term "iterative" mean?
2. Under what conditions is a DO WHILE construct used?
3. What is the index of a DO statement? Must it be an integer?
4. What is the purpose of the CONTINUE statement?
5. Under what conditions will the statements inside a DO WHILE not be executed even once?
6. Is the same thing possible for the statement inside a DO construct? Explain.
7. Describe the methods for organizing records in a data file.
8. List four reasons why a programmer might want to set up a counter in a program.
9. What is a trip counter? Why is it used?
10. What is a selector value? How is it used?
11. Describe some of the awkward features of the computed GO TO.
12. Under what circumstances would a computed GO TO be used?
13. Describe a problem where a large number of branches are involved. Make it an original problem.
14. A data file consists of 200 records, each of which contains two integer numbers representing the roll of a pair of dice. Determine how many times a seven was rolled. Determine how many times a roll of seven is followed by a roll greater than seven; less than seven; equal to seven.
15. Using the data file of exercise 14 determine how many times a pair was rolled (a pair of fours or a pair of sixes for example).

★16. For the data file in exercise 14, how many records must be read before "box cars" (double sixes) are rolled?

17. The hyperbolic arc tangent of x may be evaluated by a series expansion:

$$\tanh^{-1}x = \frac{x}{1} + \frac{x^3}{3} + \frac{x^5}{5} + \frac{x^7}{7} + \cdots$$

Write a program to read values of x from data (one value per card) and to report as output:

a. The sum of the first four terms of this series, and

b. The value of the term $x^9/9$ (which is the first term neglected).

18. Evaluate successive terms in the arc tangent equation of exercise 17 until such time as any one of the terms is less than 0.0001. Report the value of the arc tangent and the number of terms used in the evaluation.
19. Write a program to produce as output the following conversion tables:

CONVERSION TABLES (CENTIMETERS TO INCHES)

CM	INCHES	CM	INCHES	CM	INCHES
1.0	.3937	11.0	4.3307	21.0	8.2677
2.0	.7874	12.0	4.7244	22.0	8.6614
3.0	1.1811	13.0	5.1181	23.0	9.0551
4.0	1.5748	14.0	5.5118	24.0	9.4488
5.0	1.9685	15.0	5.9055	25.0	9.8425
6.0	2.3622	16.0	6.2992	26.0	10.2362
7.0	2.7559	17.0	6.6929	27.0	10.6299
8.0	3.1496	18.0	7.0866	28.0	11.0236
9.0	3.5433	19.0	7.4803	29.0	11.4173
10.0	3.9370	20.0	7.8740	30.0	11.8110

★20. An airline operates between four terminals. The X and Y coordinates of each terminal are given on separate input records. Write a program to determine the distance between terminals and report these distances by generating the table shown.

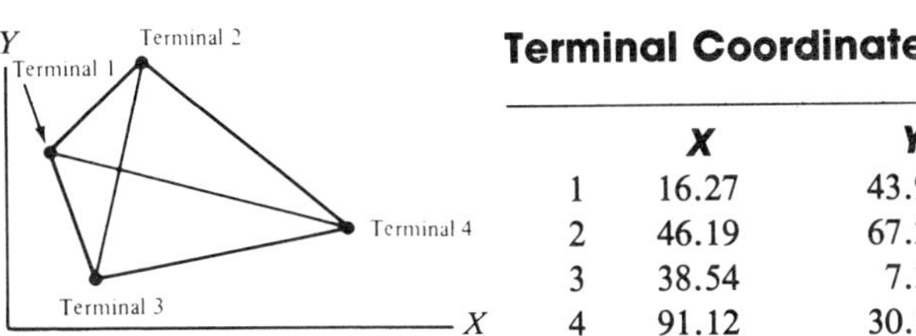

Terminal Coordinates

	X	Y
1	16.27	43.94
2	46.19	67.21
3	38.54	7.34
4	91.12	30.51

Terminal	1	2	3	4
1	0.00	37.90	42.84	76.05
2	37.90	0.00	60.36	58.01
3	42.84	60.39	0.00	57.46
4	76.05	58.01	57.46	0.00

Additional Applications

Programming Example
List by Section Number

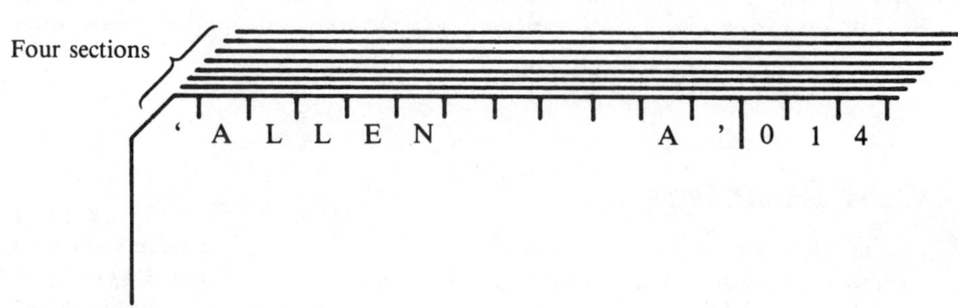

A data file contains the names of students enrolled in a FORTRAN class. There are four sections of these students. All students in Section 014 appear first, followed by the students in Section 015, followed by Sections 016 and 017. Write a program to generate a separate listing of the students in each section. This listing should start with a heading such as:

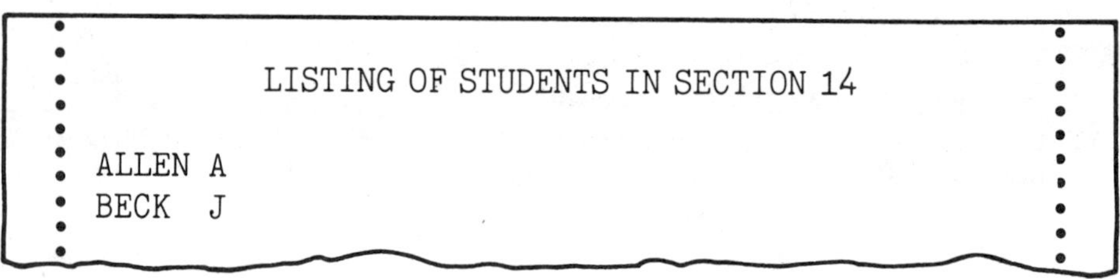

Each time a student from a new section appears, drop down three lines and PRINT an appropriate title. Your program should also count the number of students in each section. That count should be reported at the bottom of each class list:

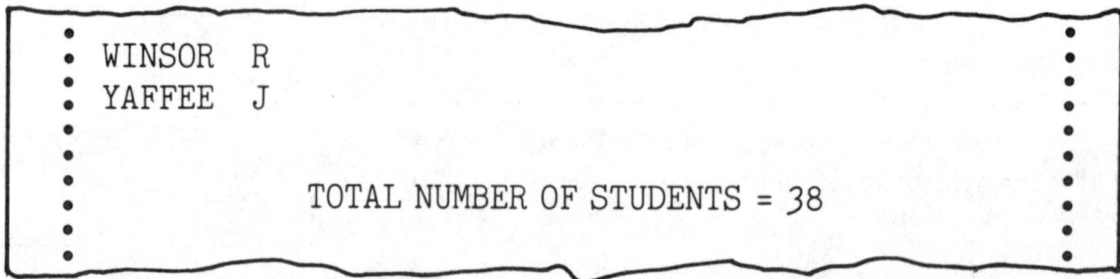

An outer loop structure will be established (a DO loop) whose index will be 14, then 15, then 16, and finally 17. Inside this loop, records are read and compared with the index (by a DO WHILE construct). If the section number matches the index, a normal posting of the student's name takes place. If the section number and the index are different, the special footings and headings just described are generated.

Programming Example–List by Section Number continued

```
C..................................................
C..   PURPOSE - PROVIDE SEPARATE LIST OF NAMES     ..
C..             FOR EACH SECTION OF STUDENTS       ..
C..................................................
C
C                ---IMPORTANT VARIABLES---
C
C     --SECTN   SECTION NUMBER FROM INPUT RECORD  --
C     --NAME    NAME OF STUDENT                   --
C     --INDEX   INDEX OF DO LOOP                  --
C     --COUNT   NUMBER OF STUDENTS IN SECTION
C                 NOW BEING PROCESSED             --
C
      CHARACTER NAME*14
      INTEGER   SECTN,INDEX,COUNT
C
      READ*,NAME,SECTN
C
      DO 200 INDEX=014,017,1
C
          PRINT*,'LISTING OF STUDENTS IN SECTION',INDEX
          PRINT*,' '
C
          COUNT=0
C
          DO WHILE (SECTN.EQ.INDEX)
C
              COUNT=COUNT+1
              PRINT*,NAME
C
              READ*,NAME,SECTN
          ENDDO
C
          PRINT*,'    TOTAL NUMBER OF STUDENTS =',COUNT
          PRINT*,' '
          PRINT*,' '
          PRINT*,' '
  200 CONTINUE
C
      STOP
      END
$
```

Programming Example
The Roll of the Dice

Each record of a data file lists two integer numbers telling what numbers came up when a pair of dice were rolled in a crap game. For the first roll the data file indicates a three and a four were rolled

Data File

```
3  4   First Record
6  3
2  2
4  6
5  1
3  2
6  6
```

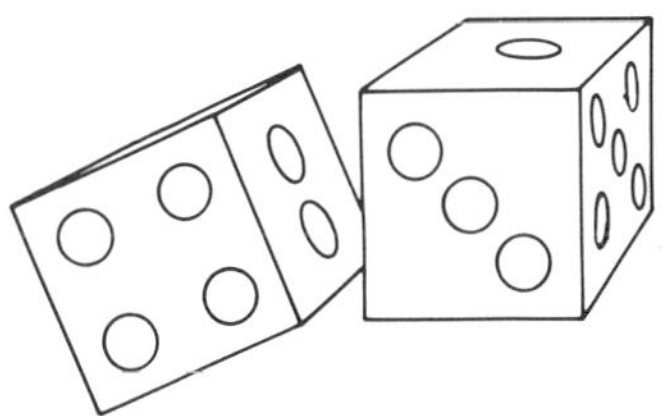

Programming Example–The Roll of the Dice continued

Part A: If this roll totals seven, issue the message:

FIRST ROLL 3 4 THE ROLL IS 7. YOU WIN.

If this roll is other than seven (five for example), issue the message:

YOUR POINT IS 5.

Part B: If the first roll is other than seven, read additional records (like the first one) and issue messages such as:

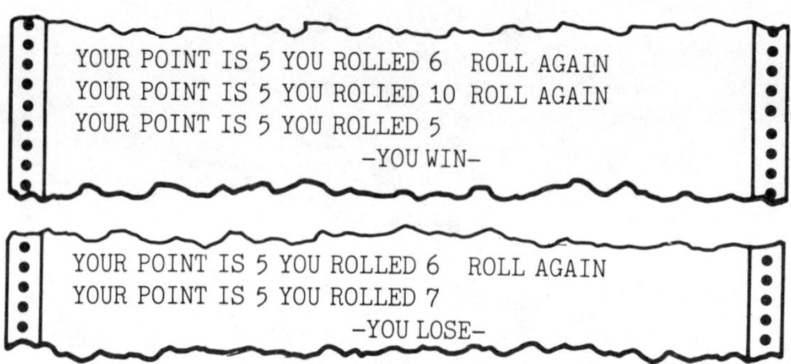


```
C.......................................................................
C..   PURPOSE - SIMULATE ACTION IN A DICE GAME.                          ..
C.......................................................................
C
C             ---IMPORTANT VARIABLES---
C
C      --N1,N2    NUMBERS ON TWO DICE                                    --
C      --TOTAL    SUM OF THESE NUMBERS                                   --
C      --POINT    NUMBER SHOOTER IS TRYING TO GET                        --
C
      INTEGER N1,N2,TOTAL,POINT
C
      READ (5,*) N1,N2
C
C     .....IS FIRST ROLL A 7 ?.....
C
      IF(TOTAL.EQ.7) THEN
C
          PRINT *, 'THE ROLL IS 7, YOU WIN!'
          STOP
      ELSE
C
C         .....ESTABLISH POINT FOR REMAINING ACTION.....
C
           POINT=TOTAL
           PRINT *,'YOUR POINT IS',POINT
      ENDIF
C
C     ********************
C     * REMAINING ACTION *
C     ********************
C
   40 READ (5,*) N1,N2
      TOTAL=N1+N2
```

Programming Example–The Roll of the Dice continued

```
C
      IF(TOTAL.EQ.POINT) THEN
          PRINT *, 'YOUR POINT IS',POINT
          PRINT *, 'YOU ROLLED',TOTAL
          PRINT *, 'YOU ARE A WINNER'
          STOP
      ENDIF
C
C     .....DID PERSON ROLL CRAPS.....
C
      IF(TOTAL.EQ.7) THEN
          PRINT *, 'YOUR POINT IS',POINT
          PRINT *, 'YOU ROLLED',TOTAL
          PRINT *, 'YOU LOSE'
          STOP
      ELSE
          PRINT *, 'YOUR POINT IS',POINT
          PRINT *, 'YOU ROLLED',TOTAL
          PRINT *, 'ROLL AGAIN'
          GO TO 40
      ENDIF
C
      END

C
```

7 More on Arithmetic Assignment Statements

Your background in programming techniques is expanding rapidly. You are perhaps not fully aware of how capable a programmer you are becoming. It will be the purpose of this chapter to demonstrate the extent of your newly acquired skills. At the same time, several additional topics associated with arithmetic assignment statements need coverage. Indexing statements, accumulators, flags, mixed mode operations, and library functions are new material covered in this chapter.

7.1 Indexing Statements

One of the topics treated in the last chapter was the concept of counting. As you will recall, three statements were needed to accomplish this special **counting** effect (see the following illustration). An initialization statement presets the counter at some starting value. An indexing or incrementing statement is positioned inside a loop and causes the counter to advance through some ordered sequence. A test statement controls the upper limit of the counter. The following table shows that these same techniques can be applied to real mode variables, such as the variable *X*.

Statement Type	Integer	Real
Initialization	COUNT=0	X=0.0
Indexing	COUNT=COUNT+1	X=X+0.2
Test	IF(COUNT.LT.40)	IF (X.LE.40.0)

For example, assume that it is necessary to have the variable *X* start at an initial value of 0.0 and then assume an ordered sequence of values until *X* is greater than 40.0. The desired sequence of intermediate values might be:

0.0, 0.2, 0.4, 0.6, 0.8, . . ., 39.4, 39.6, 39.8, 40.0

An initialization statement is again used to preset the initial value of the variable. The statement of major interest, however, is the indexing statement because it is producing the desired special effect (causing *X* to advance or index by increments of 0.2):

```
X = X + 0.2
```
Indexing Statement

With this statement positioned inside a loop, consider what happens to X. Each time the indexing statement is executed, the expression portion of the statement causes the present value of X and the value 0.2 to be added together. The result of the calculation is then returned to memory location X producing the desired incrementing of the variable. A typical application of this technique is shown in the following programming example.

Programming Example
Math Tables

Write a program that controls the value of X so that it takes on the values shown on the left of the following table. For each value X, compute and report X^2, X^3, $\sqrt{X}$, $\sqrt{X}$, $1/X$. Make the output exactly as shown in the illustration.

TABLE OF FUNCTIONAL VALUES

X VALUE	X SQUARE	X CUBE	SQUARE ROOT	CUBE ROOT	RECIPROCAL
1.0	1.00	1.00	1.0000	1.0000	1.0000
1.1	1.21	1.33	1.0488	1.0323	0.9091
1.2	1.44	1.73	1.0954	1.0627	0.8333
1.3	1.69	2.20	1.1402	1.0914	0.7692
1.4	1.96	2.74	1.1832	1.1187	0.7143
1.5	2.25	3.37	1.2247	1.1447	0.6667
1.6	2.56	4.10	1.2649	1.1696	0.6250
1.7	2.89	4.91	1.3038	1.1935	0.5882
1.8	3.24	5.83	1.3416	1.2164	0.5556
1.9	3.61	6.86	1.3784	1.2386	0.5263
2.0	4.00	8.00	1.4142	1.2599	0.5000
9.6	92.16	884.74	3.0984	2.1253	0.1042
9.7	94.09	912.67	3.1145	2.1327	0.1031
9.8	96.04	941.19	3.1305	2.1400	0.1020
9.9	98.01	970.30	3.1464	2.1472	0.1010
10.0	100.00	1000.00	3.1623	2.1544	0.1000

One aspect of this program is to control the value of X so that it goes from 1.0 to 10.0 in steps of 0.1. Based on the material just covered, the necessary statements would be:

```
X = 1.0
X = X + 0.1
IF (X.LE.10.0)
```

To obtain the five functional values needed for each line in the table, five arithmetic statements must be formed:

```
ANS1 = X**2
ANS2 = X**3
ANS3 = X**0.5
```

Programming Example–Math Tables continued

```
ANS4 = X**(1./3.)
ANS5 = 1.0/X
```

As a final detail, we must use a little care in writing the output statement needed to generate each of the numerous lines in the main body of this table. Each of these lines contains six values (the value of *X* and five functional values). This means there must be six names in the *list* of the output statement:

```
PRINT*,X, ANS1,ANS2,ANS3,ANS4,ANS5
       List
```

If, however, we want the output to appear as shown in the illustration, we must exercise format control. If we decide that each of the output values is to be allowed a field width of 12 columns, it is now only necessary to control the degree of accuracy to which each value is to be printed. The format codes would be:

```
F12.1  F12.2  F12.2  F12.4  F12.4  F12.4
```

The output statement would then be formed as follows:

```
    PRINT 10, X,ANS1,ANS2,ANS3,ANS4,ANS5
10  FORMAT (F12.1,F12.2,F12.3,F12.4,F12.4,F12.4)
```

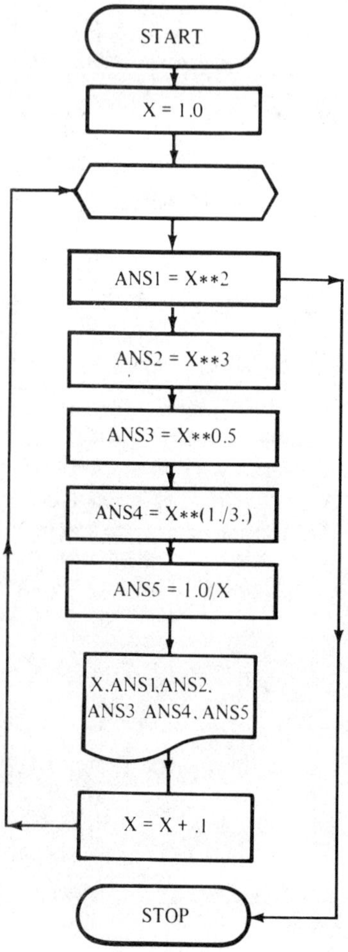

START
X = 1.0
ANS1 = X**2
ANS2 = X**3
ANS3 = X**0.5
ANS4 = X**(1./3.)
ANS5 = 1.0/X
X,ANS1,ANS2,
ANS3 ANS4, ANS5
X = X + .1
STOP

```
C.........................................................
C..    PURPOSE - DEMONSTRATE INDEXING STATEMENTS AND     ..
C..              PRODUCE TABLE OF VALUES.                ..
C..                (HEADINGS OMITTED)                    ..
C.........................................................
C
      REAL X,ANS1,ANS2,ANS3,ANS4,ANS5
C
      X = 1.0
C
C             .....LOOP ENTRY POINT .....
C
      DO WHILE (X.NE.10.0)
C
          ANS1 = X**2
          ANS2 = X**3
          ANS3 = X**0.5
          ANS4 = X** (1.0/3.0)
          ANS5 = 1.0/ X
C
          PRINT*, X,. ANS1, ANS2, ANS3, ANS4, ANS5
C
          X = X + 0.1
C
      ENDDO
C
      STOP
      END
```

This program provides an opportunity to drive home an important point about real calculations. Although these calculations are performed to a high degree of accuracy, there is nonetheless, some error associated with them. If you do many real calculations involving the same real variable, the error will build up. To provide a specific example, take a look at the WHILE statement used in our last program. Would you be shocked to learn that the loop never terminates? The STOP statement will probably never be executed. The difficulty starts with the use of the number 0.1 in our indexing statement. It is an innocent-looking number, but that is because your mind is trained in the decimal system. In binary, the number 0.1 has no finite representation.

Decimal	**Binary**
0.1	.00011001100110011001 1 . . .

When this number is stored in memory, we store as much of the number as will fit in a single word of memory, but a portion of the number (admittedly a small portion) will not be stored. This is called a truncation error, and it means that the value in memory is just slightly smaller than what we want. However, this truncation error is subject to magnification. Consider the effect of repeatedly executing the statement:

```
X = X + 0.1
```

By the time X approaches 10.0, this statement has been executed 90 times. This causes an accumulation of the truncation error. As a result, the value of X is not precisely 10.0 but has a value something like:

9.99999999999372

For most calculations this is close enough to 10.0, but it is not exactly 10.0. With this in mind, look at the way the WHILE statement is written. The loop terminates when X equals 10.0—*exactly 10.0*! There is no room for error. The WHILE statement should be written as:

```
DO WHILE (X.LE.10.0)
```

Now there is a whole range of values that causes the termination of the loop, *not just one value*.

> **Programming Style**
>
> **LOGICAL EXPRESSIONS using real numbers—use with caution**
>
> Calculations involving real numbers are susceptible to small errors that are usually of minor consequence. Such errors or inaccuracies can have a serious effect when constructing the LOGICAL expression of an IF or WHILE statement.

7.2 Accumulators

You have seen arithmetic statements used in the following unique ways:

Counting: `COUNT=COUNT+1`
Indexing: `X=X+.1`

In both these uses, the quantity added or subtracted is a constant. We now present a third type:

Accumulator: `SUM=SUM+X`

When the quantity added or subtracted is a variable (in this case, the variable *X*), the statement becomes an accumulator which can be used to add up a string of numbers. For example, assume there is a series of input records where each record contains a single real value which will be assigned the name X. Figure 7.1 suggests the procedure of using an accumulator for determining the sum of these X values.

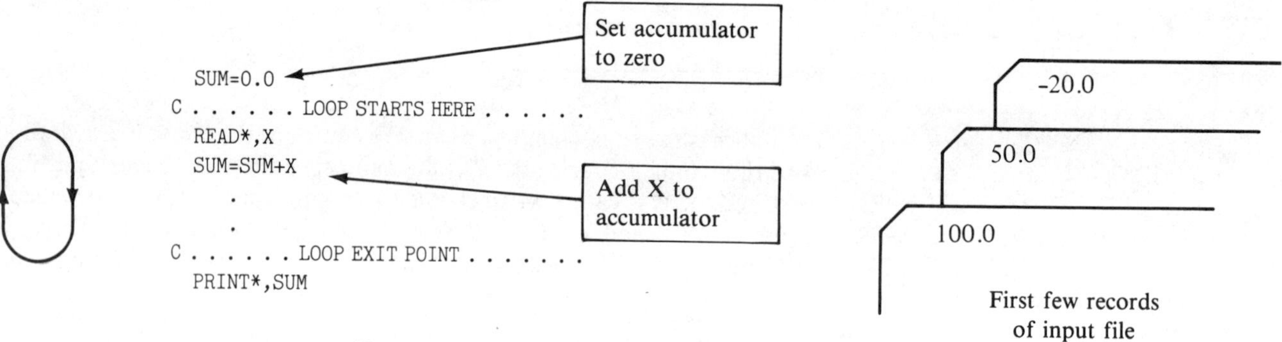

Figure 7.1 Use of accumulators

The statement:

```
SUM=0.0
```

sets the initial value of the accumulator to zero before the loop is entered. (Just as a counter or an indexing statement must be given an initial value, so too, an accumulator must be initialized).

Inside a loop, the statement:

```
SUM=SUM+X
```

increases the contents of memory location `SUM` by the value X read from the first input record. Assume the first record contains the value 100.0 (see Figure 7.1). The accumulating statement causes this value of X to be added to the present value of `SUM` (the numbers 0.0 and 100.0 are added together and the result sent to memory location `SUM`).

On the second time around the loop, the `READ` statement defines X to 50.0, and the accumulator is reached again.

```
SUM=SUM+X
   100.0  50.0
```

The values 100.0 and 50.0 are added together and the result (150.0) sent to `SUM`. The accumulator now holds the first two X values. On the next sweep X is −20.0 and `SUM` changes to 130.0.

A practical application of this type of statement would be to monitor bank transactions. Each deposit or withdrawal (X value) should cause an appropriate change in the individual's bank balance (`SUM`). This will be demonstrated in the next programming example. Accumulating statements are used to adjust inventory levels, balance checkbooks, and so on.

7.3 Flags

Programmers do strange things with arithmetic statements, one of which is pretending that they represent flags on a flag pole (see Figure 7.2).

In programming, a flag is used to record if a particular event occurred. The general procedure is to set the condition of the flag at the beginning of the program by putting the flag in the down position. As the program is running, tests are made to determine if the event being monitored ever occurs. When the event occurs, the flag is raised. At the end of the program, the condition of the flag (up or down) provides the information needed. For example, we will soon be processing the deposits and withdrawals made to a checking account for the purpose of providing a monthly statement. If, at any time during the month, the balance in the account drops below \$100.00, a service charge of \$2.00 is authorized.

Figure 7.2 Flag condition

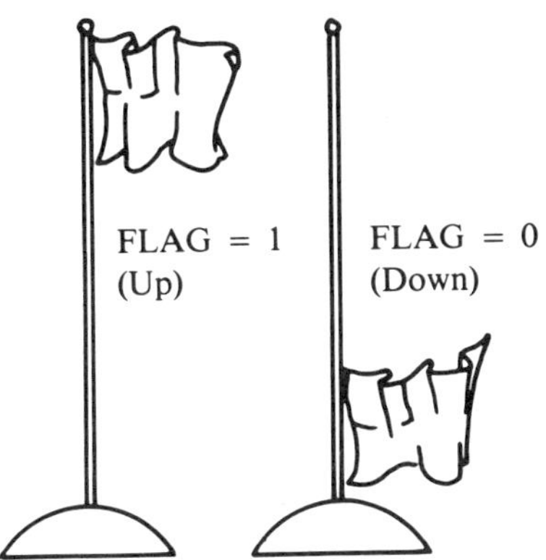

Flags record an event: we need to know at the *end* of the program if something happened during the program, in this case, a low balance. As the program starts, a zero is placed in an integer memory location called FLAG, which means the flag is down (no low balance detected yet). As the various transactions are posted, each new balance is tested to see if the balance is above \$100.00. If a low balance is detected, the flag is raised.

```
IF(BALNCE.LT.100.00) FLAG=1
```

After all the transactions are posted, a test is made to determine if an additional \$2.00 service charge is appropriate.

```
IF(FLAG.EQ.1)BALNCE=BALNCE-2.00
```

Note that this is considerably different from writing

```
IF(BALNCE.LT.100.00)BALNCE=BALNCE-2.00
```

at the end of the program. Using this IF test, only one value of BALNCE would be tested, namely the one at the end of the month.

Quiz 12 Accumulators and Flags

1. We wish to have the real variable X start at an initial value of +100 and go to −100 in steps of −0.5.
   a. Write the initialization, indexing, and test statements to accomplish this task.
   b. Could this same control be accomplished by a DO statement?
   c. If the answer is yes, write the DO statement.
2. The number 1.0 divided by 3.0 has no finite representation in the decimal system. What does the term "finite representation" mean and why are we concerned about it?
3. What does the term "truncation error" mean?

4. What is the purpose of an accumulator? How does an accumulator differ from a counter?
5. What is the purpose of a flag? Give two examples of how a flag might be used.
6. A data file lists 30 temperatures, one per record. Use a flag to determine if the temperature ever reached a value of 100° or over during the report period. Call your flag: HOT.
7. For problem 6, use a counter to determine how many times the temperature was 100° or over. Use an accumulator to determine the average temperature during the report period.

Programming Example
Monthly Statement

Write a program to produce monthly bank statements as follows.

```
                    ACCOUNT NUMBER 12345

                      WILFRED P. RULE
                      84 COUNTY ROAD
                      READING, MASS.

BALANCE AS OF JUNE 1, 1990 .......................  178.62

WITHDRAWAL ..........  50.00                         128.62
DEPOSIT ............. 100.00                         228.62
DEPOSIT .............  25.00                         253.62
DEPOSIT .............  20.00                         273.62
WITHDRAWAL .......... 200.00                          73.62

BALANCE AS OF JUNE 30, 1990 ......................   73.62
CHARGE FOR BALANCE BELOW $100.00                       2.00

          FINAL BALANCE ..........................   71.62
```

The purpose of this problem is to pull together many of the programming techniques you have learned. Your ability to handle a "complex" problem has grown substantially. Each of the requirements outlined will be explained as the solution is developed. The list is being presented to show the scope of problems you are presently capable of handling.

Requirements	**Meaning**
Carriage Control	Cause the line printer to advance to the top of a page before each new depositor's transactions are processed.
Special Headings	Produce headings at the top of the page that include the depositor's account number and mailing address.
Flag for Low Balance	Use a flag to detect the occurrence of a low balance during the month.
Use of Accumulator	Use an accumulator to keep track of the depositor's balance as various deposits and withdrawals are made.
Check for Correct Account Number	Before posting a deposit or a withdrawal, make sure the transaction is being posted to the correct account.
Deposit or Withdrawal Message	When listing a transaction, include the message "DEPOSIT" or "WITHDRAWAL," as appropriate.
Applying Service Charge	Use flag to apply a $2.00 service charge if a low-balance condition is encountered.

Programming Example–Monthly Statement continued

Problem Statement

Each month a bank must issue a statement to its depositors such as the one shown. The program that generates this statement is not a simple one, but it is one that is within your capabilities to write. Assume there is a large data file and that each customer is represented in that file by a series of records as suggested here:

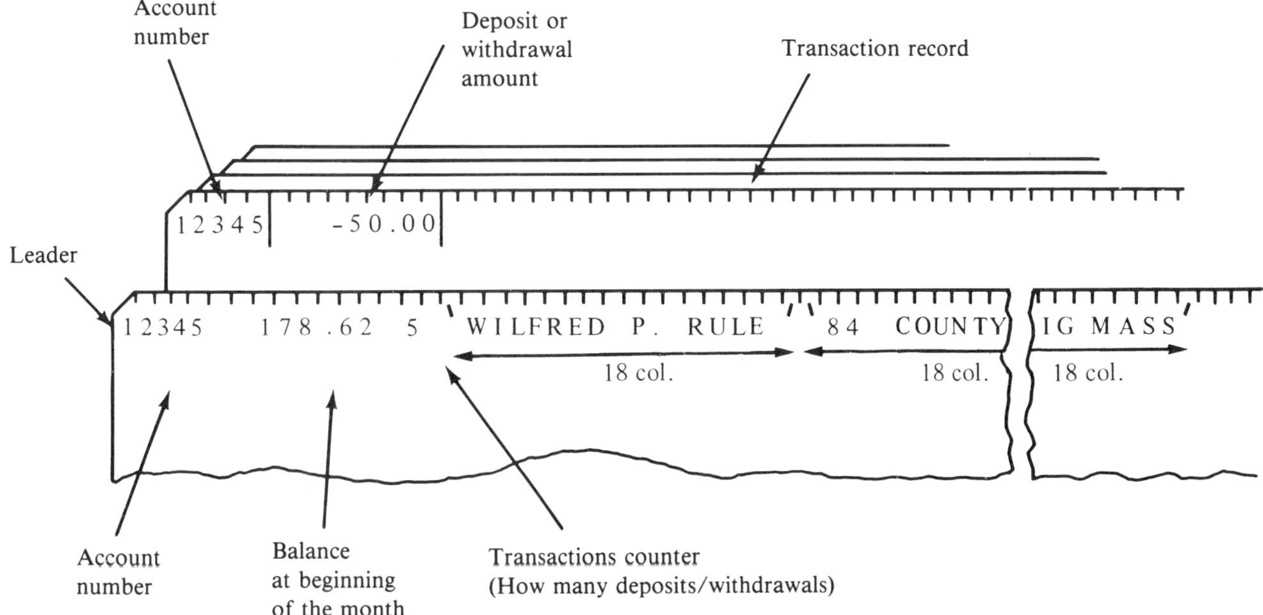

The first record is a leader record giving initial information needed concerning the depositor, such as the account number, the balance at the beginning of the month, and the number of transactions made during the month. The remainder of this record contains character information, namely the depositor's name, street address, and town. Each of these last three items is handled separately as an 18-character field. The records that follow the leader record are called transaction records. They contain an account number and the amount of a deposit or a withdrawal.

Step 1: Getting the Headings

The input data file for this program is a relatively complicated one. Many depositors are represented in the file and the number of records for each depositor is variable. However, you should recognize the use of a leader record to control the file and be able to take the Transactions Counter value given on the leader record and put it to use in a *counting* loop structure.

As the leader record of each depositor is detected, it will be necessary to read the whole record and then transfer the account number being processed and the mailing address information to the output sheet. However, before this heading information is printed, we will want to cause a "page eject" of the line printer so that each bank statement starts on a new sheet of paper. This will allow us to separate the individual statements at the end of the computer run.

When these statements are mailed, the address portion of the output sheet (the three lines under the account number) will be seen through the window of the mailing envelope. Assume that the programmer is required to leave the first 12 columns of the address output lines blank and start each line in column 13 so that the address

Programming Example–Monthly Statement continued

will be seen through the window. We covered a similar situation in Section 4.4 when we were generating information for a paycheck. Covering the topic again will reinforce the method used.

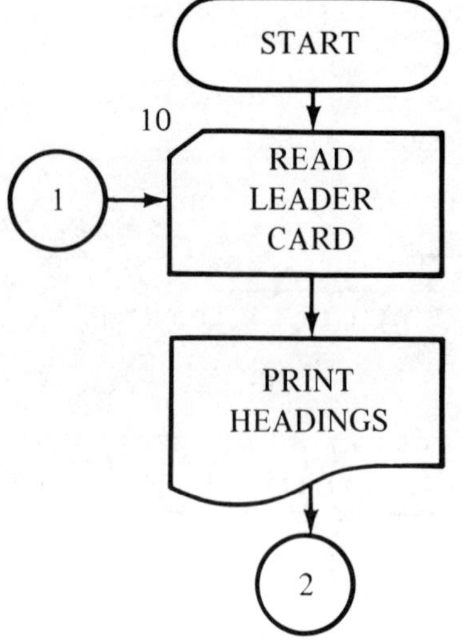


```
C.........................................................
C..   PURPOSE - (1) PRODUCE BANK STATEMENT                ..
C..             (2) DEMONSTRATE USE OF FLAGS              ..
C..             (3) DEMONSTRATE USE OF ACCUMULATORS       ..
C.........................................................
C
C              -----IMPORTANT VARIABLES-----
C
C     --AMOUNT  AMOUNT OF EACH DEPOSIT OR WITHDRAWAL   --
C     --BALNCE  CUSTOMER'S BANK BALANCE (ACCUMULATOR) --
C     --MASTER  ACCOUNT NUMBER FROM LEADER RECORD      --
C     --NUMBER  ACCOUNT NUMBER FROM TRANSACTION RECORD--
C     --NAME    CUSTOMER'S NAME                        --
C     --STREET  CUSTOMER'S STREET ADDRESS              --
C     --TOWN    CUSTOMER'S TOWN ADDRESS                --
C     --COUNT   TRANSACTIONS COUNTER                   --
C     --FLAG    LOW BALANCE INDICATOR (FLAG)           --
C           FLAG = 0    LOW BALANCE NOT DETECTED
C           FLAG = 1    LOW BALANCE DETECTED
C - - - - - - - - - - - - - - - - - - - - - - - - - - - -
C
      CHARACTER NAME*18, STREET*18, TOWN*18
      INTEGER MASTER, NUMBER, COUNT, FLAG, I
      REAL AMOUNT, BALNCE
C
  10   READ *, MASTER, BALNCE, COUNT, NAME, STREET, TOWN
C
C          ******************************
C          ** MOVE TO TOP OF NEW PAGE **
C          ******************************
C
       PRINT 15
 15    FORMAT('1')
C
C        PRODUCE HEADINGS AND ADDRESSS LINES
C
       PRINT *,'            ACCOUNT NUMBER', MASTER
       PRINT *,'              ',NAME
       PRINT *,'              ',STREET
       PRINT *,'              ',TOWN
C
```

Step 2: Set Flag and Process Transactions

The next step in the solution is to set up a loop construct to process the transaction records. Before doing this, we must accomplish one more activity before entering the loop. If at anytime during the month the balance drops below $100.00, a $2.00 service charge is made. We use a flag called `FLAG` to keep track of this. The value of `FLAG` is set to zero prior to entering the loop. If a balance of less than $100.00 is detected inside the loop, `FLAG` is set at 1, otherwise it is not redefined.

The most appropriate loop construct is a counting loop:

```
DO 40 I = 1, COUNT, 1
```

Programming Example–Monthly Statement continued

where the value of COUNT is that defined on the leader record. Inside the loop:

1. READ a transaction record.
2. See if the account number on the transaction record agrees with the number on the leader record. (If it does not, print an error message ''RECORDS OUT OF ORDER'' and terminate the program).
3. Otherwise update the balance to reflect the transaction.
4. Post the transaction on the output sheet and use an IF test to determine if the transaction is a DEPOSIT or a WITHDRAWAL (print message as appropriate).
5. See if new balance is below minimum. If yes, raise flag.

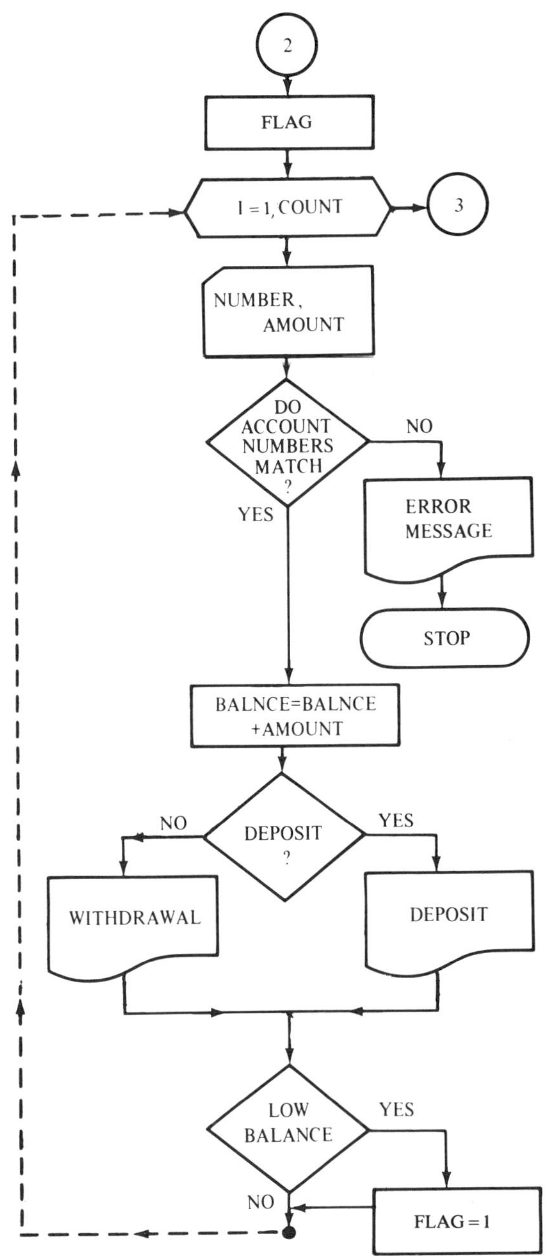

Programming Example–Monthly Statement continued

```
C       INDICATE BALANCE AT BEGINNING OF REPORT PERIOD
C
         PRINT 20,BALNCE
 20      FORMAT(' BALANCE AS OF JUNE 1,1990.........',F9.2)
C
C              ***************************
C              ** SET LOW BALANCE FLAG **
C              **    LOOP ENTRY POINT    **
C              ***************************
C
         FLAG = 0
C
         DO 40 I = 1, COUNT, 1
C
         READ *, NUMBER, AMOUNT
         IF (NUMBER .NE. MASTER) THEN
             PRINT *, 'RECORDS OUT OF ORDER'
             STOP
         ENDIF
C
         BALNCE = BALNCE + AMOUNT
C
          IF (AMOUNT .GT. 0.00) THEN
             PRINT 25, AMOUNT, BALNCE
 25          FORMAT(' DEPOSIT...........',F9.2,F20.2)
          ELSE
             PRINT 30, AMOUNT, BALNCE
 30          FORMAT(' WITHDRAWAL........',F9.2,F20.2)
          ENDIF
C
C               ****************************
C               ** CHECK FOR LOW BALANCE **
C               ****************************
C
           IF(BALNCE .LT. 100.00) FLAG = 1
C
 40     CONTINUE
```

Step 3: Closing Balance

Having processed all the transaction records, it is now necessary to post the closing balance. In the process, examine the flag to see if an additional charge of $2.00 is appropriate. If it is, the balance is decreased and the final balance posted.

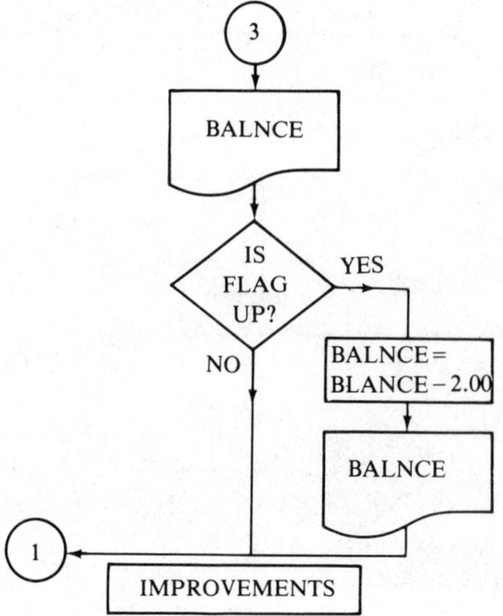

Programming Example-Monthly Statement continued

```
C
C          PRODUCE END OF STATEMENT MESSAGES
C
      PRINT 45,BALNCE
 45   FORMAT('BALANCE AS OF JUNE 30, 1990..........',F12.2)
C
C          --CHECK FOR LOW BALANCE DURING MONTH--
C
      IF (FLAG .EQ. 1) THEN
C
C              --LOW BALANCE DETECTED--
C
           BALNCE = BALNCE - 2.00
C
           PRINT *, 'CHARGE FOR BALNCE BELOW $100.00.......2.00'
           PRINT 50,BALNCE
 50        FORMAT('          FINAL BALANCE............',F12.2)
C
        ENDIF
C
        GO TO 10
C
        STOP
        END
```

Improvements

This program could be improved in many ways. The dates of JUNE 1, 1990 and JUNE 30, 1990 change for each run of the program. They should not be part of the logic. An additional leader record could be used to specify these values.

This program is not equipped to handle an inactive account. The logic assumes at least one transaction card for each account. That is not reasonable. The whole idea of recording transactions on data cards (that must be sorted) is not realistic. Transactions should be recorded on a disk file, not data cards. The statements to read a disk file are not much different from the ones to read a card file.

The use of the GO TO statement at the end of the program is a poor method of setting up the needed outer loop. An outer WHILE statement and the use of a sentinel record at the end of the input file would be considered more professional.

7.4 Top—Loop—Bottom

The various programming examples you have been dealing with exhibit a common and recurring structure. Statements appearing early in the program are executed once. They produce headings on output, establish initial values of counters or accumulators, set flags, and so on. This frequently is referred to as the "initialization" section of the program.

The next group of statements are those that are executed over and over again. This is the loop portion of the program.

Ultimately, the loop is terminated and control passes to a final group of statements that accomplish the "wrap-up" activity. This part of the program computes and reports various summary results (final value of counters and accumulators).

Comment statements should be used to clearly display this basic structure.

Programming Style
Display:
Loop entry point
Loop exit point

Show the basic structure of your program as clearly as possible. Isolate the initialization statements from those inside a loop. Show where the loop ends. Try to limit the number of exit points.

7.5 Mixed Mode Expression

When the compiler starts processing an arithmetic assignment statement, the right-hand portion of the statement should be written in a consistent mode. All the terms (the constants and the variables) should be real or integer, but *not* a mixture. *Mixed modes should not occur within an expression.*

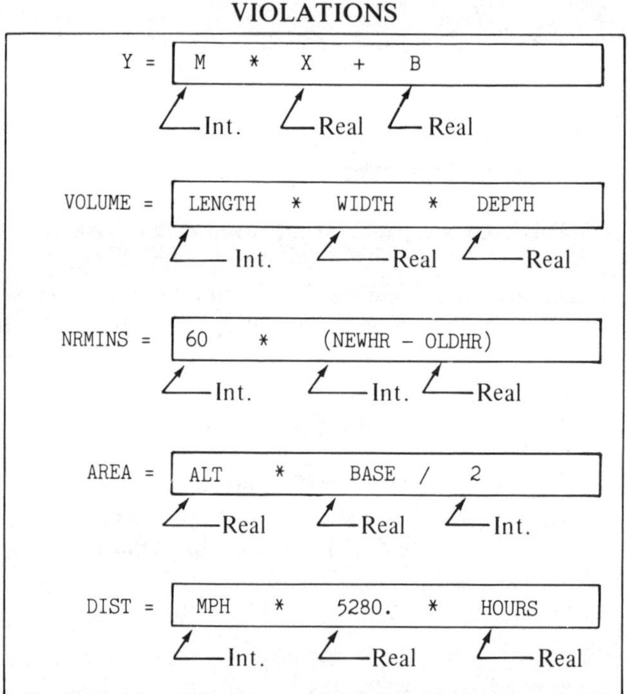

Figure 7.3 Mixed mode violations

You can save yourself a lot of difficulty by checking each expression to make sure it is written in a consistent mode. If you inadvertently forget a decimal point or are careless in naming a variable, most compilers will not "crash" your program. An attempt will be made to correct the error. The mixed expressions will be interpreted as described in the following examples.

Consider the processing of the statement:

```
AREA=1./3*RADIUS
```

The first operation performed is division. The compiler looks to the left and to the right of the divide operator to determine if this operation should be performed in the integer or real mode. Note that the quantity to the left and right of the operational symbol (divide) are called operands.

1. *Real operands.* If both values are real, division is in the real mode.
2. *Integer operands.* If both values are integer, division is in the integer mode.
3. *Mixed operands.* If the values are mixed, the integer is converted to real and division is in the real mode.

This means that the quantity 3 (integer) will be converted to 3.0 (real) and the statement will be processed as the programmer probably intended.

A less fortunate situation results in the interpretation of the statement:

```
A=RADIUS**(1/3)
```

The first operation performed again is division (to clear out the expression inside parentheses). The values on either side of the divide operator are integer and, therefore, integer division takes place producing the value 0. This obviously is not the value intended. To compound the difficulties, it is possible that no error message will be given. Two ways to guard against this difficulty are:

1. Write expressions in a consistent mode.
2. Use test data to check for the correct interpretation of your equations.

FLOAT and IFIX

Two special functions are useful in avoiding mixed mode expressions:

FLOAT (integer argument)
IFIX (real argument)

The function FLOAT is used in a real expression to permit the appearance of an integer variable without a mixed mode error. Assume for example, a program to simulate a war game (like BATTLESHIP) which uses an integer counter called NOHITS. If the value of the counter is needed in a real expression, one solution is to make a real copy of the counter by the statement:

```
COPY = NOHITS
```

The quantity COPY could now be used in place of NOHITS in the real expression. This is a little awkward and can be accomplished more directly as follows:

```
AVE = FLOAT(NOHITS) / 100. * FACTOR
```

The function FLOAT causes its integer argument NOHITS to be treated as a real value inside the real expression in which it is used.

The function IFIX accomplishes just the opposite action. It is used in integer expressions to permit the appearance of a real variable without incurring a mixed mode infraction. The statement:

```
I=M+6*IFIX(ANS1)
```

uses the real variable ANS1 in an integer expression. The function IFIX causes its real argument ANS1 to be truncated and treated as an integer inside this expression.

Note that it is only the expression portion of an arithmetic statement that should be written in a consistent mode. There is no requirement that the expression and the variable name to the left of the replacement operator be of the same mode.

Statements such as:

```
J=X/3.+4.7      or      X=(I+3)/(M-1)
```

are valid. The expression portion of each statement is in a consistent mode. The result of each calculation is sent to a memory location of the opposite mode. This is perfectly legal and was used in Chapter 6 to convert a student's grade into an integer for use as a selector value in a computed GO TO statement.

```
J=GRADE/10.
```

The Exception to the Rule

There is an exception to the rules concerning mixed mode expressions. It has to do with **exponentiation** (raising to a power). Under certain circumstances exponentiation can be accomplished by a repetitive multiplication process. At other times it is necessary to use logarithms. The programmer controls the method of computation by the mode used in expressing the exponent, as follows.

```
ANS=X**3 ←—— integer
ANS=X**3.←—— real
```

Specifying the exponent as a real value directs the computation to be accomplished by logarithms. If, however, the exponent is written in the integer mode, an entirely different method of evaluation is used. This involves a repetitive multiplication process that is usually faster and has other advantages, which we will cover shortly. The point now is that the mode of the exponent is being used in a very special and unique way. For this reason, its mode can be opposite to that of the expression in which it appears without causing a mixed mode infraction. Accordingly the following statements are not considered mixed mode:

```
AREA=PI*RADIUS**2
SCALE=10.*X**(N-1)
```

There is an exception to the mixed mode rule: when exponentiation is involved, the power may be expressed as a real or an integer. There is another advantage to expressing the power as an integer value.

```
Y=X**2
```

If the value of X is negative (like minus 4), repetitive multiplication will compute Y as +16. If the power had been specified as real, the program would terminate immediately because this implies taking the log of a negative number, which is impossible.

Quiz 13 Arithmetic Assignment Statements

Part 1: Answer the following questions.

1. Why is there any difficulty about storing a simple decimal number such as the number 0.1?
2. Flags and accumulators are devices used by programmers. Are flags and accumulators hardware or software components?

3. What are some of the typical activities accomplished in the initialization portion of a program?
4. What does the term "mixed mode" mean? Does it apply to the whole statement or just to the expression portion of the statement?
5. What are the quantities to the left and to the right of the operational symbol of an arithmetic expression called?
6. Give an example of a mixed mode expression where the mixed mode does *not* affect the intended value of the expression.
7. Give an example of a mixed mode expression where the mixed mode *does* affect the intended value of the expression.
8. How is test data used to help detect an error induced by a mixed mode expression?
9. What is the purpose of the library function FLOAT?
10. Will both these mixed mode expressions result in an error?

```
Y=(X-6.)**(1/3)
Y=(X-6)**(1.0/3)
```

Part 2: Write a Program (Is the Wheel Honest?)

11. When placing a bet at the roulette table, you may bet on the numbers 1 through 36. To test the honesty of the wheel, 200 spins are made and the winning number recorded. For our test we will divide these numbers in three groups: low, middle, and high numbers.

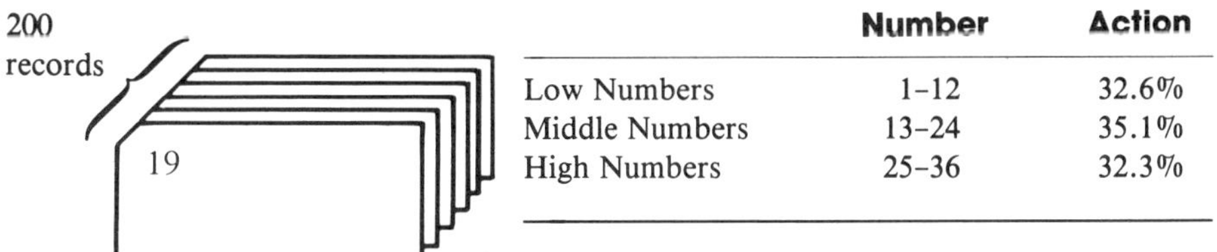

	Number	Action
Low Numbers	1–12	32.6%
Middle Numbers	13–24	35.1%
High Numbers	25–36	32.3%

Write a program to determine what percent of the time a low number (1 to 12) came up and what percent of the time a high number (25 to 36) won.

Special: you have been playing the number 16 all night long. Is it true this number never came up?

7.6 Library Functions

The following table lists the mathematical functions that are used so frequently in everyday computations that they are given special treatment in FORTRAN. By now you are familiar with the fact that these functions are implemented by software techniques. The coding necessary to evaluate each of those quantities has been written (usually in machine language) and stored on the system library. Much like reference books in a conventional library, these preprogrammed sets of instructions are stored in the processor available for use by the programmer whenever necessary. They are called **library functions**. The table is just a partial list of the more commonly used functions. A more exhaustive list is contained in appendix G.

Note that each function has a name that identifies to the processor which of the many functions the programmer wants to use. Immediately following the function name are parentheses containing what is called the argument(s) of the function.

Commonly Used Library Functions

Function	Function Name	Example	Statement
square root	SQRT	$y=\sqrt{X-6}$	Y=SQRT(X-6.)
sine	SIN	$y=R\sin\theta$	Y=R*SIN(THETA)
cosine	COS	$x=R\cos\theta$	X=R*COS(THETA)
arc tangent	ATAN	$\theta=\tan^{-1}\left(\frac{Y}{X}\right)$	THETA=ATAN(Y/X)
arc tangent	ATAN2	$\theta=\tan^{-1}\left(\frac{Y}{X}\right)$	THETA=ATAN2(Y,X)
		Note: Value of angles must be in radians	
natural log	ALOG	$y=\ln X$	Y=ALOG(X)
common log	ALOG10	$y=\log_{10}(X+3)$	Y=ALOG10(X+3)
absolute value	ABS	$y=\lvert X-8\rvert$	Y=ABS(X-8.)
exponential	EXP	$y=e^x-1$	Y=EXP(X)-1.

The following examples demonstrate that this argument can be a constant, a variable or an expression:

```
Y=SQRT (8.0)        Y=SQRT (X)        Y=SQRT (X**2+Y**2)
      Constant          Variable            Expression
```

The rules for the form of an argument are quite liberal. An argument may even include another Library Function:

```
Y=SQRT(SIN(X))
```

Each of the functions listed in the table will be discussed separately, but for the moment let us examine how the computer processes an arithmetic statement involving several library functions. Consider the equation:

$$Y = \frac{1/4 \log_{10}(A + B)}{\sqrt{A} + \sqrt{B}}$$

The appropriate arithmetic statement would be:

```
Y=(ALOG10(A+B)/4.)/(SQRT(A)+SQRT(B))
```

In processing this statement, the compiler eventually encounters the function name ALOG10. Since its argument is in the form of an expression, instructions will be generated as follows:

1. Fetch a copy of memory location A and send it to the arithmetic unit.
2. Fetch a copy of memory location B and send it to the arithmetic unit.
3. Add these values together.

At this point the argument of ALOG10 is considered reduced to a specific value, and what is needed now is a set of instructions telling how to work on this value (A + B) for the purpose of determining its common logarithm. These instructions will be provided by the system library.

The name ALOG10 is recognized as the name of a library function. Accordingly, a copy of the set of instructions associated with the name ALOG10 is taken from the library and inserted into your program. If it takes a large number of instructions to define a function, it may be more efficient to transfer control to the instructions in the system library. These instructions would, of course, include a mechanism for linking back (returning) to your program.

As processing of this statement continues, the library function SQRT is encountered *twice*. On each encounter, a copy of the instructions associated with the name SQRT will be taken from the library and inserted in your program. It is as simple as that.

SIN/COS

The two library functions provided for dealing with trigonometry problems are SIN and COS. Both require that the argument specifying the angle be expressed in *radians*. Here are two examples:

Equation	Statement
$y = \sin(45°)$	`Y=SIN(45./57.3)`
$y = \cos(x + 30°)$	`Y=COS((X+30.)/57.3)`

The constant 57.3 is being used to convert angles specified in degrees to radians.

Any other trigonometric function (like tangent or secant) must be derived from SIN and COS by the programmer:

Equation	Statement
$y = \dfrac{\tan x}{4.}$	`Y=(SIN(X/57.3)/COS(X/57.3))/4.`
$y = \csc(25°)$	`Y=1./SIN(25./57.3)`

ATAN/ATAN 2

Arc functions are used when the sides of a triangle are known and we are asked to determine the angle. It is expressed mathematically as:

$$\theta = \tan^{-1}\left(\frac{Y}{X}\right)$$

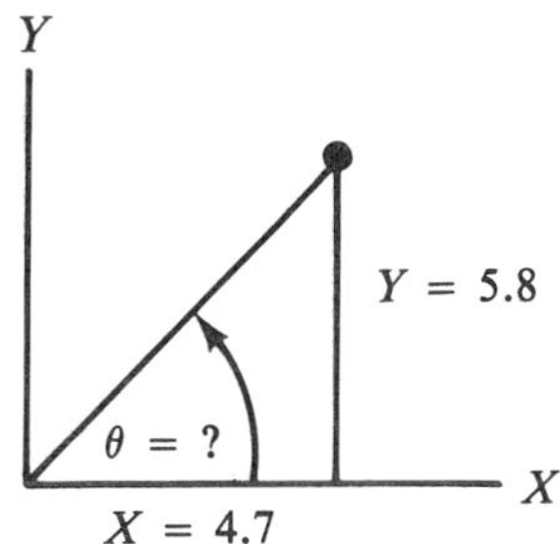

In the example shown, both X and Y are positive so the angle theta (θ) will be in the first quadrant. Since Y is just a little larger than X, the angle will be larger than 45°, but remember the functions deal in *radians*.

```
     X = 4.7
     Y = 5.8
 THETA = ATAN (Y/X)
DEGREE = THETA*57.3
```

The angle returned by this function is between 0 to 90° if the argument is positive and between 0 and −90° if the argument is negative. This means you must determine the true quadrant yourself.

ATAN2 is a similar function but has the feature of keeping track of the correct quadrant. This library function has two arguments.

```
ATAN2(Y,X)
```

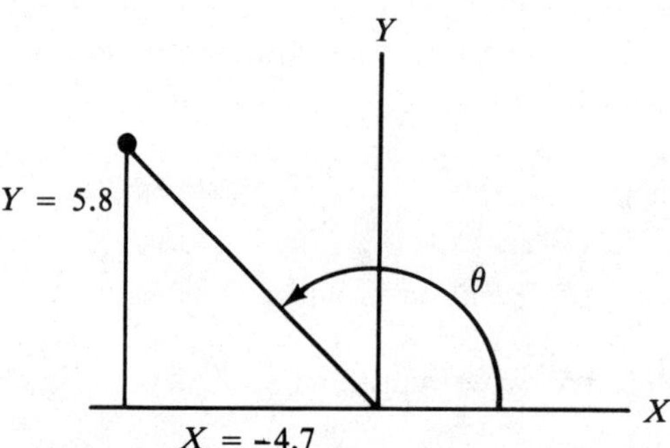

If the value of X and Y are as shown in the illustration, the angle could be determined by the statement:

```
ANGLE = 57.3*ATAN2(5.8,-4.7)
```

When a library function requires multiple arguments, they appear inside the parentheses but separated by commas.

ALOG/ALOG10

When dealing with logs, there are two types: **common logs** (logs to the base 10) and **natural logs** (logs to the base *e*).

Equation	Statement
$y = \log_{10}(x + 1)$	Y=ALOG10(X+1.0)
$y = \ln(6)$	Y=ALOG(6.0)

ABS

The absolute value function is used to strip the sign from a value. If the value is negative, it is changed to positive. If it is already positive, no action is taken.

Equation	Statement
$y = \lvert x - 6 \rvert$	Y=ABS(X-6.)
$y = \dfrac{\cos^2(X)}{\lvert X \rvert}$	Y=COS(X)**2/ABS(X)

EXP

This function is best displayed by showing several examples.

Equation	Statement
$y = e^x - 6$	`Y=EXP(X)-6.`
$y = \frac{e^x - e^x}{2}$	`Y=(EXP(X) - EXP(-X))/2.`

7.7 Other Functions

There are a few other library functions that may prove useful.

Function	Meaning
`AMAX1 (A,B,C, . . .)`	Find maximum element of list of real arguments.
`AMIN1 (A,B,C, . . .)`	Find minimum element of list of real arguments.
`MAXO (I,J,K,L, . . .)`	Find maximum element of list of integer elements.
`MINO (I,J,K,L, . . .)`	Find minimum element of list of integer elements.

These functions allow for as many arguments as you want. They search for the largest or the smallest element. Note that the name of the function is indicative of the mode of the value it returns.

7.8 DATA Statement

The portion of a program preceding any loop entry point frequently involves setting the initial value of many variables (counters and accumulators). This often requires a large number of relatively trivial statements. In the next program, for example, there are:

1. Two counters (`LOW` and `HIGH`) that must be set at zero.
2. Two accumulators (`SUMLOW` and `SUMHI`) that must be cleared.
3. A card counter that must be set at 100.

The `DATA` statement provides a quick and efficient method of assigning an initial value to each of a list of variables as the following suggests.

Old **New**

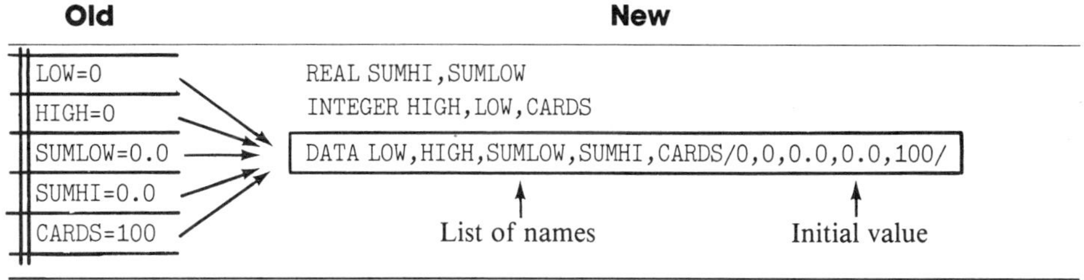

Note the one-to-one matching of name to value. The usual restrictions apply; that is, the sequence of names must agree in number and mode with the sequence of constants appearing in the initial value list. An alternate form of this statement is as follows:

```
DATA LOW,HIGH/0,0/,SUMLOW,SUMHI/0.0,0.0/,CARDS/100/
```

Caution: Commas needed

General Form

DATA list of names/list of value/

or

DATA $list_1$ of names/$list_1$ of values/, $list_2$ of names/ $list_2$ of values/, $list_3$ . . .

When the value to be assigned to a number of variables is the same, a repetition factor may be used in the initial value list as shown in the following.

```
DATA LOW,HIGH/2*0/,SUMLOW,SUMHI/2*0.0/
```

Repetition factor

Review Exercises

★ 1. Does the statement:

```
X=SIDE1**2
```

represent a mixed mode infraction? Why not?

2. What does the term "argument of a function" mean? In what form may the argument be given?

3. If your systems software only provides SIN and COS trigonometric functions, how are all the other trigonometric functions determined (for example, tangent)?

★ 4. In the statement:

```
Y=R*SIN(THETA)
```

should the angle THETA be expressed in degrees or radians?

5. A variable called X contains a negative number. Which of the following statements can be used to determine X cube? Explain.

```
Y = X**3.0
Y = X**3
```

★ 6. You have been told to exercise caution when using IF tests involving real numbers. Explain why the following STOP statement may not be executed even though the value of X is 25.0:

```
IF(SQRT(X).EQ.5.0)STOP
```

7. Describe two instances in which it would be necessary to use a flag while writing a program.

8. What are some typical activities that are accomplished in the termination section of a program?

★ 9. What is the purpose of the DATA statement?

10. Write a DATA statement that makes use of a repetition factor in assigning the same value to two or more variables.

11. A data file consists of 200 records, each containing a dollar amount representing deposits or withdrawals at a bank. Negative values represent withdrawals. Positive values represent deposits. Determine how many deposits were made and the total value of these deposits. Provide similar information concerning the withdrawals.

12. Write a program to produce the table of trigonometric values shown.

	SIN	COS	TAN	COT	SEC	CSC
0.0	.0000	1.0000	.0000	–	1.0000	.0000
1.0	.0175	.9998	.0175	57.29	1.0002	57.14
2.0	.0349	.9994	.0349	28.64	1.0006	28.65
3.0	.0523	.9986	.0523	19.08	1.0014	19.12
178.0	.0349	.9994	.0349	28.64	1.0006	28.65
179.0	.0175	.9998	.0175	57.29	1.0002	57.14
180.0	.0000	1.0000	.0000	–	1.0000	.0000

13. The first portion of a data file defines a list of X values recorded one to a record. A leader record contains an integer telling how large the list is. The remainder of the file defines a second list of X values.

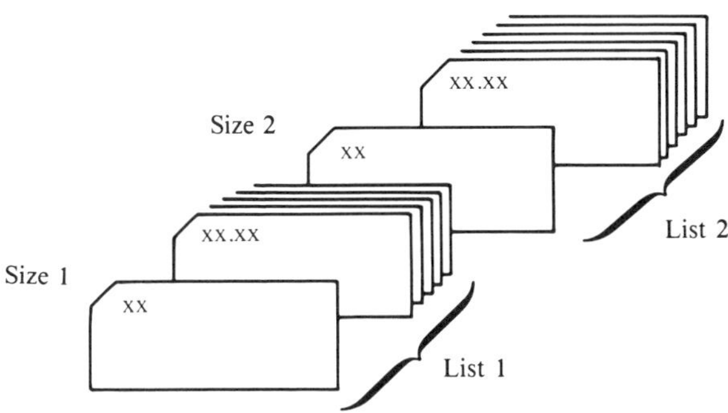

Determine and report the sum of X values in list 1 and list 2.

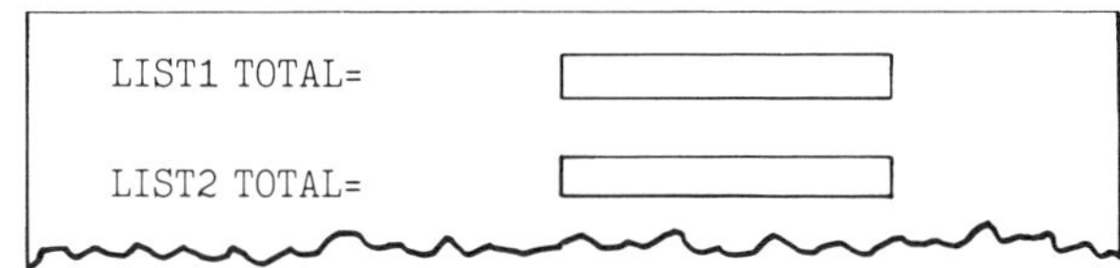

★ 14. Repeat exercise 13 except report only one sum, whichever is the larger. Have the output appear as follows:

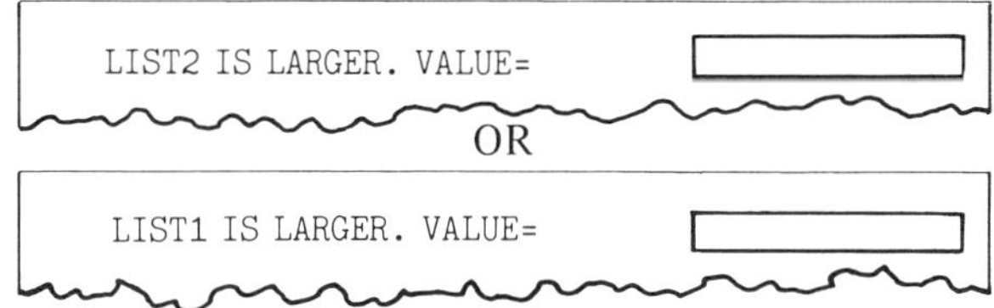

15. The goverment requires that all new cars meet a minimum efficiency rating (like 25 miles/gallon) and that rating will be increased periodically. The first record in a file defines the present requirements; the next 20

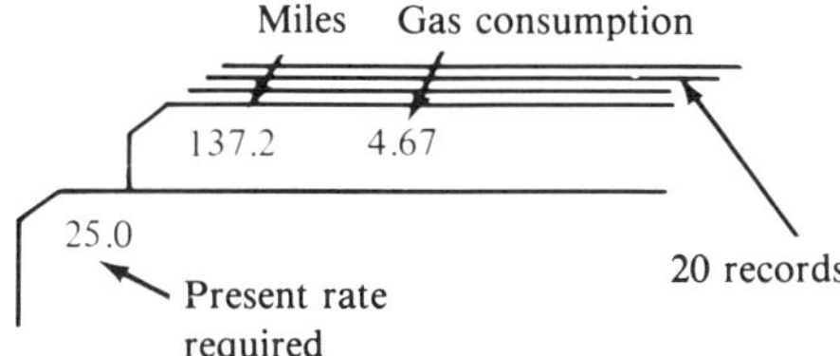

records give the results (miles driven and gas consumed) in 20 test runs on a specific model of car. Write a program that computes the mileage rating for each test run and compare each value with the government standard. Print as output one of two messages:

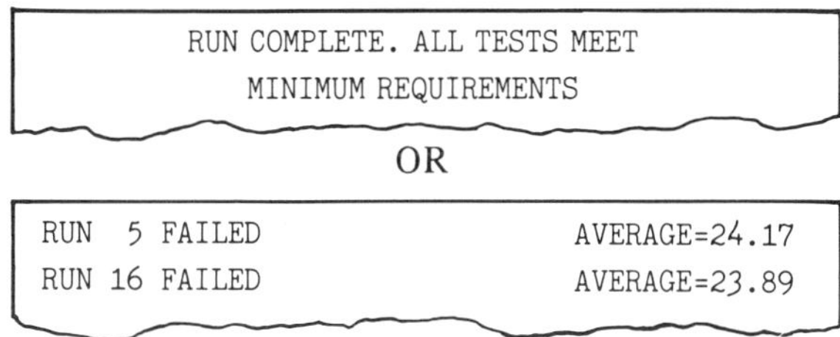

16. Repeat exercise 15 except consider the test unsuccessful if no more than 10% of the cars (2 cars) fall below the minimum imposed provided that the average "miles/gallon" for the 20 cars meet government standards. Have output appear as:

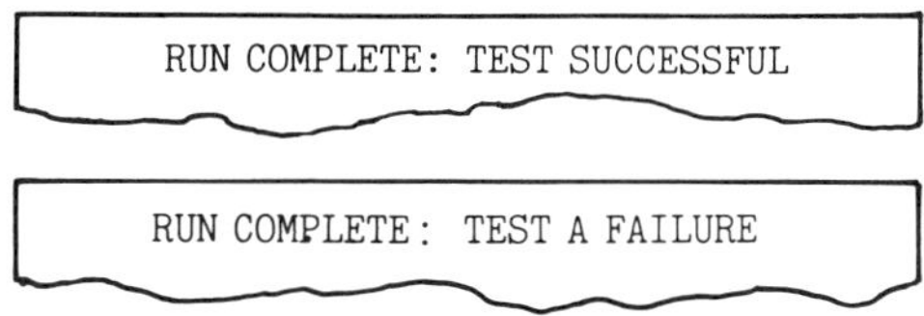

Show what intermediate output values a cautious programmer would generate to assure the program is working well.

17. The navigator of a ship is asked to plot a proposed course change. The following information is provided:

New heading: 135.0°
Proposed speed: 20.0 miles/hr.
Time on this course: 126.0 minutes

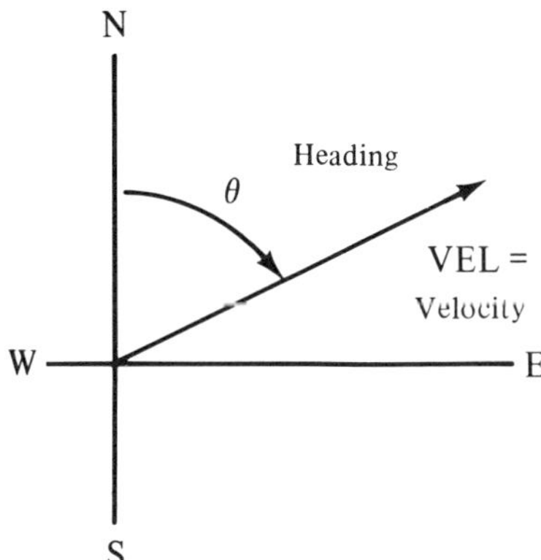

Write a program to read these three values from an input file and determine:

a. Total distance traveled
b. N-S component
c. E-W component

18. The first record of a data file gives the magnitude and inclination (degrees) of a vector (V_1); a second record gives the magnitude and inclination of a second vector (V_2):

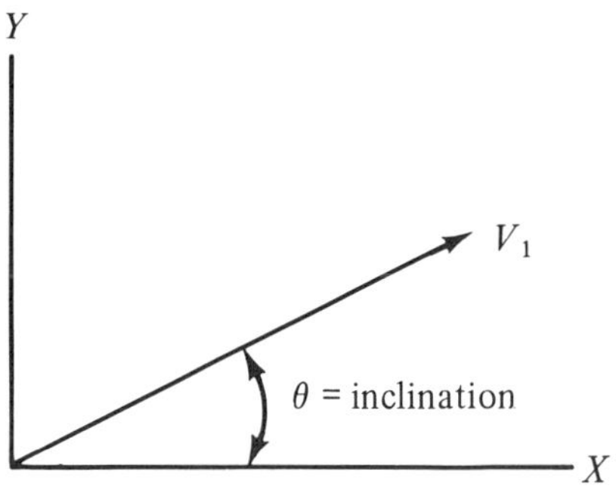

Part A: Write a program to determine the X and Y components of each vector.

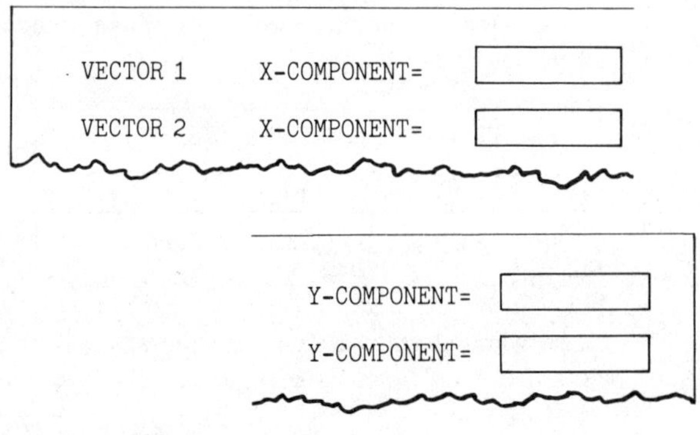

Part B: Add statements to the program that will add the two X-components together in a memory location called `SUMX`. Add the two Y-components together and label this `SUMY`. Report these two values.

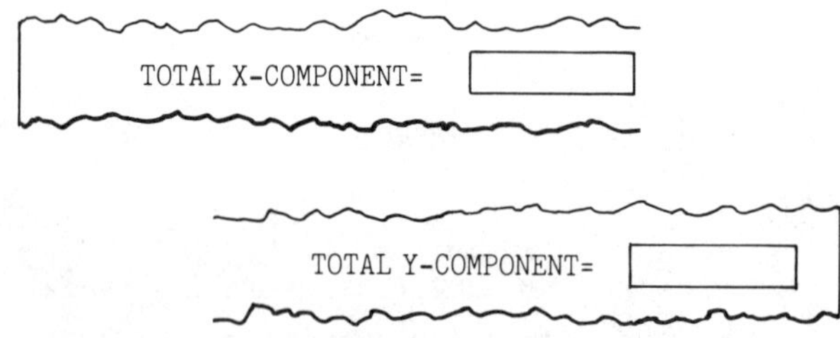

Part C: Determine the magnitude and inclination of the vector V_R whose X and Y components are `SUMX` and `SUMY`. The total program will thereby compute the vector sum of V_1 and V_2.

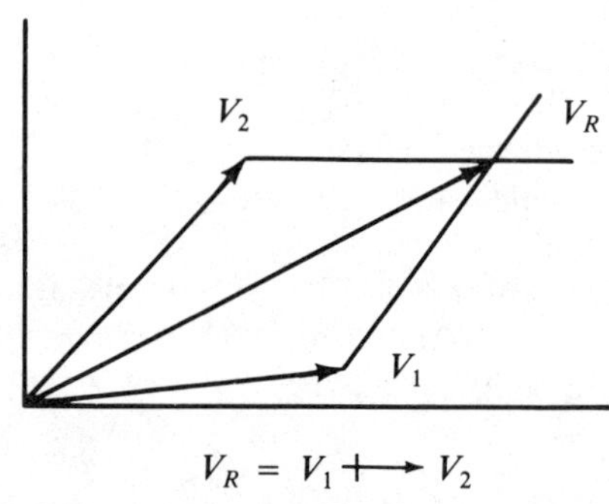

$$V_R = V_1 \overset{+}{\longrightarrow} V_2$$

19. Repeat exercise 18 except reverse the sign of the X and Y components of the second vector thereby accomplishing vector subtraction:

$$V_R = V_1 \overset{-}{\longrightarrow} V_2$$

20. Combine the features of exercises 18 and 19 into one program that involves a single input record.

CODE:
1 = Addition
2 = Subtraction

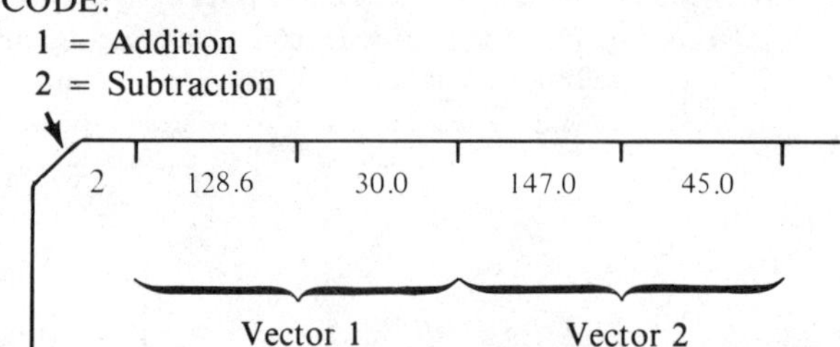

The first digit of the input record determines if the two vectors are to be added or subtracted.

★ 21. Determine the minimum and maximum value of the equations shown between X = 1 and X = 10.

$$y = \log_{10}(x + 4) + |(x^3 - 64)|$$

22. Determine and report the X and Y value of 360 equally spaced points around the periphery of a circle of radius R (read from input). Cause a memory location called `THETA` to take on the following sequence of values:

0.0,1.0,2.0,3.0,4.0,. . .,358.0,359.0,360.0

For each value of `THETA` compute X and Y from the equation:

$$X = R \cdot \cos\theta$$
$$Y = R \cdot \sin\theta$$

23. We wish to evaluate the equation:

$$y = e^x(\ln(x + 1) - 4)$$

between two limits of X to be read from data:

```
   16.0  28.0
XMIN         XMAX
```

Write a program that reads these values and computes the total range of X they span. Divide this range by 100 defining a "stepping value." Set a memory location called X at `XMIN`, and then increase X by the computed "stepping value" until `XMAX` is reached. For each value compute and report Y.

24. Read 8 real numbers from a data file. Report the largest and smallest value using the library functions listed in Section 7.7.

25. A data file consists of 100 records, each containing the X and Y of successive points on a curve (values of X are sequential). Determine the average value of Y. Determine the largest difference in X between successive data points.

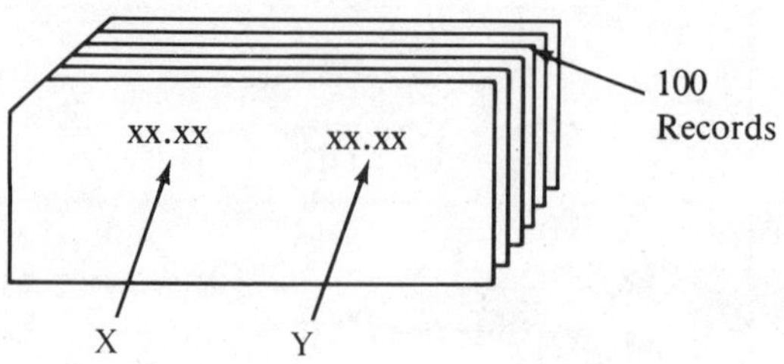

Additional Applications

Programming Example
Folding a Number

811	249	125

Social Security Number

Workers' pay records are stored in a file cabinet using their social security numbers. To speed up the filing process, the cabinet was equipped with a series of folders numbered 000, 001, 002, 003, . . ., 997, 998, 999 and to file records using only three digits of the workers' social security numbers.

First Attempt: Initially, records were stored using the *first* 3 digits, but that procedure did not work well. Some folders had hundreds of records while others were empty, because of the way in which social security numbers are issued.

Second Attempt: The process was modified by shifting to the *last* 3 digits of the number, but the results were again not satisfactory.

Third Attempt: Write a program to allow *all* digits to be used in generating the three-digit filing number as follows:

1. Divide the nine-digit number into three equal parts.
2. Add these parts together.
3. Take the last three digits of this sum as the filing number.

This is called **folding the number**.

```
C..........................................................
C..    PURPOSE - MODIFY A 9 DIGIT SOCIAL SECURITY NUMBER    ..
C..              AS DIRECTED                                ..
C..........................................................
C
C            - - - - - IMPORTANT VARIABLES - - - - -
C
C     --N1,N2,N3    THREE EQUAL PARTS OF SOCIAL SECURITY     --
C                   NUMBER                                   --
C     --SUM         SUM OF THESE PARTS                       --
C     --FILE        FILE NUMBER RESULTING FROM PROCESS       --
C     --FIRST       FIRST DIGIT OF THE VALUE SUM             --
C
      INTEGER SUM, FILE, N1, N2, N3, FIRST
C
      READ 10,N1,N2,N3
   10 FORMAT(I3,I3,I3)
C
      SUM = N1 + N2 + N3
```

Problem: The addition of these numbers may produce a four-digit result. When this happens we must determine the first digit and adjust the value of SUM appropriately.

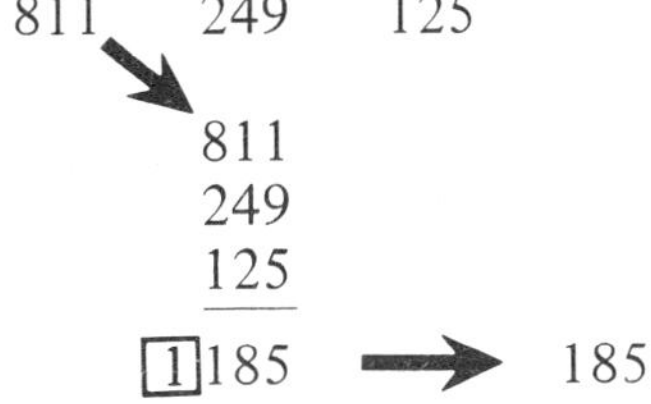

Programming Example–Folding a Number continued

```
C
      IF (SUM.GT.999)THEN
C
          FIRST=SUM/1000
C
C         REDUCE BY APPROPRIATE VALUE
C
          FILE = SUM-FIRST*1000
C
      ELSE
C
          FILE = SUM
C
      ENDIF
C
      PRINT*, FILE
C
      STOP
      END
```

FIRST will contain the value 1 for example shown above

Programming Example
Report Median Value (String of Five Digits)

To determine the median value of a string of numbers, you must first order the string (put values in numeric order). If the string consists of an odd number of values, the median is the middle number (see following illustration). If the string consists of an even number of values, the median is the average of the middle two numbers.

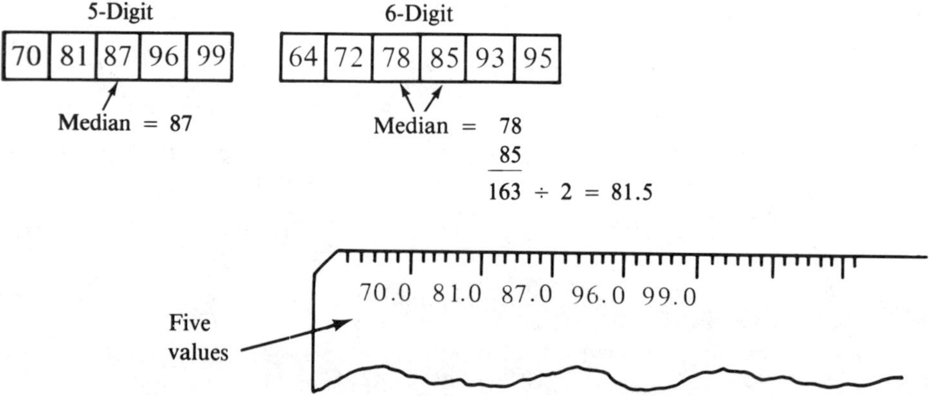

An input record contains a string of five real numbers. Verify that these numbers are in order, and then report the median value of the string.

```
C.....................................................
C..  PURPOSE - VERIFY THE ORDER - REPORT THE MEDIAN  ..
C.....................................................
C
C            ---- IMPORTANT VARIABLES -----
C
C    - - X1 TO X5 NUMBERS IN THE NUMBER SET         --
C
      READ*,X1,X2,X3,X4,X5
C
      IF(X1.GT.X2)PRINT*, 'FIRST TWO NUMBERS OUT OF ORDER'
```

Programming Example–Report Median Value (String of Five Digits) continued

```
C
      IF(X2.GT.X3)PRINT*, ' SECOND AND THIRD NUMBER OUT OF ORDER'
C
      IF(X3.GT.X4)PRINT*, ' THIRD AND FOURTH NUMBER OUT OF ORDER'
C
      IF(X4.GT.X5)PRINT*, ' FOURTH AND FIFTH NUMBER OUT OF ORDER'
C
      PRINT*,X3
C
      STOP
      END
```

Programming Example: Median Value (General)

Write a more general program for reporting the median of a string of real numbers. The first record of a data file provides an integer telling the size of the string (with the maximum number of elements being 9). Use a computed GO TO to reach one of two bodies of FORTRAN code to handle an odd or even set of elements.

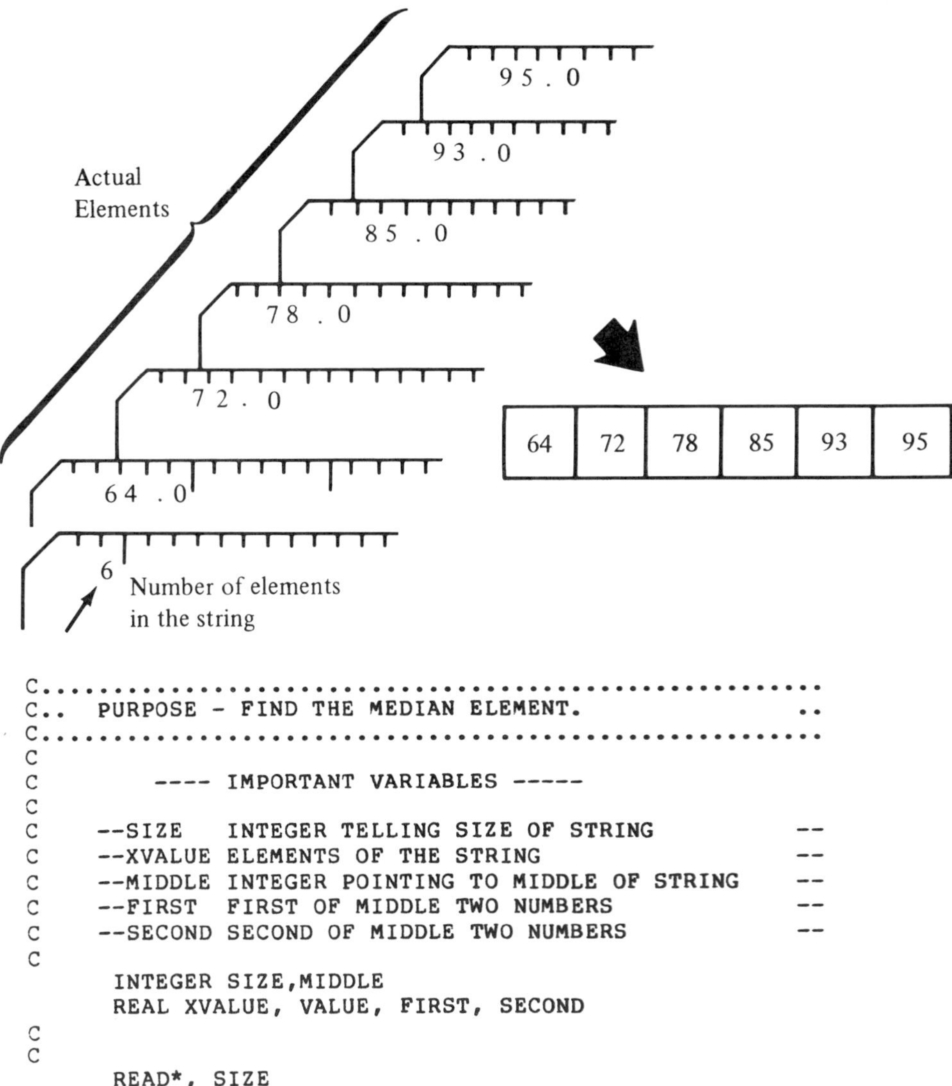


```
C.....................................................
C..  PURPOSE - FIND THE MEDIAN ELEMENT.             ..
C.....................................................
C
C         ---- IMPORTANT VARIABLES -----
C
C    --SIZE   INTEGER TELLING SIZE OF STRING          --
C    --XVALUE ELEMENTS OF THE STRING                  --
C    --MIDDLE INTEGER POINTING TO MIDDLE OF STRING    --
C    --FIRST  FIRST OF MIDDLE TWO NUMBERS             --
C    --SECOND SECOND OF MIDDLE TWO NUMBERS            --
C
      INTEGER SIZE,MIDDLE
      REAL XVALUE, VALUE, FIRST, SECOND
C
C
      READ*, SIZE
```

Programming Example–Median Value (General) continued

```
C
      GO TO(1,2,1,2,1,2,1,2,1),SIZE
C
C        MODULE 1 - HANDLE ODD NUMBER OF ELEMENTS
C
    1 MIDDLE=SIZE/2+1
C
      DO 10 I = 1, MIDDLE-1, 1
C
C        CLEAR OUT ELEMENTS BEFORE MEDIAN
C
         READ*, XVALUE
C
   10 CONTINUE
C
C     ...READ NEXT ELEMENT....IT IS THE MEDIAN....
C
      READ*, XVALUE
      PRINT*,'THE MEDIAN VALUE IS ', XVALUE
      STOP
C
C
C
C             MODULE 2 - HANDLE EVEN NUMBER OF ELEMENTS
C
C
C
C
    2  MIDDLE = SIZE/2
C
       DO 20 I = 1, MIDDLE - 1, 1
C
C         ....CLEAR OUT ELEMENTS IN FRONT....
C
           READ*, XVALUE
C
   20  CONTINUE
C
C             ************************************************
C             ** NEXT TWO ELEMENTS INVOLVED IN COMPUTATION **
C             **              OF MEDIAN VALUE               **
C             ************************************************
C
        READ*, FIRST
        READ*, SECOND
C
        VALUE=(FIRST + SECOND)/2.0
C
        PRINT*, 'THE MEDIAN VALUE = ',VALUE
C
        STOP
        END
```

Programming Example
Odd or Even

Write a program to read an integer from an input file and determine if the number is odd or even.

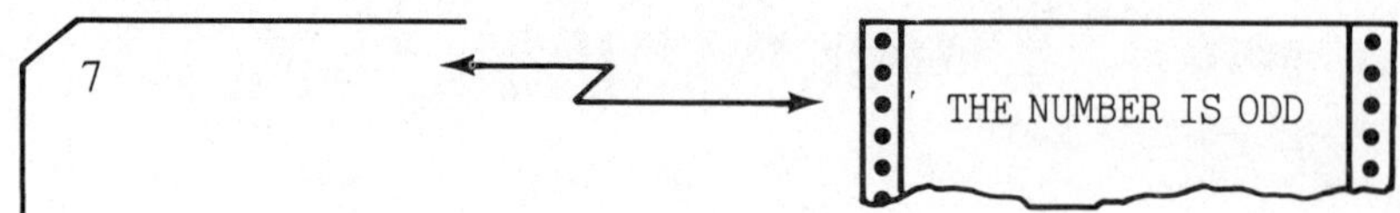

Programming Example–Odd or Even continued

When an odd number is divided by 2 in the integer mode, truncation takes place. We can use this information as follows:

1. Make a copy of the number.
2. Divide the copy by 2.
3. Multiply the copy by 2.

If the copy and the original number are now different, truncation has occurred, and the original number was odd.

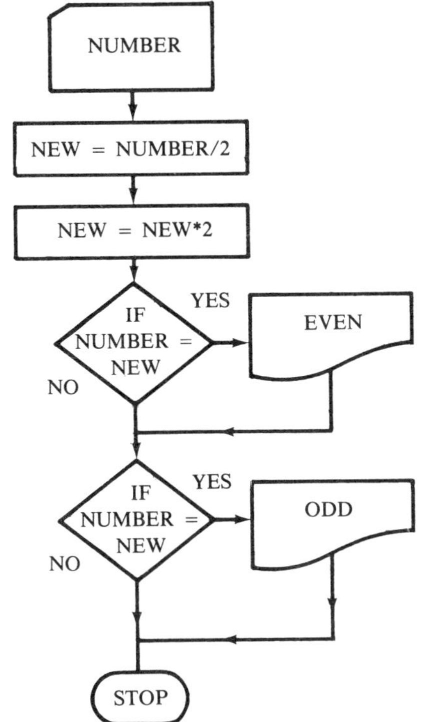


```
C.......................................................
C..    PURPOSE - DETERMINE IF A NUMBER IS EVEN OR ODD ..
C.......................................................
C
       INTEGER NEW, NUMBER
       READ*, NUMBER
C
       NEW = NUMBER/2
       NEW = NEW*2
C
       IF(NEW.EQ.NUMBER) PRINT*,' THE NUMBER IS EVEN.'
C
       IF(NEW.NE.NUMBER)PRINT*, 'THE NUMBER IS ODD.'
C
      STOP
      END
```

Programming Example
Polar to Cartesian

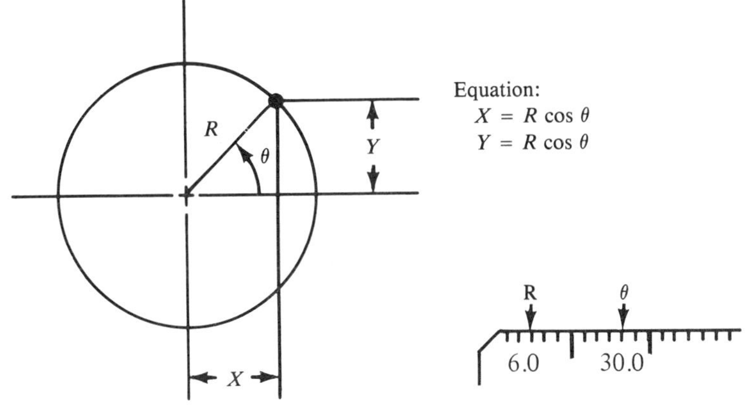

Programming Example–Polar to Cartesian continued

The location of the point can be specified in polar coordinates as follows:

Given: $R = 6$
$\theta = 30°$

The X and Y coordinates (cartesian) can be found by using the equations shown. Write a program to accept from data the polar coordinates of a point and compute the corresponding cartesian coordinates.

```
C.............................................................
C..    PURPOSE - CONVERT POLAR TO CARTESIAN COORDINATES    ..
C.............................................................
C
C                ----IMPORTANT VARIABLES----
C      --RADIUS    RADIUS OF POINT                          --
C      --THETA     ANGLE (DEGREES)                          --
C      --X,Y       CARTESIAN COORDINATES OF POINT           --
C
       REAL RADIUS, THETA, X, Y
C
       READ*,RADIUS,THETA
C
       X = RADIUS*COS(THETA/57.3)
       Y = RADIUS*SIN(THETA/57.3)
C
       PRINT*,'X=', X, 'Y=', Y
C
       STOP
       END
```

Programming Example
Either Way**
(see previous problem)

Given: R, θ
Req'd: X, Y

$X = R \cos \theta$
$Y = R \sin \theta$

OR

Given: X, Y
Req'd: R, θ

$R = \sqrt{X^2 + Y^2}$
$\theta = \tan^{-1}(Y/X)$

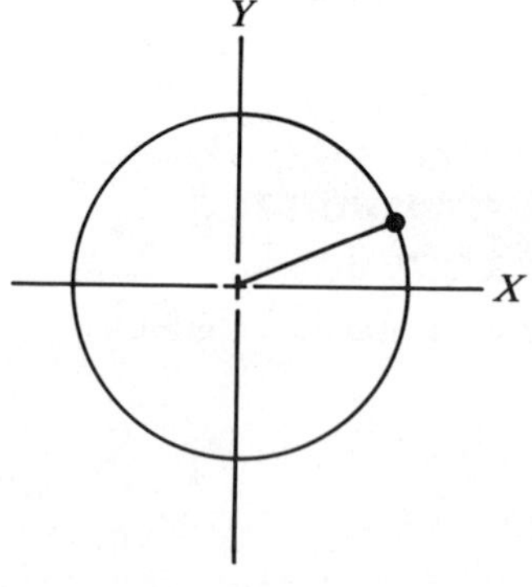

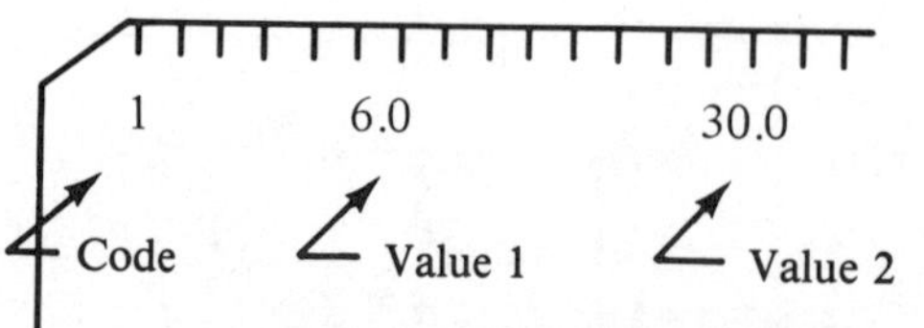

Write a program that can accept as input the cartesian coordinates of a point and compute the polar coordinates as output (CODE=1), or accept the polar coordinates and compute the corresponding cartesian coordinates (CODE=2).

Programming Example–Either Way continued

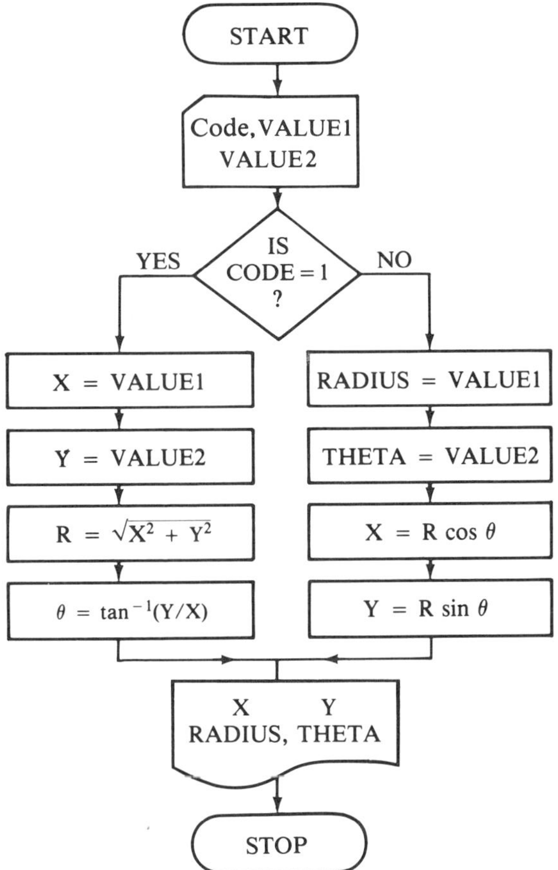


```
C.............................................................
C..     PURPOSE - CODE = 1 CONVERT POLAR TO CARTESIAN       ..
C                 CODE = 2 CONVERT CARTESIAN TO POLAR       ..
C.............................................................
C
C              ----IMPORTANT VARIABLES----
C       --CODE              SELECTOR VALUE                    --
C       --R,THETA           POLAR VALUES                      --
C       --X,Y               CARTESIAN VALUES                  --
C       --VALUE1,VALUE2     VALUES READ FROM INPUT RECORD     --
C
C
        INTEGER CODE
        REAL R, THETA, X, Y, VALUE1, VALUE2
C
        READ*, CODE, VALUE1, VALUE2
C
C       ...TEST CODE VALUE...
C
        IF(CODE.EQ.1) THEN
C
C               CONVERT POLAR TO CARTESIAN
C
```

Programming Example–Either Way continued

```
                    RADIUS = VALUE1
                    THETA = VALUE2
                    X = RADIUS*COS(THETA/57.3)
                    Y = RADIUS*SIN(THETA/57.3)
C
        ELSE
C
C                   CONVERT CARTESIAN TO POLAR
C
                    X = VALUE1
                    Y = VALUE2
                    RADIUS = SQRT(X**2 + Y**2)
                    THETA = ATAN2(Y,X)
C
        ENDIF
C
C                   OUTPUT MODULE
C
        PRINT*,'X=',X,'Y=',Y,'RADIUS=',RADIUS,'THETA=',THETA
C
        STOP
        END
```

Programming Example
Poor Grades

The college board scores of 1000 randomly selected students are to be analyzed to see if students from low-income families perform as well as students from affluent families. Determine:

1. The number of students coming from families having incomes less than $8000.
2. The average score achieved by this group.
3. The number of students coming from families having incomes of $25,000 or more.
4. The average score achieved by this group.

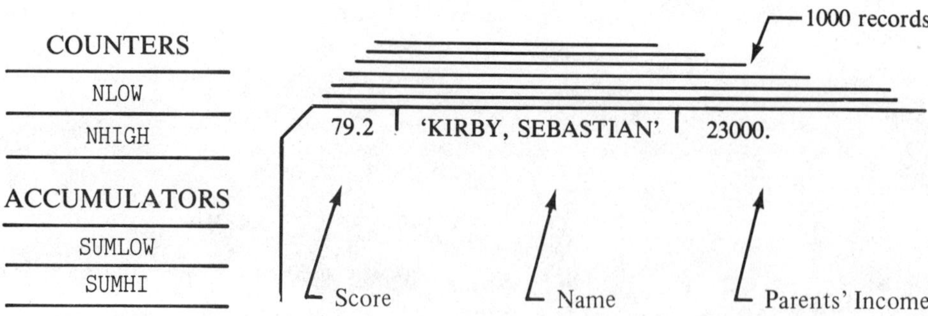

Programming Example–Poor Grades continued

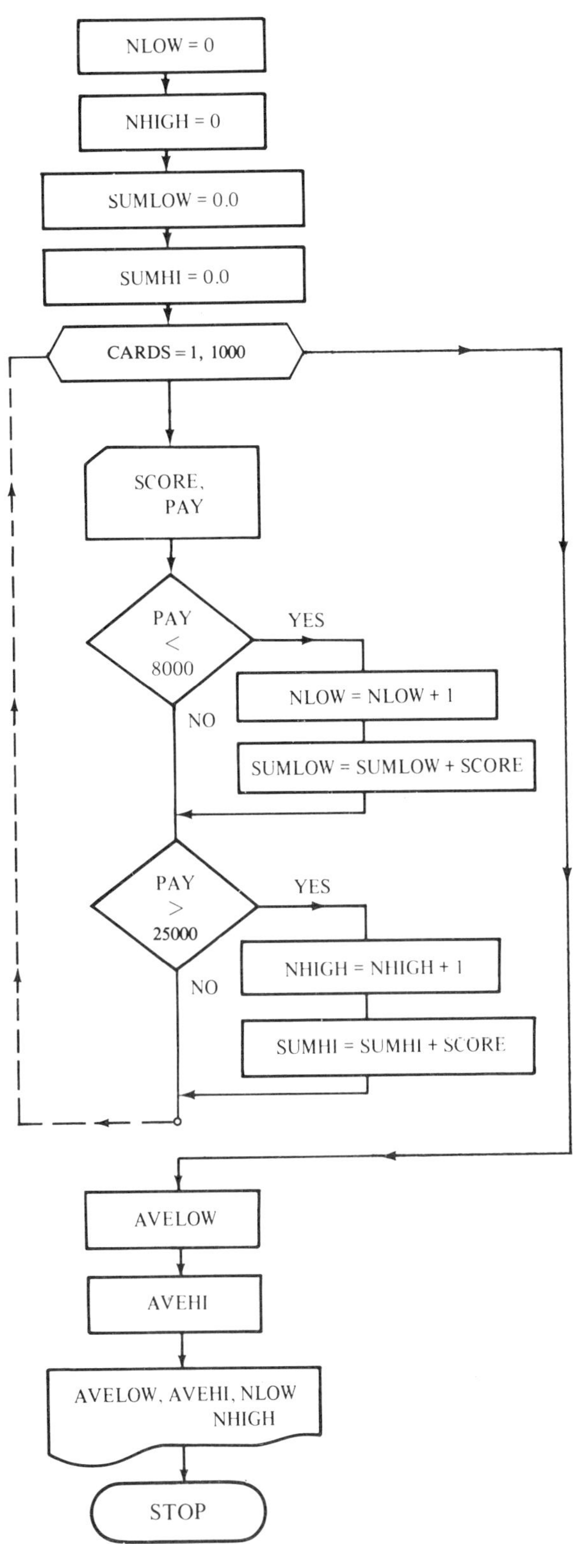

Programming Example–Poor Grades continued

```
C..........................................................
C..     PURPOSE - ANALYZE THE EFFECT OF LOW VS.HIGH FAMILY ..
C..               INCOME ON STUDENT'S GRADES               ..
C..........................................................
C
C             ----IMPORTANT VARIABLES----
C
C     --NLOW          NUMBER OF LOW INCOME FAMILIES          --
C     --NHIGH         NUMBER OF HIGH INCOME FAMILIES         --
C     --PAY           PARENT'S YEARLY INCOME                 --
C     --SCORE         STUDENT'S BOARD SCORES                 --
C     --SUMLOW        LOW SCORE ACCUMULATOR                  --
C     --SUMHI         HIGH SCORE ACCUMULATOR                 --
C     --CARDS         CARD COUNTER                           --
C
C             INITIALIZATION SECTION
C
      REAL SUMHIGH, SUMLOW, PAY, AVELOW, AVEHI
      INTEGER NLOW, NHIGH, CARDS, SCORE
C
      NLOW=0
      NHIGH=0
C
      SUMLOW=0.0
      SUMHI=0.0
C
```

A single DATA statement can be used in place of these four statements

```
 DATA NLOW,NHIGH/0,0/,SUMLOW,SUMHI/0.0,0.0/
```

```
      DO 50 CARDS = 1, 1000, 1
C
C          .....LOOP ENTRY POINT.....
C
           READ*, SCORE,PAY
C
C          SEE IF HIGH OR LOW INCOME
C
           IF(PAY.LT.8000.) NLOW = NLOW + 1
           IF(PAY.LT.8000.) SUMLOW = SUMLOW + SCORE
C
           IF(PAY.GT.25000.) NHIGH=NHIGH +1
           IF(PAY.GT.25000.) SUMHI= SUMHI+SCORE
C
 50   CONTINUE
C
C         LOOP EXIT POINT
C
C         COMPUTE AND REPORT AVERAGES
C
        AVELOW = SUMLOW/FLOAT(NLOW)
        AVEHI = SUMHI/FLOAT(NHIGH)
C
        PRINT*,   NLOW,NHIGH,AVELOW,AVEHI
C
        STOP
        END
```

Programming Example
Trig Tables

The table shown was prepared for a math book. It gives trigonometric functions for angles between 0° and 90° at one degree increments. It has been decided to expand the table by using one-half degree increments (θ = 0.0, 0.5, 1.0, 1.5, 2.0, 2.5, etc.).

Programming Example–Trig Tables continued

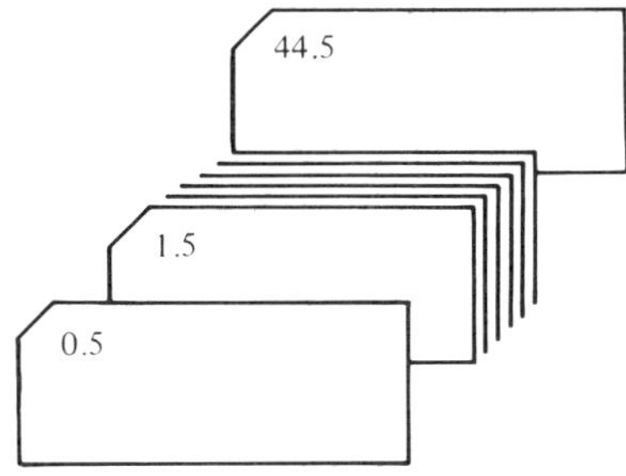

Degrees	sin	cos	tan	cot	
0°	.0000	1.000	.0000	–	90°
1°	.0175	.9998	.0175	57.29	89°
2°	.0349	.9994	.0349	28.64	88°
3°	.0523	.9986	.0524	19.08	87°
4°	.0698	.9976	.0699	14.30	86°
5°	.0872	.9962	.0875	11.43	85°
6°	.1045	.9945	.1051	9.514	84°
7°	.1219	.9925	.1228	8.144	
8°	.1392	.9903	.1405		
38°				1.280	52°
39°	.6293	.7771	.8098	1.235	51°
40°	.6428	.7660	.8391	1.192	50°
41°	.6561	.7547	.8693	1.150	49°
42°	.6691	.7431	.9004	1.111	48°
43°	.6820	.7314	.9325	1.072	47°
44°	.6947	.7193	.9657	1.036	46°
45°	.7071	.7071	1.000	1.000	45°
	cos	sin	ctn	tan	Degrees

Write a program to determine and report the *additional* values needed to expand the table. Report these values in a form similar to the existing table.

In developing the logic of this program, one of the first considerations is controlling a memory location (possibly called THETA) so that it will take on the desired sequence of values (0.5, 1.5, 2.5, . . ., 44.5). One approach is to read values of THETA from data, but you now have a more direct way of controlling THETA.

```
C......................................................
C..     PURPOSE - COMPUTE ADDITIONAL TRIGONOMETRIC VALUES..
C..               MAKE THE TABLE MORE COMPLETE.          ..
C......................................................
C
C                  ----IMPORTANT VARIABLES----
C       --THETA         ANGLE (DEGREES)                     --
C       --ANS1          FIRST OUTPUT VALUE - SINE VALUE     --
C       --ANS2          SECOND OUTPUT VALUE - COS VALUE     --
C       --ANS3          THIRD OUTPUT VALUE - TAN VALUE      --
C       --ANS4          COMPLEMENT OF THE ANGLE             --
C       --COMP          COMPLEMENT OF ANGLE                 --
C
        REAL THETA,ANS1,ANS2,ANS3,ANS4,COMP
C
C             ...LOOP ENTRY POINT...
C
        DO 50 THETA = 0.5, 45.0, 0.5
C
            ANS1=SIN(THETA/57.3)
            ANS2=COS(THETA/57.3)
            ANS3=ANS1/ANS2
            ANS4=1.0/ANS3
            COMP= 90.0 - THETA
C
C               PUBLISH LINE OF OUTPUT
```

Programming Example—Trig Tables continued

```
C
              PRINT*,THETA,ANS1,ANS2,ANS3,ANS4,COMP
C
   50   CONTINUE
C
C                  ... LOOP EXIT POINT...
C
        STOP
        END
```

Programming Example
New Highway

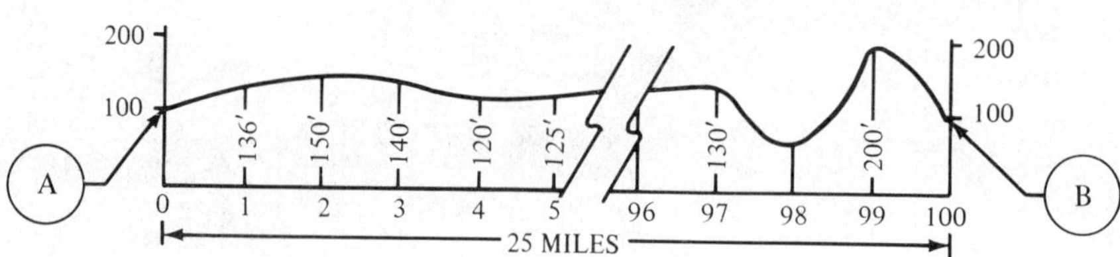

A 25-mile stretch of highway is being planned to connect point A and B shown above. The elevation of the land at 100 equally-spaced points along the route is determined and recorded. We are interested in locating those points along the highway where the change in elevation is excessive (greater than 20 ft.)

Read the first two records. If the change in elevation between these points is greater than 20 feet, report this as a trouble area.

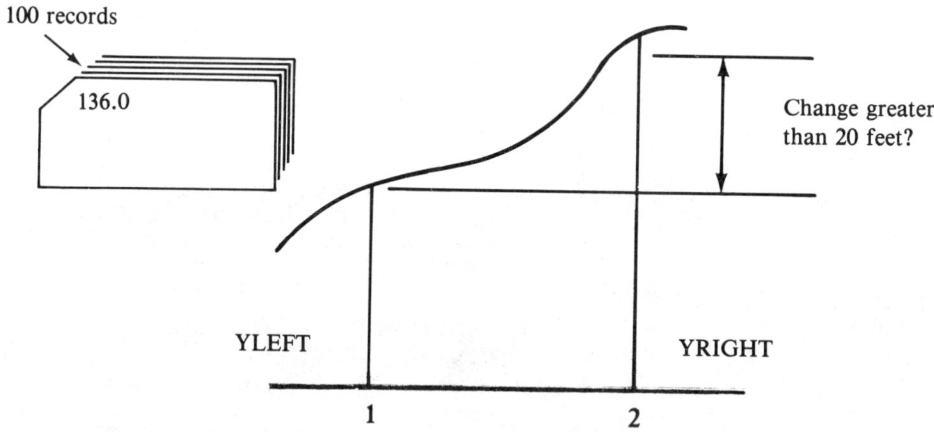

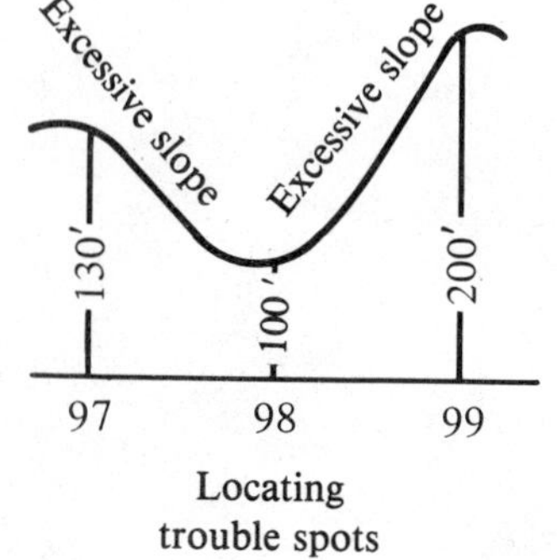

Locating trouble spots

```
C
         READ*, YLEFT
C
         READ*, YRIGHT
C
         CHANGE = ABS(YRIGHT - YLEFT)
C
         IF(CHANGE.GT.20.0) THEN
C
              PRINT*,'TROUBLE SPOT LOCATED BETWEEN POINT ',
     1              POINT,' AND POINT ',NEXT,'DIFFERENCE IS '
     2              CHANGE,' FEET.'
C
```

Programming Example–New Highway continued

Repeat this logic to determine the change in elevation between points 2 and 3, then between 3 and 4, and so on. *Report any trouble spots.*

Note: Set a flag called FLAG at the start of the program. If no trouble spots are located, use the flag to issue the printout: NO TROUBLE SPOTS LOCATED.

```
C...............................................................
C..     PURPOSE - LOCATE TROUBLE SPOTS ALONG A HIGHWAY.       ..
C...............................................................
C
C                     ----IMPORTANT VARIABLES----
C
C       --POINT     INTEGER TELLING POINT IN HIGHWAY UNDER STUDY--
C       --NEXT      POINT JUST BEYOND LOCATION POINT            --
C       --CHANGE    DIFFERENCE IN ELEVATION BETWEEN TWO POINTS  --
C       --YLEFT     ELEVATION AT LOCATION POINT                 --
C       --YRIGHT    ELEVATION AT LOCATION NEXT                  --
C       --FLAG      FLAG MARKING TROUBLE SPOT                   --
C                       FLAG = 0  NO TROUBLE SPOT               --
C                       FLAG = 1  TROUBLE SPOT LOCATED          --
C
      INTEGER POINT, NEXT, FLAG, I
      REAL YLEFT, YRIGHT, CHANGE
C
      POINT = 1
      FLAG =0
C
C
      READ*, YLEFT
C
C                 .....LOOP ENTRY POINT.....
C
      DO 20 I = 1, 99, 1
C
          READ*, YRIGHT
C
          CHANGE = ABS(YRIGHT - YLEFT)
C
          IF(CHANGE.GT.20.0) THEN
C
              NEXT= POINT + 1
              PRINT*,'TROUBLE SPOT LOCATED BETWEEN POINT ',
     1               POINT,' AND POINT ',NEXT,'DIFFERENCE IS '
     2               CHANGE,'FEET.'
C
              FLAG=1
C
          ENDIF
C
C                 ADVANCE POINT   REDEFINE YLEFT
C
      POINT = POINT + 1
      YLEFT = YRIGHT
C
   20 CONTINUE
C                 .....LOOP EXIT POINT.....
C
      IF (FLAG.EQ.0) PRINT*,' NO TROUBLE SPOTS LOCATED.'
C
      STOP
      END
```

Programming Example
Throw Darts**

A data file consists of 1000 records each containing two random numbers chosen by pure chance whose values are between 0 and 1. Each pair of random numbers will be used to specify the X and Y coordinates of where a dart landed when thrown randomly at the target area shown on the right of the following illustration. If these are truly random numbers, the darts will be evenly distributed throughout the target area.

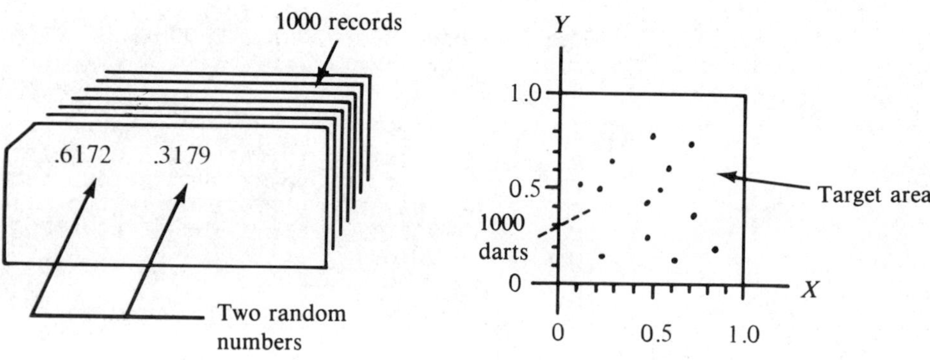

A more meaningful use of this technique is suggested by the following illustration. It is 40 units tall and 12 units wide and contains the plot of the function $y = X^2 + 12X$.

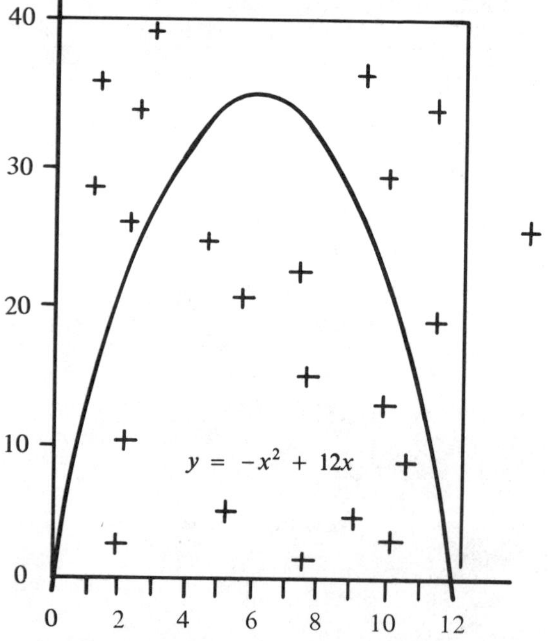

The area under this curve (the value of the integral) could be evaluated by again throwing darts and keeping track of the percentage of darts that fall below the curve. If 50% fall below the curve, the desired area is 50% of the 40-by-12 unit target area.

Consider some of the problems in writing a program to do all this. Each random number will have to be multiplied by 40 or 12 to compensate for the larger target area. Next, two counters will be needed (NYES and NNO) to keep track of how

Programming Example–Throw Darts continued

many darts fall above and below the curve. Finally, a means of determining if a dart fell below the curve will have to be found. Use the following steps:

1. Substitute the X coordinate of the dart into the equation $y = -X^2 + 12X$.
2. Call this value YEQ.
3. If the Y coordinate of the dart is greater than YEQ, the dart landed above the curve.
4. If the Y coordinate of the dart is less than YEQ, the dart landed below the curve.

```
C.......................................................
C..     PURPOSE - EVALUATE AN INTEGRAL BY RANDOM NUMBER...
C..               TECHNIQUE                             ..
C.......................................................
C
C                        ----IMPORTANT VARIABLES----
C
C        NYES     NUMBER OF DARTS THAT FELL UNDER THE CURVE      --
C        NNO      NUMBER OF DARTS THAT FELL ABOVE THE CURVE      --
C
C        X        RANDOM NUMBER CONTROLLING X LOCATION OF DART   --
C        Y        RANDOM NUMBER CONTROLLING Y LOCATION OF DART   --
C        XDART    ACTUAL X LOCATION OF WHERE DART LANDED         --
C        YDART    ACTUAL Y LOCATION OF WHERE DART LANDED         --
C        YEQ      CUT OFF VALUE OF Y (FROM EQUATION)             --
C
         INTEGER NYES, NNO, I
         REAL X, Y, XDART, YDART, YEQ
C
         DATA NNO,NYES/ 0, 0/
C
C                LOOP ENTRY POINT
C
          DO 40 I = 1, 1000, 1
C
                 READ*,X,Y
C
C                SCALE THESE VALUES
C
                 XDART = X*12.0
                 YDART = Y*40.0
C
C                COMPUTE CUT OFF VALUE
C
                 YEQ = XDART ** 2 + 12.0 * XDART
C
                 IF(YDART.GT.YEQ)NNO =NNO+1
                 IF(YDART.LT.YEQ)NYES = NYES +1
C
   40    CONTINUE
C
C                ALL DARTS THROWN  COMPUTE AVERAGE
C
   25    AVE = NYES/ (NNO + NYES)
C
         PRINT*, AVE
C
         STOP
         END
```

Take another look at statement 25. Is that the way it should be written? Using integer arithmetic will produce the value zero. The library function FLOAT is needed.

8 Program Structure Programming Style

THE BAD NEWS

Most FORTRAN programs do not work correctly the first time they are run. Very often they do not work correctly on the second, third, and fourth run. Up to half the time needed to produce a properly functioning program is spent on locating and correcting errors.

THE GOOD NEWS

It is possible to identify and organize a careful, consistent method of approach to solving each and every problem on the computer which will markedly increase the likelihood of an early successful program. It may even be possible to have a successful run on the very first try! It is the purpose of this chapter to identify these procedures.

8.1 Structure Your Approach

There is no such thing as a standard method of solving problems on the computer. We would like nothing better than to provide a check-off list that, if rigidly followed, would guarantee success. On the other hand, there are specific steps that can be applied in a consistent and orderly fashion. You are advised to structure your approach to solving each and every problem on the computer in the following way:

1. Learn what steps and recommendations have proven useful to other programmers.
2. Develop the habit of applying these steps to each problem (no matter how simple the problem may be) in a consistent way.

To get you started in this process, let us look at a special group of recommendations or steps. The list of recommendations are considered special because they are the steps most useful when first *starting* to develop a problem's algorithm. These steps concentrate on correct problem definition.

Group 1 Recommendations: Getting Started

- Logic first—details later
  - Resist the temptation to start writing code immediately
    - Problem statement—do not start until you are sure
      - Get a firm grasp on the problem's input
        - Separate the familiar from the unfamiliar

The underlying theme of these recommendations is obvious. A solution must evolve slowly, after a series of refinements. The process starts by some top-level determinations as to exactly what the problem is all about and how it can be subdivided into a series of well-defined subtasks. Some students are exceptionally capable of performing this important management function. They are able to release themselves from the petty details of implementing a program and focus immediately on the broad strategies and plan of attack for the problem. These students have learned to fight one battle at a time—the big ones first, the little ones later (rather than all battles at once).

The end product of this phase of analysis is a less-than-perfect (and certainly not detailed) set of subtasks expressed in block diagram form (pseudocode). It is from this diagram that the refinement process begins. The only requirement imposed at this time is that no major operation be overlooked and omitted.

The next step is a simplification/familiarization process. Having identified the basic tasks (modules) that are involved in the solution, examine the flow of data *into and out of each module*. For many of these modules, you will have a good idea of how to accomplish the particular task involved. The various programming examples presented in this text should help in this regard. They have been presented to develop your experience in handling operations (tasks) that are frequently encountered in processing digital information.

There is a strong temptation to start writing FORTRAN code for these simpler modules. That is a mistake for several reasons:

1. It will take your attention away from the overall strategy of solving the problem.
2. Getting down to details this early may commit you to a method of solution that is good for this particular module but not best for the problem as a whole.
3. It is possible that you will wind up with several blocks of code that prove difficult to fit together.

Handling the Harder Modules

Do not expect to uncover a direct and simple solution to each and every module. The difficult modules will require further processing. Realize that this is just the first step in the solution. It is only important to get a clear identification of the *function* of each module at this time. The specific method of implementation comes later.

If you have difficulty identifying all the steps in a particular solution: *do a hand calculation of one or more typical applications of the algorithm.* This suggestion is being made to cut down on the number of abstractions you must face at any one time. It is easier to develop a "general" algorithm after several specific solutions have been worked out. It is part of the organized (structured) approach we are promoting.

8.2 The Refinement Process

Programming Style

Algorithm check list

1. Detailed
2. Exact
3. Effective
4. Efficient

Ultimately, an algorithm must be evolved that has the following features:

1. *Detailed:* Each and every aspect of the problem solution must be identified, labeled, and dealt with in detail. Special conditions that force alternative solutions or processing must be covered explicitly and integrated into the general solution.
2. *Exact:* The algorithm must be well organized. It must present a methodical and unambiguous definition of what factors affect the solution to the problem and of how each of these factors are to be handled (accommodated) as the solution progresses.
3. *Effective:* An algorithm must be based on sound mathematical or logical procedures that lead to a correct solution or a close approximation of the solution.
4. *Efficient:* An algorithm should express a closed solution to the problem. It should consist of a finite number of steps that converge on the final solution as rapidly as possible.

Transforming the existing block diagram into a completed algorithm having the properties just described starts with a reexamination of the individual blocks. For each block the following information has already been established:

1. What data this block receives as input.
2. What function (transform) takes place inside the block.
3. What output is generated as a result of the transform.

If the block is relatively simple and within your ability to program, document its logic with a skeleton flowchart. This need not be a very elaborate diagram. Just show the type of statements and the type of constructs to be used within the block or module.

If a block is too difficult to program, it is either too big or not sufficiently well defined. Try to sharpen your understanding of what function (transform) is to take place inside the block. Attempt to further subdivide the block by listing a number of specific actions that must be taken to accomplish the block's major function.

If any of these blocks need further refinement, the breakdown would be shown in a similar fashion (the diagram develops like the root of a tree). Ultimately, the process should bring the problem into clearer focus and result in steps that are relatively simple to program.

The concept of successive refinement is extremely important. To make sure you really understand the process, take a careful look at Figure 8.1. The block on the left provides the useful information that at a particular point in a program a module is needed to "Compute a Worker's Pay Amount." The reason this is useful information is because it provides an initial *functional definition* of what the module must accomplish. The blocks on the right, however, go a step further by *firming up* how the overall assignment will be accomplished. By "firming up" we mean, "reducing the level of vagueness associated with the solution of this subtask."

Figure 8.1 Refinement process

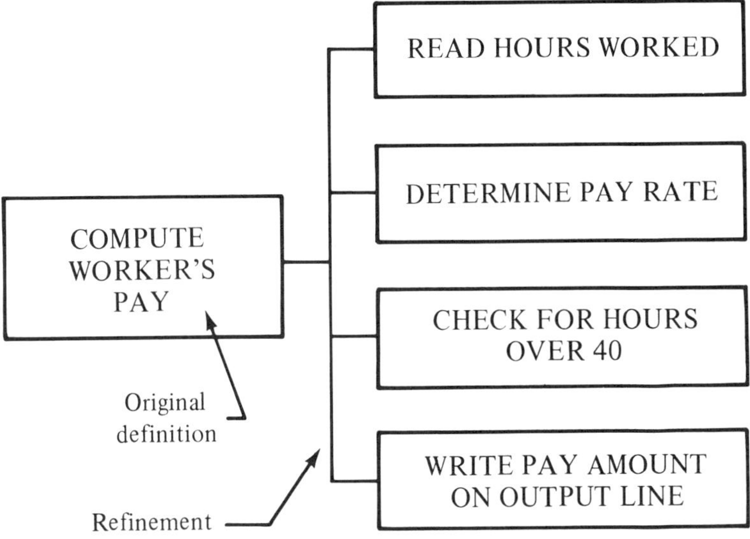

Flowcharts

> ### Programming Style
> **Flowcharts**
> **1. Top to bottom**
> **2. Don't jump around**
> **3. Parallel block structure**
>
> A flowchart should start at the top of a page and basically flow to the bottom of the page in linear fashion. This should parallel the linear structure of the block diagram or pseudocode. Do not jump around any more than is necessary. Where binary or multiple decisions are made, set up parallel paths close to one another to highlight the logic.

In constructing a flowchart, keep a few things in mind. First, remember that there is no substitute for clarity. If you are wondering how to express the logic of an IF test, or the equation of an arithmetic statement, or the indexing of a counter, *use whatever method makes it clearer.*

Try to flowchart in the same "block form" used in developing the pseudocode. Generally speaking, these blocks will be one of three basic types:

1. A *processing* block consists of a fixed series of assignment statements that accomplish a sequence of calculations (data transforms).
2. A *decision* block contains alternative groups of statements as typified by the `IF-THEN-ELSE` construction.
3. A *loop* block is a group of statements that will be executed a number of times.

Use comment statements to make these blocks stand out as clearly as possible. Design the flowchart to move from one block to the other in a simple (linear) fashion. If possible:

1. Enter a block through the top statement only.
2. Exit the block through the last statement only.

Finally, do not expect a perfect flowchart on the first attempt. Keep an eraser handy. It is all part of the refinement process.

This completes the recommendations offered for use when starting the algorithm for solving a problem. What follows next is a series of *intermediate* recommendations that are useful when you reach the point of actually writing the program (writing the individual FORTRAN statements).

Group 2 Recommendations: Forming The Modules

- Use highly descriptive names for variables—keep a table
- Avoid tricks—do not get fancy
- Use comment statements—make them meaningful
- Logical IF—preferred
- Syntax—if you are not sure, look it up
- Parenthesize to avoid ambiguity
- Restrict the use of `GO TO` statements

The programming examples of this text have been written in a special way. Comment statements consisting of a blank line are used to highlight important parts of the program. Other comment statements separate various blocks of code and provide brief descriptions of their functions. Each program starts with statements that describe the purpose of the program and the names for all important variables.

Correct habits in writing clear and easy-to-follow FORTRAN codes are very important. They are part of **programming style**. It is difficult for a student to fully appreciate the importance of programming style. For short programs, it may not be all that important. However, if you ever are required to make "updates" to a long program written by someone else, you will find programming style a life-saving feature. You are encouraged to develop a programming style of your own. Many times it makes the difference between "just a program" and "a first-class program."

Programming style starts when the individual statements are written out longhand on a coding form. Make them look as close to a computer listing as possible. Use capital letters. Be careful about spacing and indentation. Be generous in the use of comment statements, but make the comments as meaningful as possible. Check to make sure you have been consistent in the spelling of each variable name used.

8.3 Desk Check: An Important Step in the Process

The time spent carefully examining each line of code for missing commas, duplicate statement numbers, missing operators, and so forth is called a **desk check**. This is the last phase in the process. Now your attention should be totally focused on details. We have been concentrating on the avoidance of making *big* mistakes. Now is the time to be careful about making *little* ones—the so-called stupid mistakes. They are just as fatal.

A desk check should involve a very slow line-by-line examination of the program. Take your time and do a thorough, fastidious job. This phase of program preparation really is very important and should not be slighted.

Programming Style

Desk check

1. **Syntax scan**
2. **Logic scan**
3. **Data test**

At this stage of the programming effort details are the most important item. Each line of code you have written should be scanned line by line for syntax errors, missing commas, unpaired parentheses, duplicate statement numbers, missing format statements, and so on. This should not be a casual scan. Take the assignment seriously. A substantial number of compiler errors can be traced to an insufficient desk check of the program.

A logic scan follows next. To accomplish this, you assume the role of a computer. Examine the first statement in your program. Do what it tells you to do—nothing more and nothing less. Execute the next instruction exactly as you are told. If a calculation is involved, compute the value (as you are told) or aproximate it. This may help you to detect errors in the logic of your program.

8.4 Debug Techniques

As discouraging as it may seem, it is possible to go through the long and tedious procedures described in this chapter and still wind up with errors. Errors are an inevitable part of programming. Professional programmers build into their programs defensive mechanisms to cope with this annoyance. The basic tool is: Print! Print! Print!

Programming Style

Debug techniques

1. **Echo trace**
2. **Arithmetic trace**
3. **Path (logic) trace**

Programmers can do a lot to ease the job of error detection and isolation if they dismiss an ego-inspired confidence that "all will go well" and adopt a more sensible defensive attitude in writing programs. The single most powerful weapon in defensive programming is temporary, intermediate printouts. They are used in three important ways.

1. *Echo trace:* An intermediate printout positioned after each input statement to display (echo) the values just read. The statement verifies that each data value has been read correctly.
2. *Arithmetic trace:* An intermediate printout positioned after a series of arithmetic operations. The statement is used to monitor the change in key variables as the program progresses.
3. *Path trace:* An intermediate printout positioned at the top or bottom of a block of code. The statement is used to signal that a specific block has been reached and thereby to show the basic path that a program is following.

The use of extra printouts can reduce the frustration of trying to locate an error in your program. These extra print statements almost guarantee firm control over the execution of a program. Omitting them leaves the programmer helpless and invites disaster.

A properly written program consists of well-defined modules or blocks of code. It is important to know if these blocks are being executed in the sequence intended. **Path traces** can provide this information. They consist of statements such as:

```
PRINT*,'PASSING CHECK POINT 1'
PRINT*,'ENTERING PAY CALCULATION MODULE'
```

strategically placed throughout the program. Each block should have at least one trace statement. A more elaborate procedure is to include the value of key variables as part of the output message. This provides a combination of arithmetic and path trace features.

Assume your program aborts with the error message: DIVIDE FAULT-DIVISION BY ZERO. Usually it is not clear which statement caused the error. If you used only one PRINT statement at the end of the program, the error could be anywhere. If, on the other hand, you used four or five path traces, the error is reasonably well isolated. The path trace tells which blocks were executed successfully. You should be able to identify which block was the last entered before disaster struck. If you still have difficulty locating the error, you can add more trace statements to the troublesome block to help pinpoint the faulty statement.

Assume a program has been compiled and executed with test data, and the results are incorrect. If you used four or five combination path and arithmetic traces, you can examine these traces to see at what point the calculations went wrong. Each of these temporary printouts should indicate where in the program the print statement is located. The statement might include the message: PASSING STATEMENT 100 or PASSING CHECK POINT 1. Usually it is helpful to distinguish all the normal output from the temporary traces. One technique is to have the output of the trace statements appear on the right side of the output sheet and the normal output appear on the left, as shown in the following sample.

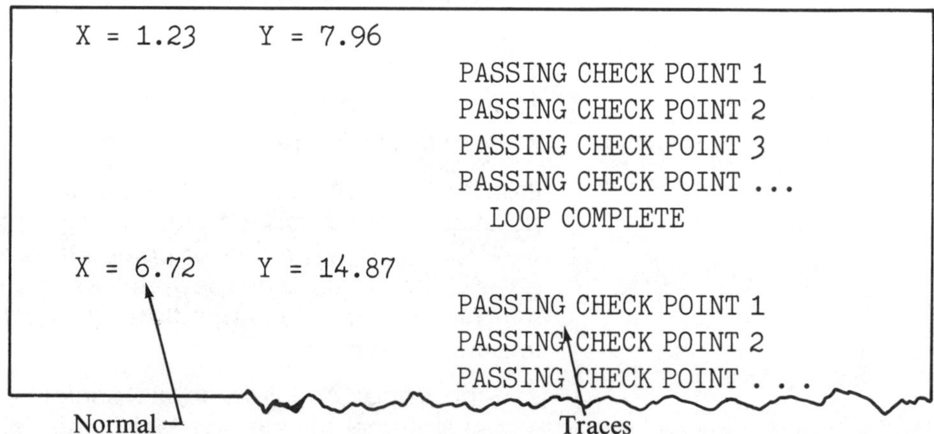

When a program is exceptionally short, perhaps there is some justification for not going to all the extremes suggested in this section. If, after two trial runs of a program, errors still exist, your only recourse is to fall back on these debugging procedures. Nothing disturbs an instructor more than the following situation:

1. Student complains of working for hours to get a program to run properly.
2. Instructor looks at program and finds no *echo* traces, no *arithmetic* traces, and no *path* traces.

Space limitation prevents the inclusion of traces in each and every example program in this text. We will compromise by showing the technique periodically in the programming examples.

8.5 Getting Help

If you are unable to understand a particular error, look for help, but be careful. Get professional help. Asking another student may or may not provide the answer. A student who starts a massive rewrite of your program is *not* doing you a service. Usually, there are people at the computation center trained to give you assistance. They are your best source of help. Bring your flowchart and any other documentation. If they see you have approached the problem in a professional (well-documented) way, you will get good help. If you bring a program with no flowchart, no listing of variable names, no comment statements, and no printouts except the one at the end of the program, you will not get (and do not deserve) much help at all.

Quiz 14 Programming Style

Part 1: Answer the following questions.

1. Why should you resist the temptation to start writing FORTRAN code as the initial step in solving a problem?
2. An algorithm should be efficient. What does that mean?
3. A flowchart should show the flow of control from the top of a program to the bottom. As much as possible, that flow should be what?
4. What action should take place during a desk check?
5. When writing a module of FORTRAN code, what three basic types of blocks are recommended?
6. What one statement is most often carelessly used and causes an interruption of the desired linear flow of control?
7. A block of code should be entered at one point and exited from another point. Identify these points.
8. Why are highly descriptive variable names helpful?
9. What is wrong with having just one PRINT statement in your program?
10. What does the term "syntax" mean regarding a FORTRAN statement?

Part 2: Writing a Program (The Mode of a Set)

11. The mode of a set of numbers is the number that occurs most frequently in the set.

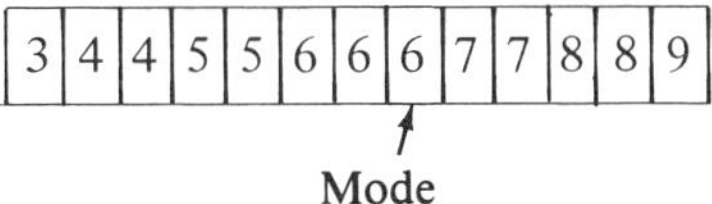

We have rolled a pair of dice 1000 times and recorded the results in the data file shown. The sum of the two numbers recorded on each record will range from a low of 2 to a high of 12. We would like to know the mode of these rolls.

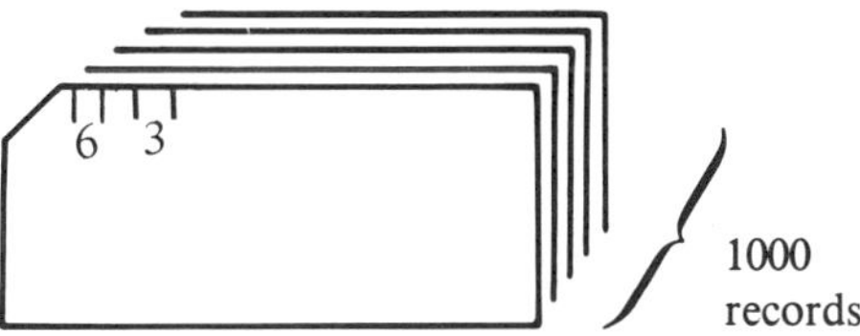

You are given even money odds that the mode is the number 7 and four to one odds that the mode is the number 6 or 8. Which is it?

```
C.........................................
C..  PURPOSE - DETERMINE IF THE MODE OF A SET ..
C..            OF 1000 NUMBERS IS 6, 7 or 8.  ..
C.........................................
C
C            --IMPORTANT VARIABLES--
C
C      -N1,N2    NUMBERS READ FROM EACH RECORD     --
C      -NO6S     NUMBER OF 6'S ROLLED              --
C      -NO7S     NUMBER OF 7'S ROLLED              --
C      -NO8S     NUMBER OF 8'S ROLLED              --
C      -SUM      SUM OF N1 AND N2                  --
```

8.6 Structured Programming

- No GO TOs
- Limit size of each module (60 lines)
- Single entry
- Single exit
- No wild detours
- Three constructs only:
  —SEQUENTIAL
  —DECISION
  —LOOP
- Top-down design
- Declare type of construct in the header statement

Figure 8.2 Attributes of structured program

In many ways, the objectives of structured programming and the objectives of programming style are quite similar. Both attempt to bring a high order of discipline and organization into:

1. The way in which an algorithm is developed.
2. The way in which FORTRAN code is written.

Structured programming, however, has a much broader, far reaching control over the way in which a program is written. Structured programming embodies the concept of rigid discipline at two distinct levels: program design and program implementation.

At the implementation level, structured programming places numerous restrictions on the way in which individual blocks of code may be written. First each block must be controlled in *length* (number of statements). A commonly accepted length is 60 lines, which will fit on one page of computer paper. Large blocks of complex code are just not allowed. Next, each block must conform to one of three permitted forms or *constructs:* sequence, decision, or loop construct. The type of construct being used is declared by the first statement in the block. Each construct may be entered at one point only, *through the top statement*, and can have only one exit point, *the bottom statement*. Transfer of control within the block is severely restricted. It must be linear in fashion with no lateral transfers permitted. (The use of `GO TO` statements is all but forbidden.)

Programs written according to these tight restrictions are programs in which there are never any surprises, no wild detours, and no unexpected branches. In structured programming everything is more precise, more controlled, and more predictable. This aspect of structured programming will be the main concern of the rest of this chapter.

At the program design level, structured programming provides an invaluable tool or methodology by which project managers can maintain a well-organized, highly efficient control over large-scale computer projects. It is sometimes difficult for student programmers to grasp the scope of complexities involved in even a modest computer project. As a result, they usually underestimate the importance of programming style and programming structure. There is a reason for this. A student is usually asked to solve a relatively small and well-defined problem. Because only one person is involved in the assignment, there are no scheduling, coordinating, or interface problems. The situation facing a project manager is considerably different. The problems are magnified a hundredfold.

Consider the typical assignment: Develop a software package to be used in screening the accuracy of Federal Income Tax Returns for a six-state region. Just attempting to identify the many subtasks involved in this project is a challenge in itself. For each task identified, a clear set of specifications must be written. These specifications must tell the number and size of the various data bases representing input to this module and what transformations are to be accomplished inside this module. A set of performance standards should be included that defines a number of sets of test data to which the module must satisfactorily respond. An estimate must be made of when in the production schedule work should be started on this module, and how many days or months will be needed to write and debug the module.

Because many modules will share the same data bases, a strict organizational control must be established. Transfer of control from one module to another must be tightly regulated. It is at this point that the design implications of structured programming play a dominant role. Structured programming imposes a strict *top-down, successive refinement* approach.

The Old Way: Bottom-Up Approach

Prior to the development of structured programming techniques, the tendency was to use a somewhat *bottom-up* approach. Many of the simple (low-level) modules of a project were written to "get things started." The more difficult modules were either set aside for the moment or given a deferred priority. Using this approach, a programmer may not know exactly when or where her particular module will be inserted into the overall program. Frequently, important design decisions were made that might have been correct for the little (low-level) module being written but were totally incorrect as far as the overall project was concerned.

This approach invites all kinds of difficulties when it comes time to try to tie all the lower-level modules together into an integrated package. It often takes more time to find out why two modules will not run well together than it took to write the modules in the first place. The difficulty with the bottom-up approach is obvious: it addresses the problem of coordination too late in the project.

The New Way: Top-Down Approach

Structured programming forces organizational control to be defined at the beginning of a project. The function, input, output, and performance criteria for the top-level modules are defined first. From this a controlled series of successive refinements is applied to define equally tight specifications for a series of second- and third-level modules. At each level, more concern is given to describing the function of each module than to the FORTRAN code that might be used. An organization chart is produced. This chart resembles the ones used in large companies to show who reports to whom in the company. The top line shows the company president. The next line shows the vice presidents who report to the president. The next level shows who reports to each vice president.

The purpose of this chart and structured programming is to focus attention on matters of major importance at the beginning of the project, *not* at the end. Problem definition, coordinating and transfer of control, data base management, and performance criteria are considered from the outset. A disciplined, rather rigid approach is applied.

The best way to demonstrate all this is to set up a relatively large problem involving a number of discrete events or activities and then apply the structured top-down approach to its solution. Don't panic over the statement of the problem—the structured approach was specifically designed to handle problems such as this.

PROBLEM STATEMENT

Numerous students work for our department as graders, teaching assistants, programming assistants, and so on. Not all students work for a single professor. A given student might work for two or three professors.

Each student is assigned a pay rate code (1 to 6) depending on the skills needed to perform the job assigned.

Present Pay Rates

Code	Pay Rate (per hour)
1	$3.75
2	$4.25
3	$4.80
4	$5.15
5	$5.50
6	$6.00

The rate for each code classification changes as the minimum wage rate changes.

Each week a student is required to fill out a work card for each professor. The following information must be supplied:

Work Card

Field	
1	Student's Social Security Number
2	Student's Name (20 characters)
3	Pay Rate Code (1 to 6)
4	Name of Professor (20 characters)
5	Hours Worked

The head of our department is concerned with the amount of money being spent by some professors. The chairman has asked that we assemble the work cards for last year and determine how much money each professor in the department has spent. The names of the 30 professors in the department are given as part of the input file associated with this problem.

DESCRIPTION OF DATA FILE

The first record lists six real numbers indicating the present rates for each of the six pay classifications. The next portion of the data file (30 records) gives the names of the various professors in the department. The remainder of the file consists of work card records. There are a large number of these records and the end of the file is signalled by a work card record on which the number of hours worked is a negative amount.

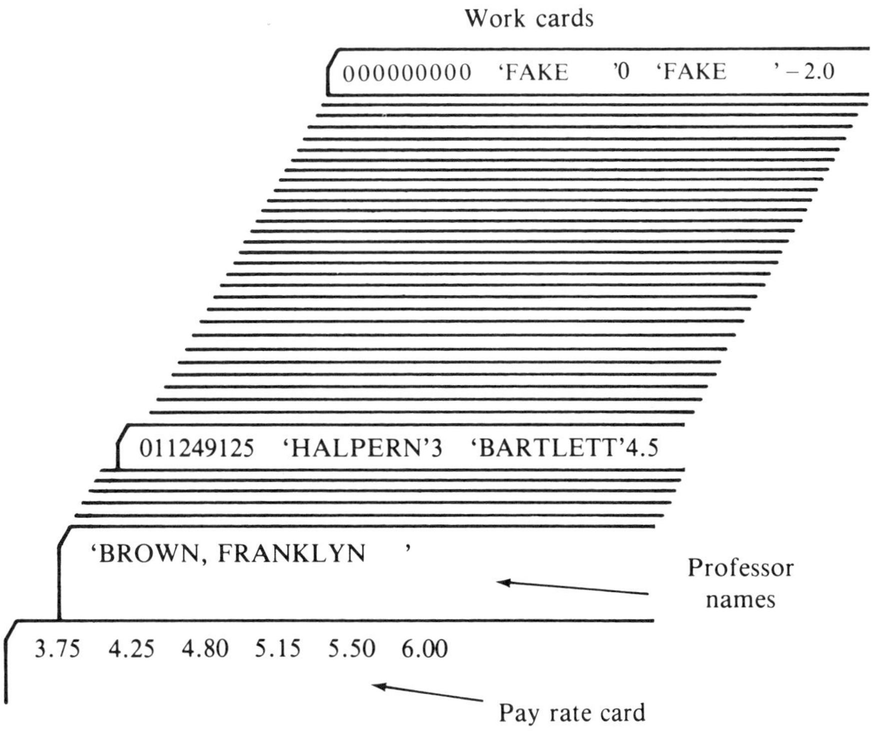

STARTING THE CHART

In starting the top-down solution to this problem we construct what is called a hierarchy chart. To establish the first and second level of this chart, we look for:

1. Some single definition of what the whole problem is about.
2. A breakdown of what subtasks are needed to accomplish the overall solution.

For this problem the chart might look like the one shown in Figure 8.3.

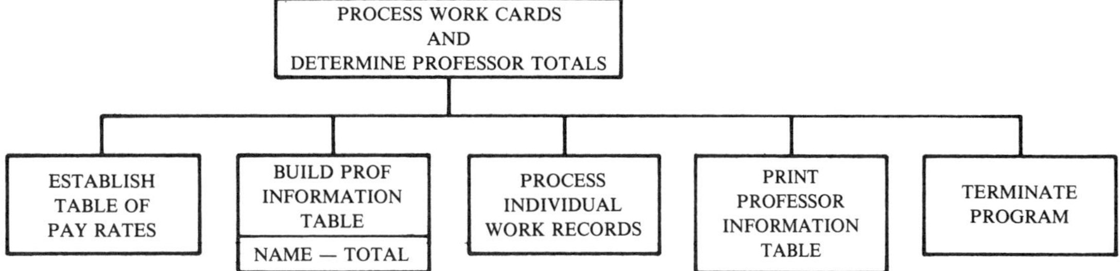

Figure 8.3 Starting hierarchy chart

It is now time to start thinking about the third level of this chart. This means taking each of the modules defined in the second level and making a judgment as to whether the module is sufficiently refined or whether that module must be further broken down. This is demonstrated by breaking down several of the more complex modules in our existing chart (see Figure 8.4).

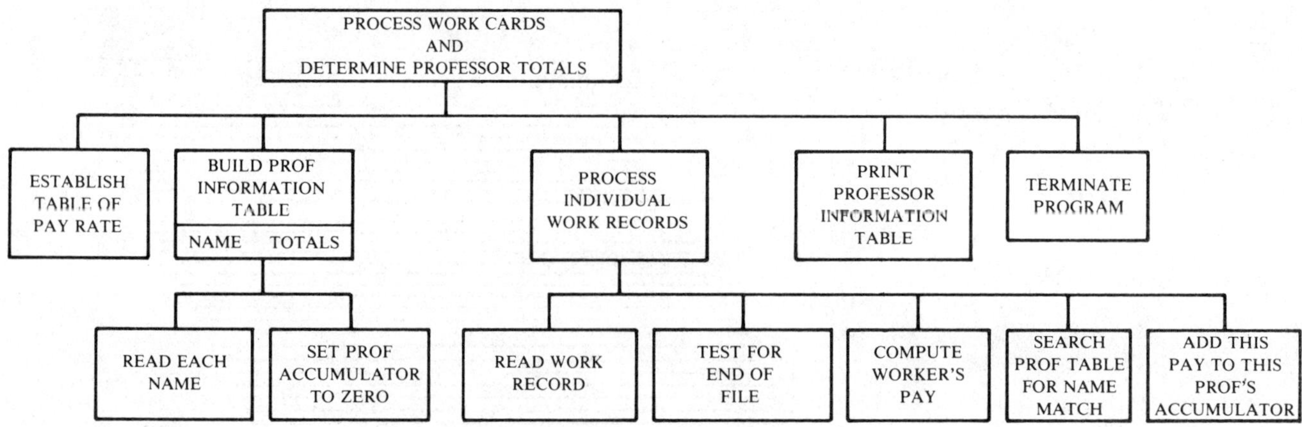

Figure 8.4 Another level of refinement

As you can see, this chart grows like an upside down tree. As more and more levels are added to the chart, the clarity of how to solve the problem takes shape. Remember that the most important advantage to this method is that it starts at the top. It forces control over the "master strategy of solution" before any of the details are considered. If any one module is exceptionally difficult to solve, it can be charted in a separate diagram. That is, this task can be passed to one of the work groups on a project and treated by this group as their primary assignment. Accordingly, some test specifications would be written and some test data agreed upon. In this way, we can bring some degree of order and organization into what is sometimes a chaotic endeavor.

This completes the presentation of how to apply structure when setting up the algorithm for solving a problem. We now move on to show how structure can be applied to writing the individual FORTRAN statements to implement the various modules you have just defined.

8.7 Structured Programs

When a student is first learning how to program a computer, it is perhaps necessary to allow that student a good deal of freedom in writing the individual statements that make up the program. As your ability increases, however, it becomes necessary to impose some standards as to how a program is written. This is called structure at the programming level.

When programs are not structured, it becomes painfully obvious that programmers are allowed to "do their own thing." FORTRAN statements are put together in any and all possible combinations. The size of a module can vary from just a few statements to hundreds of statements. Entry into the module can be at several different points and exit from the module can be almost anywhere. There is a single word for this type of programming, it is called "chaotic." Simply stated, structure at the programming level is an attempt to bring a degree of order to what otherwise is a sea of random activity.

Structured programming starts by asking each programmer to be careful in building each block or module of code. To start, make sure it matches one of a limited set of constructs: sequence, decision, or loop construct. These constructs represent the fundamental building blocks of a well-structured program. Make sure the type of construct being used in a module is immediately recognizable. This is done by using an appropriate *header* statement. The header statements are:

DO statement
DO WHILE statement
IF-THEN-ELSE statement

Be sure to clearly show the appropriate *terminating* statement to indicate where the construct ends. The terminating statements are:

CONTINUE statement
ENDDO statement
ENDIF statement

Those familiar with structured programming will then know immediately what pattern of statements to expect inside the block.

Each construct will have a single entry point and a single exit point. As stated before, there should be no surprises in structured programming. A construct is entered through the first or header statement and exited from the last or terminal statement. Inside the construct the transfer of control is regulated to flow in linear fashion from the top statement to the bottom statement. Use of nonstructured IFs and GO TOs are just not allowed. Branching, backtracking, and premature exits are not allowed because they generate what is called "spaghetti logic." You will probably object to making your programs fit into a specific mold, but soon you will find that although a little freedom is lost, there is a considerable gain in clarity and readability of the program.

Next, make use of comment statements and blank lines to make each module readily identifiable as a separate entity. Using "block like" titles for the major modules not only makes the program look nice, but will be of great value if it is necessary to expand or revise a large program. It is no longer sufficient to write a program what works (although that helps). Industrial firms have recognized the high costs associated with making updates to nonstructured programs. Your programs must work and they must be easy to read and follow.

Quiz 15 Structured Programming

Answer the following questions:

1. When starting a large project having many modules or blocks of code, what is wrong with writing a few of the simpler modules first and deferring the writing of the more difficult modules until later?
2. What information is conveyed by the top two or three levels of a hierarchy chart?
3. What is the purpose of moving deeper and deeper in the hierarchy chart? When should this refinement process stop?
4. What are the advantages of top-down structured approach to problem solving?
5. When writing a structured program, why is it so important to declare the type of each module by a clearly defined header statement?
6. Once inside a module, describe the only permitted flow of logic (execution of statements).
7. Why does the GO TO statement interrupt the linear flow of logic and destroy the single entry, single exit set up?
8. In structured programming is there any limit set on the number of statements permitted in a single block of code? Why?
9. Industry is not just satisfied with programs that work. What else are they looking for and why?
10. The following program reads a name from a header record and then searches the remainder of the file of names and social security numbers looking for a name match. As soon as the match takes place, a GO TO is used to leave the DO loop so that further searching does not go on. This is called a premature exit of the DO. Rewrite the program using a WHILE construct to avoid the use of the GO TO.

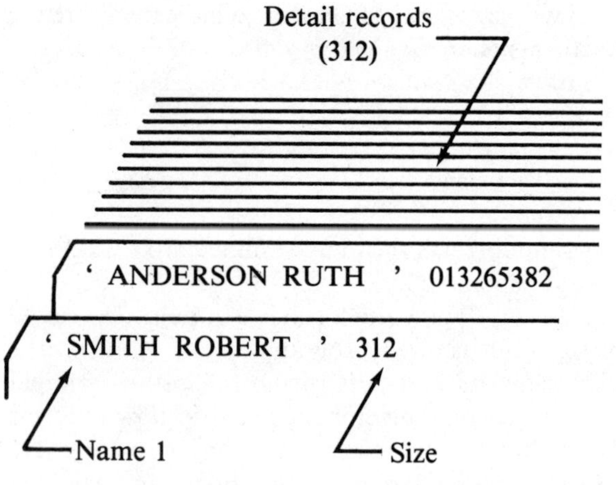

Problem: Search a file for a name. Search name and file size given on header record.

```
C     NAME1 - NAME READ FROM HEADER RECORD
C     NAME2 - NAME READ FROM DETAIL RECORD
C     SSNO  - SOCIAL SECURITY NUMBER
C     SIZE  - NUMBER OF DETAIL RECORDS IN FILE
C
      CHARACTER NAME1*20, NAME2*20
      INTEGER SSNO, SIZE, I
C
C        ....READ SEARCH NAME AND FILE SIZE....
C               FROM HEADER RECORD
C     READ*, NAME1, SIZE
C
C               ....SET UP SEARCH LOOP....
C
      DO 40 I = 1, SIZE, 1
C
         READ*NAME2, SSNO
         IF(NAME1.EQ.NAME2) GO TO 50
C
 40   CONTINUE
C
      PRINT*,'SEARCH COMPLETE. NAME NOT FOUND'
      STOP
C
 50   PRINT*,'THE SOCIAL SECURITY NUMBER IS',SSNO
```

Review Exercises

1. When first addressing a problem, what are some of the steps that should be taken to make sure the problem solution evolves slowly and methodically?
2. At what point in a problem solution do the strategy concepts dominate the solution? In what form? When do the details come into play? In what form?
★ 3. What are some of the characteristics of a well-developed algorithm?
4. The process of stepwise refinement is suggested in the accompanying illustration. At what point should the refinement process be considered complete?

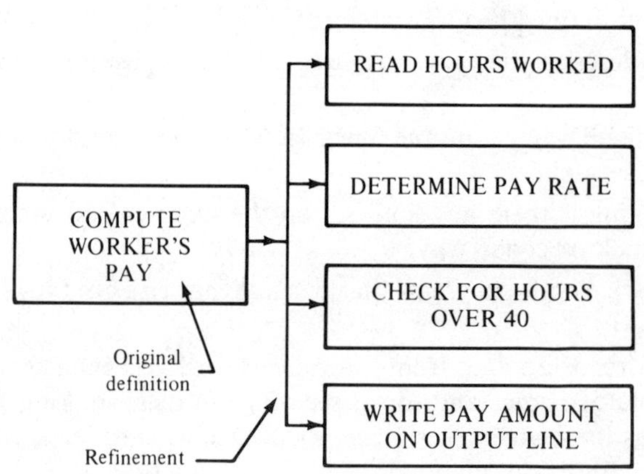

5. The flowchart of a properly structured program has well-defined features. What are they?
6. In accomplishing a desk check of your program, what activities are involved? Describe the three separate types of errors that can be detected.
★ 7. What is the single most effective method of detecting and isolating errors that might occur in the running of your program?
8. What is the difference between an arithmetic trace and a path trace? Give specific examples of each.
9. How can the trace statements and the normal output be separated one from the other?
10. Comment statements are useful to show the structure and documentation of a program. Describe at least three ways comment statements accomplish this important function.
★ 11. What is the purpose of restricting the number of statements (lines of FORTRAN code) associated with any one module or block of code?
12. Give an explanation of the following programming style recommendations:

Programming Style

Desk check

1. Syntax scan
2. Logic scan
3. Data test

> **Programming Style**
> Flowcharts
> 1. Top to bottom
> 2. Don't jump around
> 3. Parallel block structure

> **Programming Style**
> Restrict the use of GO TO statements

13. When writing out your program longhand, how should the program be made to appear? What is the purpose of coding forms in this activity?

★ 14. What is a syntax error and when is the best time to catch such errors?

15. How do you locate execution errors in your program?

16. If a program has been compiled and has no execution errors, is this a guarantee that the program is correct? What else must be done to make sure the program is correct?

17. A program has been divided into a series of subtasks. For each task, a module of FORTRAN code will be written. What are the advantages of this modular approach?

★ 18. Most modules will be one of three basic types. What are these types?

19. Where should a module or block code be entered? Where should it be exited?

20. Why is it more advisable to write FORTRAN code in easy-to-follow and relatively short steps as opposed to brief, highly concentrated code?

21. When a desk check is made of a program, what activities are involved?

★ 22. Describe a typical *execution* error. How do you know which statement in your program caused the error?

23. How can comment statements be used to make the various modules of a program easy to identify and understand? Give examples.

★ 24. When entering one of the basic constructs allowed in structured programming, how do you know which type of construct you are dealing with?

Additional Applications

Programming Example
Controlling Fuel Deliveries

The first record of a data file lists the average temperatures for each day in a given week (seven real values). Those numbers will be used to determine when heating oil should be delivered to your home to run the furnace.

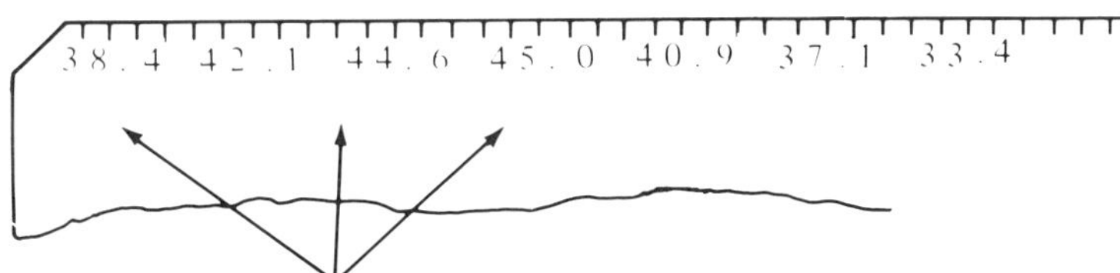

Temperatures during the week

Each day the temperature is below 60°, your furnace will use some oil. When the temperature is one degree below 60°, that is called a "1-degree-fuel day." When the temperature is two degrees below 60°, it is called a "2-degree-fuel day."

Part A: Write statements that will determine the number of degree-fuel days experienced in the week reported.

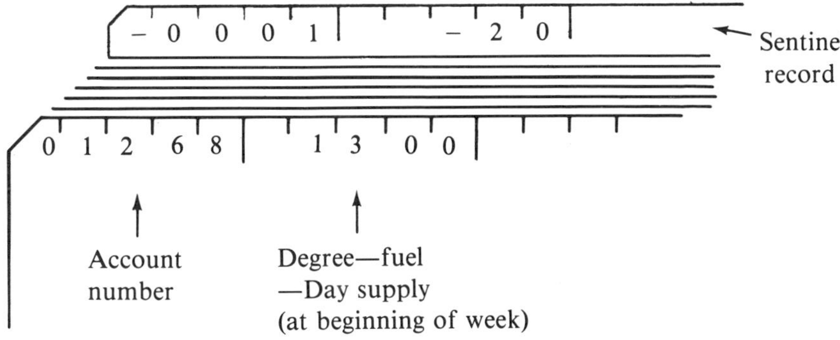

Programming Example–Controlling Fuel Deliveries continued

After determining the amount of fuel needed during a given week, the fuel company uses a computer program to determine which of its customers are getting low on fuel oil.

The remaining records in the data file give the account number and remaining fuel supply (in degree days) of customers of a local fuel dealer.

Part B: For each customer, subtract the fuel used due to the temperatures reported on the header card, thereby determining the present fuel supply. If any customer has less than a 600-degree-day's supply, mark that customer for a fuel delivery.

```
C.......................................................
C..  PURPOSE - COMPUTE NEW FUEL SUPPLIES - DETERMINE  ..
C..            WHO SHOULD GET DELIVERIES.             ..
C.......................................................
C
C              ---- IMPORTANT VARIABLES -----
C
C         --TEMP1 - TEMP7 TEMPERATURE ON EACH DAY OF THE WEEK --
C         --DDAY          DEGREE-FUEL-DAY FOR A PARTICULAR    --
C                         DAY OF THE WEEK                     --
C         --SUM           TOTAL DEGREE-DAYS FOR THE WEEK      --
C         --OLD           FUEL SUPPLY AT BEGINNING OF THE WEEK--
C         --NEW           FUEL SUPPLY AT THE END OF THE WEEK  --
C
          REAL NEW, OLD, SUM, DDAY, TEMP1, TEMP2, TEMP3, TEMP4
          REAL TEMP5, TEMP6, TEMP7
C
          SUM =0.0
C
          READ*, TEMP1,TEMP2,TEMP3,TEMP4,TEMP5,TEMP6,TEMP7
C
          IF (TEMP1.LT.60.)THEN
                DDAY = 60. - TEMP1
                SUM = SUM + DDAY
          ENDIF
C
          IF (TEMP2.LT.60.)THEN
                DDAY = 60. - TEMP2
                SUM = SUM + DDAY
          ENDIF
C
          IF(TEMP3.LT.60.)THEN
                DDAY = 60.-TEMP3
                SUM = SUM +DDAY
          ENDIF
C
          IF(TEMP4.LT.60.)THEN
                DDAY = 60.-TEMP4
                SUM=SUM+DDAY
          ENDIF
C
          IF(TEMP5.LT.60.)THEN
                DDAY = 60.-TEMP5
                SUM=SUM+DDAY
          ENDIF
C
          IF(TEMP6.LT.60.)THEN
                DDAY = 60.-TEMP6
                SUM=SUM+DDAY
          ENDIF
C
          IF(TEMP7.LT.60.)THEN
                DDAY=60.-TEMP7
                SUM=SUM+DDAY
          ENDIF
```

Programming Example–Controlling Fuel Deliveries continued

```
C
        READ*, NUMBER, OLD
C
        DO WHILE (NUMBER.GT.0)
C
            NEW=OLD-SUM
C
            IF(NEW.GT.600.)PRINT*,NUMBER,NEW,'NO DELIVERY'
            IF(NEW.LT.600.)PRINT*,NUMBER,NEW,'MAKE DELIVERY'
C
            READ*, NUMBER, OLD
C
        ENDDO
C
 60     STOP
        END
```

Programming Example Emergency Service

The fuel company of the previous problem must provide "Emergency Service" to your furnace if it breaks down on the weekend or on a holiday. The following five names on the input record provide this service on a *rotating* basis. This week Mr. Jones is on duty; next week it is Mr. Halpern.

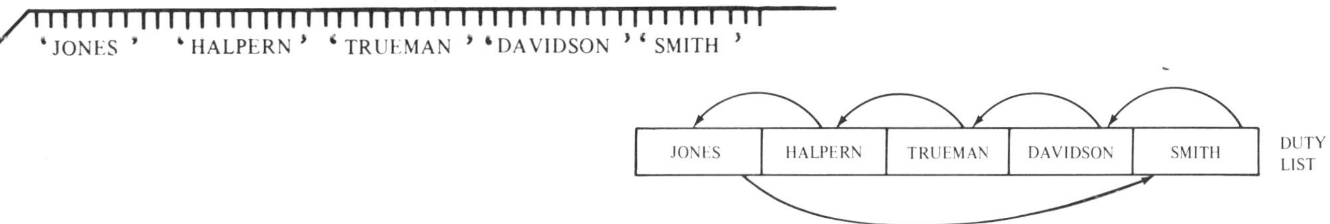

Write a program to read the five names into five different memory locations (NAME1 to NAME5). Have the program move all the names up one position and put the name at the front of the list to the back of the list.

```
C..........................................................
C..    PURPOSE - MOVE NAMES UP ONE POSITION TO           ..
C..              SHOW NEW DUTY LIST.                     ..
C..........................................................
C      SPECIAL   PROBLEM - IF WE MOVE JONES             --
C                TO THE END OF THE LIST USING           --
C                THE STATEMENT NAME5 = NAME1,           --
C                THIS WILL WIPE OUT THE NAME SMITH.     --
C
C             - - - - - IMPORTANT VARIABLES - - - - -
C
C        --NAME1 TO       NAME OF PERSON IN POSITION 1   --
C        --       NAME5   TO NAME OF PERSON IN POSITION 5 --
C        --HOLD           FIRST NAME UNTIL ALL OTHER     --
C                            NAMES HAVE BEEN MOVED       --
C
        CHARACTER*20, HOLD,NAME1,NAME2,NAME3,NAME4,NAME5
C
        READ*, NAME1,NAME2,NAME3,NAME4,NAME5
C
```

Programming Example–Emergency Service continued

```
C                STORE FIRST NAME TEMPORARILY
C
      HOLD=NAME1
C
C                MOVE UP THE NAMES
C
      NAME1=NAME2
      NAME2=NAME3
      NAME3=NAME4
      NAME4=NAME5
C
C                NOW HANDLE LAST NAME
C
      NAME5=HOLD
C
      PRINT*, NAME1,NAME2,NAME3,NAME4,NAME5
C
      STOP
      END
```

Programming Example
Records by Date (where in the file)

The Town Clerk's office records all transfers of deed titles, which are then filed (sorted) according to the *date of transfer*.

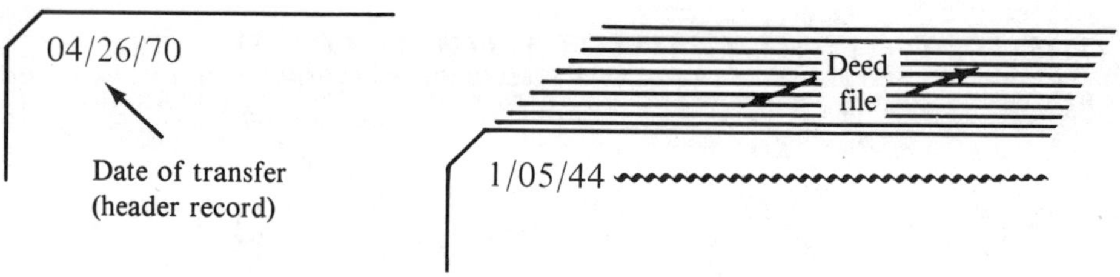

We wish to find who was the legal owner of a piece of property on a certain date. Read a header telling the DATE OF TRANSFER and report where in the deeds file the transfers for that date are listed.

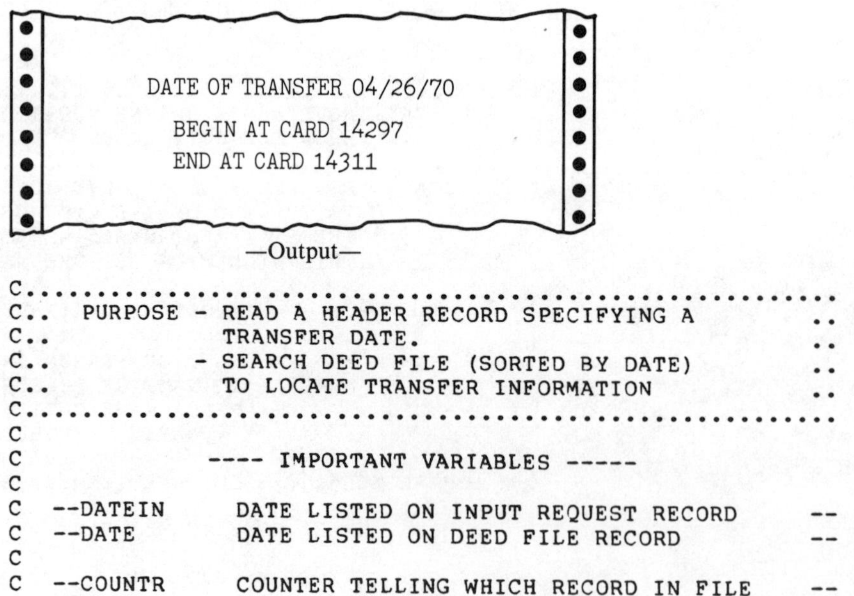

—Output—

```
C.........................................................
C..  PURPOSE - READ A HEADER RECORD SPECIFYING A          ..
C..            TRANSFER DATE.                             ..
C..          - SEARCH DEED FILE (SORTED BY DATE)          ..
C..            TO LOCATE TRANSFER INFORMATION             ..
C.........................................................
C
C              ---- IMPORTANT VARIABLES -----
C
C   --DATEIN     DATE LISTED ON INPUT REQUEST RECORD      --
C   --DATE       DATE LISTED ON DEED FILE RECORD          --
C
C   --COUNTR     COUNTER TELLING WHICH RECORD IN FILE     --
```

Programming Example–Records by Date continued

```
C
      INTEGER COUNTR
      CHARACTER DATEIN*8, DATE*8
C
C             ... READ HEADER RECORD..
C
      READ*, DATEIN
C
C              ...READ FIRST DEED RECORD...
      READ*, DATE
      COUNTR=1
C

      DO WHILE (DATEIN.NE.DATE)
C             ... SEARCH LOOP STARTS HERE...
C
C.........................................................
C..             PROGRAM MUST DETECT FIRST RECORD WHERE   ..
C..                     A MATCH IN DATES OCCURS          ..
C.........................................................
C
          READ*, DATE
          COUNTR=COUNTR+1
C
C             THIS IS NOT THE RECORD
C
      ENDDO
C
C             FIRST RECORD FOUND
C
              PRINT*, '     BEGIN AT RECORD ', COUNTR
C
C.........................................................
C..             NOW OPPOSITE ACTIVITY IS PERFORMED       ..
C..             PROGRAM MUST NOW DETECT WHEN DATES ARE   ..
C..             NO LONGER THE SAME.                      ..
C.........................................................
C
      DO WHILE (DATEIN.EQ.DATE)
C
              READ*,DATE
C
              COUNTR=COUNTR+1
C
C                     THIS IS NOT THE RECORD
C
      ENDDO
C
C                     - DATE CHANGED -
C
              COUNTR = COUNTR -1
C
              PRINT*,'        END AT RECORD', COUNTR
C
      STOP
      END
```

Additional Applications: Review of Chapters 1–8

This completes the presentation of introductory topics that constitute the basics of programming. The following programming examples show some relatively advanced applications of the topics covered in Part 1. These case studies attempt to show the power of the language and the diverse and creative way in which it can be used to solve a cross section of problems.

Programming Example
Limited Vector Addition

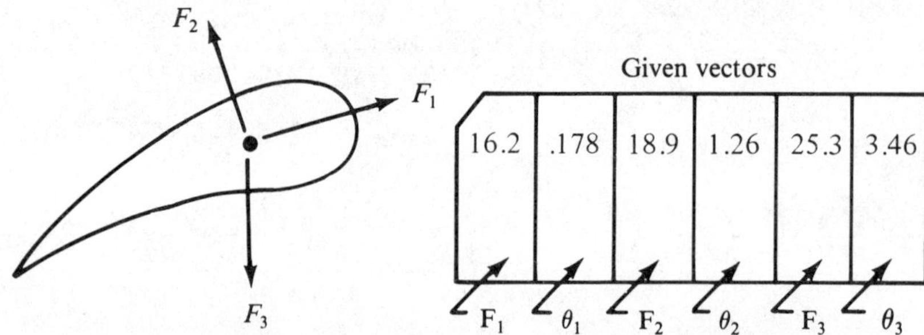

Note: Angles Expressed in Radians

Assume there is a repeated need to determine the sum of three force vectors acting on a wing profile. Because these are vector quantities, each force must be described by giving its magnitude and direction. In like fashion, the resultant or vector sum of these forces must be identified as to magnitude and direction.

The input consists of the three vectors described on a single record, which gives F_1 followed by θ_1, followed by F_2, etc. Values of force are given in pounds; values of angles are given in radians.

Input Variables

Symbol	Meaning
F1 F2 F3	Magnitudes of the three input vectors (value in pounds).
ANG1 ANG2 ANG3	Angles (inclination) of three input vectors (value given in radians).

Because the forces are vector quantities, they may not be added directly.

1. The forces must be resolved into their X and Y components:

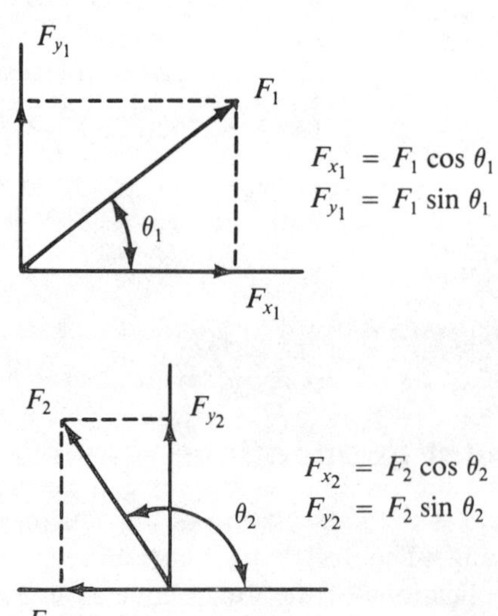

Programming Example–Limited Vector Addition continued

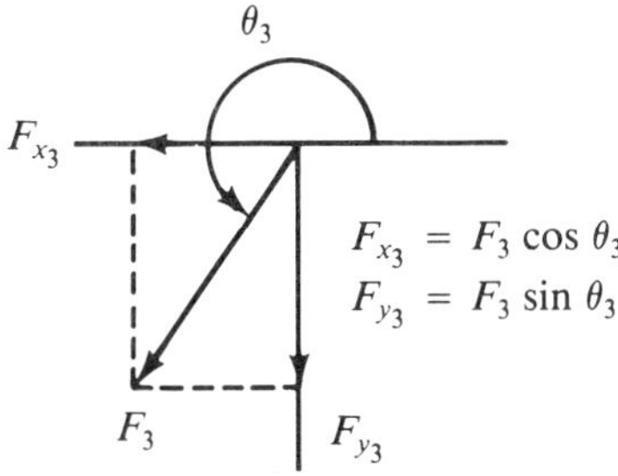

2. Then the X and Y components are added together:

   $\Sigma F_X = F_{X_1} + F_{X_2} + F_{X_3}$ $\qquad$ $\Sigma F_X = F_{y_1} + F_{y_2} + F_{y_3}$

3. The magnitude and inclination of the resultant are determined

   $R = \sqrt{(\Sigma F_x)^2 + (\Sigma F_y)^2}$

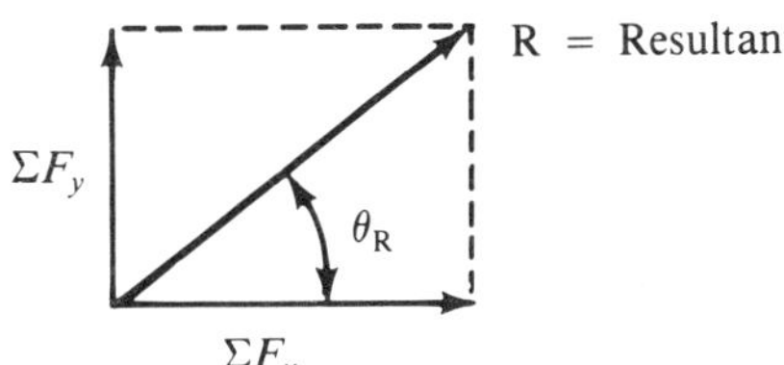

Determination of angle: $\theta_R = \tan^{-1}\left(\dfrac{\Sigma F_y}{\Sigma F_x}\right)$

Internal Variables

Symbol	Meaning
FX1, FX2, FX3	X-component of the three input vectors
FY1, FY2, FY3	Y-component of the three input vectors
SUMFX	Sum of the X-components
SUMFY	Sum of the Y-components

Output Variables

Symbol	Meaning
R	Magnitude of resultant
ANGR	Inclination of resultant

The computer program for this problem follows the mathematics rather closely and also demonstrates descriptive variable naming and the use of comment statements. The input record is read and a series of arithmetic statements is used to resolve the vectors. The sum of all the X components is then determined and stored as SUMFX. The sum of all the Y components is similarly determined and stored as SUMFY. The resultant is computed and the inclination of the resultant found. These are then printed.

Programming Example–Limited Vector Addition continued

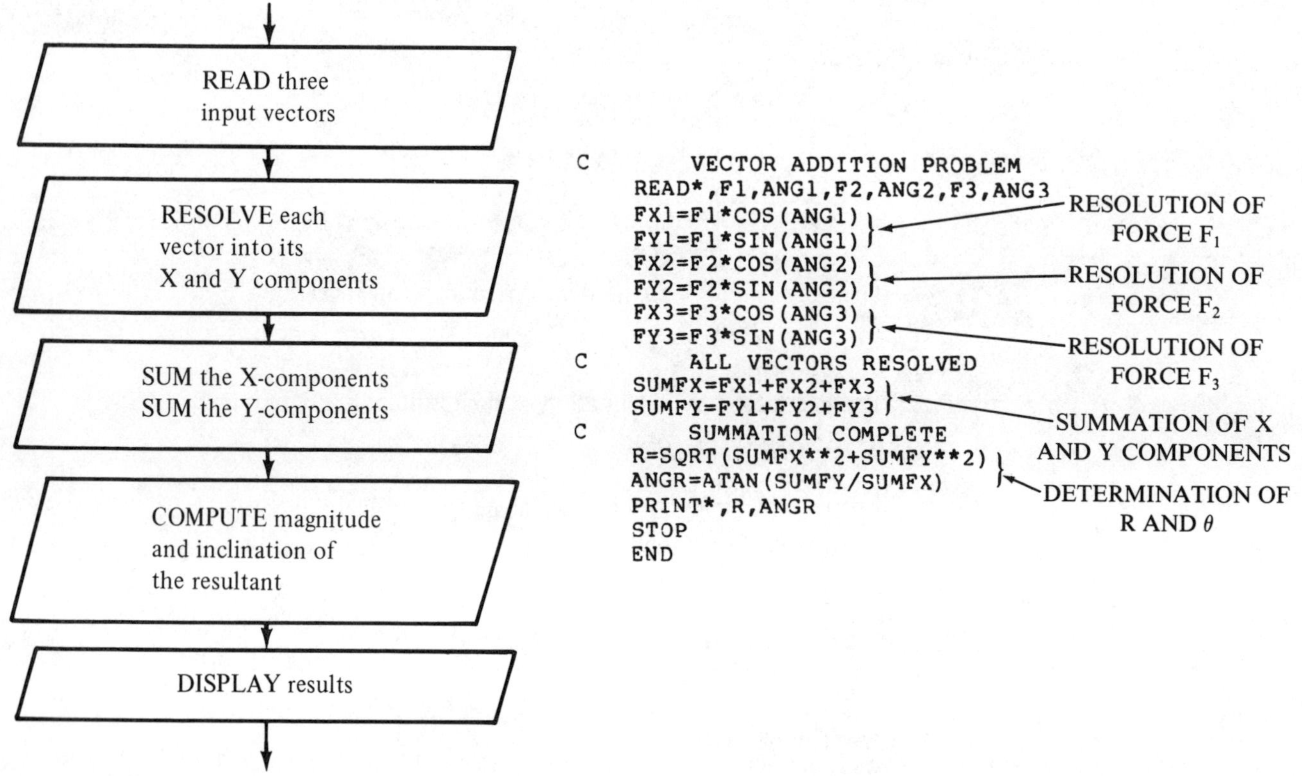

The test data is:

$F_1 = 100 \quad F_2 = 100 \quad F_3 = 100$
$\theta_1 = 90° \quad \theta_2 = 0° \quad \theta_3 = 180°$

Although the preceding program gets the problem solved, it provides no protection to the programmer if anything goes wrong. The program will be rewritten with the extra printouts that would supply the vital information to locate where and why the program failed.

```
C.....................................................
C          PURPOSE - ACCOMPLISH LIMITED VECTOR ADDITION.   ..
C.....................................................
C
C          READ MAGNITUDE AND INCLINATION OF VECTORS
C                 (VERIFY BY ECHO CHECK)
C
      READ*, F1,ANG1,F2,ANG2,F3,ANG3
      PRINT*, F1,ANG1,F2,ANG2,F3,ANG3
C
C                RESOLVE VECTORS INTO X AND Y COMPONENTS
C
      FX1 = F1*COS(ANG1)
      FY1 = F1*SIN(ANG1)
C
      FX2 = F2*COS(ANG2)
      FY2 = F2*SIN(ANG2)
C
      FX3 = F3*COS(ANG3)
      FY3 = F3*SIN(ANG3)
C
      PRINT*,'                    CHECK POINT 1 - VECTORS RESOLVED'
      PRINT*,'                    ',FX2,FY1,FX2,FY2,FX3,FY3
```

Programming Example–Limited Vector Addition continued

```
C
C              .............. ADD X AND Y COMPONENTS........
C
      SUMFX = FX1 + FX2 + FX3
      SUMFY = FY1 + FY2 + FY3
C
      PRINT*,'CHECK POINT 2 SUMFX =',SUMFX,' SUMFY = ',SUMFY
C
      R = SQRT(SUMFX**2 + SUMFY**2)
      ANGR = ATAN(SUMFY/SUMFX)
C
      PRINT*,'  MAGNITUDE =',R,' ANGLE =',ANGR,' RADIANS'
C
      STOP
      END
```

Programming Example
Vector Addition Expanded

Expand the previous case study to add vectorially any number of coplanar force vectors and provide as output the magnitude and inclination of the resultant. Each vector is described on an input record by giving its magnitude and inclination. The first record of the input file contains an integer number indicating how many vectors are to be added and, therefore, how many records follow this leader record.

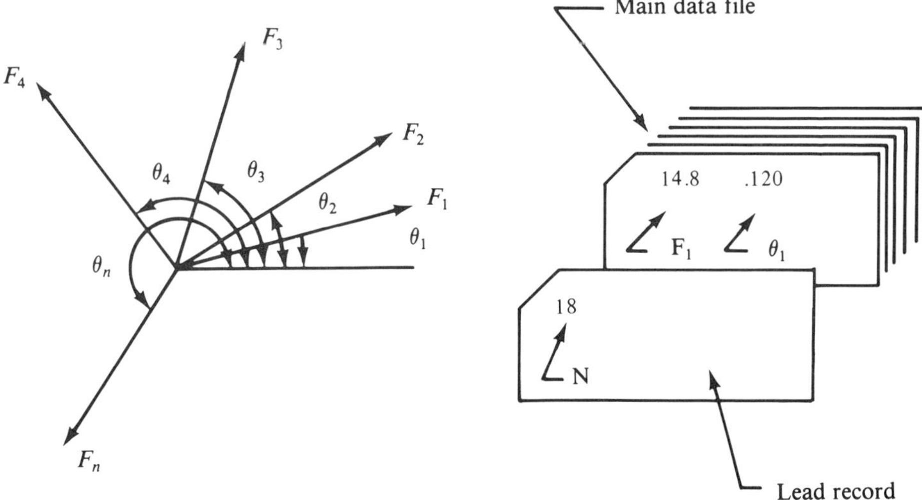

This program will be used to demonstrate the technique of dividing the total logic into a series of subtasks and then addressing those subtasks that are familiar to cut the problem down to size. The three groups of statements in the table that follows represent such a breakdown. Each group accomplishes the following subtasks:

GROUP 1: Deck Control

GROUP 2: Vector Resolution

GROUP 3: Accumulation of Components

Once the statements for these three groups are established, the remainder of the problem is relatively easy to handle.

Programming Example–Vector Addition Expanded continued

Development of Program

GROUP 1 Deck Control	GROUP 2 Vector Resolution	GROUP 3 Accumulation of Components	COMPLETE PROGRAM
READ*,N			READ*,N
		SUMFX=0.	SUMFX=0.
		SUMFY=0.	SUMFY=0.
DO 10I=1,N			DO 10 I=1,N
	READ*,F,ANG		READ*,F,ANG
	FX=F*COS(ANG)		FX=F*COS(ANG)
	FY=F*SIN(ANG)		FY=F*SIN(ANG)
		SUMFX=SUNFX+FX	SUMFX=SUMFX+FX
		SUMFY=SUMFY+FY	SUMFY=SUMFY+FY
10 CONTINUE			10 CONTINUE
		R=SQRT(SUMFX**2+SUMFY**2)	R=SQRT(SUMFX**2+SUMFY**2)
			ANGR=ATAN(SUMFY/SUMFX)
			PRINT*,R,ANGR
			STOP
			END

A program such as the one just written is not trivial, either in the programming concepts required or in the mathematics involved. If this program were to be made available for general use, it would overwhelm most users as it is now written. All programs should be accompanied by detailed documentation. The documented version of the program follows. It is written with tracer statements that should be removed as soon as the program is proven to work correctly.

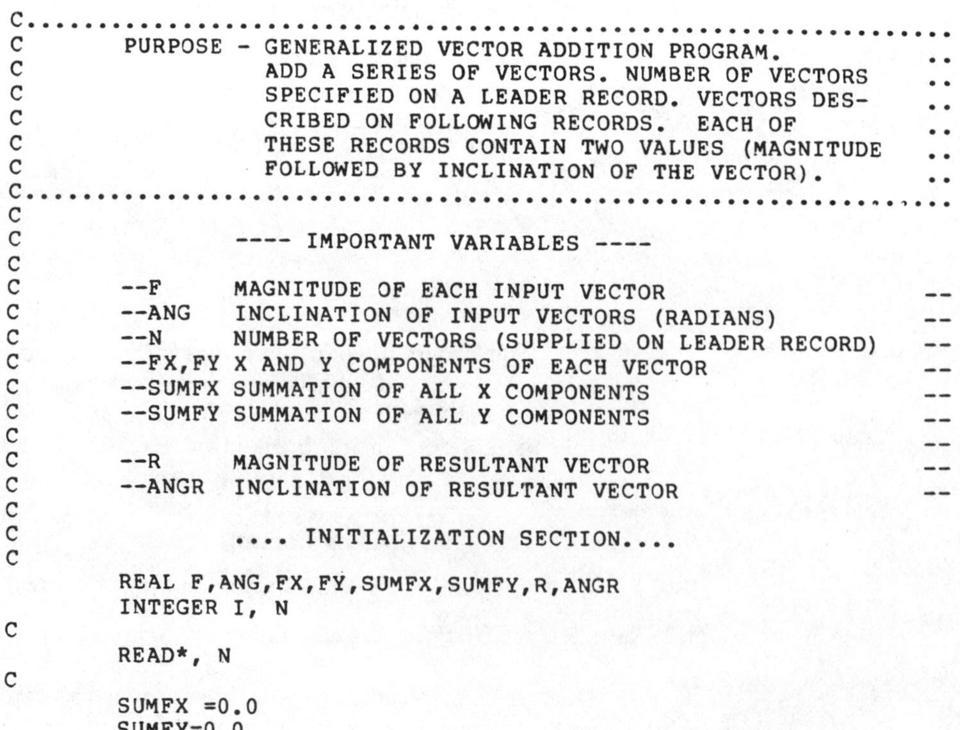

```
C.....................................................................
C        PURPOSE - GENERALIZED VECTOR ADDITION PROGRAM.              ..
C                  ADD A SERIES OF VECTORS. NUMBER OF VECTORS        ..
C                  SPECIFIED ON A LEADER RECORD. VECTORS DES-        ..
C                  CRIBED ON FOLLOWING RECORDS.  EACH OF             ..
C                  THESE RECORDS CONTAIN TWO VALUES (MAGNITUDE       ..
C                  FOLLOWED BY INCLINATION OF THE VECTOR).           ..
C.....................................................................
C
C              ---- IMPORTANT VARIABLES ----
C
C       --F      MAGNITUDE OF EACH INPUT VECTOR                      --
C       --ANG    INCLINATION OF INPUT VECTORS (RADIANS)              --
C       --N      NUMBER OF VECTORS (SUPPLIED ON LEADER RECORD)       --
C       --FX,FY  X AND Y COMPONENTS OF EACH VECTOR                   --
C       --SUMFX  SUMMATION OF ALL X COMPONENTS                       --
C       --SUMFY  SUMMATION OF ALL Y COMPONENTS                       --
C                                                                    --
C       --R      MAGNITUDE OF RESULTANT VECTOR                       --
C       --ANGR   INCLINATION OF RESULTANT VECTOR                     --
C
C              .... INITIALIZATION SECTION....
C
        REAL F,ANG,FX,FY,SUMFX,SUMFY,R,ANGR
        INTEGER I, N
C
        READ*, N
C
        SUMFX =0.0
        SUMFY=0.0
```

Programming Example–Vector Addition Expanded continued

```
C
C              .....LOOP ENTRY POINT.....
C
        DO 10 I = 1, N, 1
C
            READ*, F, ANG
C
C               RESOLVE VECTORS    ACCUMULATE COMPONENTS
C
            FX= F * COS(ANG)
            FY= F * SIN(ANG)
C
            SUMFX = SUMFX + FX
            SUMFY = SUMFY + FY
C
C
            PRINT*, FX,FY,SUMFX,SUMFY
C
C
   10   CONTINUE
C               ..... LOOP ENDS HERE....
C
        R = SQRT(SUMFX**2 + SUMFY**2)
        ANGR= ATAN(SUMFY/SUMFX)
C
        PRINT*,'MAGNITUDE=', R,'INCLINATION=' ,ANGR
C
        STOP
        END
```

Programming Example
Tracking Problem

The initial position of a ship which is underway is given by X_0 and Y_0, its X and Y coordinates on a plotting chart. One minute later its position is X_1 and Y_1. Write a program to predict the track this ship will follow if it maintains course and speed. Determine at what distance and at what time it will pass closest to the lighthouse located at X_{LH}, Y_{LH}. The values X_0, Y_0, X_1, Y_1, X_{LH} and Y_{LH} are given by the single input record shown.

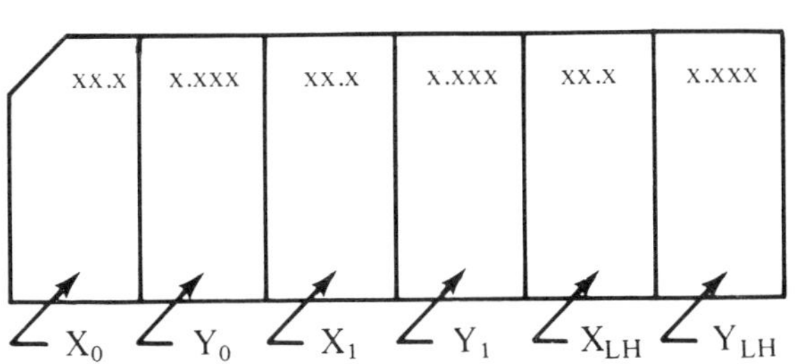

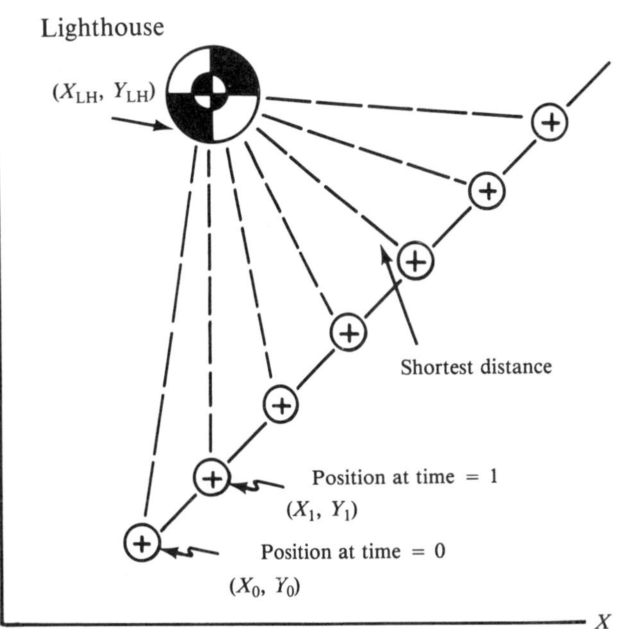

Programming Example–Tracking Problem continued

The logic of this problem will be easier to establish if a set of simplified input values (ship's position, lighthouse position) are assumed and a hand solution worked out. For example, assume the initial position of the ship is at the origin:

Time	Position	
$t = 0.0$	$X = 0.0$	$Y = 0.0$

If the ship moves to the position $X = 1.0$, $Y = 1.0$ in one minute, all future positions of the ship are easy to predict,

Time	Position	
$t = 1.0$	$X = 1.0$	$Y = 1.0$

Stationing the lighthouse at $X = 0.0$, $Y = 5.0$ makes the first (and subsequent) distance calculation easy to perform. The basic point is that simplified data and a partial hand calculation will help make it easier to develop the generalized solution.

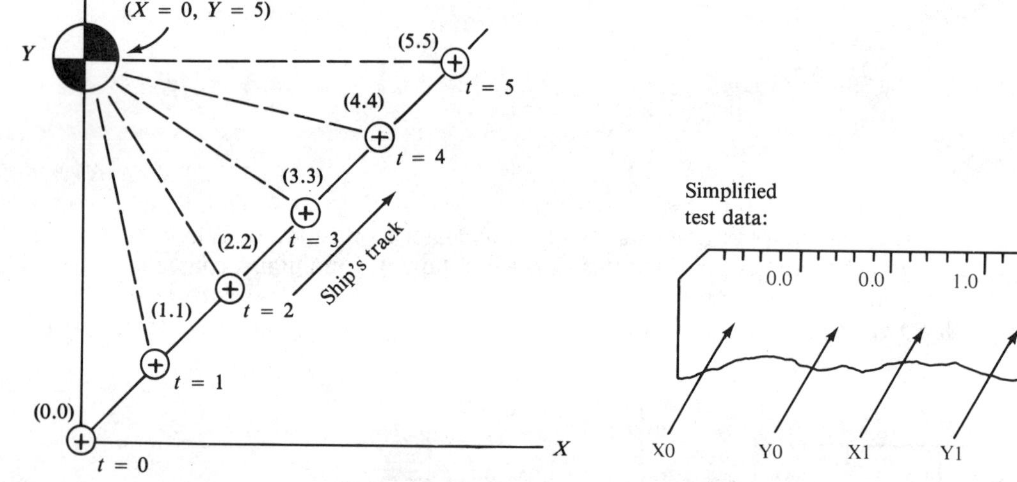

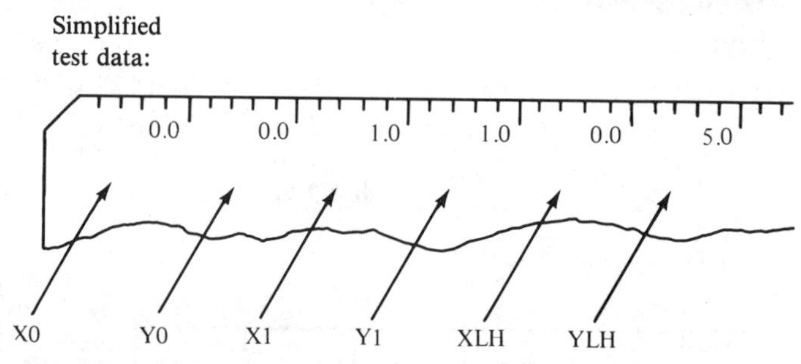

By comparing the ship's position at time = 1 minute and time = 0 minutes, we can determine the change in X position and the change in Y position that the ship is able to accomplish in one minute.

$$\text{change in } X = \Delta X = X_1 - X_0$$
$$\text{change in } Y = \Delta Y = Y_1 - Y_0$$

The ship's position at any time t is given by

$$X = X_0 + t\Delta X$$
$$Y = Y_0 + t\Delta Y$$

Programming Example–Tracking Problem continued

The distance to the lighthouse at any time *t* is:

$$\text{DIST} = -\sqrt{(X_{\text{LH}} - X)^2 + (Y_{\text{LH}} - Y)^2}$$

To predict future positions of the ship, the program uses a memory location called TIME to serve as a time clock. The statement:

```
TIME = 1.0
```

sets the clock with a value needed to calculate the first position. The statement:

```
TIME = TIME + 1.0
```

advances the clock for future calculations.

A unique aspect of this program is the way in which it determines when the ship is closest to the lighthouse. It is done by comparing two sequential values of the distance to the lighthouse (DIST and DNEW).

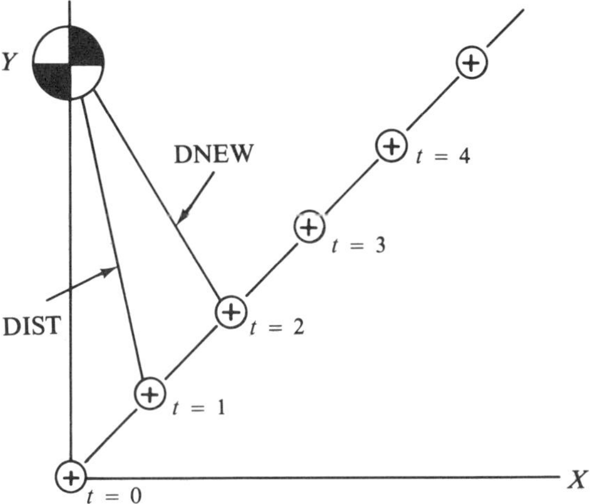

Under normal conditions, DNEW will be slightly smaller than DIST. This means we are moving closer to the lighthouse and should continue our calculations (advance the time clock and go through the loop again). The first time DNEW is larger than DIST it means we have passed the critical point (closest point) and are now starting to move away from the lighthouse. The calculation loop should be terminated.

We will use a flag called FLAG which is set at an initial value of 0 when the program starts and is shifted to a value of 1 when DNEW is larger than DIST.

```
IF(DNEW.GE.DIST) THEN
    PRINT*,DIST, TIME, X, Y
    FLAG = 1
ELSE
    TIME = TIME + 1.0
ENDIF
```

FLAG will be used in a while construct to control looping as has been described. The pseudocode and flowchart further describe this action.

Programming Example–Tracking Problem continued

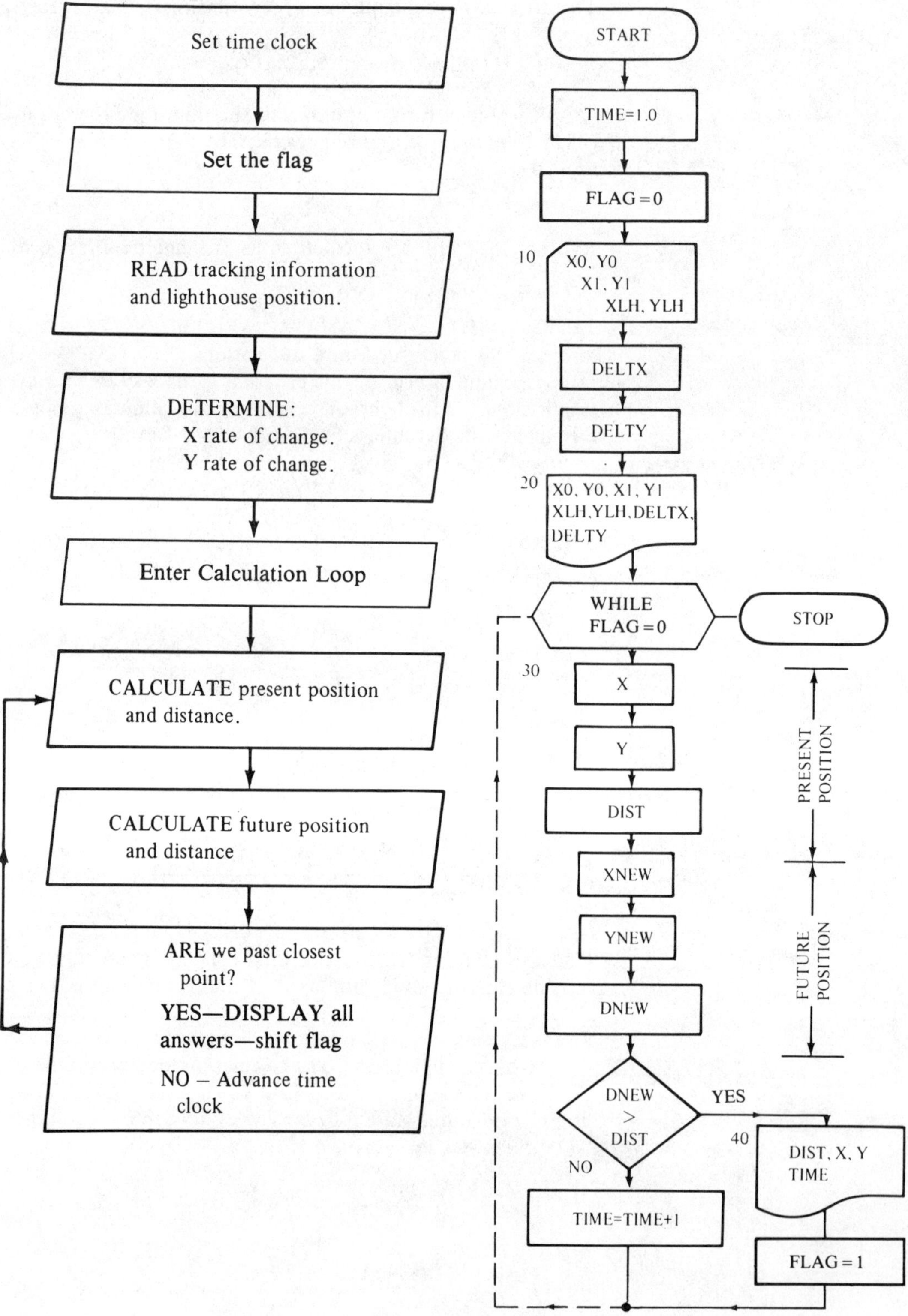

Programming Example–Tracking Problem continued

```
C.......................................................
C       PURPOSE - PREDICT THE TRACK OF A MOVING SHIP AND..
C                 DETERMINE HOW CLOSE IT WILL COME TO A ..
C                  LIGHTHOUSE.                          ..
C.......................................................
C
C                -----IMPORTANT VARIABLES------
C
C       --X0,Y0          INITIAL POSITION OF SHIP          --
C       --X1,Y1          POSITION ONE MINUTE LATER         --
C       --XLH,YLH        LOCATION OF  LIGHTHOUSE           --
C       --DELTX          X DISPLACEMENT IN ONE MINUTE      --
C       --DELTY          Y DISPLACEMENT IN ONE MINUTE      --
C
C       --X,Y            LOCATION OF MOVING SHIP           --
C       --DIST           DISTANCE AWAY FROM  LIGHTHOUSE    --
C       --TIME           VALUE OF TIME CLOCK               --
C       --FLAG           FLAG FOR LOOP CONTROL             --
C
C       XNEW,YNEW        NEXT LOCATION OF SHIP             --
C       DNEW             NEXT DISTANCE TO  LIGHTHOUSE      --
C
C       ............. INITIALIZATION SECTION............
C
        REAL X0,Y0,X1,Y1,XLH,YLH,DELTX,DELTY,X,Y
        REAL XNEW,YNEW,DNEW,DIST
C
        TIME = 0.0
        FLAG = 0
C
   10   READ*, X0,Y0,X1,Y1,XLH,YLH
C
        DELTX = X1-X0
        DELTY = Y1-Y0
C
   20   PRINT*,'INITIAL POSITION=',X0,Y0
        PRINT*,'POSITION AT TIME T = 1',X1,Y1
        PRINT*,' LIGHTHOUSE LOCATION=', XLH,YLH
        PRINT*,'RATE OF MOVEMENT', DELTX,DELTY
C
C..................................................
C...            LOOP ENTRY POINT            .........
C..................................................
        DO WHILE(FLAG.EQ.0)
C
C                COMPUTE PRESENT POSITION
C
  30        X= X0 + TIME * DELTX
            Y= Y0 + TIME * DELTY
C
C
            DIST = SQRT((XLH-X)**2 + (YLH-Y)**2)
C
C               COMPUTE FUTURE POSITION
C
            XNEW=X0+(TIME +1.) * DELTX
            YNEW=Y0+(TIME+1.) * DELTY
            DNEW= SQRT((XLH-XNEW)**2 + (YLH-YNEW)**2)
C
C               HAVE WE PASSED CLOSEST POINT OF APPROACH
C
            IF(DNEW.GE.DIST) THEN
C
C               PASSED POINT
C
  40            PRINT*,'DISTANCE=', DIST
                PRINT*,'TIME OF CLOSEST APPROACH=',TIME
                PRINT*,'OUR POSITION WILL BE',X,Y
                FLAG = 1
```

Programming Example–Tracking Problem continued

```
C
              ELSE
C
C                   POINT STILL AHEAD OF US
C
                    TIME = TIME +1.0
C
              ENDIF
C
          ENDDO
C
          STOP
          END
```

Programming Example
Optimal Shape

Very often the computer is used in the solution of design problems to allow the evaluation of many alternative design configurations and thereby permit the designer to select the best solution. The next problem is an exceptionally simplified example of this process.

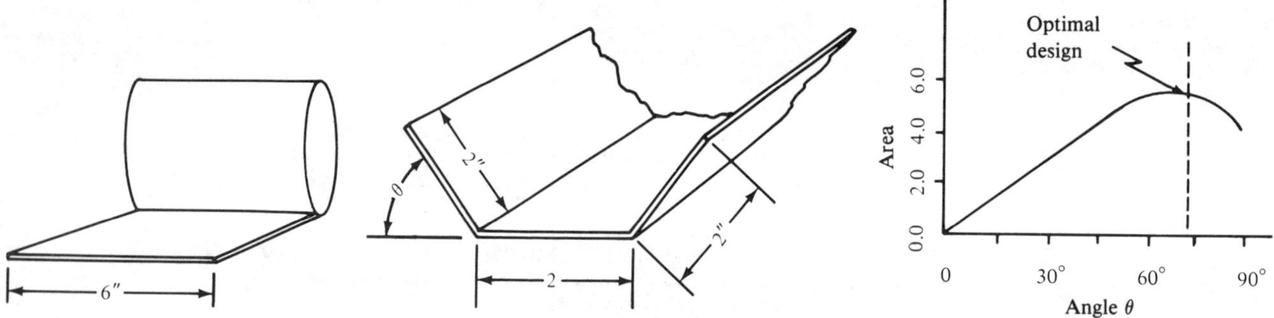

A 6″-wide roll of sheet metal is to be bent to form a trough for a rain gutter. The angle of bend, θ, affects the amount of liquid the trough is capable of handling. The computer will be used to determine the best shape for the trough. Assume the three sides of the trough are made equal (2″), determine what angle of bend, θ, gives the largest cross-sectional area.

The graph shows the cross-sectional area of the trough for various angles of bend. When the sides are vertical ($\theta = 90°$), the cross-sectional area is 4 square inches. If θ is decreased slightly, the area increases. As θ is decreased further, the cross-sectional area continues to increase until a maximum value is reached (optimal shape). If θ is decreased beyond this point, the area decreases rapidly. When θ reaches zero, the trough is flat and the area is also zero. The maximum cross-section occurs somewhere between $\theta = 0°$ and $\theta = 90°$. The problem is to find where.

Working with a unit length of trough, we can divide the cross-section into three simple shapes (one rectangle and two triangles). See the following object breakdown.

Programming Example–Tracking Problem continued

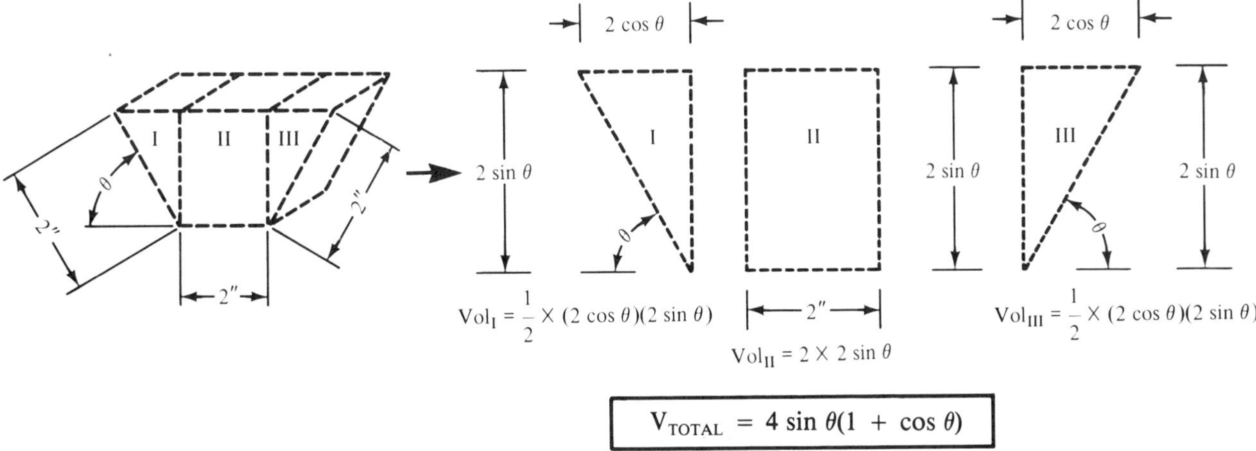

The preceding figure computes the volume of each of these individual shapes and presents an equation that expresses the total volume as a function of theta. We must evaluate this equation for various angles of theta. Write a program to evaluate the volume of this unit section of channel for various angles of θ. Start θ at 90° and decrease it by 1° increments until θ equals zero. For each value of θ, compute the volume.

Do not report all values of volume, but rather include statements in the program that will identify and report the largest volume (VMAX) and the corresponding angle (THEMX) only.

The program starts by giving an initial value to VMAX and THEMX. Inside the loop, THETA is decremented and a new value of volume computed. If this value of volume is greater than VMAX, a redefinition takes place. Note that the redefinition statements are indented to show they are under the control of the IF test:

```
      IF(VOL.GT.VMAX)THEN
          VMAX=VOL
          THEMX=THETA
      ENDIF
```

Note also that on each redefinition of VMAX it is necessary to redefine THEMX to save that value of THETA that produced this maximum value.

Note finally that those who know calculus realize that the maximum volume could be computed by taking the derivative of the volume equation with respect to θ and setting that equation equal to zero. This is a classic minimum/maximum calculation. This higher-level mathematical procedure can be approximated by the simpler equations of the preceding graph and the repeated procedures of this program.

Programming Example–Optimal Shape continued

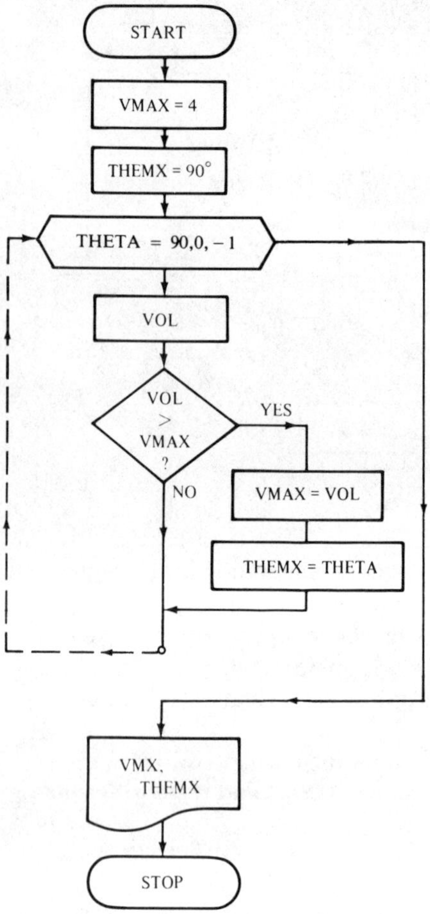

START
VMAX = 4
THEMX = 90°
THETA = 90,0, −1
VOL
VOL > VMAX ?
YES
NO
VMAX = VOL
THEMX = THETA
VMX, THEMX
STOP

```
C.......................................................................
C.. PURPOSE - OPTIMAL DESIGN PROBLEM.  DETERMINE MAXIMUM..
C             VOLUME OF CROSS SECTION OF RAIN GUTTER ..
C.......................................................................
C
C                 -----IMPORTANT VARIABLES ----
C
C         --VOL    VOLUME OF SECTION                          --
C         --THETA ANGLE OF INCLINATION                        --
C         --VMAX   LARGEST VOLUME DETECTED                    --
C         --THEMX ANGLE AT LARGEST VOLUME                     --
C
C                 ....INITIALIZATION SECTION......
C
          REAL VOL,THETA,VMAX,THEMX
C
          VMAX =4.0
          THEMX =90.0
C
C                 ....LOOP ENTRY POINT....
C
          DO 20 THETA = 90.0, 0.0, -1.0
C
              VOL = 4.*SIN(THETA/57.3)*(1.0+COS(THETA/57.3))
C
C         IF VOLUME JUST COMPUTED IS LARGER, REDEFINE VMAX
C
              IF(VOL.GT.VMAX)THEN
                   VMAX=VOL
                   THEMX=THETA
C
               ENDIF
C
C
   20     CONTINUE
C                 ..... LOOP EXIT POINT....
C
          PRINT*,'LARGEST VOLUME DETECTED=',VMAX
          PRINT*,'ANGLE AT LARGEST VOLUME=',THEMX
C
          STOP
          END
```

Programming Example
Root Determination**

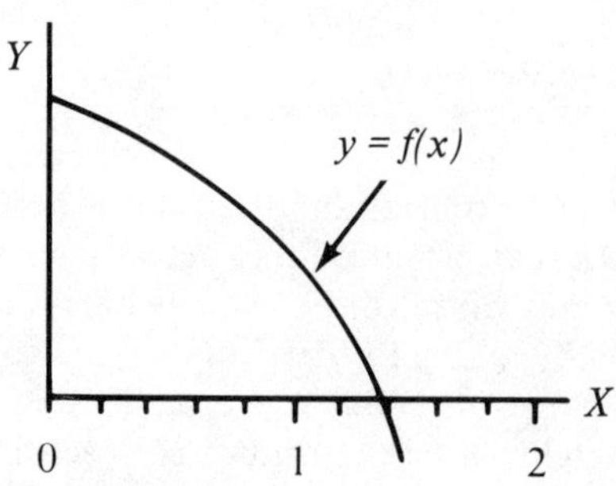

Write a program to determine the first positive root of the equation:

$$y = x^3 + 5x^2 - \ln(x + 1) + 12$$

Programming Example–Root Determination continued

Unlike the quadratic equation that was solved in Chapter 2, this equation cannot be solved by a simple formula such as:

$$x = \frac{-b \pm \sqrt{b^2 - 4ac}}{2a}$$

It can be solved, however, by a trial and error method.

This program is presented as the last case study because it places exceptional demands on the creativity of the programmer. The problem will be solved by "walking down" the X axis using large incrementing steps until we get close to the root. We then will use smaller stepping increments to get even closer to the root and then even smaller steps until we find the root to whatever accuracy we want.

At $X = 0$ the value of Y is positive and large, but as X increases, negative terms in the equation cause the value of Y to decrease until it crosses the X axis (the point of crossing is the root). This fact can be used to direct the solution of the problem.

Step	Meaning	Statement
1	SET X at an initial value of zero	X = 0.0
2	SET an incrementing value of 1.0	DELTX = 1.0
3	INDEX X at this stepping rate until Y goes negative . . . We have passed the root.	Y=-X**3+5.*X**2-ALOG(X+10.)+12.0 IF(Y.LE.0.0)
4	CORRECT for the "overshoot" by stepping back to the previous value of X	X = X-DELTX
5	DECREASE the stepping rate by a factor of ten	DELTX = DELTX/10.0
6	REPEAT steps 3 through 5 (until the stepping rate is sufficiently accurate)	DO WHILE (DELTX.GT.ACC)

Note the statement that causes X to take a step backward when the root is "overshot" (Step 4). Note the statement that cuts the stepping rate to a fraction of what it was before (Step 5).

The program has a single data record that describes how accurate the root is to be determined.

```
C.........................................................
C..PURPOSE - DETERMINE THE ROOT OF AN EQUATION USING A..
C..              TRIAL AND ERROR STEPPING PROCEDURE    ..
C.........................................................
C
C              -----IMPORTANT VARIABLES ----
C
C       --X      VALUE OF INDEPENDENT VARIABLE         --
C       --Y      VALUE FROM EQUATION                   --
C       --DELTX  STEPPING (INDEXING) RATE              --
C       --ACCRCY ACCURACY OF SOLUTION DESIRED          --
C
C              ........INITIALIZATION SECTION.....
C
        REAL X,Y,DELTX,ACCRCY
C
        READ*, ACCRCY
C
        X=0.0
        DELTX=1.0
```

Programming Example–Root Determination continued

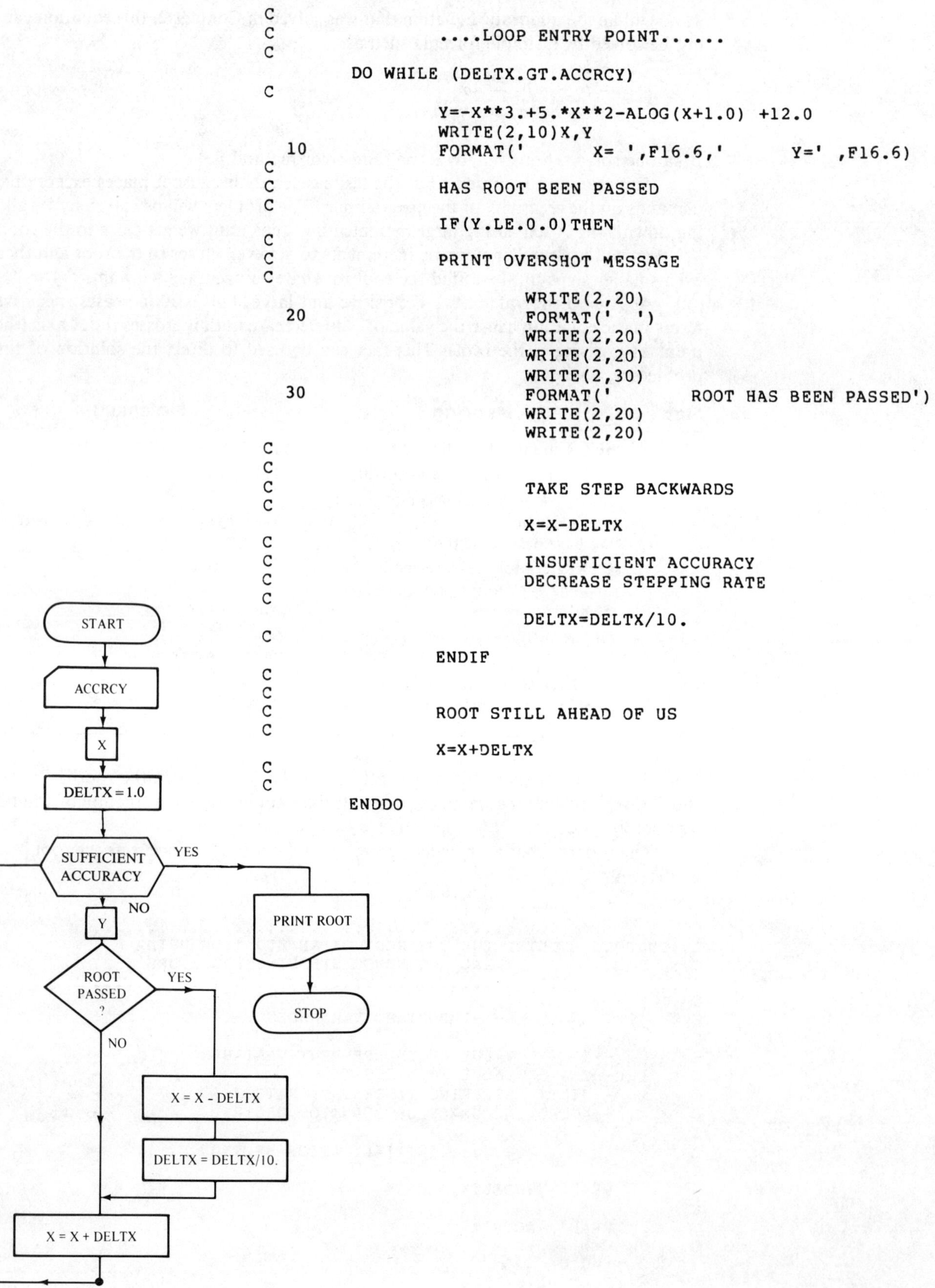

```
C
C           ....LOOP ENTRY POINT......
C
      DO WHILE (DELTX.GT.ACCRCY)
C
            Y=-X**3.+5.*X**2-ALOG(X+1.0) +12.0
            WRITE(2,10)X,Y
   10       FORMAT('       X= ',F16.6,'         Y=' ,F16.6)
C
C           HAS ROOT BEEN PASSED
C
            IF(Y.LE.0.0)THEN
C
C           PRINT OVERSHOT MESSAGE
C
                  WRITE(2,20)
   20             FORMAT(' ')
                  WRITE(2,20)
                  WRITE(2,20)
                  WRITE(2,30)
   30             FORMAT('          ROOT HAS BEEN PASSED')
                  WRITE(2,20)
                  WRITE(2,20)
C
C
C                 TAKE STEP BACKWARDS
C
                  X=X-DELTX
C
C                 INSUFFICIENT ACCURACY
C                 DECREASE STEPPING RATE
C
                  DELTX=DELTX/10.
C
            ENDIF
C
C
C           ROOT STILL AHEAD OF US
C
            X=X+DELTX
C
C
      ENDDO
```

Programming Example–Root Determination continued

The following output sheet for this problem shows the stepping procedure, the step back activity, and the final solution. Note that X starts with an incrementing rate of 1.0. As X increases, the Y term slowly decreases. At a value of $X = 6.0$, the value of Y turns negative. A message is given that the root has been passed. A step back to a value of 5.0 takes place and the stepping rate reduced to 0.1.

The process is repeated. X goes from 5.1 to 5.4 when another overshoot occurs. Another step back and another reduction in stepping rate takes place. The process continues until the root is determined to the desired degree of accuracy.

```
X=        0.000000      Y=       12.000000
X=        1.000000      Y=       15.306853
X=        2.000000      Y=       22.901388
X=        3.000000      Y=       28.613705
X=        4.000000      Y=       26.390562
X=        5.000000      Y=       10.208233
X=        6.000000      Y=      -25.945927


 ROOT HAS BEEN PASSED


X=        5.100000      Y=        7.590713
X=        5.200000      Y=        4.767446
X=        5.300000      Y=        1.732433
X=        5.400000      Y=       -1.520330


 ROOT HAS BEEN PASSED


X=        5.310000      Y=        1.417050
X=        5.320000      Y=        1.099503
X=        5.330000      Y=        0.779699
X=        5.340001      Y=        0.457747
X=        5.350001      Y=        0.133661
X=        5.360001      Y=       -0.192772


 ROOT HAS BEEN PASSED


X=        5.351001      Y=        0.101110
X=        5.352001      Y=        0.068527
X=        5.353001      Y=        0.035884
X=        5.354001      Y=        0.003378
X=        5.355000      Y=       -0.029250


 ROOT HAS BEEN PASSED
```

9 Forming a Data Base

The introductory phase of computer programming is over. You are about to take a rather substantial step forward in the complexity and type of problem you will be able to solve. We are going to become involved in what students call "real data crunching." These new problems will have two basic characteristics:

1. The amount of data associated with the problem will be relatively large.
2. The data must be stored in such a way that it can be processed over and over again, not just once.

A typical problem may ask, for example, that a thousand values of X be read and a search made to find and report the largest value. When this assignment is complete, you will be asked to search for the next largest value and report it, then the next largest value, and so on.

Problems such as this require a considerable amount of looping and also require a better way of storing and addressing data. Both the loop control and the more efficient method of storing data (as a subscripted variable) are accomplished by the expanded use of the DO statement.

9.1 Subscripting a Variable

Certain problems require subscripting of one or more variables while other problems require no subscripting at all. It is important that you *never* resort to subscripting unless it is absolutely necessary. What this means is that it is just as important to know *when* to subscript as it is to know *how* to subscript a variable. We will, therefore, use the following problem to demonstrate the following.

1. Under what conditions it is necessary to subscript a variable.
2. How the index of a DO statement can be used to provide a subscript.

The Problem: A class consisting of 20 students is given an examination and the grades received by each student are recorded on a data file. Determine the class average on this exam.

Scale the Grades: If the class average is less than 60, determine how many points must be added to each student's grade to raise the average to 75. Add these points and report the new grade.

The first part of this solution is simple enough. We merely read each of the grades, total them up as we go, and at the end divide through by 20 to get the average:

$$AVE = \frac{\sum_{i=1}^{20} X_i}{20}$$

As we start to handle the second part of this problem, the hidden difficulty emerges. We need one *complete* examination of the values in our data file to compute the class average and another complete examination of these values to scale the grades. This is the first time you have been presented with a problem that requires more than one examination of the values in your input data file.

Hidden Difficulty: The values in the data file must be processed twice:

1. Once to compute the class average.
2. Once to scale the grades, if necessary.

If you still do not fully grasp the difficulty we are facing, ask yourself, ''What is the status of the input data file as we start to solve the scaling of the grades part of the problem?'' The answer is that we are at the end-of-file condition. The data file is depleted. If we want to add a few points to the first student's grade, that grade will have to be in memory because if we execute a command read we will get an end-of-file error. The same holds true for all the other grades. Let's take a look at one possible, but awkward, solution.

First Level Solution: The Hard Way

In the first level solution we will attempt to show how difficult it is to deal with even a small data base using conventional methods.

First Level Solution

```
      READ* ,X1,X2,X3,X4,X5,X6,X7,X8,X9
     +      ,X10,X11,X12,X13,X14,X15,X16
     +      ,X17,X18,X19,X20

      SUM = X1+X2+X3+X4+X5+X6+X7+X8+X9+X10
     +      +X11+X12+X13+X14+X15+X16+X17+
     +      X18+X19+X20

15    AVE = SUM / 20.

      IF(AVE.LT.60.0) THEN

         ADD = 75.0 - AVE
         X1 = X1 + ADD
         X2 = X2 + ADD
         X3 = X3 + ADD
         X4 = X4 + ADD
         .    .    .
         .    .    .
         .    .    .
         PRINT*, X1,X2,X3,X4,X5.....X19,X20

      ENDIF
```

The awkward aspect of this solution is that each time we deal with the data base (the 20 grades) a long list of variable names must be written. Twenty names are required following the READ command and are required again in the arithmetic expression determining the SUM. The situation gets even worse when we attempt to add points to each student's grade. Twenty individual assignment statements would be needed. Obviously this method of addressing the data base is intolerable, and the situation would be even worse if 200 or 2000 grades were involved. What we need is a solution similar to this one, but one in which not so much writing is involved.

Using an Accumulator—Loop Control

To start the second level solution, we will concentrate on solving the first half of the problem (finding the class average) but without involving so much writing. We resort to a loop control structure (the DO statement) and the use of an accumulator. We then modify this solution to include the concept of subscripting.

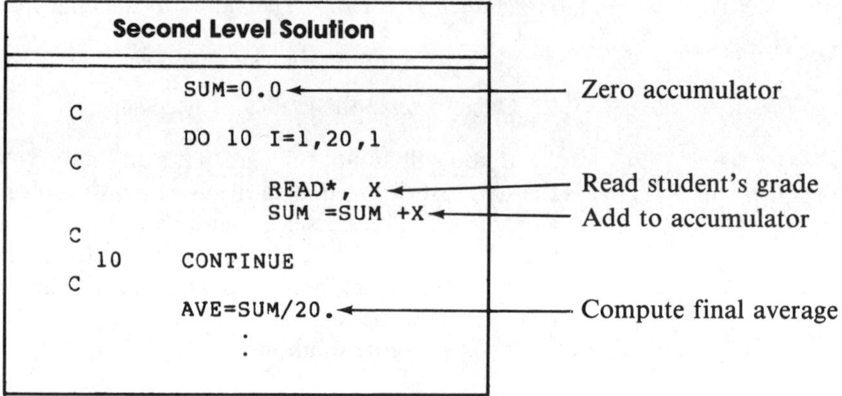

Second Level Solution

```
      SUM=0.0            <-- Zero accumulator
C
      DO 10 I=1,20,1
C
         READ*, X        <-- Read student's grade
         SUM =SUM +X     <-- Add to accumulator
C
   10 CONTINUE
C
      AVE=SUM/20.        <-- Compute final average
         .
         .
```

In moving from the first to the second level solution, we have used a loop and an accumulator to avoid having to write the name of each variable over and over again each time we want to process the data base. The trouble now is that there is only one memory location called X and therefore only one value of X is known at any given time. When the statement to compute the average is reached, only one grade is in memory, namely the grade of the last student. Our data base is *lost.*

Subscripting

We now make only a slight modification to our second level solution that will cause each and every value of X to be retained in memory. We will be back to the status of things in the first level solution, but without all the hard work.

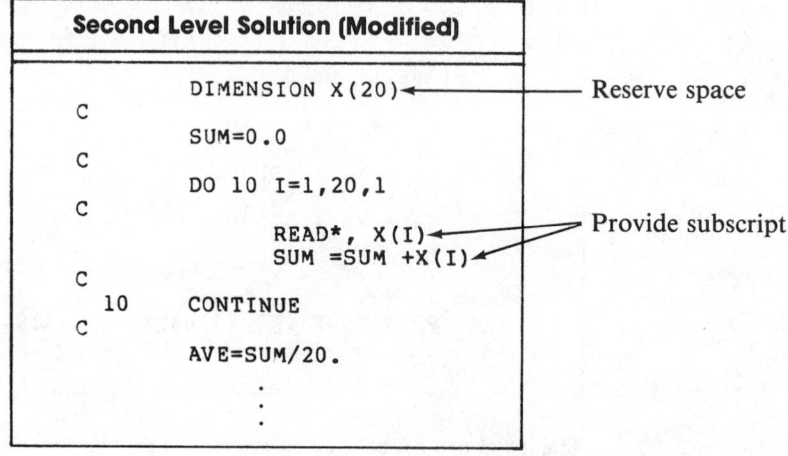

Second Level Solution (Modified)

```
      DIMENSION X(20)    <-- Reserve space
C
      SUM=0.0
C
      DO 10 I=1,20,1
C
         READ*, X(I)     <-- Provide subscript
         SUM =SUM +X(I)  <--
C
   10 CONTINUE
C
      AVE=SUM/20.
         .
         .
         .
```

Use of the Index

You have seen how the DO statement can be written to provide an index whose primary purpose is to count the number of times a series of statements is executed. Frequently the index is used for another important purpose. It can be used to provide a subscript when it becomes necessary to subscript a variable.

On those occasions (when it is necessary to retain all the values associated with a data base) we can implement a procedure that closely parallels the variable-naming technique used in the first level solution. Recall that 20 variables had the basic name X but with some added characteristics, such as a 1, a 2, or a 3, to distinguish one X value from another.

Different Naming Techniques

First Level Solution	New Techniques
`READ*,X1,X2,X3,X4,X5,...`	`DO 10 I=1,20,1`
`....X17,X18,X19,X20`	`READ*,X(I)`

The index of a DO statement can be combined with the variable name X to provide this distinguishing characteristic as suggested in the right column of the preceding table. The variable

```
X(I)
  └── Subscript
      provider
```

uses the DO loop's index I to provide a number following the variable X. Using this technique, it is possible to have all the advantages of the first level solution with all the efficiencies of the second level solutions. Let us go over this again.

The whole notion of when and how to subscript a variable takes some time to develop. When a subscript is needed, however, it can be provided by the index of a DO. FORTRAN allows a variable name to be followed by a pair of parentheses enclosing an integer constant or variable, which serves as a subscript. This integer subscript frequently is provided by the *index* of a DO statement. Permissible forms of subscripted variables include:

```
X(1)   X(20)   X(I)   NUMBER (35)
VALUE (J+1)   GRADE (200)   Y(K)
```

When subscripting takes place, the identity of each element of the data base is retained.

Subscripting a Variable

Identity Lost	Identity Retained
`DO 10 I = 1, 20, 1`	`DO 10 I = 1, 20, 1`
`READ*, X`	`READ*, X(I)`

In the READ statement on the right, the index I provides a subscript so that values of X will be read and stored as:

```
X(1);X(2);X(3); . . . X(19);X(20)
```

Collectively these values of X are called an **array**. The term array implies that a large number of variables are to be stored under a common name (in this case, the name X).

Caution: When an array is to be stored in memory, the programmer must first declare how many memory locations are needed to accommodate the various elements of the array, that is, he must give the size of the array. This is accomplished by a `DIMENSION` statement:

```
DIMENSION X(20)
```

The complete solution to the problem is now presented. The only new variable used is the quantity `ADD`, which will contain the extra points needed to bring the class average up to 75.

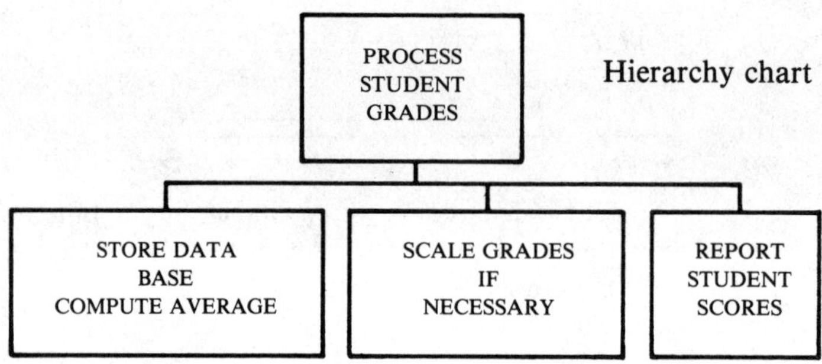

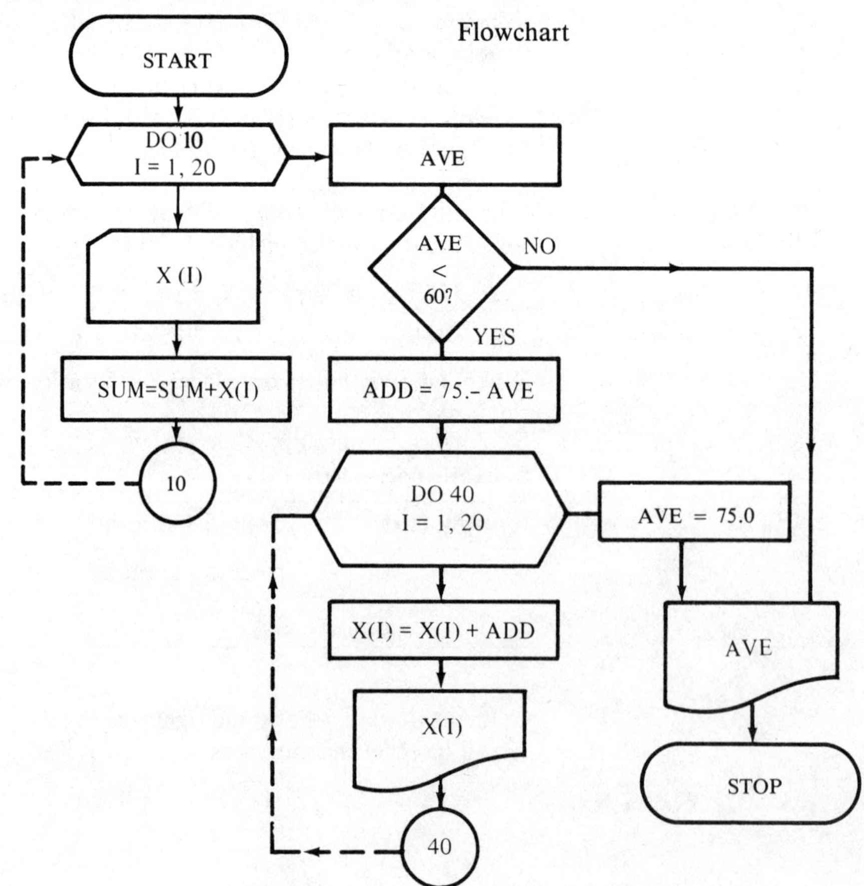

```
C.................................................................
C..     PURPOSE - 3 RD LEVEL SOLUTION                           ..
C.................................................................
C
        DIMENSION X(20)
        REAL    X, SUM, ADD, AVE
        INTEGER I
C
        SUM=0.0
C
C                ************************************
C                ** READ TWENTY GRADES - STORE AS **
C                ** SUBSCRIPTED QUANTITIES - ADD   **
C                ** ELEMENTS TO ACCUMULATOR "SUM" **
C                ************************************
C
        DO 10 I=1,20,1
             READ*,  X(I)
             SUM= SUM+X(I)
  10    CONTINUE
C
        AVE=SUM/20.
C
        IF(AVE.LT.60.0) THEN
C
C                ***********************************************
C                **..........SCALE GRADES IF NECESSARY.......**
C                ***********************************************
C
               ADD=75.0- AVE
C
C
               DO 40 I=1,20,1
                   X(I)=X(I) + ADD
                   PRINT*, I, X(I)
  40           CONTINUE
C
               AVE=75.0
C
        ENDIF
C
C                ........... TERMINATION SECTION............
C
        PRINT*,' THE AVERAGE SCORE IS ', AVE
C
        STOP
        END
```

Subscripting has been made as simple as possible to implement in FORTRAN and very often makes a difficult task easy to perform. When all the grades are in subscripted form, the data base becomes remarkably easy to deal with. For example, assume the class average turns out to be 50 and you must add 25 points to each student's grade. Using the old first level solution, it would take 20 assignment statements to accomplish the grade adjustment. Note how much easier it is to accomplish the task when the grades are subscripted.

Old Method	New Method
X1 = X1 + 25.0	DO 40 I = 1, 20, 1
X2 = X2 + 25.0	X(I) = X(I) + 25.0
X3 = X3 + 25.0	40 CONTINUE
X4 = X4 + 25.0	
X5 = X5 + 25.0	
⋮ ⋮ ⋮	
X19 = X19 + 25.0	
X20 = X20 + 25.0	

9.2 Problems Dealing with Large Arrays

Students who have worked with subscripted variables before write them off as "no big deal." If you have not dealt with them before, you will usually take a small amount of time to adjust to this higher level device for storing information. You will be just a little unsure of how subscripting of a variable fits into the type of problems you face on a day-to-day basis. In the interest of making this adjustment period as brief as possible, we defer the writing of complete programs in favor of showing several brief examples of where and when arrays can be used to advantage.

Multiple Choice Exam

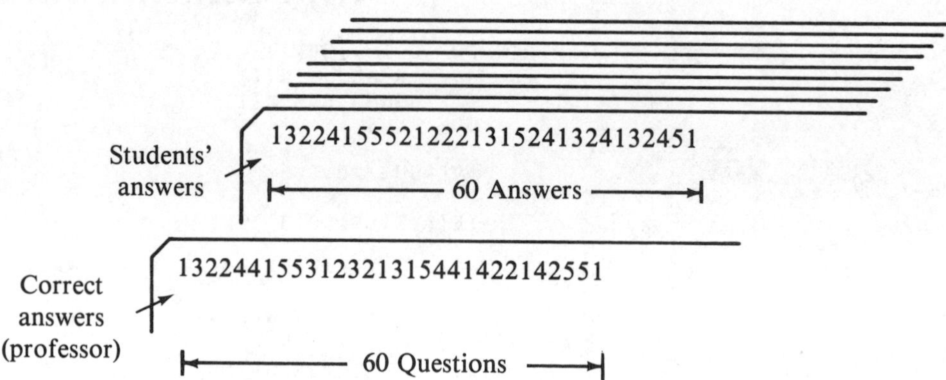

A professor gives a multiple choice exam having 60 questions. There are five possible responses (1, 2, 3, 4, and 5) to each question, and the student must select the correct one. These answers are recorded on "mark sense" cards so that they can be read directly into the computer. Assume a data file in which the first or leader record gives the correct answers as provided by the instructor. The remaining records represent the responses given by the students. Write a program to determine the number of correct answers and the appropriate score or average for each student.

It would be convenient to store the 60 correct answers provided on the leader record under a single common name such as PROF and be able to address individual elements by using an appropriate subscript. The answers given by a student could be stored the same way in an array called ANS. (See Figure 9.1.)

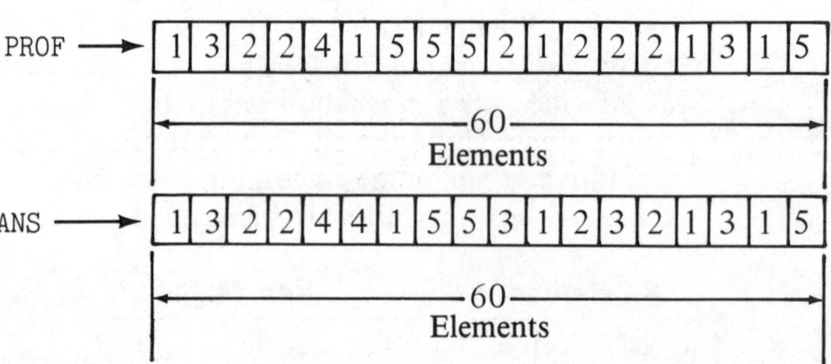

Figure 9.1 Display of data base

A DIMENSION statement can be used to reserve sufficient space in memory for these two arrays, and then a simple DO statement can be used to compare corresponding elements of the two arrays to see if a correct answer was given.

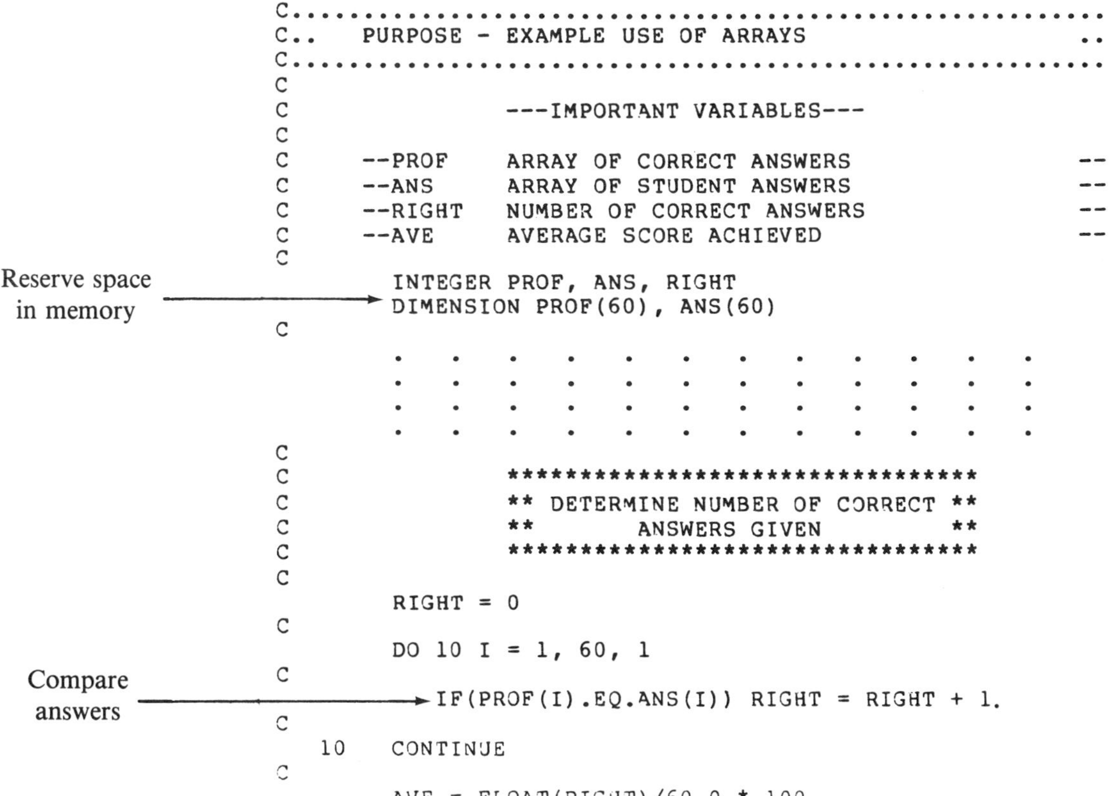

```
C.........................................................
C..   PURPOSE - EXAMPLE USE OF ARRAYS                    ..
C.........................................................
C
C               ---IMPORTANT VARIABLES---
C
C     --PROF    ARRAY OF CORRECT ANSWERS                 --
C     --ANS     ARRAY OF STUDENT ANSWERS                 --
C     --RIGHT   NUMBER OF CORRECT ANSWERS                --
C     --AVE     AVERAGE SCORE ACHIEVED                   --
C
      INTEGER PROF, ANS, RIGHT
      DIMENSION PROF(60), ANS(60)
C
      .   .   .   .   .   .   .   .   .   .   .   .
      .   .   .   .   .   .   .   .   .   .   .   .
      .   .   .   .   .   .   .   .   .   .   .   .
      .   .   .   .   .   .   .   .   .   .   .   .
C
C               *********************************
C               ** DETERMINE NUMBER OF CORRECT **
C               **       ANSWERS GIVEN         **
C               *********************************
C
      RIGHT = 0
C
      DO 10 I = 1, 60, 1
C
         IF(PROF(I).EQ.ANS(I)) RIGHT = RIGHT + 1.
C
   10 CONTINUE
C
      AVE = FLOAT(RIGHT)/60.0 * 100
```


Establish Pay Rate Table

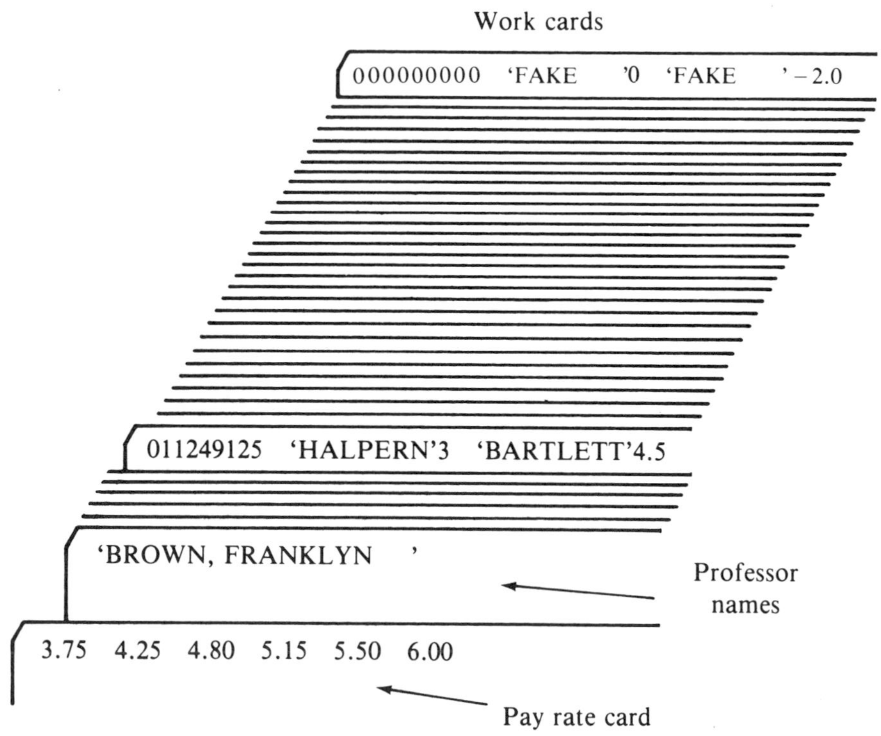

The first record of a data file gives the pay rate for six different classifications of jobs. Read these values and establish a table (array) called RATE. To make sure the table has been established properly, print out the first and last pay rate. Now, read the next 30 records giving a professor's name (20 characters). Store this information as an array called NAME. Finally, create an array called TOTAL having 30 elements, each of which is a real number whose initial value is to be set at 0.0. The picture of the data base you are establishing is as follows:

Rate	Name	Total
3.75	BROWN, FRANKLYN	0.00
4.25	CULLINANE, THOMAS	0.00
4.80	HALPERN, PAM	0.00
5.15	LEHMKULE, NONNA	0.00
5.50	⋮	⋮
6.6	⋮	⋮
	RULE, WILFRED	0.00
	SMITH, WALTER	0.00
	WOODARD, KEN	0.00

```
C.......................................................
C..   PURPOSE - EXAMPLE USE OF ARRAYS                 ..
C.......................................................
C
C                ---IMPORTANT VARIABLES---
C
C     --RATE     A TABLE OF PAY RATES                 --
C     --NAME     TABLE OF PROFESSORS' NAMES           --
C     --TOTAL    TOTAL COST OF STUDENT                --
C                HELP FOR EACH PROFESSOR              --
C
      REAL RATE, TOTAL
      CHARACTER NAME*20
C
      DIMENSION RATE(6), TOTAL(30), NAME(30)
C
      READ*,RATE(1),RATE(2),RATE(3),RATE(4),RATE(5),RATE(6)
C
C                ......ECHO CHECK FIRST AND LAST......
C
      PRINT*,'FIRST RATE = ', RATE(1)
      PRINT*,'LAST RATE = ', RATE(6)
C
C                **********************************
C                ** READ EACH NAME - SET EACH    **
C                ** ELEMENT OF TOTAL TO ZERO     **
C                **********************************
C
      DO 10 I = 1, 30, 1
C
         READ*, NAME(I)
         TOTAL(I) = 0.0
C
   10 CONTINUE
```

Table Search

By now you probably recognize this problem as the one initiated in Chapter 8—the one involving the processing of student work records. We will carry the solution one step further. Read the first work card record. It turns out that this student has a class 3 job rating and worked 4.5 hours for Prof. Bartlett.

1. Compute the pay for this work record.
2. Search the table for Prof. Bartlett's name.
3. When the name is found in the table, use the value of the subscript at that time to advance (increase) the element of TOTAL with the same subscript by the pay computed in step 1.
4. Stop the program.

```
C                ---NEW VARIABLES---
C      --SSNO    SOCIAL SECURITY NUMBER                        --
C      --STUDNT  STUDENT'S NAME                                --
C      --PROF    PROFESSOR'S NAME ON WORK CARD                 --
C      --CODE    JOB RATING CODE                               --
C      --HOURS   HOURS WORKED                                  --
C
        CHARACTER STUDNT*20, PROF*20
        INTEGER SSNO, CODE, I
        REAL HOURS, PAY
C
        READ*, SSNO, STUDNT, CODE, PROF, HOURS
C
        PAY = RATE(CODE) * HOURS
C
        DO 10 I = 1, 30, 1
C
C       *******************************************
C       ** SEARCH TABLE OF PROFESSORS' NAMES FOR **
C       **    THE NAME ON THE WORK CARD RECORD   **
C       *******************************************
C
           IF(PROF.EQ.NAME(I)) THEN
C
                TOTAL(I) = TOTAL(I) + PAY
                STOP
C
           ENDIF
C
   10   CONTINUE
```

Inventory Control

Our company sells 400 different automotive parts. Each part is described on an input data record by giving the following information:

1. Part number
2. Quantity on hand
3. Unit price

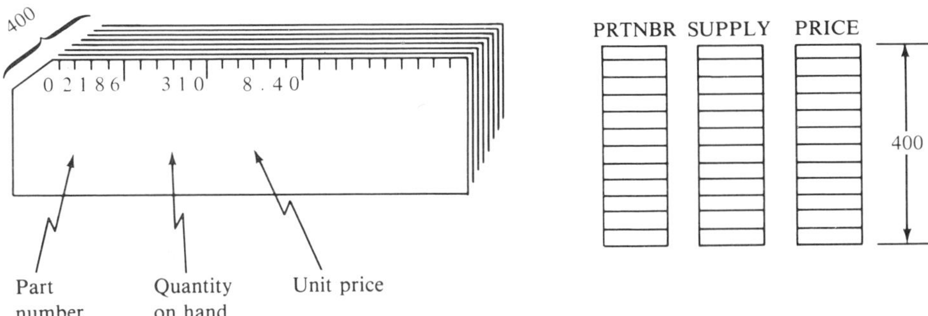

Write statements that read this information and store the values as three one-dimensional arrays.

```
C.......................................................
C..   PURPOSE - READ DATA BASE DESCRIBING AN          ..
C..             INVENTORY OF 400 AUTOMOTIVE           ..
C..             PARTS.                                ..
C.......................................................
C
C                  ---IMPORTANT VARIABLES---
C
C       --PRTNBR  ARRAY OF PART NUMBERS               --
C       --SUPPLY  NUMBER OF PARTS ON HAND             --
C       --PRICE   UNIT PRICE OF EACH PART             --
C
        REAL PRICE
        INTEGER PRTNBR, SUPPLY, I
        DIMENSION PRTNBR(400), SUPPLY(400), PRICE(400)
C
C          **************************************
C          ** READ INFORMATION FROM DATA FILE **
C          ** STORE AS THREE ONE-DIMENSIONAL   **
C          ** ARRAYS                           **
C          **************************************
C
        DO 10 I = 1, 400, 1
C
           READ*, PRTNBR(I), SUPPLY(I), PRICE(I)
C
   10   CONTINUE
```

Unit Price Changes

From time to time it is necessary to change the unit price that one or more parts sell for. The next group of records in the data file has a header record telling how many parts are to be given a new selling price. For each record that follows, search the data base for the appropriate part and change the corresponding element of the array price. For efficiency sake, assume these transaction records are in order by part number. Assume the original data base was also given in order of part number.

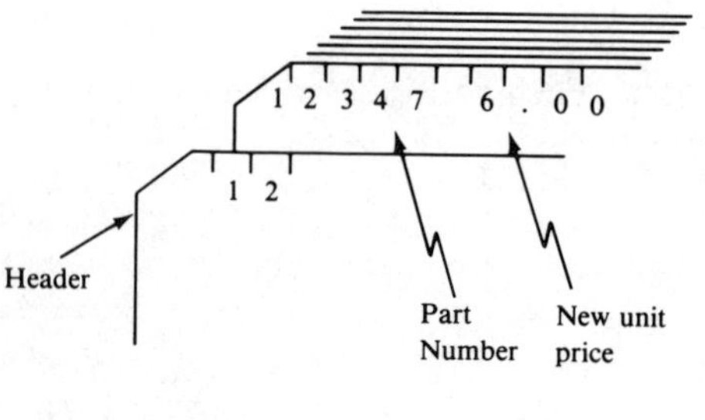


```
C     -----NEW VARIABLES-----
C
C     --PARTTC   PART NUMBER FROM TRANSACTION CARD RECORD --
C     --SIZE     NUMBER OF RECORDS IN THIS PORTION OF FILE--
C     --NEW      NEW UNIT PRICE                           --
C
      REAL NEW
      INTEGER SIZE, PARTTC
C
C             ....READ HEADER RECORD....
C
      READ*, SIZE
C
C           ....READ FIRST TRANSACTION....
C
      READ*, PARTTC, NEW
C
C             ****************************
C             ** SET UP SEARCH ACTIVITY **
C             ****************************
C
      DO 20 I = 1, 400, 1
C
         IF(PARTTC.EQ.PRTNBR(I)) THEN
C
            PRICE(I) = NEW
            SIZE = SIZE - 1
```

```
C                 ....THIS TRANSACTION COMPLETE....
C                 ......ANY MORE TRANSACTIONS?.....
                  IF(SIZE.GT.0) READ*, PARTTC, NEW
C
             ENDIF
C
   20    CONTINUE
```

Customer Order Transactions

The final portion of the input data file represents orders received from various customers for a specified number of a given part. The first order shown is for 100 of our parts numbered 23456. These order transaction records are again sorted by part number. For each transaction, make sure we have enough parts on hand to fill the order. If we do not have sufficient supply on hand, print an appropriate message.

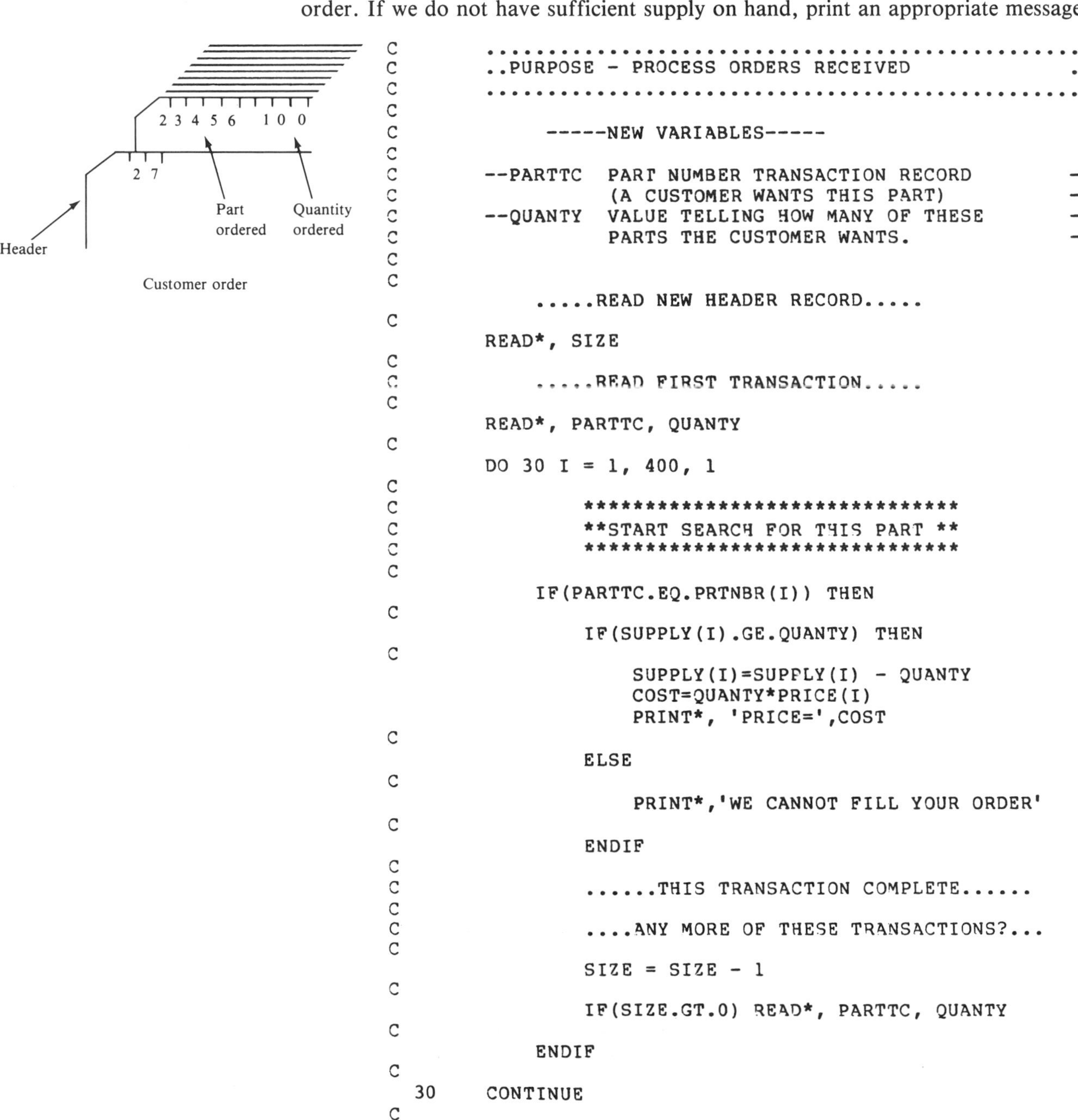

Customer order

```
C         ..............................................
C         ..PURPOSE - PROCESS ORDERS RECEIVED            ..
C         ..............................................
C
C              -----NEW VARIABLES-----
C
C         --PARTTC  PART NUMBER TRANSACTION RECORD       --
C                   (A CUSTOMER WANTS THIS PART)         --
C         --QUANTY  VALUE TELLING HOW MANY OF THESE      --
C                   PARTS THE CUSTOMER WANTS.            --
C
C
C              .....READ NEW HEADER RECORD.....
C
          READ*, SIZE
C
C              .....READ FIRST TRANSACTION.....
C
          READ*, PARTTC, QUANTY
C
          DO 30 I = 1, 400, 1
C
C                  *******************************
C                  **START SEARCH FOR THIS PART **
C                  *******************************
C
              IF(PARTTC.EQ.PRTNBR(I)) THEN
C
                  IF(SUPPLY(I).GE.QUANTY) THEN
C
                      SUPPLY(I)=SUPPLY(I) - QUANTY
                      COST=QUANTY*PRICE(I)
                      PRINT*, 'PRICE=',COST
C
                  ELSE
C
                      PRINT*,'WE CANNOT FILL YOUR ORDER'
C
                  ENDIF
C
C                 ......THIS TRANSACTION COMPLETE......
C
C                 ....ANY MORE OF THESE TRANSACTIONS?...
C
                  SIZE = SIZE - 1
C
                  IF(SIZE.GT.0) READ*, PARTTC, QUANTY
C
              ENDIF
C
   30     CONTINUE
C
          STOP
          END
```

9.3 Various Forms of the Data Base

Figure 9.2 shows some of the many options available for storing data. When only one value is involved, only one memory location is needed, and a simple variable is used. The next option is to link a series of memory locations together, forming a singly subscripted variable. This arrangement of data is graphically depicted as a string to convey its one-dimensional form or layout.

Sometimes an input variable will be basically two-dimensional in form, like these:

1. Depth of water in the area surrounding an off-shore drilling sight.
2. Radiation levels in the vicinity of a nuclear reactor.
3. Distribution of population in a high crime district.

This information (depth, radiation, and population) essentially maps itself on a two-dimensional surface. To represent this input, it is possible to organize a sequence of memory locations as if they were not just one string but a number of strings stacked one on top of the other. This produces a two-dimensional or block effect.

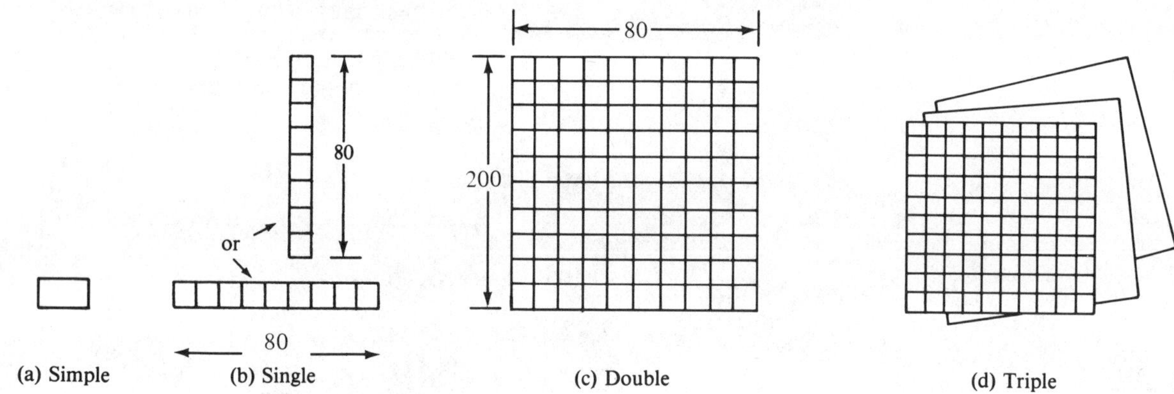

Figure 9.2 Various data forms

Each string becomes one row of the data base that can be identified by a single variable name followed by two subscripts. It is called a **doubly subscripted variable.**

The vast majority of problems do not involve input any more complicated than the forms just described. A program that deals with weather predictions might possibly need to store the three-dimensional temperature and three-dimensional pressure distribution in the atmosphere. Figure 9.2 suggests that this would be like having a number of two-dimensional arrays (blocks) stacked one behind the other like pages in a book. This would involve a subscripted variable having three subscripts.

Which Form Should I Use?

There usually is no difficulty deciding which form is best suited for storing the data associated with a given problem. Let us take a specific example to show how the choice is made. Assume you are going to operate a computer dating service. Each participant is asked to complete an 80-question questionnaire in which each question requires a multiple-choice response of 1 through 9. This generates a data base consisting of 80 separate values, and it is necessary to request 80 integer memory locations to hold the data (see Figure 9.3).

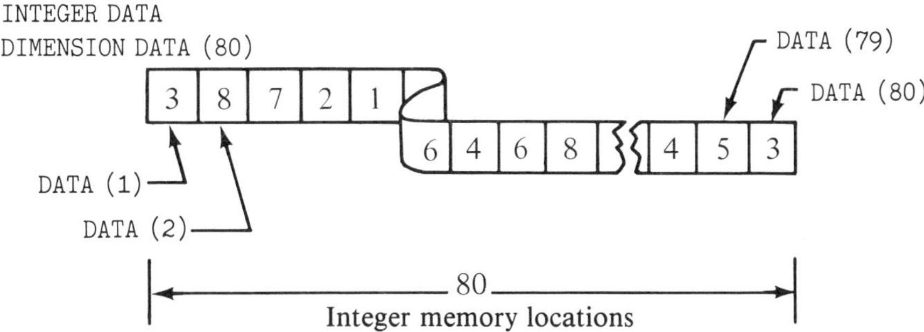

Figure 9.3 Single subscript

Information stored this way is often refered to as a **vector** or a **one-dimensional array** of values.

This form of storage exactly suits the situation and allows the programmer easy control over the data base.

The answer to question 23 is in memory location `DATA(23)`.

The answer to question 48 is in memory location `DATA(48)`.

The answer to question 67 is in memory location `DATA(67)`.

The answer to question 79 is in memory location `DATA(79)`.

To demonstrate the next higher level of data complexity, assume that 200 people have volunteered for the dating service project. The number of data values has just increased:

$$\underbrace{200}_{\text{participants}} \times \underbrace{80}_{\text{questions}} = \underbrace{16{,}000}_{\text{data values}}$$

One solution might be to expand the `DIMENSION` statement to provide additional room for the data, but this will prove to be inconvenient:

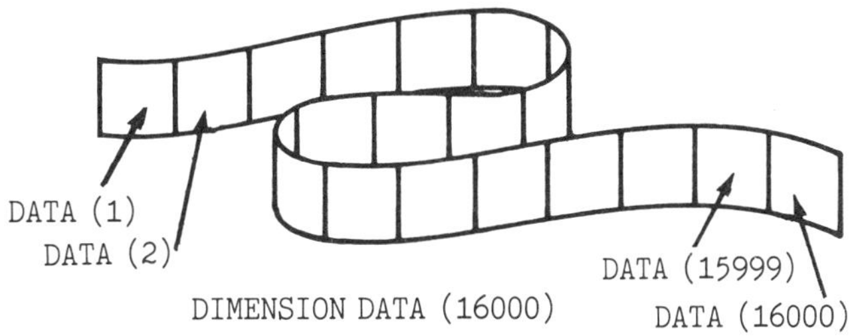

Awkward Representation

If someone asks what is stored in memory location `DATA (79)`, the answer is easy: the response of person 1 to question 79. On the other hand, if someone asks what is in memory location `DATA (1472)`, the answer is less obvious. We need a better way of storing the data.

Assume that the data base represents responses made by females. We would like a string of 80 memory locations to represent the responses given by girl 1, a string of 80 memory locations to represent the responses given by girl 2, and so on, to a string of 80 memory locations to represent the responses given by girl 200. As suggested previously, it is possible to think of each of these 80-location strings as being positioned one on top of the other, forming row after row of values (one for each girl).

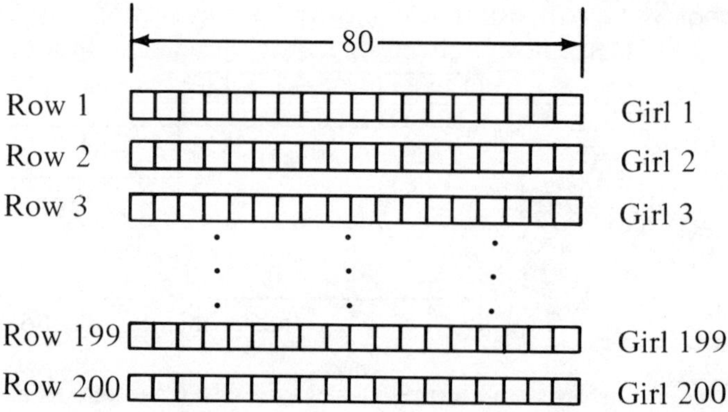

By using a slightly different `DIMENSION` statement:

```
DIMENSION DATA (200, 80)
```

(Double subscript)

we in effect ask that the 16,000 memory locations be broken down into 200 segments or rows, each containing 80 memory locations. Internally the data is in one long string, but you can deal with it just as if it were in block form as shown in Figure 9.4.

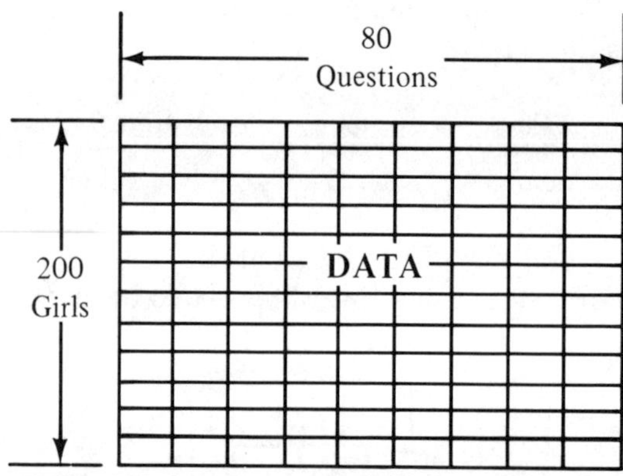

Figure 9.4 Double subpscript

All 16,000 memory locations have the name `DATA`, but individual elements of `DATA` must be qualified by a double subscript:

`DATA (1, 80)`	Answer of girl 1 to question 80
`DATA (16, 5)`	Answer of girl 16 to question 5
`DATA (200, 1)`	Answer of girl 200 to question 1

For reasons to be explained shortly, the first subscript tells which row (girl) gave the response and the second subscript tells which column (question). The important point is that this block or two-dimensional form is a better way of representing the data base and is available in FORTRAN.† Data stored in this way is often called a **matrix** or **two-dimensional array**.

† The FORTRAN '77 standards require the subset language compiler to accommodate one-, two- and three-dimensional arrays. The full language compiler must be able to accommodate arrays with up to seven subscripts.

9.4 Choose the Simplest Form Possible

Always store data in the simplest form possible. Stated another way: don't subscript unless it's absolutely necessary. When you *do* subscript, don't use any more complicated form than necessary. Just because a problem involves a considerable amount of data doesn't mean that subscripting is inevitable. Ask yourself the question, "How much of the data must be in memory at any one time?" The answer to this question decrees to what extent subscripting is necessary. Beginning programmers often get into a lot of trouble because they subscript everything in sight.

If subscripting is required, the next decision is, "Should you use single or double subscripts?" This is usually revealed by the statement of the problem. For example, an airline reservation problem may talk about a data file containing the names of people booked on any one of 147 different flights operated by the company with each flight capable of accommodating up to 216 passengers.

If the problem requires all names to be in memory at once, the choice of a double subscript is obvious. If NAME were other than a CHARACTER variable, we would use a DIMENSION statement such as:

```
DIMENSION NAME(147,216)
```

We can convey the type (character type) and the size of the array NAME in the following CHARACTER statement.

```
CHARACTER NAME(147,216)*20
```

While the size of an array is usually given in a DIMENSION statement, this example shows that a type statement (INTEGER, REAL or CHARACTER) is capable of reserving space in memory for subscripted variables.

```
CHARACTER NAME (147,216)*20
```

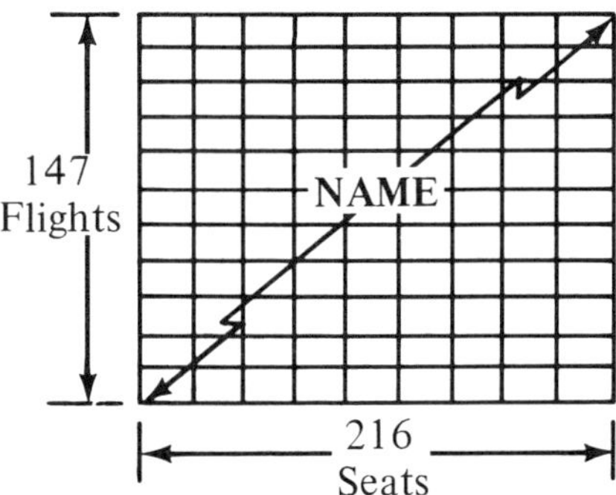

If a careful reading of the problem reveals that all that is wanted is an alphabetical list of the passengers on each flight, all names need not be in memory at any one time (only those associated with a single flight). We can decrease considerably the amount of memory needed.

```
CHARACTER NAME (216)*20
```

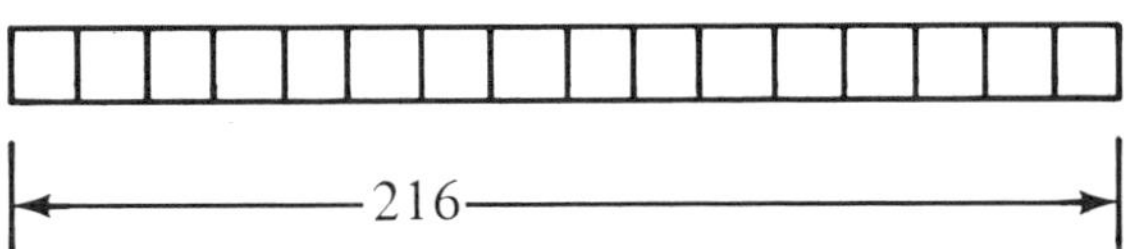

The problem can be solved by reading the names of passengers on flight 1 and sorting them. After printing the output, read and sort the names associated with the next flight. Print these and continue.

9.5 Other Typical Uses

By now, you should begin to recognize the frequency with which subscripted variables are used to represent all but the most trivial problems. To fully appreciate how computers can be used to solve a diverse cross-section of problems, we must consider other more complex applications of subscripted variables.

Returning to the airlines problem, consider all the additional information that might be needed to monitor the scheduling of arrivals and departures of these planes.

Dispatcher's Office

For each of the 147 flights we might need such information as

1. Time of departure
2. Point of departure
3. Time of arrival
4. Destination
5. Pilot's name

SCHEDULING INFORMATION

	TIME	START	ARRIVE	DEST	PILOT
	12:35	BOST	12.58	MAINE	RULE
	6:10	NEW	6:50	BOST	LANG
	9:42	L.A.	11:00	CHIC	BROWN
	21:30	DEN.	23:55	N.J.	JONES
147	16:44	N.Y.	17:30	BOST	HALPIN
	2:00	CHIC	5:15	L.A.	WALK
	7:45	SANF	9:12	PORT	HERTE
	6:18	PORT	10:45	N.Y.	FINK

This scheduling information could be stored as a series of one-dimensional arrays, each 147 long.

```
CHARACTER*20 START(147), DEST(147), PILOT(147)
REAL TIME(147), ARRIVE(147)
```

Control Tower

People in the control tower are faced with a different situation, namely keeping track of all the aircraft stacked up waiting to land and others waiting in line ready to taxi onto the runway. The first plane ready to land might be a 747, American Airlines flight 102. The next plane is Delta flight 16, a DC-10. Each time one of these planes lands or takes off, the information contained in these arrays would have to be "moved up one" to represent the new situation. We will solve this problem later.

	INBOUND		OUTBOUND	
	CARRIER	FLIGHT NO. – TYPE	CARRIER	FLIGHT NO. – TYPE
1	AMERICAN	102-747	WESTERN	224-DC6
2	DELTA	16-DC10	AMERICAN	001-747
3	EASTERN	214-707	ALLEGHENY	194-707
4	PACIFIC	013-DC9	DELTA	613-DC10
5	T.W.A.	102-707	AMERICAN	014-727
6	DELTA	408-747	EXECUTIVE	016-LEAR
7	PAN. AM.	011-727		
8	SWISSAIR	183-747		

Stock Market

Consider all the information associated with monitoring transactions on the stock market. As each stock is traded, the number of shares involved must be added to the previous share traded to determine the total value of sales. The stock's selling price is recorded and then compared to see if that price is higher than it has ever been recently (last 12 months) or lower than it has been recently. At the end of the day these data are summarized to give the total volume of sales, number of new highs, number of new lows, number of gains of the day, and number of losses on this day.

NAME	VOLUME (No. of shares)	HIGH	LOW	LAST
AM. MOT.	13617	44.75	36.10	38.47
ALCOA	491310	25.50	19.25	22.91
BAXTER	1720	87.16	62.30	67.72
DOW CHEM.	61721	27.08	9.41	12.85
•	•	•	•	•
•	•	•	•	•
•	•	•	•	•
•	•	•	•	•
U.S. STEEL	31286	47.25	35.00	39.42
XEROX	1017	60.87	41.93	52.56
ZEBART	391571	8.41	6.37	7.72

Construction

A 25-mile stretch of highway is being planned to connect two points (*A* and *B*) on either side of the mountain. The computer can be used to:

1. Estimate cost of construction.
2. Evaluate different route configurations.
3. Identify dangerous sections of the roadway.

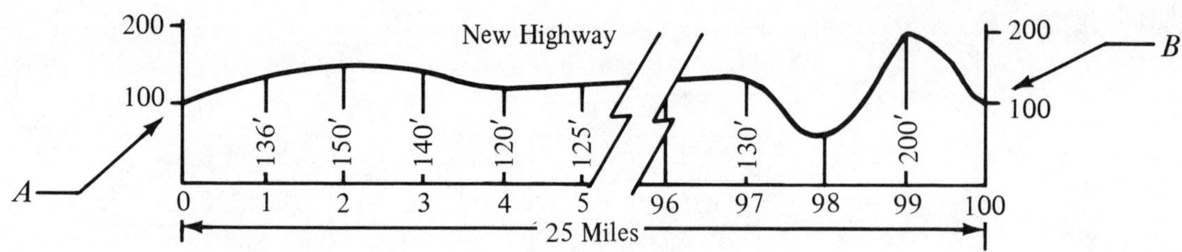

We must somehow "describe" the mountain to the computer. As a start, the elevation of the mountain at 100 equally spaced points between A and B is determined and formed into a one-dimensional array called ELEV.

ELEV

100.0	136.0	150.0	140.0	120.0	125.0	114.0	108.0	115.0	126.0	130.0	89.0	200.0	100.0

Comparing the adjacent elements of this array approximates the slope of the terrain, thereby identifying sections excessively steep.

The computer usually needs a better description of the terrain since the one-dimensional array gives only one profile. A topographic map or aerial photograph could be used. Here we divide the land surface into a large number of equally spaced grid points and determine the elevation at each point in the grid. If the grid spacing is such that there are 100 rows in the grid and 100 columns, we are talking about a two-dimensional array of elevations.

```
DIMENSION ELEV (100,100)
```

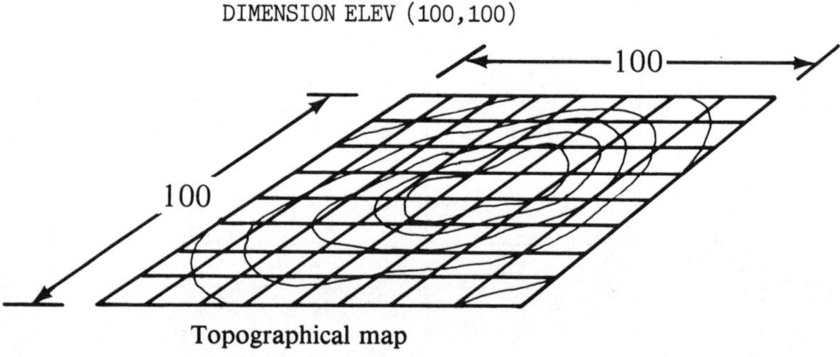

Topographical map

9.6 Input/Output of Arrays

One of the first adjustments you must make in dealing with arrays is the special input/output statements that may be required when transferring the array to and from memory. When the number of elements in the array is relatively small, it is feasible to record these elements one per record in the input file. This allows the old and familiar READ operation shown in the following Method 1 illustration.

Method 1

```
      DO 10 I = 1, 80, 1
         READ*, DATA(I)
   10 CONTINUE
```

More often, however, the sheer size of most arrays force us to pack as many elements as possible on each record of the input file. Take, for example, the

80-question questionnaire we have been talking about. Since each question has a single-integer response, we could get 40 responses on an input record if we decided to use list directed input or we can get all 80 responses on a record if FORMAT controlled input (80I1 code) is used.

Assume we decide to go with FORMAT controlled input. Recognize that the Method 1 READ operation will no longer work. Do you see why? These statements issue the READ instruction 80 times. That would consume 80 input records. Only one value would be taken from each record, namely the first one. All others would be ignored.

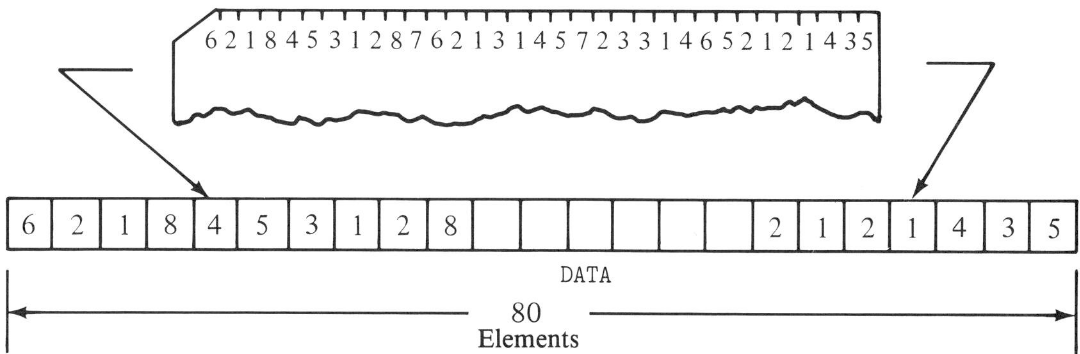

What we need is an input statement that contains a single READ command which is followed by 80 variable names, DATA(1), DATA(2), DATA(3), DATA(4), . . ., DATA(79), DATA(80). This type of READ is provided by the following Method 2 and Method 3 READ statements.

Method 2	**Method 3**
`   READ 30, (DATA(I),I=1,80)` `30 FORMAT (80I1)`	`   READ 30, DATA` `30 FORMAT (80I1)`

Method 3 is the easiest to explain. Normally the name of an array (DATA, for example) should be followed by a subscript to identify which element of the array is being referenced. However, the name of an array may on special occasions appear without a subscript. One of those occasions is in a READ/WRITE operation.

Note: When the name of an array appears in a input/output list without a subscript, the reference is to the *whole* array. This means that the Method 3 READ has in effect 80 names following the READ command.

To understand the Method 2 solution, we must review some of the features associated with the DO statement, namely:

1. Creating an indexing variable name.
2. Setting its initial value.
3. Setting its final value.
4. Controlling the incrementing rate.

```
DO 10 | I = 1, 100, 2   |  <- Index control features
DO 20 | JOB = 2, 20, 1  |
Do 30 | M = 1, 500      |
```

These index control features are allowed in conjunction with statements other than the DO statement. They are allowed in READ/WRITE statements to provide a subscript so that the names DATA(1), DATA(2), DATA(3), . . ., DATA(79), DATA(80), can be expressed in a "shorthand" fashion.

```
READ 30, (DATA(I),I=1,80,1)
                  ↖       ↖
                   Index control feature
```

The preceding single READ command is in effect followed by a list of 80 names. These names are written in a special way. The generalized name DATA(I) is used, which is then followed by those parameters that cause I to cycle from 1 to 80. This feature is called an **implied DO index.**

```
READ 30, (DATA(I),I=1,80)
```

is equivalent to

```
READ 30,DATA(1),DATA(2),DATA(3),DATA(4) . . .
                              DATA(78),DATA(79),DATA(80)
```

This is admittedly a somewhat advanced technique that requires additional explanation. The topic of subscripted variables is being presented in steps. The first step is to learn why and how subscripted variables are used in programming. That step is completed. The next step is to learn how to form READ/WRITE statements for transferring large arrays to and from memory. The next programming examples will concentrate on that one topic only.

9.7 Additional Examples

In a psychological experiment a subject is given a controlled amount of an experimental drug. To determine the effect of that drug, the subject is asked to fire at a moving target and the average error is computed. There will be 1000 shots fired giving X,Y values locating the target and 1000 X,Y values locating the subject's response (4000 values in all). These values can be recorded in the input data file in several alternative ways. Each different arrangement would require a different READ statement. We will examine several of these alternatives and, in so doing, strengthen your understanding of how to input arrays.

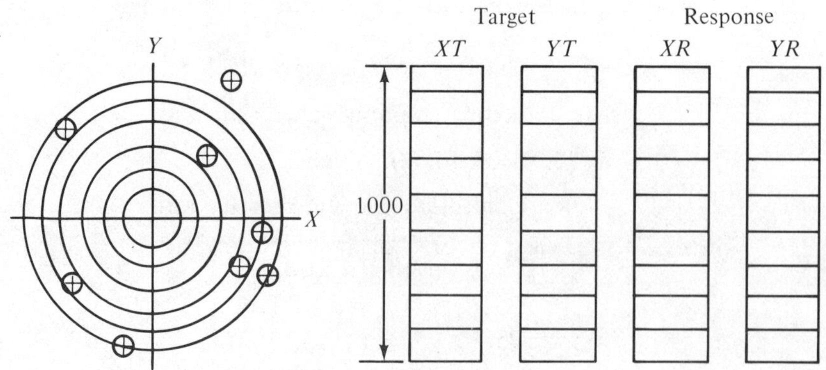

Target Values First

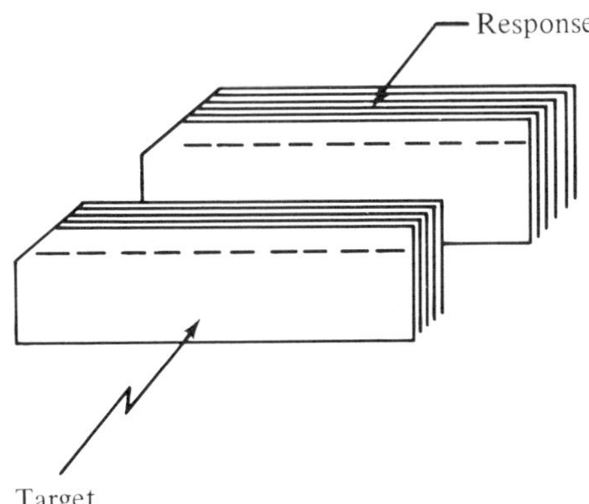

In the first arrangement assume all the target values are presented first, followed by all the subject's response positions. All values are real numbers and we can get 10 values or 5 points defined on each input record. Point 1 is defined first by giving `XT(1)` and `YT(1)`, followed by `XT(2)` and `YT(2)`.

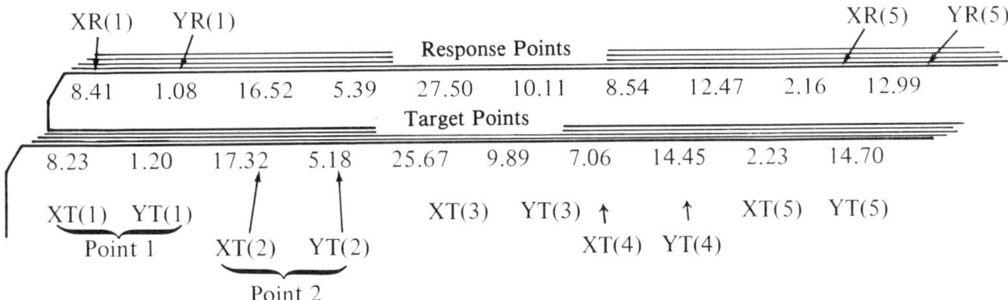

Since each record defines 5 points, it will take 200 records to define the target position, followed by 200 records to define the responses.

You are now faced with the problem of writing `READ` statements that will generate a sequence of variable names that matches the sequence in which the data is being presented. The best approach is to either recite verbally or write out longhand the first and last few names of each sequence needed. To receive the target array, the sequence is:

```
XT(1),YT(1),XT(2),YT(2) . . . XT(999),YT(999),XT(1000),YT(1000)
```

To receive the response array, the sequence is:

```
XR(1),YR(1),XR(2),YR(2) . . . YR(999),YR(999),XR(1000),YR(1000)
```

To generate the same sequence of names, but in shorthand fashion, you merely resort to the use of an index inside a `READ` statement as follows:

```
READ*, (XT(I),YT(I), I = 1, 1000)
READ*, (XR(I),YR(I), I = 1, 1000)
```

This procedure is worth reviewing because it represents an orderly way in which `READ/WRITE` statements can be written to transfer large data bases to and from memory.

1. Examine the deck and see in what sequence the individual values are being presented.
2. Either recite verbally or write out longhand enough of the variable names required so that the pattern or sequence is well defined.
3. Duplicate this sequence by writing the names in a general form (one that references an INDEX).
4. Control the INDEX to cycle through the appropriate range of values.

To show how efficient this operation can be, the whole data base could be read by a single READ statement as follows:

```
READ*, (XT(I),YT(I), I = 1, 1000), (XR(I),YR(I), I = 1, 1000)
```

This statement shows that it is possible to reset the index whenever it is necessary to start a new list of names. This particular READ statement is the equivalent of the READ command followed by 4000 names.

Alternating Values

Another possible arrangement of data is to present a target position, followed by a response position, followed by a target position, and so on.

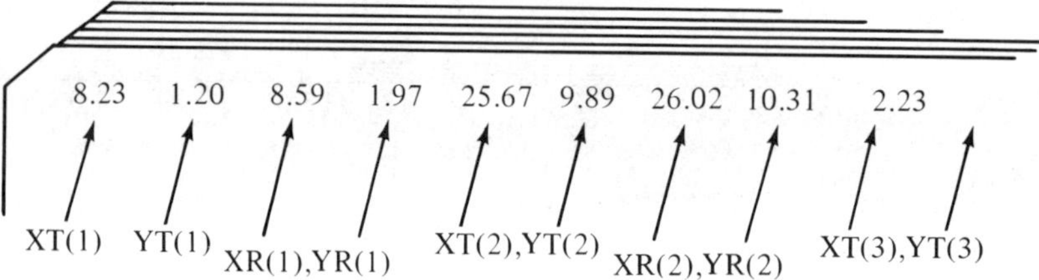

The sequence of names needed to process this arrangement of data is:

```
XT(1),YT(1),XR(1),YR(1),XT(2),YT(2),XR(2) . . .
                    XT(999),YT(999),XR(999),YR(999)XT(1000),YT(1000),
                         XR(1000),YR(1000)
```

The corresponding READ statement would be:

```
READ*, (XT(I),YT(I),XR(I),YR(I), I = 1, 1000)
```

9.8 Reading Two-Dimensional Arrays

The process of reading a two-dimensional array is basically the same except that two subscripts are involved. What is the best way of representing these three simultaneous equations?

Equation 1: $9.0X_1 + 6.5X_2 + 3.5X_3 = 27.75$

Equation 2: $4.5X_1 + 2.2X_2 + 1.5X_3 = 10.50$

Equation 3: $6.7X_1 + 3.0X_2 + 1.0X_3 = 12.25$

Note that the coefficients preceding each X term are just naturally distributed in a two-dimensional fashion. The statement:

```
DIMENSION A(3,3)
```

gives these coefficients the common name A and allows individual elements of A to be addressed by a double subscript.

The only remaining values needed to define these equations are the three right-hand constants. The statement:

```
DIMENSION C(3)
```

sets up a one-dimensional array called C to store these values.

Array [A]	Array {C}
column ↓ $\begin{bmatrix} A_{11} & A_{12} & A_{13} \\ A_{21} & A_{22} & A_{23} \\ A_{31} & A_{32} & A_{33} \end{bmatrix}$ ←row	$\begin{bmatrix} C_1 \\ C_2 \\ C_3 \end{bmatrix}$
$\begin{bmatrix} 9.0 & 6.5 & 3.5 \\ 4.5 & 2.2 & 1.5 \\ 6.7 & 3.0 & 1.0 \end{bmatrix}$	$\begin{bmatrix} 27.75 \\ 10.50 \\ 12.25 \end{bmatrix}$

When dealing with a two-dimensional array, the first subscript tells what *row* the element is in; the second subscript gives the *column* position.

$A_{2,3}$

Column position

Row position

Applying this notation to our simultaneous equations, the preceding element is in Equation 2. It is the coefficient preceding X_3. Double subscripts allow the programmer an easy way to deal with a two-dimensional data base. For example, assume you are asked to print out the terms associated with Equation 3. The appropriate WRITE statement would be:

```
WRITE(2,*)A(3,1),A(3,2),A(3,3),C(3)
```

If you were told to multiply each term in Equation 2 by 6.7, the statements would be:

```
      DO 7 I=1,3
         A(2,I)=6.7*A(2,I)
    7 CONTINUE
      C(2)=C(2)*6.7
```

The point being made is that dealing with a doubly subscripted variable is really not that difficult.

Forming Arrays

Assume the original set of three equations is represented in the data file as suggested in Figure 9.5(a).

Figure 9.5

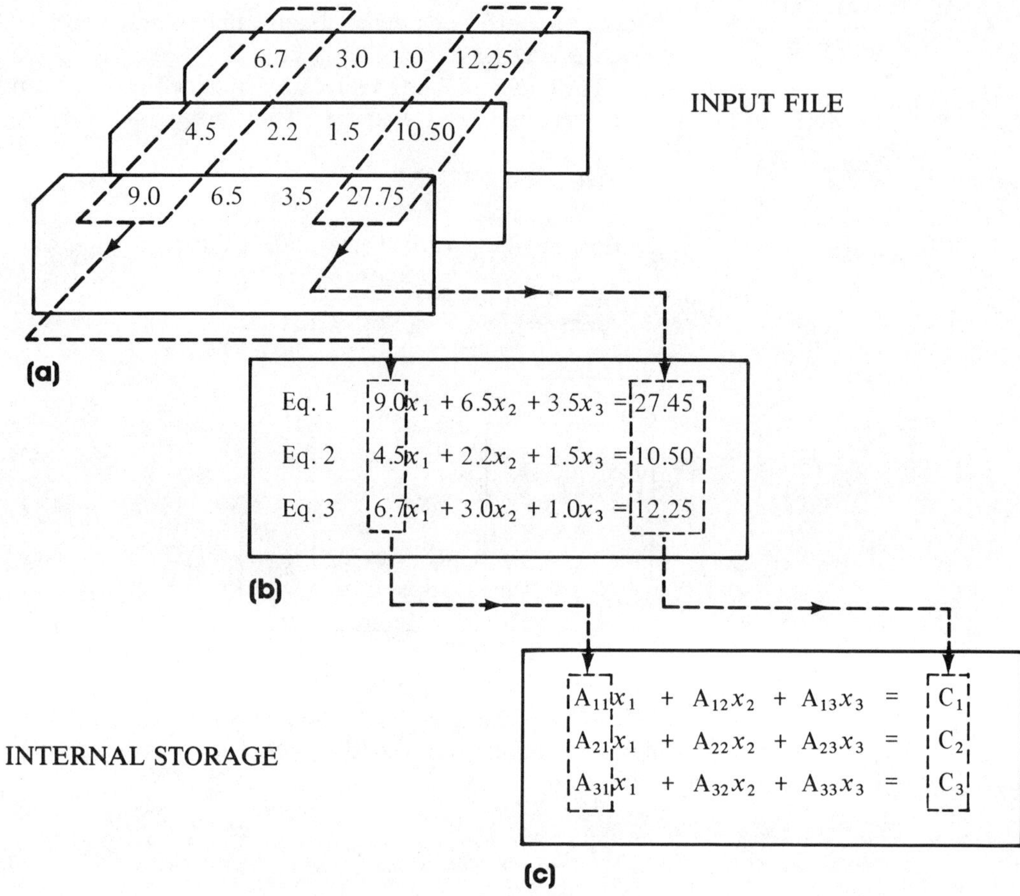

Each record represents one equation by giving the coefficients of X_1, X_2, and X_3, and the constant C in that order. Write a program to read these records and form the array A and the array C in memory. The READ command will be executed three times to process the file. On each execution, we are back to the same old problem: defining a sequence of variable names to match the sequence of values in the input data file.

```
      DIMENSION A(3,3), C(3)
C
C                ESRABLISH LOOP TO READ THREE RECORDS
C
      DO 10 I = 1, 3, 1
C
         READ*, A(I,1), A(I,2), A(I,3), C(I)
C
   10 CONTINUE
C
      WRITE(2,*) A(1,3), A(3,2), A(2,1), C(2)
C
```

Consider the position of the preceding READ statement. It is inside a DO loop whose index is I. The READ command is executed three times in rapid succession. On the first execution, I has the value 1. The names in the list of the READ statement are interpreted as A(1,1), A(1,2), A(1,3), and C(1).

Note: When a subscript appears other than as an integer constant, A(I,1) for example, the subscript is evaluated before the name is read. That is, the element of A we are reading is A(1,1), A(2,1) or A(3,1), depending on the value of I. The names

A(I,J) and A(L,M) may be identical names referring to the same element. This is true when:

1. I has the same value as L.
2. J has the same value as M.

Returning to the READ statement in the DO loop, on the second execution of the loop I equals 2 and the names in the list of the READ statement are identified as A(2,1), A(2,2), A(2,3), and C(2).

The WRITE statement is used to sample elements of A and C to randomly check the proper storage of the two arrays. Finally, the first statement of this program is a DIMENSION statement needed because A and C are arrays.

9.9 Arrays in FORTRAN

Arrays are groups of related numbers. In math/science applications, an array contains a group of real numbers or a group of integer numbers but usually not a mixture of each. The mode of these numbers is reflected by the array name. To name the array we follow the same rules for naming a nonsubscripted variable. This name is followed by a pair of parentheses enclosing the subscripts. A one-dimensional array requires a single subscript. Two- and three-dimensional arrays require multiple subscripts separated by commas. You will usually find it convenient to express a subscript as either a simple integer constant or an integer variable. Occasionally, however, a subscript may take on a slightly more complex form, namely an integer mode arithmetic expression such as:

```
A ( I + 2)  or  A ( 2 * I - 6 )
```

Integer expression

Some compilers restrict the complexity of the expression used to define a subscript. The permitted forms are shown in the following table. The FORTRAN '77 standards are much more permissive and allow almost any form of expression including array elements and function references.

Possible Subscript Restrictions

Subscript Form	General Form	Example
Constant	(C)	A(6)
Variable	(V)	A(I)
Expression		
Variable plus a constant	(V+C)	A(I+6)
Variable minus a constant	(V−C)	A(I−6)
Constant times a variable	(C*V)	A(6*I)
Constant times a variable plus a second constant	(C*V+D)	A(6*I+2)
Constant times a variable minus a second constant	(C*V−D)	A(6*I−2)

When dealing with a subscripted variable, the value of a subscript is usually a positive, nonzero value. Zero and negative subscripts are not very common. The new standards make it possible to have subscripts of this form, but such usage will not be shown in this text.

9.10 The DIMENSION Statement

Whenever a program uses a subscripted variable, the compiler must be informed through the use of one or more DIMENSION statements. A DIMENSION statement must appear at the very beginning of the program, usually before the first executable statement. It directs the computer to allocate sufficient memory space for the storage of all arrays by providing the following information:

1. The names of variables to be subscripted.
2. The number of subscripts each will have.
3. The guaranteed maximum value of each subscript.

Consider the following DIMENSION statement:

```
DIMENSION A(10,12),B(10),X(12,25)
```

This statement informs the computer that:

1. A,B, and X are subscripted variables.
2. B is declared as a one-dimensional array, whereas A and X are two-dimensional arrays.
3. Array B has 10 possible elements, requiring 10 positions in memory to store this array.
4. Array A may have up to 10 rows and 12 columns, requiring 120 positions in memory to store this array.
5. Array X has a maximum of 12 rows and 25 columns, requiring 300 positions in memory to store this array.

As a consequence of this DIMENSION statement, 430 memory locations are set aside to store these arrays.

Caution: Whenever a subscripted variable appears in a program, the value of its subscript must not exceed that given in the DIMENSION statement; the DIMENSION statement expresses a guarantee on the maximum values of all subscripts in the program.

The following table shows other DIMENSION statements and indicates the information they convey.

Sample DIMENSION Statements

Statement	Meaning
DIMENSION NUM(9,5),A(8)	NUM is a two-dimensional array of integer numbers. A is a one-dimensional array consisting of up to 8 real numbers.
DIMENSION X(25), Y(25), Z(25),I(50)	X, Y, Z, and I are one-dimensional arrays; I is an integer array; 125 positions in memory are needed to store these arrays. The subscripts of arrays X, Y, and Z may not exceed 25. I's subscripts may not exceed 50.
DIMENSION M(6, 10, 4)	M is a three-dimensional array. It consists of 4 planes. Each plane holds a 6 x 10 group of numbers (6 rows and 10 columns).

Type statements discussed in Chapter 3 may also serve the same purpose as a DIMENSION statement. For example, the statement:

```
REAL ITEM (100)
```

accomplishes two actions: it declares ITEM to be a real name, and it sets up 100 memory locations for this variable, that is, makes ITEM a one-dimensional array of 100 elements.

The value expressing the size of an array in a DIMENSION statement must be an *integer constant:*

```
DIMENSION A (10,3) , C(100)
              ↑          ↑
              └─ Integer ─┘
                 constant
                   only
```

Variables or expressions are *not* allowed. The reason for this is that the array size is needed during the compiling of the program (to control how much memory is to be allocated for each array). At compiling time, the computer can translate an expression, but it cannot *evaluate* the expression. Evaluation is possible only when the program is executed. *The subscripts appearing in the main program should not exceed the value declared in the* DIMENSION *statement.*

The storing of arrays consumes vital memory space, and care must be exercised not to exceed available memory capacity.

Once an array has been identified in a DIMENSION statement as a one-, two-, or three-dimensional array, all other reference to this array must be consistent. If an array is declared to be a two-dimensional array in a DIMENSION statement and later in the main program the array is referred to as a one-dimensional array, an error will result.

9.11 Nonexecutable Statements

Most FORTRAN statements are called executable because they cause the activation of one or more hardware components. A limited number of statements are more passive in nature. They belong to the specification group described in Chapter 1. These statements supply supportive information needed by the compiler to effectively translate the executable statement. This usually means providing bookkeeping details such as how to interpret the various columns on a data card or how much room is needed to hold variables other than simple variables.

Type statements (INTEGER, REAL) and the DIMENSION and FORMAT statements fall into this nonexecutable classification. A complete list of nonexecutable statements is given in Appendix D.

Quiz 16
Subscripting a Variable

Part 1: Answer the following questions.

1. Correct the statement: It makes no difference if you store an array as a one-, two-, or three-dimensional array; they are all just as easy to work with.
2. How many rows are there in the array ITEM:

```
DIMENSION ITEM (100,50)
```

3. When reading arrays with many elements, the list of names is often written with an implied DO index. Give an example.
4. May a Type statement (REAL or INTEGER) be used to reserve space in memory for an array?
5. What is wrong with the following statements:

```
   DO 20 I=1,100
   READ(5,10)X(I)
10 FORMAT(10F8.2)
20 CONTINUE
```

6. What is wrong with the following DIMENSION statement:

```
DIMENSION X(N,M)
```

7. Define a nonexecutable statement.
8. What must the DIMENSION statement look like if the size of an array A varies as follows:

   a. Sometimes there are 60 elements.
   b. Sometimes there are only 10 elements.
   c. Once in a while there are 120 elements.

9. Is it possible for these two elements of the array A to be the same?

```
A(M)      A(N)
```

10. What is wrong with the following statements?

```
DIMENSION A(200)
READ*, (A(I),I=1,300)
```

Part 2: Writing a Program

11. The price of 200 stocks at the beginning and end of a report period are listed as shown.

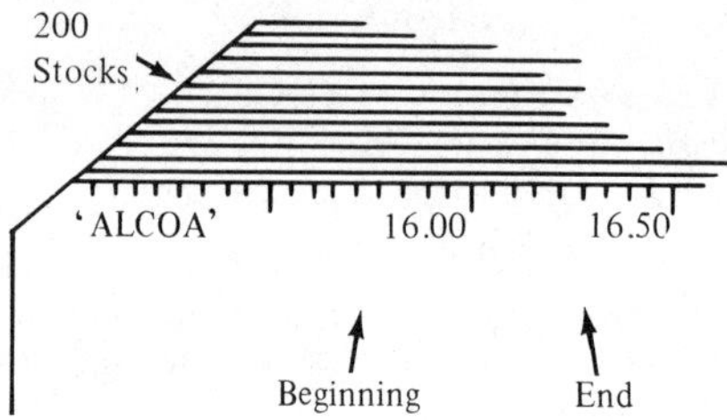

   a. Provide a list of all stocks that increased 10% or more in value.
   b. Provide a list of all stocks that decreased 10% or more in value.

9.12 Some Practice with Subscripted Variables

The next step in dealing with subscripted variables is to perform basic mathematical operations with them. This usually means setting up a loop structure in which each element of a data base contributes some small value toward the final solution.

Programming Example
Locating the Center of Gravity

A missile has 1000 component parts. Each part is identified by a record giving part weight (W_n) and part location (X_n) from the tip of the missile.

Write a program to read 1000 records and form a one-dimensional array called W and a one-dimensional array called X, each containing 1000 elements.

When the arrays are formed, write a program to determine the total weight of the missile:

$$\text{Weight} = W_1 + W_2 + W_3 + W_4 + \cdots + W_{998} + W_{999} + W_{1000} = \Sigma W$$

Programming Example–Locating the Center of Gravity continued

Next, multiply each weight by the corresponding value of X to determine the individual moments (force times distance) each weight imposes on the missile.

$$\text{Moment} = W_1X_1 + W_2X_2 + W_3X_3 + \cdots + W_{999}X_{999} + W_{1000}X_{1000} = \Sigma WX$$

Finally, divide the total moment by the total weight and determine the location of the center of gravity of the missile.

$$\text{Center of Gravity} = \frac{W_1X_1 + W_2X_2 + W_3X_3 + \cdots + W_{1000}X_{1000}}{W_1 + W_2 + W_3 + \cdots + W_{1000}} = \frac{\Sigma WX}{\Sigma W}$$

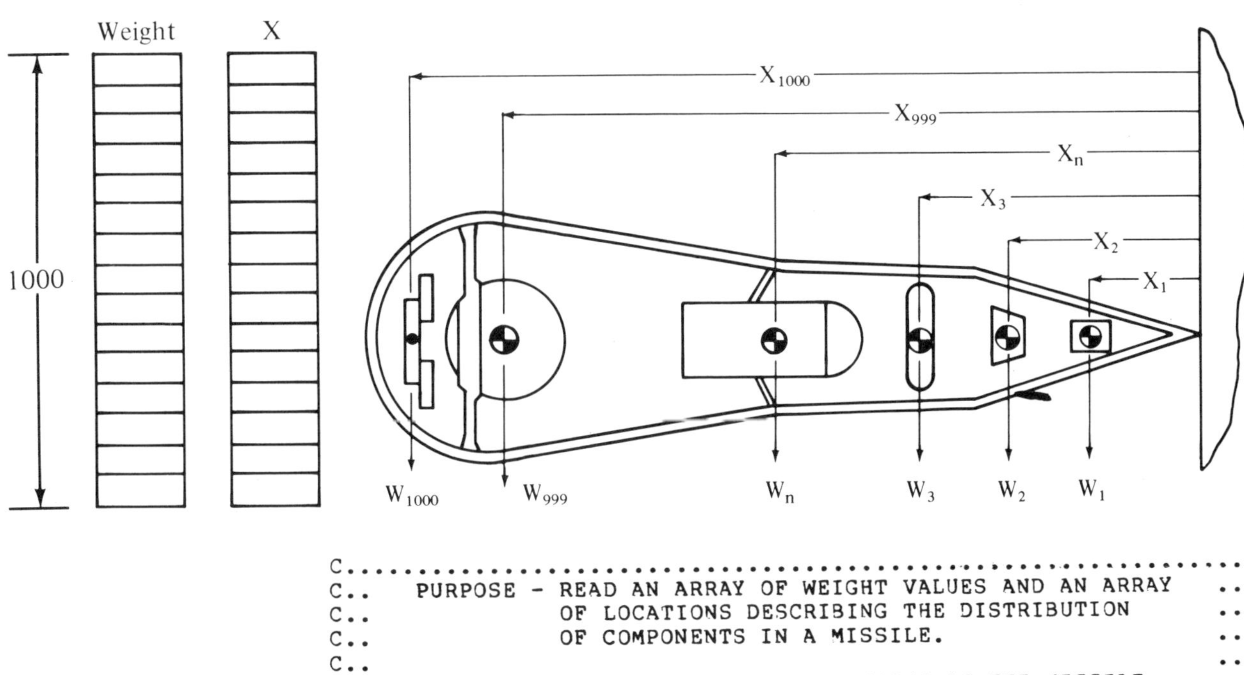


```
C...................................................................
C..    PURPOSE - READ AN ARRAY OF WEIGHT VALUES AND AN ARRAY      ..
C..              OF LOCATIONS DESCRIBING THE DISTRIBUTION         ..
C..              OF COMPONENTS IN A MISSILE.                      ..
C..                                                               ..
C..              DETERMINE THE TOTAL WEIGHT OF THE MISSILE        ..
C..              AND THE LOCATION OF ITS CENTER OF GRAVITY.       ..
C...................................................................
C
C               ---IMPORTANT VARIABLES---
C
C      --WEIGHT   ARRAY OF COMPONENT WEIGHT (LBS)                 --
C      --X        ARRAY OF COMPONENT LOCATIONS (IN.)              --
C      --SUMW     ACCUMULATOR (TOTAL WEIGHT)                      --
C      --SUMM     ACCUMULATOR (TOTAL MOMENT)                      --
C      --CG       SIMPLE VARIABLE TELLING LOCATION OF THE
C                 CENTER OF GRAVITY.                              --
C
C      .....RESERVE ROOM IN MEMORY FOR THE TWO ARRAYS.....
C
       INTEGER I
       REAL    WEIGHT(1000), X(1000), SUMW, SUMM, CG
C
       DO 10 I= 1, 1000
          READ *,WEIGHT(I),X(I)
   10  CONTINUE
C
C      .....INITIALIZE VALUE OF TWO ACCUMULATORS.....
C
       SUMW = 0.0
       SUMM = 0.0
```

Programming Example–Locating the Center of Gravity continued

```
C
C       .....LOOP ENTRY POINT.....
C
        DO 20 I = 1, 1000
C
            SUMW = SUMW + WEIGHT(I)
            SUMM = SUMM + WEIGHT(I)  * X(I)
C
   20   CONTINUE
C
        CG = SUMM /SUMW
C
        PRINT *, 'THE TOTAL WEIGHT =',SUMW,'CENTER OF GRAVITY =',CG
C
        STOP
        END
```

Programming Example
Move Up One

A one-dimensional array called LAND has 20 elements and represents the landing sequence at a busy airport. Each element uses a six-character alphanumeric symbol to represent the airline and flight number of each aircraft in the landing pattern.

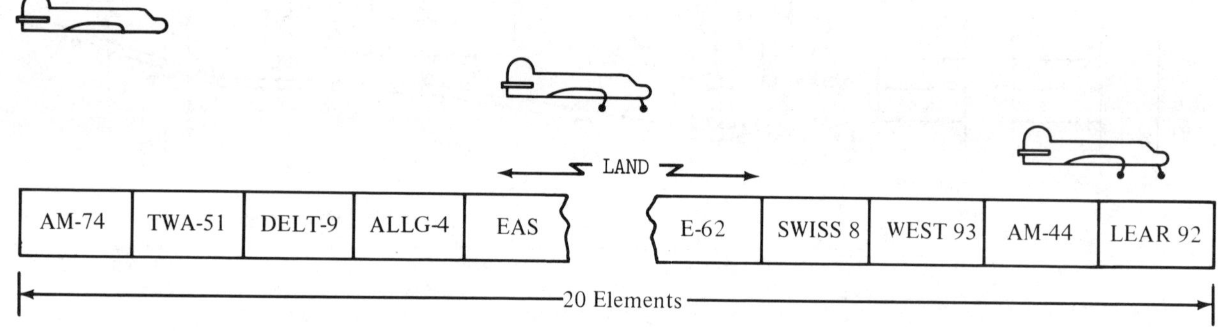

Part A (Read In): Write statements to READ the elements of this array from a data file (one element per record) and form the array LAND. Display this waiting list as suggested in the following illustration. Note that two aircraft are given per line of output. On line 1 are aircraft 1 and 11; on the next line are aircraft 2 and 12.

WAITING LIST

NO.	SYMBOL	NO.	SYMBOL
1	AM-74	11	SWISS2
2	TWA-51	12	DELT63
3	DELT-9	13	LEAR15
4	ALLG-4	14	AM-49
9	TWA-08	19	AM-44
10	EXEC15	20	LEAR92

Programming Example–Example Up One continued

```
C...............................................................
C..   PURPOSE - READ A ONE DIMENSIONAL ARRAY REPRESENTING     ..
C..             LANDING AIRCRAFT - DISPLAY AS REQUESTED.      ..
C...............................................................
C
C                 ---IMPORTANT VARIABLES---
C
C     --LAND      ARRAY OF CODED INFORMATION                  --
C     --I         SUBSCRIPT OF LEFT HAND COLUMN               --
C     --M         SUBSCRIPT OF RIGHT HAND COLUMN              --
C
      CHARACTER LAND(20)*8, NEXT
      INTEGER   I, M
C
C     .....READ ALL ARRAYS INTO MEMORY.....
C
      READ *, (LAND(I), I = 1, 20)
C
C     .....MOVE TO TOP OF PAGE.....
C
      PRINT 20
   20 FORMAT ('1',40X,'WAITING LIST')
C
C     .....PRINT COLUMN HEADINGS.....
C
      PRINT 30
   30 FORMAT ('   NO.      SYMBOL      NO.      SYMBOL')
C
C     .....DISPLAY ELEMENTS OF ARRAY.....
C
      DO 50 I = 1, 10
C
          M = I + 10
          PRINT *, I, LAND(I), M, LAND(M)
C
   50 CONTINUE
```

Part B (Move Elements): Write statements to advance each element of the array up one position (a plane has landed). Read the next record (record 21) from the input file and place that symbol in the last position of array LAND.

```
C
C...........................................................
C..   PURPOSE - MOVE EACH ELEMENT UP ONE . FILL LAST      ..
C..             ELEMENT WITH THE NEW AIRCRAFT WAITING.    ..
C...........................................................
C
C                 ---IMPORTANT VARIABLES---
C
C     --NEXT      SIMPLE VARIABLE- NEXT AIRCRAFT IN LINE  --
C
C     .....MOVE EACH ELEMENT UP ONE POSITION.....
C
      DO 60 I =1, 19
          LAND(I) = LAND(I+1)
   60 CONTINUE
C
C     .....READ AIRCRAFT TO BE ADDED TO LIST.....
C
      READ*, NEXT
C
C     .....ADD TO END OF LIST.....
C
      LAND(20) = NEXT
C
      STOP
      END
```

Review Exercises

★ 1. The simplest way in which information can be stored is as a simple variable. In order of complexity, describe the other alternative ways of storing information.

2. What does the term "vector" mean?

3. When a variable is doubly subscripted, it is considered as having a number of rows and a number of columns. Which subscript, first or second, provides the row descriptor?

★ 4. The following DO loop defines a one-dimensional array called X having 400 elements:

```
    DO 20 I=1,400
       READ*,X(I)
20 CONTINUE
```

Write a READ statement that uses an implied DO index that is the equivalent of the preceding statements.

5. Write statements that will define a matrix of size 10 by 10, each element having a value equal to the sum of its row and column position.

★ 6. What is the error in the following statements?

```
M=6
N=4
DIMENSION ARRAY(M,N)
```

7. Describe the allocation of memory associated with the following DIMENSION statement:

```
DIMENSION A(10,10),B(200),C(6)
```

8. Provide the definition of a problem that requires the use of a one-dimensional array called NAME and a one-dimensional array called AMOUNT.

9. What is wrong with the following statements?

```
REAL X(200),Y(200)
INTEGER NUMBER(50)
DIMENSION X(20,40)
```

10. What does the term "nonexecutable statement" mean? Give several examples.

11. Twenty values of X are given on a single input record. Read this array of X values and determine the sum of the even elements and the sum of the odd elements of the array.

6.7 10.1 19.3 4.2 1.6 -8.7 9.4 6.2 −1.5

Array *X*

6.7	10.1	19.3	4.2	1	7	9.4	8.7	6.2	-1.5

20 Elements

12. A data file consists of three records similar to the record described in exercise 11.

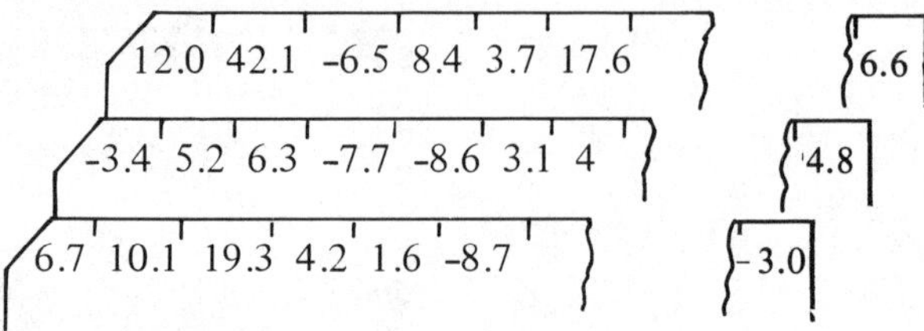

Use these records to define three arrays called X1, X2, and X3. Now define an array called BIG, each element of which is the largest of the corresponding elements of X1, X2, and X3.

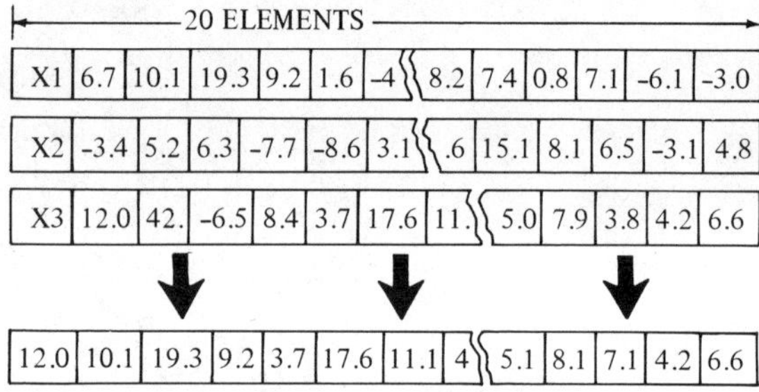

★ 13. Determine the average value of each of the arrays in exercise 12 (arrays X1, X2, and X3). Now report how much each element of an array is above or below this average value.

14. The shape of a turbine shaft is defined by an array of X values and an array of R values. The shaft is considered to be a connected series of cylinders where each R value defines the radius of a cylinder and each X value defines its height or thickness.

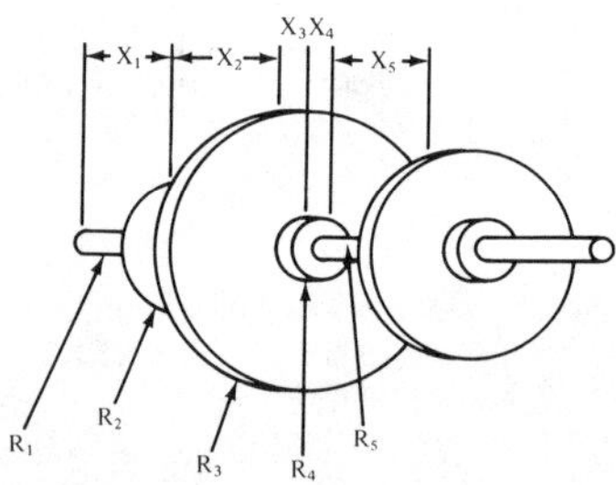

If each array contains 200 elements and the shaft is made of steel (density = 0.3 lb/in^3), determine the weight of the shaft.

15. Repeat exercise 14 except that the number of elements in each array is a number N, which is less than 200. The value of N is given by a lead record as shown. Determine the weight and center of gravity of the shaft.

★ 16. An array called X has 100 elements that are in ascending order of magnitude. Define an array Y whose elements are the same as the elements of X except in descending order. Y(1) will have the value of X(100), Y(2) will have the value of X(99), and so on.

17. The name, gross income, and federal taxes paid of 1000 suspected tax evaders are stored as three one-dimensional arrays as shown.

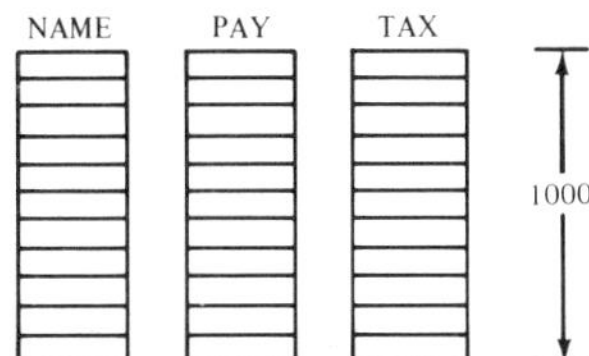

Determine what percentage of this group earned over $80,000 and paid less than $1,000 in taxes.

18. Expand the analysis of the data described in exercise 17 to provide the following information:

	Tax paid				
	No tax paid	>$500	>$1000	>$2000	>$3000
Earned over → $80,000					

19. The equation:

$$y = x^5 - 3x^3 + 6x - 1$$

is to be analyzed between $X = X_{initial}$ and $X = X_{last}$. Write a program to evaluate the equation at 100 equally spaced points between these limits of X (to be read from data).

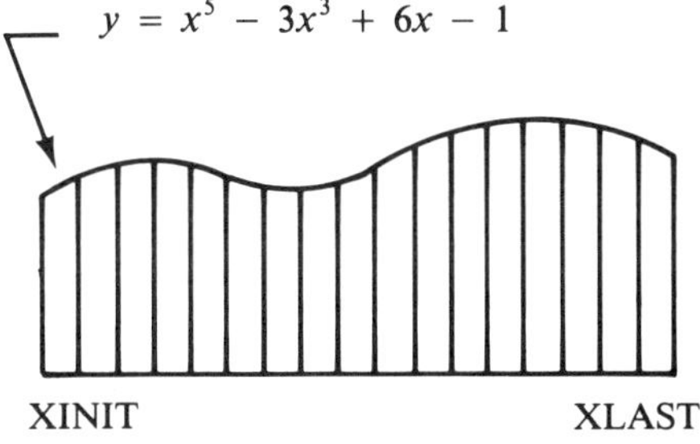

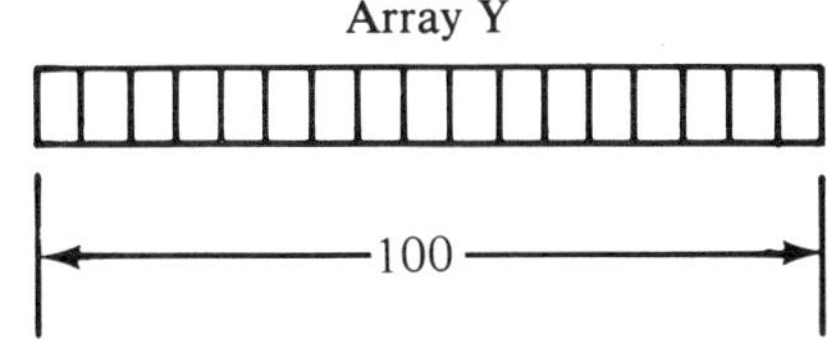

Each value of Y thus obtained is to form an element of a one-dimensional array to be called Y.

★ 20. An array called X has 100 elements which are in ascending order of magnitude. Values of X are given 10 values per input record. Read this array and then *remove element 50*, that is, the element that was in position 51 should now be in position 50, the element in position 52 should be in position 51, and so on.

21. Repeat exercise 20 except that an element is to be *added* to the array called X. Read this additional element from input. Locate where in the array this element belongs. Starting at the end of the array, move elements up one position to make room for this new element. Finally, position the new element in the array and print the array.

22. The government monitors the price of 200 food items on a month-to-month basis. The array called START gives the cost of each item at the beginning of the year. Arrays PRICE1, PRICE2, and PRICE3 give the price of these items at the end of the first, second, and third months of the year.

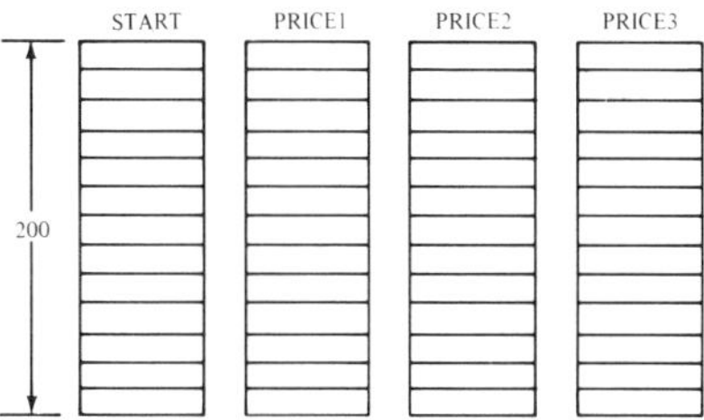

a. How many items increased in cost for three consecutive months?
b. How many items sold for less in the third month than they did at the beginning of the year?
c. Determine the average increase in the cost of food during month 1, month 2, and month 3.

23. An array called X has 100 elements (10 rows and 10 columns) and represents the radiation level surrounding a nuclear power plant. Values of X appear in a data file, one per record in row order.

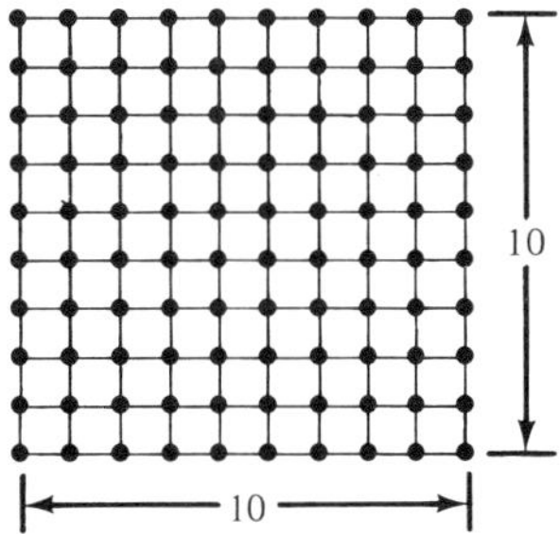

a. Determine the average radiation level around the perimeter of the plant.
b. Determine the average level inside the perimeter.

24. The elements of X in exercise 23 are divided into four quadrants as shown.

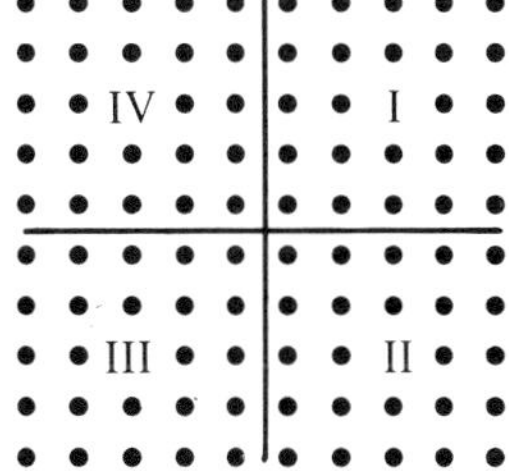

Determine the average radiation level in each quadrant.

★ 25. LIST1 and LIST2 are both arrays of integer numbers. Determine if any number in LIST1 also appears in LIST2.

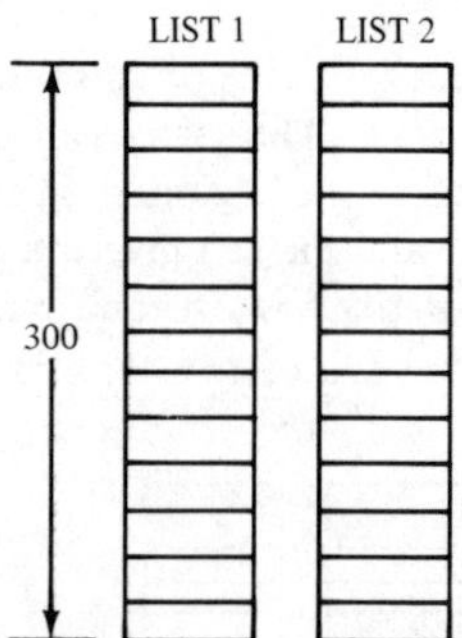

Determine if the first number in LIST1 appears anywhere in LIST2. Output should be the message:

or the message:

26. Repeat the search accomplished in exercise 25 for each element in LIST1.

27. An array called CARS has 5 rows and 5 columns and is used to keep track of the number of police cars in various sectors of a large metropolitan city.

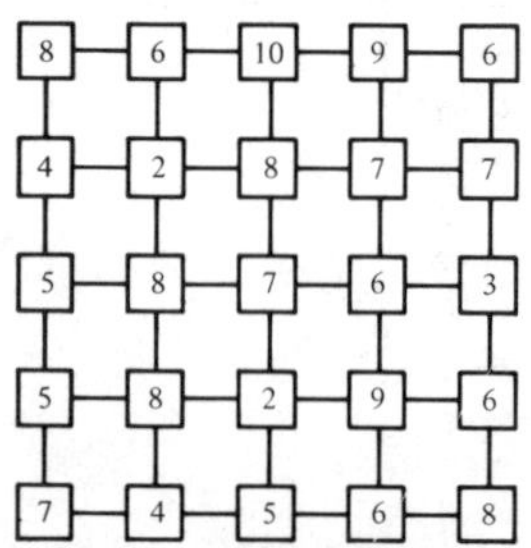

Design an algorithm to account for a car leaving one sector and entering another.

28. For the array shown in exercise 27, design an algorithm to tell how many cars are in a given sector and all the sectors immediately adjacent to this sector.

29. A parcel of land 150 ft. by 100 ft. is divided into 10 ft. squares, and the elevation (above sea level) of each square is determined. Use these elevations to form a two-dimensional array called A. Values of A are given in a data file, one value per record in row order.

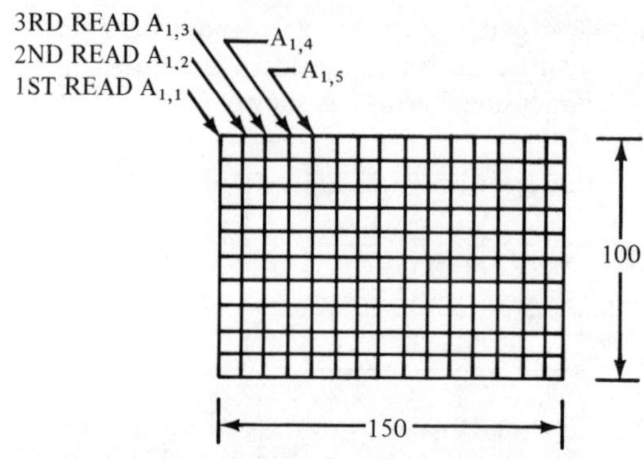

30. After forming the array A in exercise 29, determine the average elevation of the land.

31. By comparing adjacent elements of array A in exercise 29, it is possible to determine the local slope of the ground. Write a program to determine the maximum grade or slope of the land. (This is a reasonably difficult program for a beginner to write.)

32. Arrays A and B are both two-dimensional, having 9 rows and 10 columns. Assume these arrays have already been read from data. Write a program to compare each element of A with the corresponding element of B and print the larger of the two elements.

★ 33. Repeat exercise 32, but use the larger of the two corresponding elements to form an element of an array to be called C. Array C will be the same size as A or B, and each element of C will be equal to or greater than the corresponding element in A or B.

★ 34. A two-dimensional array called M is to have 10 rows and 10 columns. All elements of M have the value 0, except those on the "main diagonal." Elements of the main diagonal are those whose row and column numbers are identical. These elements are each to have value 1. Write a program to form this array. Values of M are *not* to be read from data.

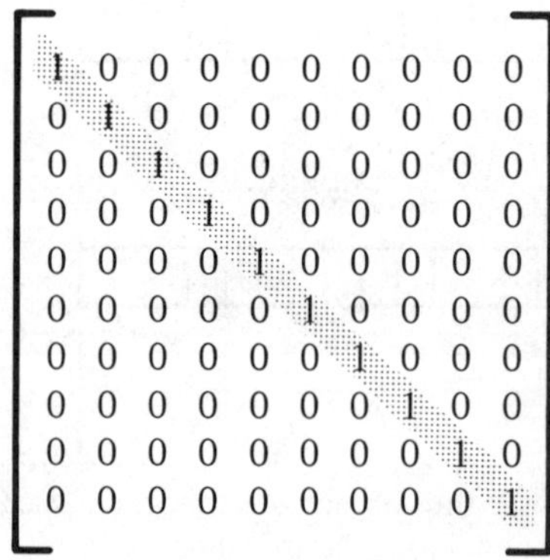

Additional Applications

Programming Example
Cargo Loading

Each record of a data file describes a piece of cargo to be loaded on a plane. The first two numbers on each record indicate the weight of the item and the number of the cargo bay (1, 2, or 3) it has been assigned to. Write a program to determine how many pieces of cargo are represented in the file and the total weight of this cargo. Also compute the weight of cargo in each of the three cargo bays.

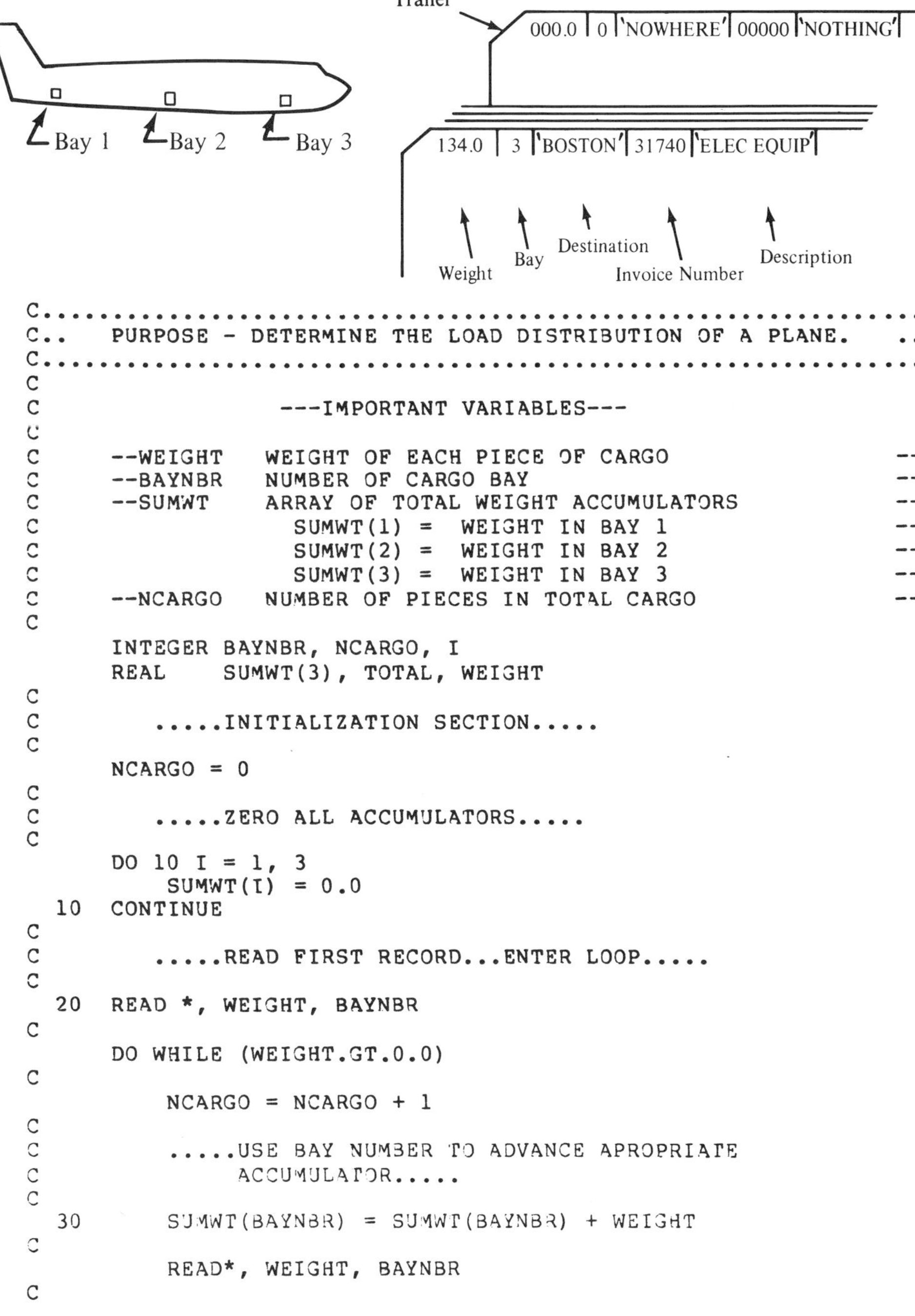


```
C.................................................................
C..    PURPOSE - DETERMINE THE LOAD DISTRIBUTION OF A PLANE.    ..
C.................................................................
C
C                  ---IMPORTANT VARIABLES---
C
C      --WEIGHT    WEIGHT OF EACH PIECE OF CARGO                  --
C      --BAYNBR    NUMBER OF CARGO BAY                            --
C      --SUMWT     ARRAY OF TOTAL WEIGHT ACCUMULATORS             --
C                    SUMWT(1) =  WEIGHT IN BAY 1                  --
C                    SUMWT(2) =  WEIGHT IN BAY 2                  --
C                    SUMWT(3) =  WEIGHT IN BAY 3                  --
C      --NCARGO    NUMBER OF PIECES IN TOTAL CARGO                --
C
       INTEGER BAYNBR, NCARGO, I
       REAL    SUMWT(3), TOTAL, WEIGHT
C
C         .....INITIALIZATION SECTION.....
C
       NCARGO = 0
C
C         .....ZERO ALL ACCUMULATORS.....
C
       DO 10 I = 1, 3
          SUMWT(I) = 0.0
   10  CONTINUE
C
C         .....READ FIRST RECORD...ENTER LOOP.....
C
   20  READ *, WEIGHT, BAYNBR
C
       DO WHILE (WEIGHT.GT.0.0)
C
          NCARGO = NCARGO + 1
C
C         .....USE BAY NUMBER TO ADVANCE APROPRIATE
C              ACCUMULATOR.....
C
   30     SUMWT(BAYNBR) = SUMWT(BAYNBR) + WEIGHT
C
          READ*, WEIGHT, BAYNBR
C
```

Programming Example–Cargo Loading continued

```
      ENDDO
C
C     .....ALL RECORDS PROCESSED.....
C
   40 TOTAL = SUMWT(1) + SUMWT(2) + SUMWT(3)
      PRINT *, NCARGO, TOTAL, SUMWT(1), SUMWT(2), SUMWT(3),
C
      STOP
      END
```

Note: The selection of which accumulator to advance could have been accomplished by three IF statements:

```
IF(BAYNBR.EQ.1)SUMWT(1)=SUMWT(1)+WEIGHT
IF(BAYNBR.EQ.2)SUMWT(2)=SUMWT(2)+WEIGHT
IF(BAYNBR.EQ.3)SUMWT(3)=SUMWT(3)+WEIGHT
```

Statement 30 does all this testing with only one statement. We will use a similar statement to save rather exhaustive testing (100 tests) in the next programming example.

Programming Example
Frequency Charts

The array called GRADE has 1000 elements. Scores on a college entrance exam are to be stored in the array. The scores are recorded on 250 records of a data file, four elements per record.

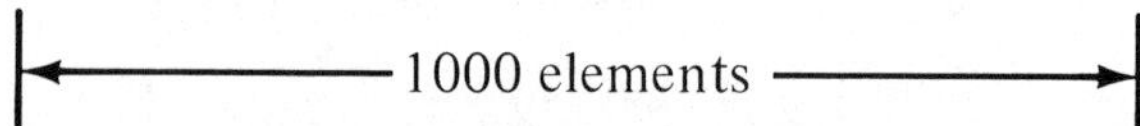

Part A: Read the scores, and store them in the GRADE array.

```
      INTEGER GRADE(100)
C     .....READ VALUES FOUR PER RECORD....
C
      DO 10 I = 1, 1000,4
C
         READ*, GRADE(I),GRADE(I+1),
     1            GRADE(I+2),GRADE(I+3)
C
   10 CONTINUE
```

or

```
      INTEGER GRADE(1000)
C
C     ....USE MORE EFFICIENT READ....
C
      READ*, (GRADE(I),I=1,1000,1)
C
```

Programming Example–Frequency Charts continued

Score	Number of students
100	0
99	0
98	1
97	2
96	4
95	7
94	6
32	3
31	1
30	0

Part B: The ultimate goal of this program is to obtain a chart that shows the distribution of grades on the exam. It is technically called a **frequency chart**. It tells how many people scored 100, how many scored 99, and so on. To start, we would like to know what was the highest score and what was the lowest score, that is, what was the *range* of scores.

```
C          .......THE HARD WAY.....THE HARD WAY......
           DO 40 I = 1, 1000, 1
                IF(GRADE(I).EQ.FREQ(1)) FREQ(1) = FREQ(1) + 1
                IF(GRADE(I).EQ.FREQ(2)) FREQ(2) = FREQ(2) + 1
                IF(GRADE(I).EQ.FREQ(3)) FREQ(3) = FREQ(3) + 1
                    .                   .                 .
                    .                   .                 .
                    .                   .                 .
               IF(GRADE(I).EQ.FREQ(99)) FREQ(99) = FREQ(99) + 1
               IF(GRADE(I).EQ.FREQ(100))FREQ(100)= FREQ(100)+ 1
```

Part C: Go through the array GRADE and determine how many students scored the highest grade, next highest grade, and so on.

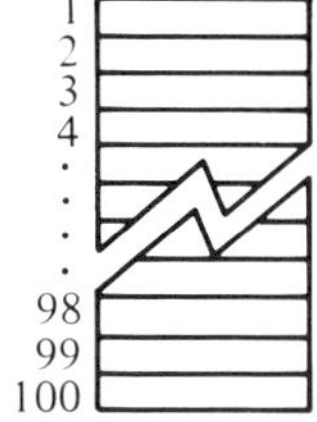

To accomplish this requirement, a 100 element array of frequency counters called FREQ will be set up to function as follows: FREQ(100) will count how many students scored 100; FREQ(99) will count the 99's; FREQ(98) will count the 98's; etc. These statements set up the FREQ array and initialize its elements at 0.

```
C          ......THE EASY WAY.....THE EASY WAY.......
C
           DO 40 I = 1, 100
                K = GRADE(I)
                FREQ(K) = FREQ(K) + 1
   40      CONTINUE
```

Score	Number of students
98	1
97	2
96	4
95	7
94	6
37	3
36	0
35	2

One possible (but unreasonably long) approach to counting the frequency of grades is this:

```
C       .....DETERMINE RANGE OF GRADES.....
C
        BIG = GRADE(1)
        SMALL = GRADE(1)
C
        DO 20 I = 1, 1000
C
             IF (GRADE(I).GT.BIG) BIG = GRADE(I)
             IF (GRADE(I).LT.SMALL) SMALL = GRADE(I)
C
   20   CONTINUE
```

The previous approach would have resulted in 100 IF statements. An obviously more efficient scheme would be this:

```
C
C       .....ZERO FREQUENCY ARRAY.....
C
        DO 30 I = 1, 1000
C
             FREQ(I) = 0
C
   30   CONTINUE
```

Part D: Produce the frequency chart that has been suggested. The chart should start at the highest grade and end at the lowest grade.

Programming Example–Frequency Charts continued

```
C...............................................................
C..   PURPOSE - PROVIDE A FREQUENCY CHART OF EXAM SCORES      ..
C..             STARTING WITH THE HIGHEST SCORE AND ENDING    ..
C..             WITH THE LOWEST SCORE.                        ..
C...............................................................
C
C                ---IMPORTANT VARIABLES---
C
C     --GRADE    ARRAY OF 1000 EXAM SCORES                      --
C     --BIG      HIGHEST GRADE ACHIEVED ON EXAM                 --
C     --SMALL    LOWEST GRADE ACHIEVED ON EXAM                  --
C     --FREQ     AN ARRAY OF COUNTERS                           --
C                  FREQ(100) = HOW MANY SCORE 100               --
C                  FREQ(99)  = HOW MANY SCORE 99                --
C                  FREQ(98)  = HOW MANY SCORE 98                --
C
      INTEGER GRADE(1000), FREQ(100), BIG, SMALL, I, K
C
C     .....READ DATA BASE EXAM SCORES.....
C
      DO 10 I = 1, 1000, 4
C
         READ *, GRADE(I), GRADE(I+1), GRADE(I+2), GRADE(I+3)
C
   10 CONTINUE
C
C     .....DETERMINE RANGE OF GRADES.....
C
      BIG = GRADE(1)
      SMALL = GRADE(1)
C
      DO 20 I = 1, 1000
C
         IF (GRADE(I).GT.BIG) BIG = GRADE(I)
         IF (GRADE(I).LT.SMALL) SMALL = GRADE(I)
C
   20 CONTINUE
C
C     .....ZERO FREQUENCY ARRAY.....
C
      DO 30 I = 1, 1000
C
         FREQ(I) = 0
C
   30 CONTINUE
C
C     .....PROCESSING LOOP STARTS HERE.....
C
      DO 40 I = 1, 1000
C
         K = GRADE(I)
         FREQ(K) = FREQ(K) + 1
C
   40 CONTINUE
C
C     .....OUTPUT VALUES STARTING AT THE TOP.....
C
      DO 60 I = BIG, SMALL, -1
C
         PRINT *, I, FREQ(I)
C
   60 CONTINUE
C
      STOP
      END
```

Programming Example
Pollution Control

The pollution level for the first 28 days of each month in the year 1982 have been measured and are to be formed into a two-dimensional array called BAD82 having 28 rows and 12 columns. These values are recorded 10 values per record in column order.

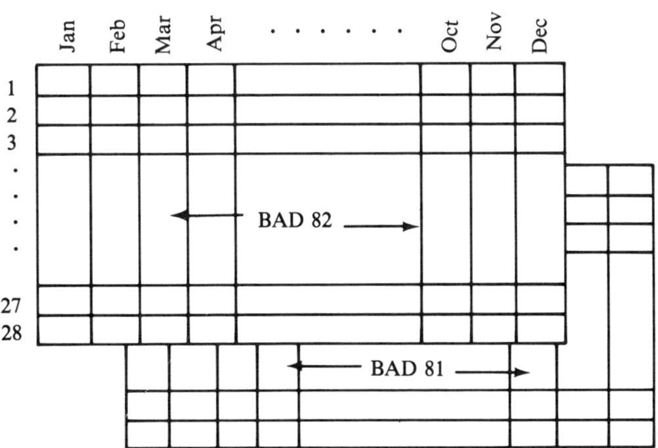

A similar set of records have been prepared for 1981. Their contents are to be stored in an array called BAD81.

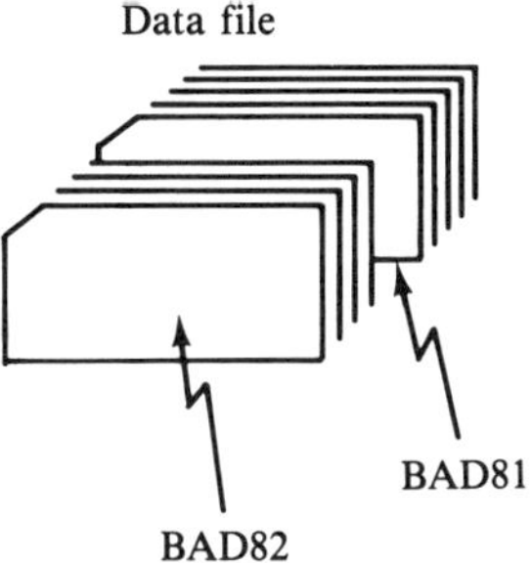

Part A: Write statements that read in the data and form the arrays BAD82 and BAD81.

```
      INTEGER    I, J, K
      REAL       BAD82(28,12), BAD81(28,12), SUM81, SUM82,
C                AVE81, AVE82
      READ *, ((BAD81(I,J), I = 1, 28), J = 1, 12)
      READ *, ((BAD82(K,J), K = 1, 28), J = 1, 12)
```

Part B: Write statements that compute the average pollution level for the month of February 1981.

```
      SUM = 0.0
C
      DO 10 I = 1, 28
         SUM = SUM + BAD81(I,2)
   10 CONTINUE
```

Programming Example–Pollution Control continued

Part C: Write statements that compute and report the average for each month of the year 1982.

```
      DO 20 J = 1, 12
C
         SUM = 0.0
C
         DO 30 K = 1, 28
C
            SUM = SUM + BAD82(K,J)
C
   30    CONTINUE
C
         AVE = SUM / 28.0
C
         PRINT*, AVE
C
   20 CONTINUE
C
      STOP
      END
```

Final Program: Write a complete program to compute all the averages suggested in the simulated output sheet shown.

POLLUTION REPORT	1981	1982
AVERAGE POLLUTION LEVEL FOR JAN.	4.62	5.73
AVERAGE POLLUTION LEVEL FOR FEB.	3.93	6.08
AVERAGE POLLUTION LEVEL FOR MAR.	3.70	4.81
AVERAGE POLLUTION LEVEL FOR APR.	4.55	5.64
AVERAGE POLLUTION LEVEL FOR MAY	5.19	6.22
AVERAGE POLLUTION LEVEL FOR JUNE	4.09	5.17
AVERAGE POLLUTION LEVEL FOR JULY	4.42	5.38
AVERAGE POLLUTION LEVEL FOR AUG.	4.93	5.11
AVERAGE POLLUTION LEVEL FOR SEP.	5.20	6.31
AVERAGE POLLUTION LEVEL FOR OCT.	5.00	6.19
AVERAGE POLLUTION LEVEL FOR NOV.	5.61	6.72
AVERAGE POLLUTION LEVEL FOR DEC.	6.11	7.43

To obtain the months of the year on the output sheet as shown, they were first read in character form from a record such as:

'Jan.' 'Feb.' 'Mar.' 'Apr.' 'May' 'June' 'July' 'Aug.' 'Sep.' 'Oct.' 'Nov.' 'Dec.'

These values are stored as a one-dimensional array called MONTH containing 12 elements to be used later in the program in the following output statement.

```
C.....................................................................
C..   PURPOSE - PRODUCE MONTHLY COMPARISON OF POLLUTION             ..
C..             LEVELS.                                             ..
C..             FOR YEARS 1981 AND 1982                             ..
C.....................................................................
C
      CHARACTER MONTH*6(12)
      INTEGER   I, J, K
```

Programming Example–Pollution Control continued

```
      REAL     BAD82(28,12), BAD81(28,12), SUM81, SUM82, AVE81, AVE82
C
      READ *, ((BAD81(I,J), I = 1, 28), J = 1, 12)
      READ *, ((BAD82(K,J), K = 1, 28), J = 1, 12)
C
C     .....READ MONTHS OF YEARS FROM RECORD AT END OF DECK.....
C
      READ *, (MONTH(I), I = 1, 12)
C
C     .....PUT HEADINGS ON OUTPUT SHEET.....
C
      PRINT *,'                POLLUTION REPORT            1981    1982'
      PRINT*,' '
      PRINT*,' '
C
C     .....OUTER COMPUTATIONAL LOOP.....
C
      DO 40 J = 1, 12
          SUM81 = 0.0
          SUM82 = 0.0
C
          DO 20 I = 1, 28
              SUM81 = SUM81 + BAD81(I,J)
              SUM82 = SUM82 + BAD82(I,J)
   20     CONTINUE
C
          AVE81 = SUM81 / 28.0
          AVE82 = SUM82 / 28.0
C
          PRINT *,'AVERAGE POLLUTION LEVEL FOR  'MONTH(J), AVE81, AVE82
   40 CONTINUE
C
      STOP
      END
```

Programming Example
Half Interval Search**

A relationship between X and Y has been established experimentally by the 64 data points shown. A table of these X,Y values has been stored in the computer as a one-dimensional array called X and a one-dimensional array called Y, each containing 64 elements.

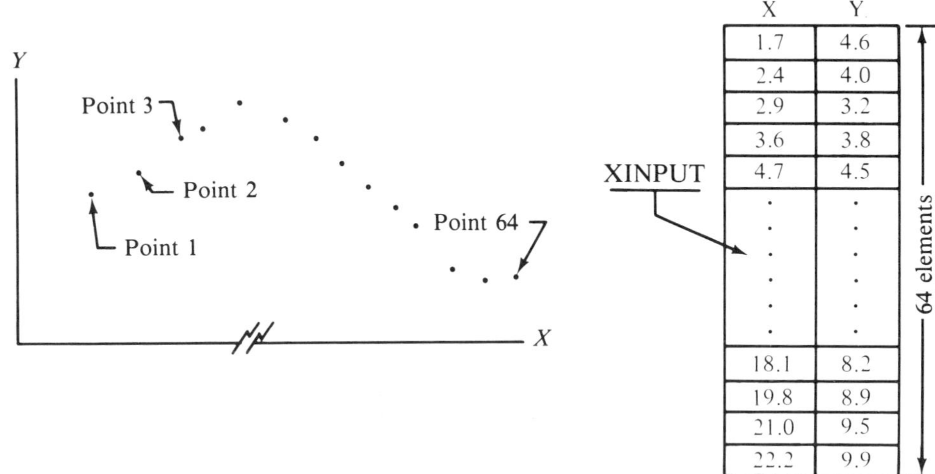

Programming Example–Half Interval Search continued

Assume it is necessary to enter the table and see if a specific value of X is listed in the table and to print the corresponding value of Y if it does.

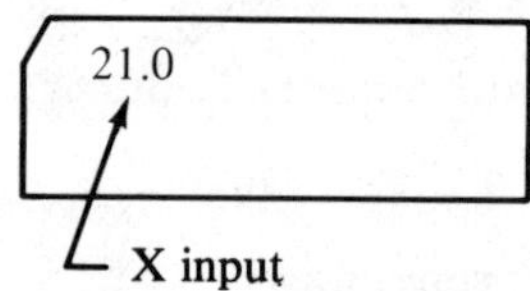

Part A: Write a series of statements to read XINPUT from input and determine if it falls within the range of the table. If it does not, print the message "NOT IN THE RANGE OF THE TABLE."

```
C......................................................................
C..      PURPOSE  - PROGRAM SEGMENT TO SEE IF A VALUE LIES ..
C..                  WITHIN THE RANGE OF A TABLE            ..
C......................................................................
C
C                ----IMPORTANT VARIABLES----
C
C     --XINPUT    INPUT VALUE TO BE CHECKED IF WITHIN RANGE--
C     --X         ARRAY OF X VALUES (64 ELEMENTS)           --
C
      REAL X(64), XINPUT
C
      READ*, XINPUT
C
C         IS VALUE TOO LOW?
C
      IF(XINPUT.LT.X(1))PRINT*,'NOT IN RANGE OF TABLE
C                                              ....TOO LOW'
C          IS VALUE TOO HIGH?
C
      IF(XINPUT.GT.X(64))PRINT*,'NOT IN RANGE OF TABLE
C                                              ....TOO HIGH'
      STOP
      END
```

Part B: Assuming XINPUT falls in the range of the table, it is now necessary to search for it. One method is to start at X(1) and move down the table sequentially. If XINPUT is 21.0 (a value way at the end of the table), this will be a long search. A better method (the half interval search) starts by determining if XINPUT lies in the upper or lower half of the table. This immediately eliminates 32 elements of the table. Write statements that do this.

```
C  IS VALUE IN FIRST HALF OF TABLE?
      IF(XINPUT.LT.X(32)) PRINT*,'POINT LIES IN FIRST HALF'
C
C  IS VALUE IN SECOND HALF OF TABLE?
      IF(XINPUT.GE.X(32)) PRINT*,'POINT LIES IN SECOND HALF'
C
```

Part C: The technique continues by dividing each surviving interval into two parts. The convergence is very rapid. The following chart shows how many elements remain in the interval after each pass. The maximum number of passes is 6.

Write a complete program that will keep dividing the table into smaller and smaller "halves" until the value is located. The variables START, END, and MIDDLE will be used to define the interval that remains to be divided in half on the next pass of the logic.

Programming Example–Half Interval Search continued

PASS	REMAINING INTERVAL SIZE
1	32
2	16
3	8
4	4
5	2
6	1

```
C..............................................................
C..    PURPOSE - DEMONSTRATE BASIC TECHNIQUE OF HALF INTERVAL  ..
C..              SEARCH.                                       ..
C..............................................................
C
C                ---IMPORTANT VARIABLES---
C      --START    SUBSCRIPT OF FIRST ELEMENT OF REMAINING HALF --
C      --END      SUBSCRIPT OF LAST ELEMENT OF REMAINING HALF  --
C      --MIDDLE   SUBSCRIPT OF MIDDLE ELEMENT OF REMAINING HALF--
C
      INTEGER START, END, MIDDLE, I
      REAL    X(64), XINPUT
C
      READ *,(X(I), I = 1, 64)
C
      READ *, XINPUT
C
C     .....ESTABLISH INITIAL LIMITS OF TABLE.....
C
      START = 1
      END = 64
      MIDDLE = 32
C
C     .....VALUE SHOULD BE FOUND IN SIX PASSES.....
C
      DO 100 I = 1, 6
C
          IF (XINPUT.LT.X(MIDDLE)) THEN
C
C             .....VALUE IN FIRST HALF OF TABLE
C                  ADJUST SEARCH PARAMETERS ACCORDINGLY.....
C
              END = MIDDLE
C
          ELSE
C
C             .....VALUE IN SECOND HALF OF TABLE.....
C
              START = MIDDLE
C
          ENDIF
C
C         .....REDEFINE MIDDLE OF TABLE.....
C
          MIDDLE = START + ((END - START) / 2)
C
C         .....VALUE FOUND YET.....
C
          IF (XINPUT.EQ.X(START)) THEN
              PRINT*,X(START), START
              STOP
          ENDIF
C
  100 CONTINUE
C
  140 PRINT *, 'VALUE NOT FOUND IN TABLE'
C
      STOP
      END
```

Caution: This program represents an extremely simplified version of a complex algorithm. The program uses a convenient number of tabular values to show how the algorithm works. A program that accommodates a *variable* number of tabular values would be considerably more difficult to write.

10 Functions/Subroutines/Subprograms

In the early days of computers, the major technological advances concentrated pretty much on hardware development. We needed faster machines that could process several programs at once. We needed more memory and higher transfer rates. Costs had to be reduced. The situation today is considerably different. The majority of new advances are software oriented. The cost of hardware has become almost trivial, while the cost of programming and program management is skyrocketing. Why is this?

A textbook deals with relatively simple programs requiring 20 to 25 lines of FORTRAN code. Government and industry, on the other hand, have problems requiring up to 20 or 25 *thousand* lines of code. Teams of programmers and years of program development are involved. When programs are this large, certain new techniques are needed to handle them. These new techniques are the subject covered in this chapter. Just as subscripted variables provided an efficient means of dealing with high volumes of data, **subprogramming** allows us to deal efficiently with problems having large volumes of complex, interrelated (and often repeated) FORTRAN code.

Subprogramming involves the concept of dividing a program's algorithm into manageable parts (modules) where each part accomplishes a subsidiary task of the overall problem. Each of these parts (subprograms) can be written, compiled and tested *independently*, making error detection, verification, and program management much more efficient. Each subprogram can even be written by a different person, if necessary.

Assume, for example, that you are involved in a large scientific project, and as part of the overall programming effort it is necessary to solve several large sets of simultaneous equations (such as those in Chapter 9). Subprogramming techniques allow you to write the FORTRAN code necessary to accomplish this subsidiary task. When the code is written, it can be compiled as a *separate item* and tested *independently*. When the subprogram is found to be working correctly, it can easily be merged with other subprograms for use by the main program. This will prove to be an invaluable "divide and conquer" technique so important to modern software development. Further, as more and more subprograms (like your simultaneous equation one) are written, we start to develop a library of subprograms that considerably broaden our computational capabilities. We develop what is called a **software library**.

10.1 Types of Subprograms

Subprograms fall into two basic categories: **FUNCTION subprograms** and **SUBROUTINE subprograms**. If the purpose of a subprogram is to compute or define a *single* value (like the root of an equation or the tangent of an angle or the area under a curve), a FUNCTION subprogram usually is used. When a subprogram has to compute or define more than one value, a SUBROUTINE subprogram should be used.

There is a strong similarity between writing a main program and defining a subprogram. Figure 10.1 demonstrates this point by writing (side by side) the FORTRAN code for computing the tangent of an angle, first as a program and then as a FUNCTION subprogram.

Figure 10.1 Subprogram conversion

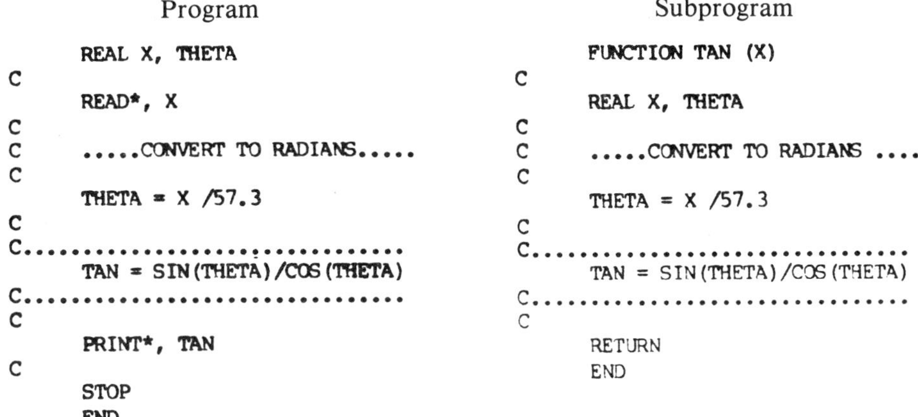

Program	Subprogram
`      REAL X, THETA`	`      FUNCTION TAN (X)`
`C`	`C`
`      READ*, X`	`      REAL X, THETA`
`C`	`C`
`C     .....CONVERT TO RADIANS.....`	`C     .....CONVERT TO RADIANS .....`
`C`	`C`
`      THETA = X /57.3`	`      THETA = X /57.3`
`C`	`C`
`C.............................`	`C..............................`
`      TAN = SIN(THETA)/COS(THETA)`	`      TAN = SIN(THETA)/COS(THETA)`
`C.............................`	`C..............................`
`C`	`C`
`      PRINT*, TAN`	`      RETURN`
`C`	`      END`
`      STOP`	
`      END`	

Very shortly, we will explore in detail the difference between a program and a subprogram, but for the moment note the following:

1. The subprogram has as its first statement a title statement, which declares the type and name of the subprogram.
2. The subprogram does not use a READ statement to define the input value X or a PRINT statement to output the value TAN.
3. The subprogram uses a RETURN statement in place of the STOP statement used in the main program.

Of these three differences, the easiest to explain is why a RETURN statement is used in place of a STOP statement.

Execution of a STOP statement signals that the program is completed; there are no more statements to execute; and the CPU (central processing unit) is released. While it is not impossible for a subprogram to issue a STOP instruction, that is an activity more typically accomplished in the main program. The subprogram is supposedly written to determine some intermediate value. When this value is found, we must somehow pass control from statements in the subprogram back to statements in the main or invoking program. That is what the RETURN statement accomplishes.

Differences Between Programs and Subprograms

We can identify three main differences between programs and subprograms.

Difference No. 1: The STOP statement does not normally appear in a subprogram. In place of the STOP statement, use the RETURN statement. It accomplishes the control transfer you want without releasing the CPU (stopping execution.)

Difference No. 2: READ and WRITE statements may appear inside a subprogram, but they are not the conventional and most convenient way to provide input/output to a subprogram. The next difference is that data values usually are not communicated to or from a subprogram by READ/WRITE operations. There is reason for this. Consider how inconvenient it would be if the subprogram SIN or SQRT contained READ or WRITE statements. Each time you wanted to use these functions, an input record would be required and extraneous (usually unwanted) lines of output generated. The more conventional way of passing information to a subprogram is by using an argument list. In Figure 10.1, the input value X is passed to subprogram TAN as an argument. The idea of communicating values by using one or more arguments is not new to you. You have done it before many times when communicating with library functions such as:

```
SIN(X)          ALOG10(B)          ATAN2(Y,X)
```

SIN(X): X — Input argument; ALOG10(B): B — Input argument; ATAN2(Y,X): Y, X — Input arguments

Difference No. 3: A subprogram must have a title or identification statement that declares the type of subprogram, the name of the subprogram, and the parameters of the subprogram. When defining a subprogram, the title or identification statement is required as the first statement. We already have indicated that this statement declares the name of the subprogram and tells whether it is a FUNCTION subprogram or a SUBROUTINE subprogram. The title statement serves one more purpose: it defines the value(s) that must be provided as input for the subprogram to operate on.

```
FUNCTION      TAN       (X)
```

FUNCTION — Type; TAN — Name; (X) — Argument list

The variable name or names appearing in the argument list define the number and mode of the input values that must be provided in order to initiate the subprogram.

It may be easier for you to understand the argument list this way. Whatever variable names you previously would place after the READ command to provide input to a main program, these same names will now appear in the argument list to provide input to the subprogram. The normal procedure is to allow the main program to define (READ, if necessary) all the input values and then pass them to the subprogram through the argument list. These input values are more correctly called the **parameters** of the subprogram. They are the names used in the definition of the subprogram. The term **argument** is used for the corresponding variable names used by the invoking program.

Output from a function subprogram is transmitted through the function name. The name declared in the title statement of a function subprogram serves two purposes:

1. It is the name or title given to the block of FORTRAN code that defines the function.
2. It is the name of a memory location in the invoking or using program that will be loaded each time the block of code is executed.

For example, the name TAN identifies the series of statements that computes this trigonometric value, and it is also the name of a memory location (in the main program) that will be loaded each time these statements are executed. Because the name of a function subprogram serves as a **carrier** (holds the output generated by the subprogram), that name must be given a value somewhere inside the subprogram (usually by an assignment statement). This means that the name TAN must appear again somewhere between the title statement and the RETURN statement. This is the way the output of a function subprogram is transmitted back to the invoking program.

The title statement has already been described in some detail. It must be the first statement in the subprogram.

10.2 Driver (Test) Program

Now that we have written (defined) our first subprogram, the next step is to write a short main program (driver) that will test its correct performance. If the subprogram is found to be working correctly, we can release it for general use in whatever large program it was intended for.

Figure 10.2 Test driver program

```
C.................TEST PROGRAM ........... TEST PROGRAM..........
C..   PURPOSE - A SHORT DRIVER PROGRAM TO TEST THE ACCURACY     ..
C..                   OF THE FUNCTION TAN.                      ..
C...............................................................
C
      REAL ANS1, ANS2, ANS3, TAN
C
      ANS1 = TAN (45.0)          <-------- Subprogram TAN used
      ANS2 = TAN (30.0)                    (tested) three times
      ANS3 = TAN (00.0)
C
      PRINT*, ANS1, ANS2, ANS3   <-------- Output test results
C
      STOP                       <-------- Release CPU
      END
```

Output:

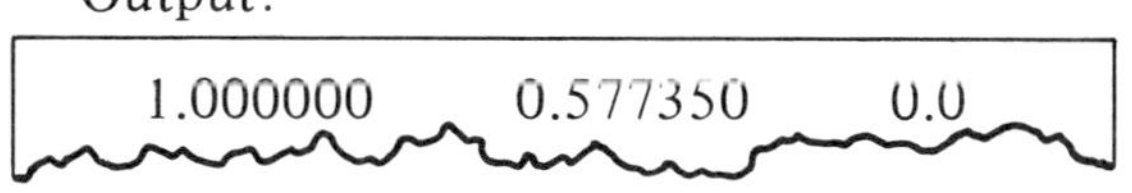

The statements in Figure 10.2 are merely a brief main program that uses subprogram TAN three times. Although the sample test data is not as extensive as it should be, it is sufficient to detect any major flaw.

Deck Layout

When one or more subprograms are used in solving a problem, the usual procedure is to place the statements defining each subprogram immediately after the statements defining the main program.

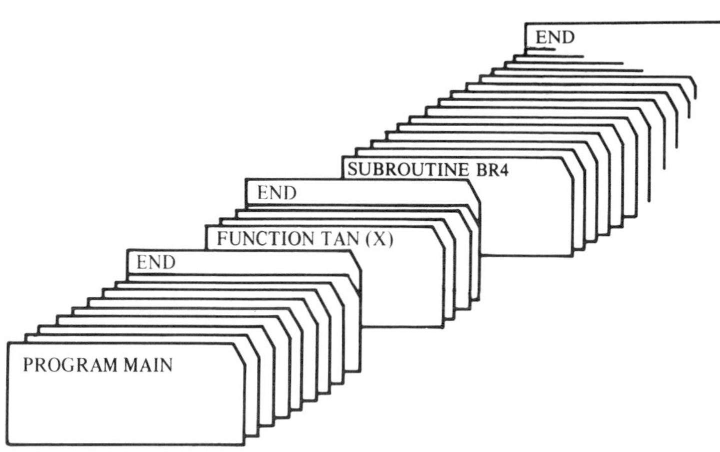

The main program and the various subprograms will be listed and compiled separately. If no compiling errors are detected, the execution process starts by passing control to the first statement in the main program. Whenever the name of one of your subprograms appears in the main program, control immediately leaves the main program and passes to statements inside the subprogram. These statements are executed until a RETURN statement is reached. At that time control passes back to the main (invoking) program.

For the driver program shown in Figure 10.2, that process takes place three times. Each time the function TAN appears in the main program, the argument enclosed in parentheses is passed to the subprogram. The subprogram operates on this value until the quantity TAN is defined. A RETURN statement is then reached, which passes control back to the main program where TAN is used to define ANS1, ANS2, or ANS3. A PRINT statement displays all these values, and the STOP statement is executed. The program terminates.

10.3 Root of an Equation

We have dealt almost exclusively with functions that have a single variable in their argument or parameter list. We now present a problem requiring a larger list.

Write a FUNCTION subprogram that determines *one* root of a quadratic equation.

General Form	Basic Equation	Input
$ax^2 + bx + c = 0$	$\text{root} = \dfrac{-b + \sqrt{b^2 - 4ac}}{2a}$	A, B, C

For the moment only one root will be determined. That accomplished, the solution can be expanded to include both roots, thereby forcing a conversion to a SUBROUTINE subprogram.

To demonstrate that a subprogram *can* contain a READ or WRITE statement, assume the following additional requirement is imposed: if the equation does not have real roots, issue the following error message:

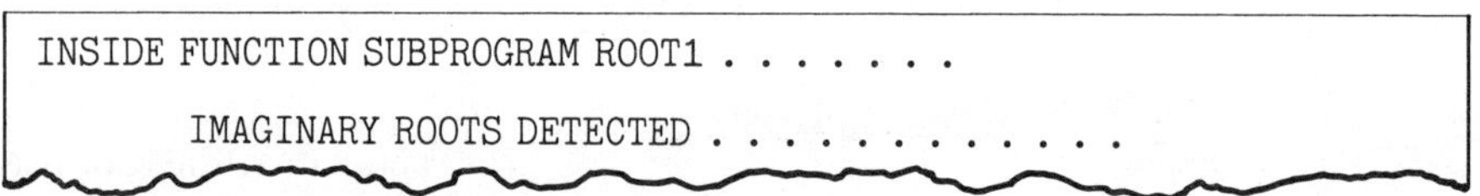

Do not attempt any further calculation.

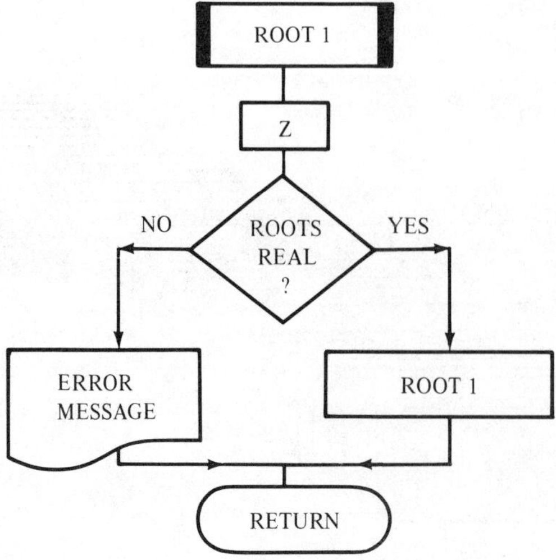

```
      FUNCTION ROOT1 (A, B, C)
C...................................................................
C..   PURPOSE - DETERMINE ONE OF THE ROOTS OF A QUADRATIC          ..
C..             EQUATION. DEMONSTRATE AN ARGUMENT LIST             ..
C..             HAVING MORE THAN ONE ARGUMENT.                     ..
C...................................................................
C
C             ---IMPORTANT VARIABLES---
C
C     --ROOT1    NAME OF FUNCTION SUBPROGRAM                       --
C     --A,B,C    COEFFICIENTS DEFINING THE EQUATION                --
C
      REAL A, B, C, Z, ROOT1
C
C     .....TEST FOR REAL OR IMAGINARY ROOTS.....
C
      Z = B**2 - 4.0*A*C
C
      IF (Z.GE.0.0) THEN
C
C         .....ROOTS ARE REAL.....
C
          ROOT1 = (-B + SQRT(Z)) / (2.0*A)
C
      ELSE
C
C         .....ROOTS ARE IMAGINARY.....
C
          PRINT *,'..... INSIDE FUNCTION SUBPROGRAM ROOT1 .....'
          PRINT *,'......... IMAGINARY ROOTS DETECTED .........'
C
      ENDIF
C
      RETURN
      END
```

The parameter list in the title statement declares that three values are needed to initiate this subprogram. These arguments (parameters) are separated by commas. A statement inside the subprogram uses these parameters to define the value Z. The variable Z is called a **local variable** meaning that it is an intermediate quantity needed or used by the subprogram in the computational process.

Z is tested to determine if an imaginary root is involved. If the root is imaginary, an error message is generated. If the root is real, the variable ROOT1 (which is also the name of the function) is defined, after which control is returned to the using program.

10.4 Converting to a Subroutine

If both roots of the quadratic equation are wanted, the easiest solution is to convert to a SUBROUTINE subprogram. The first modification is in the title statement. It would now be:

```
SUBROUTINE ROOTS (A,B,C,ROOT1,ROOT2)
```

(A,B,C: Sending; ROOT1,ROOT2: Receiving)

The most noticeable difference in this title statement (other than the word SUBROUTINE) is that the argument list contains both input (sending) and output (receiving) variable names. Since a subroutine is expected to return more than one output value, the name of the subroutine is used for identification purposes *only*. It is *not* used to hold any of the output values. Names associated with the output of a subroutine simply are added to the parameter list. The complete subroutine now would be as follows.

```
      SUBROUTINE ROOTS (A, B, C, ROOT1, ROOT2)
C.........................................................................
C..   PURPOSE - COMPUTE BOTH ROOTS OF EQUATION.  DEMONSTRATE           ..
C..             SUBROUTINE SUBPROGRAM AND SHOW THE DIFFERENCE          ..
C..             IN THE ARGUMENT LIST OF THIS TYPE OF SUBPRO-           ..
C..             GRAM.                                                  ..
C.........................................................................
C
C               ---IMPORTANT VARIABLES---
C
C     --A,B,C     COEFFICIENTS DEFINING THE EQUATION                    --
C     --ROOT1     OUTPUT DEFINING ONE OF THE ROOTS                      --
C     --ROOT2     OUTPUT DEFINING THE OTHER ROOT                        --
C
      REAL A, B, C, Z, ROOT1, ROOT2
C
C     .....TEST FOR REAL OR IMAGINARY ROOTS.....
C
      Z = B**2 - 4.0*A*C
C
      IF (Z.GE.0.0) THEN
C
C         .....BOTH ROOTS ARE REAL.....
C
          ROOT1 = (-B + SQRT(Z)) / (2.0*A)
          ROOT2 = (-B - SQRT(Z)) / (2.0*A)
C
      ELSE
C
C         .....ROOTS ARE IMAGINARY.....
C
          PRINT *,'..... INSIDE  SUBROUTINE ROOTS .....'
          PRINT *,'..... IMAGINARY ROOTS DETECTED .....'
C
      ENDIF
C
      RETURN
      END
```

As you can see, the difference in defining a subroutine and a function subprogram is not substantial. It is basically the matter of providing additional entries in the parameter list of the subroutine to accommodate more than one output value.

10.5 Formal Definitions

Now that you have a general understanding of subprogramming, we present some tighter, more formal definitions. It is important for you to know that there actually are four types of subprograms in FORTRAN.

1. Library Functions
2. Arithmetic Statement Functions
3. FUNCTION Subprograms
4. SUBROUTINE Subprograms

Library functions are the easiest to understand and the simplest to use. They represent a series of predefined function subprograms that are provided as part of the compiler/processor software. The list of library functions available on your system is provided in its reference manual. They cover the more common mathematical operations. If the mathematics you want to perform are not available as a library function, you can design a "home-made" function by means of one of the other three types of subprograms.

If you are computing a single value and that value can be determined by a *single arithmetic statement*, you can use the **arithmetic statement function** subprogram. Because this type of subprogram is so brief (consisting of only one arithmetic statement), it is handled in a special way. It does not require a separate block of code and a title statement. It does not require a RETURN statement or an END statement. This type of subprogram is merged more simply into the using or evoking program as will be shown shortly.

If you are computing a single value but many statements are needed, you could use the FUNCTION subprogram. Finally, if you are computing many values (obviously requiring many statements), the SUBROUTINE subprogram is most appropriate.

10.6 Definition versus Use

Definition and use are two distinctly different operations involved when dealing with any subprogram. We have been concentrating on the definition of a subprogram, which starts by writing the title statement. The next step is to write the defining code. During this process, the programmer selects variable names, statement numbers, and sequence of statements with all the freedom previously used when writing a main program.

If you decide to number some of the statements in your subprogram with the numbers 10, 20, and 30, you need not be concerned that some other subprogram or that the main program might be using these same statement numbers. If you use the variable names X and Y in defining your subprogram, the names X and Y can be used by other subprograms (or by the main program) to represent entirely different variables and *no conflict will arise.* Each X and Y will have its own memory location. When you use the name X in your subprogram, you will get the X memory location tied to your subprogram and not some other X value. The reason for this is that each subprogram is *independent* of either the main program or any other subprogram. The END statement appearing as the last statement in each block of code signals the compiler to treat the block as a separate entity. It is to have its own statement numbers, its own variable name table, its own object code. *It is to be compiled separately.*

When a number of subprograms have been written and individually tested, all of them can be put together as shown in Figure 10.3.

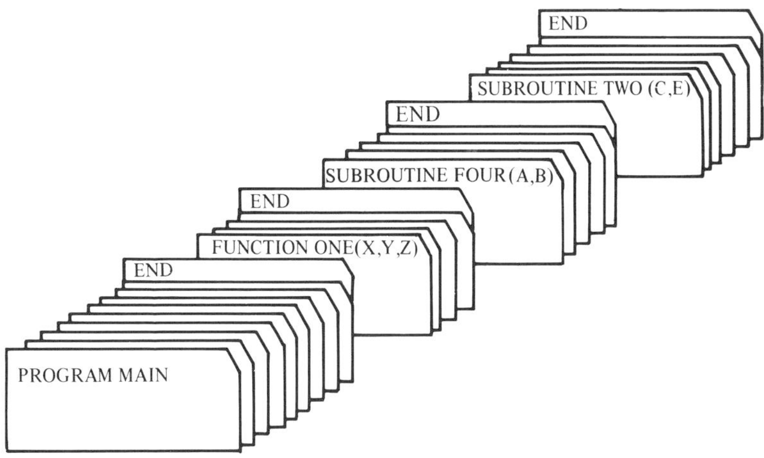

Figure 10.3 Deck configuration

Using a Subprogram

Now that you see how to *define* a subprogram, it is necessary to start talking about the very much separate and distinctly different activity of *using* a program. In the case of FUNCTION subprograms, very little additional explanation will be needed.

Using a `SUBROUTINE` subprogram, however, is something you have not seen before and will require considerable explanation. Because no numeric value is associated with the name of a subroutine, the subroutine name is not used in arithmetic statements in the same way a function subprogram is used. A separate `CALL` **statement** is necessary, the details of which we will cover shortly.

A `CALL` statement can appear almost anywhere. One subroutine can `CALL` another (which could, in turn, `CALL` another). A `CALL` statement can appear inside a `FUNCTION` subprogram. About the only restriction imposed is that a subprogram cannot `CALL` itself. Realize, however, that a `CALL` involves a transfer of control and that transfer should be shown in the simplest most easy-to-follow way.

A Structured Approach

As the complexity of a program increases, there must be an increase in the *disciplined approach* you use in writing the program. You must learn to modularize your solution, that is, to identify the program in terms of a number of related subtasks. Each of these subtasks can then be written as a somewhat independent (isolated) subprogram, usually a subroutine.

The main program is then given the responsibility for making `CALL`s to the various subroutines as they are needed. In this way, the main program takes on a supervisory or executive role and does not become involved in any of the petty calculations. If the main program is primarily responsible for making sequential calls to the various subprograms, it becomes almost like an organizational chart, showing in what order the various modules (subprograms) are used in the overall solution of the problem.

In the problems that follow, the main program will:

1. Control or supervise the input and storage of data values. (Establish the problem's data base.)
2. Make successive calls to the various subprograms. (Pass data to subprograms—receive data from subprograms.)
3. Output important values and generate any final reports.

Some of these functions even can be assigned to a subprogram, but, for the moment, let the main program handle the input, output, and most of the calls. Let the subprograms do all the work.

Transfer of Values

When a subprogram is used, the variables supplied as input by the invoking program (those in the argument list) must be coupled (bound) to the corresponding variable names used in the definition of the subprogram (those in the parameter list). The coupling process is accomplished in two different ways: **substitution by value** and **substitution by address**. Both methods will be described in detail in Chapter 11.

In one case, the present value of an input variable (variable defined in the invoking program) is passed to the subprogram. In the second (and more frequently used) method, an address is passed. It tells which memory location in the invoking program holds the value wanted by the subprogram. In either method, there should be a consistency in number and mode between the variable names in the argument list and the parameter list. If the parameter list calls for a one-dimensional array of real numbers in its *defining* statement, the using program must oblige by providing a one-dimensional array of real numbers when the subprogram is *used*. Any variation almost surely will result in an error.

There are a few other things to learn before you can use a subprogram effectively, but these considerations will be deferred just a little longer.

10.7 Arithmetic Statement Function (In Detail)

The arithmetic statement function has a great deal in common with library functions. It returns only *one* value to the point in the program where it was used. Depending on the mode of its name, that value will be either real or integer. The function can have one argument or many arguments. Once it has been properly defined *within a block of code* (a main program or a subprogram), it can be used in arithmetic expressions *within that particular block of code only*! You might say, it has "local" meaning (meaning within the block). All other subprograms have "global" meaning (can be used by all blocks).

The name of this function must conform to the same rules used for naming a variable:

1. The name can contain no more than six characters.
2. The first character must be a letter and all other characters are restricted to letters and numbers.
3. If the first letter is I, J, K, L, M, or N, it is an integer function and will return an integer result; otherwise, it is a real function.

The need for this type of subprogram might develop in the following way. Assume you are writing a program or subprogram where two equations keep cropping up.

Equation 1 $f(x,y) = \dfrac{x^4 - y^4}{xy} - 1$

Equation 2 $f(x,y) = \dfrac{(x - y)^4}{xy} - 1$

Because it is annoying to keep writing these equations over and over each time they occur, you elect to set up two arithmetic statement functions called EQ1 and EQ2. The defining statements would be:

```
EQ1(X,Y)=(X**4-Y**4)/(X*Y)-1.0
EQ2(X,Y)=(X-Y)**4/(X*Y)-1.0
```

Name — Dummy arguments — Defining expression

These defining statements must appear at the top of the block of code they are to be used in (before any executable statement in that block). These statements show the function names, arguments, and method of evaluation (how to compute the function based on the input arguments provided).

With these definitions established, statements such as:

```
ANS1 = EQ1(3.0,4.0) - EQ2(3.0,4.0)
```

can be written. Wherever X and Y appear in the definition of these functions, the values 3.0 and 4.0 will be substituted. Equation 1 is evaluated, then Equation 2. The difference is stored as ANS1.

Figure 10.4 shows several other arithmetic statement function definitions. The first defines a function called TAN that has a single argument called X. The defining arithmetic expression shows how to use X to compute a value, which you should recognize as the tangent of X. This is a quicker way of doing what we did in Figure 10.1. Both techniques result in a function called TAN, but the one in Figure 10.4 could only be used in the block of code in which this defining statement occurred. It would have local meaning only. The one defined in Figure 10.1 (a function subprogram) could be used by any block of code.

Figure 10.4 Sample arithmetic statement function

```
TAN(X) = SIN(X/57.3)/COS(X/57.3)
SIND(X) = SIN(X/57.3)
COSD(X) = COS(X/57.3)
SECD(X) = 1.0/COS(X/57.3)
CSCD(X) = 1.0/SIN(X/57.3)
```

The next four examples in Figure 10.4 could be used in a program that dealt with several trigonometry problems. They not only provide a secant and cosecant function, but also functions where the argument is in degrees, not radians.

Conflicting Names

What happens if you inadvertently name an arithmetic statement function the same as a library function? This situation should be avoided. In most systems, your definition will take precedence. It is a matter of how the compiler does its searching. If it searches for subprograms you have defined before those predefined by the processor, your error will be corrected. As a final example, take a look at these two definitions:

```
ROOT1 (A,B,C) = (-B+SQRT(B**2-4.*A*C))/(2.*A)
ROOT2 (A,B,C) = (-B-SQRT(B**2-4.*A*C))/(2.*A)
```

We opened this chapter by determining these roots in FUNCTION subprograms. They then were combined into a SUBROUTINE subprogram. Now we are using an ARITHMETIC STATEMENT subprogram. All three forms are allowed in FORTRAN. Each has certain advantages over the other. This latter form is the quickest and easiest to define, but it is not global. The subroutine is more complex to define, but it is global and can include internal checking for imaginary roots.

Rules for Defining the Arithmetic Statement Function

Example: `ROOT2 (A,B,C)=(-B-SQRT(B**2-4.*A*C))/(2.*A)`

Name **Parameter List** **Defining expression**

The Name: ROOT2

The name must obey the rules for naming a variable and be consistent with the mode of the value it is to supply.

The Parameters: A,B,C

1. These are the defining parameters. They are **dummy variables** (see section 10.8).
2. They are separated by commas when more than one.
3. They are enclosed in parentheses.
4. Subscripted variables are not allowed as parameters in the definition. (Only simple variables can be used.)

The Defining Expression: (-B-SQRT(B**2-4.*A*C))/(2.*A)

1. It establishes a relationship among the parameters.
2. It may include constants, variables other than parameters, library functions, and other defined subprograms whose definition precedes this one.
3. It may not include subscripted variables in definition.

Special Location

As mentioned before, the unique nature of this subprogram (only one statement long) allows special positioning of its defining statement. It is located in the declarative portion of the program or subprogram in which it is to be used. The declarative portion is that part that lies before the first executable statement in the program. This defining statement is itself a nonexecutable statement; it just provides a definition. Other statements that are found in the declarative portion include REAL, INTEGER, DIMENSION, etc. (See Appendix D for a complete list and preferred sequence of presentation.)

10.8 Dummy Variables

The defining parameters (variables) of this type of function are *not* true variables in that they do not cause the assignment of new memory locations. They are called **dummy variables** and simply serve to establish a relationship between each variable name's position in the parameter list and its position or positions within the defining expression. They are *place holders.* Since these defining variables are providing positional information only, they should be simple variables. Subscripted variables are not allowed in the definition.

When the function is used, the situation is entirely different. In the place of each defining (dummy) variable, a specific constant, the name of a variable (simple or subscripted) or an expression may be used. Remember the consistency requirements: the arguments in the using statement must agree in number, order and mode (but not in *name*) with the arguments in the defining statement or subprogram.

Using Different Names

Beginning programmers do not like the idea of using one set of variable names when defining a function and another set of names when using it. It is regarded as a purposeless confusion factor. "I don't care what they say," the programmer grumbles, "to avoid confusion, I'm always going to use the same names in the argument list that were used in the parameter list when the function was defined."

The point is well taken. When there is nothing to be gained in a different name, confusion *can* be avoided by using identical names. There are times, however, when this isn't practical. The library function SIN is probably *defined* in terms of a parameter called X. It would be a serious handicap if all *uses* of this function required X as an argument. We want more flexibility than that. The obvious solution is to allow any value when the function is used and to represent that value by the name X in the definition.

There are times when the name of the argument and the name of the corresponding parameter *must* be different.

Consider a main program that must deal with three quadratic equations. A value of A, B, and C is needed to define each equation. Accordingly the names A1, B1, and C1 are used to define the first equation; and A2, B2, and C2 are used to define the second equation; and A3, B3, and C3 are used to define the third equation.

$$\text{Equation 1}\quad \underset{\downarrow}{\overset{A_1}{}}3x^2 + \underset{\downarrow}{\overset{B_1}{}}6.5x - \underset{\downarrow}{\overset{C_1}{}}7.2$$

$$\text{Equation 2}\quad \underset{\downarrow}{\overset{A_2}{}}5.8x_1 - \underset{\downarrow}{\overset{B_2}{}}3.6x_2 - \underset{\downarrow}{\overset{C_2}{}}2.9$$

$$\text{Equation 3}\quad \underset{\downarrow}{\overset{A_3}{}}4.0x^2 - \underset{\downarrow}{\overset{B_3}{}}2.0x - \underset{\downarrow}{\overset{C_3}{}}18.3$$

The arithmetic statement subprograms we were dealing with a minute ago can now be used for solving these equations as follows:

```
ROOT1 (A,B,C) = (-B+SQRT(B**2-4.*A*C))/(2.*A)
ROOT2 (A,B,C) = (-B-SQRT(B**2-4.*A*C))/(2.*A)
```

To find the desired roots, it is only necessary to substitute a set of the new coefficients (A1, B1, and C1 for example) in place of those used in the definition.

```
ANS1 = ROOT1(A1, B1, C1)
ANS2 = ROOT2(A1, B1, C1)

ANS3 = ROOT1(A2, B2, C2)
ANS4 = ROOT2(A2, B2, C2)

ANS5 = ROOT1(A3, B3, C3)
ANS6 = ROOT2(A3, B3, C3)
```

Rules for Using the Arithmetic Statement Function

Example: `ROOT1(A,B,C) = (-B+SQRT(B**2-4.*A*C))/(2.*A)`
`ROOT2(A,B,C) = (-B-SQRT(B**2-4.*A*C))/(2.*A)`

Equation: $3x^2 + 6.5x - 7.2$

A_1 B_1 C_1

Use: `ANS1 = ROOT1(3.0,6.5,-7.2)`
`ANS2 = ROOT1(A1,B1,C1)`

Other Uses: `DIFF = ROOT1(6.0, 2.*B, C(6))`

Constant Expression Subscripted variable

The Arguments:

1. They are program variables (that is, not dummies). They must agree in number, order, and mode with the arguments in the defining statement, but their actual names need not agree.
2. They may be subscripted variables.
3. They may be expressions.
4. They may be constants.

10.9 The Function Subprogram

When the topic of FUNCTION subprograms was first introduced, somewhat trivial examples were given so as not to obscure how they operate. It is time to show their true potential by developing more substantial applications. In the process, the topic of defining versus using arguments will be discussed in more detail.

Assume you have just been hired by a group that is involved in graphically displaying data. You are constantly being given a series of X and Y values and required to plot them (either by hand or by a computer-controlled plotter). The values are almost always too big or too small to plot directly. The first operation is to scale the data (determine a factor by which each value must be multiplied so that the data fits on the specified plotting surface).

As a simple example, assume you have been asked to plot the X-Y values representing a sine curve (Figure 10.5). They are to be plotted so that the physical height of the plot (`YSIZE`) is 8 inches and the width (`XSIZE`) is 12 inches. Since the largest value of Y is +1 and the smallest value is −1, plotting Y directly would give a plot 2 inches in height, and, therefore, a scale factor of 4.0 is needed. The values of X range from 0.0 to 360. and these values will have to be scaled also—in this case, scaled down.

When processing unfamiliar data, it would be necessary to search for the largest value, search for the smallest value, define the range, and then compute the scale factor. This is just the type of assignment a subprogram is designed to accomplish.

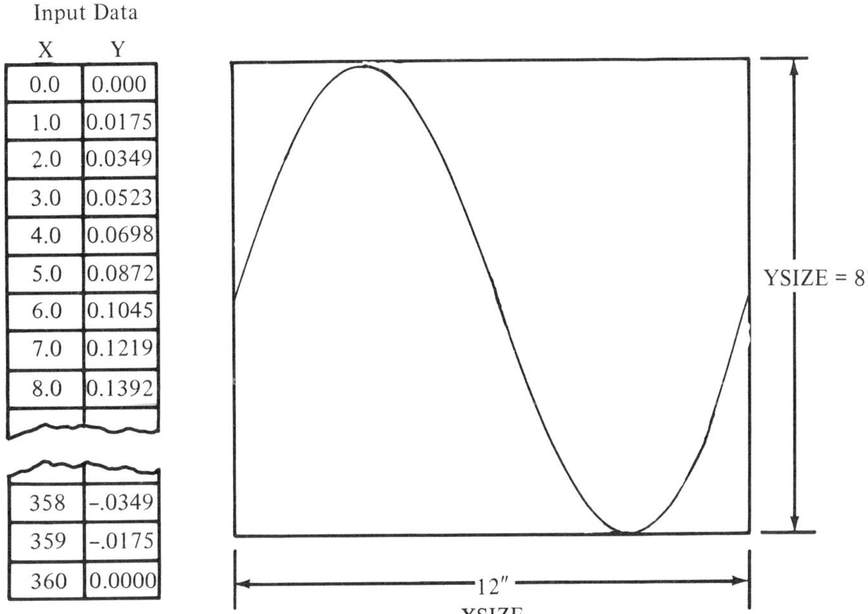

Figure 10.5 Typical plot of a graph

You need to write a `FUNCTION` subprogram called `SCALE` that receives as input:

1. `ARRAY`—the name of a one-dimensional array of data to be scaled.
2. `NSIZE`—an integer telling the number of elements in this `ARRAY`.
3. `SIZE`—the physical size (in inches) of the plotting surface.

The purpose of this subprogram is to compute a single real value called `SCALE`. This is the value that all elements in `ARRAY` should be multiplied by to get the data in a form that can be plotted directly.†

For the moment, assume that the maximum size of the input vector `ARRAY` is 1000 elements. Of course, the subprogram should be able to handle arrays of varying size, and that is the reason for the parameter `NSIZE`. Inside subprogram `SCALE` the data will be scanned to determine the largest and smallest element. Once these are known, the scale factor is computed by simple division.

† To adjust the values of Y as required in Figure 10.5, the value of `SCALE` would be 4.0.

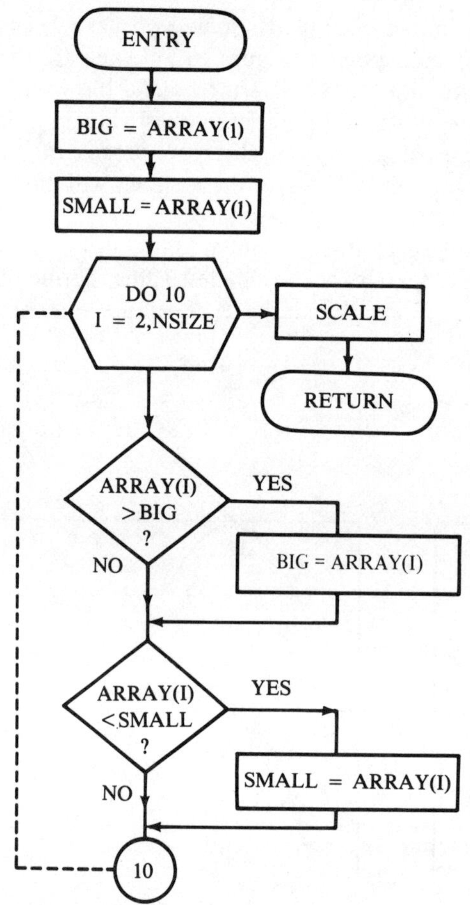


```
      FUNCTION SCALE (ARRAY, NSIZE, SIZE)
C.................................................................
C..   PURPOSE - SEARCH A ONE DIMENSIONAL ARRAY (VECTOR) AND        ..
C..             DERTERMINE A SCALE FACTOR TO ALLOW THE DATA       ..
C..             TO BE PLOTTED WITHIN A SPECIFIC AREA.              ..
C.................................................................
C
C                  ---IMPORTANT VARIABLES---
C
C     --ARRAY      ARRAY OF DATA TO BE SEARCHED                     --
C     --NSIZE      NUMBER OF ELEMENTS IN ARRAY (1000 MAX)           --
C     --BIG,SMALL LARGEST AND SMALLEST ELEMENT OF ARRAY             --
C
      INTEGER NSIZE
      REAL    SIZE, BIG, SMALL, ARRAY(100)
C
C     INITIALIZE SEARCH ACTIVITY
C
      BIG = ARRAY(1)
      SMALL = ARRAY(1)
C
      DO 10 I = 2, NSIZE
C
         IF (ARRAY(I).GT.BIG) BIG = ARRAY(I)
         IF (ARRAY(I).LT.SMALL) SMALL = ARRAY(I)
C
   10 CONTINUE
C
C     .....COMPUTE SCALE FACTOR.....
C
      SCALE = SIZE / (BIG - SMALL)
C
      RETURN
      END
```

In the process of testing this subroutine, we can give a specific example of the requirement that arguments in the *using* statement must agree in number, type, order, and mode with those established in the definition statement.

The test data will be X-Y values representing a sine curve (the data shown in Figure 10.5). These values are easily generated inside the main or driver program by statements such as:

```
C.............................................................
C..   PURPOSE - MAIN PROGRAM TO TEST THE EFFECTIVENESS OF       ..
C..             FUNCTION SCALE. TEST DATA WILL BE SINE CURVE    ..
C.............................................................
C
C                      ---IMPORTANT VARIABLES---
C
C     --X         ARRAY OF 361 VALUES REPRESENTING ANGLES
C                         (0 TO 360)                              --
C     --Y         ARRAY OF 361 VALUES REPRESENTING SINE(X)        --
C
      INTEGER I
      REAL    SCALE, X(361), Y(361), XSCALE, YSCALE
C
C     .....SET UP LOOP TO DEFINE BOTH ARRAYS.....
C
      DO 10 I = 1, 361
C
          X(I) = FLOAT (I-1)
          Y(I) = SIN  (X(I)  / 57.3)
C
   10 CONTINUE
```

The following statements invoke function SCALE twice: once to get the X-scale factor and once to get the Y-scale factor.

```
C
C
      XSCALE = SCALE  (X, 361, 12.0)
C
C
      YSCALE = SCALE  (Y, 361, 8.0)
C
```

In both these examples, the first argument is a real one-dimensional array, the second is a simple integer, and the last is a simple real variable. When the name X appears in the first use of SCALE, the name X and the name ARRAY are linked. The next time SCALE is used, the name Y is linked to the name ARRAY.

Now that the two scale factors are known, statements in the main (or driver) program can be written to modify each value of array X and array Y so that the elements of each can be plotted directly.

```
C     .....SCALE BOTH ARRAYS.....
C
      DO 40 I = 1, 361
C
          X(I) = X(I)  * XSCALE
          Y(I) = Y(I)  * YSCALE
C
   40 CONTINUE
C
C     .....ALL ELEMENTS ARE READY FOR PLOTTING.....
C
```

Passing an Array Name

This is the first time you have seen the name of an array passed as an argument. There is nothing terribly difficult about this except that an inexperienced programmer is tempted to put a subscript after the array's name:

```
C
      XSCALE = SCALE (X(I), 361, 12.0)
C                        ↑
      STOP
      END            Incorrect use of subscript
```

(Most often you get in trouble when you do *not* provide a subscript; here, you get in trouble if you do.) When a subscript is provided after the name of an array, you are no longer referencing the whole array, just one element of the array. An array name followed by a subscript is the equivalent of a simple variable.

Note: If the subprogram asks for the whole array, *give the name only*. If a subscript is provided, the corresponding defining argument must be a simple variable.

10.10 Defining and Using Arguments

For every different variable name appearing in a main program, the compiler automatically assigns a memory location for that variable and uses a variable name table to keep track of where in memory each value is located (its address). In the case of subscripted variables, the table records only where the first element is located. It is called the **base address** of the array. All other elements of the array can be found using this base address.

Variables in a subprogram are handled pretty much in the same way. Each subprogram has its own variable name table, and, as each new variable occurs, a new memory location is assigned and posted in the table.

Exception: Variables that appear in the argument list (its parameters) are not treated in exactly the same way. They are listed in the variable name table, but they are not assigned addresses (locations in memory) of their own. Instead, they wait to take on the *address* of the variable they are to be related to in the calling program. This means that BIG or SMALL have their own memory location, but the names ARRAY, NSIZE, and SIZE do not. The name ARRAY will pick up the base address of the array X on the first use of SCALE and the base address of Y on the second call. Although we need this feature to couple the two programs, a definite danger is involved. The subprogram now is able to get directly at memory locations that are supposed to be under the control of (assigned to) the main program only. This could lead to difficulties.

A statement such as:

```
ARRAY (10) = 0.0
```

appearing in the subprogram in effect zeros out the tenth element of X or the tenth element of Y in the main program.

A clever programmer can use this information to change many values in the invoking program when a function is called (not just the single value associated with the function name). For example, the whole array X could be modified in one call to the function SCALE. All you would have to do is modify each element of ARRAY and you are thereby modifying the X array. Any variable in the argument list is vulnerable to redefinition in this way.

Warning: *This is not a recommended procedure.* If the original intent is to modify more than one variable, a subroutine should be used. When defining a subprogram, be careful in making changes to any variables in the parameter list. These changes have a direct effect on the corresponding variable in the invoking program. It may be convenient to think about some variables (parameters) as input variables or output variables, but both are capable of modifying memory locations in the using program because of the way in which correspondence of arguments is being accomplished (substitution by address), *any* argument is subject to change.

There is one last comment on this programming example. Based on what you have just been told, it would be possible to establish the identity of vector ARRAY in the subprogram by using the following DIMENSION statement:

```
FUNCTION SCALE(ARRAY,NSIZE,SIZE)
DIMENSION ARRAY(1)
```

Room for base address only

This DIMENSION statement establishes the fact that ARRAY is a subscripted variable and provides sufficient room for accepting the base address of the one-dimensional array of the calling program. The reason for pointing this out is that this technique is often used in commercially prepared subprograms as will be shown in Chapter 13. When you see a DIMENSION statement like this for the first time, you might well be concerned that an error has been made and that the array is too small.

Warning: When passing multidimensional arrays, it is necessary to pass more than just the base address of the array. For this reason, the technique used above only applies for one-dimensional arrays.

Quiz 17 Subprograms

Part 1: Answer the following questions.

1. Why is subprogramming so important when writing exceptionally large, complex programs?
2. Does the RETURN statement accomplish the same action that the STOP statement does?
3. Usually, input and output to a subprogram is accomplished by other than READ/WRITE operations. Explain.
4. What two purposes does the name of a FUNCTION subprogram serve?
5. What is a "Test Driver" program? What is it used for?
6. Describe the difference between the argument list of a FUNCTION and a SUBROUTINE subprogram.
7. What are the four types of subprograms allowed in FORTRAN?
8. Variables names used in a subprogram are said to be *independent* of variable names used in the main or other subprograms. What does this mean to you, the programmer?
9. What is the purpose of a CALL statement?
10. What are the rules for naming a subprogram?

Part 2: Writing a Subprogram (Median Value).

A FUNCTION subprogram called MEDIAN receives as input arguments:

ARRAY—a one-dimensional array of values sorted in ascending order of magnitude.

SIZE—an integer telling the size of ARRAY (maximum value to be 100)

11. The subprogram verifies that ARRAY has been sorted properly and then returns the median value of the array—the middle element.

10.11 The SUBROUTINE Subprogram

The SUBROUTINE subprogram is a most useful type of subprogram because it is specifically designed to handle more complex problems requiring the return of many values to the evoking program. The whole concept of software package development would not be possible without this basic building block.

As you will recall, the argument list of a subroutine contains both sending and receiving variables. These serve as ''carriers'' of values needed to initiate the subroutine and *clearly* return the output of the subroutine. In constructing the argument list:

```
SUBROUTINE ROOTS(A,B,C, ROOT1, ROOT2)
                 \___/  \__________/
                 Input     Output
```

many programmers list the input or sending arguments first, followed by the output or receiving arguments. This is just a matter of style, but it makes things clearer and easier to follow. These arguments are like the arguments in a FUNCTION subprogram. They are not assigned memory locations of their own, but, rather, assume the address of the corresponding memory locations used when the subprogram is evoked. The same warning applies. Changing any of these variables (input or output) cause changes in the evoking program.

Perhaps this is a good time to get a few things straight. The more capable student (and sometimes the more devious student) will say, ''There is no such thing as an input or output argument. They are all the same. I can compute many values inside a function and return them to the using program. What do I need a subroutine for?''

The cost of software is as high as it is because some people cannot resist the temptation to be tricky. They will do such things as use a variable as an input argument and then use it to hold output also. All these things are possible but, in the long run, not very smart.

Keep it Simple

We are about to write a large, somewhat involved program. It should be written as clearly and as simply as possible. People who get exceptionally clever when writing any program probably do not have any more errors than anyone else, but these errors are often much more difficult to track down.

10.12 Use of a Subroutine

To evoke (use) a SUBROUTINE subprogram, a separate CALL statement is needed.

```
CALL ROOTS (6.0,7.2,-1.0,FIRST,SECOND)
```

The word CALL is followed by the name of the subprogram being evoked. This is followed by the argument list. In those positions where input or sending values are required, a constant, defined variable, or expression may appear. In those positions where output or receiving values are required, you put the name of the memory locations in the invoking program that is to be loaded as a result of this call. The preceding CALL statement loads memory locations FIRST and SECOND with the two roots to the equation:

$$6x^2 + 7.2x - 1.0 = 0$$

As part of the definition of a subroutine, considerable documentation should be provided to make the use of this routine as easy as possible. The required input arguments and their position in the argument list should be shown. The same for output arguments. The purpose of the routine should be stated, and sometimes a typical CALL statement is shown. This can be accomplished by a series of comment statements as will be shown in the next programming example.

Programming Example
Correct the Exams

A professor gives a multiple choice exam. To each question there are five possible responses (1, 2, 3, 4, or 5), and the student must select the correct response.

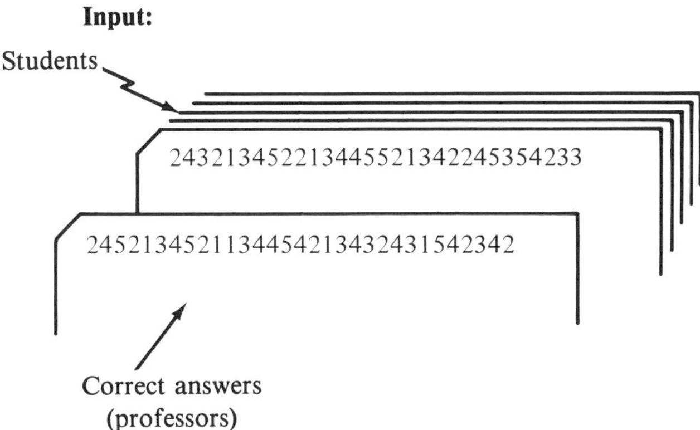

Write a subroutine called GRADER that compares the answers given by a student and the answers given by the professor to determine:

1. Number correct
2. Number wrong
3. Score this student achieved

The subroutine should be able to process exams of varying length (that is, number of questions.)

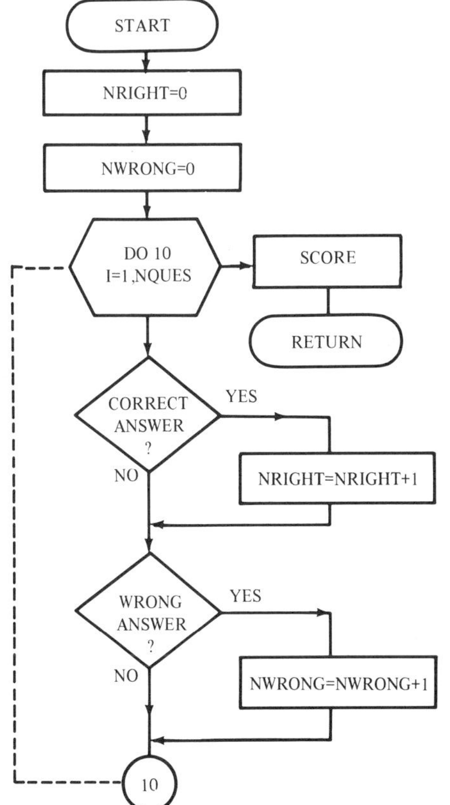

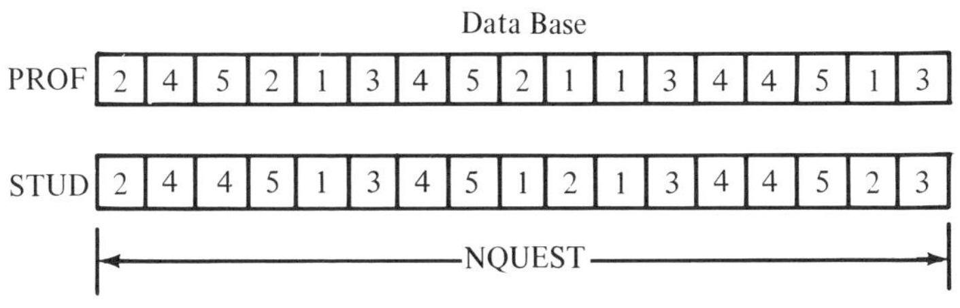

Programming Example–Correct the Exams continued

```
      SUBROUTINE GRADER(PROF,STUD,NQUEST,NRIGHT,NWRONG,SCORE)
C..................................................................
C..   PURPOSE - THIS SUBROUTINE COMPARES THE ANSWERS OF A        ..
C..             SINGLE STUDENT AND THE ANSWERS PROVIDED BY       ..
C..             THE TEACHER.                                     ..
C..................................................................
C
C                      ---IMPORTANT VARIABLES---
C
C     --PROF     INPUT ARRAY OF CORRECT ANSWERS (SIZE = NQUEST) --
C     --STUD     INPUT ARRAY OF STUDENT ANSWERS (SIZE = NQUEST) --
C     --NQUEST   INTEGER TELLING NUMBER OF QUESTIONS            --
C     --NRIGHT   OUTPUT VALUE, NUMBER OF CORRECT ANSWERS        --
C     --NWRONG   OUTPUT VALUE, NUMBER OF INCORRECT ANSWERS      --
C     --SCORE    OUTPUT VALUE, OVERALL SCORE ON THE EXAM        --
C
      INTEGER PROF(1), STUD(1), NRIGHT, NWRONG, NQUEST, I
      REAL    SCORE
C
C     .....CLEAR ALL COUNTERS.....
C
      NRIGHT = 0
      NWRONG = 0
C
C     .....LOOP ENTRY POINT.....
C
      DO 10 I = 1, NQUEST
C
          IF (STUD(I).EQ.PROF(I)) NRIGHT = NRIGHT + 1
          IF (STUD(I).NE.PROF(I)) NWRONG = NWRONG + 1
C
   10 CONTINUE
C
C               .....COMPUTE AVERAGE.....
C
      SCORE = FLOAT(NRIGHT) / FLOAT(NQUEST) * 100.0
C
      RETURN
      END
```

Use of Grader: Subroutine GRADER will now be used to score the two exams. The first record in the data file indicates the number of questions and the number of students who have taken the first exam. The next record gives the correct answers to the exam. The student answers follow.

A second set of records describes exam 2 in a similar fashion. Assume the number of questions and the number of students are different. Write a main program to process both exams. Assume that the maximum number of questions is 80.

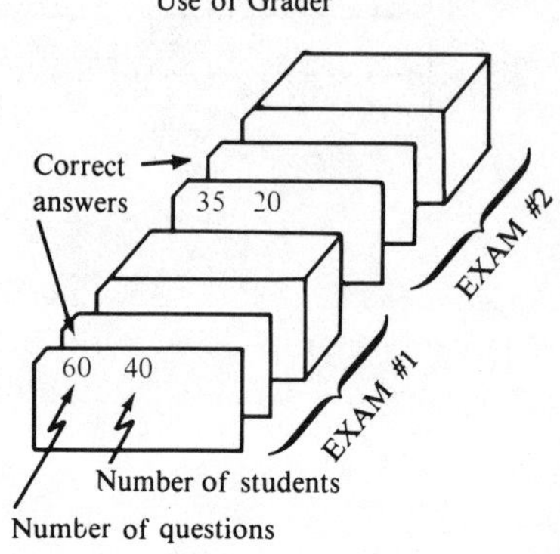

Programming Example–Correct the Exams continued

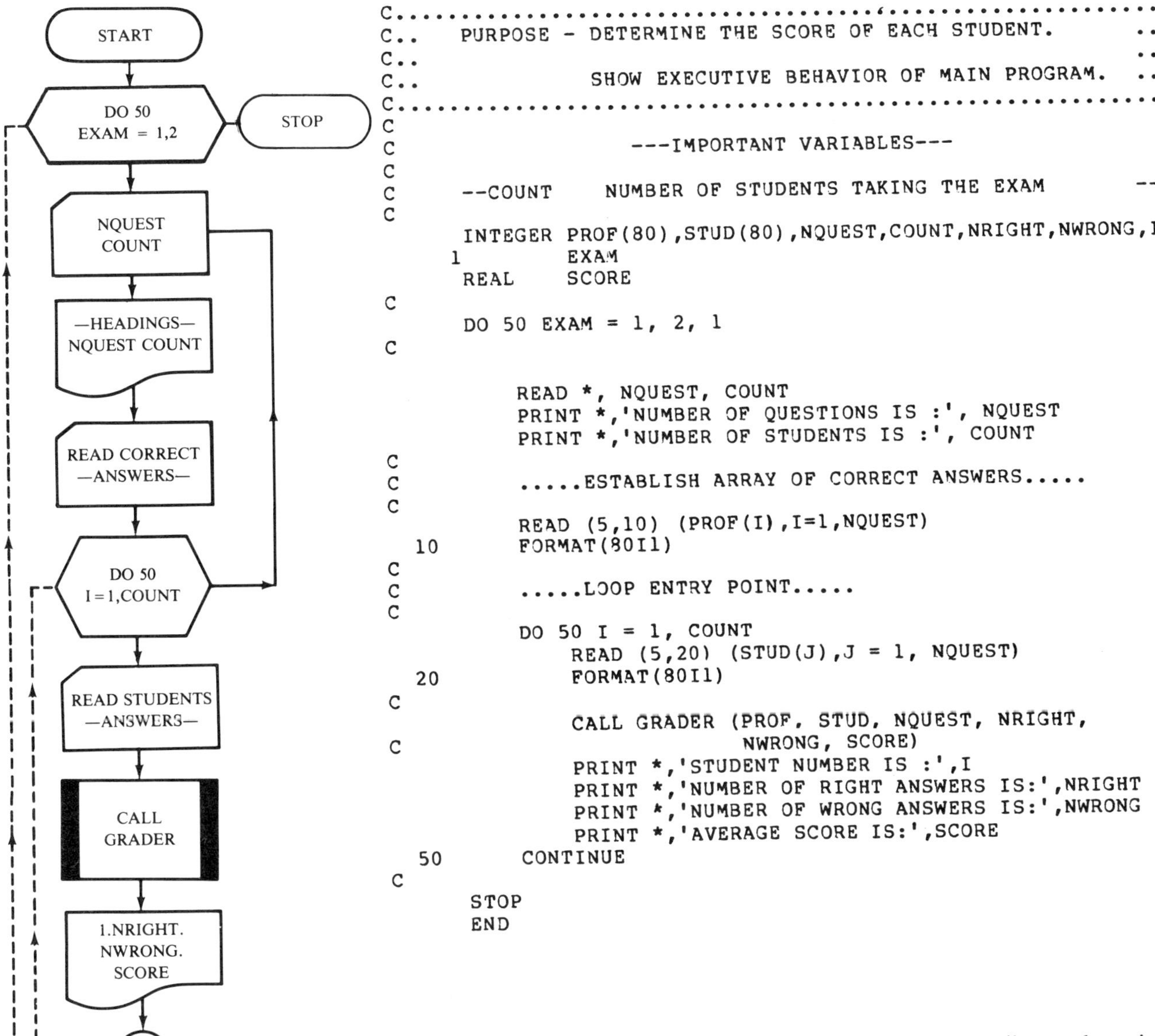


```
C.............................................................
C..    PURPOSE - DETERMINE THE SCORE OF EACH STUDENT.       ..
C..                                                         ..
C..              SHOW EXECUTIVE BEHAVIOR OF MAIN PROGRAM.   ..
C.............................................................
C
C                  ---IMPORTANT VARIABLES---
C
C      --COUNT    NUMBER OF STUDENTS TAKING THE EXAM          --
C
       INTEGER PROF(80),STUD(80),NQUEST,COUNT,NRIGHT,NWRONG,I
      1        EXAM
       REAL    SCORE
C
       DO 50 EXAM = 1, 2, 1
C

            READ *, NQUEST, COUNT
            PRINT *,'NUMBER OF QUESTIONS IS :', NQUEST
            PRINT *,'NUMBER OF STUDENTS IS :', COUNT
C
C           .....ESTABLISH ARRAY OF CORRECT ANSWERS.....
C
            READ (5,10) (PROF(I),I=1,NQUEST)
   10       FORMAT(80I1)
C
C           .....LOOP ENTRY POINT.....
C
            DO 50 I = 1, COUNT
               READ (5,20) (STUD(J),J = 1, NQUEST)
   20          FORMAT(80I1)
C
               CALL GRADER (PROF, STUD, NQUEST, NRIGHT,
C                           NWRONG, SCORE)
               PRINT *,'STUDENT NUMBER IS :',I
               PRINT *,'NUMBER OF RIGHT ANSWERS IS:',NRIGHT
               PRINT *,'NUMBER OF WRONG ANSWERS IS:',NWRONG
               PRINT *,'AVERAGE SCORE IS:',SCORE
   50       CONTINUE
C
       STOP
       END
```

This main program reads the input data, makes successive calls to subroutine GRADER, and controls the output of the final results. Names in the main program and in the subprogram have been made identical. These names could, of course, be different (see next example). In the main program, the arrays PROF and STUD must be of sufficient size to take in the largest number of questions possible. In the subroutine, these arrays are dimensioned at one. (Note the new symbol in the flowchart. The processing box with thick vertical sides is frequently used to represent the use of a SUBROUTINE subprogram.)

It would be nice if each student could get a list of the questions he or she failed to answer correctly as well as the correct answers. This could be accomplished inside subroutine GRADER. It might be nice if each student got a sheet of output with the professor's answers across the top, with the student's answers directly below, with the wrong responses suitably marked, and with the final SCORE printed at the bottom. The student is invited to expand subroutine GRADER appropriately to accomplish these tasks.

Programming Example
A Large-Scale Problem (Aircraft Controller)

To demonstrate the more complex use of subroutines, we are going to become aircraft controllers at a busy airport. Our responsibility is to keep track of where aircraft are on a radar screen, how close they are getting to each other, and to issue appropriate warnings and corrective action if they get too close. This will be a complicated task so we will break it into parts, each accomplished by a separate subroutine.

Subroutine TRACK: One of the first problems will be to track the planes on radar (for the moment we will ignore altitude variations). Accordingly, a subroutine `TRACK` is to be written whose input arguments are the X and Y position of an aircraft when first sighted (X0,Y0) and its position one minute later (X1,Y1). (This is like the lighthouse tracking problem in Chapter 8.) The subprogram will use the four input values to predict the flight path of the plane. We want the output to be a vector `XARRAY` and a vector `YARRAY`, each containing 60 elements representing the expected X-Y positions of the plane at one-minute intervals for the next 60 minutes. Once subroutine `TRACK` is defined, we will test it twice. The first test simulates a National Airlines flight departing from the airport, and the second test simulates an American Airlines flight passing nearby. The input test data has been specifically chosen to allow easy recognition of the path both these planes will have.

Figure 10.6 Radar screen

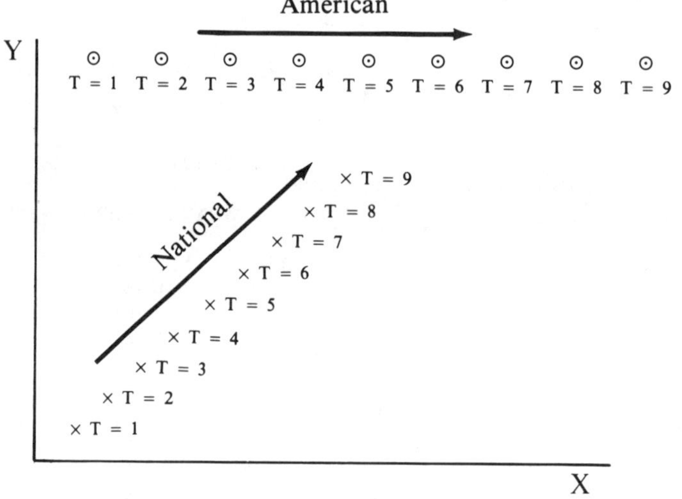

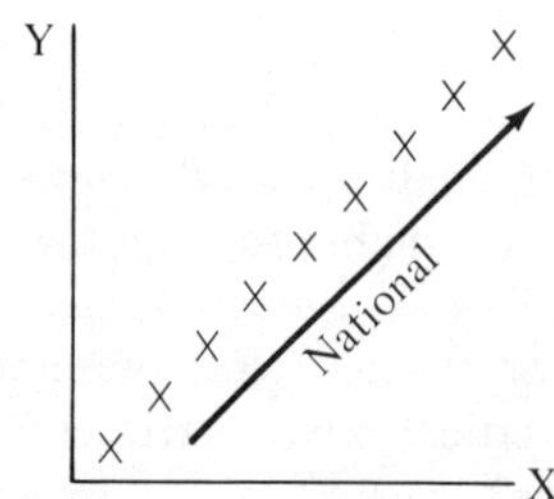

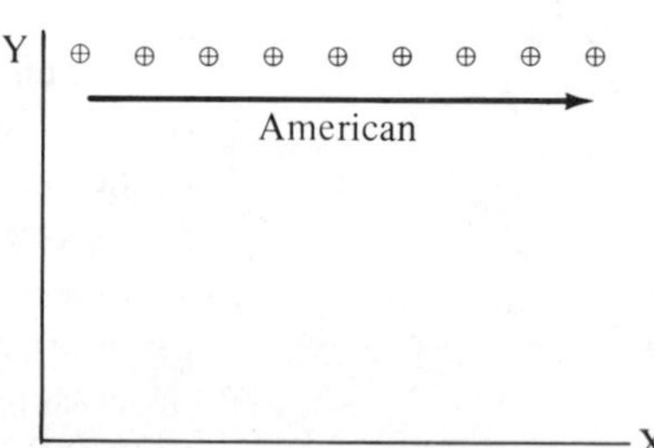

First Input Test Data

TIME=0	TIME=1
X0 = 0.0	X1 = 1.0
Y0 = 0.0	Y1 = 1.0

The output of this call represents a National Airlines plane.

Second Input Test Data

TIME=0	TIME=1
X0 = 0.0	X1 = 1.0
Y0 = 20.0	Y1 = 20.0

The output of this call represents the American Airlines plane.

Programming Example–A Large-Scale Problem continued

By making two calls to TRACK, we are computing four vectors representing the X-Y paths of two different aircraft on the radar screen. These positions can be displayed on the screen to assist the controller, but they will serve another important purpose in the next subroutine.

Subroutine CPA: The purpose of tracking these planes is to determine how close they will get to each other if they maintain course and speed. A little mental computation will reveal that these planes are on a collision course if they are at the same altitude. The minimum distance at which they will pass is called CPA (closest point of approach). Write a subroutine with the same name (CPA) that receives as input the projected path of two planes, and determine how close they will get to each other and when that will happen.

Inside subroutine CPA, compute a one-dimensional array called DIST representing the separating distances of the planes (again assuming the same altitude) at one-minute intervals for 60 minutes. Have subroutine CPA search DIST for its minimum element (call it SMALL) and the position of this element (subscript) in the array (call it TIME). SMALL tells how close the planes get to each other. TIME tells how many minutes into the flight this will take place.

Subroutine WARNING: If the value of SMALL is less than one mile, a possible dangerous situation is developing. The altitude of the two aircraft should be verified by radar or by voice communication or both. A warning message should be issued and, if the separating altitude turns out to be less than 1000 feet, a course change, speed change, or altitude change made. Finally, the whole process should be repeated to assure safe passing of these two planes. This could be accomplished by subroutine WARNING. Any number of additional tasks could be involved, but we already have a sizable job in front of us.

Writing Subroutine TRACK: Given:

X0,Y0–X and Y locations at time 0.
X1,Y1–X and Y locations at time 1.

Required:

XARRAY }
YARRAY } –X and Y locations for next 60 minutes.

The first calculation inside subroutine TRACK is to determine the change in X for the first minute of flight and store that value as DELTAX. The corresponding change in Y should be determined and stored as DELTAY. To determine where the aircraft will be, say, five minutes into the flight, it will be 5 times DELTAX and DELTAY away from where it was originally sighted.

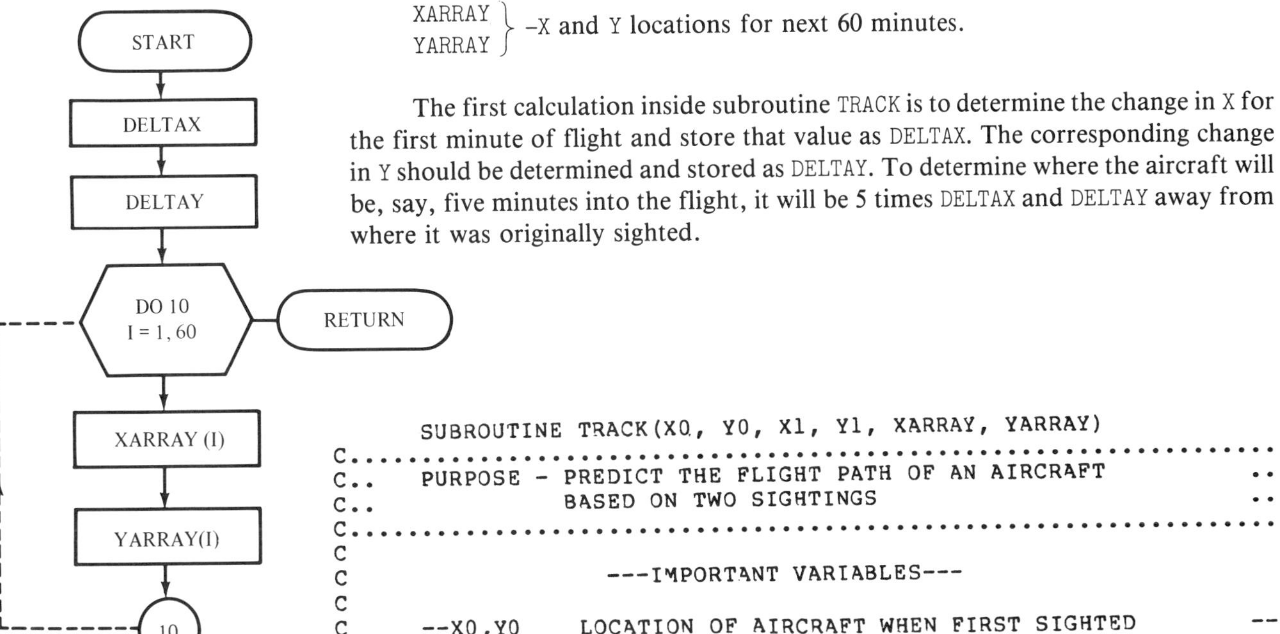


```
      SUBROUTINE TRACK(X0, Y0, X1, Y1, XARRAY, YARRAY)
C.................................................................
C..   PURPOSE - PREDICT THE FLIGHT PATH OF AN AIRCRAFT          ..
C..             BASED ON TWO SIGHTINGS                          ..
C.................................................................
C
C                ---IMPORTANT VARIABLES---
C
C     --X0,Y0    LOCATION OF AIRCRAFT WHEN FIRST SIGHTED        --
C     --X1,Y1    LOCATION OF AIRCRAFT ONE MINUTE LATER          --
```

Programming Example–A Large-Scale Problem continued

```
C
C      --XARRAY,YARRAY
C                   OUTPUT LOCATION ARRAY...X AND Y LOCATIONS
C                     FOR A SIXTY MINUTE PERIOD.                   --
C
      INTEGER I
      REAL     X0, Y0, X1, Y1, DELTAX, DELTAY
      REAL     XARRAY(1), YARRAY(1)
C
C     .....COMPUTE RATE INFORMATION.....
C
      DELTAX = X1 - X0
      DELTAY = Y1 - Y0
C
C     .....DEFINE ELEMENTS OF OUTPUT ARRAY.....
C
      DO 10 I = 1, 60
C
          XARRAY(I)  = X0 + FLOAT(I)  * DELTAX
          YARRAY(I)  = Y0 + FLOAT(I)  * DELTAY
C
   10 CONTINUE
C
      RETURN
      END
```

The next step in the solution is to write a main program that calls TRACK twice: once for the National flight and once for the American flight. Recognizing that both flight paths will be needed for the next phase of the problem (writing and testing CPA), the main program must provide room in memory to store both flight paths. The output should appear as follows:

NATIONAL		AMERICAN	
X	Y	X	Y
1.0	1.0	1.0	20.0
2.0	2.0	2.0	20.0
3.0	3.0	3.0	20.0
4.0	4.0	4.0	20.0
5.0	5.0	5.0	20.0
59.0	59.0	59.0	20.0
60.0	60.0	60.0	20.0

```
C.....................................................................
C..   PURPOSE - MAIN PROGRAM TO DEFINE THE FLIGHT PATH OF           ..
C..             TWO AIRCRAFT.                                        ..
C.....................................................................
C
C                      ---IMPORTANT VARIABLES---
C
C     --XNAT           ARRAY OF X-POSITIONS (NATIONAL FLIGHT)   --
C     --YNAT           ARRAY OF Y-POSITIONS (NATIONAL FLIGHT)   --
C     --XAM            ARRAY OF X-POSITIONS (AMERICAN FLIGHT)   --
C     --YAM            ARRAY OF Y-POSITIONS (AMERICAN FLIGHT)   --
C
      REAL     XNAT(60), YNAT(60), XAM(60), YAM(60)
      INTEGER I
```

Programming Example–A Large-Scale Problem continued

```
C
C             DEFINE NATIONAL ARRAY
C
      CALL TRACK(0.0, 0.0, 1.0, 1.0, XNAT, YNAT)
C
C             DEFINE AMERICAN ARRAY
C
      CALL TRACK(0.0, 20.0, 1.0, 20.0, XAM, YAM)
C
      PRINT 10
 10   FORMAT(1H1, 6X,'NATIONAL',51X,'AMERICAN')
C
      PRINT 11
 11   FORMAT(4X,'X',12X,'Y',45X,'X',12X,'Y',//)
C
C             .....DUMP ARRAYS....
C
      PRINT 12,(XNAT(I), YNAT(I), XAM(I), YAM(I), I = 1,60)
 12   FORMAT(1X,2F10.1,35X,2F10.1)
C
      STOP
      END
```

On the first call to TRACK, the four input arguments are specified as constants. Then the names XNAT and YNAT are specified, which are both array names. These are the memory locations the subprogram will be loading as a result of this first call to TRACK. On the second call to TRACK, the one-dimensional arrays XAM and YAM are defined.

Writing Subroutine CPA: Under the direction of the main program (it is acting like a supervisor) subroutine CPA will be passed the data generated by the two calls to subroutine TRACK. We will use subroutine CPA to suggest how several different programmers can be involved in writing different portions of a large program.

Assume for a moment that you have been completely isolated from any part of this problem description. You know nothing about a National or American Airlines flight—the fact that they are on a collision path or any of the variable names or calculations that have taken place thus far. All you have been told is that you will be given a number of arrays defining the position of two aircraft at one-minute intervals. You are told to use this information to produce an array defining the separating distance between the aircraft at each interval. You are further asked to determine the smallest element of this array and its position (location) in the array.

As you start to solve your part of the problem, you have the right to give the four input arrays any variable names you choose. Since you are dealing with the 60 X,Y values of two different planes, it is possible you would select names as follows:

```
DIMENSION X1(60),Y1(60),X2(60),Y2(60)
```

Even though the variable names X1 and Y1 have been used in another block of code (they are simple variables in subroutine TRACK), this is of no concern to you. *Any names you choose while writing* CPA *will be independent of any other names in other subprograms.*

Figure 10.7 shows how the distance between the two (test) aircraft keeps decreasing. The computation of any one value of DIST (like at time T = 10) is a relatively simple one. The difference in X location of the two aircraft is computed (and called SIDE1) and the difference in the Y location of the two aircraft is computed (and called SIDE2). Squaring these sides and taking the square root will compute one of the elements of the array DIST. After 60 distances are computed, we will search array DIST for the smallest value and its position in the array.

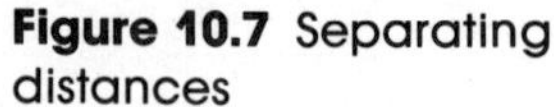

Programming Example–A Large-Scale Problem continued

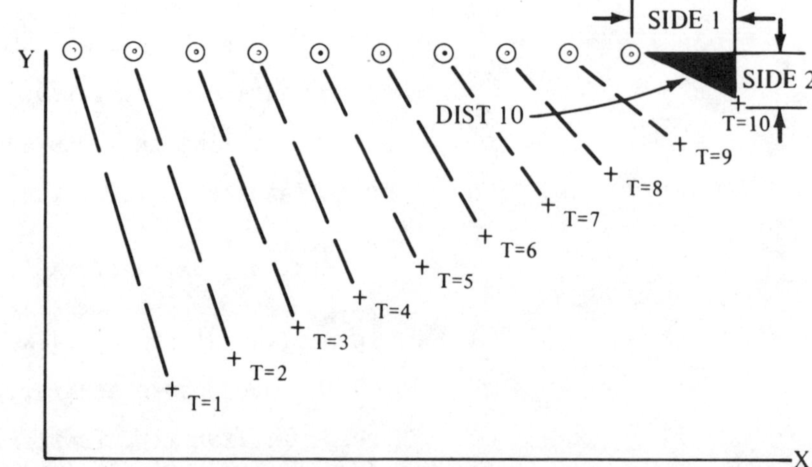

Figure 10.7 Separating distances

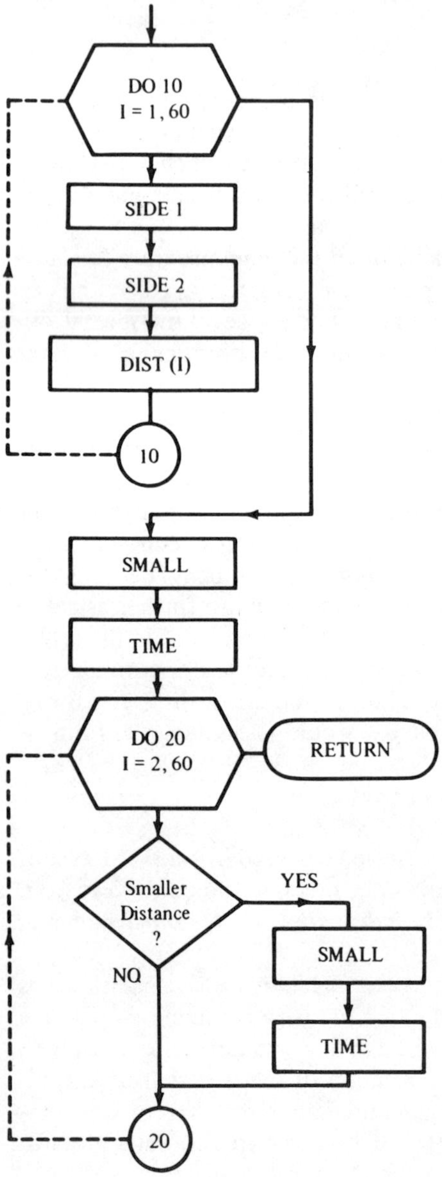

DO 10
I = 1, 60
SIDE 1
SIDE 2
DIST (I)
10
SMALL
TIME
DO 20
I = 2, 60
RETURN
Smaller Distance ?
YES
NO
SMALL
TIME
20

```
C.............................................................
C..   PURPOSE - DETERMINE THE CLOSEST POINT OF                ..
C..             APPROACH OF TWO AIRCRAFT IF THEY              ..
C..             MAINTAIN COURSE AND SPEED.                    ..
C.............................................................
C
      SUBROUTINE CPA(X1,Y1,X2,Y2,SMALL TIME)
C
C                    ---IMPORTANT VARIABLES---
C
C     --X1,Y1     ARRAYS GIVING POSITION OF FIRST PLANE  --
C     --X2,Y2     ARRAYS GIVING POSITION OF OTHER PLANE  --
C     --DIST      ARRAY OF SEPARATING DISTANCES          --
C     --SMALL     SMALLEST ELEMENT OF ARRAY DIST         --
C     --TIME      TIME OF CPA                            --
C
      REAL DIST(60),X1(1),X2(1),Y1(1),Y2(1)
      REAL SIDE1, SIDE2
C
C     .....COMPUTE DIST ARRAY.....
C
      DO 10 I = 1, 60, 1
C
         SIDE1 = X2(I) - X1(I)
         SIDE2 = Y2(I) - Y1(I)
         DIST(I) = SQRT(SIDE1**2 + SIDE2**2)
C
   10 CONTINUE
C
C     .....SEARCH FOR SMALLEST ELEMENT.....
C
      SMALL = DIST(1)
      TIME = 1
C
      DO 20 I = 2, 60, 1
C
         IF(DIST(I).LT.SMALL) THEN
C
            SMALL = DIST(I)
            TIME = I
C
         ENDIF
C
   20 CONTINUE
C
      RETURN
      END
```

Programming Example–A Large-Scale Problem continued

Note that the array called DIST is dimensioned as having 60 elements, whereas all the other arrays are dimensioned at one. Do you know why? The array DIST is not a parameter. It is a block of memory used inside of CPA to hold 60 intermediate values. All the other arrays are parameters. For the sake of programming style, it would really be better to dimension all the arrays to a value of 60.

Statements can now be added to the main program that will pass the arrays representing the flight paths of the National and American flights to subroutine CPA.

```
C......................................................................
C..    PURPOSE - SHOW STATEMENTS IN MAIN PROGRAM THAT PASS          ..
C..              FLIGHT PATH INFORMATION TO SUBROUTINE CPA          ..
C..              AND THEN RECEIVE OUTPUT FROM CPA.                  ..
C......................................................................
C
         REAL XNAT(60),YNAT(60),XAM(60),YAM(60)
         INTEGER WHEN
C
   10    CALL TRACK(0.0,0.0,1.0,1.0,XNAT,YNAT)
   20    CALL TRACK(0.0,20.0,1.0,20.0,XAM,YAM)
C
C        .....PASS ARRAYS TO CPA.....
C
   30    CALL CPA(XNAT,YNAT,YAM,XAM,ANS,WHEN)
C
         PRINT*,ANS, WHEN
C
         STOP
         END
```

If you understand argument transfer, you will see that subroutine CPA receives the base address of XNAT and YNAT that binds these arrays to the names X1 and Y1 (arrays). It also received XAM and YAM base addresses. When the RETURN statement in CPA is reached, a value called SMALL and a value called TIME will have been defined. Each time these variables names are dealt with in the subprogram, memory locations ANS and WHEN (locations in the main program) are defined.

An interesting feature of this problem is that in actual operation the initial X and Y positions are not read from data cards or typed on a terminal. A light pen is attached to the radar screen. The operator holds the light pen over the aircraft's position on the screen, and special electronics determine where on the screen the light pen is pointing. The X and Y of the pen is fed to the computer just as if a conventional READ statement had been executed.

We have carried this problem as far as we should, except that statements might be added to subroutine CPA that issue a special warning (in the form of a printout) if the value SMALL (minimum separating distance) is less than 1 mile. The last few statements of CPA are repeated here with the extra print statement added.

```
C
         DO 20 I = 2, 60
C
            IF(DIST(I).LT.SMALL) THEN
C
               SMALL = DIST(I)
               TIME = I
C
            ENDIF
C
   20    CONTINUE
C
```

Programming Example–A Large-Scale Problem continued

```
C       .....SEE IF PLANES TOO CLOSE.....
C
        IF(SMALL.LT.1.0) PRINT*,'WARNING.......WARNING',
     1       'PLANES TOO CLOSE   DISTANCE = ',SMALL,
     2       ' AT TIME ', TIME
C
        RETURN
        END
```

Review Exercises

1. Subprogramming involves the concept of dividing a program's algorithm into manageable parts or modules. Why are these modules described as being "more manageable"?
★ 2. Is a STOP statement absolutely forbidden in a subprogram?
3. The name of a FUNCTION subprogram serves a purpose not provided by the name of a SUBROUTINE subprogram. What is that purpose?
4. Explain how to test a subprogram you have written prior to merging it with many other subprograms in a large computer project.
5. Provide an example where it is necessary to have names in the argument list of the using statement different from the names in the parameter list of the defining statement of a subprogram.
★ 6. As the complexity of a computer project increases, the function of the main program is usually restricted to three major tasks. What are these tasks?
7. Discuss the terms "local" vs. "global." Give an example of each.
★ 8. Discuss the term "dummy variable" and show what is meant by "a place holder."
9. When passing the name of a whole array in an argument list, should a subscript follow the name of the array?
★ 10. Discuss the term "base address" as it applies to arrays. Why is this quantity so important when passing an array in an argument list?
11. Write a FUNCTION subprogram called COUNT that will examine a one-dimensional array and determine how many times a specific value appears in the array:

    FUNCTION COUNT (ARRAY, NSIZE, VALUE)

    ARRAY—Name of Array being searched

    NSIZE—Number of elements (size) of ARRAY

    VALUE—Specific value we are looking for.

    COUNT—Number of times VALUE appears in ARRAY.

12. A one-dimensional array called X consists of whole numbers between 1.0 and 10.0:

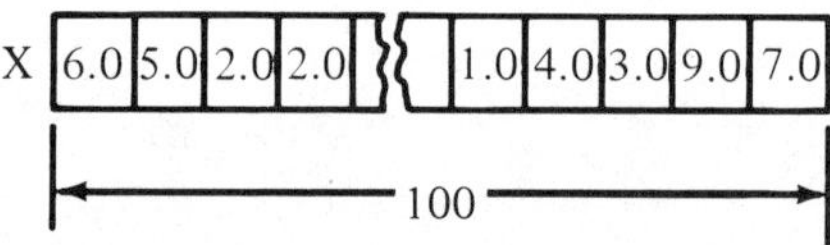

If the array X has 100 elements, use the subprogram in exercise 11 to determine how many times the number 6.0 appears in the array.

13. Repeat exercise 12, except determine how many times each of the whole numbers appears in the array. Report the number that occurs most frequently, that is, the mode of the array.
14. Write a FUNCTION subprogram called BIG that will examine a one-dimensional array called DATA (of size NSIZE) and determine the largest element of array DATA.
★ 15. Write a FUNCTION subprogram called LOCATN that will examine the array called DATA of exercise 14 and determine where the largest element of this array is located, that is, determine the subscript of the largest element.
16. Write a SUBROUTINE subprogram called BOTH that determines the two quantities requested in exercises 14 and 15. That is, examine an array called DATA (of size NSIZE) and determine the largest element of the array and its location in the array:

    SUBROUTINE BOTH(DATA, NSIZE, BIG, LOCATN)

★ 17. The mechanism shown consists of a rotating crank, a connecting rod, and a piston. Crank R rotates at one revolution per second driving the piston P. The position of the piston is related to the position of the crank as follows:

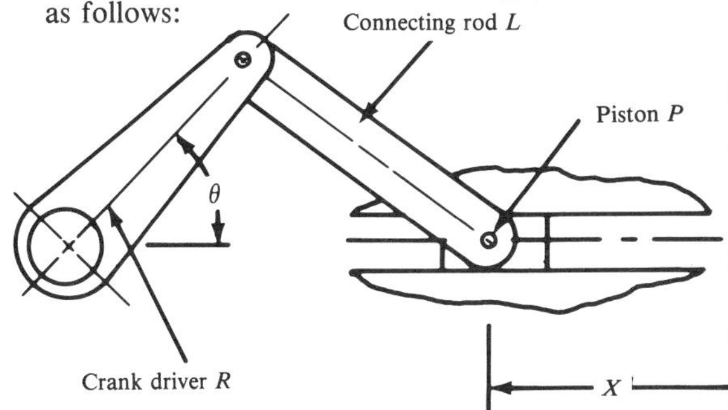

$$X = R(1. - \cos\theta) + L(1. - \sqrt{1. - (R/L)^2 \sin^2\theta})$$

where $R = 12''$ X = Position of Piston
$L = 24''$ θ = Position of Crank

Write an arithmetic statement function to compute X as a function of θ.

18. After the arithmetic statement function in exercise 17 is defined, compute the position of the piston (the value of X) for θ equal to 0, 1, 2, 3, 4, . . ., 358, 359, 360 degrees.

★ 19. The sine of an angle can be obtained by evaluating the series:

$$\sin(X) = X - \frac{X^3}{3!} + \frac{X^5}{5!} - \frac{X^7}{7!} + \cdots$$

Write a subprogram to compute the first ten terms of this series. The argument of this function is to be X.

20. Write a subroutine to read a two-dimensional real array having N columns and M rows (N or M not to exceed 20) and determine the row and column position of the largest elements of the array.

★ 21. Write a subprogram to compute the area under any curve whose equation is of the form:

$$Y = X^A$$

between the limits $X_{initial}$ and X_{final}. Input arguments should be:

a. $X_{initial}$ b. X_{final} c. A

22. The equation

$$y = x^3 + 6x^2 + 10x - 12$$

is to be integrated from X = 0 to X = 10. The area under this curve is equal to the area under the curve $y = x^3$ plus six times the area under the curve $y = x^2$; etc. Use the subprogram in exercise 21 (several times) to evaluate the desired area.

23. Write a subprogram to determine all combinations of three integers whose product is N (N is an argument of the subprogram).

24. A projectile is fired with an initial velocity $V_{initial}$ and travels at constant acceleration a for t seconds. Write a subprogram to determine the distance traveled.

$$S = V_{initial}t + 1/2at^2$$

25. An aircraft fires a projectile at an initial velocity of 1000 ft/sec. This projectile is self-propelled and has an acceleration of 10 ft/sec^2. At firing time the speed of the aircraft is 800 ft/sec. The aircraft makes a 90° turn and accelerates at 16 ft/sec^2. Use the subprogram in exercise 24 to determine when the aircraft and projectile are 10 miles apart.

★ 26. Write a subprogram to search a one-dimensional array and determine:

a. The largest element and its location if an integer variable M is positive.
b. The smallest element and its location if the integer variable M is negative or zero.

Store the desired element in `ELMT` and its location in `LOC`. The array contains 100 elements. Arguments of the subprogram are the array and the integer variable M.

27. Each year every pilot working for an airline must take a test to evaluate his reaction time in performing 40 tasks. An array called `TIME` having 40 elements records a given pilot's performance on these tasks. The maximum time he is allowed is 12 seconds on any one task and 400 seconds for all 40 tasks. Write a subroutine called `TEST` that receives the array `TIME` and returns the sum of the elements in array `TIME` as well as the number of elements that are less than 12.0.

28. Write a `FUNCTION` subprogram called `AREA` that approximates the area under a curve. The curve is defined by a one-dimensional array called X and a one-dimensional array called Y (which are input arguments). The final input argument is `NDIM`, which tells how many data points there are and is the size of both arrays (`NDIM` not to exceed 100).

a. Write this program on the assumption that the points are equally spaced.
b. Write this program assuming the spacing between points is variable.

29. Write a subroutine that divides each element in a specified row of a two-dimensional array by the real value `XDIVID`. Input arguments should be:

`A`	The name of the array.
`NROW`	The number of rows in A.
`NCOL`	The number of columns in A.
`XDIVID`	The value to divide.
`NROWSP`	The row to be modified.

Additional Applications

Programming Example
Data Analysis (Standard Deviation)

DATA ANALYSIS
(STANDARD DEVIATION)

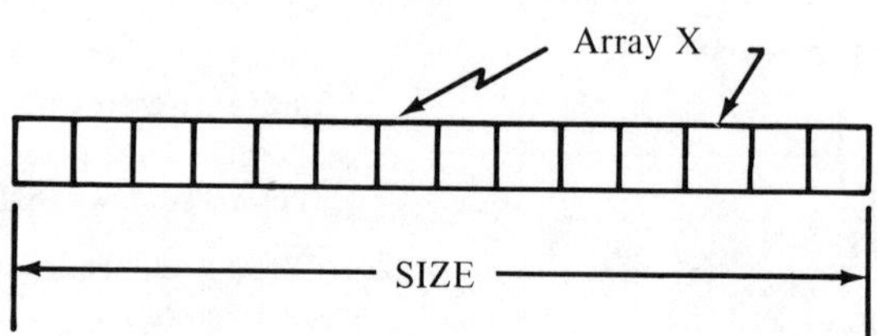

Very often a series of data values will all be relatively close to one another in value. Any one element of an array X is not much above or below the average value of X. An example of this is when an exam is given and all the students get about the same grade—the data values do not spread out very much.

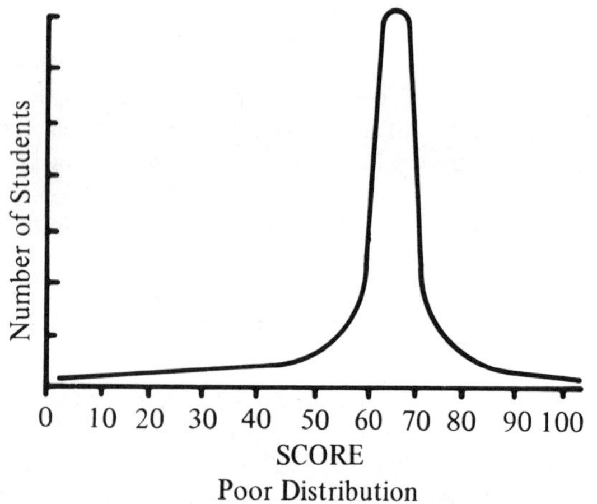

Poor Distribution

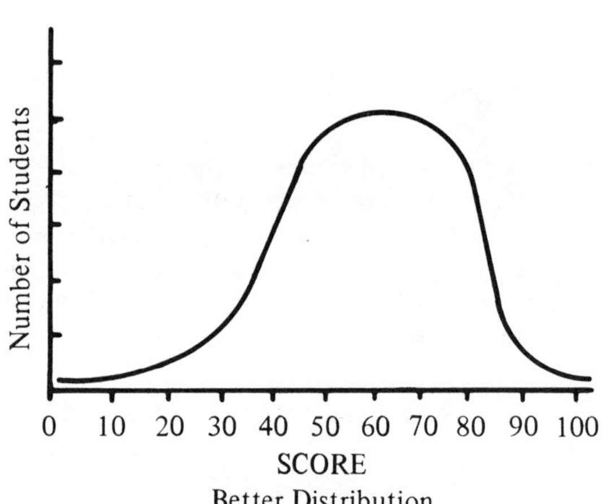

Better Distribution

One way to determine how much the data spreads out is to compute the average value of the array X and then go back and compute the deviation of each element of X from this average value:

$$\text{Deviation}_i = |X_i - (X_{AVE})|$$

By summing up these individual deviations and dividing by the number of elements in array X, the value obtained is one way to express how much the data spreads out:

$$\text{Average Deviation} = \frac{\sum_{i=1} |(X_i - X_{AVE})|}{\text{SIZE}}$$

where: X_{AVE} = Average value of array X
SIZE = Number of elements in array X.

This is not the conventional way to determine the deviation of data. We will revise the calculation shortly.

Programming Example–Data Analysis (Standard Deviation) continued

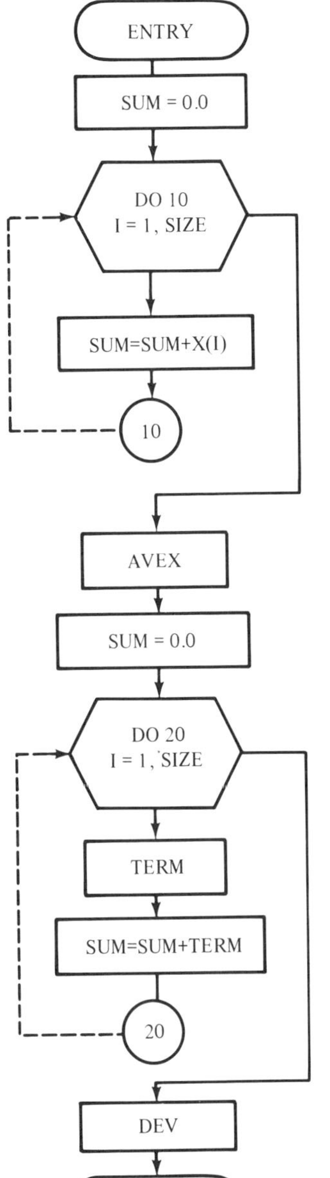


```
      FUNCTION DEV (X, SIZE)
C.............................................................
C..   PURPOSE - EXAMINE AN ARRAY OF DATA VALUES. FIND THE       ..
C..             AVERAGE VALUE. DETERMINE THE AVERAGE DEV-       ..
C..             IATION.                                         ..
C.............................................................
C
C                  ---IMPORTANT VARIABLES---
C
C     --X        ARRAY OF INPUT DATA                              --
C     --SIZE     SIZE OF ARRAY (INPUT)                            --
C     --AVEX     AVERAGE VALUE OF ARRAY (INTERNAL)                --
C     --DEV      AVERAGE DEVIATION OF ARRAY (OUTPUT)              --
C
      INTEGER I, SIZE
      REAL    SUM, AVEX, DEV, TERM, X(1)
C
C     .....COMPUTE AVERAGE VALUE OF ARRAY X.....
C
      SUM = 0.0
C
      DO 10 I = 1, SIZE
C
          SUM = SUM + X(I)
C
   10 CONTINUE
C
      AVEX = SUM / FLOAT(SIZE)
C
C     .....COMPUTE AVERAGE DEVIATION.....
C
      SUM = 0.0
C
      DO 20 I = 1, SIZE
C
          TERM = ABS(X(I) - AVEX)
          SUM = SUM + TERM
C
   20 CONTINUE
C
      DEV = SUM / FLOAT(SIZE)
C
      RETURN
      END
```

The more accepted way to determine the dispersal of data is given by the equation:

$$\text{Standard Deviation} = \sqrt{\frac{(X_1 - X_{AVE})^2 + (X_2 - X_{AVE})^2 + \cdots + (X_n - X_{AVE})^2}{n - 1}}$$

$$\text{Standard Deviation} = \sqrt{\frac{\sum_{i=1}^{SIZE} (X_i - X_{AVE})^2}{SIZE - 1}}$$

This equation requires each individual deviation to be squared before being accumulated. When this action is completed, exit the DO loop, compute the average value of these squared terms and take the square root of this average. The resulting value is defined as the standard deviation. The section of code following the computation of the average value of the X array would now be slightly modified to obtain this new value.

Programming Example–Data Analysis (Standard Deviation) continued

```
C
      AVEX = SUM / FLOAT(SIZE)
C
C     .....COMPUTE STANDARD DEVIATION.....
C
      SUM = 0.0
C
      DO 20 I = 1, SIZE
C
         TERM = (X(I) - AVEX) ** 2
         SUM = SUM + TERM
C
   20 CONTINUE
C
      DEV = SQRT(SUM / FLOAT(SIZE-1))
C
      RETURN
      END
```

Programming Example
Data Screening

DATA SCREENING

Data In

6.2	7.5	8.3	11.4
14.3	6.2	18.4	7.6
10.2	13.4	−4.1	9.9
3.6	4.7	8.9	12.1
21.2	9.9	11.6	5.8

→

Data Out

0.0	7.5	8.3	0.0
0.0	0.0	0.0	7.6
10.2	0.0	0.0	9.9
0.0	0.0	8.9	0.0
0.0	9.9	0.0	0.0

Write a subroutine called SCREEN that will examine all the elements of a two-dimensional array of real numbers and set to 0 any element that does not lie within a specified range (between XMIN and XMAX inclusive). Input arguments of subroutine SCREEN are to be:

DATA A two-dimensional array to be screened, containing up to 20 rows and up to 20 columns.

NROW, NCOL } Integers specifying the actual number of rows and columns.

XMIN, XMAX } Two real numbers specifying the acceptable range of each element (in the preceding example, XMIN=7.5 and XMAX=10.2).

The output argument is

OUT A two-dimensional output array of size NROW by NCOL containing the screened array.

Demonstrate the use of this subroutine in a main program that reads from data an array called HOT. The program is to pass the array to subroutine SCREEN and receive in return an array called COLD containing values in the range of 13.6 to 24.8 only. It should be set to handle HOT and COLD arrays of up to 20 by 20 elements in size, but should read from a header record the exact number of rows and columns to be processed in any particular run. The COLD array is to be printed after screening.

Programming Example–Data Screening continued

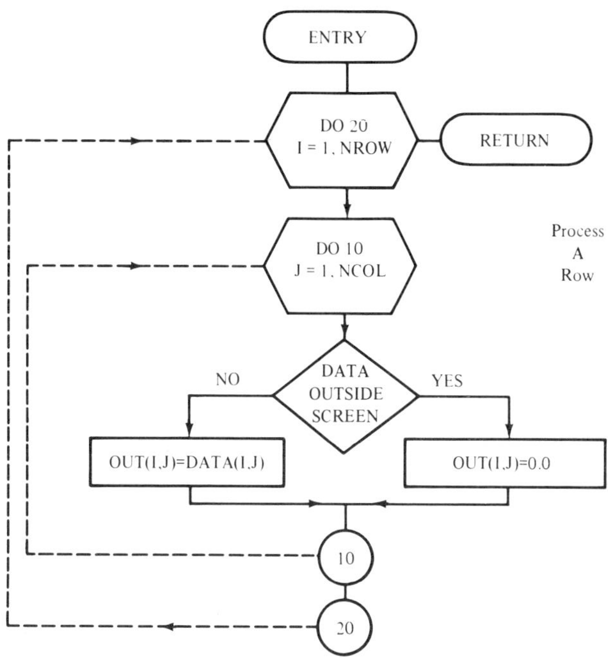

The subroutine is as follows.

```
      SUBROUTINE SCREEN (DATA, NROW, NCOL, XMIN, XMAX, OUT)
C.....................................................................
C..   PURPOSE - SCREEN AN ARRAY CALLED DATA. GENERATE AN            ..
C..             OUTPUT ARRAY CALLED OUT, HOLDING ALL THE            ..
C..             SCREENED VALUES.                                    ..
C.....................................................................
C
      INTEGER I, J, NROW, NCOL
      REAL    DATA(NROW,NCOL), OUT(NROW,NCOL), XMIN, XMAX
C
C     .....THE SIZE OF THIS DIMENSION STATEMENT MUST AGREE IN SIZE
C          WITH THE DIMENSION STATEMENT IN THE MAIN PROGRAM.....
C
C     .....PROCESS ARRAY IN ROW ORDER.....
C
      DO 20 I = 1, NROW
C
          DO 10 J = 1,NCOL
C
              IF (DATA(I,J).LT.XMIN.OR.DATA(I,J).GT.XMAX) THEN
C
C                 .....DATA VALUE OUTSIDE SCREEN.....
C
                  OUT(I,J) = 0.0
C
              ELSE
C
C                 .....DATA VALUE INSIDE SCREEN.....
C
                  OUT(I,J) = DATA(I,J)
C
              ENDIF
C
   10     CONTINUE
C
   20 CONTINUE
C
      RETURN
      END
```

Programming Example–Data Screening continued

The main program is as follows.

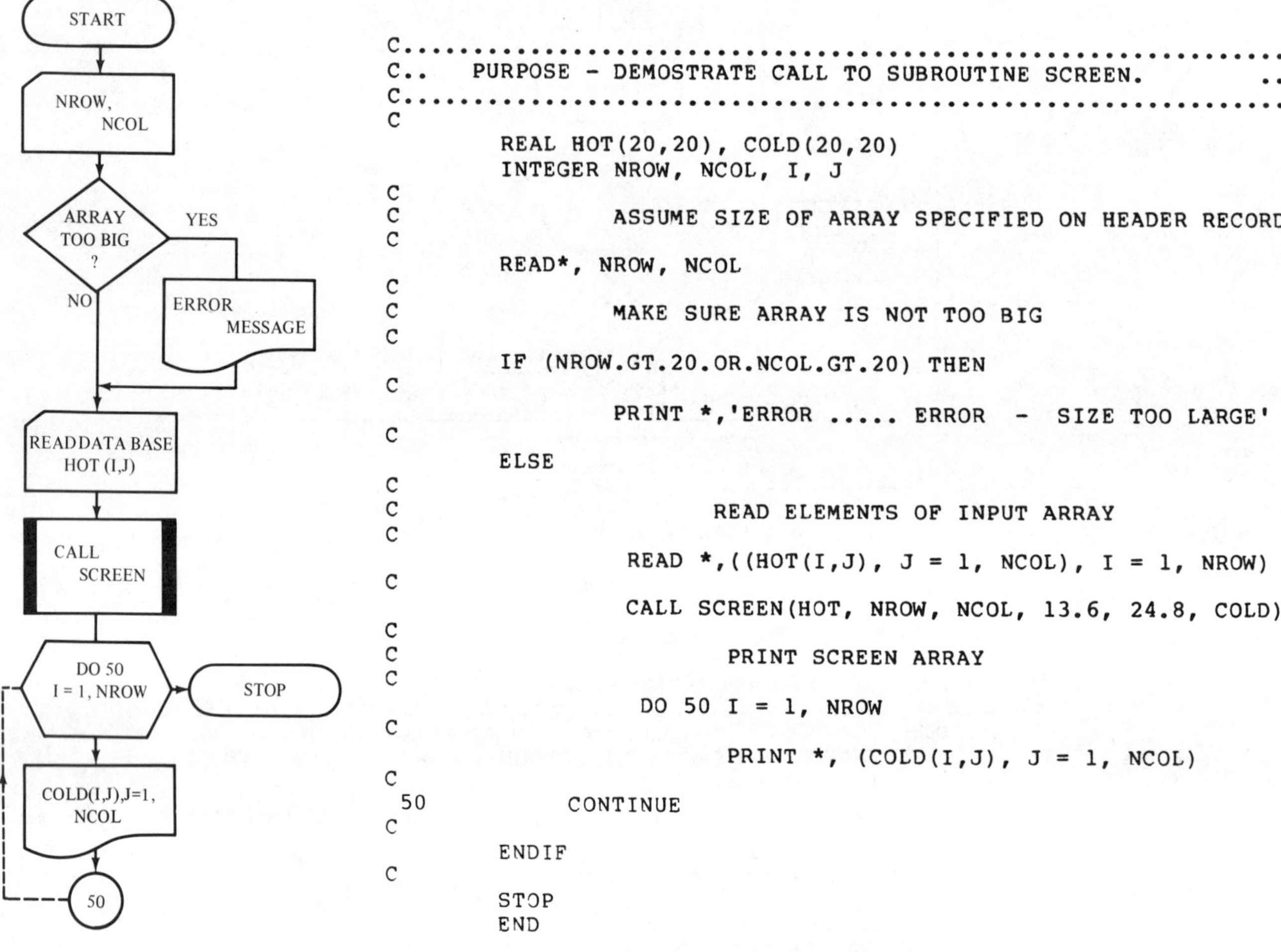


```
C.................................................................
C..   PURPOSE - DEMOSTRATE CALL TO SUBROUTINE SCREEN.           ..
C.................................................................
C
         REAL HOT(20,20), COLD(20,20)
         INTEGER NROW, NCOL, I, J
C
C                 ASSUME SIZE OF ARRAY SPECIFIED ON HEADER RECORD
C
         READ*, NROW, NCOL
C
C                 MAKE SURE ARRAY IS NOT TOO BIG
C
         IF (NROW.GT.20.OR.NCOL.GT.20) THEN
C
                  PRINT *,'ERROR ..... ERROR  -  SIZE TOO LARGE'
C
         ELSE
C
C                        READ ELEMENTS OF INPUT ARRAY
C
                   READ *,((HOT(I,J), J = 1, NCOL), I = 1, NROW)
C
                   CALL SCREEN(HOT, NROW, NCOL, 13.6, 24.8, COLD)
C
C                         PRINT SCREEN ARRAY
C
                    DO 50 I = 1, NROW
C
                          PRINT *, (COLD(I,J), J = 1, NCOL)
C
 50             CONTINUE
C
         ENDIF
C
         STOP
         END
```

Programming Example
Searching Data

Write a subroutine called SEARCH that will receive as input arguments:

DATA A one-dimensional array containing up to 100 elements.

N An integer specifying the actual size of the array.

The purpose of this routine is to find the largest element in the array and to transfer it to the end of the array by swapping its position with the nth element of the array.

One technique is to compare the first element of the array with the last element. If the first is bigger, swap the two; if it is not, compare the second element with the last element; then the third with the last, and so on. This would involve an excessive number of swaps. A better technique is to search the array for the location of the largest element. When this element is located, swap it with the last element. Make sure you do not lose the value of the last element during the swap activity.

Programming Example–Data Screening continued

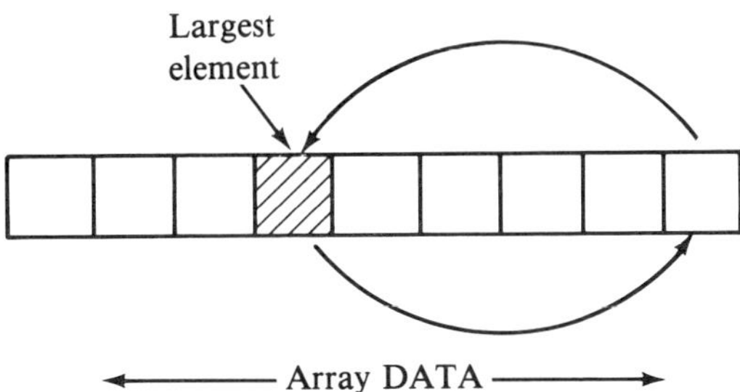

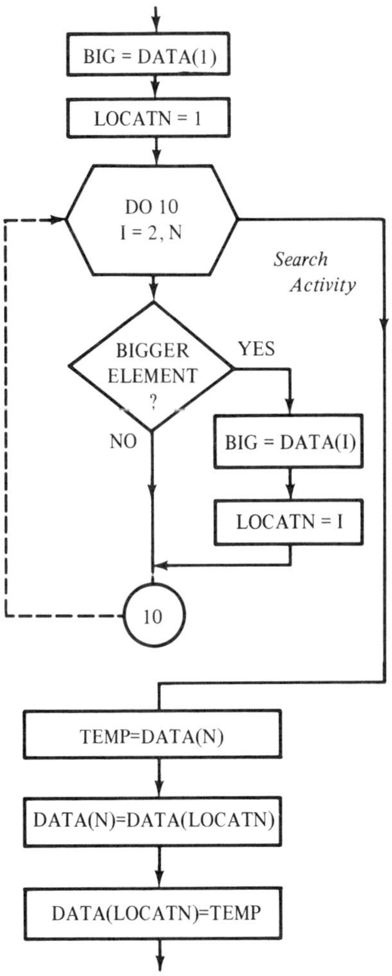

```
      SUBROUTINE   SEARCH( DATA, N)
C
C.............................................................
C..  PURPOSE - SEARCH AN ARRAY AND FIND THE LARGEST ELEMENT  ..
C..            MOVE THIS ELEMENT TO THE END OF THE ARRAY.    ..
C.............................................................
C
C                     ---IMPORTANT VARIABLES---
C
C     --DATA     NAME OF VECTOR ARRAY TO BE SEARCHED         --
C     --N        SIZE OF ARRAY DATA                          --
C     --BIG      NAME WITH LARGEST NUMBER EQUIVALENCE        --
C     --LOCATN   WHERE THIS NAME IS LOCATED IN THE LIST      --
C
      INTEGER I, N, LOCATN
      REAL    DATA(1), BIG, TEMP
C
C     .....ASSUME FIRST ELEMENT IS THE LARGEST.....
C
      BIG = DATA(1)
      LOCATN = 1
C
C     .....SEARCH REMAINING ELEMENTS.....
C
      DO 10 I = 2, N
C
          IF (DATA(I).GT.BIG) THEN
C
              BIG = DATA(I)
              LOCATN = I
C
          ENDIF
C
   10 CONTINUE
C
C     .....SWAP STATEMENTS FOLLOW.....
C
      TEMP = DATA(N)
      DATA(N)=DATA(LOCATN)
      DATA(LOCATN) = TEMP
C
      RETURN
      END
```

Programming Example Sorting Data

If an array called DATA had 60 elements and the previous subroutine, SEARCH, was called as follows:

```
CALL SEARCH(DATA,60)
```

Programming Example–Sorting Data continued

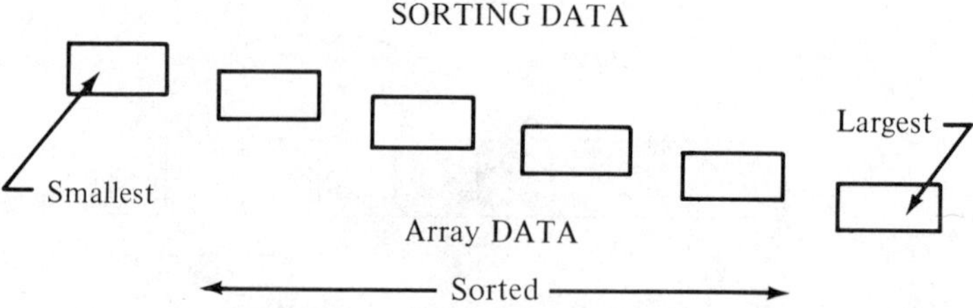

the largest element of DATA should now be in position 60. What would happen if a second call to SEARCH was made but with N indexed down by one to 59?

```
CALL SEARCH(DATA,59)
```

Clearly only the first 59 elements of DATA would be searched and the largest of these would be in position 59.

Write a subroutine called SORT that receives as input arguments:

DATA A one-dimensional array containing up to 100 elements.

N An integer specifying the actual size of the array.

This routine should sort elements of data in descending order of magnitude so that the smallest element is in position 1 and the largest element is in the *n*th position.

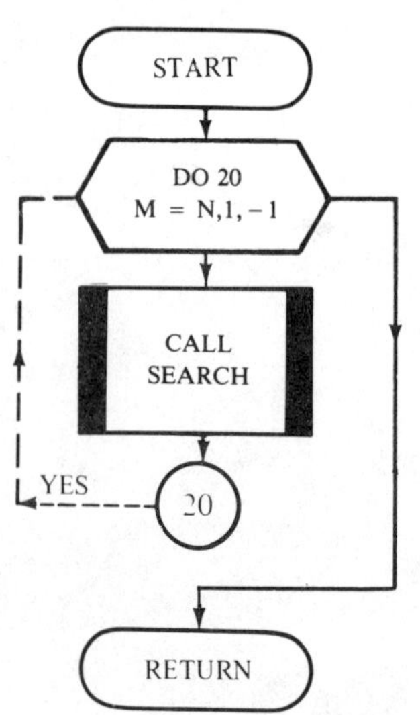


```
      SUBROUTINE SORT( DATA, N)
C.............................................................
C..   PURPOSE - MAKE SUCCESSIVE CALLS TO SUBROUTINE SEARCH     ..
C..             -----------------------                        ..
C..             ON EACH CALL TO SORT, THE SIZE OF THE ARRAY    ..
C..             WILL BE DECREASED BY ONE. THE ARRAY WILL       ..
C..             EVENTUALLY BE TOTALLY SORTED                   ..
C.............................................................
C
      INTEGER N, M
      REAL    DATA(1)
C
      DO 20 M = N, 1, -1
C
          CALL SEARCH (DATA,M)
C
C
   20 CONTINUE
C
C     .....ARRAY COMPLETLY SORTED.....
C
      RETURN
      END
```

11 Advanced Topics—Additional Subprogramming Facilities

When a program requires the use of one or more doubly subscripted variables, we must set up what is called a *nested* loop (one DO loop inside another). This nesting is needed to control the two subscripts involved. In this chapter we will study the behavior of the index of each DO loop and learn the techniques for reading and processing multidimensional arrays. We will also examine the special treatment required when these arrays are used in a subprogram.

11.1 Nested Loops

It is sometimes necessary to nest one DO loop inside another. FORTRAN allows the nesting of DOs, but does not permit overlapping of DO loops. Figure 11.1(a) shows that one loop may lie inside another. It is also possible to have several loops that terminate on the same CONTINUE statement as in Figure 11.1(b). Figure 11.1(c) shows a forbidden situation, namely an overlapping loop. The inner loop does not lie wholly inside the range of the outer DO loop; the loops overlap one another. This configuration is not allowed.

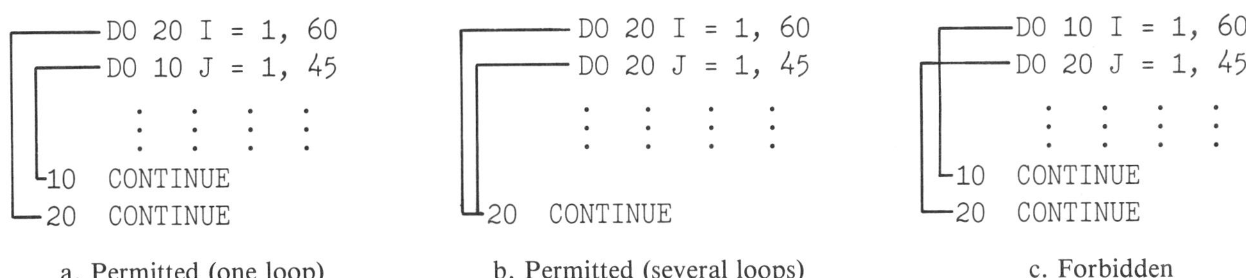

```
a. Permitted (one loop)
      DO 20 I = 1, 60
      DO 10 J = 1, 45
        :  :  :  :
   10 CONTINUE
   20 CONTINUE

b. Permitted (several loops)
      DO 20 I = 1, 60
      DO 20 J = 1, 45
        :  :  :  :
   20 CONTINUE

c. Forbidden
      DO 10 I = 1, 60
      DO 20 J = 1, 45
        :  :  :  :
   10 CONTINUE
   20 CONTINUE
```

Figure 11.1 Nested loops

Behavior of the Index in Nested DOs

When two DO loops are nested as suggested in Figure 11.2, one of the indices will index rapidly (the index of the inner DO), whereas the other index will change slowly.

Let's see why. When the first DO statement is executed, the value of I is set equal to 1. Executing the second, or inner, DO statement sets the value of J equal to 1. The program now continues until statement 10 is reached. This completes the first execution of all the statements in the range of the *inner* DO. (The outer DO is not complete because statement 20 has not been reached.) Therefore the index J is advanced to value 2 while the index I remains at 1 and control passes to the top of the inner DO. Execution of statements inside the inner DO continues (four iterations) until J reaches its test value. Control is then allowed to pass statement 10, reaching statement 20 for the first time. Because this is the last statement of the *outer* DO, the index I is advanced to 2. The trip counter of the outer DO will be incremented. Control then passes to the top of the outer DO. Because this is a DO statement, its index J is reset to 1 and the inner loop counter is set to its initial value.

Figure 11.2 Nest of DOs

```
┌───────DO 20 I = 1, 20
│ ┌─────DO 10 J = 1,  4
│ │        : :  :  :
│ └─10
└───20
```

Looping continues until the inner DO is once again satisfied. Control passes statement 10 reaching statement 20. I changes from 2 to 3, and the outer trip counter is updated. Note that the index of the inner DO is changing rapidly, whereas the index of the outer DO changes slowly.

The same sequence of indexing takes place for the "Nest of DOs" shown in Figure 11.3. When several DO loops end on the same statement, control is passed back to the top of the innermost uncompleted DO loop. Many programmers prefer to avoid using a single CONTINUE statement to terminate multiple DO loops. Instead, each loop is given its own CONTINUE statement to avoid any confusion.

Figure 11.3 Similar nest of DOs

```
┌───────DO 20 I = 1, 20
│ ┌─────DO 20 J = 1,  4
│ │        : :  :  :
└─┴─20  CONTINUE
```

Nested DOs and Two-Dimensional Arrays

Nested DOs frequently are used to provide the needed subscript control when processing two-dimensional arrays. The individual elements of two-dimensional arrays are processed in either *row* order or in *column* order:

1. *Row Order*—elements in row 1 are processed first, followed by the elements in row 2, followed by the elements in row 3, and so on.
2. *Column Order*—elements in column 1 are processed first, followed by the elements in column 2, followed by the elements in column 3, and so on.

Consider the array A shown in Figure 11.4. Assume we wish to find the sum of all these elements and we decide to process the array in row order (Figure 11.5). All the elements in row 1 are processed, followed by all the elements in row 2, and so on until all rows are processed.

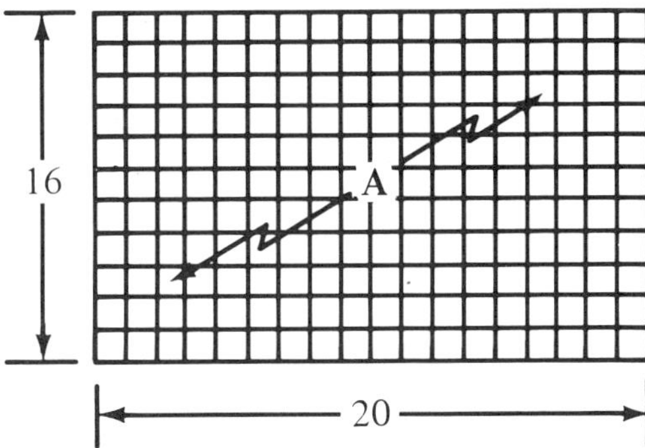

Figure 11.4 Typical two-dimensional array

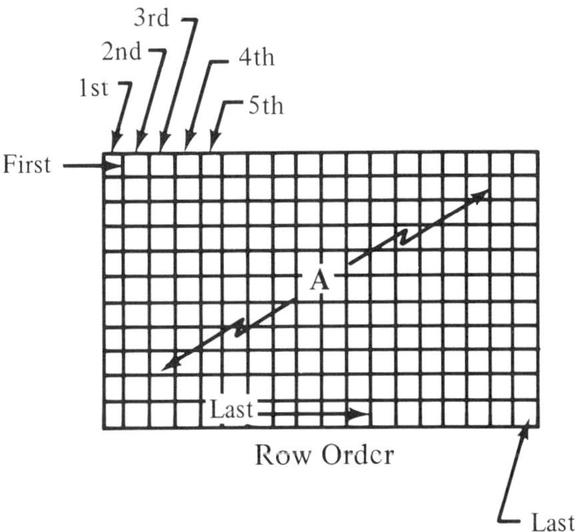

Figure 11.5 Row order

Step 1: *Process the first row.* Set up a DO loop to process all the elements in row 1 of the array only.

```
      DIMENSION A(16,20)
C
C
C...............................
      SUM = 0.0
C...............................
C
      DO 10 J = 1, 20, 1
C
          SUM = SUM + A(1,J)
C
   10 CONTINUE
C
C
C..............................
```

The sequence of variable names generated inside the loop is:

```
A(1,1),A(1,2),A(1,3),A(1,4), . . ., A(1,19),A(1,20)
```

The first subscript defines which row is being processed. Its value stays at 1 while the second subscript cycles through all the elements in that row.

Step 2: *Process all rows.* Now set up another DO loop, an outer loop, that repeats this ''row processing'' activity and process all 16 rows.

```
C...............................
      SUM = 0.0
C...............................
C
      DO 20 I = 1, 16, 1
C
         DO 10 J = 1, 20, 1
C
            SUM = SUM + A(I,J)
C
   10    CONTINUE
C
   20 CONTINUE
C
```

There is one change to the statement inside the inner DO. The index I has been substituted for the constant 1 in the first subscript position. For the first 20 executions of this statement, I has the value 1, and the sequence of names is the same as in step 1. When statement 20 is reached, I advances to 2 (row 2 is to be processed next). J is set back to 1 and starts to cycle again. The elements of A are being accumulated in the sequence intended.

An Alternate Form of Processing: Column Order

Sometimes the programmer has no choice as to what sequence in which to process an array. Assume, for example, you are told that the array A is given in the data file, one value per record in column order.

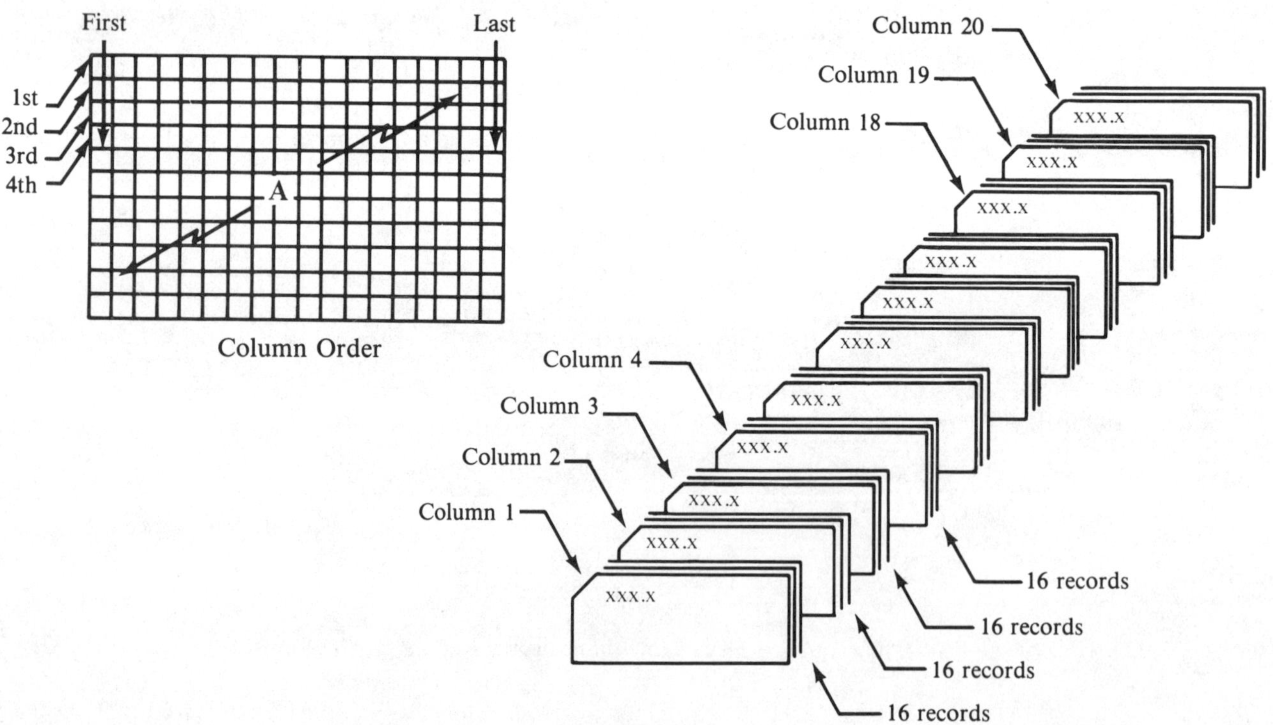

Figure 11.6 Column order

All elements in column 1 of the array must be read first, followed by all the elements in column 2, and so on. As before, you are advised to handle the subscript control problem in steps. In this instance, we would first concentrate on setting up statements that read in column 1 of the array:

```
C..............................
      SUM = 0.0
C..............................
C
      DO 20 J = 1, 16, I
C
          READ*, A(J,1)
C
          SUM = SUM + A(J,1)
C
   20 CONTINUE
C
C
C.............................
```

The sequence of names being generated is:

A(1,1),A(2,1),A(3,1),A(4.1), . . . , (A15,1),A(16,1)

Since the second subscript defines the column location, it should hold at 1 while the first subscript runs through the number of elements in a column (16 elements). Having this portion of the problem out of the way, we set up an outer loop to repeat this process for the remaining columns (20 in all). The constant 1 is replaced by the index of this new loop as shown in the following.

```
      DIMENSION A(16,20)
C..............................
      SUM = 0.0
C..............................
C
      DO 30 I = 1, 20, 1
C
          DO 20 J = 1, 16, 1
C
              READ*, A(J,I)
C
              SUM = SUM + A(J,I)
C
   20     CONTINUE
C
   30 CONTINUE
```

Both DO loops could terminate on the same statement. The program has been written with two CONTINUE statements to avoid confusion.

Whenever you are dealing with double subscripts, go at things slowly. Determine if the data must be processed in row order or column order. Set up a statement that handles the first row or the first column only. Do not try to handle the total array all at once.

When these foundation statements are complete, *generalize* them by setting up an outer DO that processes *all* rows and *all* columns. This usually involves substituting the index of the outer DO where a constant was used before.

11.2 Input/Output of Large Arrays

Recall that when reading one-dimensional arrays, several methods of subscript control were allowed. These options are shown in Figure 11.7. The subscript can be provided by a DO statement or by an implied index. The Method 3 option is the final alternative where the system provides the subscript control.

Figure 11.7 Forms of READ statement

Method 1

```
    DO 10 I = 1. 10
         READ*, B(I)

10 CONTINUE
```

Method 2

```
READ*, (B(I),I=1, 200)
```

Method 3

```
READ*, B
```

Figure 11.8 shows a similar sequence of input statements for two-dimensional arrays. Assume the data is presented in column order and we are again dealing with the array A(16,20). Each method generates 320 names needed to process the whole array, but one method does it best.

Figure 11.8 Column order in two-dimensional READ statements

Method 1

```
   DO 30 I = 1, 20, 1
     DO 20 J = 1, 16, 1
       READ*, A(J,I)

20     CONTINUE
30 CONTINUE
```

Method 2

```
    DO 30 I = 1, 20, 1
          READ*, (A(J,I),J=1, 16)

30 CONTINUE
```

Method 3

```
READ*, ((A(J,I),J=1, 16),I=1, 20)
```

Method 4

```
READ*, A
```

Method 1 is not very realistic. Because only one name follows the READ command, 320 records would be required. Method 2 is a little more efficient in that each execution of the READ command brings in one column of the matrix. There is an even more efficient READ statement, however. Method 3 is the preferred method. It executes a single READ command followed by all 320 names. The subscript J cycles between 1 and 16. The subscript I cycles between 1 and 20 (it is like a DO loop inside a DO loop). The index J is obviously the inner index (it cycles fast). The index I is the outer index (it cycles slowly). Take a minute to make sure you understand this. It is important.

Now let's turn things around. Assume the data is in row order. What should the READ statement look like?

```
READ*,((A(J,I),I=1,20),J=1,16)
READ*,((A(M,N),N=1,20),M=1,16)
```

Any statement where the second subscript cycles fast and the first cycles slowly is basically correct.

The `READ` statement in Method 4 causes the transfer of the whole array automatically. The array is transferred in column order. Transferring arrays by using `READ/WRITE` statements that have self-contained subscript control features is called **implicit transfer** or **implied `DO` transfer**.

Quiz 18
Nested DO Loops

1. Describe a nested `DO`.
2. If two loops are nested, the index of which `DO` changes faster?
3. What is meant by overlapping `DO`s? Are they allowed?
4. May more than one `DO` loop terminate on the same `CONTINUE` statement?
5. What does the term ''row'' order mean?
6. A two-dimensional array called B has 5 rows and 8 columns. Write a single `READ` statement that uses the implied index method to input the array. The array is given in row order.
7. May the name of a two-dimensional array appear in an input/output statement without a subscript and thereby cause the transfer of the whole array? If the answer is yes, in what order is the array transferred?
8. A two-dimensional array called C has 10 rows and 12 columns. Write statements that will print the first and last row of the array on separate lines of output.
9. Repeat question 8 except print the first and last column of the array in its natural form (have column 1 appear on the left side of the output sheet and column 12 appear on the right side).
10. In the following `READ` statement, which subscript cycles faster, `L` or `K`?

```
READ*,(A(K,L),L=1,18),K=1,20)
```

11.3 Multidimensional Arrays as Arguments

We have presented numerous examples in which one-dimensional arrays have been passed as arguments between the using and defining subprogram. Because of the simple way in which one-dimensional arrays are stored in memory, using them as arguments is a relatively straightforward process. It just involves passing of the ''base address'' of the array.

The storage of multidimensional arrays (two-dimensional and three-dimensional) is not as simple, and passing them as arguments is more complicated in that the following restriction is imposed: When multidimensional arrays are passed as arguments, the *size* of the array in the using program must be the *same* as the *size* of the array in the defining program. This means that the array B of the program shown on the right of Figure 11.9 could not be used as an argument to supply values for an array called A in the subroutine `SCALE` because they are of different size. One is 3 by 3, the other is 10 by 10.

Figure 11.9

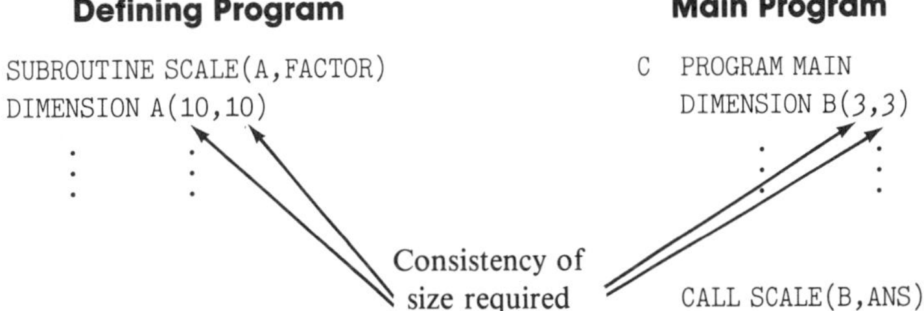

Stated another way, subroutine `SCALE` (as presently written) can only process arrays of a fixed size, namely 10 by 10. This would be a serious obstacle if it were not for the fact that DIMENSION statements describing arrays of a subprogram are allowed to have two special forms. Recall that in a main program only *integer constants* are permitted when specifying the size (maximum subscript) of an array. The same restriction is applied to DIMENSION statements used in a subprogram if the purpose of the DIMENSION statement is to reserve large areas of memory needed for *local* variables of that subprogram. The following statement demonstrates the main program restriction.

```
DIMENSION A(10,10),B(16,14),C(20)
```

Integer constants

Arrays that are *arguments* do not fall in this category and are not bound by this restriction. For these variables there is no need to set up large areas of memory of their own. These variables share the areas established by the DIMENSION statement in the evoking (using) program. Under these special circumstances, a DIMENSION statement need only show that a particular variable represents a subscripted quantity. For each of these variables, only the following information is needed:

1. The base address of the corresponding array in the calling program.
2. The size of the array if the array is multidimensional (number of rows, number of columns, for example).

Under these conditions, the size of these arrays can be expressed as *integer variables* provided that these integer variables are defined in the argument list of the subprogram.

This is just the relief needed to meet the ''same size'' requirements imposed on multidimensional arrays. The procedure is to use a DIMENSION statement that specifies the array size using variables like M or N. These names are added to the list of arguments with the requirement that their values be defined when the CALL is made. The end result is that both arrays appear to be of the same size (see the programming example that follows). By defining M or N, the subprogram can locate where beyond the base address a particular element of a two-dimensional array is located. These *adjustable dimensions* provide a convenient way to satisfy the consistency of size requirements.

```
DIMENSION A(M,N),OUT(14,12), D(N)
```

Integer variable allowed
if array is an argument

Note that a second method is available on some systems that is even more direct in obtaining this "matching of size" condition:

```
DIMENSION A(*,*),OUT(*,*),D(*)
```

It involves placing an asterisk in place of size descriptions. The appearance of the asterisk causes the compiler to examine the DIMENSION statement of the calling program to define the information (SIZE) usually supplied in that position.

Programming Example
Scale a Matrix

It is getting more and more difficult these days to avoid problems involving matrix operations. One of the simpler operations is to **scale a matrix**. This merely means to multiply each element of a two-dimensional array by a specific value like 2.0, 3.8, or 1.6 (the scale factor). By writing a subroutine to accomplish this operation, we will

Programming Example–Scale a Matrix continued

be dealing with a relatively simple subprogram but one that requires the two-dimensional matrix to be consistent in size with the evoking program. To be effective, this subroutine must be capable of accepting matrices of varying sizes.

Write a subroutine called SCALE that receives as input:

A	Name of the matrix.
NROW	Number of rows in the matrix.
NCOL	Number of columns in the matrix.
FACTOR	Value by which each element is to be multiplied.

Output of this subroutine is the modified form of the array A. To test this subroutine, we write a main program that scales two different arrays. The first is array B of size 3 by 3. Each element of B is set at 2.0 and a scale factor of 4.0 used. The second array, array C, is a 4 by 5 array. Each element is set at −1.0, and the scale factor is −8.0. If subroutine SCALE works properly, all elements in both arrays will wind up with the value 8.0

```
      SUBROUTINE SCALE(A, NROW, NCOL, FACTOR)
C...............................................................
C..   PURPOSE - TO SCALE A MATRIX OF SIZE NROW BY NCOL.       ..
C...............................................................
C
C           ----IMPORTANT VARIABLES----
C
C     --A        THE MATRIX TO BE SCALED                      --
C     --NROW     NUMBER OF ROWS IN THE MATRIX                 --
C     --NCOL     NUMBER OF COLUMNS IN THE MATRIX              --
C     --FACTOR   THE SCALING FACTOR                           --
C
C              ....THE OUTPUT IS THE SCALED MATRIX A....
C
C     EXAMPLE OF VARIABLE DIMENSION
C
      REAL A(NROW,NCOL)
C
      DO 10 I = 1, NROW
C
          DO 20 J = 1, NCOL
C
              A(I,J) = A(I,J) * FACTOR
C
   20     CONTINUE
C
   10 CONTINUE
C
      RETURN
      END
```

	ARRAY B			**ARRAY C**				
Size	3 by 3			4 by 5				
Input	2.0	2.0	2.0	−1.0	−1.0	−1.0	−1.0	−1.0
	2.0	2.0	2.0	−1.0	−1.0	−1.0	−1.0	−1.0
	2.0	2.0	2.0	−1.0	−1.0	−1.0	−1.0	−1.0
				−1.0	−1.0	−1.0	−1.0	−1.0
Scale Factor	4.0			−8.0				
Output	8.0	8.0	8.0	8.0	8.0	8.0	8.0	8.0
	8.0	8.0	8.0	8.0	8.0	8.0	8.0	8.0
	8.0	8.0	8.0	8.0	8.0	8.0	8.0	8.0

Programming Example–Scale a Matrix continued

```
C...........................................................
C..    PURPOSE - A MAIN PROGRAM THAT TESTS SUBROUTINE SCALE  ..
C..                                                          ..
C..            THE PROGRAM GENERATES TWO SETS OF TEST DATA ..
C..            AND THEN MAKES TWO CALLS TO SUBROUTINE SCALE..
C...........................................................
C
C                    ---IMPORTANT VARIABLES---
C
C      --B         FIRST TEST ARRAY... SIZE (3, BY 3)...ALL
C                  VALUES OF ARRAY B INITIALLY SET AT 2.0      --
C
C      --C         SECOND TEST ARRAY... SIZE (4 BY 5)...ALL
C                  VALUES OF ARRAY C INITIALLY SET AT -1.0     --
C
      REAL B(3,3), C(4,5)
C
C     .....DEFINE ALL ELEMENTS OF ARRAY B.....
C
      DO 10 I = 1, 3
C
          DO 10 J = 1, 3
C
              B(I,J) = 2.0
C
   10 CONTINUE
C
C         .............................
C         .....FIRST CALL TO SCALE.....
C         .............................
C
      CALL SCALE(B,3,3,4.0)
C
C     .....DISPLAY SCALED ARRAY.....
C
      WRITE(2,20) ((B(I,J),J=1,3),I=1,3)
   20 FORMAT(3X,3F12.1)
C
C     .....DEFINE ALL ELEMENTS OF ARRAY C.....
C
      DO 30 I = 1, 4
C
          DO 30 J = 1,5
C
              C(I,J) = -1.0
C
   30 CONTINUE
C
C         ...................................
C         .....MAKE SECOND CALL TO SCALE.....
C         ...................................
C
      CALL SCALE(C,4,5,-8.0)
C
C     .....DISPLAY CALLED.....
C
      WRITE(2,40) ((C(I,J),J=1,5),I=1,4)
   40 FORMAT(3X,5F12.1)
C
      STOP
      END
```

11.4 Understanding Array Storage

Subprogramming has many advantages that we will continue to exploit in detail. For a moment, however, we must at least suggest a serious disadvantage: *the concept of subprogramming involves the sharing of memory, which can be dangerous.*

To understand the full implications of this warning, you must know how the computer stores two-dimensional arrays. The following presentations show how a 3 by 3 array called B is stored internally and how a 10 by 10 array called A is stored. We then will show what would happen if these arrays were linked in a subprogram.

Recall the arrays suggested in Figure 11.9. If a main program declares a two-dimensional array of size 3 by 3, nine consecutive memory locations are assigned to hold this array. The first three locations hold column 1 of the array, the next three locations hold column 2 and the last three hold column 3. That is, the array is stored in *column order.*

Figure 11.10 Illustration of column order storage

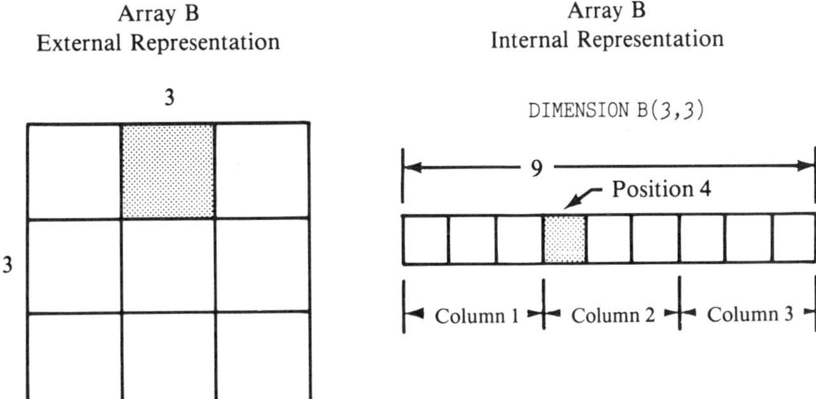

Each time any element of this array is referenced, it is necessary to determine where in the string of nine memory locations this particular element is located. Take, as an example, the element B(1,2). Since it is the first element of column 2, it is located in the fourth memory location. Remember, we are storing in column order.

Now consider the array A of the subprogram that is declared to be of size 10 by 10. If this array was assigned memory locations of its own, the first 10 locations would hold column 1 of the array, the next 10 locations would hold column 2, and so on. An element such as A(1,2) would be 11 elements beyond the base address.

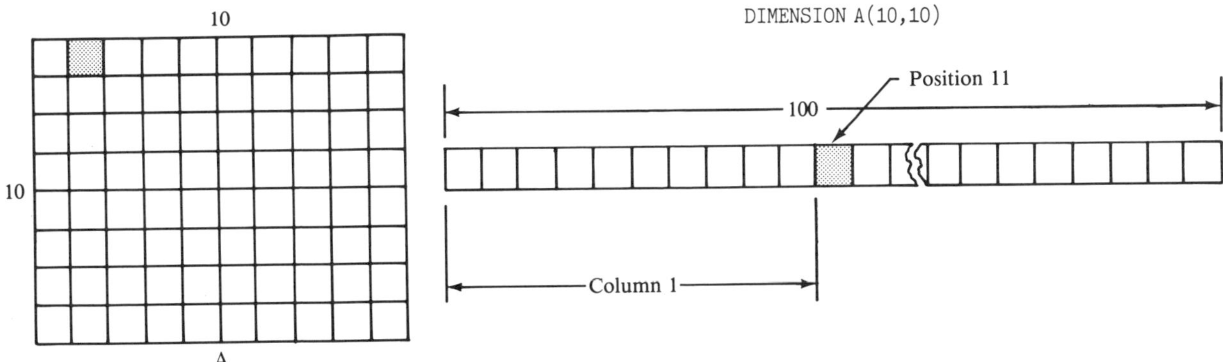

Do you see why these arrays cannot be equated? If the arrays were both the same size, A(1,2) and B(1,2) would be referencing the same elements of the two arrays. When the dimension statements are different, this is not true. A(1,2) is referencing a memory location 11 positions into the array, but the array (in the main program) is only 9 elements long. You would be referencing a memory location two positions beyond array B. If the statement A(1,2) = 0.0 were made, some variable two locations beyond array B would be redefined. Errors like this are rather sophisticated in nature and sometimes very difficult to find.

Using subprograms requires a better understanding of memory management because of this "sharing of memory" effect.

11.5 The Equivalence Statement

The EQUIVALENCE statement is a nonexecutable statement that allows the programmer to exercise control over the assignment of memory locations. The EQUIVALENCE statement allows a single memory location to be identified by more than one variable name. How would one use this feature? Assume a program (or subprogram) has been written, and that the programmer has inadvertently used the names IMAX, MAX, and IBIG to represent the same value. It would be desirable to correct this error without rewriting all the statements that involve those variable names. The correction can be accomplished by adding (usually in the declarative section) the EQUIVALENCE statement:

```
EQUIVALENCE (IMAX,MAX,IBIG)
```

This causes the three variable names contained within the parentheses to refer to a single memory location, thereby correcting the error. The name IMAX, MAX, and IBIG all will point, so to speak, to the same memory location.

An equivalence can be set up between more than one group of names. The statement:

```
EQUIVALENCE (IMAX,MAX,IBIG), (X,Y,Z), (D,E)
```

First group Second group Third group

establishes the names IMAX, MAX, and IBIG as being equivalent, whereas the names X, Y, and Z are another group of names equated. Finally, D and E are made equivalent to each other. *The names within each pair of parentheses are equated to each other.*

The EQUIVALENCE statement can be used in an entirely different way. Assume that A, B, and C represent rather large arrays within a program, but that only one of these arrays

```
DIMENSION A(100), B(100), C(100)
```

is needed at any given time in the program. The array A may be in active use early in the program. The array B is needed only for a short time in the middle of the program and array C is needed late in the program. We describe this situation by saying there is "no overlap in need" for these arrays. A single set of 100 memory locations could be used to store all values but referenced by three different names, thereby conserving memory. It is possible to establish an equivalence between these arrays by the statements:

```
DIMENSION A(100), B(100), C(100)
EQUIVALENCE (A(1), B(1), C(1))
```

While it appears that the equivalence statement is equating only three variables (the first element of each array), actually, the effect is much larger. Arrays are always stored in successive memory locations. This is accomplished automatically by the compiler. Aligning or equating the first element of these arrays automatically aligns or equates the remaining elements of the arrays. This relationship is shown in Figure 11.11. The shaded location is the only location referred to in the EQUIVALENCE statement. Using this technique has reduced the amount of memory consumed from 300 to 100.

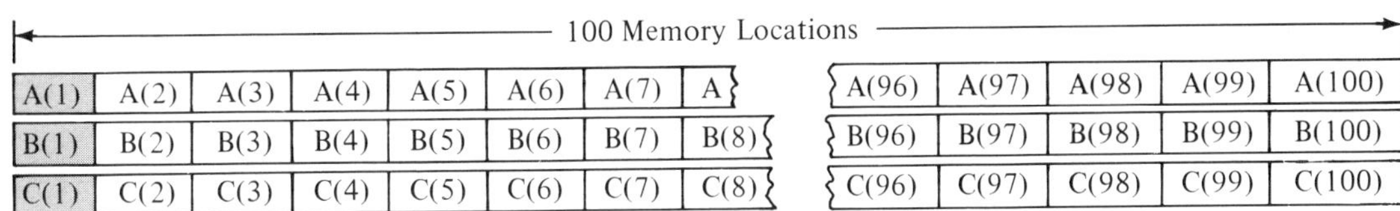

Figure 11.11 Equating whole arrays

While it is true we could go back and use a single variable name for all arrays (like A), this would involve rewriting the program and would reduce the ease and clarity with which the program can be read.

One does not often preplan the equating of large arrays. It most often happens on an after-the-fact basis, namely when a program will not fit into the memory space available. It is then that the programmer starts shopping around to see what space can be saved. This is one method of making the program shorter.

The following example is offered to reinforce or clarify the alignment procedure that takes place when subscripted variables appear in EQUIVALENCE statements.

Figure 11.12 A second example

```
DIMENSION A(5), B(4), C(2)
EQUIVALENCE (A(3), B(2), C(1))
```

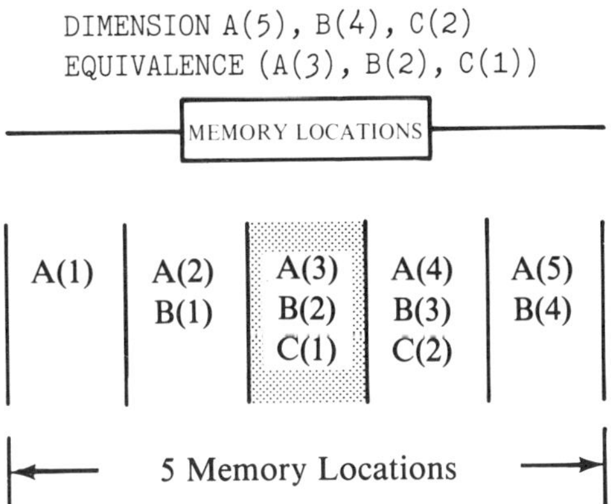

The arrays A, B, and C are declared as being of size 5, 4, and 2, respectively. The equivalence statement aligns A(3), B(2), and C(1) as the shaded block shows. Then all other elements are positioned as shown. After this aligning, the variables A(4), B(3), and C(2) all refer to the same memory location.

Reminder: When referencing a subscripted variable in an EQUIVALENCE statement, the subscript must be expressed as a constant.

11.6 The COMMON Statement

The EQUIVALENCE statement coordinates variable naming within a single program or subprogram. The COMMON statement allows the coordination of variable naming between a main program and one or more subprograms. It can be used to conserve memory and to allow the sharing of data by means other than an argument list.

Most computers reserve a specific amount of memory for the running of a program. The compiler uses this block of memory in the following way. Starting at the beginning of the block, memory is allocated sequentially to the variables and arrays of the main program and then to those of the various subprograms. The variable names used within each subprogram to identify these locations are, of course, independent of each other.

Normally, when this is completed, there will be some unused memory at the end of the block. We will take advantage of this to set up a special segment of memory, which starts at the end of the block and works forward. This area is called COMMON **storage** and is under your control through the use of the COMMON statement. This area is unique in that it is accessible to any of the subprograms and to the main program (it can be shared) by evoking the COMMON statement and then declaring what names the sequential memory locations in this area are to be assigned. The statement:

```
COMMON A,X,BOY,I          In the Main Program
```

appearing in the main program says, in effect, that the main program intends to participate in the sharing of common storage. It declares the names A, X, BOY, and I as those to be used in the main program to reference the first four locations in common storage. The statement:

```
COMMON B,Y,GIRL,M          In the Subprogram
```

appearing in a subprogram indicates that this subprogram will also share these four memory locations, but that they are to be called B, Y, GIRL, and M in this subprogram.

If, at any time in the main program, the variables A, X, or I are defined, the corresponding locations in common storage are loaded, and, as a consequence, the variables B, Y, or M in the subprogram will automatically become defined (known). On the other hand, defining B, Y, or GIRL in the subprogram automatically defines A, X, or BOY in the main program. A second subroutine could participate in the sharing process by using the statement:

```
COMMON X1, Y1, Y2, J
```

It now has access to these four locations in common storage using the names that the subprogram finds most appropriate, namely X1, Y1, Y2, and J. If it becomes necessary, COMMON storage can be expanded.

Returning to the main program, consider these statements:

Old	**New**
COMMON A,X,BOY,I	COMMON A,X,BOY,I COMMON OUT(100),SALES(60)

The appearance of the second COMMON statement has extended common storage. In addition to the four original memory locations, 160 more real memory locations have been added on. The first 100 of these is an array called OUT followed by 60 locations to be called SALES.

This allocation of memory could have been accomplished by a single COMMON statement as follows:

```
DIMENSION OUT(100),SALES(60)
COMMON A,X,BOY,I,OUT,SALES
```

When constructing the list of variable names following the word COMMON in a program or the various subprograms that share common storage, a consistency of *mode* must be observed. The last COMMON statement declares that the first three locations in common storage are to be real in mode, followed by a single integer mode, followed by 160 real locations. You may, of course, set up any pattern of reals and integers you want, but once established *all other* COMMON *statements must conform to the same pattern.*

The correspondence in mode consistency is displayed in the following example:

Main Program	Subprogram
`DIMENSION J(4),X(35)` `COMMON J,X`	`DIMENSION A(10),B(25)` `COMMON K,L,M,N,A,B,`

Both lists of names declare that the first four locations in common storage are to be treated as integers and the next 35 as real.

Note that it is possible to declare the size of arrays within the COMMON statement and eliminate the DIMENSION statement. The previous statement could be written more efficiently as:

Main Program	Subprogram
`COMMON J(4),X(35)`	`COMMON K,L,M,N,A(10),B(25)`

J(1) in the main program is identified as K in the subprogram, J(2) is identified as L, and so on. Since the "address determination" for a subscripted variable takes longer than for a simple variable, the subprogram is accessing data more quickly than the main program.

Both the EQUIVALENCE and COMMON statements are nonexecutable statements and are best positioned in the declarative block of your program (those before any executable statement).

11.7 Advantages of Common Storage

It should be obvious that the EQUIVALENT statement is *local* in nature and can be used to conserve memory within a given program or subprogram. The COMMON statement is said to be *global* and can be used to conserve memory between the main program and its subprograms. This is because the appearance of each COMMON statement does not cause the allocation of additional memory. It just allows the same area in common storage to be called by different names.

Common storage has another and perhaps more important application. Values that must be shared by a program and various subprograms do not have to be passed using an argument list. These values can be placed in common storage (usually by the main program) and then used or accessed by the various subprograms. In complex problems, the argument list tends to become long and cumbersome. The argument list can be made more manageable (that is, reduced in size) by placing some of the variables in common storage. In the case of a subroutine, the argument list can even be eliminated altogether. A function subprogram, however, must have at least one argument. Using common storage to pass arguments of a subprogram is called **implicit transfer of arguments.**

The next programming example involves a large data base that must be accessible to four or five subroutines. These subroutines accomplish various tasks associated with an airline reservation problem. Because the people using these routines will have little or no programming experience, it is essential that the argument list be as simple and as small as possible. Accordingly, the data base is stored in common storage. Each subroutine can access the information in the data base, but the name of the data base does not have to be a part of any argument list.

In large projects where many subprograms are involved, each with a different argument list, those arguments that the subprograms have in common are usually placed in common storage. The other arguments (those unique to each subprogram) are left in the argument list.

Programming Example
Airline Reservation

An airline operates 128 flights each week and for simplicity's sake we will assume all flights have a seating capacity of 214 seats. As part of an "airlines reservation program," we must keep track of the names of passengers booked on each flight and what seat they have been assigned. These names will be stored in an array called RESERV forming a large data base that will be operated on (shared) by several subroutines.

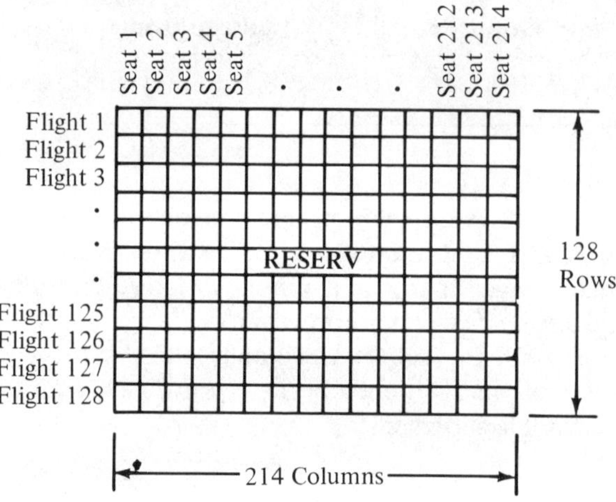

Each row of the array called RESERV is to represent a given flight. Each of the 214 elements in any row represents a seat on that flight. An element contains either the name of the passenger booked on that flight (and in that seat) or the word "EMPTY" (to signal the seat is available). The word size of each memory location is assumed to be 8 characters in length.

Figure 11.13 Typical row in the data base

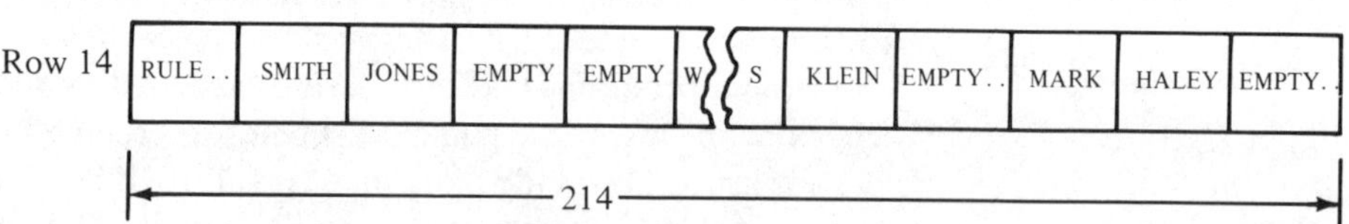

Part A: Unreserved Seats One of the subroutines we will be writing should be able to examine any row of the data base and determine how many seats are still unreserved (empty) for that specific flight, assuming the array RESERV already has been read and placed in common storage.

Write a subroutine called AVAIL that has a single input argument, FLIGHT. This number tells which flight a passenger is asking information about. For the moment, have this subroutine return a single argument, NSEATS, telling how many seats are still available. This subroutine examines one row of the data base to see if any of the elements contains the word EMPTY. Since each element contains 8 alphabetic characters, we need to know if the 8 characters are 'EMPTY___'. This will be accomplished by an IF test, but in a slightly new way: using an alphabetic constant.

Programming Example–Airline Reservation continued

Figure 11.14 Two types of IF statements

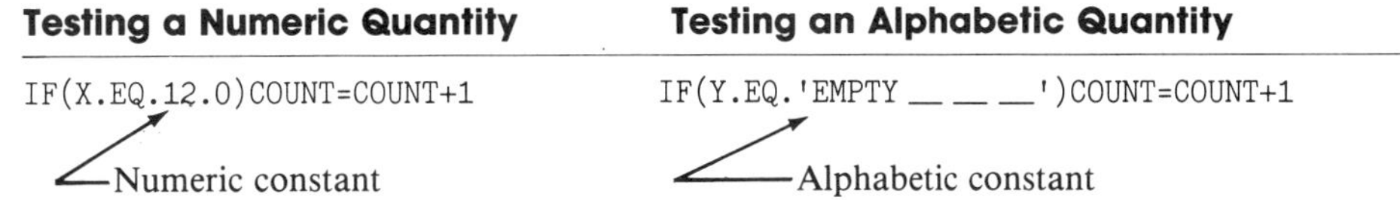

The IF tests shown in Figure 11.14 are of two distinctly different types. You are more familiar with the first IF test shown. It tests to see if the memory location X contains the *numeric* value 12.0. The other IF test is used to see if the memory location Y contains a specific *aphabetic* value, namely 'EMPTY _ _ _'. The presence of quotation marks identifies an alphabetic constant as being the object of this IF test.†

```
      SUBROUTINE AVAIL(FLIGHT, NSEATS)
C
C.........................................................
C..    PURPOSE - DEMONSTRATE THE  USE OF COMMON STORAGE.    ..
C..              DETERMINE THE NUMBER OF EMPTY SEATS ON A   ..
C..              SPECIFIC FLIGHT.                           ..
C.........................................................
C
C                    ---IMPORTANT VARIABLES---
C
C      --RESERV   DATA BASE OF NAMES (IN COMMON STORAGE)    --
C      --FLIGHT   NUMBER OF FLIGHT BEING SEARCHED           --
C      --NSEATS   NUMBER OF EMPTY SEATS ON THAT FLIGHT      --
C
      CHARACTER*8 RESERV
      INTEGER  FLIGHTS,NSEATS
      COMMON   RESERV(128,214)
C
C
      NSEATS = 0
C
C     .....SET UP LOOP TO SEARCH ROW FLIGHT.....
C
      DO 10 I = 1, 214
C
          IF(RESERV(FLIGHT,I).EQ.'EMPTY  ') NSEATS = NSEATS + 1
C
   10 CONTINUE
C
      RETURN
      END
```

Part B: Specific Seat Numbers. If there are sufficient seats on a flight, the next step is to determine the specific seat numbers of unreserved seats. This is to be accomplished by subroutine SEATS. Its input arguments are:

1. FLIGHT—the flight we are booking.
2. NUMBER—the number of seats we want.
3. NSTART—where in the plane the search for empty seats should start.

The last argument allows the passenger to locate approximately where in the plane he or she would like to sit. Subroutine SEATS should print as output *twice* the number of seat numbers being requested to give the passenger a choice.

† Without the quotation marks, EMPTY would be interpreted as the name of a simple variable.

Programming Example–Airline Reservation continued

```
      SUBROUTINE SEATS(FLIGHT, NUMBER, NSTART)
C.................................................................
C..   PURPOSE - PRINT OUT AVAILABLE (EMPTY) SEATS ON A          ..
C..             SPECIFIC FLIGHT STARTING WITH SEAT NUMBER ..
C..             NSTART                                          ..
C.................................................................
C
C                    ---IMPORTANT VARIABLES---
C
C     --NUMBER   NUMBER OF SEATS REQUESTED                      --
C     --NSTART   WHERE IN PLANE SEARCH STARTS FROM              --
C
      CHARACTER RESERV*8
      INTEGER   FLIGHT,NUMBER,NSEATS
      COMMON    RESERV (128,214)
C
C     REDEFINE NUMBER TO TWICE VALUE REQUESTED...GIVE CUSTOMER
C               A LARGE CHOICE OF SEATS
C
      NUMBER = NUMBER * 2
C
C     .....SEARCH LOOP STARTS HERE.....
C
      DO 20 I = NSTART, 214
C
          IF(RESERV(FLIGHT,I).EQ.'EMPTY   ') THEN
C
              PRINT*, I
              NUMBER = NUMBER -1
              IF(NUMBER.EQ.0) RETURN
C
          ENDIF
C
   20 CONTINUE
C
      PRINT*,'THESE ARE THE ONLY',NSEATS,'SEATS AVAILABLE'
C
      RETURN
      END
```

Part C: Reserving Seats The next subroutine to be written is called SOLD. It allows the booking agent to reserve specific seats. We will make the subroutine conversational in mode in that all the agent must do is enter the statement "CALL SOLD" and control passes to the subroutine, which then gives directions for providing the necessary input. This assumes that the input/output is via terminals.

```
      SUBROUTINE SOLD
C..........................................................
C..   PURPOSE - DEMONSTRATE CONVERSATIONAL MODE          ..
C..             PROGRAMMING. BOOK INDIVIDUAL             ..
C..             SEATS ON THE AIRCRAFT.                   ..
C..........................................................
C
      CHARACTER*8 PASNGR, RESERV
      INTEGER   FLIGHT, NSEATS, N
      COMMON    RESERV(128,214)
C
      PRINT*,'ENTER THE FLIGHT NUMBER'
C
      READ*, FLIGHT  <------------------------------  Requesting flight
C                                                     number
      PRINT*,'ENTER PASSENGER NAME'
C
      READ*, PASNGR  <------------------------------  Requesting passenger's
C                                                     name
```

Programming Example–Airline Reservation continued

```
C     .....DETERMINE NUMBER OF SEATS WANTED.....
C
      PRINT*,'HOW MANY SEATS ARE YOU BOOKING?'
      READ*, NSEATS
C
      DO 40 I = 1, NSEATS
C
C         .....READ SEAT NUMBERS.....
C
          PRINT*, 'TYPE IN SEAT NUMBER ONE PER LINE'
C
          READ*, N<-------------------------------- Requesting seat
C                                                    number
C         BOOK PASSENGERS NAME INTO DATA BASE
C
          RESERV(FLIGHT,N) = PASNGR<--------------- Making reservation
C
   40 CONTINUE
C
      STOP
      END
```

Many other subroutines would be needed to complete this package. When a flight departs, it would be necessary to change all elements in one row of the data base to 'EMPTY___ ___ ___' to set up for future booking of this flight. Passengers often try to shift from one flight to another or have to cancel out. All these can be written by separate subroutines that operate on the data base stored in common storage.

11.8 Labeled Common

We have shown that common storage can be used to share large arrays with one or more subprograms. Common can also be used to avoid long argument lists between subprograms. Common storage is so useful, especially when a large number of subprograms are involved, that it has been found advisable to allow the programmer to set up more than one area of common storage. These areas are similar to the common storage just described (to be called **unlabeled common** from now on) except that they must be given an identifying name and are, therefore, called **labeled common**. The statement:

```
COMMON/A/X, Y, Z(10)
```

creates a labeled common storage area named A. It assigns the names X and Y to the first two locations in the area and the name Z to the next ten areas (Z is a subscripted variable). If the statement:

```
COMMON/A/C, D, B(10)
```

appears in the subprogram, it identifies the variable names used by that program to identify successive memory locations in common storage A.

It is possible to identify memory locations in both labeled and unlabeled common with a single common statement. Consider the following statements:

Main Program	**Subprogram**
`COMMON A, B, C/Z1/D, E, F(10)/Z2/M, N`	`COMMON R, S, T/Z1/U, V, W(10)/Z2/I, J`

The first portion of these statements declares the names to be used in identifying the first three locations in unlabeled common storage. The name A in the main program and the name R in the subprogram both identify the first location in unlabeled common storage. The next sequence of names identifies locations in labeled common Z1. This labeled common area has 12 locations containing two nonsubscripted variables, followed by a one-dimensional array called F in the main program and W in the subprogram. Finally, labeled common Z2 is created containing two integer locations.

11.9 The EXTERNAL Statement

Until now, the names appearing in an argument list of a subprogram have represented memory locations exclusively—they represent simple variables or arrays. A name in the argument list of a subprogram can, however, represent an entirely different quantity; it can represent the *name of another subprogram*. The implication is that one subprogram needs information contained within the other subprogram to function properly.

Assume you have been asked to write a subroutine called AREA.

```
SUBROUTINE AREA(XLEFT,XRIGHT,Y,ANS)
```

The purpose of this subroutine is to determine the area under a curve between two limits of X defined by XLEFT and XRIGHT.

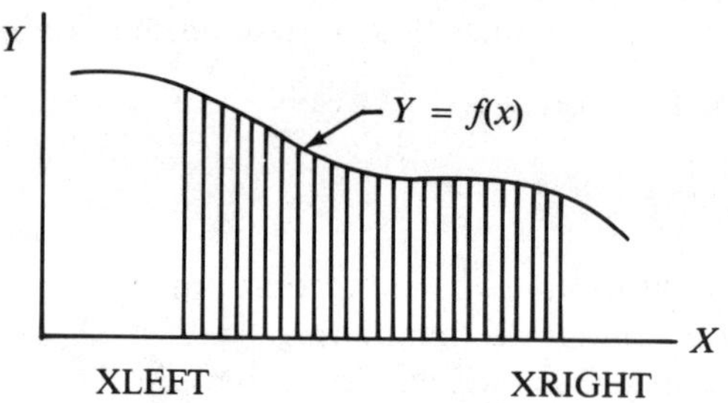

The argument ANS returns the computed area to the calling program. The remaining argument, Y, is used to define the curve. The curve may be known in two possible ways:

1. As a series of data points.
2. As an equation.

If the curve is defined by a series of data points (by an array called Y), we would use a DIMENSION statement to show the special attribute of the name Y—to show it is an array.

If the curve is defined by an equation, we are allowed to define a function subprogram containing that equation, give it the name Y, and include it in the argument list of subroutine AREA (just as we did before). We must again somehow show the special attribute of the name Y—to show it is the name of a subprogram. The EXTERNAL statement serves that purpose:

```
EXTERNAL Y
```

As a specific example, assume we are dealing with a curve whose equation is:

$$y = x^6 - x^2 + \ln(x + 4)$$

The new procedure would suggest setting up the following function subprogram.

```
      FUNCTION Y (X)
C
C......................................................
C..   PURPOSE - TO HOLD THE EQUATION OF THE CURVE    ..
C......................................................
C
      Y = X**6 - X**2 + ALOG(X+4.0)
C
      RETURN
      END
```

We now write subroutine AREA, which is capable of receiving this function name (in the third argument position) and of computing the area. The method of solution will be to:

1. Divide the span of X into 100 equal parts,

$$\Delta X = \frac{(\text{XRIGHT} - \text{XLEFT})}{100}$$

2. Starting at XLEFT, evaluate the equation at each point in the span (by repeatedly invoking the function subprogram Y).
3. Determine the average value of the equation in the span and multiply this by (XRIGHT − XLEFT). This approximates the area.

```
      SUBROUTINE AREA (XLEFT, XRIGHT, Y, ANS)
C...............................................................
C..   ARGUMENT Y IS THE NAME OF A FUNCTION SUBPROGRAM THAT    ..
C..   EXPRESSES THE EQUATION WE ARE DEALING WITH.              ..
C...............................................................
C
      DELTX = (XRIGHT - XLEFT) / 100.
C
      SUM = 0.0
C
      X = XLEFT
C
      DO 10 I = 1, 101
C
   5     SUM = SUM +Y(X)
C
         X = X + DELTX
C
  10  CONTINUE
C
      AVEAL = SUM / 101
C
      ANS = AVEAL * (XRIGHT - XLEFT)
C
      RETURN
      END
```

Statement 5 is the key to the whole procedure. It invokes the subprogram Y for various values of X. Each time this statement is reached, control passes to the function subprogram to evaluate the equation. Had we placed our equation inside subroutine AREA, statement 5 would appear as follows:

```
5 SUM=SUM+X**6-X**2+ALOG(X+4.)
```

The resulting area would be the same, but the subroutine would no longer be general. Placing the specific equation inside subroutine AREA destroys its effectiveness. It becomes almost worthless. Allowing the equation to be referenced by the name Y (the name of a subprogram external to AREA) makes the subroutine invaluable.

Having written subroutine AREA, we would want to test it. Figure 11.15 shows two exceptionally simple curves that might be used:

1. A straight line passing through the origin whose slope is 45°.

   Equation: $y = x$

2. A horizontal line whose y value is constant.

   Equation: $y = \text{constant} = 8$

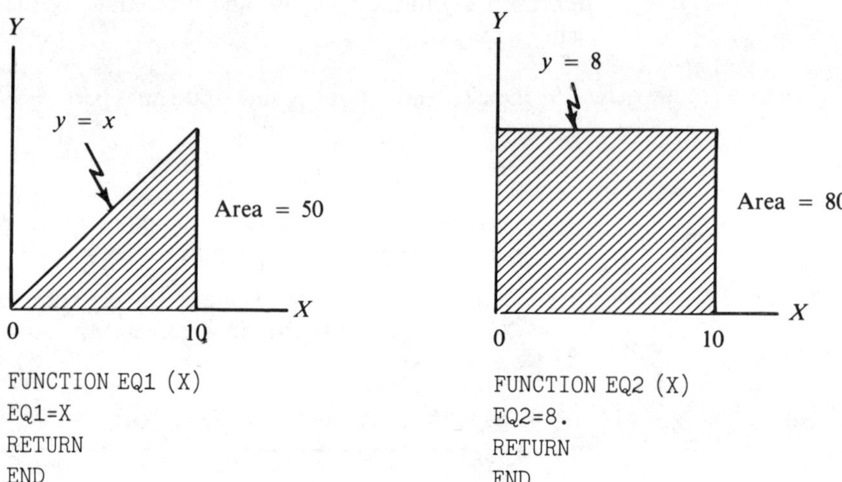

Figure 11.15 Testing by using two simple areas

```
FUNCTION EQ1 (X)
EQ1=X
RETURN
END
```

```
FUNCTION EQ2 (X)
EQ2=8.
RETURN
END
```

Because we have two curves, we must set up two function subprograms: EQ1 and EQ2. By choosing equally simple limits on x, say 0.0 and 10.0, we can compute the areas by inspection. For the triangle it is 50. For the rectangle it is 80.

```
C         .....MAIN PROGRAM TO TEST SUBROUTINE AREA.....
C
          EXTERNAL EQ1, EQ2
C
          CALL AREA (0.0, 10.0, EQ1, ANS1)
          CALL AREA (0.0, 10.0, EQ2, ANS2)   <---- Subroutine AREA called twice
C
          PRINT*, ANS1, ANS2
C
          STOP
          END
```

```
          FUNCTION EQ1 (X)
C
C         .....DERIVE 45 DEGREE LINE.....
C
          EQ1 = X   <---- Defines first equation
C
          RETURN
          END
```

```
      FUNCTION EQ2 (X)
C
C     .....DEFINE HORIZONTAL LINE.....
C
      EQ2 = 8.0   <------------------ Defines second equation
C
      RETURN
      END
```

We call subroutine AREA twice. On the first call, the name EQ1 is placed in the third argument position so that our first test equation will be evaluated. The name EQ1 will be identified with the name Y in the definition. On the second call to AREA, the name EQ2 is substituted so that the second function subprogram will be linked to Y.

You have learned that the DIMENSION statement is used to warn the compiler that certain variable names are special in that they represent arrays. The names representing subprograms are also special, and we warn the compiler through the use of the EXTERNAL statement. This statement appears at the top of the test program and declares EQ1 and EQ2 as the names of subprograms external to the main program. The EXTERNAL statement is needed whenever a CALL is made to a subprogram that has within its argument list the name of another (external) subprogram.

Programming Example
Merge Two Lists

LIST1 and LIST2 are both arrays of integer numbers. Each list has been sorted (smallest element first, largest element last). The size of each list is specified by an integer variable, NSIZE1 and NSIZE2.

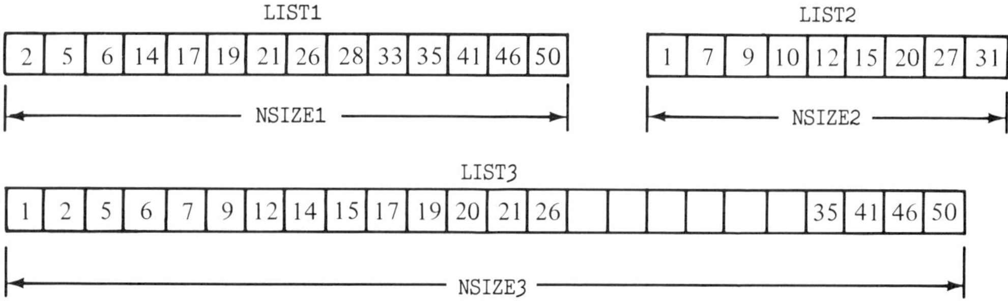

Write a subroutine called MERGE that will merge these two arrays into a single list of sorted numbers.

The logic of the subroutine is to compare the first element of LIST1 and LIST2. If the LIST1 element is smaller:

1. Move that element into LIST3.
2. Advance the LIST1 and LIST3 subscript.

If the LIST2 element is the smaller:

1. Move that element into LIST3.
2. Advance the LIST2 and LIST3 subscripts.

Continue this basic process until either LIST1 or LIST2 is depleted. When one list becomes depleted, pass control to statements that will "dump" the remainder of the other list directly into LIST3.

Programming Example–Merge Two Lists continued

```
      SUBROUTINE MERGE(LIST1,NSIZE1,LIST2,NSIZE2,LIST3,NSIZE3)
C.........................................................
C..   PURPOSE - MERGE TWO SORTED LISTS INTO A SINGLE     ..
C..             (COMBINED) SORTED LIST.                   ..
C.........................................................
C
C                    ---IMPORTANT VARIABLES---
C
C     --LIST1    NAME OF FIRST SORTED LIST                 --
C     --L1       SUBSCRIPT USED WHEN DEALING WITH LIST1    --
C     --LIST2    NAME OF SECOND SORTED LIST                --
C     --L2       SUBSCRIPT USED WHEN DEALING WITH LIST2    --
C     --LIST3    NAME OF COMBINED (OUTPUT) LIST            --
C     --L3       SUBSCRIPT USED WHEN DEALING WITH LIST3    --
C
      REAL LIST1(1), LIST2(1), LIST3(1)
      INTEGER L1,L2,L3
C
C     .....INITIAL VALUE OF INPUT ARRAY SUBSCRIPTS.....
C
      L1 = 1
      L2 = 2
C
C              .....LOOP ENTRY POINT.....
C
      DO 10 L3 = 1, NSIZE1 + NSIZE2, 1
C
C         .....DETERMINE WHICH LIST HAS SMALLEST ELEMENT.....
C
         IF (LIST(L1).LT.LIST2(L2)) THEN
C
C            .....TAKE FROM LIST1.....
C
            LIST3(L3) = LIST1(L1)
            L1 = L1 + 1
C
         ELSE
C
C            .....TAKE FROM LIST2.....
C
            LIST3(L3) = LIST2(L2)
            L2 = L2 + 1
C
         ENDIF
C
C         .....SEE IF EITHER LIST IS DEPLETED.....
C
         IF(L1.GT.NSIZE1) GO TO 20
         IF(L2.GT.NSIZE2) GO TO 40
C
   10 CONTINUE
C
      RETURN
C
C     .....THIS SECTION HANDLES LIST1
C       DEPLETION SITUATION.....
C
   20 DO 30 I3 = L3, NSIZE1 + NSIZE2, 1
C
C         .....DUMP REMAINDER OF LIST INTO LIST3.....
C
         LIST3(I3) = LIST2(L2)
         L2 = L2 + 1
C
   30 CONTINUE
C
      RETURN
C
```

Programming Example–Merge Two Lists continued

```
C     .....THIS SECTION HANDLES LIST2
C          DEPLETION SITUATION.....
C......................................................
C
  40  DO 50 I3 = L3, NSIZE1 + NSIZE2, 1
C
C          .....DUMP REMAINDER OF LIST INTO LIST3.....
C
           LIST3(L3) = LIST1(L1)
           L1 = L1 + 1
C
  50  CONTINUE
C
      RETURN
      END
```

Quiz 19
Subprogramming

1. Does the "consistency of size" requirement apply to:
   a. Local arrays?
   b. One-dimensional arrays?
   c. Multidimensional arrays that are arguments?
2. What does the term "base address" mean when dealing with arrays?
3. Are two-dimensional arrays stored in block form in internal memory? How are they stored?
4. In what order are two-dimensional array elements stored?
5. Describe one way to get around the "consistency of size" requirement when passing a multidimensional array as an argument.
6. Give two reasons why you might use the EQUIVALENCE statement.
7. How does the COMMON statement accomplish an implicit transfer of arguments?
8. What is another advantage of the COMMON statement?
9. What is the purpose of labeled common?
10. What information is conveyed to the compiler by the EXTERNAL statement?

Review Exercises

1. Does the "consistency of size" requirement in arrays that are passed as arguments apply to all arrays?
2. What are some of the ways in which this "consistency of size" requirement is satisfied when arrays are shared?
3. ★ A two-dimensional array called A is 5 by 4 in size. Describe how this array is stored in memory. In what position is the element A(3, 2) located?
4. Up until now, the size of an array as expressed in a DIMENSION statement must be provided as an integer *constant*. Under what circumstances can the size be expressed as a variable?
5. ★ An array used in a subprogram is described as a "local" array. Describe what that means. What restrictions apply to the DIMENSION statement declaring the size of this array?
6. A memory location in common storage may be known by different variable names in various subprograms. How is this accomplished?
7. Describe two situations that might require the use of the EQUIVALENCE statement.
8. ★ Several subprograms have argument lists that are very long. A number of arguments appear in each of the several argument lists. Describe how these argument lists can be made shorter.
9. The DIMENSION statement is used to declare that a variable name represents the name of an array and not a simple variable. What statement is used to declare that a name represents the name of a subprogram?
10. ★ Until now, an argument list consists of a sequence of simple variables or the names of arrays. Now an argument list may contain the name of a "user supplied" subprogram. Why is this new type of argument needed? Give an example.

11. A company is divided into 20 different divisions each manufacturing the same item. A one-dimensional array called NAME identifies the name of the supervisor of each department. A monthly record of the production output of each department is kept (units manufactured each month). The array UNITS holds this information. The cost of labor to produce these units in each department is also recorded on a monthly basis, forming another two-dimensional array. Write a subroutine to read this information and place it in common storage. Each division is represented in the data file as follows:

Record	Meaning	Representation
1	Name of supervisor	10 characters
2	Number of units produced	12I6
3	Monthly payroll	12F6.0

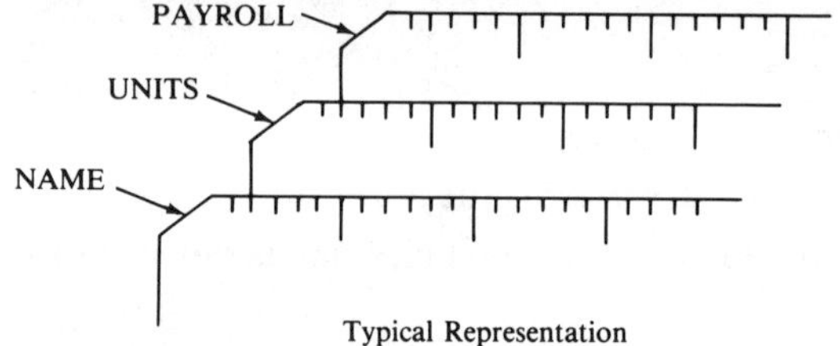

Typical Representation

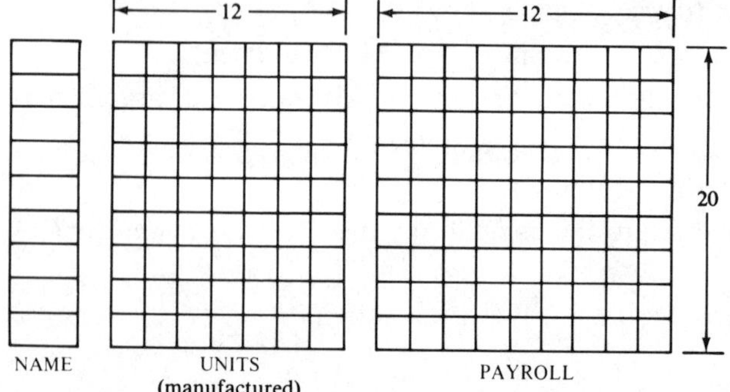

12. Using the data base established in exercise 11, write a subroutine called NUMBER that computes the number of units manufactured by each department for the year.

13. Repeat exercise 12 except have the subroutine NUMBER report the units manufactured by the most productive department first (give supervisor's name and units manufactured), then the next most productive department, and so on.

14. Write a subroutine that computes the variation in *unit cost* to produce the items described in exercise 11. This subroutine should compute a two-dimensional array called COST having 20 rows and 12 columns. Elements of COST are obtained by dividing each department's monthly payroll by the units produced. The array COST should then be searched for the largest and smallest elements.

15. A two-dimensional array called A has 14 rows and 28 columns. Write a subroutine called CHANGE that examines the elements in column 1 of each row of array A and determines which of these elements is the largest. The row containing this largest element is to be moved to the top of the array (do a row swap).

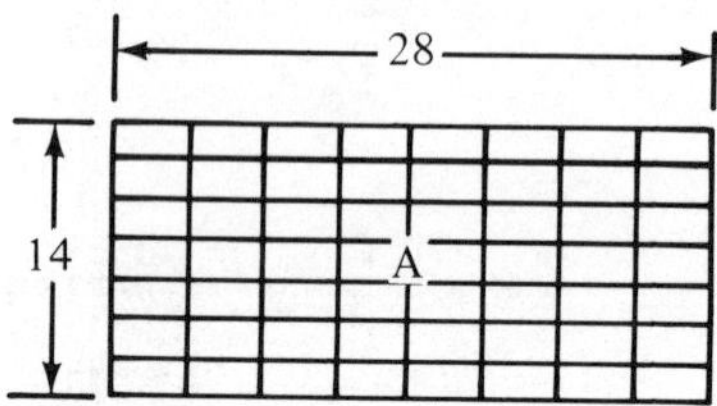

16. Repeat exercise 15 except that the size of array A is to be variable.

17. A subroutine called ROOTS receives three input arguments.

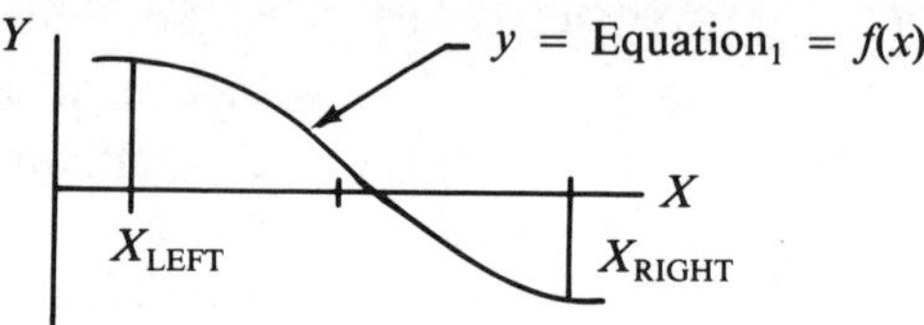

The first argument is the name of a user-supplied function subprogram containing the equation we are trying to find the root of. A typical example is:

```
FUNCTION Y(X)
Y=X**6-ALOG(X)*X**4
RETURN
END
```

The remaining two arguments are XLEFT and XRIGHT defining the interval of the expected root. Have subroutine ROOTS determine and report the value of the equation at X_{LEFT}, X_{RIGHT}, and halfway between these two values.

★ 18. In exercise 17, if the value of the equation at X_{LEFT} and at the midpoint have a different algebraic sign, the root lies to the left of the midpoint. If the value of the equation at the midpoint and at X_{RIGHT} have a different algebraic sign, the root lies to the right of the midpoint. Expand subroutine ROOTS to issue one of two messages:

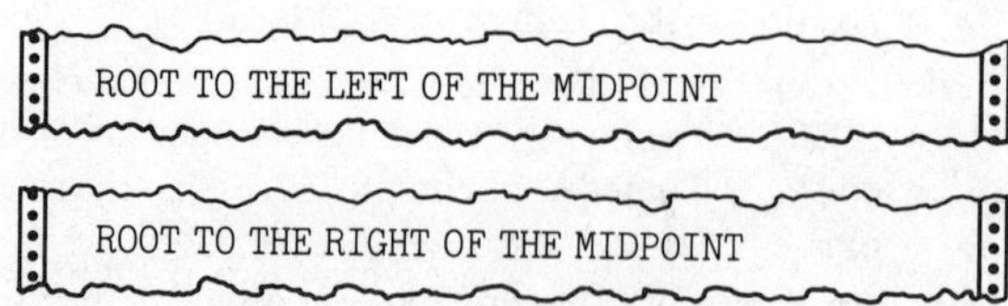

19. Exercise 18 does not account for the possibility that the algebraic sign of the equation will be the same at all three test points (no root in the interval). Expand subroutine ROOTS to accommodate this possibility.

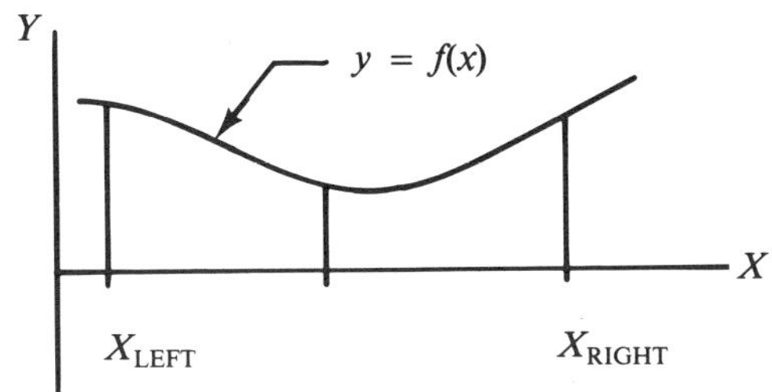

20. A unit matrix is by definition a square matrix (number of rows equals number of columns) in which elements on the main diagonal have the value 1.0. All other elements have the value 0.0. Write a subroutine called TEST that will receive as input an array called A and determine if A is a unit matrix. The output of TEST should be one of two messages:

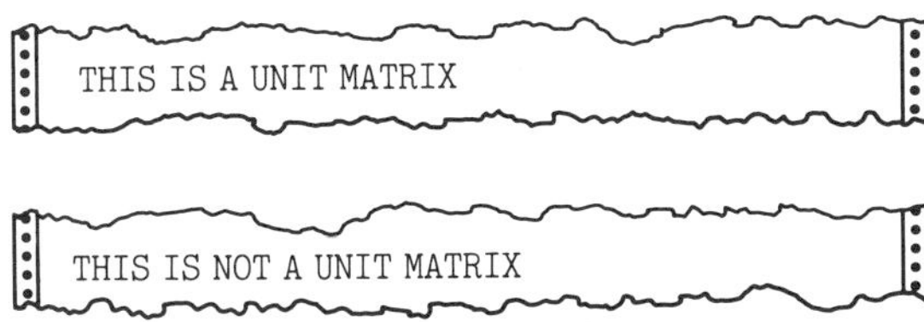

21. A series of data points are represented by a one-dimensional array called X and a one-dimensional array called Y.

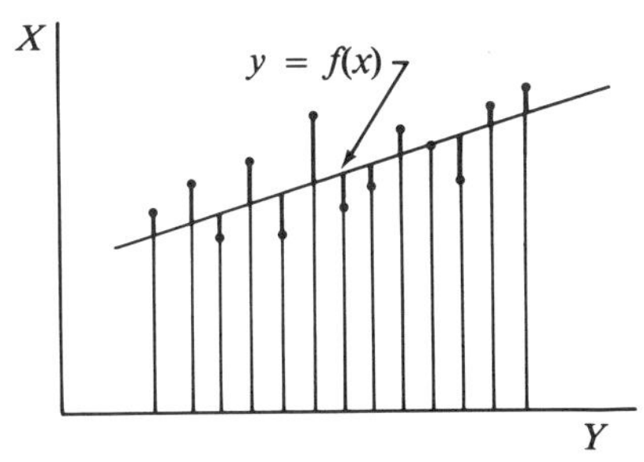

These points are to be compared to the equation of a straight line defined inside a user-supplied FUNCTION subprogram called EQ; as in this typical example:

```
FUNCTION EQ(X)
EQ=6.72*X+1.43
RETURN
END
```

Write a subprogram to determine how many points lie above the line and how many points lie below the line.

22. For each point in exercise 21 determine the distance that the point lies above or below the line. Report each distance and the average error of these points.

★ 23. An array A has NROW rows and NCOL columns. Each row of this array is to be scaled (multiplied by a value). The scale factor for each row is defined by a one-dimensional array called VALUE. Write a subroutine called SCALE that redefines all elements of array A as described.

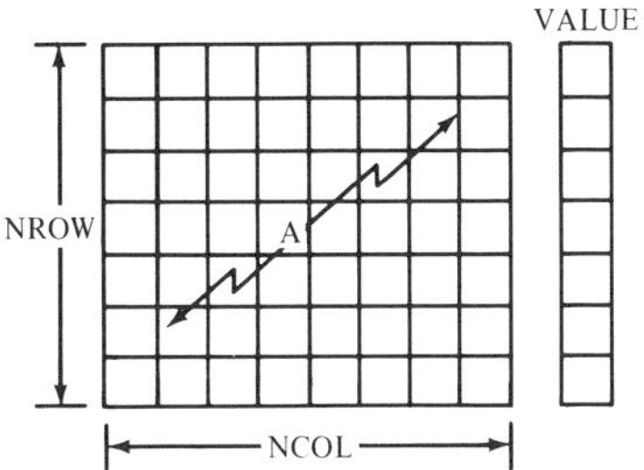

24. A user-supplied SUBROUTINE subprogram defines two equations that are both functions of X, as in this typical example:

```
SUBROUTINE Y(X,EQ1,EQ2)
EQ1 = X**3-1.4**X**2-4.
EQ2 = X**2-9.6*X+1.4
RETURN
END
```

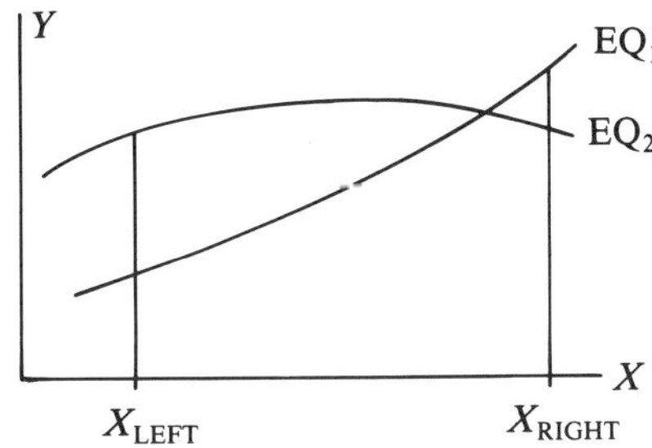

We are interested in knowing which of the two equations has the larger value at the two test points (X_{LEFT} and X_{RIGHT}). Write a subprogram called TEST that determines the desired information. Have subprogram TEST print a message such as:

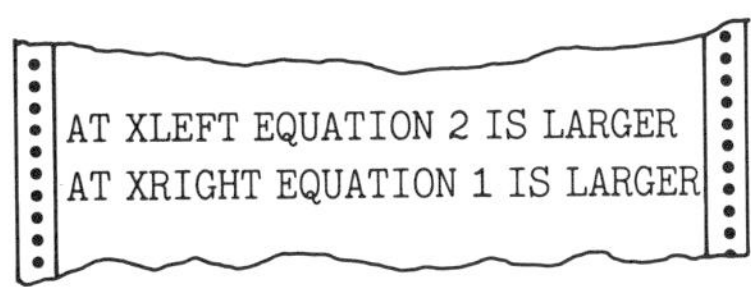

25. Repeat exercise 24, except that we do not want any printout. Instead of the printout, load a memory location called MLEFT with the value 1 or 2 depending on which equation is larger at XLEFT. Load a memory location MRIGHT with the value 1 or 2 depending on which equation is larger at XRIGHT.

26. If MLEFT and MRIGHT hold different numbers after a call to subroutine TEST, the two equations cross over (intersect) within the interval XLEFT and XRIGHT. Expand subroutine TEST to search for this point of intersection.

Additional Applications

Programming Example
Data Boundaries (Specific)

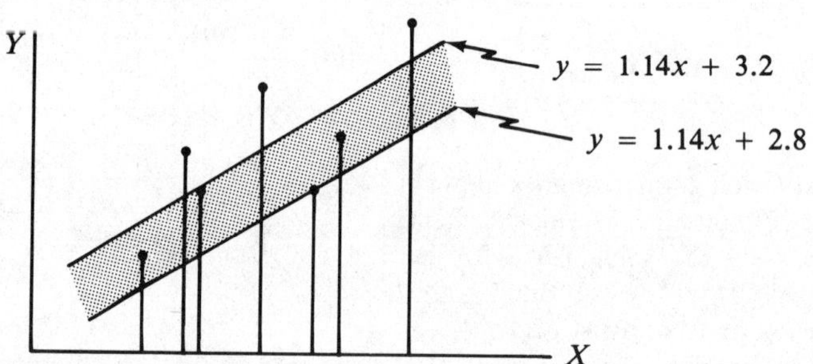

An array called X and an array called Y define a series of data points. We are interested in knowing how many of these points are bounded by (lie inside) the two straight lines shown in the illustration. Write a SUBROUTINE called BOUND that receives as input:

XARRAY	Array of X values (data points).
YARRAY	Array of Y values (data points).
NSIZE	Number of elements (data points).

Determine how many points lie inside the bounds specified by the two straight lines.

```
C...........................................................
C..    PURPOSE - DETERMINE IF DATA POINTS LIE WITHIN          ..
C..              SPECIFIC BOUNDS.                             ..
C...........................................................
C
      SUBROUTINE BOUND(XARRAY,YARRAY,NSIZE,INSIDE,PERCNT)
      INTEGER INSIDE,NSIZE
      REAL    XARRAY(NSIZE),YARRAY(NSIZE),PERCNT
C
      INSIDE = 0
C
      DO 10 I=1, NSIZE
C
C        ...COMPUTE MINIMUM AND MAXIMUM VALUE OF Y...
C
         YMAX = 1.14 * XARRAY(I) + 3.2
         YMIN = 1.14 * XARRAY(I) + 2.8
C
C        ...SEE IF DATA POINT FALLS BETWEEN THESE LIMITS...
C
         IF(YARRAY(I).LT.YMAX.AND.YARRAY(I).GT.YMIN) THEN
C
            INSIDE = INSIDE + 1
C
         ENDIF
C
   10 CONTINUE
C
      PERCNT = FLOAT(INSIDE)/FLOAT(NSIZE) * 100.
C
      RETURN
      END
```

Programming Example
Data Boundaries (General)

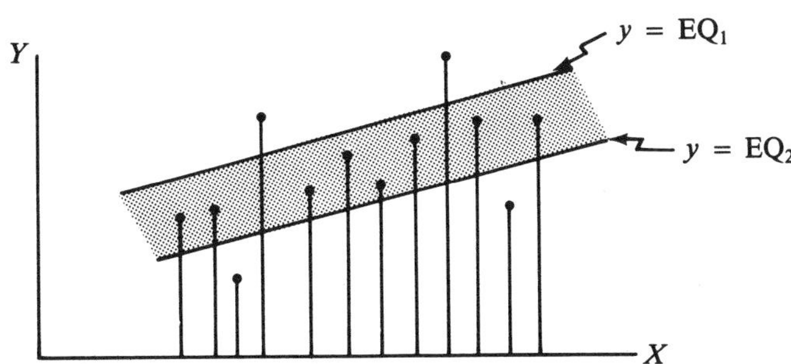

The two equations representing the data boundaries shown in the previous programming example change from time to time. Accordingly they are placed inside the following two FUNCTION subprograms.

```
FUNCTION EQ1(X)          FUNCTION EQ2(X)
EQ1 = 1.14*X+3.2         EQ2 = 1.14*X+2.8
RETURN                   RETURN
END                      END
```

Rewrite SUBROUTINE BOUND to accept the name of these two FUNCTIONS in its argument list and process the data points as before.

```
      SUBROUTINE BOUND(XARRAY,YARRAY,NSIZE,EQ1,EQ2,INSIDE,PERCNT)
C
      EXTERNAL EQ1,EQ2
C
      REAL XARRAY(NSIZE),YARRAY(NSIZE)
C
      INSIDE = 0
C
      DO 10 I=1, NSIZE
          YMAX = EQ1(XARRAY(I))
          YMIN = EQ2(XARRAY(I))
          IF (YARRAY(I).LT.YMAX.AND.YARRAY(I).GT.YMIN) THEN
              INSIDE = INSIDE +1
C
          ENDIF
C
   10 CONTINUE
C
      PERCNT = FLOAT(INSIDE)/FLOAT(NSIZE)*100
C
      RETURN
      END
```

Programming Example
Symmetric Array (Partial Check)

ARRAY

1.1	2.2	3.3	4.4	5.5	6.6	7.7
2.2	2.6	2.8	3.0	3.2	3.4	3.6
3.3	2.8	-5.2	-5.0	-4.8	-4.6	-4.4
4.4	3.0	-5.0	-0.4	-0.4	-0.2	-0.0
5.5	3.2	-4.8	-0.4	4.3	4.1	3.9
6.6	3.4	-4.6	-0.2	4.1	8.7	8.9
7.7	3.6	-4.4	-0.0	3.9	8.9	2.1

Programming Example–Symmetric Array (Partial Check) continued

A two dimensional array is said to be symmetric if:

1. The number of rows equals the number of columns (a square matrix).
2. Elements above and below the main diagonal have the same value: A(M,N) = A(N,M).

Write a subprogram called TEST that receives the following input:

A	Name of array to be checked.
NROW	Number of rows in array A.
NCOL	Number of columns in array A.

Subroutine TEST should attempt to determine if array A is symmetric as follows:

1. *Size Error:* If the number of rows does not equal the number of columns, reject the array immediately.
2. *Same Elements:* Check the elements in row 1 of the array to see if they equal the elements in column 1 of the array. If all elements are equal, issue the message "MAYBE."

```
      SUBROUTINE TEST(A,NROW,NCOL)
C.........................................................
C..   PURPOSE - MAKE A PARTIAL CHECK TO SEE IF          ..
C..             AN ARRAY IS SYMMETRIC.                  ..
C.........................................................
C
      REAL A(NROW,NCOL)
      INTEGER NROW, NCOL
C
      IF (NROW.NE.NCOL) THEN
C
          PRINT*, 'ARRAY NOT SYMMETRIC - SIZE ERROR'
          RETURN
C
      ENDIF
C
C     .....CHECK ROW/COLUMN 1.....
C
      DO 30 I=1, NROW
C
          IF(A(I,1).NE.A(1,I)) THEN
              PRINT* ,'ARRAY NOT SYMMETRIC - ELEMENTS NOT EQUAL'
              RETURN
C
      ENDIF
C
   30 CONTINUE
C
      PRINT*,'MAYBE....SUGGEST FURTHER CHECKING'
C
      RETURN
      END
```

Programming Example Symmetric Array (General)

Write subroutine TEST to check all elements of array A (all rows against all columns).

```
C.............................................................
C..    PURPOSE - MAKE GENERAL TEST TO SEE IF AN             ..
C..              ARRAY IS SYMMETRIC                         ..
C.............................................................
C
      SUBROUTINE TEST (A,NROW,NCOL)
      REAL A(NROW,NCOL)
      INTEGER NROW, NCOL
C
      IF (NROW.NE.NCOL) THEN
C
          PRINT*, 'ARRAY NOT SYMMETRIC - SIZE ERROR'
          RETURN
C
      ENDIF
C
C     .....SET UP OUTER DO LOOP.....
C
C     .....INDEX M TELLS WHICH ROW
C          INDEX I TELLS WHICH COLUMN.....
C
      DO 40 M=1, NROW
C
          DO 30 I = M, NROW
C
              IF (A(I,M).NE.A(M,I)) THEN
                  PRINT*, 'ARRAY NOT SYMMETRIC -  ELEMENTS NOT EQUAL'
                  RETURN
C
              ENDIF
C
   30     CONTINUE
C
   40 CONTINUE
C
C     .....ALL ELEMENTS CHECKED.....
C
      PRINT*, 'ARRAY IS SYMMETRIC'
C
      RETURN
      END
```

Programming Example Largest Value

We wish to know which of two equations has the largest value between two limits of X (between XINIT and XFINAL). Write a subroutine that received as input:

XINIT	Initial value of interval.
XFINAL	Final value of interval.
EQ1	Function subprogram holding first equation.
EQ2	Function subprogram holding second equation.

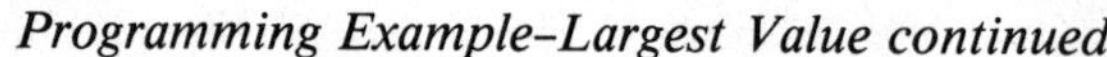

Programming Example–Largest Value continued

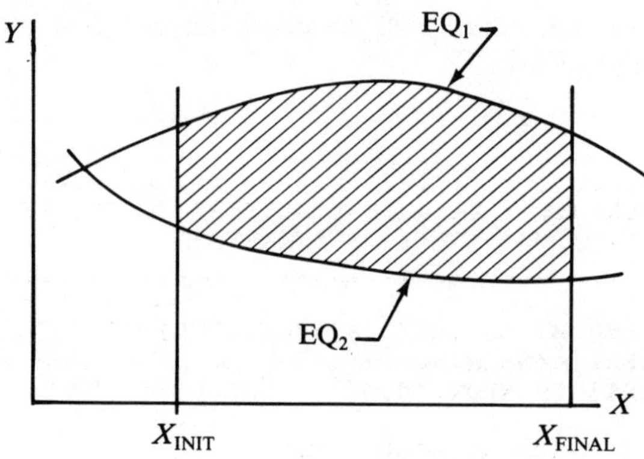

The output of this subroutine should be:

`BIGY`	Largest value in interval.
`X`	Value of X for largest Y.
`NUMBER`	Integer (1 or 2) telling which equation gives largest value.

```
      SUBROUTINE LARGST(XINIT,XFINAL,EQ1,EQ2,BIGY,X,NUMBER)
C..........................................................
C..   PURPOSE - TO FIND THE LARGEST VALUE OF Y              ..
C..........................................................
C
      EXTERNAL EQ1,EQ2
C
C     .....DIVIDE X-SPAN INTO 100 EQUAL PARTS.....
C
      DELTX = (XFINAL-XINIT) / 100.
C
C     .....DEFINE Y AT START FOR BOTH EQUATIONS.....
C
      Y1 = EQ1(XINIT)
      Y2 = EQ2(XINIT)
C
      X = XINIT
C
C     .....PROCESSING LOOP STARTS HERE.....
C
      DO 10 I=1, 101
C
C          .....CHECK FIRST EQUATION.....
C
           YNEW = EQ1(X)
C
           IF (YNEW.GT.Y1) THEN
               Y1 = YNEW
               X1 = X
           ENDIF
C
C          .....CHECK SECOND EQUATION.....
C
           YNEW = EQ2(X)
C
           IF (YNEW.GE.Y2) THEN
               Y2 = YNEW
               X2 = X
           ENDIF
C
```

Programming Example–Largest Value continued

```
C          MOVE ON TO THE NEXT VALUE OF X
C
           X = X + DELTX
C
  10  CONTINUE
C
C                END OF SEARCH LOOP
C     .....DETERMINE WHICH EQUATION HAS LARGER Y.....
C
      IF (Y1.GT.Y2) THEN
          BIGY = Y1
          X = X1
          NUMBER = 1
      ELSE
          BIGY = Y2
          X = X2
          NUMBER = 2
C
      ENDIF
C
      RETURN
      END
```

12 Complex/Logical/ Double Precision Variables

For the programming done so far, two types of variables (real and integer) have satisfied our needs reasonably well. The importance of these two basic types of variables is indicated by the fact that on some FORTRAN† systems they are the only types of variables permitted. Most FORTRAN compilers, however, allow other types, which are the subject of this chapter. For example, a *complex* variable will be introduced for use in storing and manipulating complex numbers. A *double precision* variable will be presented, which permits values to be determined and stored to at least twice the usual accuracy. Finally, a *logical* variable will be described.

From now on, variable names appearing in a program are no longer just real or integer variable names. The name may represent a complex value, a double precision value, or a logical value. It, therefore, will be necessary to declare early in the program all names used to represent these new types of variables. This is the purpose of **explicit type statements.**

12.1 Explicit Type Statements

The statements shown in the following table are explicit type statements. Note that for each type of variable (real, integer, complex, double precision, and logical) there is a corresponding type statement that explicity declares those names the programmer has chosen to be associated with each type of variable.

Sample Explicit Type Statements

```
INTEGER X, ABLE, DER
REAL M, N, ISEC
DOUBLE PRECISION A, B, VALUE, C
COMPLEX XONE, XTWO
LOGICAL A1, A2, A3, D5, REM
```

† The FORTRAN '77 standards define the features of the full language and a subset language. Complex and double precision variables are not part of the subset language.

As described in Chapter 3, integer and real values can be declared in two ways: explicitly or implicitly. Implicit definition describes the method of using the first letter of a variable name to declare it as either integer or real. Explicit definition, on the other hand, is accomplished by an explicit type statement that overrides (takes precedence over) the implicit definition.

Any name representing a double precision, complex, or logical variable must be declared in an appropriate type statement. This is the only way of declaring these names.

```
DOUBLE PRECISION )     Names must be
     COMPLEX      }    declared by a
     LOGICAL      )    type statement
```

All type statements must be placed early in the source program so that the type statement precedes the first use of the variable name. Note also that the resulting assignment of names is permanent for the remainder of that program. Once the type of a variable has been declared in a type statement, it may not be subsequently changed. Finally, a name may not appear in two different type statements. The name SETS, for example, may be declared to be an integer variable name or a complex variable name, but not both.

12.2 Variations in Compilers

At several points in this text, we have commented on minor variations in the way in which FORTRAN is implemented by various computers. These variations result from a difference in word size, memory capacity, and type of machine language instructions available on a particular system.

Prior to the FORTRAN '77 standards, these variations were rather extensive. Smaller systems would limit the number of continuation cards allowed, the number of letters in a variable name, the type of input/output statements permitted, the form of subscripted variables, and so on. These variations are known as **system characteristics** and are usually published in tabular form as follows.

System Characteristics

Characteristic	IBM 704 (8K)	IBM 360 Level D	CDC 3600
Maximum number of continuation cards allowed	4	19	No limit
Maximum magnitude of integer constants allowed	$2^{35} - 1$	$2^{31} - 1$	$2^{47} - 1$
Maximum digits of a real constant (mantissa size)	9	7	11
Maximum digits of a double precision constant		16	25
Maximum statement number allow	99999	9999	99

These variations cause problems of portability (running a program on more than one system).

The effect of the new standards is to minimize these variations. All compilers eventually will be made to meet one of two levels of certification:

1. *Full* language features (to be implemented on large systems).
2. *Subset* language features (to be implemented on smaller systems).

Double precision and complex variables are features available in the full language but not in the subset. A detailed description of the difference between the full and subset language is presented in Appendix F.

12.3 Double Precision Values

A double precision value is very much like a real value except that more space in memory is allocated for storing double precision values. The usual practice is to string two real memory locations together to form one double precision memory location. The resulting mantissa size for a double precision variable is usually at least twice that of a real variable.

Figure 12.1 Typical double precision word size

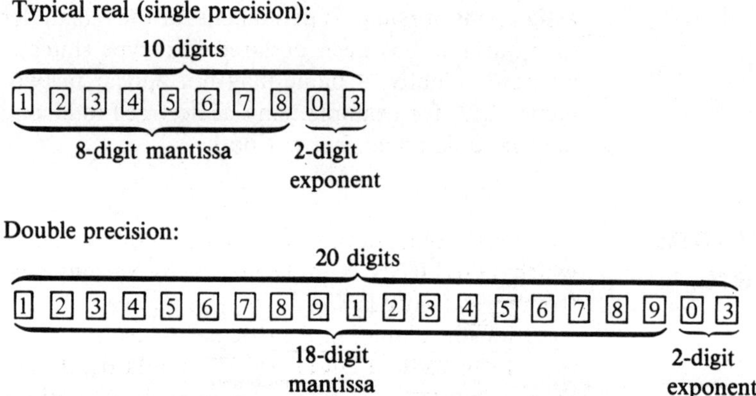

Figure 12.1 shows the internal storage of a real number in a computer using a 10-digit word size (8-digit mantissa and a 2-digit exponent). Also shown is the internal storage of the same number in double precision form, using a 20-digit word size (18-digit mantissa and a 2-digit exponent).

One obvious use of double precision is to obtain more accurate solutions. Often a program is written, compiled, and checked using real variables and constants until the program has proven itself. Then values are transformed into double precision form, and the program is run again to obtain more accurate results.

Another use of double precision is to reduce round-off errors. Consider the two real numbers stored in memory locations A and B of Figure 12.2. If these numbers are added and the result stored in real location C, the number stored in location C is identical to the number stored in memory location A. This has happened because the true result of this addition is a 16-digit number, but memory location C can accommodate only the first 8 digits. The remainder, 0.12345678, is called the round-off error, and the value stored in C is inaccurate by this amount. This error has resulted because A is so large compared to B. If the value as now stored in C is used in subsequent calculations, the effect of this error can grow.

Figure 12.2 How round-off errors are generated

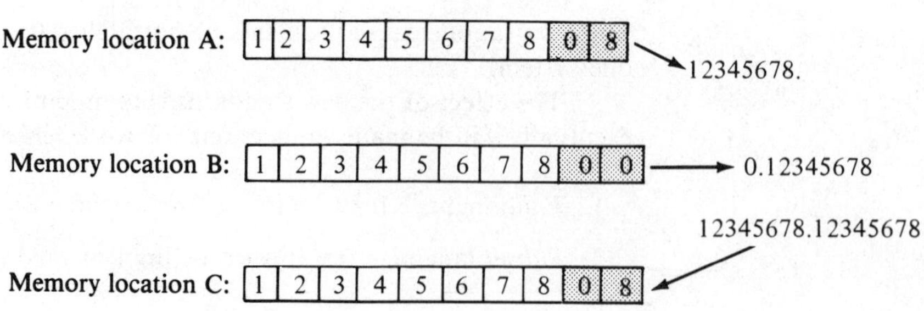

Most calculations suffer from errors, but if this error is in the eighth or ninth decimal place of a value, the error is not serious. However, any result that is obtained after a long sequence of operations (each with its own error) may suffer from an accumulation of errors (error build-up). One way to reduce these errors is to use double precision.

There is a strong similarity between the way in which real and double precision expressions are formed. The description that follows is easier to understand if this similarity is kept in mind.

Double Precision Constants

Figures 12.1 and 12.2 show that real numbers (single and double precision) are stored internally in scientific notation. This method of storage is best for handling numbers that are extremely variable (sometimes very large and sometimes very small).

Scientific Notation	Number
-8.10×10^{13}	-81,000,000,000,000.
-4.27×10^{-15}	-.00000000000000427
3.862×10^{9} (3.862 = Mantissa; 9 = Exponent)	3,862,000,000.

Scientific notation uses one or more digits written with a decimal point (called the mantissa) followed by the number 10 raised to some power (called the exponent).

To permit constants to be expressed in scientific notation, FORTRAN resorts to the following notation.

Mathematical Notation	Equivalent FORTRAN Representation (Single Precision)	Equivalent FORTRAN Representation (Double Precision)
-8.1×10^{13}	-8.1E13	-8.1D13
-4.27×10^{-15}	-4.27E-15	-4.27D-15
3.862×10^{9}	3.862E9	3.862D9

Since a FORTRAN statement must be written on one continuous line, the letter E or the letter D is used to separate the mantissa from the exponent. The letter serves as a substitute for writing the number 10 and a superscript. The letter E is used to express a single precision constant. The letter D is used to signal a double precision constant.

Double Precision Constants

Constant	Meaning
0.15967 [D+04]	(1596.7)
0.923716534487 [D-02]	(.00923716534487)
-1483767.5421D00	(-1483767.5421)
8.3 [D02]	(830.)
1.34 [D4]	(13400.)
-16. [D-8]	(-0.00000016)

The mantissa may contain from one to 16 digits written with a decimal point (located as desired) followed by the letter D and an exponent in integer form. This exponent indicates the power of ten by which the mantissa is to be multiplied. An alternate way of expressing a double precision constant is as a real number (written without an exponent) containing a sign and at least ten significant digits, as with these two examples.

```
-32.916752434        +627383.0691
```

Just as a real constant is distinguished from an integer constant by the presence or absence of a decimal point, there must be some unique feature to distinguish a double precision constant. That feature is the appearance of ten or more digits when specifying the constant.

Double Precision Variables

A double precision variable is formed by creating a name (according to the usual rules for naming a variable) and then declaring this name as being a double precision variable by using the appropriate explicit type statement.

```
DOUBLE PRECISION A, VALUE, ITEM, XRAY
```

Double precision variables may appear in the lists of input/output statements. When this happens, double precision numbers will be read from an input record or will be written on an output record. Generally speaking, it is easier to input the advanced data types discussed in this chapter using format control. (Free format can sometimes cause a problem.) The general form of the format code describing double precision numbers is:

Fw.d. If the number appears without an exponent

Dw.d. If the number appears with an exponent as described in the previous paragraphs.

This input/output procedure for double precision values will be demonstrated in the next case study.

A double precision constant(s) or variable(s) may appear in any arithmetic expression in exactly the same way that a real constant(s) or variables(s) appears. Further, single precision (real) and double precision values may appear in the *same* arithmetic expression.

When defining the mode of any arithmetic operation, the compiler looks to the left and right of the operational symbol at the operands involved.

If one is real and the other is double precision, the operation is performed in double precision. The remaining rules for forming double precision expressions are the same as the rules for single precision (real) expressions. The operational symbols (*,/,+,-,**) are the same. The hierarchy of operation, use of parentheses, and mixed mode restrictions are the same.

It should be clearly understood that the use of single precision (real) values in a double precision expression may or may not imply inaccuracy. Take, for example, the number 1.24. Just because there are only three digits in the number does not mean it can be stored with complete accuracy in a single precision (real) memory location. The method of internal representation (storage) must be considered. If this number is stored in binary (base 2), octal (base 8), or hexadecimal (base 16), it may not have finite representation. On the other hand, numbers like 124. or 6297. could be stored in single precision form with complete accuracy.

Double Precision Library Functions

Library functions such as SIN, COS, and SQRT, which have been used in the past, evaluate the desired function to single precision accuracy. Double precision calculations involving these functions require their evaluation to a higher degree of accuracy—to double precision accuracy. For this reason, the following double precision functions have been created.†

```
DSIN      DLOG
DCOS      DSQRT
DATAN     DABS
```

The argument(s) of these functions must be double precision quantities. The value returned is double precision.

12.4 Use of Double Precision

Programming Example
Double Precision Addition

Write a program to read the record shown and to determine the sum of the values listed.

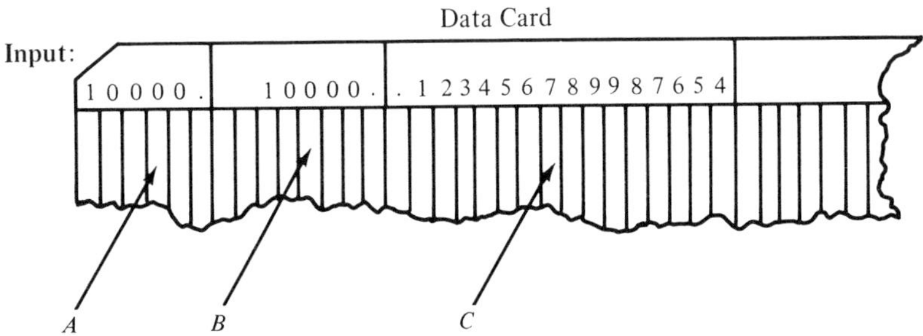

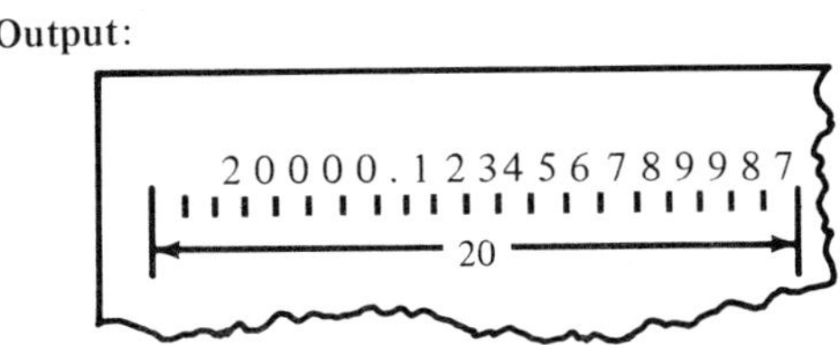

† It may not be necessary to use the special functions just described. The FORTRAN '77 standards have defined what is called a **generic function**. A generic function returns a value consistent with the mode of the argument(s) used when evoking the function. For example, the generic library functions SIN, COS, SQRT, and so on can accept a real, double precision, or complex argument. They will return a real, double precision, or complex value depending on which type of argument was used.

Programming Example–Double Precision Addition continued

```
C
      DOUBLE PRECISION C, SUM
C
   10 READ 20, A, B, C
   20 FORMAT(F6.0,F8.0,F16.15)
C
   30 SUM = A + B + C
C
      PRINT 40, SUM
   40 FORMAT(1X, F20.12)
C
      STOP
      END
```

Examining the record, we see that values A and B can be stored in single precision form, but C will require double precision. When A is added to B (in statement 30), single precision accuracy is used. The next ADD operation will be accomplished in double precision because of the appearance of the double precision variable C. To preserve this accuracy, the result should be stored (assigned) to a double precision memory location. For this reason, both C and SUM are declared as double precision values by the TYPE statement "DOUBLE PRECISION C, SUM."

Programming Example Approximating a Volume

Write a program to approximate the volume obtained by revolving the line $y = f(x)$ about the x axis between the limits $x = 0$ and $x = 6$ (see Figure 12.3).

One approximation would be to form a series of cylinders of thickness $\Delta x(\Delta v = \pi r^2 \Delta x)$ and to sum these volumes. If the number of such cylinders is large, the "omitted volume" (see Figure 12.3) will be small, thereby reducing the error of the approximation. The theories of calculus would suggest we make Δx infinitely small to obtain the best approximation.

Although increasing the number of cylinders reduces the geometric error of the approximation, it will, at the same time, increase the number of calculations that must be performed.

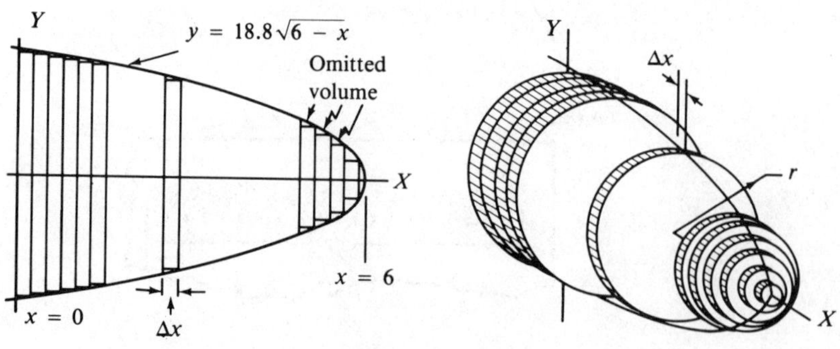

Figure 12.3 Approximation by a series of cylinders

Caution: Any result that is obtained after a long sequence of operations (each with its own error) may suffer from an accumulation of errors (error build-up).

Programming Example–Approximating a Volume continued

Causing Δx to be excessively small can create a problem as the vertex of the solid is approached (x approaches 6). The volume already determined is large in relation to the volume of each cylinder yet to be accounted for. The effect of adding a small number to a large number has been demonstrated earlier. For the reasons just stated, the following program employs double precision calculations where necessary.

```
C.............................................................
C..   PURPOSE - DEMONSTRATE DOUBLE PRECISION CALCULATIONS.   ..
C.............................................................
C
C              ---IMPORTANT VARIABLES---
C
C     --RAD        RADIUS (DOUBLE PRECISION)                  --
C     --SUMV       SUM OF THE VOLUMES                         --
C     --VOL        VOLUME OF AN INDIVIDUAL CYLINDER           --
C
      DOUBLE PRECISION SUMV, X, RAD, VOL, DELTX
C
C     .....INITIALIZATION SECTION.....
C
      DELTX = 0.01
      SUMV = 0.0
      X = DELTX
C
C     .....LOOP ENTRY POINT.....
C
      DO WHILE (X.LT.6.0)
C
   10     RAD = 18.8 * DSQRT(6.0 - X)
          VOL = 3.14159265358979 * RAD**2 * 0.01
C
          SUMV = SUMV + VOL
          X = X + DELTX
C
      ENDDO
C
C     .....LOOP TERMINATES HERE.....
C
      PRINT *, 'VOLUME = ',SUMV
C
      STOP
      END
```

The first series of statements are comment statements. The next statement declares SUMV, X, RAD, and VOL as double precision. SUMV and VOL must be double precision variables so that each value of volume may be stored and accumulated to a high degree of accuracy. The accuracy to which the volume, VOL, can be determined depends on the accuracy to which the radius, RAD, is computed. The variable RAD, therefore, must be double precision. Finally, X is made double precision so that the argument of the square root function appearing in statement 10 will be a double precision value.

Method of Solution: SUMV accumulates individual values of volume (VOL) generated as X moves from the origin to the vertex of the solid in increments of 0.01 (DELTX). The radius of each cylinder is obtained by substituting the value of X into the equation:

$$y = 18.8\sqrt{6 - x}$$

12.5 Complex Values

Complex numbers of the form $(a + bi)$ occur frequently in mathematics. They consist of an ordered pair of real numbers (a and b), the latter of which is combined with the quantity i, which has the property $i^2 = -1$. Complex numbers can be used to represent vectors (see Figure 12.4).

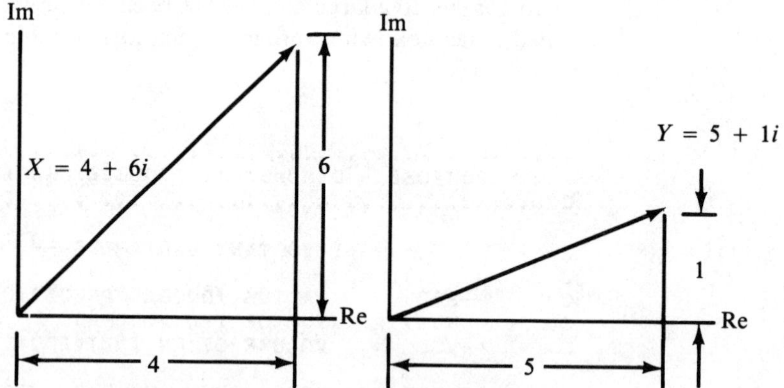

Figure 12.4 Vector representation of complex numbers

The addition of complex numbers is defined as:

$$(a + bi) + (c + di) = (a + c) + (b + d)i$$

Applying this definition to X and Y of Figure 12.4:

$$\begin{aligned} Z &= X + Y \\ &= (4 + 6i) + (5 + 1i) \\ Z &= (9 + 7i) \end{aligned}$$

The result is the complex number Z whose meaning is shown in Figure 12.5. It is the **resultant** (vector sum) of the system.

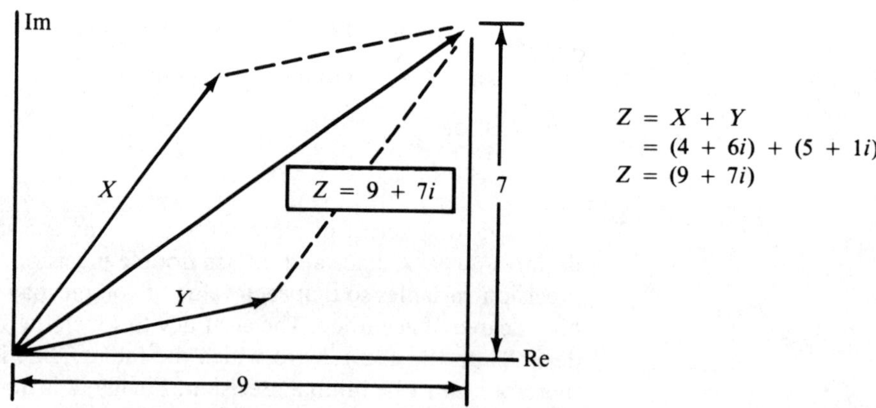

Figure 12.5 Vector representation of the resultant

The preceding example demonstrates that the arithmetic manipulation of complex numbers involves the identification and manipulation of the real and imaginary parts of these numbers. To facilitate this, "full language" compilers have been written to allow the direct storage and direct mathematical manipulation of complex values.

Specifically, if a variable is declared in a `TYPE` statement as a `COMPLEX` variable, that variable name will identify two consecutive floating point locations in memory in which the real and imaginary parts of the complex number are stored.

The real and imaginary parts are identified by a single name. In addition, if that variable name appears in an arithmetic expression, the operational symbols (+,−,*,/, etc.) will be understood to mean complex addition, complex subtraction, complex multiplication, and so on.

Consider the following program segment.

```
C...............................................................
C..   PURPOSE - PROGRAM SEGMENT TO ADD VECTORS X AND Y PRO-    ..
C..             DUCING RESULTANT VECTOR Z.                     ..
C...............................................................
C
C            ---IMPORTANT VARIABLES---
C
C     --X,Y         COMPLEX VECTORS TO BE ADDED                 --
C     --Z           RESULTANT COMPLEX VECTOR                    --
C
      COMPLEX X, Y, Z
C
C     .....READ COMPLEX VALUES FROM DATA.....
C
      READ 10, X, Y
 10   FORMAT (4F10.3)
C
C     .....DATA CARD CONTAINS FOUR VALUES.....
C
C     .....COMPLEX ADDITION THEN ACCOMPLISHED.....
C
      Z = X + Y
C
      PRINT 20,Z
  20  FORMAT(1X,2F10.2)
C
      STOP
      END
```

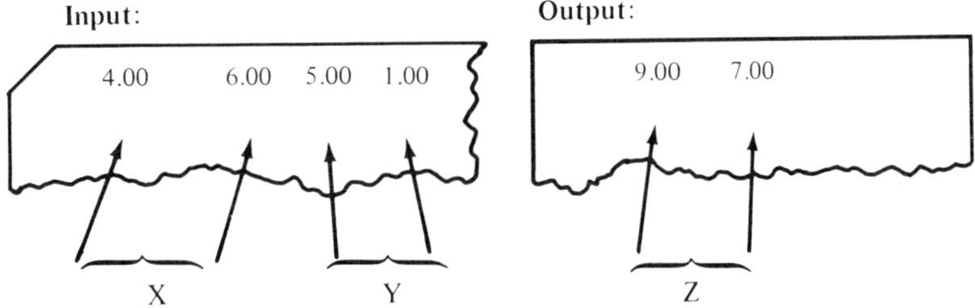

The TYPE statement is used to identify X, Y, and Z as the names of complex variables. The READ statement is executed next. Although only two names are in the list of this READ statement, four values will be read from data because X and Y have been declared as complex quantities. The statement:

```
Z = X + Y
```

will result in the formation of the complex value Z through the complex addition of X and Y. The operational symbol + is interpreted as complex addition because X and Y are complex quantities. This program segment computes the vector Z shown in Figure 12.5.

Complex Constants

A **complex constant** is formed by specifying two floating point numbers enclosed in parentheses and separated by a comma. These values represent the real and imaginary parts of the complex constant.

Example	Meaning
(6.00, 5.20)	6.00 + 5.20i
(−4.82, 16.06)	−4.82 + 16.06i
(0.00, 4.00)	0.00 + 4.00i
(5.17, 0.00)	5.17 + 0.00i
(2.00E+02, 4.10)	200.00 + 4.10i

Complex Variables

A **complex variable** is formed by creating a name (according to the usual rules for naming a variable) and then declaring that name a complex value by using the appropriate TYPE statement. For example:

```
COMPLEX X, BRN, SUM
COMPLEX A1, A2, A3
COMPLEX X, Y
```

Input/Output

INPUT/OUTPUT of complex values is accomplished in the same way real values are transferred to and from memory, except that the appearance of a complex variable name in the list of a READ/WRITE statement causes the transfer of *two floating point numbers* (the real and imaginary parts).

The controlling format statement must provide separate specifications describing each part of the complex number.

Arithmetic Expressions

Arithmetic operations involving complex numbers require special attention. The rules governing the addition, subtraction, multiplication, and division of complex numbers are shown in Figure 12.6.

Figure 12.6 Mathematics of complex operations

ADDITION	$(a + bi) + (c + di) = (a + c) + (b + d)i$
SUBTRACTION	$(a + bi) - (c + di) = (a - c) + (b - d)i$
MULTIPLICATION	$(a + bi) \times (c + di) = (ac - bd) + (bc + ad)i$
DIVISION	$(a + bi) \div (c + di) = \dfrac{(ac + bd) + (bc - ad)i}{c^2 + d^2}$

These operations are the ones that occur most frequently in arithmetic expressions involving complex quantities.

A complex expression defines a sequence of arithmetic operations to be performed involving complex constants, complex variables, real constants, and real variables. Integer values may only appear as subscripts or as exponents. Examples of complex expressions are:

```
COMPLEX Z, A, B, SUM, X
```

1. `Z = (5.28, -6.15) * (7.56, 2.28)`
2. `B = Z - (2.26, 3.39)`
3. `A = (B/Z)**2`
4. `SUM = A + B + Z`
5. `X = CSQRT ( (4.0, 3.0) )`

Although the formation of a complex expression is similar to the formation of a real expression, certain differences do exist.

1. A complex quantity may only be raised to an integer power: real and complex values may not be used as the exponent of a complex expression.
2. The result of a complex expression is a complex value and must be stored as such. If the right-hand side of an arithmetic statement is a complex expression, the variable on the left-hand side should be a complex variable.
3. Complex variables have their own library functions, which are described in the following table.†

Complex Library Functions

Name	Purpose	Remarks
CABS	Computes the absolute value of a complex number.	Argument is a single complex quantity. The result is a real value.
CMPLX	Transforms two real values into a single complex quantity.	Arguments are two real values. The result is a complex number.
REAL	Separates and returns just the *real* portion of a complex number.	Argument is a complex value. The result is a floating point number.
AIMAG	Separates and returns just the *imaginary* portion of a complex number.	Argument is a complex value. The result is a floating point number.
CONJG	Produces the conjugate of its complex argument.	Argument and result are both complex quantities.
CEXP	e^Z	Argument and result are both complex quantities.
CLOG	$\ln Z$	
CSIN	$\sin Z$	
CCOS	$\cos Z$	
CSQRT	$\sqrt{Z}$	

Some of these library functions require additional explanation.

CABS—The absolute value of a complex quantity is interpreted as the length of the vector representing the complex value. The argument of this function is a complex value. The result is a floating point number representing the physical length of the vector.

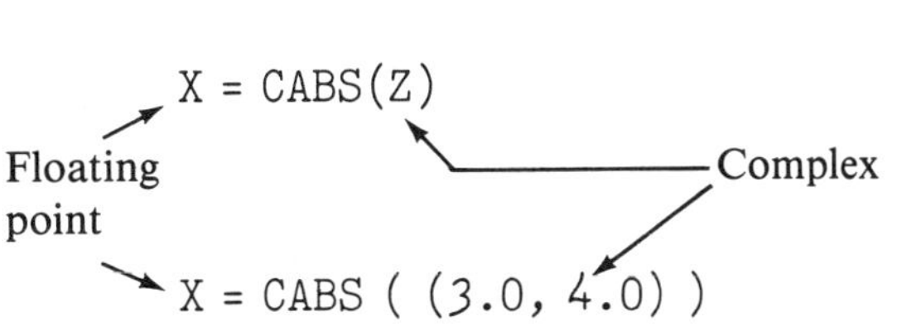

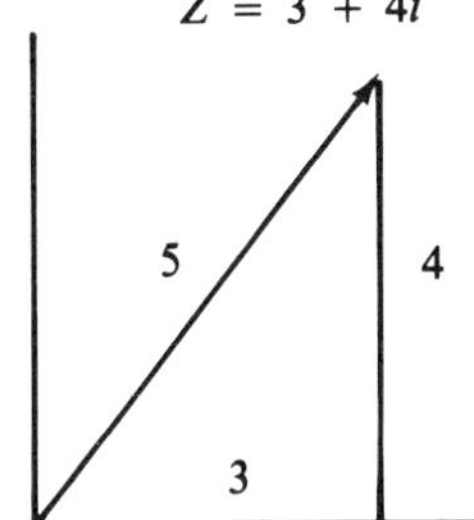

Both of the preceding expressions would result in the computation and storage of the floating point number 5 in memory location X. (Note that the argument of a function must be enclosed in parentheses. A complex constant consists of two numbers enclosed in parentheses. If the argument is a complex constant, two pairs of parentheses are needed.)

† Generic Library Functions may be available. See discussion in Section 12.4.

CMPLX—The function is designed to receive two floating point arguments as input and to form a single complex value from these. For example:

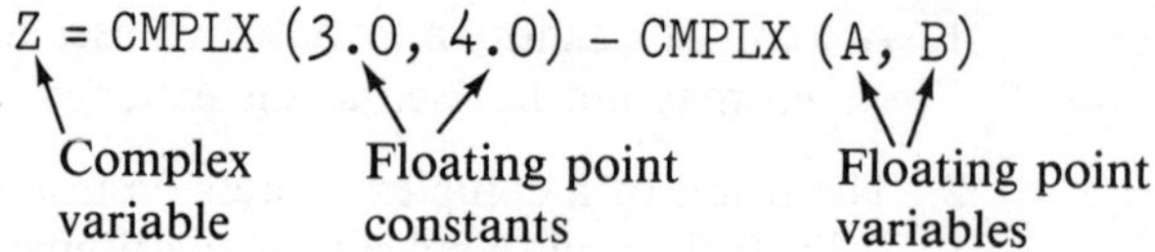

The function CMPLX is used twice to form two complex values. The floating point constants (3.0 and 4.0) are used to form one complex value; the floating point variables (A and B) are used to form the second value. These are then subtracted (complex subtraction) producing a complex result which is stored in Z.

REAL and AIMAG—Sometimes we must determine just the real or just the imaginary part of a complex value. This can be accomplished by using the REAL or AIMAG function. These functions receive a complex value as arguments and produce a single floating point value (the real or imaginary part) as output.

12.6 Use of Complex Values

Programming Example
Analysis of a Mechanism

Complex numbers can be used in the design and analysis of mechanisms such as the one shown in Figure 12.7. As depicted, the mechanism consists of a series of links. The length and angular position of each link is described on an input record (see Figure 12.8, center column). The first step in the solution will be to convert these input values (length and angle) into vectors expressed in complex notation. These vectors are shown in the last column of Figure 12.8.

Write a program to read the records shown in Figure 12.8 (containing real values) and form the complex quantities AB, BC, and CD. Determine the distance between center A and pin D of the mechanism (add vectors AB, BC, and CD and compute the absolute value).

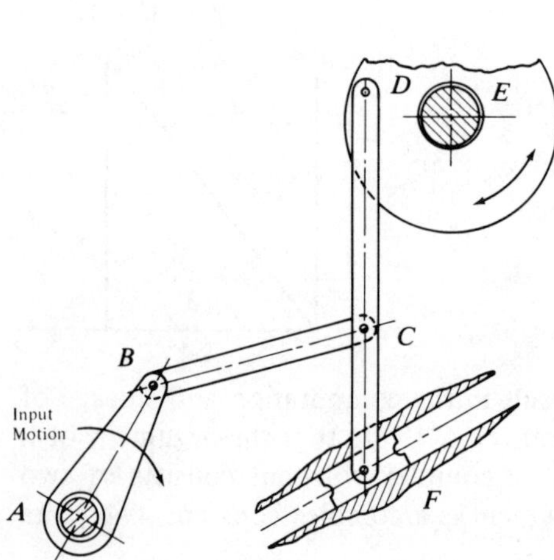

Figure 12.7 Mechanical linkage

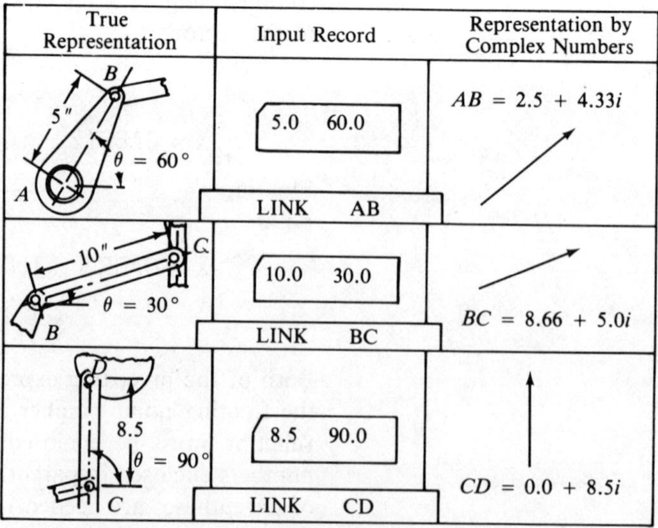

Figure 12.8 Representation of links

Programming Example–Analysis of a Mechanism continued

The program for this program proceeds as follows:

1. Read the radius and inclination of each link from data.
2. Compute two floating point numbers representing the real and imaginary portions of the equivalent complex number representation (statements 20 and 30).
3. Call the library function CMPLX to create the complex equivalent using the two floating point numbers just described as arguments.
4. Having accomplished this transformation, perform complex addition to determine the desired distance.
5. Call the library function CABS to convert the complex representation of the desired distance to a real (absolute) value.

```
C...........................................................
C..   PURPOSE - DEMONSTRATE THE USE OF COMPLEX VARIABLES,    ..
C..             DETERMINE THE POSITION OF OUTPUT CRANK.      ..
C...........................................................
C
C                      ---IMPORTANT VARIABLES---
C
C     --RE        REAL COMPONENT OF COMPLEX NUMBER               --
C     --IM        IMAGINARY COMPONENT OF COMPLEX NUMBER          --
C     --N         LINKAGE COUNTER                                --
C     --AB,BC,CD  COMPLEX NUMBER REPRESENTING THE POSITION OF    --
C                 LINKS AB, BC, AND CD RESPECTIVELY              --
C     --SUMD      RESULTANT VECTOR DETERMINING THE POSITION OF   --
C                 OUTPUT CRANK                                   --
C
      COMPLEX AB, BC, CD, SUMD
      INTEGER N
      REAL    RE, IM, R, THETA, DIST
C
      N = 0
C
C     .....LOOP ENTRY POINT.....
C
      DO WHILE (N.LT.3)
          READ 10, R, THETA
 10       FORMAT(2F12.2)
C
          N = N + 1
C
C         .....COMPUTE REAL AND IMAGINARY PARTS.....
C
 20       RE = R * COS(THETA / 57.3)
 30       IM = R * SIN(THETA / 57.3)
C
          IF (N.EQ.1) AB = CMPLX(RE,IM)
          IF (N.EQ.2) BC = CMPLX(RE,IM)
          IF (N.EQ.3) CD = CMPLX(RE,IM)
C
      END DO
C
C     .....LOOP TERMINATES HERE.....
C
C     .....COMPLEX ADDITION OF VECTORS.....
C
      SUMD = AB + BC + CD
      DIST = CABS(SUMD)
C
      PRINT *, DIST
C
      STOP
      END
```

Programming Example
AC Circuit Analysis

Complex numbers are used in AC circuit analysis. Although the current, voltage, and resistance of a DC circuit can be represented by real numbers, these same quantities require complex representation in AC circuit analysis. Similarly all calculations (such as the application of Ohm's law) require complex arithmetic.

Figure 12.9 AC and DC circuit analysis

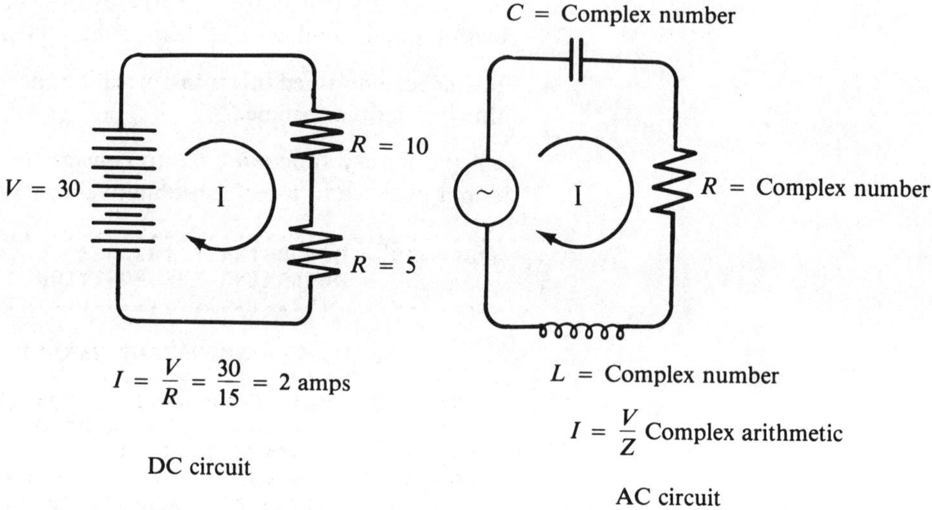

The effect of a capacitance, resistance, or inductance in an AC circuit is shown in Figure 12.10.

Figure 12.10 Representation of impedance

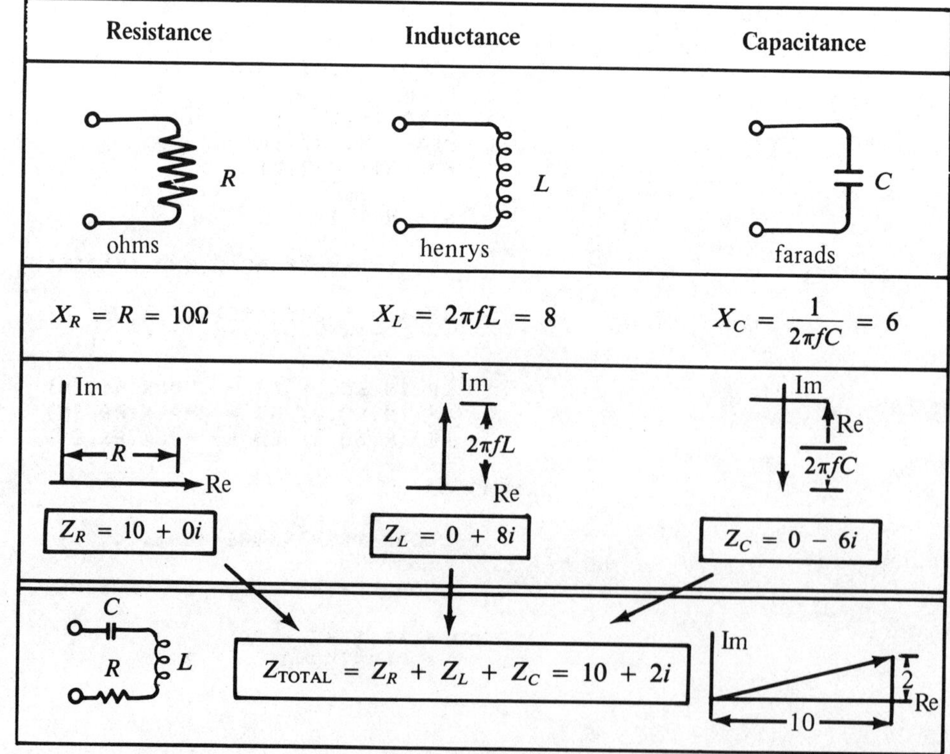

Programming Example–AC Circuit Analysis continued

Given the values of R, L, and C for series circuit, the floating point quantities X_R, X_L, and X_C may be computed. They, however, may not be added directly because of the phase (angular) differences. The complex quantities Z_R, Z_L, and Z_C must be formed and then the total impedance of the circuit can be computed. This impedance is used to relate to the current I and the voltage V according to the equation:

$$I = \frac{V}{Z}$$

This equation affords an opportunity to describe the physical significance of complex division for the purpose of making the next example more meaningful.

Figure 12.11 Computation of instantaneous current

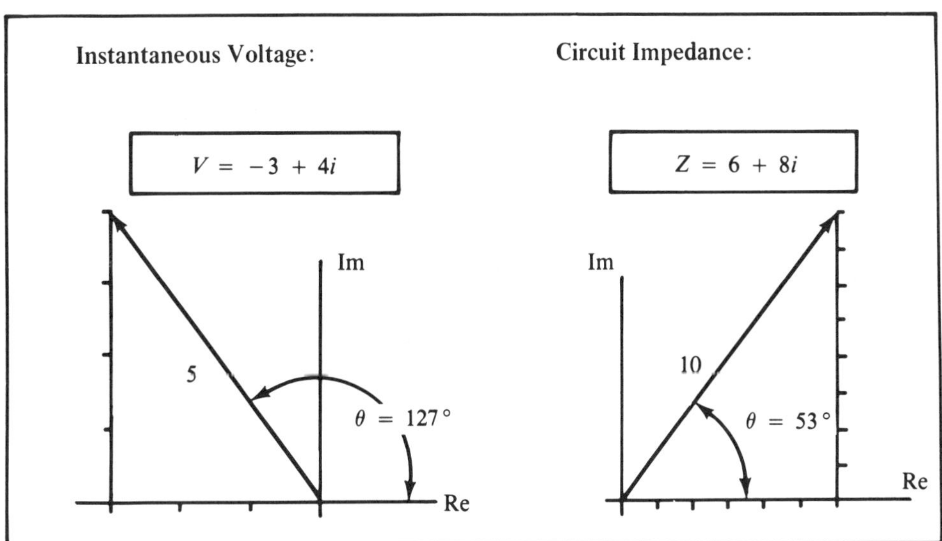

Division: $(a + bi) \div (c + di) = \dfrac{(ac + bd) + (bc - ad)i}{c^2 + d^2}$

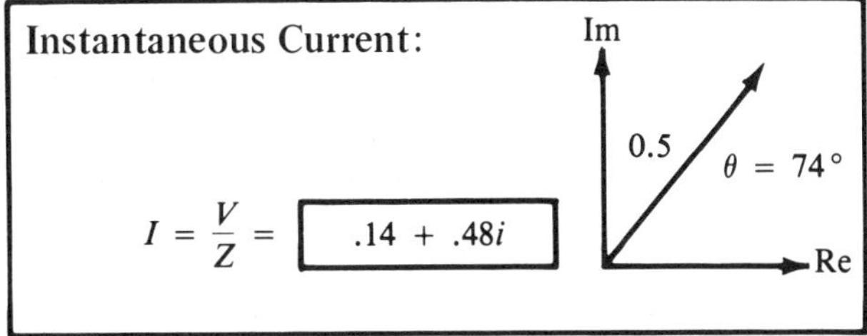

The division of two complex numbers such as V and Z produces a complex result I, whose magnitude (absolute value) equals the magnitude of V divided by the magnitude of Z and whose inclination θ_I equals the inclination of V minus the inclination of $Z(\theta_V - \theta_Z)$. The magnitude of V is 5 and θ_V equals 127°. The magnitude of Z is 10 and θ_Z equals 53° The magnitude of I equals 0.5 and θ_I equals 74°.

Programming Example–AC Circuit Analysis continued

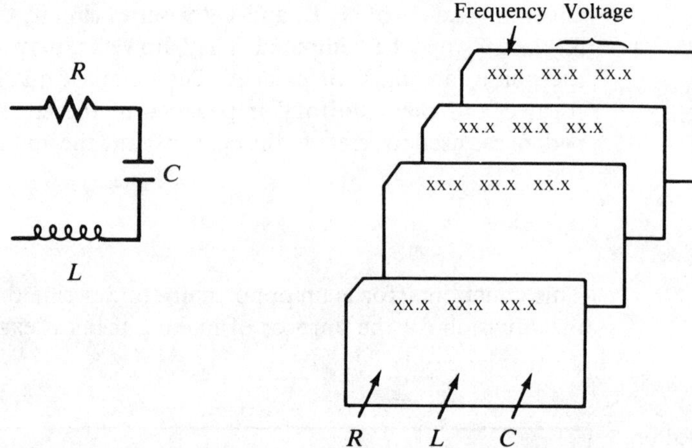

The following program reads a leader record, which specifies values for R, L, and C in the circuit shown. Each of the three remaining records specifies a frequency (real number) and the instanteous voltage (complex number) that is applied to the circuit. For each frequency, the program:

1. Computes X_R, X_C, and X_L (real values).
2. Transforms these to their complex equivalents Z_R, Z_C, and Z_L.
3. Determines the total impedance Z.
4. Determines and reports the instantaneous current.

V	Voltage (complex)
L	Inductance (real)
I	Current (complex)
IABS	Current (absolute value)
ZR, ZC, ZL	Various impedances (complex)
ZTOTL	Total impedance
F	Frequency

```
C.......................................................................
C..    PURPOSE - APPLY COMPLEX MATHEMATICS TO THE SOLUTION          ..
C..              OF AN AC CIRCUIT ANALYSIS PROBLEM.                 ..
C.......................................................................
C
C                 ---IMPORTANT VARIABLES---
C      --V          VOLTAGE (COMPLEX)                                --
C      --L          INDUCTANCE (REAL)                                --
C      --I          CURRENT (COMPLEX)                                --
C      --IABS       CURRENT (ABSOLUTE VALUE)                         --
C      --ZR,ZC,ZL   VARIOUS IMPEDANCES (COMPLEX)                     --
C      --ZTOTL      TOTAL IMPEDANCE (COMPLEX)                        --
C      --F          FREQUENCY                                        --
C
       COMPLEX V, I, ZR, ZC, ZL, ZTOTAL
       INTEGER N
       REAL    L, IABS, R, C, F
C
       N = 0
C
       READ 10, R, L, C
  10   FORMAT(3F12.2)
```

Programming Example–AC Circuit Analysis continued

```
C
C       .....LOOP ENTRY POINT.....
C
        DO WHILE (N.LT.3)
C
            READ 20, F, V
   20       FORMAT(2F12.2)
C
C           .....DETERMINE CIRCUIT IMPEDANCE.....
C
            XR = R
            XL = 2.0 * 3.1416 * F * L
            XC = 1.0 / (2.0 * 3.1416 * F * C)
C
C           .....CONVERT TO COMPLEX NOTATION.....
C
            ZR = CMPLX( XR , 0.0 )
            ZC = CMPLX( 0.0 , -XC )
            ZL = CMPLX( 0.0 , XL )
C
C           .....ACCOMPLISH COMPLEX ADDITION.....
C
            ZTOTAL = ZR + ZC + ZL
C
C           .....ACCOMPLISH COMPLEX DIVISION.....
C
            I = V / ZTOTAL
            IABS = CABS( I )
            PRINT *, I, IABS
C
            N = N + 1
        ENDDO
C
C           .....LOOP TERMINATION POINT.....
C
        STOP
        END
```

12.7 Logical Variables

So far the applications of the FORTRAN language have been restricted to those problems that readily lend themselves to exact numerical solution. Double precision and complex variables were obviously developed to augment the computing capability and convenience of the FORTRAN language in handling certain problems within this broad category.

Attention must now be turned, however, to problems that are characteristic in that they do not lend themselves to exact numerical representation. Problems in medical diagnosis, personnel selection, or analysis (identification) of chemical compounds fall into this category. Most typically, the solution to these problems must be based on the yes/no answers to such questions as:

1. Is blood pressure above normal?
2. Does the compound dissolve in sulfuric acid?
3. Is the applicant's I.Q. greater than 120 but less than 140?

Analysis of these problems is closely tied to two-value (Boolean) logic. Logical variables, constants, expressions, and IF statements have been developed to give the FORTRAN language a convenient means of storing and manipulating the yes/no or true/false information typical of these problems.

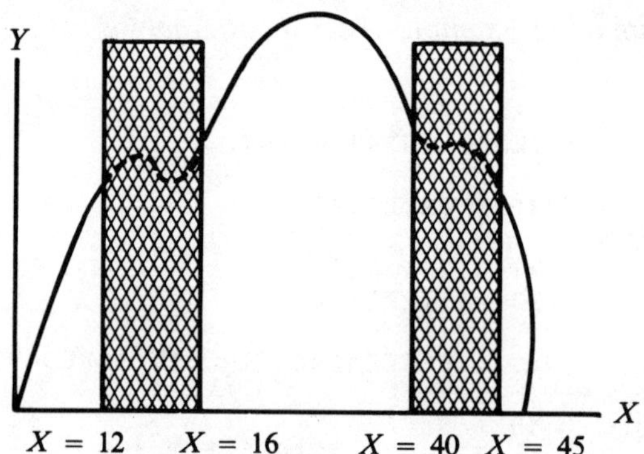

Figure 12.12 Representation of wanted data

To provide a concrete example of the use of logical variables as implemented in FORTRAN, consider the curve shown in Figure 12.12. The relationship between *X* and *Y* is well established except in the two shaded areas. Each value of *X* appearing in a program must be analyzed to determine:

1. Is *X* greater than 12 but less than 16?
2. Is *X* greater than 40 but less than or equal to 45?

If the answer to question 1 or 2 is true, special processing is necessary and control must be passed to statement 100.

With the features to be described in this section, the logical variables A and B can be created by the statement:

```
LOGICAL A, B
```

and these variables can be assigned the value "true" or "false" by the logical assignment statements:

```
A = X.GT.12.0.AND.X.LT.16.0
B = X.GT.40.0.AND.X.LE.45.0
```

Variables A and B will now contain the answers to questions 1 and 2. Finally, a logical IF statement is available to accomplish the desired transfer of control if either A or B has the value "true":

```
IF(A.OR.B) CALL PRNTER (X,Y)
```

Although the logic of this problem is not overpowering, consider the problems suggested in Figure 12.16. Two input records have been specially prepared.

Record 1 contains the results of a series of tests performed on an unknown chemical compound for the purpose of determining its composition. The compound may be dissolved by various acids, subjected to flame and precipitant tests, and so on, with the results recorded on the record shown. T indicates true (or yes) and F indicates false (or no). Record 2 shows a profile of a naval officer's qualifications. He may or may not be a qualified officer of the deck, CIC officer, and so on. In either example, it is possible to read the logical data on these records and store the information in memory. Logical expressions can be written to compare the stored information with desired or established standards. For example, on record 1, a T in columns 1, 12, 18, and 20 and an F in columns 6, 15, 19, and 21 may identify the compound as a nitrate.

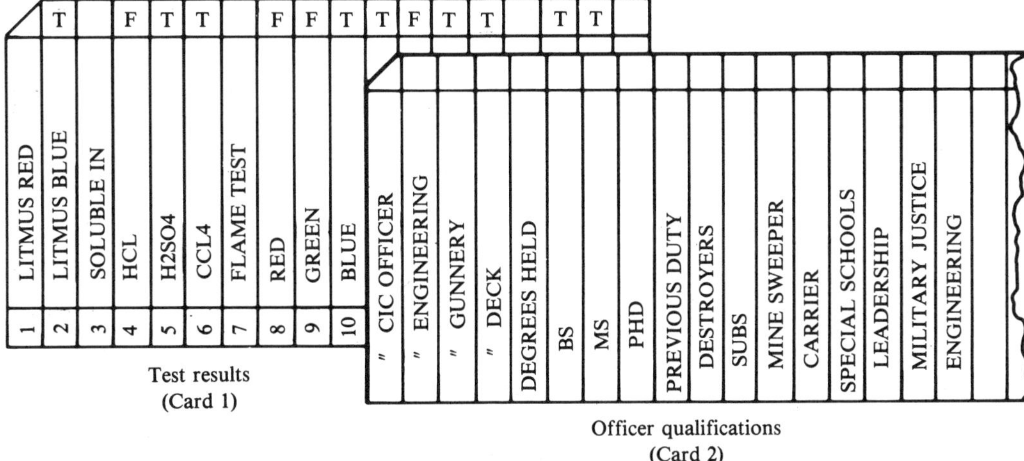

Figure 12.13 Representation of logical data

Logical Constants/Variables

Logical variables are permitted by most FORTRAN compilers. The names of variables used to represent logical values must be declared in a LOGICAL type statement.

```
LOGICAL X, Y, Z, A, BIT
```

These variables can be assigned the value "True" or "False" by the LOGICAL assignment statements:

```
X = .TRUE.
Y = .FALSE.
```

where the quantities .TRUE. and .FALSE. are logical constants.

Variables can also be assigned values from data by INPUT statements such as:

```
   READ (5,3) X, Y, Z, A, BIT
3  FORMAT (L5, L6, L1, L9, L1)
```

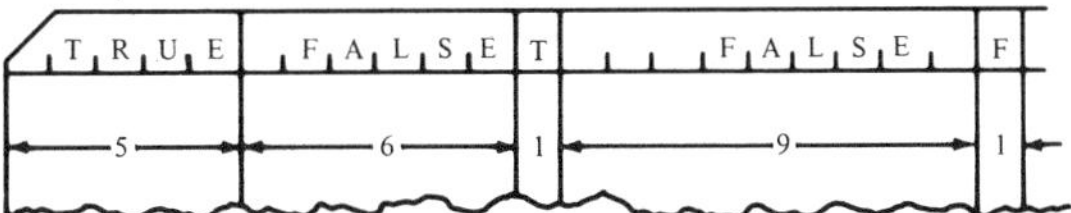

The general form of the format code controlling the INPUT/OUTPUT of logical quantities is:

```
Lw
```

where w specifies field width. On input, the first nonblank character within each specified field should be the letter T or F to indicate true or false. The remaining characters, if any, are of no importance. If the field is blank, the value False is assigned.

The following records convey the same meaning as the preceding one.

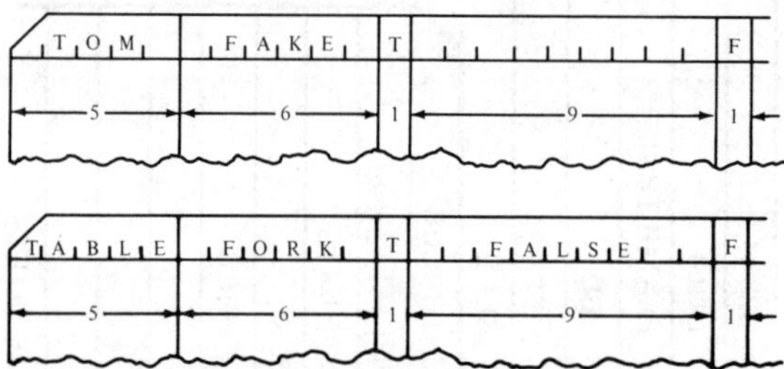

On output, only the letter T or F will be printed right justified in the specified field.

Logical Expressions

Logical expressions can be compared to arithmetic expressions in that both are used to specify a sequence or series of basic operations to be performed on various constants and variables. While the basic arithmetic operations are +,−,*,/, and so on, the basic logical operations are:

```
.NOT.        .AND.        .OR.
```

The logical expression:

```
A  .AND.  B
```

combines the logical variables A and B. The expression has the value true if both A and B are true; otherwise the expression is false. For example:

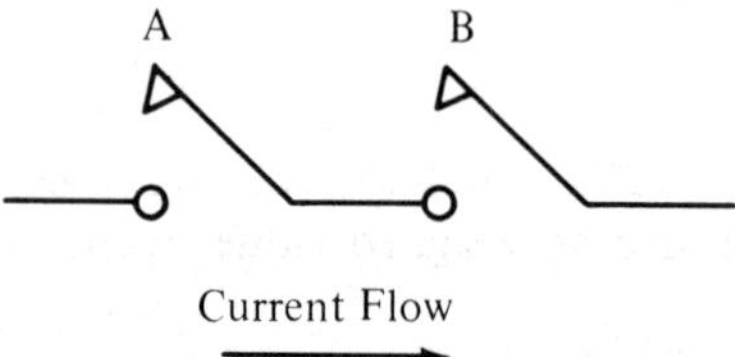

Switch A and switch B are in series. The state of each switch can be represented by a logical variable (A and B). An open switch has the value false; a closed switch has the value true. The logical expression A .AND. B tests to see if current will flow for the existing positions of the two switches.

The logical expression:

```
A .OR. B
```

combines the logical variables A and B. The expression has the value true if either A or B (or both) has the value true. For example:

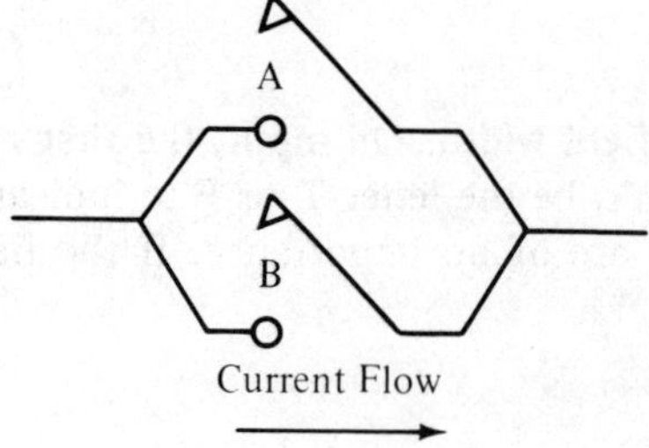

Switch A and switch B are in parallel such that current can flow if either switch A or switch B is closed. This is described by the expression `A .OR. B`.

The logical operation `.NOT.` is used to reverse the logical value. Recall the officer qualification card shown in Figure 12.13. Let logical variables `A` and `B` store the information as to whether the officer is qualified in engineering and whether he has had submarine duty. Further, assume there existed a need for an engineering officer who had not yet had submarine experience. The logical expression

```
A .AND. .NOT. B
```

expresses the desired logic. This expression will have the value true if A is true and B is false. If B is false, `.NOT.B` is true (since it reverses the logical value).

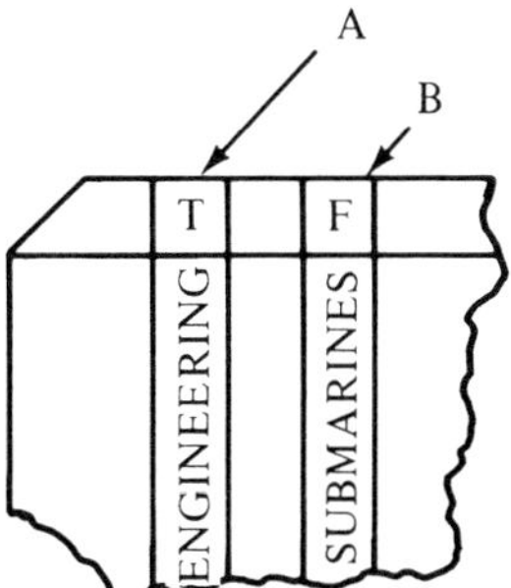

In the following examples of logical expressions, A has the value true, B has the value false, T has the value true, and F has the value false.

Expression	**Value**
.NOT. A	false
B .AND. F	false
B .OR. .NOT. F	true
A .AND. F .AND. B	false
A .OR. B .OR. F	true
A .AND. B .OR. F	false

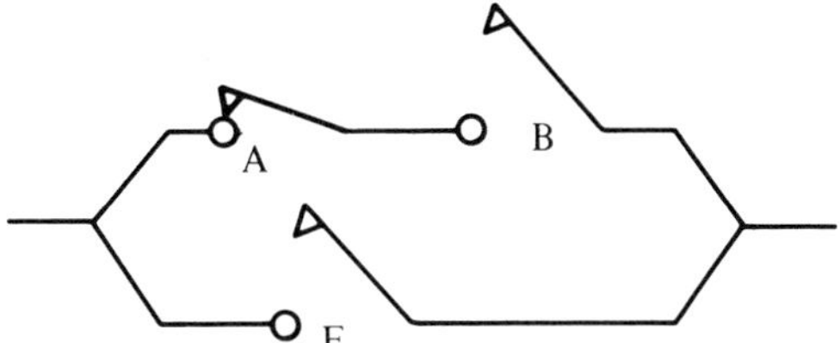

Problem: A, B, and F represent the state of three switches in the circuit shown. Write a logical expression telling under what conditions current will flow in the circuit.

Relational Operation Symbols

In some situations, numerical values may be available to establish a true/false relationship. In the following table are shown the available relational operators and their equivalent mathematical symbols.

Table of Relational Operators

Relational Operation Symbol	Meaning	Mathematical Symbol
.GT.	greater than	$>$
.GE.	greater than or equal to	$\geq$
.EQ.	equal to	$=$
.LT.	less than	$<$
.LE.	less than or equal to	$\leq$
.NE.	does not equal	$\neq$

These symbols may be used with real, double precision, or integer values as described in the following examples:

```
LET A = 1.0; B = 2.0; N = 10
```

Figure 12.14 Example statements

Logical Expression	Value
A .GT. B	false
N .LE. 10	true
B .NE. 3.0	true
1.6D03 .LT. B	false
(A**4-5) .EQ. (B/10.)	false
(A.GT.B) .AND. (B.EQ.2.0)	false

The use of parentheses in the last two examples suggests that a hierarchy of operations exists. This hierarchy now involves arithmetic, logical, and relational operators, and is shown in the following table.

Hierarchy of Operations

Arithmetic (First)
* *
*, /
+, -
Logical (Last)
.GT., .GE., .EQ., .LT., .LE., .NE.
.NOT.
.AND.
.OR.

Operations are performed left to right in cases of equal priority. Each line on the table represents a different level. For example, multiplication and division are performed before addition and subtraction. The logical operators .AND. are performed before .OR. On the basis of this, are any of the parentheses in the last two examples in Figure 12.14 needed?†

† No, but the policy of using parentheses when in doubt still applies.

Logical Assignment Statements

A **logical assignment statement** specifies a sequence of operations to be performed for the purpose of evaluating a logical expression. The true/false result is then assigned a location in memory identified by the logical variable name appearing on the left side of the statement. Consider the following examples:

```
A = 1.0; B = 2.0; T = TRUE: F = FALSE and I = 10

LOGICAL T, F, X, Y, Z

X = A .GT. 6.2 .OR. .NOT. T              X is false
X = A .LT. 6.2 .AND. .NOT. T             X is false
X = A .LT. 6.2 .AND. T                   X is true

Y = 6.7D08/B .GE. A .AND. T              Y is true
Y = 6.7D08/B .GE. A .OR. T               Y is true
Y = 6.7D08/B .GE. A .AND. .NOT. T        Y is false

Z = I - 4 .GT. (I - 6)**2                Z is false
Z = A**I-1 .EQ. B                        Z is false
Z = .NOT. (A.GT.B)
```

Review Exercises

1. Integer and real variables may be defined either implicitly or explicitly. Is this true for complex, double precision, and logical variables?
2. If a calculation is to be performed to double precision accuracy, does that mean that all values (constants and variables) in the defining expression must be stored in the double precision mode?
3. ★ What is the difference between the library functions SIN and DSIN? Which would evaluate more terms in the approximating series expansion?
4. What is the purpose of the library function CABS? Describe the input argument(s). Describe the output to this function.
5. What is meant by a generic function? How does a generic function determine what type of argument to return?
6. ★ May a variable that has been declared as a double precision one early in a program be later redefined as a logical or complex variable?
7. In the hierarchy of operations which are performed first, logical or arithmetic operations?
8. Describe the type of problem in which logical variables might be used.
9. In order for a round-off error to occur, an operation must be performed in which one of the operands is very large and the other operand is very small. Describe a situation where this might happen.
10. Evaluate the first 20 terms of the following equation for $X = 50.0$

$$Y = X + \frac{2}{X^2} + \frac{3}{X^3} + \frac{4}{X^4} + \frac{5}{X^5} + \frac{6}{X^6} + \cdots$$

Report the value of each term as a separate item. Along with this value, report the sum of all terms in the equation up to and including this term. Repeat the process using double precision.

11. ★ A job has been offered that pays one cent the first week but doubles the salary each week; that is, \$.01 the first week \$.02 the second week, \$.04 the third week, . . . $\$2^{n-1}/100$ in the nth week. Write a program that determines and reports the salary for each week and the salary paid to date for 50 weeks. Use double precision to obtain the accuracy needed for income tax purposes.
12. Write a program to determine accurately the probability of being dealt a perfect bridge hand. This may be represented by

$$\frac{13!(52 - 13)!}{52!} = \text{Probability}$$

13. Write a program to determine the value of $\int_1^{10} e^x dx$; that is, the area under the curve $Y = e^x$ from 1 to 10. Use the trapezoidal approximation

$$A = \frac{\Delta x}{2}(Y_1 + 2Y_2 + 2Y_3 + \cdots + 2Y_{n-1} + Y_n)$$

Let $\Delta x = .05$ and use both real and double precision variables. Compare answers.

14. A data file consists of 10 records, each containing 2 floating point values representing the real and complex portion of a vector. Write a program to determine the length of the largest vector represented in the input file.

★ 15. Arm AB rotates about A, and wheel BC rotates about B. For the position shown:

a. Express the position of point B as a complex number.

b. Express the position of point C as a complex number.

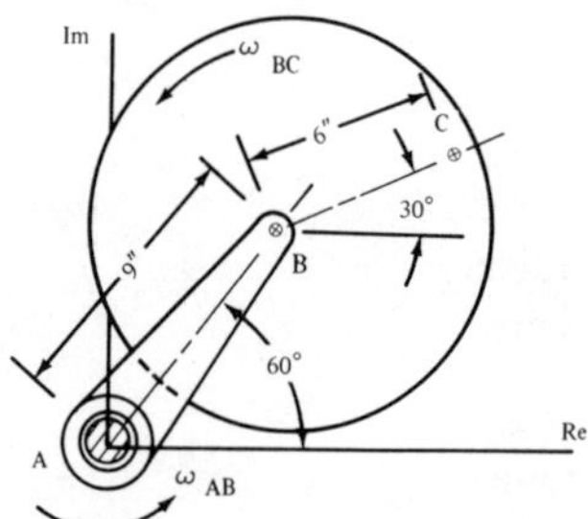

If both AB and BC rotate at one revolution per minute, report the position of B and C at one-second intervals starting from the present position.

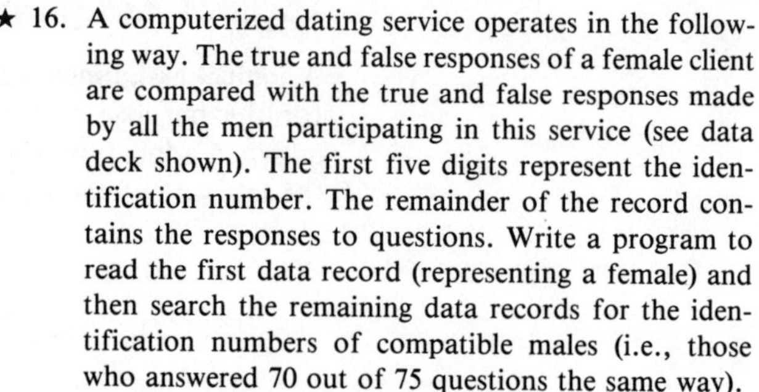
★ 16. A computerized dating service operates in the following way. The true and false responses of a female client are compared with the true and false responses made by all the men participating in this service (see data deck shown). The first five digits represent the identification number. The remainder of the record contains the responses to questions. Write a program to read the first data record (representing a female) and then search the remaining data records for the identification numbers of compatible males (i.e., those who answered 70 out of 75 questions the same way).

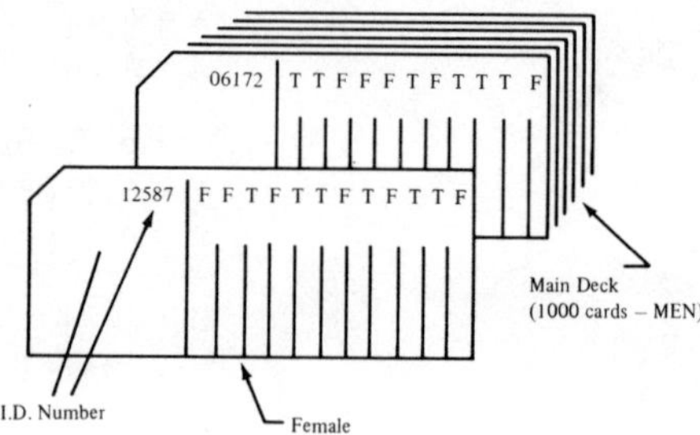

Additional Applications

Programming Example
Using a Logical Flag

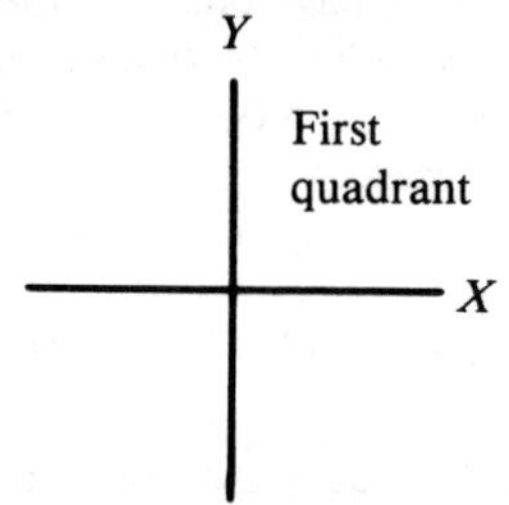

A data file consists of 40 records each containing the *X* and *Y* coordinates of a point. All points should lie in the first quadrant (Positive *X* and positive *Y*). Process all these records and print out one of the following two messages.

Message A

```
ALL POINTS IN FIRST
QUADRANT
```

Message B

```
POINT 5 NOT IN FIRST QUADRANT
POINT 9 NOT IN FIRST QUADRANT
```

The problem is to know if Message A should be printed after the 40 records are processed. Try setting a logical memory location called FLAG equal to .TRUE. early in the program. Then, if any point lies outside the first quadrant, report that point and execute the statement:

```
FLAG = .FALSE.
```

This pulls down the flag that was run up the pole at the beginning of the program. An IF statement now can be used at the end of the program (see statement 20) to check the condition of the flag (up or down) and execute or not execute Message A.

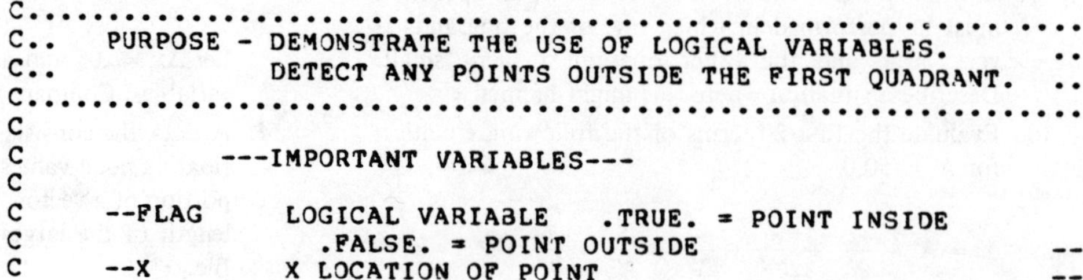

```
C.....................................................................
C..   PURPOSE - DEMONSTRATE THE USE OF LOGICAL VARIABLES.            ..
C..             DETECT ANY POINTS OUTSIDE THE FIRST QUADRANT.        ..
C.....................................................................
C
C               ---IMPORTANT VARIABLES---
C
C       --FLAG       LOGICAL VARIABLE    .TRUE. = POINT INSIDE
C                       .FALSE. = POINT OUTSIDE                      --
C       --X          X LOCATION OF POINT                             --
```

Programming Example–Using a Logical Flag continued

```
C      --Y         Y LOCATION OF POINT                                 --
C      --CARDS     CARD COUNTER                                        --
C
C      ..... RAISE FLAG BEFORE ENTERING LOOP.....
C
       INTEGER CARDS
       LOGICAL FLAG
       REAL    X, Y
C
       FLAG = .TRUE.
C
       CARDS = 0
C
C      .....LOOP ENTRY POINT.....
C
       DO WHILE (CARDS.LT.40)
C
           READ *, X, Y
C
           CARDS = CARDS + 1
C
C          .....CHECK LOCATION OF POINT.....
C
           IF (X.LT.0.0.OR.Y.LT.0.0) THEN
C
               FLAG = .FALSE.
               PRINT 10, CARDS
   10          FORMAT(8X,'POINT',1X,I4,1X,'NOT IN FIRST QUADRANT')
C
           ENDIF
C
C          .....ANY CARDS REMAINING.....
C
       ENDDO
C
C      .....LOOP EXIT POINT.....
C
C      .....SEE IF MESSAGE IS APPROPRIATE.....
C
   20  IF (FLAG) PRINT *,'        ALL POINTS IN FIRST QUADRANT'
C
       STOP
       END
```

Programming Example
Resultant Force

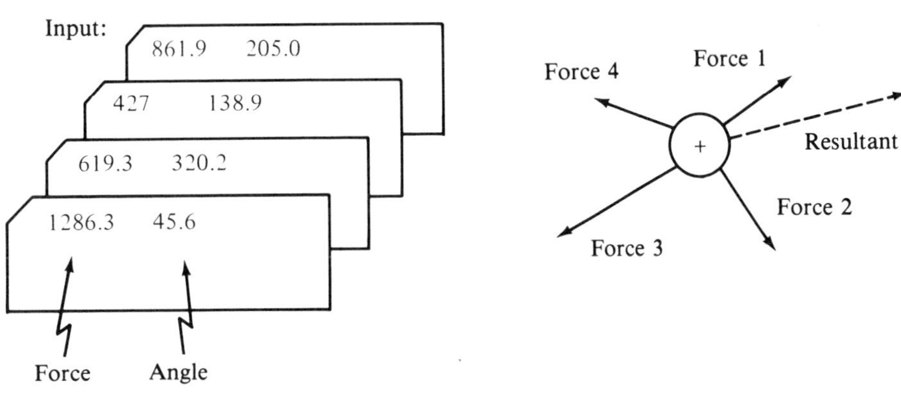

Programming Example–Resultant Force continued

Four forces are applied to a small ring. The magnitude of each force is described on a record (angle specified in degrees 0 to 360). Determine the resultant of these forces. Express the resultant in two ways:

1. Standard representation (magnitude and inclination).
2. Complex representation (real and imaginary component).

```
C.............................................................
C..   PURPOSE - EXAMPLE OF USING COMPLEX VARIABLES.         ..
C.............................................................
C
C              ---IMPORTANT VARIABLES---
C
C     --F1,F2,F3,F4
C                 MAGNITUDE OF THE FORCES APPLIED TO
C                   THE RING                                 --
C     --ANG1,ANG2,ANG3,ANG4
C                 ANGLE AT WHICH EACH FORCE IS APPLIED TO
C                   THE RING                                 --
C     --FORCE1,FORCE2,FORCE3,FORCE4
C                 COMPLEX FORCES                             --
C     --RESULT    SUM OF COMPLEX FORCES                      --
C     --FORCE     MAGNITUDE OF RESULT (|RESULT|)             --
C     --ANGLE     ANGLE OF RESULT                            --
C     --X         REAL PART OF RESULT                        --
C     --Y         IMAGINARY PART OF RESULT                   --
C
      COMPLEX FORCE1, FORCE2, FORCE3, FORCE4, RESULT
      REAL    X, Y, F1, F2, F3, F4, ANG1, ANG2, ANG3, ANG4
C
C     .....CONVERT INPUT TO COMPLEX NOTATION.....
C
      READ *, F1, ANG1
      FORCE1 = CMPLX (F1*COS(ANG1/57.3),F1*SIN(ANG1/57.3))
C
      READ *, F2, ANG2
      FORCE2 = CMPLX (F2*COS(ANG2/57.3),F2*SIN(ANG2/57.3))
C
      READ *, F3, ANG3
      FORCE3 = CMPLX (F3*COS(ANG3/57.3),F3*SIN(ANG3/57.3))
C
      READ *, F4, ANG4
      FORCE4 = CMPLX (F4*COS(ANG4/57.3),F4*SIN(ANG4/57.3))
C
C     .....ADD VECTORS OBTAIN RESULTANT.....
C
      RESULT = FORCE1 + FORCE2 + FORCE3 + FORCE4
      PRINT 10, RESULT
   10 FORMAT(2X,'COMPLEX REPRESENTATION OF RESULTANT......',10X,
     1        'REAL PART = ',F9.1,10X,'IMAGINARY PART = ',F9.1)
C
C     .....CONVERT RESULTANT TO STANDARD FORM.....
C
      FORCE = CABS(RESULT)
C
      X = REAL (RESULT)
      Y = AIMAG (RESULT)
      ANGLE = ATAN (Y/X) * 57.3
C
      PRINT *,' THE MAGNITUDE OF THE RESULTANT IS',FORCE
      PRINT *,' THE INCLINATION IS',ANGLE
C
      STOP
      END
```

Programming Example
Financial Aid (Question Analysis)

Each input record shows a series of true/false answers given to 16 questions that are used to determine if a person qualifies for financial aid.

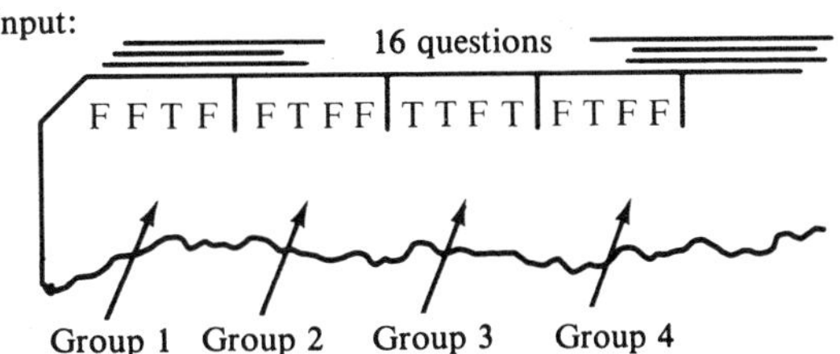

The questions are categorized into four groups consisting of four questions each. The applicant must respond "true" to at least one question in each group to qualify. Write a program to process each card and respond with the message "APPLICANT QUALIFIES" or "APPLICANT DOES NOT QUALIFY."

```
C.................................................................
C..   PURPOSE - DEMONSTRATE THE USE OF LOGICAL VARIABLES TO      ..
C..             ANALYZE TRUE/FALSE (BINARY) INFORMATION.          ..
C.................................................................
C
C              ---IMPORTANT VARIABLES---
C
C     --X1...X16 ANSWERS TO THE 16 QUESTIONS GIVEN               --
C     --GROUP1...GROUP4
C               GROUPS OF QUESTIONS BY CATEGORIES                 --
C
      LOGICAL X1, X2, X3, X4, X5, X6, X7, X8, X9, X10, X11, X12,
     1  X13, X14, X15, X16
      LOGICAL GROUP1, GROUP2, GROUP3, GROUP4
C
      READ 10, X1, X2, X3, X4, X5, X6, X7, X8, X9, X10, X11, X12,
     1  X13, X14, X15, X16
   10 FORMAT(16L1)
C
C     .....TEST GROUP SET 1.....
C
      IF (X1.OR.X2.OR.X3.OR.X4) THEN
          GROUP1 = .TRUE.
      ELSE
          GROUP1 = .FALSE.
      ENDIF
C
C     .....TEST GROUP SET 2.....
C
      IF (X5.OR.X6.OR.X7.OR.X8) THEN
          GROUP2 = .TRUE.
      ELSE
          GROUP2 = .FALSE.
      ENDIF
C
C     .....TEST GROUP SET 3.....
C
      IF (X9.OR.X10.OR.X11.OR.X12) THEN
          GROUP3 = .TRUE.
      ELSE
          GROUP3 = .FALSE.
      ENDIF
C
C     .....TEST GROUP SET 4.....
C
      IF (X13.OR.X14.OR.X15.OR.X16) THEN
          GROUP4 = .TRUE.
```

Programming Example–Financial Aid continued

```
      ELSE
         GROUP4 = .FALSE.
      ENDIF
C
C     .....TEST TOTAL GROUPS.....
C
      IF (GROUP1.AND.GROUP2.AND.GROUP3.AND.GROUP4) THEN
C
         PRINT *,'         APPLICANT QUALIFIES'
C
      ELSE
C
         PRINT *,'         APPLICANT DOES NOT QUALIFY'
C
      ENDIF
C
      STOP
      END
```

Programming Example
Water Bill

An input record gives the water meter reading of a customer at the beginning and the end of the month. The number in column 1 indicates if this is an industrial or residential user.

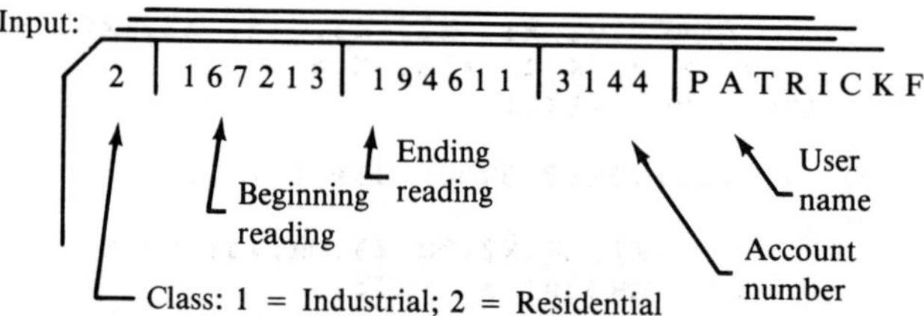

Industrial users are charged a flat rate of 0.5¢/gallon. Residential users pay 0.8¢/gallon until they reach 5000 gallons. The rate then changes to 0.6¢/gallon for all additional use.

Write statements that will determine and report a correct water bill for both types of users. Plan on a trailer card containing 0's in all fields.

Special situation: Usually, the gallons of water consumed can be determined by subtracting the "end" and "beginning" meter readings. There is a single exception, however, and that is when the meter passes through its maximum value (999999) and moves on to 000000. This is called **meter-go-round**. Include statements in your program to detect this situation and take appropriate corrective action.

Programming Example–Water Bill continued

```
C.................................................................
C..   PURPOSE - COMPUTE WATER BILL.                             ..
C.................................................................
C
C              ---IMPORTANT VARIABLES---
C
C      --NBEGIN    METER READING AT BEGINNING OF PERIOD           --
C      --NEND      METER READING AT END OF PERIOD                 --
C      --NACCT     ACCOUNT NUMBER                                 --
C      --CLASS     CLASS CODE
C                    1 = INDUSTRIAL
C                    2 = RESIDENTIAL                              --
C      --GAL       GALLONS OF WATER CONSUMED                      --
C      --BILL      AMOUNT TO PAY WITH RATE OF:
C                    CLASS 1 = 0.005
C                    CLASS 2 = 0.008. IF OVER 5000
C                    GALLONS PAY EXTRAS AT 0.006                  --
C
      INTEGER CLASS, NBEGIN, NEND, NACCT, GAL
      REAL    BILL
C
      READ *,CLASS, NBEGIN, NEND, NACCT
C
C     .....TEST FOR TRAILER CARD.....
C
      IF (NACCT.EQ.0) STOP
C
C     .....HAS METER PASSED 999999.....
C
C     .....IF YES CORRECT END READING.....
C
      IF (NEND.LT.NBEGIN) NEND = NEND + 1000000
C
C     .....CALCULATE GALLONS AND REPORT BILL.....
C
      GAL = NEND - NBEGIN
C
C     .....IF INDUSTRIAL USER APPLY FLAT RATE.....
C
C     .....(RATE = 0.5 CENTS PER GALLON).....
C
      IF (CLASS.EQ.1) BILL = GAL * 0.005
C
C     .....IF RESIDENTIAL USER CHECK FOR LOW USE.....
C
C     .....(RATE = 0.8 CENTS PER GALLON).....
C
      IF (CLASS.EQ.2.AND.GAL.LT.5000) BILL = GAL * 0.008
C
C     .....IF RESIDENTIAL AND OVER 5000 GAL.....
C
      IF (CLASS.EQ.2.AND.GAL.GT.5000) BILL = (5000 * 0.008 +
     1    + (GAL - 5000) * 0.006)
C
      PRINT *, NACCT, BILL
C
      STOP
      END
```

13 Use of Large Software Packages

Unless you become a professional programmer, the chances are that from now on you will become less involved in *writing* subprograms and more involved in *using* them. In this chapter we will show how the various subprograms of several typical software packages are organized and documented. We will try to convey the tremendous scope of these packages and explain how to use them.

The experience you have gained in writing just a few subprograms of your own will make this a relatively easy task. As powerful as these software packages are, just remember, they are not much more than a collection of FORTRAN subroutines. As such you must be prepared to provide input in two basic forms.

The majority of routines operate on pure numeric data. Accordingly the documentation will ask you to define certain *variables* and *arrays*. These will then be passed as input. This represents the first and most frequent form of input. A second group of subprograms on occasion may require an equation as input. When this happens, you will be told to write a user-supplied subprogram that holds this alternative form of input and to pass the name of that subprogram in an argument list. This is the same procedure used in Chapter 11 to pass an equation to subroutine AREA. This is the second basic form of input.

13.1 Typical Software

All computer centers maintain a file of commonly used arithmetic functions and problem algorithms to accomplish a wide variety of mathematical operations. In the early days of computers, these files were rather modest in scope and were not considered very powerful. Today the situation is entirely different. The importance of providing quality software to support existing hardware systems has been recognized and hundreds of man-years of effort have been expended to organize, code, and test a powerful and comprehensive group of subprograms. A partial list includes subprograms to:

1. Solve linear and nonlinear equations.
2. Solve systems of simultaneous equations.
3. Integrate and differentiate equations.

4. Analyze raw data (find mean, average, variance, standard deviation, minimum value, maximum value, and so on).
5. Tabulate data and determine correlation coefficients.
6. Do factor analysis of data and compute eigenvalues.
7. Solve numerically both differential and partial differential equations.
8. Do curve fitting and curve smoothing (that is, generate an equation to satisfy a series of data points).
9. Do matrix operations (such as add, subtract, multiply, divide, invert, and transpose).
10. Do regression analysis, time series, and develop nonparametric statistics on data.

This list is presented not to overwhelm you, but to show how extensive and complete these software packages are. As formidable as this list may be, it represents only a part of the software development that is going on today. Many special interest groups such as business, banking, and management have developed large scale "discipline-oriented" software to facilitate the extensive use of computers in their particular areas of interest. Deposits and withdrawals, interest calculations, check processing, mortgage payments, payroll control, accounts receivable, and accounts payable are just a few of the many day-to-day business activities accomplished by an interconnected group of subroutines.

Engineers and architects bring the power of the computer to bear on problems such as highway design, stress analysis of structures, plant layout, numeric control of machinery, maintenance scheduling, and a variety of activities too numerous to mention. Social scientists have software systems to simulate and analyze urban networks and population distributions. Medical researchers use software packages to assist in diagnostic evaluations, complex equipment control, and other health care treatment problems.

Development of software is a multibillion dollar business.

13.2 A Look at Software Documentation

To make the individual subroutines of a software package as easy to use as possible, careful attention has been given to provide clear and uniform documentation within each routine. This documentation tells you:

1. What the purpose of the subroutine is.
2. What arguments it needs.
3. Which are input, which are output.
4. How the subprogram should be called.
5. What method of solution is used.
6. Any special requirements or limitations.

Within any package, the documentation is *consistent*. That is, the documentation for any one routine is the same as for all others.

In a previous chapter, we wrote a subroutine called `AREA` that computed the area under a curve between two limits of X. This process is known in calculus as computing the integral of a function. The following subroutine (Figure 13.1) is taken from the IBM Scientific Subroutine Package and is used to show typical documentation. This subroutine is much more sophisticated than our subroutine `AREA`, but the similarity is sufficient to help you follow its documentation.

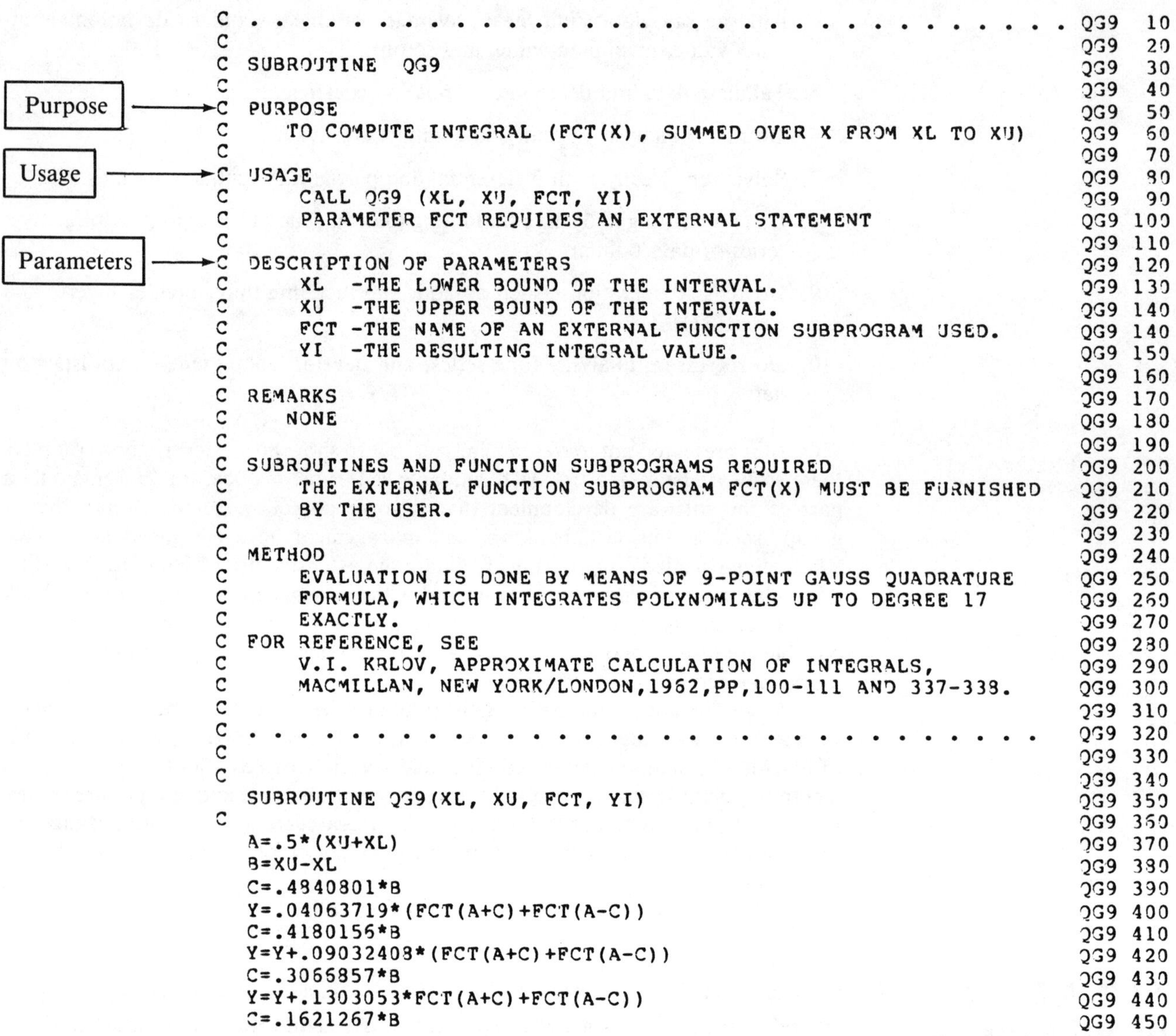


```
C . . . . . . . . . . . . . . . . . . . . . . . . . . . . . . .
C
C SUBROUTINE  QG9
C
C PURPOSE
C    TO COMPUTE INTEGRAL (FCT(X), SUMMED OVER X FROM XL TO XU)
C
C USAGE
C     CALL QG9 (XL, XU, FCT, YI)
C     PARAMETER FCT REQUIRES AN EXTERNAL STATEMENT
C
C DESCRIPTION OF PARAMETERS
C     XL  -THE LOWER BOUND OF THE INTERVAL.
C     XU  -THE UPPER BOUND OF THE INTERVAL.
C     FCT -THE NAME OF AN EXTERNAL FUNCTION SUBPROGRAM USED.
C     YI  -THE RESULTING INTEGRAL VALUE.
C
C REMARKS
C    NONE
C
C SUBROUTINES AND FUNCTION SUBPROGRAMS REQUIRED
C    THE EXTERNAL FUNCTION SUBPROGRAM FCT(X) MUST BE FURNISHED
C    BY THE USER.
C
C METHOD
C     EVALUATION IS DONE BY MEANS OF 9-POINT GAUSS QUADRATURE
C     FORMULA, WHICH INTEGRATES POLYNOMIALS UP TO DEGREE 17
C     EXACTLY.
C FOR REFERENCE, SEE
C     V.I. KRLOV, APPROXIMATE CALCULATION OF INTEGRALS,
C     MACMILLAN, NEW YORK/LONDON,1962,PP,100-111 AND 337-338.
C
C . . . . . . . . . . . . . . . . . . . . . . . . . . . . . .
C
C
      SUBROUTINE QG9(XL, XU, FCT, YI)
C
      A=.5*(XU+XL)
      B=XU-XL
      C=.4840801*B
      Y=.04063719*(FCT(A+C)+FCT(A-C))
      C=.4180156*B
      Y=Y+.09032408*(FCT(A+C)+FCT(A-C))
      C=.3066857*B
      Y=Y+.1303053*FCT(A+C)+FCT(A-C))
      C=.1621267*B
```

Figure 13.1 Integration routine

In the USAGE section, you are shown how to make a call to this subroutine, i.e., how the argument list is constructed. To further help you, each of the parameters on this list is explained in more detail in the section called DESCRIPTION OF PARAMETERS. This subroutine is one of those that must be passed an equation to operate on. Note the extreme effort that is made to make sure you handle this properly. In the PARAMETER section, you are told that an external subprogram is needed. In the USAGE section, you are reminded to use an EXTERNAL statement in the calling program. Finally, in the section entitled SUBROUTINES AND FUNCTION SUBPROGRAMS REQUIRED, you are told the type of subprogram the user must supply and what argument list should be used.

To demonstrate the use of this subroutine, assume that we wish to determine the integral of the equation:

$$y = e^x - \frac{\ln(x^2 + 1)}{X}$$

between X = 5 and X = 10. Two blocks of code would be required. The first is the main or calling program.

```
C...............................................................
C..    PURPOSE - DEMONSTRATE CALL TO SUBROUTINE QG9(IBM-SSP)   ..
C..              WHERE BASIC INPUT IS A FUNCTION SUBPROGRAM    ..
C...............................................................
C
       EXTERNAL Y
C
       CALL QG9(5.0,10.0,Y,ANSWER)
C
       PRINT*, 'ANSWER=', ANSWER
C
       STOP
       END
```

Note how extremely easy it is to take advantage of this prewritten routine.

The second item that must be supplied is the FUNCTION subprogram holding the specific equation to be integrated. We have chosen to use the name Y for that subprogram.

```
       FUNCTION Y(X)
C
C...........................................................
C..    PURPOSE - THIS IS A DEFINITION OF THE SUBPROGRAM    ..
C..              REQUESTED BY QG9. THIS SUBPROGRAM HOLDS   ..
C..              THE EQUATION THAT IS TO BE INTEGRATED.    ..
C...........................................................
C
       Y = EXP(X) - ALOG(X**2 + 1.0) / X
C
       RETURN
       END
```

13.3 Subroutine SIMQ

Subroutine SIMQ is used to find the solution to simultaneous equations such as:

Equation 1	$9.0X_1 + 6.5X_2 + 3.5X_3 = 27.75$
Equation 2	$4.5X_1 + 2.2X_2 + 1.5X_3 = 10.50$
Equation 3	$6.7X_1 + 3.0X_2 + 1.0X_3 = 12.25$

Before reading the documentation of SIMQ, it would help to anticipate what information must be passed to such a subroutine to solve equations of this form. Obviously the coefficient preceding each X term is needed, suggesting a two-dimensional array (matrix) possibly called A. The three right-hand coefficients are needed suggesting a one-dimensional array (vector) B. We must provide either the size of these arrays or an integer telling how many equations are in the set. With this as a start, let's look at SIMQ (see Figure 13.2).

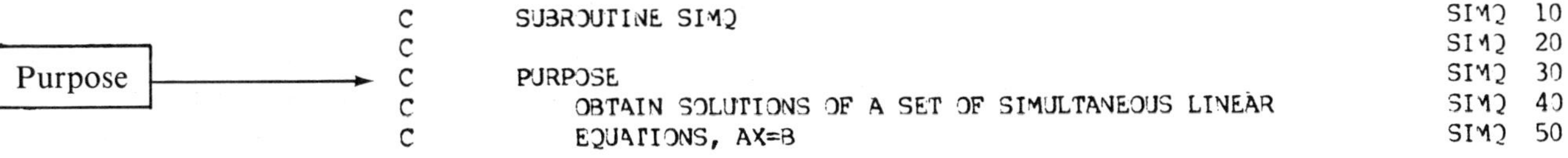


```
C      SUBROUTINE SIMQ
C
C      PURPOSE
C         OBTAIN SOLUTIONS OF A SET OF SIMULTANEOUS LINEAR
C         EQUATIONS, AX=B
```

Figure 13.2 Subroutine SIMQ documentation (continues on next page)

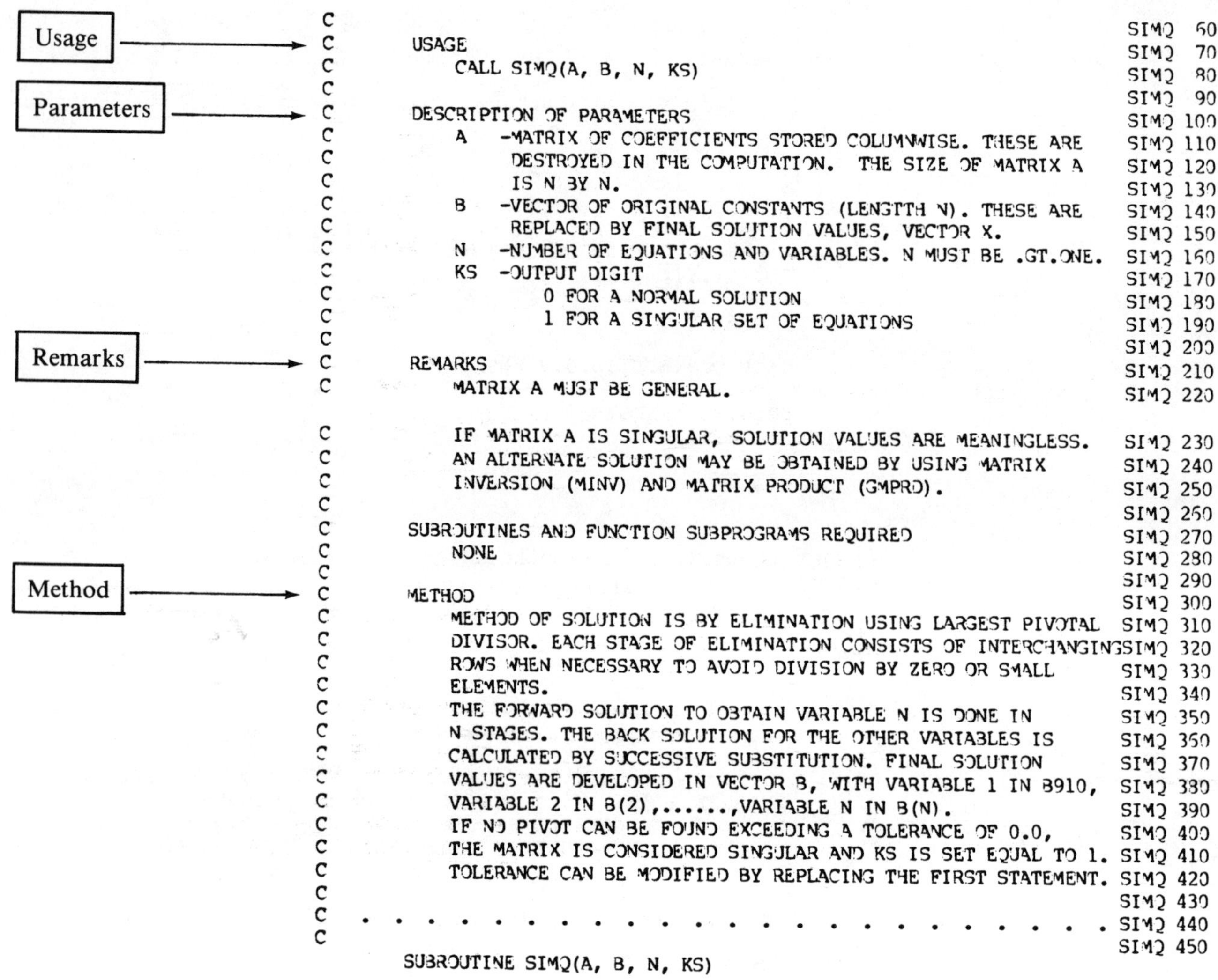


```
C
C        USAGE
C           CALL SIMQ(A, B, N, KS)
C
C        DESCRIPTION OF PARAMETERS
C           A    -MATRIX OF COEFFICIENTS STORED COLUMNWISE. THESE ARE
C                 DESTROYED IN THE COMPUTATION.  THE SIZE OF MATRIX A
C                 IS N BY N.
C           B    -VECTOR OF ORIGINAL CONSTANTS (LENGTTH N). THESE ARE
C                 REPLACED BY FINAL SOLUTION VALUES, VECTOR X.
C           N    -NUMBER OF EQUATIONS AND VARIABLES. N MUST BE .GT.ONE.
C           KS   -OUTPUT DIGIT
C                   0 FOR A NORMAL SOLUTION
C                   1 FOR A SINGULAR SET OF EQUATIONS
C
C        REMARKS
C           MATRIX A MUST BE GENERAL.

C           IF MATRIX A IS SINGULAR, SOLUTION VALUES ARE MEANINGLESS.
C           AN ALTERNATE SOLUTION MAY BE OBTAINED BY USING MATRIX
C           INVERSION (MINV) AND MATRIX PRODUCT (GMPRD).
C
C        SUBROUTINES AND FUNCTION SUBPROGRAMS REQUIRED
C           NONE
C
C        METHOD
C           METHOD OF SOLUTION IS BY ELIMINATION USING LARGEST PIVOTAL
C           DIVISOR. EACH STAGE OF ELIMINATION CONSISTS OF INTERCHANGING
C           ROWS WHEN NECESSARY TO AVOID DIVISION BY ZERO OR SMALL
C           ELEMENTS.
C           THE FORWARD SOLUTION TO OBTAIN VARIABLE N IS DONE IN
C           N STAGES. THE BACK SOLUTION FOR THE OTHER VARIABLES IS
C           CALCULATED BY SUCCESSIVE SUBSTITUTION. FINAL SOLUTION
C           VALUES ARE DEVELOPED IN VECTOR B, WITH VARIABLE 1 IN B910,
C           VARIABLE 2 IN B(2),......,VARIABLE N IN B(N).
C           IF NO PIVOT CAN BE FOUND EXCEEDING A TOLERANCE OF 0.0,
C           THE MATRIX IS CONSIDERED SINGULAR AND KS IS SET EQUAL TO 1.
C           TOLERANCE CAN BE MODIFIED BY REPLACING THE FIRST STATEMENT.
C
C     . . . . . . . . . . . . . . . . . . . . . . . . . . . . . . . .
C
      SUBROUTINE SIMQ(A, B, N, KS)
```

Figure 13.2 Subroutine SIMQ documentation (continued)

First, examine the CALL statement and the description of parameters:

```
CALL SIMQ (A,B,N,KS)
```

Note that we have predicted or anticipated the first three arguments. In the DESCRIPTION OF PARAMETERS, however, it is stated that the matrix A and the vector B are destroyed in the computation. The reason for this needs explaining.

One of the first steps in solving the problem is to get the coefficients preceding X_1 in all the equations to be the same. This is done by multiplying each row of matrix A (and an element of B) by an appropriate value. Although this does not destroy the functional relationships expressed by these equations, it does destroy their original identity.

We are also told that the final solution values (X_1, X_2, and X_3) replace the original values in vector B. Vector B is being used for both input and output. On input, B holds the right-hand constants. On output, it holds all the answers.

Usually it is not necessary to preserve the identity of the original equations. All that are needed are the solution values. If the equations must be preserved, the obvious answer would be to make a copy of both arrays and feed these copies to SIMQ.

A Mailbox

The last argument, KS, is like a mailbox and is used to signal if a normal solution is being achieved. Statements inside SIMQ are constantly checking to see if anything is going wrong. If no difficulties are encountered, the number 0 is loaded into memory location KS just before the RETURN statement is executed. This signals a normal solution.

If, however, the subroutine detects something has gone wrong (one equation is the exact multiple of another), a number other than 0 is loaded into memory location KS using a statement such as:

```
KS = 1
```

and the RETURN statement executed immediately, terminating the solution. If a number other than 0 is returned in KS, a list of "disaster" codes is provided to match the number to the difficulties encountered. You then are told to ignore any other output values. All software packages have some method of signaling the user when something has gone wrong. This is one of many techniques used.

The steps involved in writing the main program, which uses a typical predefined subroutine, are:

1. Define the variables, arrays or subprograms requested as input in the description of parameters.
2. Make the appropriate call.
3. Check for a normal solution.
4. Output results or pass values to other subprograms.

Our original set of three equations could now be solved by the following main program.

```
C.............................................................
C..     PURPOSE - DEMONSTRATE CALL TO SUBROUTINE SIMQ (IBM-SSP)..
C..               WHERE BASIC INPUT IS BY ARRAYS.             ..
C.............................................................
C
        DIMENSION A(3,3),B(3)
C
C                        READ EQUATIONS FROM DATA
C
        DO 20 I=1,3
C
            READ*,A(I,1),A(I,2),A(I,3),B(I)
C
  20    CONTINUE
C
C       ...............................................
C               CALL SIMQ(A,B,3,MAIL)
C       ...............................................
C
C       CHECK MAIL FOR SUCCESSFUL SOLUTION
C
        PRINT*,  MAIL
C
        IF(MAIL.NE.0) STOP
C
C               PUBLISH SOLUTION VALUES
C
        PRINT*, (B(I),I=1,3)
C
        STOP
        END
```

13.4 Other Software Packages (Conversational)

Consider yourself fortunate that you are competent in a computer language such as FORTRAN. Software packages are of two basic types: one for those who can program and one is for those who cannot. The packages that require no programming skill must compensate in some way. This can be achieved by making or incorporating a conversational feature inside the subprogram.

Consider the use of one such conversational subprogram called SIMULEQN in solving another set of simultaneous equations:

$$\begin{aligned} 3x + 2y + 1z &= 3 \\ 5x - 3y + 2z &= -3 \\ 4x + 16y + 5z &= 27 \end{aligned}$$

After logging in on the remote console, the interactive feature is initiated by typing the key word:

```
SIMULEQN
```

The console responds with the message:

```
DO YOU WANT INSTRUCTIONS (O=NO, 1=YES), WHICH?
```

If you now answer:

```
YES
```

you have given an incorrect response and the console patiently replies:

```
ILLEGAL INPUT.RETYPE?
```

After giving an acceptable response of 1, the following documentation is presented on the console. A complete set of instructions is provided followed by an example set of equations and the input that would be supplied for this example set.

```
S I M U L E Q N

DO YOU WANT INSTRUCTIONS (O=NO, 1= YES), WHICH? YES ILLEGAL INPUT.
RETYPE ?1

SIMULEQN SOLVES SYSTEMS OF N LINEAR EQUATIONS IN N UNKNOWNS. ALL DATA IS
ENTERED BY NUMBERED DATA STATEMENTS. THE FIRST DATA STATEMENT MUST BE
NUMBERED 10, AND MUST SPECIFY THE NUMBER OF SYSTEMS TO BE SOLVED AND THE
NUMBER OF EQUATIONS (AND HENCE THE NUMBER OF VARIABLES) IN THE SYSTEM.

DATA STATEMENTS NUMBERED FROM 11 TO 99 AS REQUIRED ARE USED TO ENTER THE
COEFFICIENTS AND RIGHT-HAND SIDE CONSTANTS.

ENTER THE COEFFICIENT MATRIX, BY ROWS, AND THEN THE RIGHT-HAND SIDE CON-
STANT TERMS. THIS PROGRAM IS SLOW. IF ADDITIONAL CASES WITH THE SAME CO-
EFFICIENT MATRIX BUT DIFFERENT RIGHT SIDES ARE TO BE RUN, THEY WILL BE
RUN AT ONCE BY SIMPLY ENTERING ADDITIONAL RIGHT-HAND CONSTANT TERMS.

FOR EXAMPLE, THE TWO SYSTEMS:
 3X + 5Y - 2Z =  9   3X + 5Y - 2Z = 19
 7X +  Y      = -3   7X +  Y      = -3
  X - 7Y + 9Z = 14    X - 7Y + 9Z =  8
COULD BE SOLVED BY TYPING:
```

```
*10 DATA 2,3
*11 DATA 3,5,-2,7,1,0,1,-7,9
*12 DATA 9,-3,14,19,-3,8
*RUN
*10 DATA 2,3
*11 DATA 3,5,-2,7,1,0,1,-7,9
*12 DATA 9,-3,14,19,-3,8
*RUN
AFTER THE COMPUTER RESPONDS WITH READY AND AN ASTERISK * ENTER YOUR DATA
STATEMENT IMMEDIATELY FOLLOWING THE ASTERISKS SUPPLIED, THEN TYPE RUN
```

Note that a set of instructions is given, followed by sample input to clarify the responses required.

Responding to all this, the first input would be:

```
10 DATA 1,3
```

indicating a desire to solve one set of three equations. The statement:

```
11 DATA 3,2,1,5,-3,2,4,16,5
```

provides the coefficient array in row order. Finally, the right-hand constants are supplied by:

```
12 DATA 3,-3,27
```

The subprogram takes over and the final results are presented as follows:

```
READY
*10 DATA 1,3
*11 DATA 3,2,1,5,-3,2,4,16,5
*12 DATA 3,-3,27
*RUN
S I M U L E Q N
SOLUTION FOR LINEAR SYSTEM OF ORDER  3
                            INDEX:
           1                  2                  3
SOLUTION VECTOR FOR CASE  1

      -.3614458          1.337349           1.409639
PROOF OF SOLUTION FOR CASE  1

           3                 -3                 27
```

This example shows the documentation and use of another typical software package.

13.5 Output Alternatives

So far, we have concentrated on how to provide *input* to some of these software routines. Figures 13.3 through 13.7 now show some of the *output* options available within certain subprograms. Figure 13.3 shows the output of a statistical subroutine used to analyze the scores of 1000 students on a college entrance exam.

Figure 13.3 Elegant output

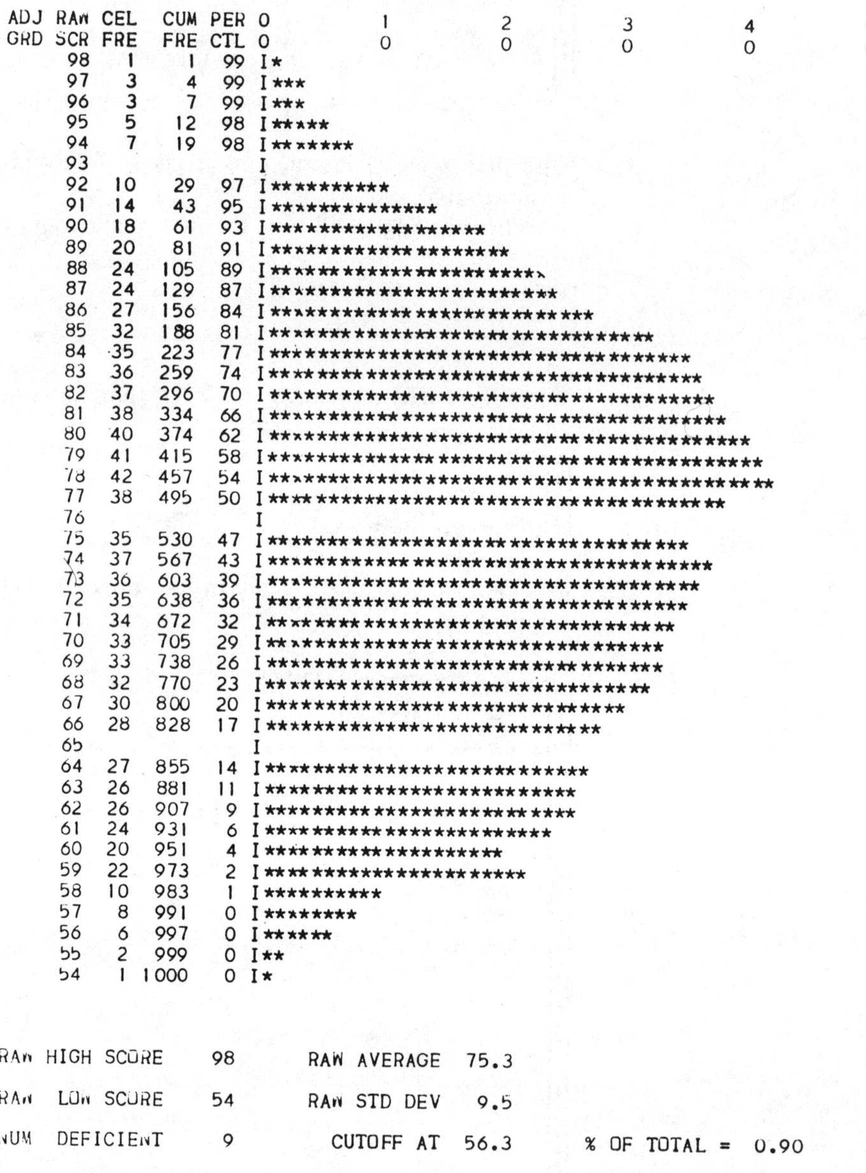

```
ADJ RAW CEL  CUM PER 0         1         2         3         4         5
GRD SCR FRE  FRE CTL 0         0         0         0         0         0
     98   1     1  99 I*
     97   3     4  99 I***
     96   3     7  99 I***
     95   5    12  98 I*****
     94   7    19  98 I*******
     93                I
     92  10    29  97 I**********
     91  14    43  95 I**************
     90  18    61  93 I******************
     89  20    81  91 I********************
     88  24   105  89 I************************
     87  24   129  87 I************************
     86  27   156  84 I***************************
     85  32   188  81 I********************************
     84  35   223  77 I***********************************
     83  36   259  74 I************************************
     82  37   296  70 I*************************************
     81  38   334  66 I**************************************
     80  40   374  62 I****************************************
     79  41   415  58 I*****************************************
     78  42   457  54 I******************************************
     77  38   495  50 I**************************************
     76                I
     75  35   530  47 I***********************************
     74  37   567  43 I*************************************
     73  36   603  39 I************************************
     72  35   638  36 I***********************************
     71  34   672  32 I**********************************
     70  33   705  29 I*********************************
     69  33   738  26 I*********************************
     68  32   770  23 I********************************
     67  30   800  20 I******************************
     66  28   828  17 I****************************
     65                I
     64  27   855  14 I***************************
     63  26   881  11 I**************************
     62  26   907   9 I**************************
     61  24   931   6 I************************
     60  20   951   4 I********************
     59  22   973   2 I**********************
     58  10   983   1 I**********
     57   8   991   0 I********
     56   6   997   0 I******
     55   2   999   0 I**
     54   1  1000   0 I*

RAW HIGH SCORE    98       RAW AVERAGE  75.3

RAW LOW SCORE     54       RAW STD DEV   9.5

NUM DEFICIENT      9         CUTOFF AT  56.3      % OF TOTAL =  0.90


                     DESCRIPTIVE STATISTICS

NUMBER OF OBSERVATIONS ....................................1000
MEAN .............................................. 7.534900E+01
MEDIAN ............................................ 7.500000E+01
RANGE ............................................. 4.400000E+01
UNADJUSTED VARIANCE ............................... 9.057687E+01
UNADJUSTED STANDARD DEVIATION ..................... 9.517188E+00
ADJUSTED VARIANCE ................................. 9.066754E+01
ADJUSTED STANDARD DEVIATION ....................... 9.521950E+00
SKEWNESS ..........................................-6.200773E-06
KURTOSIS .......................................... 2.153488E+00
```

Note the wealth of information presented. In addition to determining the highest, lowest, and average score, the subprogram determines and reports the mean, variance, and standard deviation, and the skewness of distribution. The subprogram even generates a histogram. All this output results from a single call to a subroutine called HIST1.†

Income versus Grades

If the income of the students' parents is known, a tabulation of scores achived vs. parents' income could be obtained by using a program called CROSSTABS.‡ The elegant output shown in Figure 13.4 is controlled almost entirely within the subprogram, the user providing just a few labels.

Figure 13.4 Typical SPSS output

```
                    INCOME
                    I$5001-   $10001-   $15001-   $20001-   OVER      ROW
                    I$10000   $15000    $20000    $25000    $25001    TOTAL
                    I    2.00I    3.00I     4.00I     5.00I     6.00I
GRADES      --------I--------I--------I---------I---------I---------I
            1.00    I     3  I    43  I      23 I      0  I      0  I     69
  50-60             I   4.3  I  62.3  I    33.3 I    0.0  I    0.0  I    6.9
                   -I--------I--------I---------I---------I---------I
            2.00    I     0  I    74  I     176 I      9  I      0  I    259
  61-70             I   0.0  I  28.6  I    68.0 I    3.5  I    0.0  I   25.9
                   -I--------I--------I---------I---------I---------I
            3.00    I     0  I     0  I     157 I    181  I      0  I    338
  71-80             I   0.0  I   0.0  I    46.4 I   53.6  I    0.0  I   33.8
                   -I--------I--------I---------I---------I---------I
            4.00    I     0  I     0  I       5 I    189  I     97  I    291
  81-90             I   0.0  I   0.0  I     1.7 I   64.9  I   33.3  I   29.1
                   -I--------I--------I---------I---------I---------I
            5.00    I     0  I     0  I       0 I      5  I     38  I     43
  91-100            I   0.0  I   0.0  I     0.0 I   11.6  I   88.4  I    4.4
                   -I--------I--------I---------I---------I---------I
          COLUMN          3       117       361       384       135      1000
           TOTAL         .3      11.7      36.1      38.4      13.5     100.0

CHI SQUARE =  1070.67107  WITH 16 DEGREES OF FREEDOM
CRAMER≠S V =     .51737
CONTINGENCY COEFFICIENT =    .71907
KENDALL≠S TAU B =    .76551
KENDALL≠S TAU C =    .67805
GAMMA =     .96754
SOMER≠S D =    .78580
```

Figure 13.5 shows the output of a subprogram used by chemical engineers to calculate the compressibility of a gas. The computer-aided solution includes graphical output (using the line printer) to plot the functional relationship determined.

† Program developed for the U.S.M.A. Academic Computer Center system library by Mrs. Sylvia Sands of the U.S.M.A. staff.

‡ "Statistical Package for the Social Sciences" developed by Bent, Nie and Hull in conjunction with Stanford University.

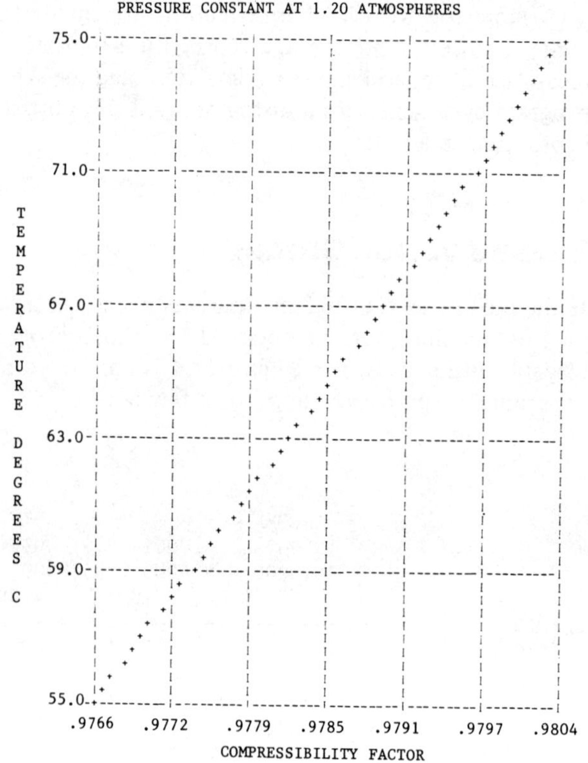

Figure 13.5 Graph using on-line printer

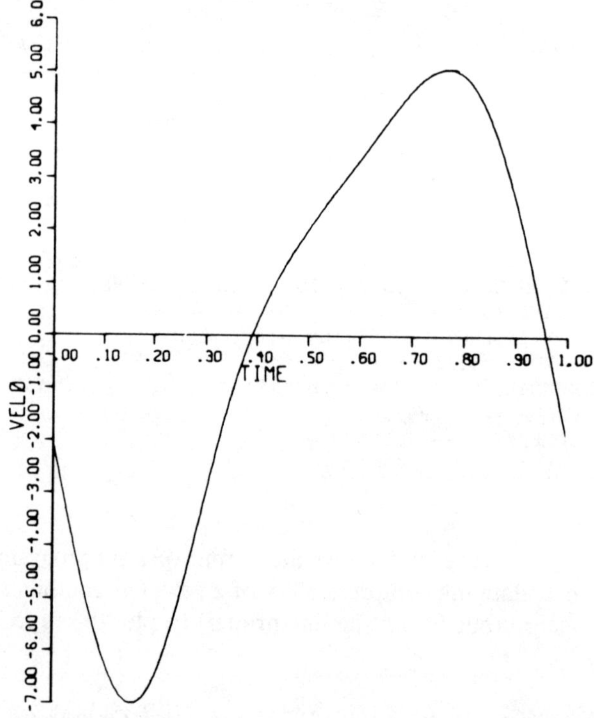

Figure 13.6 Graph using CalComp plotter

Finally, there are a number of software packages that produce graphical output on special devices, such as an incremental digital plotter. These routines are activated just like any others, that is, by passing simple variables, subscripted variables, or user-supplied subprograms. For example, the hidden lines in Figure 13.7 were generated by calls to the subroutine DASHLN:

```
CALL DASHLN(X1,Y1,X2,Y2)
```

whose arguments define the X and Y location of the beginning and end of the dashed line. The circles were drawn by subroutine SIMCIR:

```
CALL SIMCIR(X,Y,R)
```

whose argument list obviously specifies the location of the center of the circle and its radius.

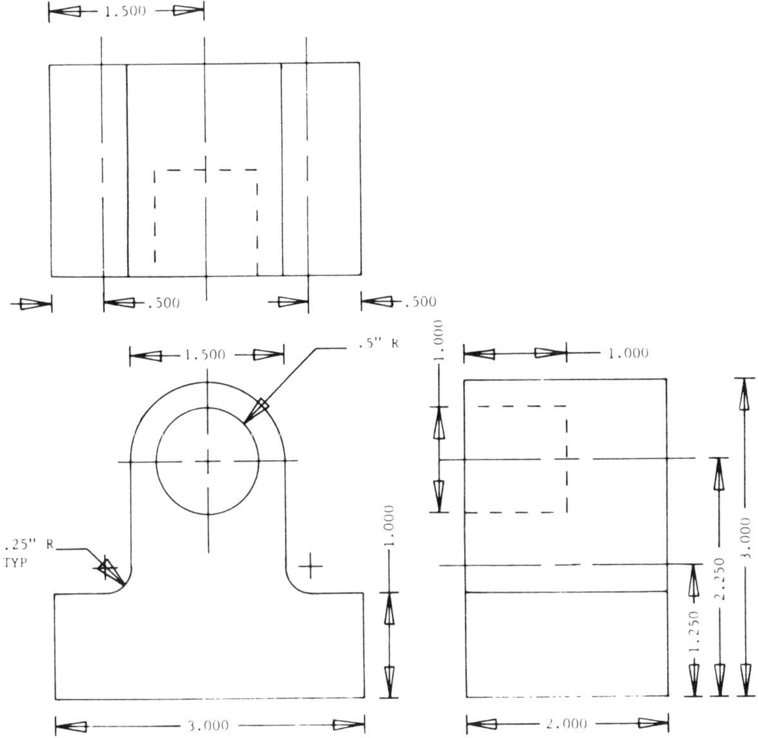

Figure 13.7 Multiview drawing (Reprinted from "Digital Computer Plotting" ©1969, courtesy of Prof. Franklyn K. Brown, Northeastern University.)

13.6 A Final Example: Numerical Methods

Not all subroutines are easy or safe to use. The examples given thus far have had relatively simple argument lists. The subroutine in this final example is more typical of what a complex argument list looks like.

There is another difficulty in using some subprograms, especially those involving complicated mathematics. Subprogramming involves a shift in responsibility for knowing the theory behind solving the problem. The person who writes a subprogram must know what he or she is doing, and *so should the user*. When that is not true, trouble cannot be far off.

Numerical methods is an area of mathematics concerned with finding better and more efficient ways of solving problems on a computer. For example, for solving simultaneous equations there are three basic numerical techniques: determinant, iteration, and elimination methods. One method may be very good if only a few equations are involved. This same method would be deadly if 50 equations were to be solved. While some amount of warning is given in the documentation, it is generally dangerous to use a routine whose theory is unknown to the user.

The Newton-Raphson Procedure

The following problem is typical of various numerical methods available in most software packages. It is the well-known **Newton-Raphson procedure** for determining the roots of nonlinear equations. Early in this text a clumsy "trial and error" procedure was used: that of letting X take on a series of values (0.1, 0.2, 0.3, 0.4, . . .) hoping a root would be nearby (see Chapter 8). The programmer was essentially guessing at successive values of X to try. It is possible to use the derivative or slope of an equation to come up with a better sequence of X values to try.

Refer to Figure 13.8 to follow the four steps of the procedure.

1. Starting with some initial guess, X_n, determine Y (the value of equation at $X = X_n$).
2. At $X = X_n$ determine the derivative (slope) of the equation.
3. Extend this slope line until it crosses the X axis. Use this intercept as the next value of X to try (X_{n+1}).
4. Repeat the process.

Figure 13.8 Newton-Raphson procedure

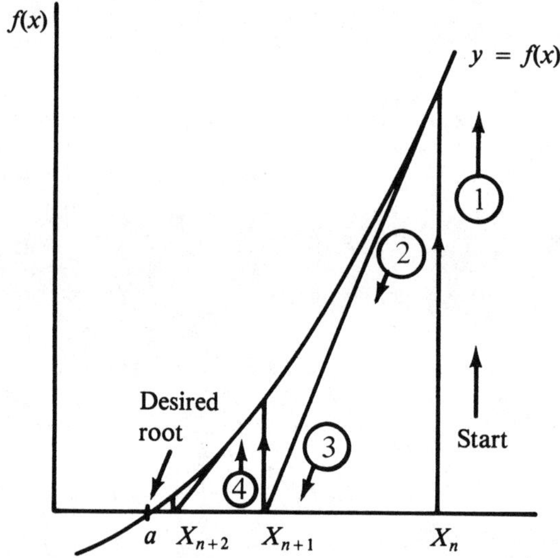

The root should be reached much faster because successive approximations to the root are *calculated*, not guessed at.

There are some dangers in using this method. If any of the values of X developed in approaching the root are in the vicinity of X_1 or X_2 of Figure 13.9, the slope or tangent line will not intersect the X axis.

Figure 13.9 Possible problems

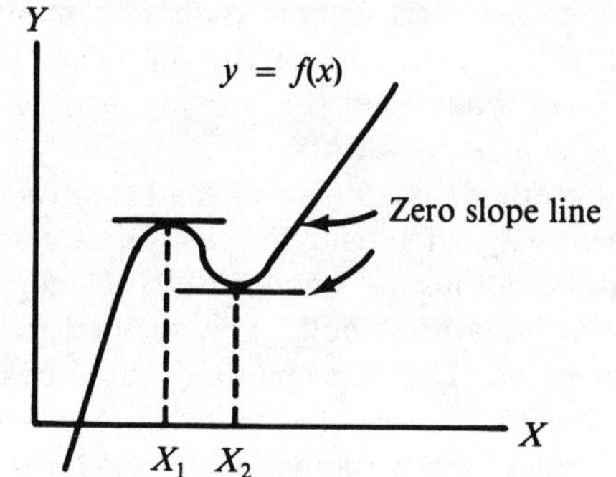

If any value of X falls between X_1 and X_2, the slope or tangent line will intersect off to the right, which is not in the direction of the root.† These situations will exist if the value of the derivative is changing rapidly in the vicinity of the root, that is, if the equation is not well behaved.

With this as background, consider the use of subroutine RTNI (Figure 13.10) for determining a root to the equation:

$$y = e^x - \ln(x^2 + 1) - \frac{1}{\sqrt{e^{-x} + 1}}$$

Although the call to RTNI seems formidable, it is really not so bad.

```
CALL RTNI(X,F,DERF,FCT,XST,EPSI,IEND,IER)
```

Consider the last four arguments. XST is the initial guess needed to start the search; EPSI asks the degree of accuracy to which the root should be determined. If EPSI is set equal to 0.001, the method is repeated until the root is known to this degree of accuracy. It may be impossible to obtain a solution to this degree of accuracy, so IEND specifies the maximum number of iterations to be performed. If the root has not been determined to the desired degree of accuracy after IEND cycles, a value of 1 is given to IER to indicate this lack of convergency. If a near-zero slope occurs at any time, IER is given a value of 2.

```
C
C      . . . . . . . . . . . . . . . . . . . . .
C
C      SUBROUTINE RTNI
C
C      PURPOSE
C         TO SOLVE GENERAL NONLINEAR EQUATIONS OF THE FORM F(X) = 0
C         BY MEANS OF NEWTON'S ITERATION METHOD.
C
C      USAGE
C         CALL RTNI(X,F,DERF,FCT,XST,EPS,IEND,IER)
C         PARAMETER FCT REQUIRES AN EXTERNAL STATEMENT.
C
C      DESCRIPTION OF PARAMETERS
C         X    -RESULTANT ROOT OF EQUATION F(X) = 0.
C         F    -RESULTANT FUNCTION VALUE AT ROOT X.
C         DERF-RESULTANT VALUE OF DERIVATIVE AT ROOT X.
C         FCT -NAME OF EXTERNAL SUBROUTINE USED. IT COMPUTES TO
C              GIVEN ARGUMENT X FUNCTION VALUE F AND DERIVATIVE
C              DERF. ITS PARAMETER LIST MUST BE X,F,DERF.
C         XST -INPUT VALUE WHICH SPECIFIES THE INITIAL GUESS OF THE
C              ROOT X.
C         EPS -INPUT VALUE WHICH SPECIFIES THE UPPER BOUND OF THE
C              ERROR OF RESULT X.
C         IEND-MAXIMUM NUMBER OF ITERATION STEPS SPECIFIED.
C         IER -RESULTANT ERROR PARAMETER CODED AS FOLLOWS
C              IER  = 0 - NO ERROR.
C              IER  = 1 - NO CONVERGENCE AFTER IEND ITERATION STEPS.
C              IER  = 2 - AT ANY ITERATION STEP DERIVATIVE DERF WAS
C                         EQUAL TO ZERO
C
C
C      REMARKS
C         THIS PROCEDURE IS BYPASSED AND GIVES THE ERROR MESSAGE IER=2
C         IF AT ANY ITERATION STEP DERIVATIVE OF F(X) IS EQUAL TO 0.
```

Figure 13.10 Root determination subroutine (continues on next page)

† RTNI will use a "mailbox" called IER to signal if difficulties are encountered while searching for the root.

```
C          POSSIBLY THE PROCEDURE WOULD BE SUCESSFUL IF IT IS STARTED
C          ONCE MORE WITH ANOTHER GUESS XST.
C
C       SUBROUTINE AND FUNCTION SUBPROGRAMS REQUIRED
C          THE EXTERNAL SUBROUTINE FCT(X, F, DERF) MUST BE FURNISHED
C          BY THE USER.
C
C       METHOD
C          SOLUTION OF EQUATION F(X)=0 IS DONE BY MEANS OF NEWTON'S
C          ITERATION METHOD, WHICH STARTS AT THE INITIAL GUESS XST OF
C          A ROOT X. CONVERGENCE IS QUADRATIC IF THE DERIVATIVE OF
C          F(X) AT ROOT X IS NOT EQUAL TO ZERO. ONE ITERATION STEP
C          REQUIRES ONE EVALUATION OF F(X) AND ONE EVALUATION OF THE
C          DERIVATIVE OF F(X). FOR TEST ON SATISFACTORY ACCURACY SEE
C          FORMULAE (2) OF MATHEMATICAL DESCRIPTION.
C          FOR REFERENCE, SEE R. ZURMUFHL, PRAKTISCHE MATHEMATIK FUER
C          INGENIEURE UND PHYSIKER, SPRINGER, BERLIN/GOETTINGEN/
C          HEIDELBERG, 1963,   PP.12-17.
C
C       . . . . . . . . . . . . . . . . . . . . . . . . . .
C
        SUBROUTINE RTNI(X,F,DERF,FCT,XST,EPS,IEND,IER)
C
C
C       PREPARE ITERATION
        IER = 0
        X = XST
        TOL = X
        CALL FCT(TOL, F, DERF)
        TOLF = 100. * EPS
C
C
C       START ITERATION LOOP
        DO 6 I = 1, IEND
        IF(F) 1, 7, 1
C
C       EQUATION NOT SATISFIED BY X
    1   IF(DERF) 2, 8, 2
C
C       ITERATION IS POSSIBLE
    2   DX = F/DERF
        X = X - DX
        TOL = X
        CALL FCT(TOL,F,DERF)
C
C       TEST ON SATISFACTORY ACCURACY
        TOL = EPS
        A = ABS(X)
        IF(A-1.) 4, 4, 3
    3   TOL = TOL * A
    4   IF(ABS(DX) - TOL)5, 5, 6
    5   IF(ABS(F)-TOLF)7, 7, 6
    6   CONTINUE
C       END OF ITERATION LOOP
C
C       NO CONVERGENCE AFTER IEND ITERATION STEPS, ERROR RETURN
        IER = 1
    7   RETURN
C
C       ERROR RETURN IN CASE OF ZERO DIVISOR
    8   IER = 2
        RETURN
        END
```

Figure 13.10 Root determination (continued)

This subroutine needs a user-supplied subprogram to obtain values and the derivative of the function for each new X value to be tried. The section entitled SUBROUTINES AND FUNCTION SUBPROGRAMS REQUIRED suggests that a subroutine called FCT be provided whose argument list includes the input value X and the output quantities F and DERF.

RTNI computes successive values of X starting from XST. For each X, a call to FCT is made to determine F and DERF. On the last call to FCT, X is the resulting approximation to the root. F is the value of the function at that X value (usually F is near zero) and DERF is the derivative at this root.

To demonstrate the use of RTNI, the following main program and user-supplied subprogram are shown for the equation suggested before:

$$y = e^x - \ln(x^2 + 1) - \frac{1}{\sqrt{e^{-x} + 1}}$$

```
C       MAIN PROGRAM
C
        EXTERNAL FCT
C
        READ*, XSTART
C
C       CALL RTNI(XROOT,Y,YPRIME,FCT,XSTART,0.0001,20,IER)
C
        PRINT*, 'ROOT=', XROOT, 'Y=', Y, 'YPRIME=', YPRIME
C
        STOP
        END
C
        SUBROUTINE FCT(X, Y, YPRIME)
C
        Y=EXP(X)-ALOG(X**2+1.)-1.0/SQRT(EXP(-X)+1.0)
C
   10   YPRIME=EXP(X)-2.*X/(X**2+1.0)-EXP(-X)*.5+
     1                (EXP(-X)**(-1.5)
C
        RETURN
        END
```

If it proved too difficult to determine the derivative of the equation by calculus (see statement 10 in subroutine FCT), a numerical technique could be used. Two adjacent values of Y would be computed and their difference divided by Δx. Obviously this will affect the accuracy somewhat. How much? The answer lies in the field of numerical methods. Those who have a background in this field can give good estimates of the probable error. For the student who does not have such background, it is enough to know that this numerical technique would result in *some* degree of error and that all results should be used with caution.

Review Exercises

1. Describe some of the documentation provided by a typical software package to make the use of any one of its routines as straightforward as possible.
2. ★ What is meant by the term "discipline-oriented" software package?
3. Describe what functions are accomplished in the main program when using one or more of these prewritten subprograms.
4. ★ Most software routines use statements inside the subprogram to determine if the solution is progressing properly. Describe at least one method of signalling the user that something has gone wrong.
5. What are some of the features unique to software packages that are written for use with terminals and employ "conversational" features?
6. Describe some of the rather exotic output that is available from some of these software routines.
7. Some software routines, like SIMQ, destroy the identity of the equations the routine is solving. Why?
8. ★ How can the identity of the original equations described in exercise 7 be retained?
9. Describe some of the software routines that could be used to make the running of a hospital more efficient. Describe a discipline-oriented software package that might be used by a police department.
10. Write a subroutine subprogram that will sort a vector of real numbers. Provide documentation of this routine similar to that used in the IBM Scientific Subroutine Package.

11. Repeat exercise 10 and provide a means of sorting the vector in either ascending or descending order depending on whether a variable called `INMAIL` has a value of 1 or 2.

★ 12. Write a subprogram that receives as input two sides of a right triangle and returns the size of the hypotenuse and angle A and angle B of the triangle.

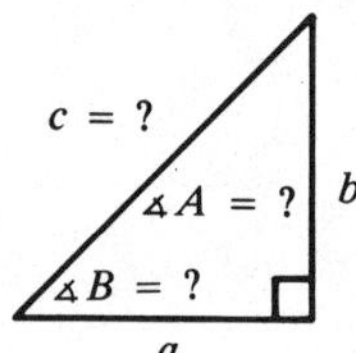

13. Generalize the subprogram in exercise 12 to receive alternate forms of input such as one side and the hypotenuse or one side and an angle. Carefully document this routine.

14. Devise one or more routines to be used on a merchant ship to assist in the navigation of that ship. For example, write a subroutine to receive as input a vector of course headings, a vector of times (number of minutes on each course heading), and a vector of speeds (ship's speed on each heading). Have the subroutine report the X and Y location of the ship at any time t.

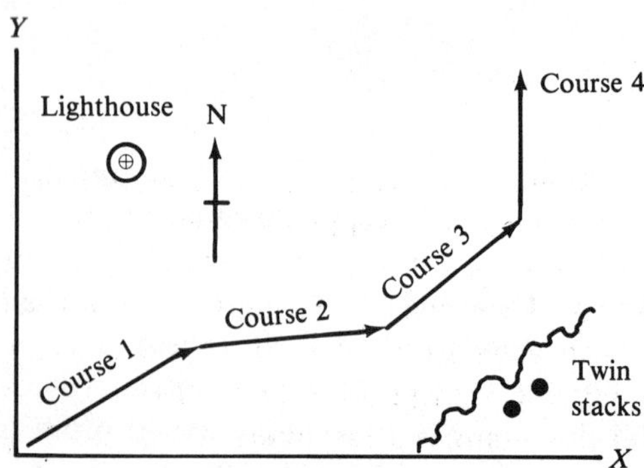

15. Expand the subroutine in exercise 14 to provide as output the bearing at which certain landmarks will appear (like a lighthouse or twin smokestacks) as the ship steams along its course.

16. Revise exercise 14 to allow for two additional input values, namely the direction and speed of the current (flow of water that will set the vessel off course if not accounted for).

★ 17. Write a root determination routine that uses a *half-interval search* technique. This routine should receive as input: the name of a user-supplied subprogram holding the equation whose root we are looking for, and `XLEFT` and `XRIGHT` defining the span of X within which the root lies. This routine should determine the sign of the function at `XLEFT`, `XRIGHT`, and at the midpoint of this span. With this information it is possible to determine if the root lies in the right or left half of the span. For example, if the root lies in the right half of the span, redefine `XLEFT` (give it the value of the present midpoint) and repeat the process.

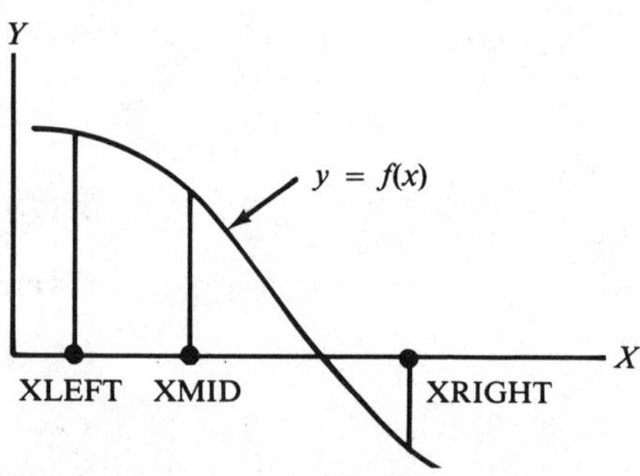

18. Repeat exercise 17, except provide *two* methods of terminating the solution similar to those used in `RTNI`. That is, allow the user to stipulate the degree of accuracy to be imposed on the root, or the maximum number of iterations of the half interval procedure to be used.

19. Repeat exercise 17, except provide means of determining if the solution runs into difficulties. The possible difficulties should include:

    a. No solution in the span designated.

    b. Solution terminated due to reaching maximum iterations.

    c. Any other difficulty this procedure might encounter (give description).

20. Describe the difficulties that would be encountered if the procedures developed in exercise 17 were used for the following functions.

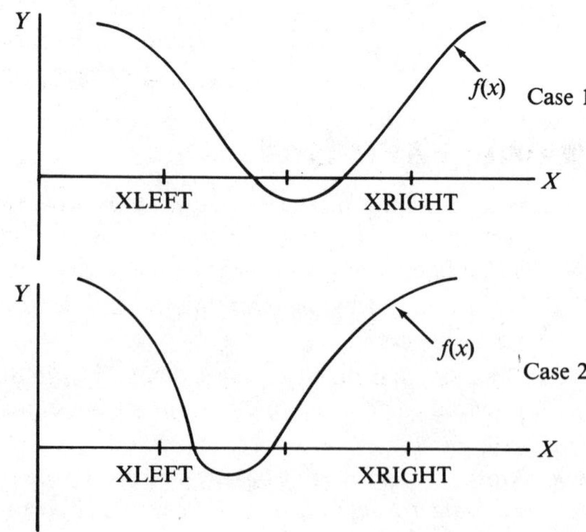

14 Format Codes

This chapter examines some of the details associated with FORMAT controlled input/output. As a start, we will set a goal of mastering I-codes, A-codes, and the codes for handling real numbers (F-codes and E-codes). These latter codes, the codes for real numbers, have not been covered in sufficient detail and are the codes that can cause the most difficulties. By ''mastering'' we mean learning what range of values a specific code can accommodate and learning any special peculiarities or difficulties associated with each of the codes.

14.1 I-Codes

I-codes have the general form:

```
Iw
```

where I identifies the integer mode and w specifies a field width. This code, like all the other format codes, tells what type of information is being processed and how many columns are used to specify the value.

When a code such as I6 is encountered in a sequence of format codes, it signals that the next quantity is an integer number and is contained in the next six columns. When constructing I-codes, watch out for these things:

1. Make the field width large enough to hold all the digits and the sign of the number (if any).
2. Make sure the number is right justified in the field.
3. Make sure the memory location (variable name) associated with this code is *integer* in mode.

Let us see what happens when these rules are not followed.

The specification I5 (controlling output) may be used to print a five-digit positive integer number or a four-digit negative integer mode number. The difference exists because all unsigned values are considered positive and on output the plus sign is omitted. If the value is negative, however, the negative sign is written which consumes one column of width. If you misuse this code and try to print a five-digit negative number, an overflow results. The operating system signals this overflow, usually by filling the field with asterisks. When you see asterisks in your output, check for insufficient field width.

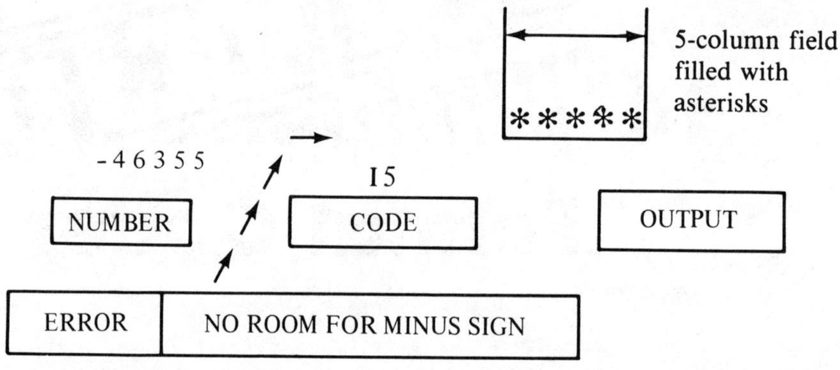

Figure 14.1 One-digit overflow

The way to avoid an overflow is to use a *large* field width, let us say I9, as shown in Figure 14.2. Note that all digits will be printed, and three blank columns will precede the number.

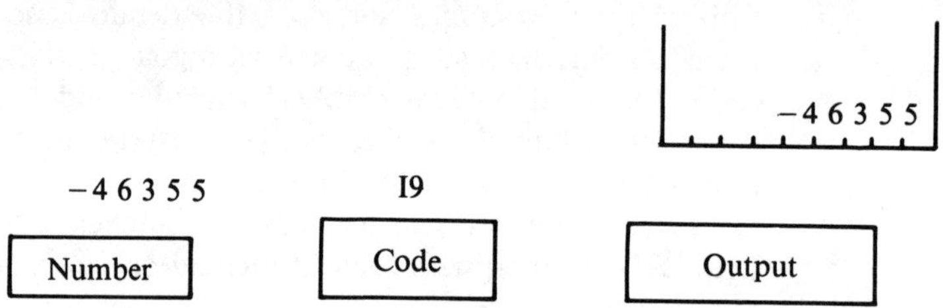

Figure 14.2 Sufficient field width

Right Justified

You have been cautioned to position integer numbers so that the extreme right-hand digit of the number is placed in the extreme right-hand column of the field. Numbers so positioned are described as right justified. The reason for this is that blanks within a FORMAT controlled field are interpreted as zeros. As shown in Figure 14.3, zeros before or after a floating point number have no effect on the way that number is interpreted by the computer. The number 42.75 can be positioned to the left or to the right of its field and the value remains the same. In contrast, the integer value 46 can only be interpreted correctly if it is right justified in its field.

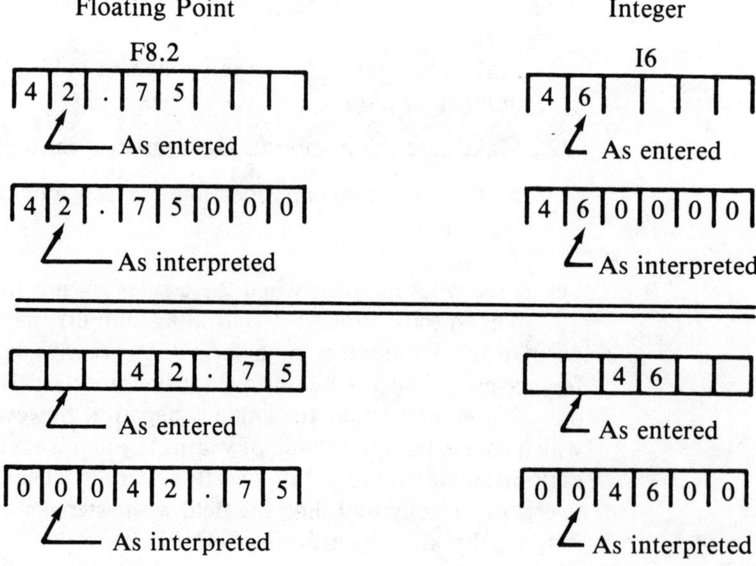

Figure 14.3 Need to right justify integers

Range of Values

Once a format code is written, there is a specific range of values that code can handle. Consider the range associated with an I4 code:

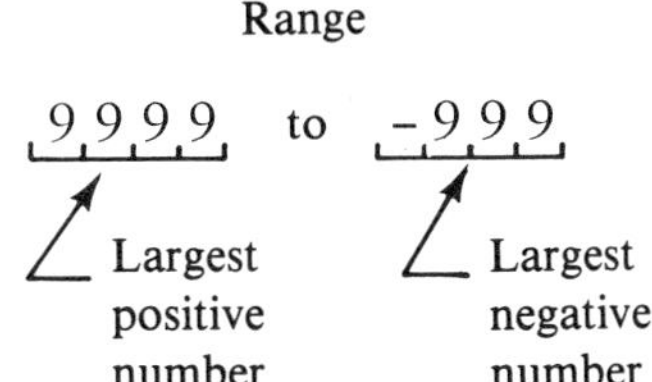

It is a relatively simple matter to determine the range of integer numbers. Look at the field width for the code to be used. Sketch a series of boxes for each column in the field. Do this twice. Now place the largest possible integer in the first series of boxes and the smallest possible number in the second series of boxes. This defines the range of the code you are using. You would be wise not to crowd yourself. Add a couple of columns to the field width if you suspect your field width is insufficient.

14.2 F-Codes

F-codes have the general form:

```
Fw.d
```

where:

- `F` signals that the data item is a floating point or real number.
- `w` defines the field width.
- `d` describes the position of the decimal point.

This code is similar to I-codes except for the "d" parameter. This extra value is required because floating point or real numbers are structured differently from integer numbers. Remember that a real memory location must be capable of accommodating a large number of digits after the decimal point to reduce truncation error. As explained in Chapter 2, it is possible for real numbers to be stored to 15- or 20-decimal digit accuracy.

A programmer is seldom interested in displaying numbers to this degree of accuracy. Usually two- or three-digit accuracy is sufficient. This is controlled by the "d" parameter, which tells how many digits are to be displayed after the decimal point. Consider how the number 13.333333333333333333 would appear when printed under the following F-codes:

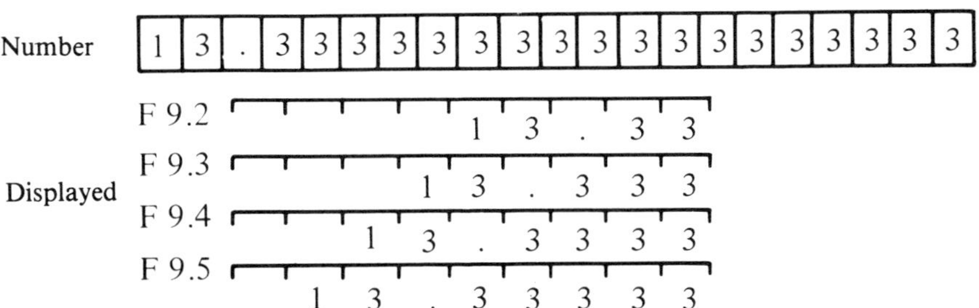

Floating point numbers require one space for the decimal point and may consume one space for the sign (as described in I-codes).

Each floating point format code accommodates a specific range of numbers. An F8.2 code can accommodate the following range of values:

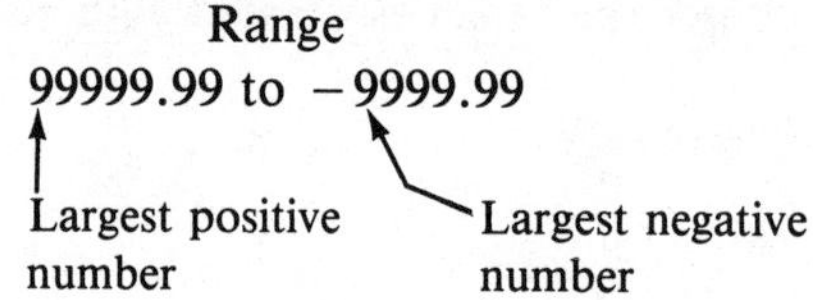

The code F8.4 consumes the same field width, but because the numbers are written to four-place accuracy, the safe range is considerably reduced.

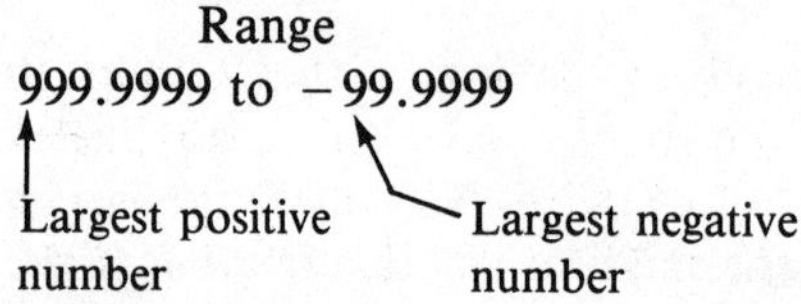

It is often very difficult to predict the size of an output value. This is especially true if the number has been obtained after long or difficult calculations. If the field width is not sufficient to hold the number, overflow results as explained previously. As before, we recommend specifying a large field width.

As a final comment about F-codes, it is possible to record these numbers in an input file without recording the location of the decimal point. As the following example shows, the number 1484.957 is recorded without a decimal point. The point is positioned by the "accuracy value" in the format code. If no point is specified, an implied location is determined (in this case the last three digits are assumed after the decimal point). If, however, the point is given, this accuracy value is not used on input. (The point as recorded is the point that is used even if it conflicts with the format code.)

```
1 4 8 4 9 5 7          F 7 . 3
```

Implied location of decimal point

14.3 Truncation versus Rounding

You will hear the terms "truncation" or "rounding" used to describe how a real number is transferred from memory to output. Consider the transfer of the number:

7	.	3	1	4	9	2	7	8	6	3

under the control of an F6.3 code. The cutoff point is between the 4 and the 9.

```
7 . 3 1 4 | 9 2 7 8 6 3
```

The printed value may appear in two possible ways:

Truncation	Rounding
7.314	7.315

Truncation implies a direct transfer of digits. If rounding is used, digits after the cutoff point are allowed to affect (by rounding up) the value being sent to output. In this case, the 9 causes a rounding up of the 4 to a 5.

14.4 E-Codes

There is an alternate form of representing real numbers sometimes needed by the programmer. You have seen this form used in mathematics to express a very large or very small number:

Scientific Notation	Number
-8.10×10^{13}	$-81{,}000{,}000{,}000{,}000.$
-4.27×10^{-15}	$-.00000000000000427$
3.862×10^{9}	$3{,}862{,}000{,}000.$
↑ Mantissa ↖ Exponent	

This notation uses one or more digits written with a decimal point (called the **mantissa**) followed by the number 10 raised to some power (called the **exponent**).

This exponent tells how many places the decimal point in the mantissa should be moved to convert to the more standard form. Since FORTRAN statements *must* be written on one continuous line, numbers in scientific notation must be represented in the following way.

Mathematical Notation	Equivalent FORTRAN Representation
-8.1×10^{13}	`-8.1E13`
-4.27×10^{-15}	`-4.27E - 15`
3.862×10^{9}	`3.862E9`

The letter E is used to separate the mantissa from the exponent. It is a substitute for writing the number 10 and a superscript. Numbers may be expressed in this form in the instruction deck and in the data deck. When reading or printing a real value expressed in this form, an E-code is used in the FORMAT statement:

```
E  1  2  .  5
```

E — Type; 12 — Field width; 5 — Accuracy of mantissa

E-codes have the general form:

```
Ew.d
```

They provide an alternate way of publishing real numbers but with the distinct advantage of *protection from overflow.* When real numbers are published using an F-code, there is always a specific range of values the code can accommodate and therefore there is the possibility of overflow. Not so with E-codes. As long as the field width is a fixed number larger than the "d" parameter, no overflow will take place. All computers have a maximum size (magnitude) of real numbers they can handle. This is usually a very large number. A typical range of magnitudes is 10^{38} to 10^{-38}. Let us see why there is no overflow with E-codes.

The quantity "d" again controls the accuracy to which the number is displayed. This time it controls the number of digits appearing after the decimal point of the mantissa.

Number	**As Printed**	**E-Code**
−0.0006275432	-0.6275E-03	E11.4
167,280,000.	0.16728E+09	E12.5
.126	0.1260E+00	E11.4

Having decided on a value of "d," we need seven additional columns to complete the number: *four* columns are needed to express the exponent (the E, the sign, and a two-digit integer) and *three* more columns to complete the mantissa (a sign, leading zero, and a decimal point).

If the field width "w" is 7 greater than the accuracy parameter "d," *all* numbers expressed by this code will be accommodated. It is much safer to make the field width larger than the minimum, but the point is that an E-code is a safe one to use if you are not sure how large or how small your data value may be.

The following table shows the way in which the number -0.12345678×10^4 would appear when printed under various E-codes.

Number	As Printed	Code	
-0.12345678×10^4	*****	E6.4	Insufficient Field Width
	******	E7.4	
	*******	E8.4	
	********	E9.4	
	*********	E10.4	
	-0.1234E 04	E11.4	
	-0.1234E 04	E12.4	
	-0.1234E 04	E13.4	
	-0.123456E 04	E15.6	
	-0.123457E 04†		

† Last digit affected by truncation or rounding

When E-FORMAT numbers are written by the programmer as input values, certain shortcuts in writing the number are allowed. We see here the number 0.16728×10^9 written as output and the equivalent acceptable input forms.

Output Form (E12.5)
0.16728E 09

Equivalent Acceptable Input Form

.16728E9	.16728E+9	+.16728E09	+.16728E+09

These shorter forms are not recommended for the beginner. One form:

```
          Blank
           /
0.16728E+9 
```

produces an error. The problem in the example shown is that, since the exponent is an integer number, it must be positioned right justified in its field. The blank in the extreme right-hand column of the field will be read as a zero. The exponent will be read incorrectly, causing the number to be 0.16728×10^{90}.

14.5 Repeat Codes

If several data values are of the same form (have the same format code), the FORMAT statement may be written in an abbreviated fashion by using what are called repeat codes.

```
  READ (5, 7)A,B,C,D,I,J,K
7 FORMAT (4F12.4,3I6)
```

Repeat code   Repeat code

The number preceding the letter in the code indicates this code (F12.4 or I6) should be repeated as many times as indicated.

The FORMAT statement:

```
7 FORMAT      (4F12.4, 3I6)
```

is the same as

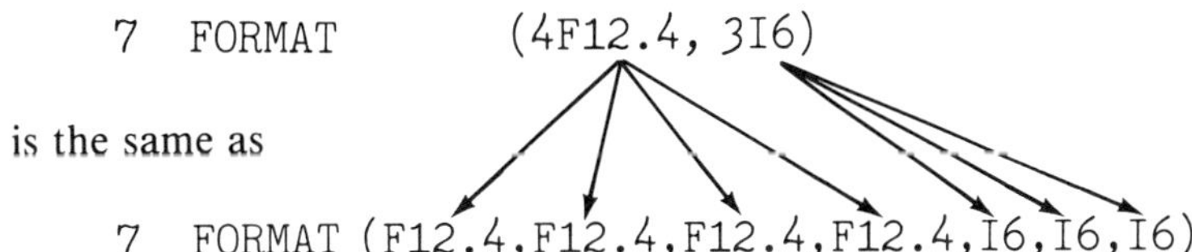

```
7 FORMAT (F12.4,F12.4,F12.4,F12.4,I6,I6,I6)
```

Common Errors

There should be agreement in number and mode of the variable names appearing in the list of a READ statement and the codes used in the supporting FORMAT statement. This recommendation is not adhered to in the following statements.

```
  READ(5,7)A,B,C,D
7 FORMAT (F8.1)
```

Note that there are four names following the READ command, but only one format code in the FORMAT statement. This is perfectly legal in FORTRAN, but would only be used in a more or less advanced application. When reading large arrays, having let's say over 100 elements, we issue a READ command and have more names in the list of the READ statement than could be recorded on one data record. Under these circumstances, the FORMAT statement is written to describe one typical input record with the understanding that as many records as necessary will be read to satisfy the list of the READ statement.

Getting back to the READ and FORMAT statements under discussion. Each time this READ is executed, four input records are consumed. The FORMAT statement informs the compiler that there is one floating point value on the record it is describing. There are actually four values on the record, but that is not what the FORMAT statement says. Accordingly the computer reads four records in order to satisfy the list of the READ statement.

Until you gain a degree of experience in dealing with FORMAT statements it is a good idea to have the number of codes in the FORMAT statement:

1. Match in number and mode the variable names in the list of the input or output statement.
2. Match in number and mode the values recorded on the input record you are processing.

When this agreement in number is not observed, the FORMAT statement is understood as describing one "typical record" and as many records of this type as needed will be processed in order to satisfy the list. The list of the READ statement is the dominant item, not the format codes.

Quiz 20 Introduction to FORMAT Statements

1. When inputting both real and integer numbers, the number must always be right justified in the specified field. Is all or part of this true?
2. Describe the error associated with the following input/output statements:

```
   READ(5,10)I,J,K
10 FORMAT (I8,I8,I8)
   WRITE (2,20)I,J,K
20 FORMAT (F8.2,F8.2,F8.2)
```

3. Describe the function of the "accuracy parameter" in the following output activity.

```
   WRITE(2,10)A
10 FORMAT (F12.2)
```

Accuracy parameter

4. How will the value shown on the following data record be interpreted? Must the decimal point be located?

```
1 2 3 4 5 6 7 8          READ(5,10)X
                      10 FORMAT (F8.3)
```

5. Show how the value read in question 4 would be printed if the following output statement were used:

```
   WRITE (2,20)X
20 FORMAT (E15.4)
```

6. What will the values of I, J, K, and L be if they are read as follows:

```
   READ(5,10)I,J,K,L
10 FORMAT(2I3,I1,I4)

6 1 7 6 0 3 5 9 1 2
```

7. Overspecifying the field width in all format codes avoids what two possible difficulties?
8. What is a repeat code and what purpose does it serve?

14.6 Elegant Output

List directed input/output has many advantages. The "free format" associated with this process is a valuable tool for the programmer. One disadvantage is that you give up control of how information appears on your output sheet. If you want to control the exact form and the exact position of each output item, you must revert to FORMAT controlled output. It is possible to get very elaborate output. Page headings at the top of a new page, column headings with several blank lines in between, double or triple spacing of your detail lines, indentation, and alignment of data are all possible with FORMAT controlled output. All this is called **elegant output**, which is the subject of this section. We now examine several new format codes that give the programmer absolute control over where and how various output values are to be printed.

New Format Codes

Code	Meaning	Example
X-code	skip columns	20X—skip 20 columns
H-code	fixed typing (count involved)	3HTHE—type three characters — THE
'-code	fixed typing	'THE' or *THE*
*-code	(no count involved)	type the characters between symbols
/-code	skip lines or cards	//// — skip 3 lines

These new codes have one feature that makes them markedly different from I-, F-, E-, and A-codes. They do not involve any exchange or interaction with memory. The purpose of these new codes is entirely different, namely to present the output in a more readable form.

X-code

The X-code is used to skip spaces. The code 20X appearing in a FORMAT statement would cause 20 spaces to be skipped. On input this would mean: "ignore the next 20 columns on the record." It would be used to jump over some unwanted input. On output, 20X would be like hitting the space bar twenty times. If this were the first code in a FORMAT statement, it would result in a 20-column margin on the left side of the output sheet. It could also be used to separate one column of data from another by 20 spaces.

/-code

The /-code causes the skipping of lines or records. The code /// means skip the next three records. If this code were used in a FORMAT statement controlling a READ operation, each slash would mean: "skip a record." On output it means: "skip a line." Each slash is the equivalent of hitting the carriage return bar on the typewriter or terminal.

Character Strings

Figure 14.4 shows an example of elegant output. The first two lines of the output are of primary interest. They are used to form titles and headings that assist in reading the numeric data that follows.

Figure 14.4 An example output page

THE ANSWERS ARE

I	X	Y	Z
21	5.2305	62.3000	.2847
82	9.2634	12.4819	.7490
8	52.9538	.2849	81.8479
124	0.0362	116.3859	54.3905
56	826.3950	6.3793	7.2933

Obtaining a message in a line of printout is by no means a new topic. Consider the statement:

```
WRITE(2,*)'ANSWER 1 =',X,'ANSWER 2=',Y
```

You should recognize that the quotation marks enclosing the message `'ANSWER 1 ='` and `'ANSWER 2='` signal that these character strings are to be included in the line of output.

To obtain the headings shown in Figure 14.4 we use a similar technique except that the character string is stipulated *inside* a `FORMAT` statement so we can tightly control where the desired character string is to be positioned on the page.

1. Skip across the line to somewhere near the middle of the page.
2. Type the words `''THE ANSWERS ARE''`.

The three ways of issuing these instructions are shown in Figure 14.5

Figure 14.5 Code for character strings

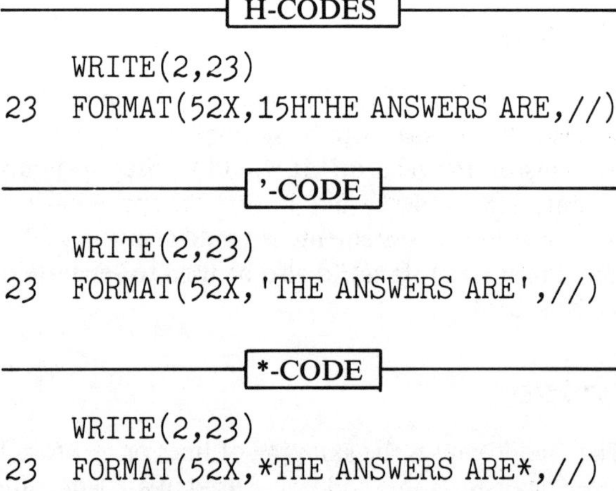

H-CODES

```
   WRITE(2,23)
23 FORMAT(52X,15HTHE ANSWERS ARE,//)
```

'-CODE

```
   WRITE(2,23)
23 FORMAT(52X,'THE ANSWERS ARE',//)
```

*-CODE

```
   WRITE(2,23)
23 FORMAT(52X,*THE ANSWERS ARE*,//)
```

In each method, the `WRITE` command is used to get control of the output device. Note that there are no variable names in the list of this `WRITE` statement. This is because the line of output can be generated without any exchange with memory. Memory comes into play only when the line of output contains a variable quantity. The contents of this line are fixed.

The first code in each `FORMAT` statement is a "skipping" code. It indicates that the first 52 columns of the output line are to be blank. The printer is now sitting at column 53 of the output line ready to process the next field, the message. Figure 14.5 shows that there are three ways of defining the message.

The middle set of instructions encloses the message between quotation marks paralleling the techniques used before. The last set of instructions shows that the asterisk can be used in place of the quotation marks.

The quotation mark or asterisk is called a **delimiter** and is used to show where the message begins and where the message ends. The asterisk becomes a very useful delimiter if the message to be printed contains an embedded quotation mark:

```
*SALESMAN'S COMMISSIONS*
```

H-Codes

The method of defining the message in the first set of instructions in Figure 14.5 is called a **Hollerith code**. It allows *any* combination of characters in the message. This code starts by giving an exact count of how many characters are in the message string. The letter H defines the type of code being used.

When the code 15H is encountered in the FORMAT statement, the computer copies the 15 characters following the letter H directly onto the next 15 columns of the output line.† The complete Hollerith code is characterized by a numeric quantity followed by the letter H followed by the message to be printed. The number preceding the letter H must be an exact count of all characters in the message including blanks.

Getting the Second Line

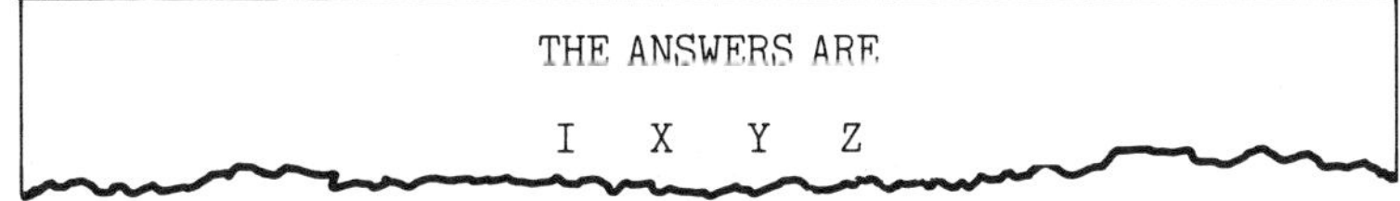

The second line of output shown above is like the first in that no exchange with memory is required. This line can be generated by the statements:

```
      WRITE(2,24)
   24 FORMAT(20X,1HI,20X,1HX,20X,1HY,20X,1HZ)
```

As usual, the format codes provide an efficient means of describing exactly the various fields needed to obtain the desired line of output:

Field	Meaning
1	A blank field of 20 columns.
2	A one-column Hollerith field in which the letter I appears.
3	A blank field of 20 columns.
4	A one-column Hollerith field in which the letter X appears.
5	A blank field of 20 columns.
6	A one-column Hollerith field in which the letter Y appears.
7	A blank field of 20 columns.
8	A one-column Hollerith field in which the letter Z appears.

† The serious disadvantage of this method is that a character count is required. If this count is not accurate, an error occurs. For this reason, H-codes are less popular than the other methods.

The remaining lines of output in Figure 14.4 contain numerical values only. The field width for each of these values would be adjusted to make the number fall under the column headings just printed.

14.7 Combining FORMAT Codes

All the FORMAT codes described thus far (A, I, F, E, X, H, *, ', /) may appear in any combination within a single FORMAT statement. Figure 14.6 shows output similar but not identical to that in Figure 14.4.

Figure 14.6 An example output page

```
                         THE ANSWERS ARE

I= 21          X=  5.2305          Y=62.7330          Z=   .6486
I= 82          X=  9.2733          Y=12.9476          Z=  1.1684
I=  8          X= 52.5321          Y=   .6488         Z= 86.8372
I=124          X=  8.0357          Y= 7.3857          Z=167.7940
I= 56          X=537.9386          Y=46.5667          Z= 20.0375
I=  5                                                 Z=  7.3950
```

Most of the output contains a mixture of Hollerith fields and blank fields interspersed with the numeric values. These lines are obtained by the statements:

```
      WRITE(2,30)I,X,Y,ZERO
30    FORMAT(14X,2HI=,I3,10X,2HX=,F8.4,10X,2HY=,
     1F8.4,10X,2HZ=,F8.4)
```

Because there are four variables in the output line, the WRITE statement contains four variable names. Statement 30 controls the format of the line. It starts by skipping 14 spaces and printing, I=. The code I3 is then reached. Because this type of code involves an exchange with memory, the computer consults the list of variable names following the WRITE statement to determine where in memory this integer value is stored.

The next two format codes are a blank and Hollerith field, respectively. The code F8.4 is the second code that involves an exchange with memory. The second name in the list of the WRITE statement determines where in memory this value is found. The process continues until the output line is complete.

Commas are used to separate the various codes in the FORMAT statement. They make the code easier to read.

14.8 Carriage Control

In Chapter 4 a brief reference was made to the fact that column 1 of any output line has a special meaning. Whatever character appears in this position will *not* be printed on the output sheet, but rather will be used to control where on the output page the line should appear. Stated another way, it controls how many lines the paper will be advanced before the printout takes place. For this reason the character in column 1 is called "the carriage control" character.

A blank in column 1 indicates the line should be printed on the next available line (advance the carriage one line before printing). By using other characters we can get double spacing, triple spacing, advancing to the middle of a page, advancing to the top of a new page, and so on. The following table lists the four most commonly used control characters and the effect they have on advancing the paper. One of these characters should be made to appear in column 1 of each line of printed output. Again realize that this character will *not* be printed on the output line.

Carriage Control Characters

Character	Effect
Blank	Paper advances a single line.
0	Paper advances two lines.
1	Paper advances to the first line on the next page.
+	Paper does not advance.

There are three techniques for getting a character into the carriage control column.

```
7  FORMAT(1H1, 6F 8.2)
              7  FORMAT(*1*, 6F 8.2)
                           7  FORMAT('1', 6F 8.2)
```

In each of the examples, a 1 has been placed in the carriage control position, which causes the line of output to appear at the top of a new page.

Other carriage control characters are not as standard as those just listed. Each computer system has its own set of characters, which are described in the User's Manual for that system.

14.9 FORMAT Statements with Internal Parentheses

Internal parentheses are allowed in FORMAT statements to cause the repeating of certain portions of the FORMAT code. For example, internal parentheses are used in the statement:

```
6  FORMAT(2F6.2,3(F12.1,I2))
```

This statement is functionally equivalent to the statement:

```
6  FORMAT(2F6.2,F12.1,I2,F12.1,I2,F12.1,I2)
```

As a second example, consider the statement:

```
7  FORMAT(2(I6,F8.3),E10.3)
```

This statement has the same meaning as:

```
7  FORMAT(I6,F8.3,I6,F8.3,E10.3)
```

Using more than two internal parentheses (parentheses inside of parentheses) is not allowed. For example:

Allowed	Not Allowed
FORMAT (2,(I6,F6.3), 10X, 4(I6,F5.1))	FORMAT (10X, 4(F12.2, 3(I4, I6)))

14.10 Summary

You are getting very close to having the ability to place output values (numeric, alphabetic, or both) anywhere on the output sheet you find appropriate. Most scientific programmers make use of these new format features to generate the clear and "pleasant to look at" output we have shown in several previous programming examples. It is called elegant output.

These new format features have another application. Consider the problem of generating the payroll check shown in Figure 14.7. The usual output paper is removed from the printer and replaced by a series of blank checks. As the programmer, you may not only be required to calculate a person's pay amount, but also be told to place that value in a specific position, namely two lines down from the top of the check and 36 columns in from the left-hand edge of the check. This would be accomplished by statements such as:

```
    WRITE(2,18) PAY
18  FORMAT(1H1,/,36X,F8.2)
```

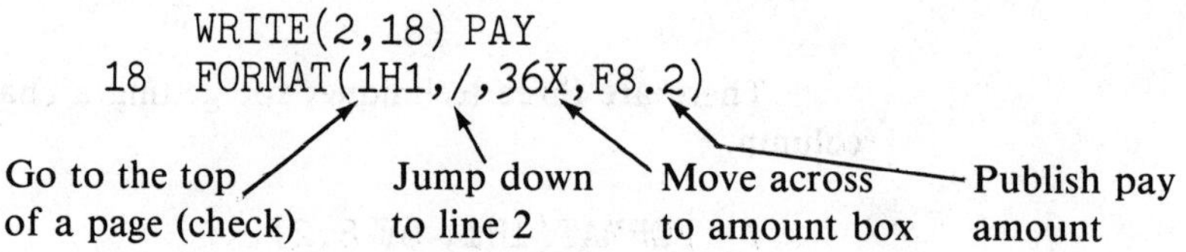

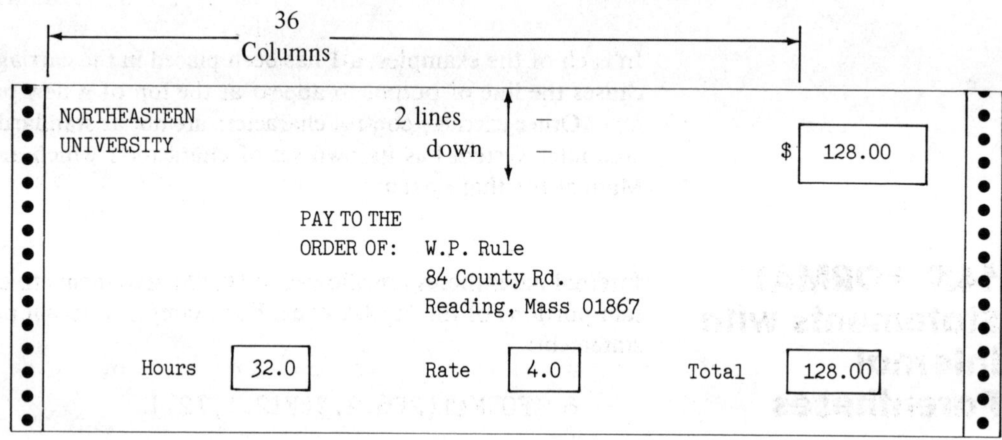

Figure 14.7 Computer generated paycheck

The next requirement might be to drop down three more lines and print the employee's name starting in column 11.

```
    WRITE(2,19)NAME
19  FORMAT(//,10X,A12)
```

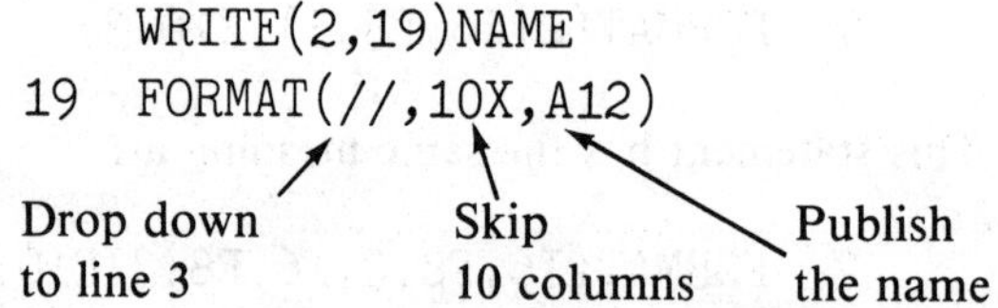

The point is that your understanding of format codes gives you considerable flexibility to meet the vast majority of problems you might be presented with.

Recall some of the elegant output used in previous programming examples. The stock report example from Chapter 3 is typical. At the time it was first presented, you did not have the ability to:

1. Start the report on a new page.
2. Center the words "STOCK REPORT" on the top of the sheet.
3. Produce the column headings.
4. Spread the individual stock listings evenly across the page.

The situation should be different now—now you have the ability.

STOCK REPORT

NAME OF SECURITY	NO.OF SHARES	PURCHASE PRICE	TOTAL COST	TODAYS PRICE	TOTAL VALUE	PROFIT (LOSS)
ALCOA	40	130.00	5200.00	138.75	5550.00	350.00
DISNEY	20	75.00	1500.00	125.00	2500.00	1000.00
DOW CHEM	100	38.65	3865.00	48.65	4865.00	1000.00
IBM	80	43.41	3472.00	42.45	3396.00	-76.80
MONSANTO	45	83.75	3768.75	38.70	1741.50	-2027.25

COL. 8 COL. 20 COL. 30 COL. 50 COL. 70 COL. 90 COL. 110 COL. 130

```
C
C        ....GO TO TOP OF NEW PAGE...PRINT REPORT HEADINGS....
C
         WRITE(2,20)
   20    FORMAT(1H1,62X,*STOCK REPORT8)
C
C        ....SKIP DOWN TWO LINES....PRINT TOP LINE OF HEADINGS....
C
         WRITE(2,30)
   30    FORMAT(//,7X,*NAME OF*,19X,*NO. OF*,15X,*PURCHASE*,14X,
      1  *TOTAL*,14X,*TODAY'S*,15X,*TOTAL*,14X,*PROFIT*)
C
C               .......PRINT BOTTOM OF COLUMN HEADING........
C
         WRITE(2,40)
   40    FORMAT(7X,*SECURITY*,18X,**SHARES*,15X,*PRICE*,15X,*COST*
      1  ,15X,*PRICE*,14X,*VALUE*,13X,*9LOSS)*)
C
C          ........SKIP DOWN AND PRODUCE LONG DASH LINE......
```

Spreading the listing of individual stocks across the output sheet can be done in two ways: using skipping codes and using large "field widths."

```
C
C        .......PRINT INFORMATION ON INDIVIDUAL STOCKS.......
C
         WRITE(2,50)NAME,NUMBER,PRICE,TCOST,VALUE,TVALUE,PROFIT
   50    FORMAT(8X,A16,I10,F20.2,F20.2,F20.2,F20.2,F20.2)
C
         STOP
         END
```

Large field widths

Realize that the codes `10X, F6.1`, and `F16.1` are very similar with regard to the positioning of a floating point number. The `F16.1` code uses a field width that is 10 larger than necessary for the number. It thereby obtains separation of fields and at the same time provides extra protection from overflow. The use of large field widths is recommended.

Quiz 21
FORMAT Codes

Part 1: Answer the following questions.

1. Describe the output generated by the following statements:

```
   WRITE(2,10)A,B,C,D,E
10 FORMAT(1X,F12.2)
```

2. Asterisks in an output field are symptomatic of what problem?
3. What does the term "unit record" mean? On input? On output?
4. What is the first column of any line of output used for?
5. In the following output statement, the letter L has been mistakenly placed in column 1. How will the output be written?

```
   WRITE(2,10)
10 FORMAT(*LARGEST VALUE*)
```

6. Write an output statement whose only function is to go to the top of a page and print the message `'PG.1'` on the right of an output page.
7. Write a single `FORMAT` code that is the equivalent of the codes:

```
10X,F6.3
```

8. What is the most important advantage of E-codes compared to F-codes?
9. What are the three ways of causing a character string (fixed message) to be included as part of a line of output?
10. Define "elegant output." What advantage does it have?

Part 2: Writing a Program

11. Write statements that will produce the heading, column headings, and the first detail line (listing WHITE incomes) similar to those of the following table.

```
* * * * * * * * * * * * * * * * * * * * * * * * * * *
* *                 CROSS TABULATION                 * *
* *      ETHNIC ORIGIN        BY      FAMILY INCOME  * *
* * * * * * * * * * * * * * * * * * * * * * * * * * *
RACE:    INCOME:
          0-4000   4001-6000  6001-8000  8001-10000   OVER    TOTAL
- - - - I - - - - I - - - - I - - - - I - - - - I - - - - I
WHITE   I    40   I    68   I   190   I   270   I   301   I   869
- - - - I - - - - I - - - - I - - - - I - - - - I - - - - I
BLACK   I    45   I    82   I   168   I   201   I   210   I   706
- - - - I - - - - I - - - - I - - - - I - - - - I - - - - I
SPANISH I    16   I    47   I    84   I   120   I   119   I   386
- - - - I - - - - I - - - - I - - - - I - - - - I - - - - I
OTHER   I     3   I     5   I     8   I    24   I    52   I    92
- - - - I - - - - I - - - - I - - - - I - - - - I - - - - I
  TOTAL     104       202       450       615       682      2053
```

Review Exercises

1. The following integer values are to be printed as output using an I3 FORMAT code. Show how these values will apear.

Value	Output
76	☐☐☐
1006	☐☐☐
+1	☐☐☐
1234	☐☐☐
−104	☐☐☐

★ 2. The statements:

```
  READ(5,8)XINIT,YINIT,XFINL,YFINL,NUM
8 FORMAT(2F8.2,2F10.3,I6)
```

are used to transfer five values from the data card shown to memory.

a. Do all values lie within their specified field width?
b. Several values are not right justified in their respective fields. Will this produce an error?
c. Which values have their decimal points located in the proper column?

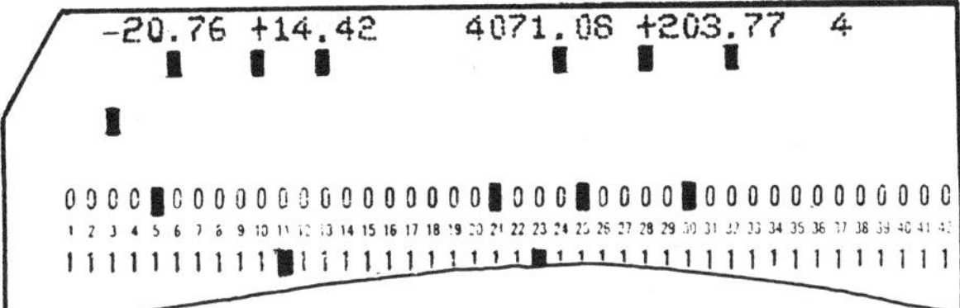

d. Is improper decimal point location a problem?
e. Show how these values would appear if printed as output under the control of FORMAT statement 8.

3. Repeat part (e) of exercise 2 for the following modified FORMAT statements:
   a. Each field width has been increased by two columns.

```
8 FORMAT(2F10.2,2F12.3,I8)
```

   b. Each field width has been increased by four columns and two additional places after the decimal points have been requested.

```
8 FORMAT(2F12.4,2F14.5,I10)
```

★ 4. Complete the table by specifying the range of values the following format code will accommodate:

Code	Range
I5	to
F8.6	to
F10.4	to
I7	to
E14.4	to

5. Write a program that will print the letter H 15 units high and 15 units wide centered on the output sheet as shown.

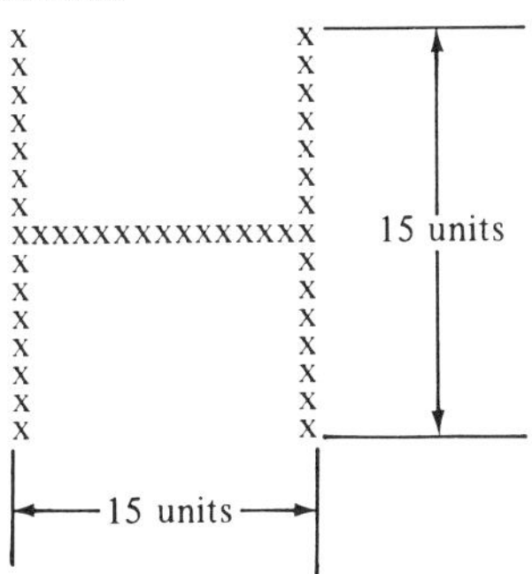

6. All field width specifications should include room for either a plus or a minus sign. True or false?
7. What does the term "carriage control character" mean? Give two examples.

★ 8. Which of these two groups of output statements is preferred? Why?

```
   WRITE(2,20)NAME1,NAME2
20 FORMAT(///,1X,2A6)

   WRITE(2,20)NAME1,NAME2
20 FORMAT(///,2A6)
```

9. How many records will be consumed by the following READ statement? Describe the location of A, B, and C.

```
   READ(5,10)A,B,C
10 FORMAT(//,3F8.1)
```

10. Describe the line of output generated by the following statements:

```
   WRITE(2,30)
30 FORMAT(1H1,///,3X,60(2H__))
```

★ 11. In the following output statement, the count of Hollerith characters is in error (it's one too large). What effect will this have regarding the correct syntax of the FORMAT statement?

```
   WRITE(2,40)
40 FORMAT(35X,7HOUTPUT)
```

12. A data file consists of records containing a single value of X. This value may be positive or negative and represents DEPOSITS or WITHDRAWALS to a checking account.

DEPOSITS	WITHDRAWALS
200.00	-16.50
10.00	-25.00

Post these transactions as shown above.

a. Provide statements to produce the column headings shown at the top of an output page.

b. Post the individual transaction amount on the left or the right of the page as appropriate.

13. Repeat exercise 12 but include the following features. You are to post no more than forty transactions on any one page. If several pages are needed to list all the transactions contained in the data deck, each page is to have its own column headings and each page should be numbered. You will need a page counter and a transaction counter.

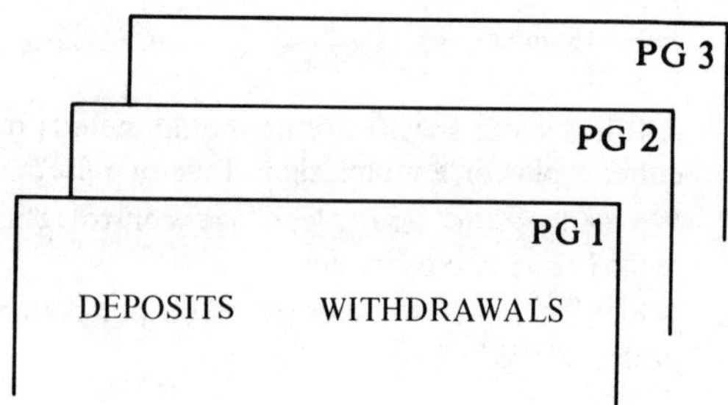

14. A fraternity wants a banner made of letters 30 lines tall and 20 characters wide. This is a tedious job of writing 30 pairs of `WRITE/FORMAT` combinations to obtain the desired output. Write the statements necessary to obtain the top two lines of the output wanted.

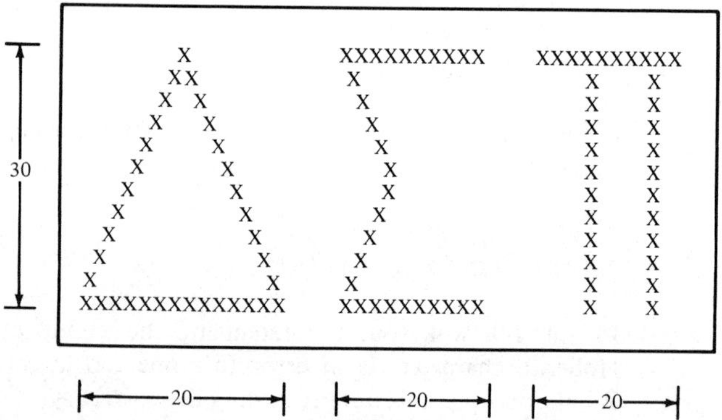

15. A video terminal is used to display the flight number of arriving and departing aircraft. Write statements to obtain the top two or three lines of this output.

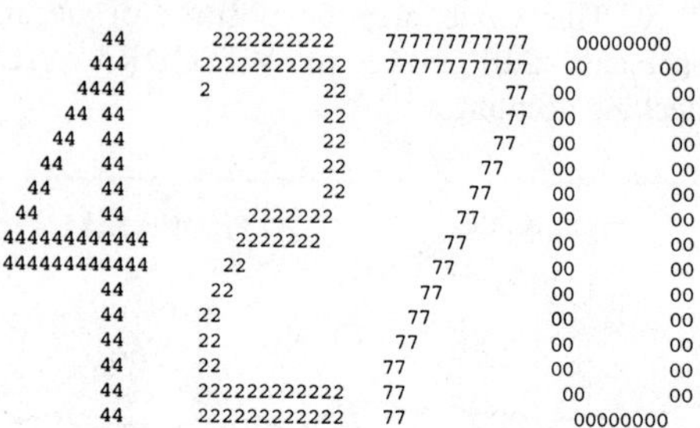

★ 16. The output of a program is to consist of several lines of output and a graph plotting this output. The graph is to be plotted by hand, but the X and Y axes of the graph are to be machine generated through the use of appropriate Hollerith codes. Write the statements needed to print the X and Y axes shown.

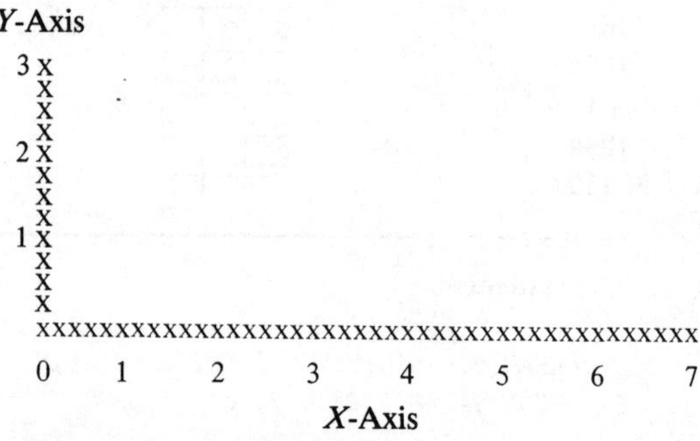

17. Write a program to produce as output the following conversion tables:

Conversion Tables: Centimeters to Inches

CM.	INCHES	CM.	INCHES	CM.	INCHES
1.0	.3937	11.0	4.3307	21.0	8.2677
2.0	.7874	12.0	4.7244	22.0	8.6614
3.0	1.1811	13.0	5.1181	23.0	9.0551
4.0	1.5748	14.0	5.5118	24.0	9.4488
5.0	1.9685	15.0	5.9055	25.0	9.8425
6.0	2.3622	16.0	6.2992	26.0	10.2362
7.0	2.7559	17.0	6.6929	27.0	10.6299
8.0	3.1496	18.0	7.0866	28.0	11.0236
9.0	3.5433	19.0	7.4803	29.0	11.4173
10.0	3.9370	20.0	7.8740	30.0	11.8110

18. A ball is positioned 10 feet above a circular table that is rotating in a counterclockwise direction at one revolution per minute. At time $t = 0$ the leading edge of the hole is at the "12 o'clock" position. The ball is at the "3 o'clock" position. At time t, to be read from a data card, the ball is dropped. Write a program to determine if the ball will pass through the hole in the table. Have the computer print `YES` or `NO`.

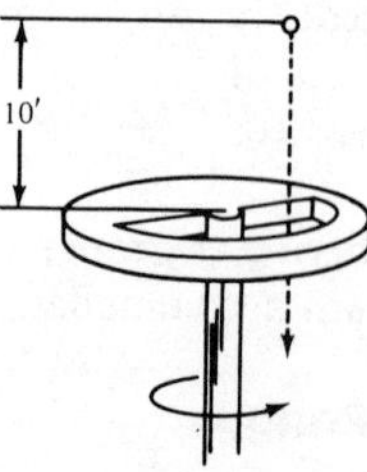

★ 19. An airline operates among four terminals. The X and Y coordinates of each terminal are given on separate data cards. Write a program to determine the distance between terminals and report these distances by generating the table shown.

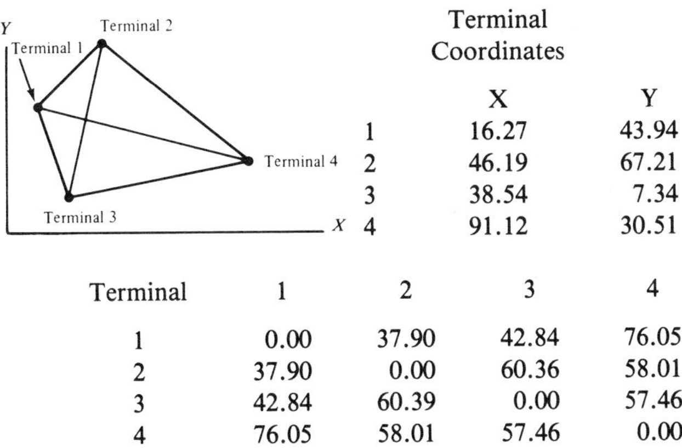

Terminal Coordinates

	X	Y
1	16.27	43.94
2	46.19	67.21
3	38.54	7.34
4	91.12	30.51

Terminal	1	2	3	4
1	0.00	37.90	42.84	76.05
2	37.90	0.00	60.36	58.01
3	42.84	60.39	0.00	57.46
4	76.05	58.01	57.46	0.00

20. A programming example in Chapter 6 involved determining how many times the number 5 appears in a data deck. Write the program again to include the elegant output suggested. Use statements early in the program to produce the headings. Use statements later in the program to generate the final message, ''RUN COMPLETE: FINAL RESULT 3''. Generate the intermediate output as well.

CARD BEING PROCESSED	VALUE READ FROM CARD	CONDITION OF COUNTER
1	6	0
2	1	0
3	5	1
4	2	1
18	7	2
19	5	3
20	3	3

RUN COMPLETE: FINAL RESULT 3

21. A toy manufacturer is considering producing a computerized tic-tac-toe game. Write software that will produce the basic game board as suggested in the illustration.

```
               X               X
               X               X
               X               X
               X               X
XXXXXXXXXXXXXXXXXXXXXXXXXXXXXXXXXXXXXXXXXXXX
               X               X
               X               X
               X               X
XXXXXXXXXXXXXXXXXXXXXXXXXXXXXXXXXXXXXXXXXXXX
               X               X
               X               X
               X               X
               X               X
```

22. A computer is used to generate inventory reports for the National Guard. Each report is 20 to 30 pages long, and there are hundreds of reports generated on one computer run. We need a convenient way to separate one report from another.

Write a program to be used at the end of each report that will generate *two* pages of output as follows, which will serve as a means of separating the reports.

```
XXXXXXXXXXXXXXXXXXXXXXXXXXXXXXXX
XXXXXXXXXXXXXXXXXXXXXXXXXXXXXXXX
XX                            XX
XX                            XX
XX                            XX
XX                            XX
XX                            XX
XX                            XX
XX                            XX
XX                            XX
XX                            XX
XX                            XX
XX                            XX
XXXXXXXXXXXXXXXXXXXXXXXXXXXXXXXX
XXXXXXXXXXXXXXXXXXXXXXXXXXXXXXXX
```

Additional Applications

Programming Example
List by Section Number

A data file contains the names of students enrolled in a FORTRAN course. There are *four* sections of these students. All students in section 014 appear first in the file, followed by the students in section 015, and so on. Write a program to provide a separate listing of the students in each section. (When the section number changes, go to the top of a new page and provide an appropriate heading.)

Programming Example–List by Section Number continued

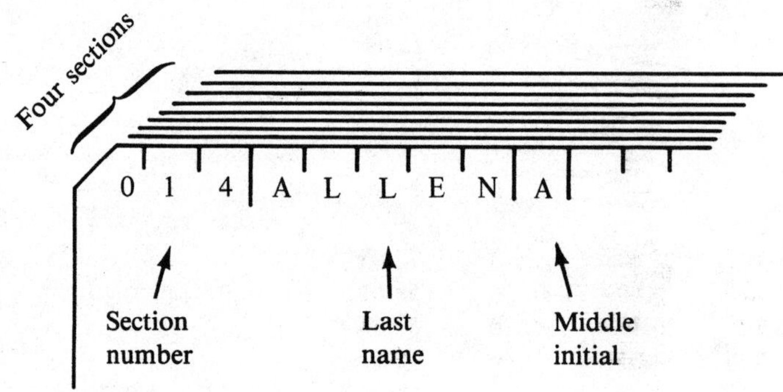


```
SECTION 014
ALLEN  A
BECK   J
BROWN  D
GELID  M
HILL   S
LANE   R
NORTON K

SECTION 015
BAKER  G
DEAN   W
HARB   A
```

```
C.............................................................
C..     PURPOSE - PROVIDE SEPARATE LIST OF NAMES            ..
C                 FOR EACH SECTION OF STUDENTS.             ..
C.............................................................
C
C                 -----IMPORTANT VARIABLES-----
C
C       --SECTN    SECTION NUMBER READ FROM INPUT RECORD  --
C       --NAME     NAME OF STUDENT (6 CHARACTERS)          --
C       --MI       MIDDLE INITIAL (1 CHARACTER)            --
C       --PRESNT   SECTION NUMBER PRESENTLY BEING PRINTED --
C
        INTEGER SECTN, PRESNT
        CHARACTER NAME*6, MI*1
C
C               SET PRESNT TO RIDICULOUS VALUE
C
        PRESNT = -9999
C
C               LOOP STARTS HERE
C
   10   READ(5,20,END=50)SECTN, NAME, MI
   20   FORMAT(I3, A6, A1)
C
        IF(SECTN.NE.PRESNT) THEN
C
C               NEW PAGE NECESSARY
C
```

Programming Example–List by Section Number continued

```
            WRITE(2,30)SECTN
   30       FORMAT(1H1, 15X, 'SECTION ', I3)
C
            PRESNT = SECTN
C
         ENDIF
C
         WRITE(2,40)NAME, MI
   40    FORMAT(5X,A6,4X,A1)
C
         GO TO 10
C
   50    STOP
         END
```

Programming Example Drunk Drivers

To keep drunks off the road, a new ignition lock is being developed that displays a four-digit number and requires the operator to respond by punching in the same four-digit number. Responding correctly three times in a row allows the car to be started.

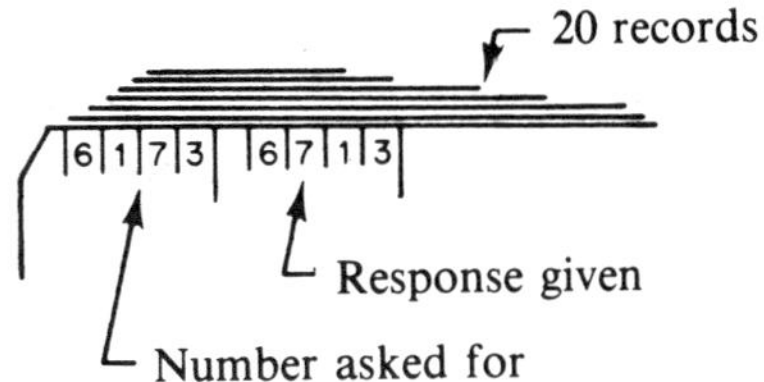

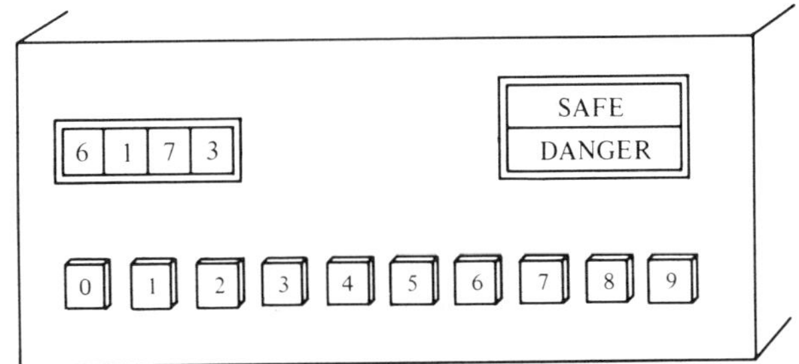

To test the system, a drunk is given 20 chances to beat the device. Write a program that determines if he ever makes three correct responses in a row. Output should be one of the messages:

1. HE BEAT THE SYSTEM
2. HE COULD NOT BEAT THE SYSTEM

Programming Example–Drunk Drivers continued

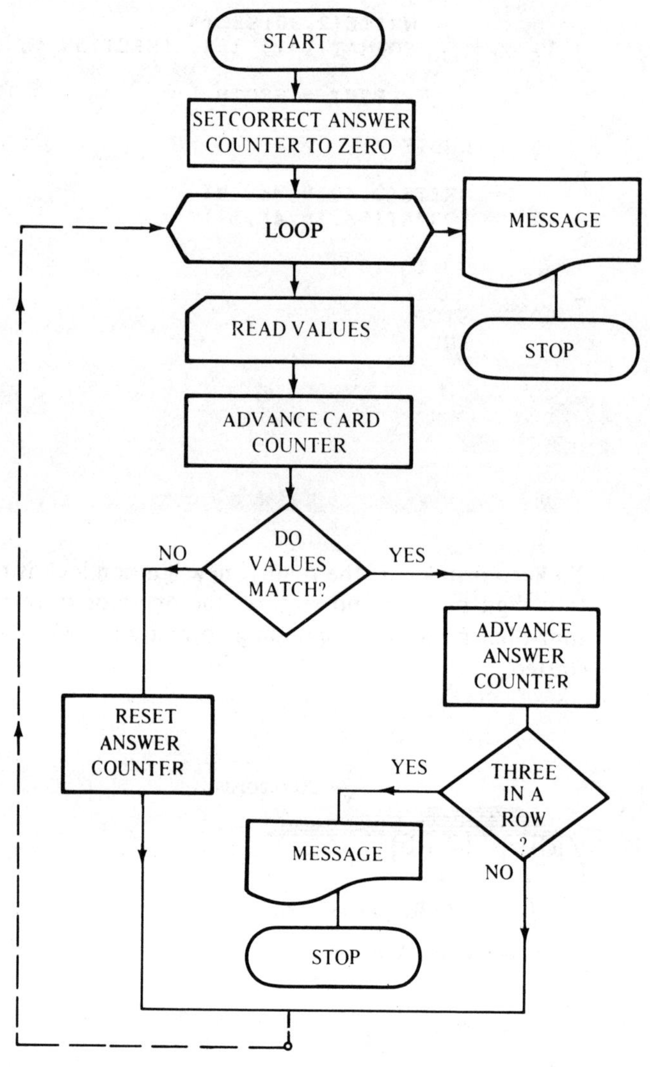


```
C.......................................................................
C       PURPOSE - TEST NEW IGNITION SYSTEM PERFORMANCE                ..
C.......................................................................
C
C               ---- IMPORTANT VARIABLES----
C
C       --NGOOD CORRECT ANSWER COUNTER
C       --CARDS CARD COUNTER
C       --NWANT NUMBER CALLED FOR
C       --NGIVEN        NUMBER GIVEN IN RESPONSE
C
        INTEGER NGOOD,CARDS,NWANT,NGIVEN
C
        NGOOD = 0
C
        DO 40 CARDS = 1, 20, 1
C
   10   READ(5,11) NWANT,NGIVEN
   11   FORMAT(2I5)
C
C
C               TEST FOR CORRECT RESPONSE
C
        IF(NWANT.EQ.NGIVEN) THEN
```

Programming Example–Drunk Drivers continued

```
C
C              CORRECT ANSWER SECTION
C
        NGOOD = NGOOD + 1
C
              IF(NGOOD.EQ.3) THEN
C
C                SYSTEM HAS BEEN BEATEN
C
                  WRITE(2,21)
   21             FORMAT(10X,'HE BEAT THE SYSTEM')
                  STOP
              ENDIF
C
        ELSE
C
C                WRONG ANSWER - RESET COUNTERS
C
             NGOOD = 0
        ENDIF
C
   40   CONTINUE
C
   30   WRITE (2,31)
   31   FORMAT(10X,'HE DID NOT BEAT THE SYSTEM')
C
        STOP
        END
```

Programming Example Separate Courses by Major

Each record in a data file gives the course number and the number of students enrolled in a particular course. Write a program to search the data file for all courses whose number starts with the digits 01. Print these courses and their enrollments on a separate sheet of output.

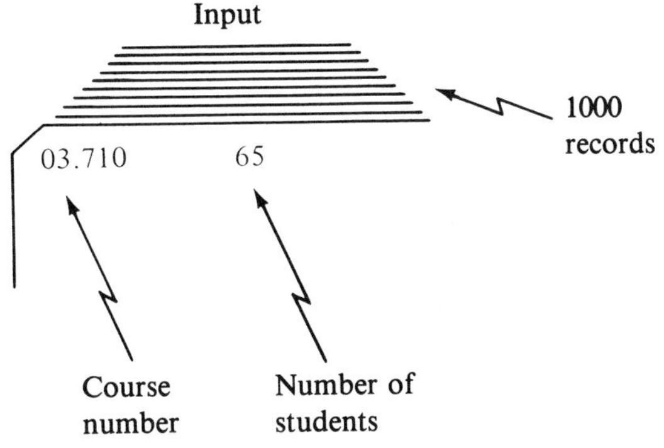

Output

Course	Number
01.824	18
01.173	72
01.242	36
Course	Number
02.010	106
02.724	12
02.865	33
02.729	64
Course	Number
03.445	19
03.191	58

Programming Example–Separate Courses by Major continued

When this is complete, make a search for all courses that start with the number 02. These starting numbers tell which department is giving the course.

Continue this search and print activity until you reach the 93 series, which is the largest department number course possible. The data base is 1000 elements called CRSNO and 1000 elements called NUMBER:

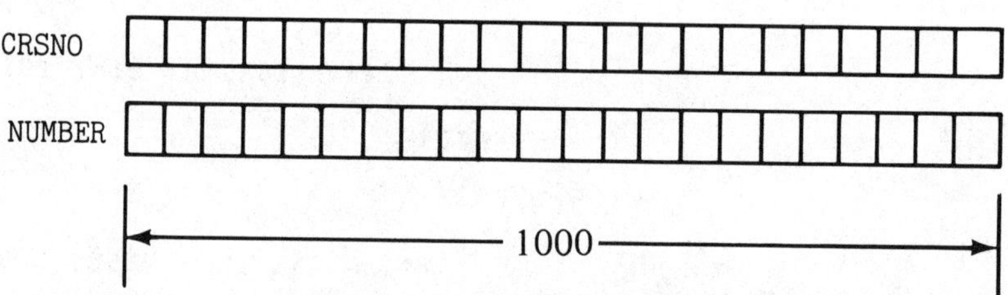

Part A: Search for 01 series courses only. The basic procedure is to examine each course number and convert the number to an integer. If that integer is 01, we have found a course number that should be printed out.

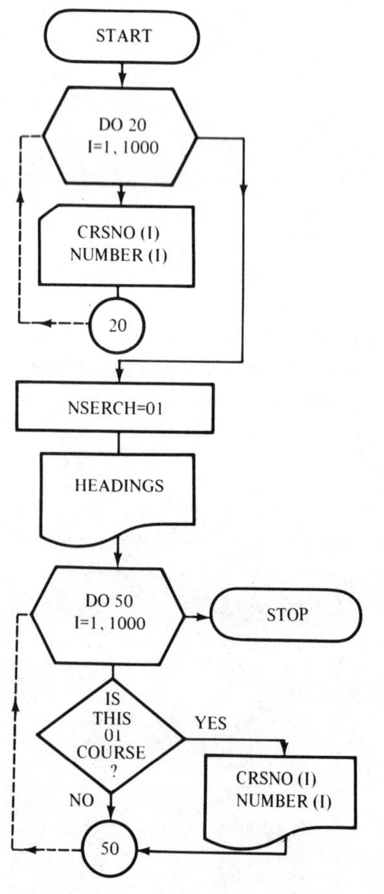


```
C.............................................................
C..     PURPOSE - READ AND STORE DATA BASE REPRESENTING 1000    ..
C..               COURSES AND THEIR STUDENT ENROLLMENT.         ..
C..                 --------------------------------            ..
C..               SEARCH FOR COURSES THAT START WITH 01         ..
C.............................................................
C
C             ---IMPORTANT VARIABLES---
C
C     --CRSNO    ARRAY OF COURSE NUMBERS                         --
C     --NUMBER   ARRAY OF STUDENT ENROLLMENTS                    --
C     --NSERCH   COURSE NUMBER BEING SEARCHED FOR (01)           --
C
      INTEGER NUMBER(1000),NSERCH
      REAL    CRSNO(1000)
C
C     .....READ DATA BASE.....
C
      DO 20 I = 1, 1000
 10      READ(5,11)CRSNO(I),NUMBER(I)
 11      FORMAT(F6.3,I3)
 20   CONTINUE
C
C     .....SET SEARCH VALUE...START SEARCH.....
C
      NSERCH = 01
C
 30   WRITE(2,31)
 31   FORMAT(1H1,20X,'COURSE',10X,'NUMBER')
C
C     .....LOOP ENTRY POINT.....
C
      DO 50 I = 1,1000
C
         M = CRSNO(I)
 40      IF(M.EQ.NSERCH)WRITE(2,41)CRSNO(I),NUMBER(I)
 41      FORMAT(10X,F6.3,13X,I3)
C
 50   CONTINUE
C
      STOP
      END
```

Programming Example–Separate Courses by Major continued

Part B: Search for 01 through 93 series. The logic of this part is merely to set up an outer DO loop that will conduct search after search after search through the data base.

As has happened before, once the logic for solving one typical search through the problem is complete, it is only necessary to establish an outer DO loop so that repetitive applications of the logic are applied to the data base. In this case this means setting up a DO loop that will search for courses in department 02, 03, 04, . . . , 92, 93.

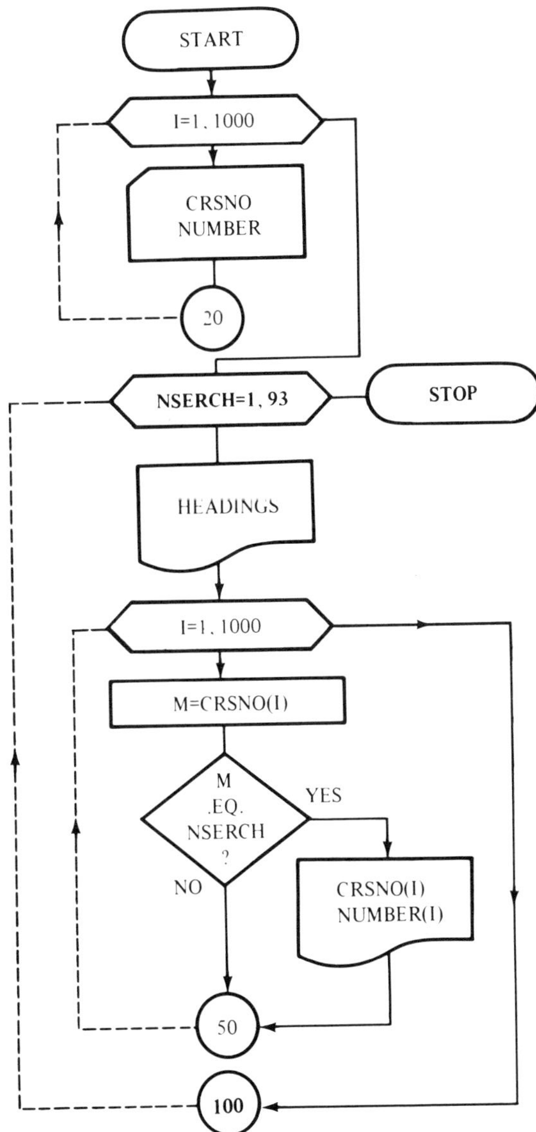

Programming Example–Separate Courses by Major

```
C.................................................................
C..   PURPOSE - PROVIDE A SEPARATE LISTING OF ALL COURSES      ..
C..             BEING OFFERED BY EACH DEPARTMENT.              ..
C..             (SEE LIST IN PREVIOUS EXAMPLE)                 ..
C.................................................................
C
      INTEGER NUMBER(1000),NSERCH
      REAL    CRSNO(1000)
C
C     .....READ DATA BASE.....
C
      DO 20 I=1,1000
  10     READ(5,11)CRSNO(I),NUMBER(I)
  11     FORMAT(F6.3,I3)
  20  CONTINUE
C
C     .....SET UP OUTER DO LOOP.....
C
      DO 100 NSERCH=1,93
C
C        .....PRODUCE HEADINGS.....
C
  30     WRITE(2,31)
  31     FORMAT(1H1,20X,'COURSE',10X,'NUMBER')
C
C        .....SET UP INNER DO TO SEARCH DATA BASE.....
C
         DO 50 I=1,1000
            M = CRSNO(I)
  40        IF(M.EQ.NSERCH) WRITE(2,41)CRSNO(I),NUMBER(K)
  41           FORMAT(10X,F6.3,I25)
  50     CONTINUE
C
C        .....THIS COMPLETES THE SEARCH......
C
 100  CONTINUE
C
      STOP
      END
```

15 Character Manipulation/ Case Studies

15.1 Processing Character Information

We have been dealing almost exclusively with the manipulation and modification of *numerical* values. It is time to cover a somewhat different set of operations, namely those that operate on *character* information. This is not a totally new topic in that you have already used character constants to produce page headings and Hollerith messages in WRITE statements that generate elegant output. Another character constant:

```
''EMPTY ___ ___ ___''
```

was used in the airline reservation problem to search for empty seats on an aircraft.

On several occasions we have read the name of a stock or the name and address of a customer (or company) and stored this character information in memory. It is now time to look at some alternative ways of declaring a character string and to examine in greater detail how character strings are stored and manipulated.

Consider the new features associated with the following two TYPE statements:

```
CHARACTER A*10, B(20)*4
CHARACTER*12 C, D, E*6
```

The variable A is declared as a character string of size 10 (we have been using this form throughout the text). B is declared as an array of character strings (20 strings) where each string is of size 4. The next CHARACTER statement shows that the size (or declared length) specification may be attached to the word CHARACTER. This means that any character variable name in the list that follows will be given this length (in our example, a length of 12) unless a different length is specified. Accordingly C and D are character variables of length 12, while E is of length 6.

Input/Output

A character variable may be read from input by either a list directed or a FORMAT controlled READ statement. When list directed input is used, the string of characters on the input record must be enclosed in apostrophes. These apostrophes are obviously delimiters to show where the string starts and where the string ends. FORMAT controlled input does not use apostrophes.

Note two things about these read operations. First, the blank between the words ALFA and ROMEO takes one space on the input record and one character position in the character string. A blank must be treated like any other character. Next, note that the length of the two input values is exactly the same as the string size. What happens when the lengths are different? The quick answer is one of the following.

1. Left justification.
2. Blank fill on the right.
3. Truncation of characters on the right.

When an input value is smaller than the string size of a variable, there will be left justification, meaning that the left-most character of the input quantity is positioned in the left-most character position of the variable. Because the input item is smaller than the string size, a number of character positions will not be filled. These will be "blank filled." The system loads the character representation of a blank into each of these positions.

When an input value is larger than the string size of a variable, there is left justification and a "truncation" of overhanging characters. All this is illustrated in the following READ examples.

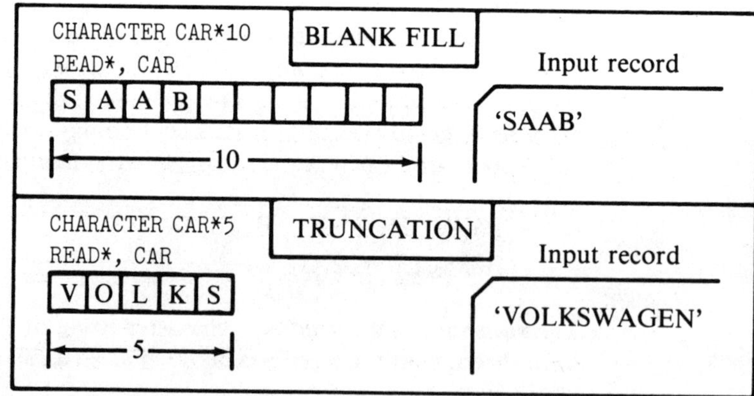

Character Constants

A character variable may be defined inside a program through the use of an assignment statement:

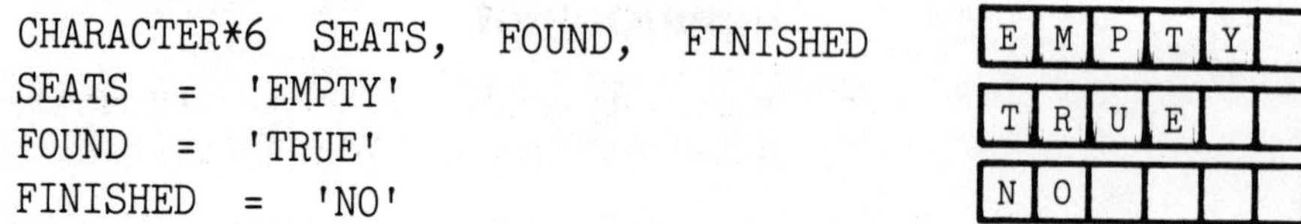

In the first example, a character variable called SEATS is declared of size 6. A character assignment statement defines the value of SEATS as equal to 'EMPTY'. Note that the size of the constant and the size of the variable are not the same. As described in the previous section, the five-character constant 'EMPTY' is expanded to the size of the receiving character variable (a blank is added to bring the size up to 6). The same process is followed for the other constants.

Logical IF Tests

If it seems we are overdoing the emphasis on equal size, there is a good reason. Assume, for example, we must test the value of memory location SEATS to see if the string 'EMPTY' is there. We would use the following statement:

```
IF(SEATS.EQ.'EMPTY') PRINT*,'TAKE THIS SEAT'
```

If the variable SEATS is six characters in size and the character constant 'EMPTY' is five characters in size, the two strings cannot be equal (they are of different length).

We warned you about the importance of a blank. It is just as important as any other character. The blank that is missing on the end of the character constant would cause the equality of the IF test to fail! With this "necessity of equality in size" in mind, this process of *blank fill* or *truncation* was developed. You will see this more clearly when we go into how strings are stored internally.

Special Case

Once in a great while it will be necessary to establish a character constant that has within it an apostrophe (for example, an apostrophe S to show possession). The title line of the following output page is an example.

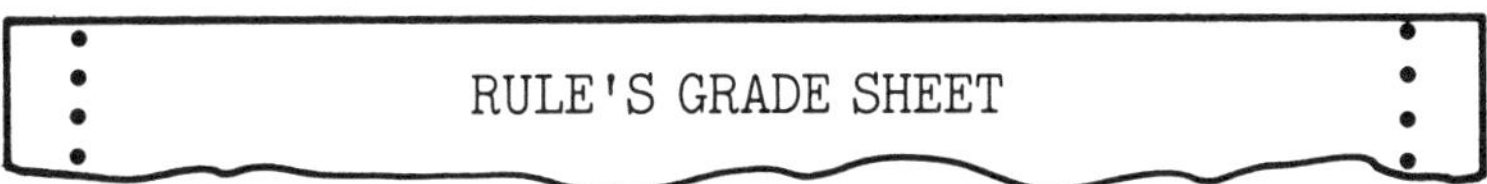

This special case is handled by using a double apostrophe as shown. The reason for using a double apostrophe is that a single apostrophe would be interpreted as the delimiter or end of the string.

```
CHARACTER*20  TITLE
TITLE  =  'RULE''S GRADE SHEET'
```

Special case

Storing Character Information

It will prove to your advantage if you have some idea as to how character information is stored in internal memory. As described in Chapter 1, memory is a series of binary storage devices called **bits**. Each bit can store a 0 or a 1. When an integer or a real number is stored in memory, it is convenient to group a number of binary bits together to form a **word** of memory. A typical word size is 32 binary bits. When we store character information, the number of binary bits needed to represent one character is grouped together (usually 8) to form what is called a **byte** of memory.

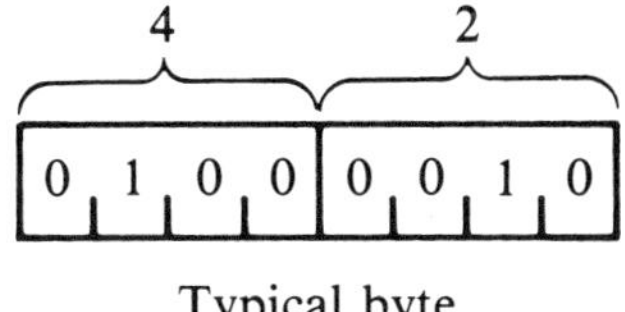

Typical byte

Using an 8-bit byte, we can represent 256 different characters. Within a byte of memory, each character is stored internally in the form of a *two-digit number code* as suggested in the following table.

Typical Character Code

Character	Internal Code	Character	Internal Code	Character	Internal Code
Blank	00	R	42	,	51
A	21	S	43	.	52
B	22	T	44	)	53
C	23	U	45	(	54
D	24	V	46	+	55
E	25	W	47	;	56
F	26	X	50	*	57
G	27	Y	51	–	60

To see how a character string is formed, consider the following. Statements such as:

```
      CHARACTER M*4
      READ(5,10) M
   10 FORMAT (A4)
```

define the variable M as a character variable. A character string, 4 bytes long,† is set up in memory to hold the string. An input record, such as the one in Figure 15.1 is read. The use of an A-code in the FORMAT statement causes each of the four characters to be read from the record and converted to its two-digit equivalent and sent to memory.

The important aspects of this procedure are:

1. All characters are represented internally according to a two-digit number code.
2. Once in memory, the binary bit pattern of a character string is just like the bit pattern of a number (they could be used in an IF test, for example).

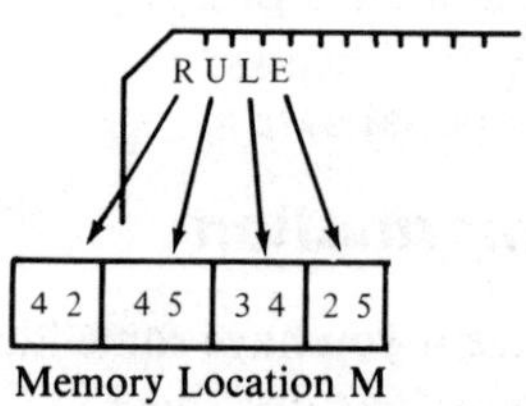

Figure 15.1 Typical conversion process

Various computers use several different character codes to represent the character set on that computer. These codes have the following features in common:

1. The number code for a blank is smaller than the code for any letter or any digit.

† If the computer is not a byte-addressable machine, each character is stored in a separate word of memory.

2. Letters in the alphabet must be in order, with the number code for the letter A the smallest.
3. The number code for digits must be in order and precede the letters† but not the blank.

This is called the **collating sequence.**

This method of number representation and the collating sequence should provide a good deal of insight as to how character manipulation is accomplished on the computer. Consider the internal representation of the following short words read from data under the content of an A3 format code.

Internal Representation (A3 code)

Word	Internal Representation		
A C E	21	23	25
A C T	21	23	44
A R E	21	42	25
A T	21	44	00
B A R	22	21	42
D C	24	23	00
W E T	47	25	44

Words beginning with an A have a smaller number code than words beginning with B. Words that are shorter than three letters are padded with blanks.

Alphabetic sorting can now be accomplished as follows. Read a group of words. Find the word with the smallest internal number code. Print it out in A-format. Look for the word with the next smallest number code. Print it out, and so on. A problem in alphabetic sorting will be covered shortly.

15.2 Alphabetic Sort

One of the more practical applications of character manipulation is the alphabetic sorting of a list of names. This operation occurs so frequently that many advanced algorithms have been developed to accomplish the sort in an efficient, high-speed fashion. The method presented in this section is not very efficient, but it is relatively easy to follow.

We accomplish the sort in two parts. The first part deals with a list of names that is fixed in size (40 names) and asks that the name with the largest number code be found and moved to the bottom of the list. For the list of names used, the name ZOTOS is the largest. It is moved from position 13 in the list to position 40.

Once the programming to accomplish this is complete, we generalize the code to:

1. Work with a list of variable size (`SIZE`).
2. Employ a `DO WHILE` loop structure to repeat the code until the list is fully sorted.

† One of the codes (`EBCDIC`) places the digits *after* the letters.

Programming Example
Sort: First Pass

A data file contains the names of 40 students not in alphabetic order. These names are eight characters in length and are presented 10 names per line of input (use a 10A8 code). Sort these names in the following way.

Part A: Read the data file and print the names, 10 per line.

```
CASWELL     GILMORE     OSMOND     ...    KING      RULE
EPSTEIN     CLIFFORD    ZOTOS      ...    RYDER     MACKEY
PENNEY      STUART      WALKER     ...    VAUGHN    MARTIN
COHEN       SCHMIDT     BAILEY     ...    FISHER    YOUNG
```

This step is used to allow the programmer to examine the original configuration of the data.

Part B: Find the name whose numerical equivalent is the largest. Print this name and its position in the array.

```
THE LARGEST NAME IS ZOTOS .IT IS IN POSITION 13.
```

This step verifies that the largest name has been detected correctly.

Part C: Move this "largest name" to the end of the array, but be careful not to lose the name already in position 40. Republish the array to see if the swap activity required above has been effective.

```
CASWELL     GILMORE     OSMOND     ...    KING      RULE
EPSTEIN     CLIFFORD    YOUNG      ...    RYDER     MACKEY
PENNEY      STUART      WALKER     ...    VAUGHN    MARTIN
COHEN       SCHMIDT     BAILEY     ...    FISHER    ZOTOS
```

```
C.......................................................
C..   PURPOSE - THIS PROGRAM WILL FIND THE LARGEST NAME IN..
C..             AN UNSORTED LIST OF 40 NAMES AND MOVE THAT..
C..             NAME TO THE BOTTOM OF THE LIST.            ..
C.......................................................
C
C            - - - - - IMPORTANT VARIABLES - - - - -
C
C     -- NAME      VECTOR OF 40 STUDENT NAMES                --
C     -- LARGE     LARGEST OF THE 40 NAMES                   --
C     -- LOC       LOCATION (SUBSCRIPT) OF LARGEST NAME      --
C
C
      CHARACTER NAME(40)*8
C
C     READ NAMES.....PRINT FOR VERIFICATION
C
      READ(5,10)(NAME(I),I=1,40)
   10 FORMAT(10A8)
C
      WRITE(2,20)(NAME(I),I=1,40)
   20 FORMAT(10(4X,A8))
C
C      ASSUME FIRST NAME IS THE LARGEST
C
      LARGE = NAME(1)
      LOC = 1
C
C    .......PROCESS REMAINING NAMES.......
C
      DO 30 I = 2, 40
```

Programming Example–Sort: First Pass continued

```
C
C               IS THIS NAME LARGER
C
            IF(NAME(I).GT.LARGE) THEN
C
                LARGE = NAME(I)
                LOC = I
C
            ENDIF
C
   30    CONTINUE
C
C        ...PART B PRINT OUT...
C
         PRINT*,'      THE LARGEST NAME IS     ', LARGE
         PRINT*,'      ITS POSITION IS        ', LOC
C
C      .......SWAP NAMES, BE CAREFUL NOT TO LOSE THE LAST NAME...
C
         ICOPY = NAME(40)
         NAME(40) = LARGE
         NAME(LOC) = ICOPY
C
C     .........VERIFY THAT SWAP HAS TAKEN PLACE.......
C
         WRITE(2,20)(NAME(I),I=1,40)
C
         STOP
         END
```

Part D: The program just written can now be generalized. At the moment we have 40 names. When the largest name is found, it is moved to the bottom of the list, to position 40. We now want to repeat the logic, but looking at a list that is 39 elements long and placing the largest element of that list in position 39. Another repeat of the logic with 38 names, then 37 names. You get the idea.

We can accomplish this without much difficulty. Look at the old program. Wherever the specific value of 40 appears, make the substitution of the variable SIZE. SIZE tells how many elements are as yet unsorted. It will be used to control looping and to tell where the bottom of the unsorted list is (the element the largest name should be sent to). We make the statement:

```
SIZE = 40
```

to start the program and cause SIZE to be reduced by 1 each time a pass through the logic is completed. A DO WHILE construct is used to maintain looping until the list is totally sorted.

```
C..........................................................
C..    PURPOSE - THIS PROGRAM REPEATS THE LOGIC OF THE        ..
C..              PREVIOUS EXAMPLE PROBLEM TO COMPLETELY SORT ..
C..              THE LIST OF 40 NAMES.                        ..
C..........................................................
C
C              - - - - - IMPORTANT VARIABLES - - - - -
C
C     --SIZE       SIZE OF LIST YET UNSORTED               --
C
C
         CHARACTER*8  NAME(40)
C
C        .....READ NAMES.....PRINT FOR VERIFICATION.....
C
         READ(5,20)(NAME(I),I=1,40)
   20    FORMAT(10(4X,A8))
```

Programming Example–Sort: First Pass continued

```
C
          SIZE = 40
C
          DO WHILE (SIZE.GT.1)
C
C                   ASSUME FIRST NAME THE LARGEST
C
                    LARGE = NAME(1)
                    LOC = 1
C
C         .....PROCESS REMAINING NAMES.....
C
                DO 30 I = 2,SIZE
C
                     IF(NAME(I).GT.LARGE) THEN
C
                              LARGE = NAME(I)
                              LOC = I
C
                     ENDIF
C
   30           CONTINUE
C
C         ............START SWAP ACTIVITY...............
C
              ICOPY = NAME(SIZE)
              NAME(SIZE) = LARGE
              NAME(LOC) = ICOPY
C
C         ............DECREASE SIZE OF UNSORTED LIST.........
C
              SIZE = SIZE -1
C
          ENDDO
C
C                        PRINT OUT SORTED LIST
C
          WRITE(2,20) (NAME(I),I=1,40)
C
          STOP
          END
```

15.3 ICHAR and CHAR Functions

When dealing with character information, sometimes we must determine where in the collation sequence a given character is positioned. For example, we might want to know where the letter "A" appears. This can be found by the statement

```
LOC = ICHAR('A')
```

The function ICHAR accepts as input a character string of length 1 and returns an integer telling where in the collation sequence that character is positioned. We sometimes refer to this as the **ordinal** value of the character.

The function ICHAR could be used to determine if letters of the alphabet appear before or after the digits 0 through 9 in the following way:

```
IF(ICHAR('A').LT.ICHAR('O')) THEN
    PRINT*,'THE LETTERS CAME FIRST'
ELSE
    PRINT*,'THE NUMBERS COME FIRST'
ENDIF
```

A companion function called CHAR performs the opposite activity. It receives as an input argument an integer expression (usually a variable or a constant) and returns the character that occupies that position in the collation sequence. The following program uses this function to determine which characters occupy positions 40 to 60 in the collation sequence of the computer the program is run on.

```
      CHARACTER OUT*1
      INTEGER I
C
      DO 10 I = 40, 60
C
              OUT = CHAR(I)
C
              PRINT*, 'I = ',I, 'CHARACTER = ', OUT
C
   10 CONTINUE
C
      STOP
      END
```

To observe some useful applications of these functions, consider the following problems. Assume you have read a character from input. You are first to determine if the character is a letter or a digit. If it turns out to be a letter, you are to indicate which letter of the alphabet it is—the first letter, the second letter, and so on.

```
      CHARACTER INPUT*1
C
      READ*, INPUT
C
      IF (INPUT.GE.'A'  .AND. INPUT.LE.'Z') THEN
C
              PRINT*, 'THIS IS A LETTER'
              LOC = ICHAR(INPUT) - ICHAR('A')
              PRINT*, 'IT IS THE ',LOC,' IN THE ALPHABET'
C
      ELSEIF (INPUT.GE.'0'.AND.INPUT.LE.'9') THEN
C
              PRINT*, 'THIS CHARACTER IS A DIGIT'
C
      ELSE
C
              PRINT*, 'THIS IS A SPECIAL CHARACTER'
C
      ENDIF
C
      STOP
      END
```

Write a program that encodes a secret message as follows. Type the characters of the message one at a time. Convert each character to a number (its collation sequence number) and report this number. To ensure the safety of your message, start the program by asking which day of the month the message is to be sent on. Add this value to each number reported. Anyone trying to decode the message would take your numbers and subtract the date from each number before asking which character the number represents. Signal the end of a message with a dollar sign.

```
C        ************************
C        ** TO SEND A MESSAGE **
C        ************************
C
         CHARACTER LETTER*1
         INTEGER DAY, NUMBER
C
         READ*, DAY
         READ*, LETTER
C
         DO WHILE (LETTER.NE.'$')
C
              NUMBER = ICHAR(LETTER)
              NUMBER = NUMBER + DAY
              PRINT*, NUMBER
              READ*, LETTER
C
         ENDDO
C
         PRINT*,ICHAR('$') + DAY
C
        STOP
        END
```

```
C        **************************
C        ** TO DECODE A MESSAGE **
C        **************************
C
         CHARACTER LETTER*1
         INTEGER DAY, NUMBER
C
         READ*, DAY
         READ*, NUMBER
         NUMBER = NUMBER - DAY
C
         DO WHILE (CHAR(NUMBER).NE.'$')
C
              LETTER = CHAR(NUMBER)
              PRINT*, LETTER
              READ*, NUMBER
              NUMBER = NUMBER - DAY
C
         ENDDO
C
         STOP
         END
```

15.4 Character Processing During Compilation

To give you some idea of how involved character processing can get, consider the problems handled by the compiler as each of your FORTRAN statements is processed. A table of key words (READ, WRITE, GO TO, WHILE, and so on) is used to detect which particular instruction is being given. Once the type is determined, each must be broken down into its component parts.

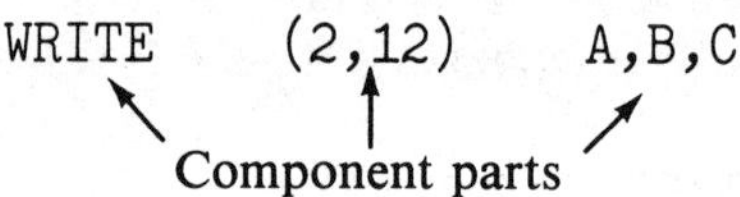

This may involve searching for an open parenthesis and a closed parenthesis and then extracting the two numbers inside.

The next programming examples suggest some simple operations that might be performed.

Programming Example
Where Does It End?

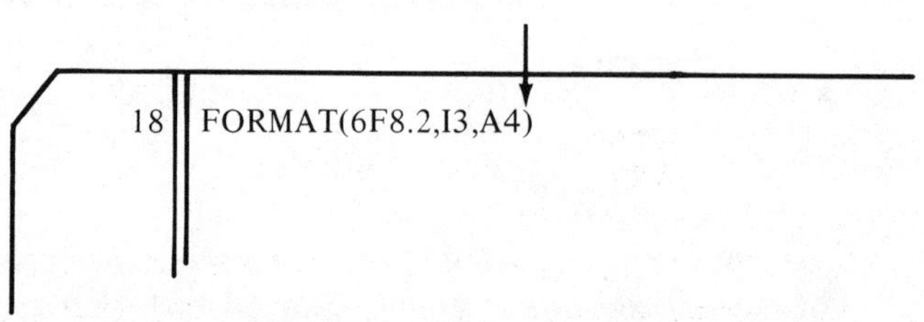

In the process of compiling a FORTRAN statement, assume that it is necessary to read a statement card (as if it were a data card) and determine in what column the statement ends. We can do this by storing the information on the card using an 80A1 code. We can then scan the card *backwards* until a nonblank character is detected.

Programming Example–Where Does It End? continued

```
C.............................................................
C..   PURPOSE - FIND IN WHAT COLUMN A STATEMENT ENDS.       ..
C.............................................................
C
C              - - - - - IMPORTANT VARIABLES - - - - -
C
C     --INPUT        ARRAY OF INPUT CHARACTERS (80A1)             --
C     --NSIZE        OUTPUT VALUE - WHERE STATEMENT ENDS          --
C     --BLANK        CHARACTER CONSTANT HOLDING A BLANK           --
C
        CHARACTER*1 INPUT(80), BLANK
        INTEGER NSIZE
C
        BLANK = ' '
C
C        READ 80 CHARACTERS FROM A CARD
C
        READ(5,10) INPUT
  10    FORMAT(80A1)
C
C        SEARCH STRING BACKWARDS
C
        DO 20 I = 80, 1, -1
C
        IF(INPUT(I).NE.BLANK) THEN
C
            NSIZE = I
            WRITE(2,15) NSIZE
  15        FORMAT(2X,'THIS STATEMENT ENDS IN COLUMN ',I3)
            STOP
C
        ENDIF
C
  20     CONTINUE
C
C           IF THIS DO LOOP SATISFIED CARD MUST HAVE BEEN BLANK
C
        WRITE(2,30)
  30    FORMAT(1X,'THE CARD WAS BLANK')
C
        STOP
        END
```

The character assignment statement loads memory location BLANK with the number code of a blank. The structured DO allows reverse subscript control from 80 backwards. The first time a nonblank element of the array INPUT is detected, a WRITE statement displays the location of the first nonblank character and the STOP statement (inside the loop) is executed. If no interruption of this loop takes place, the card must be blank. An appropriate output message is given and the program stops.

15.5 Substrings

We have performed operations that compare one character string to another. We have moved a string from one location to another. In each of these operations, the string is being processed as a whole; that is, as a separate unit. We now turn to considering operations that can be performed on individual parts of a string.

A string can be divided into parts called **substrings**. We can copy these substrings, we can test these substrings, and we can print or replace these substrings. Activities such as these are common in text processing operations.

When the name of a declared character variable is written by itself (as we have been doing) the reference is made to the whole string. It is possible to write the name of a character variable and then follow the name with two qualifiers enclosed in parentheses:

```
CHARACTER  WORD*15
    WORD(4:6)  ← Qualifiers
```

These qualifiers are very much like subscripts. They point to the substring we are interested in. The first qualifier tells at which position (in the original string) this substring starts. The second qualifier tells where the substring ends. If the original string has the value:

N	E	W	S	P	A	P	E	R		T	R	U	C	K

the substring being referenced will have the value:

S	P	A

Either substring qualifier can be an integer constant, an integer variable or an integer expression. If the first qualifier is omitted, the value 1 is assumed. If the second qualifier is omitted, the value of the string length is assumed. For example, the specification:

```
WORD(6:)
```

would be interpreted just as if the specification:

```
WORD(6:15)
```

had been written.

Programming Example
Locating a Substring

Assume a string called INPUT has a maximum of 72 characters. Assume further that the string INPUT holds a FORTRAN statement, such as:

```
10 READ (5,20) A, B, C
```

Write statements that will determine where in this string the word READ appears. Load an integer called FRONT with the starting position of the substring. Load an integer called BACK with the end position. If the word READ does not appear, load FRONT with the value 0. If the substring does appear, see if it starts and ends between columns 7 and 72.

Programming Example–Locating a Substring continued

```
      CHARACTER INPUT*72
      INTEGER I, FRONT, BACK
C
      READ*, INPUT
C
      DO 30 I = 1, 69
C
          IF(INPUT(I:I+3).EQ.'READ') THEN
C
              FRONT = I
              BACK = I + 3
              PRINT*, 'STRING STARTS AT ',FRONT
              PRINT*, 'STRING ENDS AT ',BACK
              IF(FRONT.GE.7.AND.BACK.LE.72)THEN
                  PRINT*,'IN PROPER POSITION'
              ELSE
                  PRINT*,'OUT OF POSITION'
              ENDIF
              STOP
C
          ENDIF
C
   30 CONTINUE
C
      FRONT = 0
      PRINT*, 'READ NOT DETECTED IN STRING', FRONT
C
      STOP
      END
```

15.6 INDEX Function

When dealing with substrings, we frequently need to search a character string for the appearance of a specific substring. (In the last example problem, we searched a character string called INPUT for the location of the substring READ.)

The function INDEX has been designed to perform this operation. It has, as you might expect, two arguments. The first is the name of the character string to be searched. The second argument defines the "target substring" (the string we are searching for).

INDEX (string, substring)

The function INDEX returns an integer number telling where in the string the target substring starts. If the value returned in INDEX were the value 5, for example, the target substring does appear in the string and its first appearance starts at character position 5 of the string.

Note: If the target substring does not appear in the string, INDEX will be assigned the value 0.

The INDEX function will now be shown in a program that suggests how a *text editor* works. The following program allows a user to type a line of text, like a line of a business letter or a line of a manuscript. After typing the line, the text editor should display the line so that any errors in the line can be detected. Assume, for example, when the line is displayed it looks like this:

As you can see the word SHOULD has been typed incorrectly. The text editor asks if any changes are desired? An answer of yes starts a process whereby:

1. A request is made to identify the incorrect word.
2. The program locates where in the string the faulty word is located.
3. A request is made for the desired substitution (for the correct word).
4. The faulty portion of the string, a substring, is redefined.

In the following program, INPUT will be used to hold the original line of text. The character variable ERROR will hold the incorrect word if any.

```
      CHARACTER INPUT*80, ERROR*5, NEW*5, RESPNS*3
C
      PRINT*,'PLEASE ENTER A LINE OF TEXT'
C
      READ*,INPUT
C
C     ....DISPLAY FOR POSSIBLE CORRECTION....
C
      PRINT*,INPUT
C
      PRINT*,'DO YOU WISH TO MAKE CORRECTIONS TO THIS LINE?'
      READ*,RESPNS
C
      DO WHILE (RESPNS.EQ.'YES')
C
         PRINT*,'PLEASE ENTER THE FAULTY WORD IN THE LINE.'
         READ*, ERROR
C
C                    ******************************************
C                    **FIND WHERE INCORRECT WORD IS LOCATED**
C                    ******************************************
C
  10     LOC = INDEX(INPUT,ERROR)
C
         PRINT*,'PLEASE ENTER THE CORRECT WORD'
C
C                    ******************************************
C                    ** MAKE DIRECT CHANGE TO STRING INPUT **
C                    ******************************************
C
  20     READ*,INPUT(LOC:LOC+4)
C
         PRINT*,INPUT
         PRINT*,' DO YOU WISH TO MAKE ANOTHER CHANGE?'
         READ*,RESPNS
C
      ENDDO
C
      STOP
      END
```

The interesting part of this program starts at statement 10. We use the function INDEX to locate at what character position the faulty word starts. Statement 20 is also important. It reads the correct spelling of the word, but more importantly it reads these characters *directly* into INPUT (the original line of text). Because the name following the command READ is a substring name (a substring of INPUT), that portion of INPUT starting at character position LOC and continuing to LOC + 4 will be redefined. Although this is a good example of the use of a substring name, you probably recognize that the program will only work if the number of characters in ERROR and NEW is exactly 5.

In order to generalize the program we must be prepared to replace any length substring ERROR with any other (and possibly different) length substring NEW. For example, assume the original line of text were typed as follows:

To correct this error, we have to reconstruct the string INPUT. We join together:

1. The first part of the string (the part up to the error).
2. A substring representing the correct spelling of the word SHOULD.
3. The last part of the string (the part after the error.)

If LOC and LENTH are known, part 1 is the substring INPUT(1:LOC-1), part 2 is the substring NEW, and part 3 is the substring INPUT(LOC+LENTH-1:)

One of the purposes of this section is to focus your attention on substrings and how to specify a substring name. Take a look at the two preceding substring names. Make sure you see the portions of the string INPUT these names point to.

The idea of joining together several substrings to form a new string is called **concatination**. Determining the length of a substring and the topic of concatination are the topics of the next section.

15.7 Concatination

In character manipulation, it is possible to join together one or more strings of characters to form a new string. This is called concatination and the concatination operator is a double slash (//). Consider the following simple examples:

```
NAME = 'MRS.' // FIRST // LAST
DATE = MONTH // DAY // '1984'
DOC = 'DR.' // NAME(12:24)
```

In each of the examples, a new character variable is formed by joining together specific character constants, variables, or substrings. The usefulness of this feature to solve our text editing problem of the previous section should be immediately obvious. The statement:

```
INPUT = INPUT(1:LOC-1) // 'SHOULD' // INPUT(LOC+LENTH-1:)
```

would cause the desired redefinition. The idea, however, of specifying the correct spelling of the word as a constant is not realistic. It was just done to show how concatination works.

To make the text editor work, we must increase the size of the string variables ERROR and NEW so that they can handle variable length words (not just the five-letter words of the previous solution). This presents a problem. When the error and the

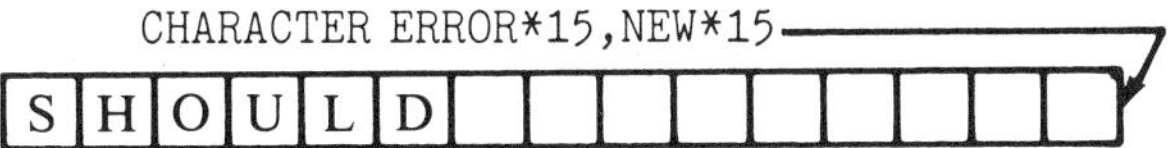

correction are read from input, they are positioned in their respective variables as shown, that is, left justification and blank fill of the remaining character positions. In our solution we need to know how many nonblank characters are in each string. This is the quantity LENTH in all our diagrams.

There is a system-supplied function called LEN, which receives a single input argument, the name of a character string variable, and returns the length of that variable:

LEN (character variable or expression)

If the argument of this function were NEW or ERROR, the value returned in LEN would be the number 15, the defined length of the character strings. Since this function is not providing the information we want, a new function called LENTH is written that searches the argument string backwards looking for the first nonblank character. This function solves all our problems.

```
      FUNCTION LENGTH (STRING)
C
      CHARACTER STRING*(*)
C
      LENGTH = LEN(STRING)
C
      DO WHILE (STRING(LENGTH:LENGTH).EQ.' ')
C
          LENGTH = LENGTH - 1
C
      ENDDO
C
      RETURN
      END
```

The function LENTH receives as its only argument the quantity STRING. A CHARACTER statement identifies STRING as a character variable. Since STRING is an argument, its size does not have to be specified as an integer constant, but rather we can use the method allowed with subscripted variables, namely specifying the size with an asterisk. The size is then the same as the argument used in the evoking of the function.

We then determine the length of STRING by using the system-supplied LEN function. This value is needed so we can scan the character string backwards. The WHILE statement examines a substring of STRING of size 1 to see if that substring is a blank. If the answer is yes, the value of LENTH is decreased by 1 and a check for a blank continues. When the first nonblank character is reached, the WHILE terminates and the function returns this important value.

We conclude this topic by using this function in an updated version of the text editor.

```
      CHARACTER INPUT*80, ERROR*15, NEW*15, RESPNS*3
      INTEGER SIZE1, SIZE2
C           ____________________________________
C     SIZE1 AND SIZE2 ARE THE NUMBER OF CHARACTERS IN
C           THE ERROR WORD AND THE CORRECT WORD
C
C           ____________________________________
      PRINT*,'PLEASE ENTER A LINE OF TEXT'
C
      READ*,INPUT
C
C     ....DISPLAY FOR POSSIBLE CORRECTION....
C
      PRINT*,INPUT
```

```
C
      PRINT*,'DO YOU WISH TO MAKE CORRECTIONS TO THIS LINE?'
      READ*,RESPNS
C
      DO WHILE (RESPNS.EQ.'YES')
C
           PRINT*,'PLEASE ENTER THE FAULTY WORD IN THE LINE.'
           READ*, ERROR
C
C                     ****************************************
C                     **FIND WHERE INCORRECT WORD IS LOCATED**
C                     ****************************************
C
   10      LOC = INDEX(INPUT,ERROR)
C
           PRINT*,'PLEASE ENTER THE CORRECT WORD'
C
C          HOW LARGE IS THE CORRECTION....SIZE OF ERROR
C
           SIZE1 = LENTH(ERROR)
C
C
   20      READ*,NEW

C
C          HOW LARGE IS THE NEW WORD.....SIZE OF CORRECT WORD
C
           SIZE2 = LENTH(NEW)
C
C          .....CONCATINATE THE THREE PARTS....
C
           INPUT=INPUT(1:LOC-1)//NEW(1:SIZE1)//INPUT(LOC+SIZE2-1:)
C
           PRINT*,INPUT
           PRINT*,' DO YOU WISH TO MAKE ANOTHER CHANGE?'
           READ*,RESPNS
C
      ENDDO
C
      STOP
      END
```

15.8 Evaluating an Integral

The remainder of this chapter shows several programming examples that fall in the area called **numerical analysis**. They attempt to show how the computer is used to solve relatively high-level mathematical problems. These examples will provide an opportunity to demonstrate some of the new structured programming constructs we have just presented.

Programming Example
Evaluate an Integral

Write a program to evaluate the integral shown:

$$\int_{x=1}^{x=10} (x^2 + 2x + 3)\,dx$$

The value of this integral is first found by what is called a trapezoidal approximation as shown in the following illustration. We then use a slightly more advanced method—Simpson's Rule—to gain a better approximation of the integral.

Programming Example–Evaluate an Integral continued

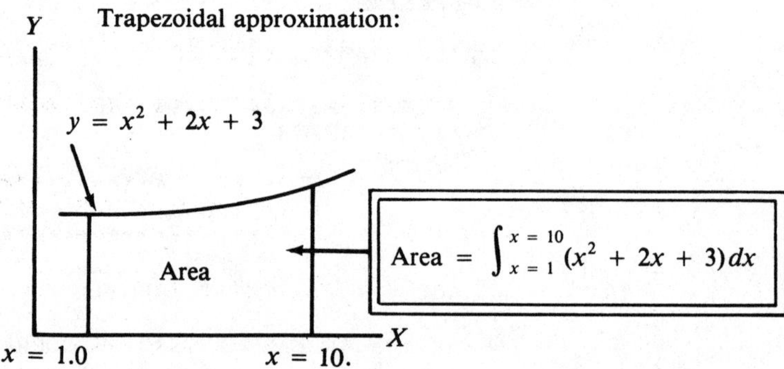

Step 1: Divide the total area under the curve into a number of small differential areas (thin strips, 0.1 inches wide).

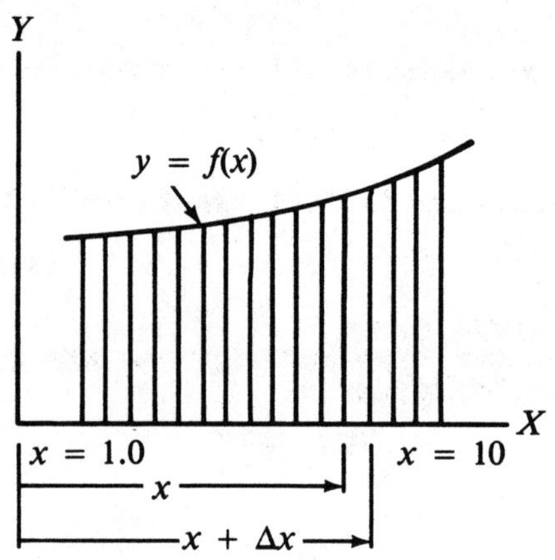

Step 2: The area of each strip can be approximated by the area of a trapezoid whose geometry is as shown in the accompanying figure. The values of y and $y + \Delta y$ are obtained by substituting x and $x + \Delta x$, respectively, into a given equation.

$y = f(x)$

$$\text{Width} = \Delta x = 0.1$$

$$\text{Average Height} = \frac{(y + \Delta y) + (y)}{2}$$

y $\quad$ $y + \Delta y$

Δx

Step 3: Compute the area of each differential strip.

$$\Delta \text{A} = \frac{[(y + \Delta y) + y]}{2} \Delta x$$

Differential area — Area of trapezoid

Step 4: Determine the sum of these differential areas.

$$\text{AREA} = \Sigma \Delta \text{A} = \int_{x=1}^{x=10} (x^2 + 2x + 3)dx$$

Programming Example–Evaluate an Integral continued

What is being accomplished by this solution is shown graphically in Figure 15.2. This is called the **trapezoidal method** because each of the differential areas is being evaluated as if it were a trapezoid.

Figure 15.2 How small areas are formed

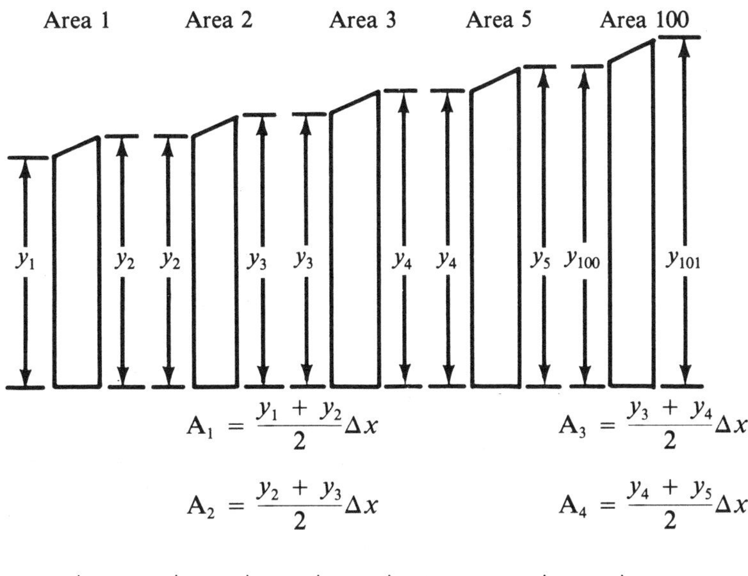

$$A_1 = \frac{y_1 + y_2}{2}\Delta x \qquad A_3 = \frac{y_3 + y_4}{2}\Delta x$$

$$A_2 = \frac{y_2 + y_3}{2}\Delta x \qquad A_4 = \frac{y_4 + y_5}{2}\Delta x$$

$$\text{Area} = A_1 + A_2 + A_3 + A_4 + \cdots + A_{99} + A_{100}$$

Eq. 15.1

$$\text{Area} = \frac{1}{2}(y_1 + 2y_2 + 2y_3 + 2y_4 + 2y_5 + \cdots + 2y_{99} + 2y_{101} + y_{101})\Delta x$$

```
C...........................................................
C..   PURPOSE - DETERMINE THE AREA UNDER A CURVE (INTEGRATE) ..
C..             BY THE CLASSIC TRAPEZOIDAL APPROXIMATION     ..
C..             METHOD.                                      ..
C...........................................................
C
C              - - - - - IMPORTANT VARIABLES - - - - -
C
C     --AREA        VALUE OF ACCUMULATED AREA                --
C     --X           VALUE OF INDEPENDENT VARIABLE            --
C     --DELTX       WIDTH OF EACH TRAPEZOID                  --
C     --YPLUS       VALUE OF Y AT X = X + DELTX              --
C-----------------------------------------------------------
C
C               ....INITIALIZATION SECTION....
C
        DATA AREA,DELTX / 0.0, 0.1 /
C
C               USE INDEX OF DO LOOP TO CONTROL X
C
        DO 10 X = 1.0, 10.0, 0.1
C
           Y = X**2 + 2.0*X + 3.0
           YPLUS = (X+DELTX)**2 + 2.0* (X+DELTX) + 3.0
           AREA = AREA + DELTX * (YPLUS + Y) / 2.0
C
  10    CONTINUE
C
C
        PRINT*,'  AREA =    ', AREA
C
        STOP
        END
```

Three major improvements should be made to this program to make it at all acceptable.

1. Remove reference to a specific equation. (The value of the equation is obtained by invoking a user-supplied function subprogram.)
2. Make the limits of integration variable (read from data).

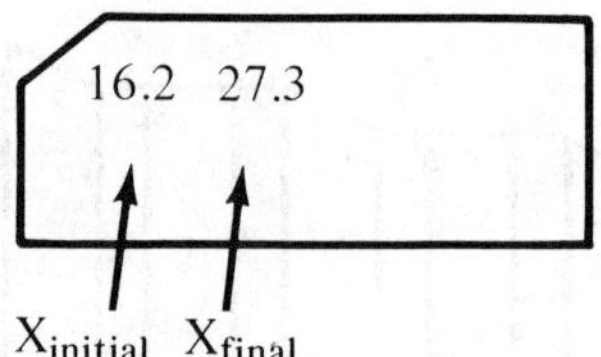

3. Use a more accurate approximation technique.

In the previous program, the equation being integrated was approximated by a series of straight lines (first order equations.) If the curve (equation) is of second or higher order, an inaccuracy occurs as suggested in Figure 15.3. This error can be reduced by connecting any two points with a second order curve (a parabola) instead of a straight line. This reduces the approximation error and involves the concept of using a point upstream or downstream of the specific differential area to define the correct parabola to use. This is suggested in Figure 15.4 and when worked out mathematically requires the evaluation of an equation only slightly more complicated than the one used before (Eq. 15.1).

$$\text{Area} = \frac{\Delta x}{3}(y_1 + 4y_2 + 2y_3 + 4y_4 + \cdots + 2y_{99} + 4y_{100} + y_{101}) \quad \textbf{Eq. 15.2}$$

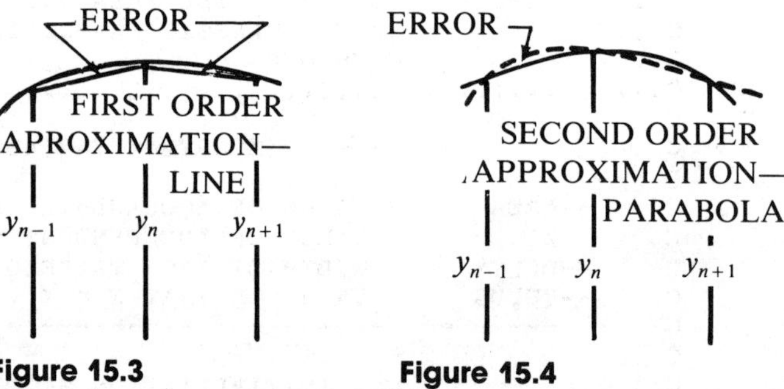

Figure 15.3 **Figure 15.4**

This method of approximation is called **Simpson's Rule**. The procedure is:

1. READ the data record defining the limits of integration $X_{initial}$ and X_{final}.
2. Divide this interval into 100 strips of equal width (ΔX). (See Figure 15.5.)
3. Define an array called Y consisting of 101 elements by invoking the user-supplied program 101 times.
4. Use this array as directed by Eq. 15.2 to determine the desired AREA (integral).

One of the complications in Eq. 15.2 is that all the even subscripted elements of Y should be multiplied by 4 and all the odd terms (except the first and last) should be multiplied by 2.

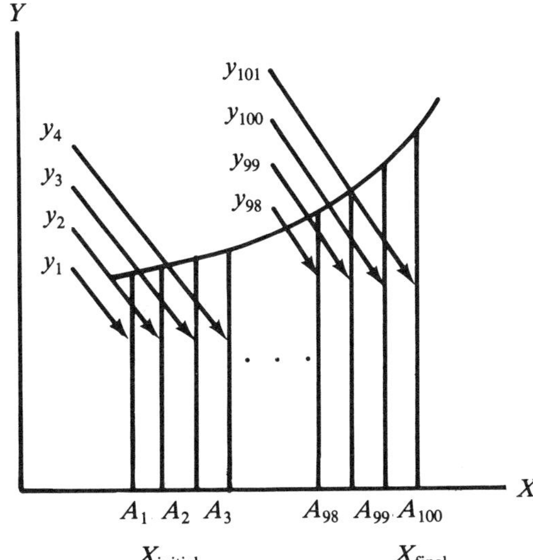

Figure 15.5 Dividing the interval

```
C..............................................................
C..   PURPOSE - WRITE A MORE GENERAL INTEGRATION PROGRAM     ..
C..             USING SIMPSONS'S RULE OF APPROXIMATION.      ..
C..............................................................
C
C               - - - - - IMPORTANT VARIABLES - - - - -
C
C     -- XINTL     INTITIAL LIMIT OF INTEGRATION             --
C     -- XFINL     FINAL LIMIT OF INTEGRATION                --
C     -- DELTX     WIDTH OF DIFFERENTIAL AREAS               --
C     -- EQ        USER SUPPLIED (EXTERNAL) FUNCTION         --
C                  SUB PROGRAM DEFINING THE FUNCTION.        --
C     -- Y         ARRAY OF 101 ELEMENTS REPRESENTING THE    --
C                  EQUATION IN DIGITAL FORM.                 --
C     -- ODD       ACCUMULATOR OF MAJORITY OF ODD TERMS      --
C     -- EVEN      ACCUMULATOR OF MAJORITY OF EVEN TERMS     --
C     -- AREA      VALUE OF INTEGRAL
C
      DIMENSION Y(101)
C
      EXTERNAL EQ
C
C               DETERMINE LIMITS OF INTEGRATION.
C
      READ*, XINTL, XFINL
C
C               DEFINE ARRAY OF Y VALUES
C
      DELTX = (XFINL - FINTL) / 100.0
      X = XINTL
C
      DO 20 I = 1, 101
C
         Y(I) = EQ(X)
         X = X + DELTX
C
   20 CONTINUE
C
C     ACCUMULATE THE MAJORITY OF EVEN SUBSCRIPTED Y ELEMENTS
C
      EVEN = 0.0
C
      DO 30 I = 2, 100,2
C
         EVEN = EVEN + Y(I)
C
   30 CONTINUE
```

```
C
C
C
C         ACCUMULATE THE MAJORITY OF ODD SUBSCRIPTED Y ELEMENTS
C
          ODD = 0.0
C
          DO 40 I = 3, 99, 2
C
             ODD = ODD + Y(I)
C
   40     CONTINUE
C
C                 ADD IN THE FIRST AND LAST TERMS
C                 (USE PROPER WEIGHTING FACTORS)
C
          AREA = DELTX/3.0*(Y(1)+4.0*EVEN+2.0*ODD+Y(101))
C
C
          PRINT*, '      AREA =     ', AREA
C
          STOP
          END
C
```

Each equation to be integrated is placed inside the FUNCTION subprogram (supplied by the user) as suggested in the following.

```
C.........................................................
C..    PURPOSE - USER SUPPLIED SUBPROGRAM DEFINING THE    ..
C..              EQUATION THAT IS TO BE INTEGRATED        ..
C.........................................................
C
          FUNCTION EQ(X)
C
          EQ = X**2 + 2.0*X + 3.0
C
          RETURN
          END
```

15.9 Simulation: Bouncing Ball

There is a large area of application in which the computer is made to simulate some complex model or situation. As an example of this usage, assume we are asked to determine under what conditions a ball fired into the chamber shown in Figure 15.6 will fall through the hole in the floor positioned as shown. A ball enters a chamber with an initial velocity $V_0 = 10.0$ ft./sec. acting at angle $\theta = 45°$.

Figure 15.6 Bouncing ball problem

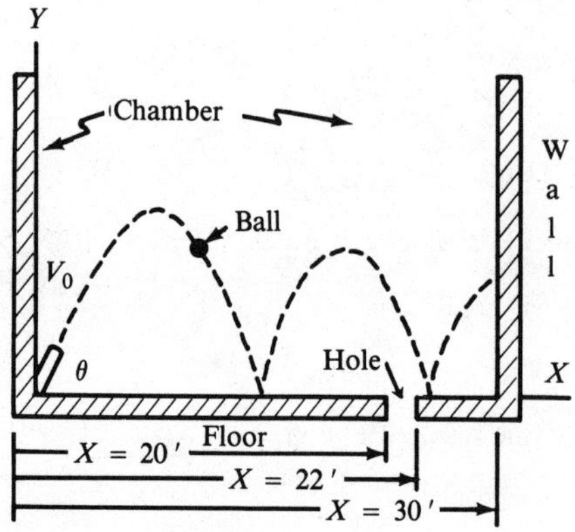

Interesting parts of this solution are:

1. To determine the equation of motion of the ball.
2. To determine when the ball is about to bounce off the floor.
3. To either redirect the motion of the ball if it does not hit the hole or signal a successful traverse if the ball does reach the hole.

Equations of Motion for Parts 1 and 2

Displacement in *X* Direction	**Displacement in *Y* Direction**
$X = V_{X_0} \cdot t$ (constant velocity)	$Y = V_{Y_0} \cdot t - \frac{1}{2} gt^2$ (constant acceleration)

where $V_{X_0} = V_0 \cos \theta$ and $V_{Y_0} = V_0 \sin \theta$

Part 1

Write a program to determine the *X* and *Y* coordinates of the ball at time increments of 0.01 seconds until the ball impacts with the floor for the first time.

First the initial velocity and entry angle of the ball (VZERO and ANGLE) are read from data. Then the X and Y components of this velocity are computed. All that remains now is to evaluate the displacement equation over and over again for various values of time. A memory location called TIME is created and given an initial value of 0.01. The first X and Y location values are computed. Memory location TIME is indexed by 0.01 and another X and Y value computed. This process continues as long as the ball is still in the air (Y has a positive value). When Y becomes zero or negative, looping is interrupted and control passes to the WRITE statements that give the time and location of this first bounce.

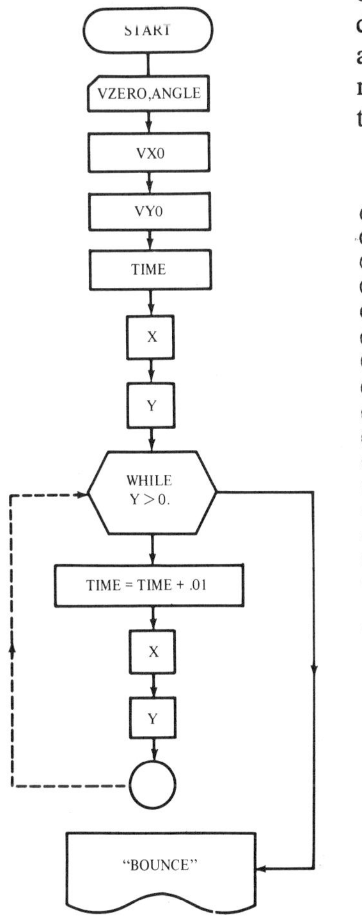


```
C.................................................................
C..   PURPOSE - SIMULATE THE MOTION OF A BOUNCING BALL.         ..
C.................................................................
C
C             - - - - - IMPORTANT VARIABLES - - - - -
C
C     -- VZERO      INITIAL VELOCITY OF THE BALL                 --
C     -- ANGLE      ANGLE OF ENTRY                               --
C     -- VXO        X COMPONENT OF INITIAL VELOCITY              --
C     -- X          X POSITION OF THE BALL                       --
C     -- VYO        Y COMPONENT OF INITIAL VELOCITY              --
C
C     -- TIME       TIME CLOCK
C
C        DETERMINE X AND Y VELOCITY COMPONENTS
C
         READ*, VZERO, ANGLE
C
         VXO = VZERO * COS(ANGLE / 57.3)
         VYO = VZERO * SIN(ANGLE / 57.3)
C
C            SET TIME CLOCK...COMPUTE INITIAL X AND Y VALUES
C
         TIME = 0.01
C
         X = VXO * TIME
         Y = VYO * TIME - 32.2 / 2.0 * TIME ** 2
C
C                ....ESTABLISH COMPUTATIONAL LOOP....
```

```
C
      DO WHILE (Y.GT.0.0)
C
         TIME = TIME + 0.01
         X = VX0 * TIME
         Y = VY0 * TIME - 32 / 2.0 * TIME ** 2
C
      ENDDO
C
C              ....BALL HAS HIT THE FLOOR....
C
      PRINT*, 'BALL HAS HIT THE FLOOR. TIME =', TIME
C
      PRINT*, 'LOCATION IS X = ', X,'Y = ', Y
C
C
C
      STOP
      END
```

Part 2

Expand the program to determine if the ball falls through the hole in the floor—(assume an infinitely small ball). To improve accuracy, index time at a *slower* rate (0.001 sec.) when the ball is close to impact ($Y \leq 1$ ft).

Two additional requirements have been imposed by the Part 2 solution. To obtain a more accurate solution when impact is imminent, the time clock (TIME) should be incremented at a slower rate, 0.001 seconds, when the ball is less than one foot off the floor. Therefore, these statements will be incorporated into the solution.

```
IF(Y.GT.1.0) THEN
    TIME=TIME+0.01
ELSE
    TIME=TIME+0.001
ENDIF
```

We must also detect if the ball has by chance fallen into the hole.

```
IF(X.GE.20.0.AND.X.LE.22.0) THEN
    PRINT*, 'BALL WENT IN THE HOLE, TIME=' TIME
ELSE
   PRINT*, 'JUST MAKING A BOUNCE, TIME=' TIME
ENDIF
```

The flowchart and FORTRAN code are updated to incoporate these features.

```
C...........................................................
C..   PART II   UPDATE   -  PROCESSING A BOUNCE           ..
C...........................................................
C
C     .......NEW COMPUTATIONAL LOOP.........
C
      DO WHILE (Y.GT.0.0)
C
         IF (Y.GT.1.0) THEN
C
            TIME = TIME + 0.01
C
         ELSE
C
            TIME = TIME + 0.001
C
```

```
            ENDIF
C
            X = VXO * TIME
            Y = VYO * TIME - 32.2 / 2.0 * TIME ** 2
C
         ENDDO
C
C
C              ...BALL HAS REACHED THE FLOOR...
C
C           ...TEST FOR LOCATION OF BALL WITH RESPECT TO HOLE...
C
         IF(X.GE.20.0.AND.X.LE.22.0) THEN
C
            PRINT*,  'BALL HAS GONE INTO THE HOLE, TIME = ', TIME
C
            STOP
C
         ELSE
C
            PRINT* ,'BALL BOUNCED. TIME = ', TIME
            PRINT*, 'LOCATION X= ', X,'Y= ', Y
C
         ENDIF
C
         STOP
         END
```

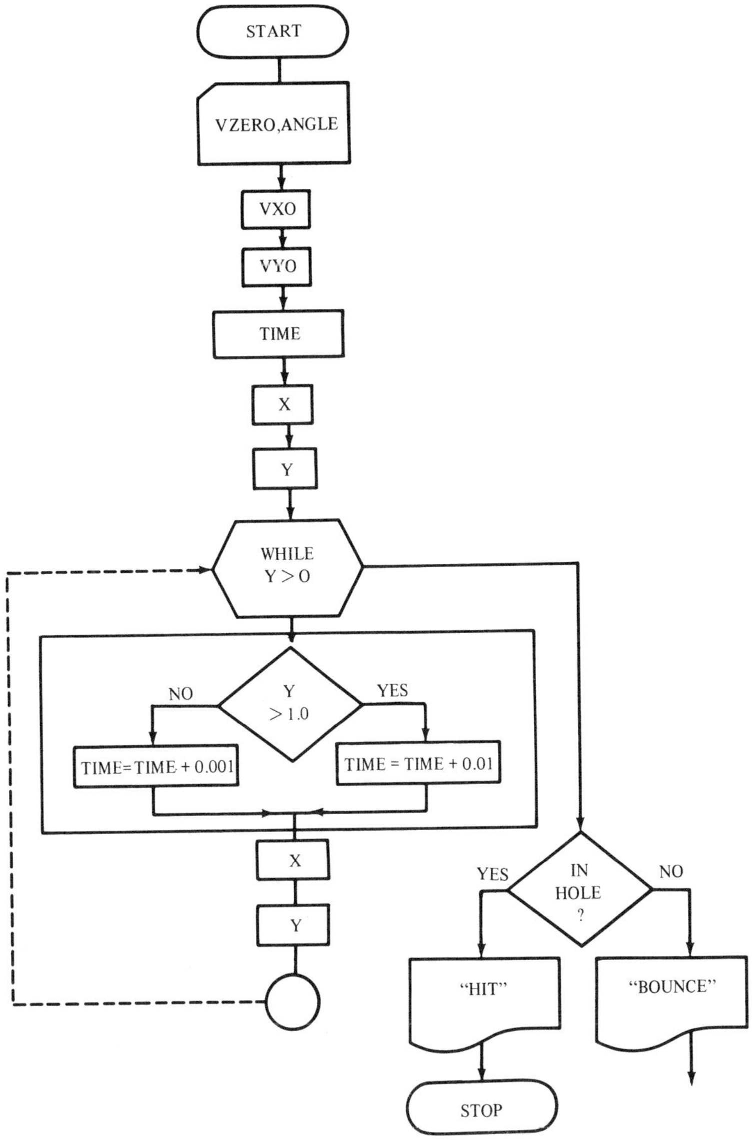

START
VZERO,ANGLE
VXO
VYO
TIME
X
Y
WHILE Y > 0
NO
Y > 1.0
YES
TIME=TIME + 0.001
TIME = TIME + 0.01
X
Y
YES
IN HOLE ?
NO
"HIT"
"BOUNCE"
STOP

Part 3

If the ball does not pass through the hole, our program must account for a bounce (impact). The major adjustments are as follows:

1. If the floor is assumed to be frictionless, the horizontal velocity is unaffected by impact. Displacement computations continue as before.
2. The vertical velocity component must be reversed and decreased in magnitude by a value called the **coefficient of restitution.**

This part of the solution demonstrates a simple but very important method of analysis. It is called the **method of superposition.** The complex motion of this ball can be treated as one simple motion superimposed on another simple motion. The X motion is one of constant velocity. The computation of this motion remains the same throughout the problem.

Figure 15.7 Analysis of motion

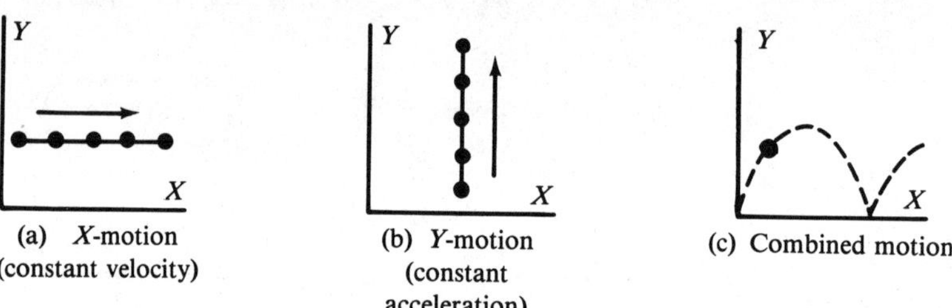

(a) X-motion (constant velocity) (b) Y-motion (constant acceleration) (c) Combined motion

We can now concentrate on the remaining, more complex Y motion. At each impact or bounce we must:

1. Compute the Y component of velocity prior to impact.

   $V_Y = V_{Y_0} - \text{at}$

2. Change the sign (direction) of the velocity and decrease its magnitude (by 85% – coefficient of restitution.)

   $V_{Y_0} = -.85 \cdot V_Y$

3. Set a new time clock (TNEW) back to zero on each impact (as if a new problem were starting all over again).

   TNEW = 0.0

   The statements to accomplish this are:

```
C..........RECOMPUTE VELOCITY DUE TO IMPACT.............
C                VELOCITY PRIOR TO IMPACT
      VY = VYO - 32.2 * TNEW
C                REVERSE AND DIMINISH VELOCITY
      VYO = -0.85 * VY
C                RESET TIME CLOCK
      TNEW = 0.0
```

These statements are executed each time a bounce occurs. This allows for a continuous solution until the ball hits the far wall.

The problem must now use two time clocks. `TIME` is used for the *X*-motion calculations and runs continuously. `TNEW` is for the *Y*-motion calculations and is reset to zero each time a bounce takes place.

The complete program is now presented.

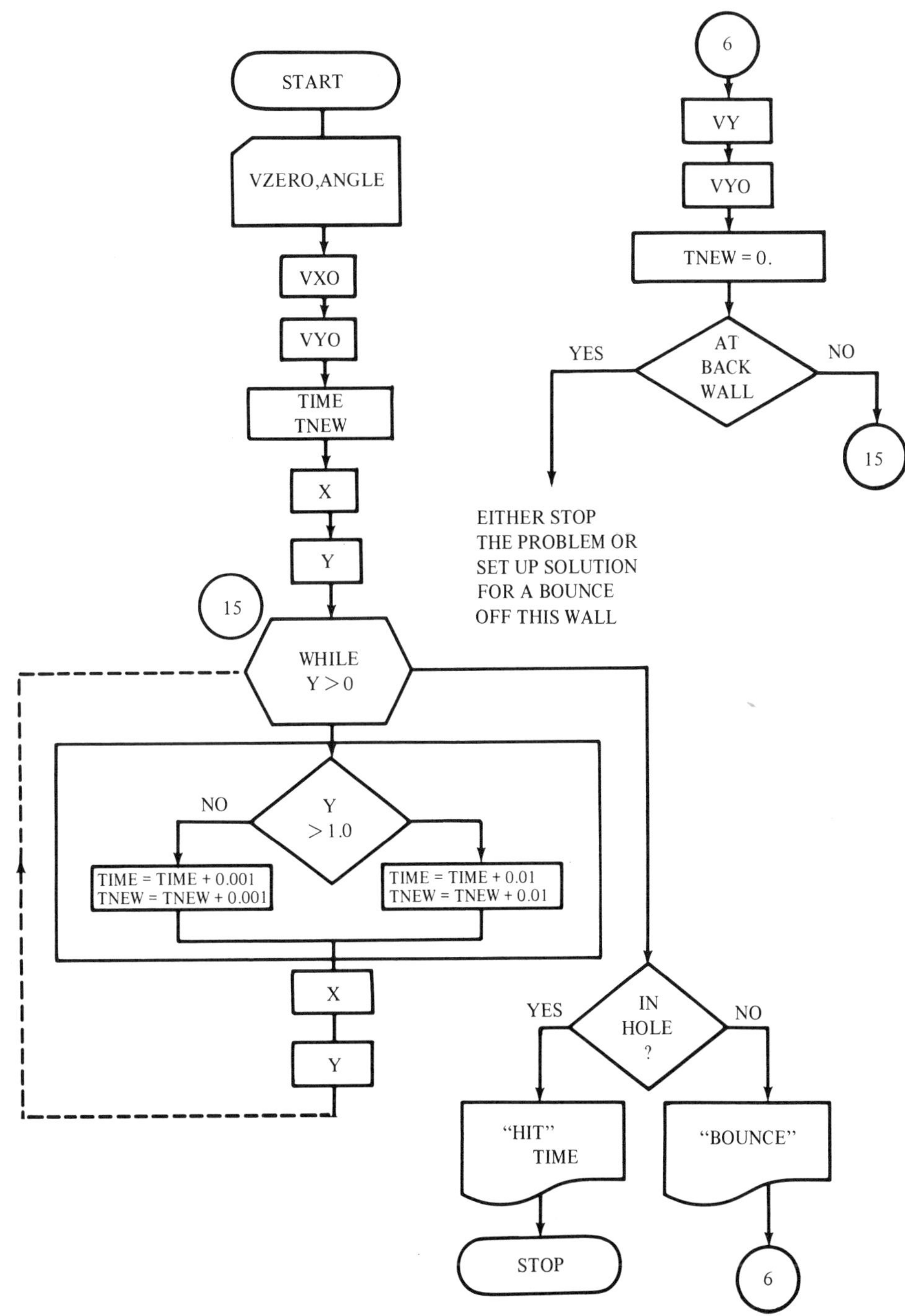

```
C.......................................................................
C..   PURPOSE - PART III SOLUTION.....REDEFINITION OF                ..
C..             VELOCITIES WHEN BALL IMPACTS WITH FLOOR.              ..
C.......................................................................
C
C              - - - - - IMPORTANT VARIABLES - - - - -
C
C     -- TNEW        NEW TIME CLOCK FOR Y MOTION                  --
C     -- VY          VELOCITY JUST PRIOR TO ANY IMPACT WITH --
C                    FLOOR.                                           --
C
C             COMPUTE X AND Y COMPONENTS OF VELOCITY
C
      READ*, VZERO, ANGLE
C
      VX0 = VZERO * COS(ANGLE / 57.3)
      VY0 = VZERO * SIN(ANGLE / 57.3)
C
C             SET BOTH TIME CLOCKS
C
      TIME = 0.01
      TNEW = 0.01
C
C             COMPUTE INITIAL X AND Y LOCATIONS
C
      X = VX0 * TIME
      Y = VY0 * TNEW - 32.2/2.0*TNEW**2
C
C             SET UP COMPUTATIONAL LOOP
C
   15 DO WHILE (Y.GT.0.0)
C
C             NEAR IMPACT
C
         IF (Y.GT.1.0) THEN
            TIME = TIME + 0.01
            TNEW = TNEW + 0.01
         ELSE
            TIME = TIME + 0.001
            TNEW = TNEW + 0.001
         ENDIF
C
C             COMPUTE BALL LOCATION
C
         X = VX0 * TIME
         Y = VY0 * TNEW - 32.2/2.0*TNEW**2
C
      ENDDO
C
C             BALL HAS REACHED THE FLOOR
C
      IF (X.GE.20.0.AND.X.LE.22.0) THEN
C
         PRINT*, 'BALL HAS GONE INTO THE HOLE, TIME = ', TIME
C
         STOP
C
      ELSE
C
C             RECOMPUTE Y MOTION DUE TO IMPACT
C             VELOCITY JUST PRIOR TO IMPACT
C
         VY = VY0 - 32.2 * TNEW
C
C             REVERSE AND DIMINISH VELOCITY
C
         VY0 = 0.85 * VY
C
C             RESET TIME CLOCK FOR Y MOTION
C
         TNEW = 0.0
```

```
C
C          HAS BALL REACHED FAR WALL YET
C
       IF (X.GT.30.0) THEN
C
          PRINT* ,'BALL AT BACK WALL. TIME = ', TIME
C
          STOP
C
       ELSE
C
          GO TO 15
C
          ENDIF
C
      ENDIF
C
     STOP
     END
```

15.10 Solving Simultaneous Equations

The solution of simultaneous equations is another example of numerical methods. It provides a good opportunity to review operations dealing with two-dimensional arrays. We will start by representing the general form of equations in the following way:

$$
\begin{aligned}
a_{11}x_1 + a_{12}x_2 + a_{13}x_3 + \cdots + a_{1n}x_n &= c_1 \\
a_{21}x_1 + a_{22}x_2 + a_{23}x_3 + \cdots + a_{2n}x_n &= c_2 \\
a_{31}x_1 + a_{32}x_2 + a_{33}x_3 + \cdots + a_{3n}x_n &= c_3 \\
\cdots\cdots\cdots\cdots\cdots\cdots\cdots\cdots\cdots \\
a_{n1}x_1 + a_{n2}x_2 + a_{n3}x_3 + \cdots + a_{nn}x_n &= c_n
\end{aligned}
\qquad \textbf{Eq. 15.3}
$$

Coefficients preceding the terms in (X) were stored as a two-dimensional array called A. The right-hand coefficients are stored as a one-dimensional array called C.

$$
[A] = \begin{bmatrix} a_{11}a_{12}a_{13} \ldots a_{1n} \\ a_{21}a_{22}a_{23} \ldots a_{2n} \\ a_{31}a_{32}a_{33} \ldots a_{3n} \\ \cdots\cdots\cdots \\ \\ a_{n1}a_{n2}a_{n3} \ldots a_{nn} \end{bmatrix} \qquad [C] = \begin{bmatrix} c_1 \\ c_2 \\ c_3 \\ \cdot \\ \cdot \\ \cdot \\ c_n \end{bmatrix}
$$

The method of solving these equations will be easier to follow if we deal with a specific set of equations, namely the set introduced in Chapter 9.

Equation 1 $9.0x_1 + 6.5x_2 + 3.5x_3 = 27.75$
Equation 2 $4.5x_1 + 2.2x_2 + 1.5x_3 = 10.50$
Equation 3 $6.7x_1 + 3.0x_2 + 1.0x_3 = 12.25$

Step 1: First Reduction

This solution starts by eliminating x_1 from all equations except equation 1. We obtain a new equation 2 in which the coefficient preceding x_1 is zero as follows:

1. Divide each term in equation 1 by 9.0 and then multiply by 4.5.

2. Subtract each of these terms from the corresponding term in equation 2, to get the new equation 2 as shown here:

$$9.0x_1 + 6.5x_2 + 3.5x_3 = 27.75 \qquad \text{Equation 1}$$

$$4.5x_1 + 2.2x_2 + 1.5x_3 = 10.50 \qquad \text{Equation 2}$$

$$\left(\frac{4.5}{9.0}\right) \rightarrow 4.5x_1 + 3.25x_2 + 1.75x_3 = 13.875$$

$$0.0x_1 - 1.05x_2 - 0.25x_3 = -3.37 \qquad \text{New Equation 2}$$

Subtraction

Write statements that will accomplish steps 1 and 2. In the process, redefine elements of array A and array C associated with equation 2, but not those associated with equation 1.

```
C.......................................................................
C..   PURPOSE - OBTAIN A NEW EQUATION  NO. 2                          ..
C.......................................................................
C
      FACTOR = 4.5 / 9.0
C
C              .....LOOP ENTRY POINT.....
C
      DO 5 I = 1, 3, 1
C
         TERM = FACTOR * A(1,I)
         A(2,I) = A(2,I) - TERM
C
    5 CONTINUE
C
C              ....REDEFINE ELEMENT OF C....
C
      TERM = FACTOR * C(1)
      C(2) = C(2) - TERM
C
```

We can eliminate x_1 from equation 3 by an almost identical process.

$$9.0x_1 + 6.5x_2 + 3.5x_3 = 27.75 \qquad \text{Equation 1}$$

$$6.7x_1 + 3.0x_2 + 1.0x_3 = 12.50 \qquad \text{Equation 3}$$

$$\left(\frac{6.7}{9.0}\right) \rightarrow 6.7x_1 + 4.8x_2 + 2.6x_3 = 20.66$$

$$0.0x_1 - 1.8x_2 - 1.6x_3 = -8.16 \qquad \text{New Equation 3}$$

This time terms in equation 1 are multiplied by 6.7/9.0 and then subtracted from equation 3.

Write statements that will define a new equation 3, but deal with the general equation 3 (not the specific equation).

Block 1 appears as follows:

```
C.............................................................
C..   PURPOSE - OBTAIN A NEW EQUATION NO. 3 (GENERAL)        ..
C.............................................................
C
         FACTOR = A(1,3) / A(1,1)
C
C                ......LOOP ENTRY POINT.....
C
         DO 10 I = 1, NOEQS, 1
C
            TERM = FACTOR * A(1,I)
            A(3,I) = A(3,I) - TERM
C
   10    CONTINUE
C
C                ....REDEFINE ELEMENT OF C.....
C
         TERM = FACTOR * C(1)
         C(3) = C(3) - TERM
```

Note that the multiplication factor is expressed in general terms and is equal to the coefficient of x_1 in the equation we are redefining divided by the coefficient of x_1 in equation 1. The only other difference is in the number of equations in the set. The variable NOEQS replaces the constant 3.

Repeating the code just written (block 1) for all the remaining equations will cause a redefinition of almost the whole array A and array C as follows:

$$
\begin{aligned}
a_{11}x_1 + a_{12}x_2 + a_{13}x_3 + \cdots + a_{1n}X_n &= c_1 \\
0 + a'_{22}x_2 + a'_{23}x_3 + \cdots + a'_{2n}x_n &= c'_2 \\
0 + a'_{32}x_2 + a'_{33}x_3 + \cdots + a'_{3n}x_n &= c'_3 \\
\cdots\cdots\cdots\cdots\cdots\cdots\cdots\cdots \\
0 + a'_{n2}x_2 + a'_{n3}x_3 + \cdots + a'_{nn}x_n &= c'_n
\end{aligned}
\qquad \textbf{Eq. 15.4}
$$

The FORTRAN code used to accomplish the large volume of computations involved is remarkably concise:

```
C.............................................................
C..   PURPOSE - ELIMINATE X1 FROM ALL EQUATIONS EXCEPT       ..
C..             EQUATION ONE.                                ..
C.............................................................
C
C
C                           REPEAT PREVIOUS LOGIC
C
C
         DO 20 COUNT = 2, NOEQS, 1
C
C
            FACTOR = A(1,COUNT) / A(1,1)
C
C                ....INNER LOOP ENTRY POINT....
C
            DO 10 I = 1, NOEQS
C
               TERM = FACTOR * A(1,I)
               A(COUNT,I) = A(COUNT,I) - TERM
C
   10       CONTINUE
C
C                ....REDEFINE ELEMENT OF C....
C
            C(COUNT) = C(COUNT) - TERM
C
   20    CONTINUE
```

This new block of code has very efficiently eliminated x_1 from all equations (except equation 1) by setting the original code in a simple DO loop.

Step 2: Further Reduction

The next move is to eliminate x_2 in all equations except equation 2, then eliminate x_3 from all equations except equation 3, and so on. All this will be accomplished by setting the code already written inside another DO loop. The end result will redefine arrays A and C as follows:

$$\begin{array}{ccccccc} a''_{11}x_1 + & 0 + & 0 + 0 + \cdots + & 0 & = c''_1 \\ 0 + & a''_{22}x_2 + & 0 + 0 + \cdots + & 0 & = c''_2 \\ 0 + & 0 + & a''_{33}x_3 + 0 + \cdots + & 0 & = c''_3 \\ \cdots & \cdots & \cdots & \cdots & \cdots \\ 0 + & 0 + & 0 + 0 + \cdots + & a''_{nn}x_n & = c \end{array} \qquad \text{Eq. 15.5}$$

Step 3: Back Substitution

In this form all elements of A except those on the main diagonal are zero, which is convenient because any value of x can then be determined by simple division.

$$x_1 = \frac{c''_1}{a''_{11}}; \quad x_2 = \frac{c''_2}{a_{22}}; \quad x_3 = \frac{c''_3}{a''_{33}}; \quad \ldots; \quad x_n = \frac{c''_n}{a''_{nn}}$$

These solution values would be obtained by the following statements:

```
C
C                BACK SUBSTITUTION FOR THE FINAL ANSWERS
C
      DO 40 I = 1, NOEQS, 1
C
         X(I) = C(I) / A(I,I)
C
         PRINT*, X(I)
C
   40 CONTINUE
C
      STOP
      END
```

Implementing Step 2

To accomplish the logic in step 2, we start by letting equation 2 assume the dominant role previously played by equation 1. That is, equation 2 is multiplied by various factors so that, when subtracted from the other equations (1, 3, 4, 5, and so on), a new equation will be formed in which x_2 has been eliminated. x_2 is to be retained in equation 2 only. Equation 2 becomes what is called the **pivot equation.**

For example, to eliminate x_2 from equation 1, the multiplication factor is:

$$\frac{a_{12}}{a_{22}}$$

To eliminate x_2 from equation 3, the factor is:

$$\frac{a'_{32}}{a'_{22}}$$

In the program segment that follows, an integer variable called PIVOT is used to identify which equation is the PIVOT equation. When PIVOT is 1, equation 1 dominates the mathematics to eliminate x_1. When PIVOT is 2, equation 2 dominates and x_2 is being eliminated.

This programming is obviously getting rather complex. Without extensive documentation, it would be almost impossible to follow.

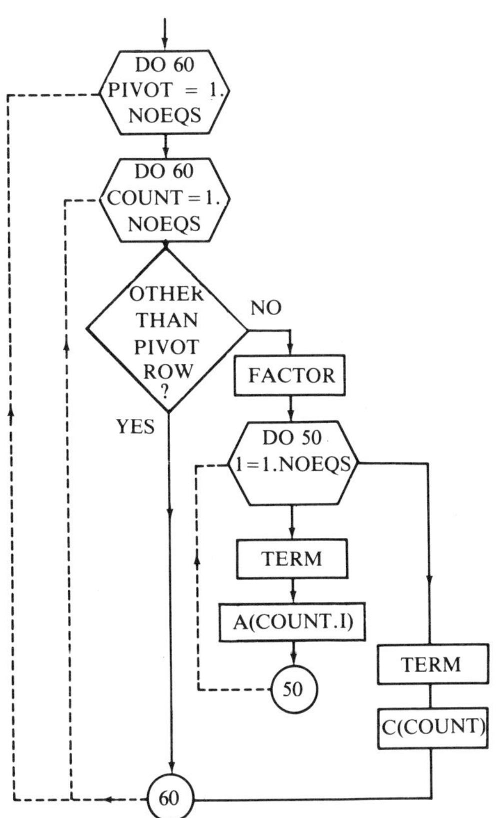


```
C...............................................................
C..   PURPOSE - SOLVE A SET OF LINEAR SIMULTANEOUS EQUATIONS..
C...............................................................
C
C            - - - - - IMPORTANT VARIABLES - - - - -
C
C     -- PIVOT      AN INTEGER TELLING WHICH EQUATION IS    --
C     --            THE PIVOT EQUATION                      --
C
      INTEGER PIVOT
C
C               SET UP OUTER MOST LOOP
C               (INDEX NAME IS PIVOT)
C
      DO 60 PIVOT = 1, NOEQS
C
C         FOR EACH PIVOT EQUATION WE MUST PROCESS ALL OTHER
C         EQUATIONS EXCEPT THE PIVOT EQUATION TO ELIMINATE
C         X(PIVOT) FROM EACH OF THESE EQUATIONS.
C
            DO 60 COUNT = 1, NOEQS
C
C         WE ARE NOW AT THE INDIVIDUAL EQUATION LEVEL
C         AND MUST ASK THE QUESTION, ' DOES COUNT EQUAL
C         PIVOT' IF YES - DO NOT REDUCE THIS EQUATION
C                IF NO  - REDUCE THIS EQUATION
```

```
C
                  IF (COUNT.NE.PIVOT) THEN
C
                     FACTOR = A(COUNT,PIVOT)/A(PIVOT,PIVOT)
C
                     DO 50 I = 1, NOEQS
C
C           WE ARE NOW AT THE LEVEL OF MODIFYING
C           INDIVIDUAL TERMS IN THE EQUATION.
C
                        TERM = FACTOR * A(PIVOT,I)
                        A(COUNT,I) = A(COUNT,I) - TERM
C
   50                CONTINUE
C
                        TERM = FACTOR * C(PIVOT)
                        C(COUNT,I) = C(COUNT,I) - TERM
C
   60      CONTINUE
C
C              BACK SUBSTITUTION SECTION
C
           DO 80 I = 1, NOEQS
C
              X(I) = C(I) / A(I,I)
              PRINT*, X(I)
C
   80      CONTINUE
C
C.........................................................................
C...   CAUTION - THIS SOLUTION IS STILL NOT COMPLETE IN THAT ..
C..               IT DOES NOT CHECK FOR THE CONDITION OF       ..
C..               A(PIVOT,PIVOT) BEING EQUAL TO  ZERO.  WHEN   ..
C..               THIS  CONDITION OCCURS A ROW SWAP IS         ..
C..               NECESSARY.                                   ..
C.........................................................................
C
           STOP
           END
```

No mention has been made of possible pitfalls in this solution. One very obvious one is the possibility of division by zero (or near zero) values. If any of the pivot terms (a_{11}, a'_{22}, a''_{23}) are zero, this solution "blows up." To avoid this, we might test any pivot term for a near zero value and accomplish an equation interchange if one is detected.

Another problem is the number of operations required as the number of equations increases. These and other aspects of the solution would be covered in a course called "*Numerical Analysis.*"

15.11 Curve Fitting

In this final case study, we will form a set of simultaneous equations the solution of which defines an equation that best represents a series of data points. This is called **curve fitting.**

The world of science and engineering is as much experimental in nature as it is analytic. It is often difficult to theoretically derive exact mathematical models (sets of equations) that correctly describe each and every situation or problem that needs solving. It is often necessary to resort to empirical methods and techniques. The design of a space capsule, for example, involves new and complex aerodynamic, structural, and thermodynamic relationships. It is fair to say that the state of the art in these fields does not provide exact theory to solve each new problem that occurs. In these situations, laboratory experimentation and test flights become an important aspect of the total design effort. This case study shows how the multiplicity of data values (that are typical of this empirical approach) can be reduced to a more convenient form, namely reduced to an equation. This is called *curve fitting* and concentrates on generating equations (curves) that best represent the experimentally obtained data. This is an exceptionally powerful analytic tool.

An experiment is conducted (see Figure 15.8) and M data points are established. The X and Y coordinates of each point are recorded on a data card forming the data deck shown.

Figure 15.8 Experimentally obtained data

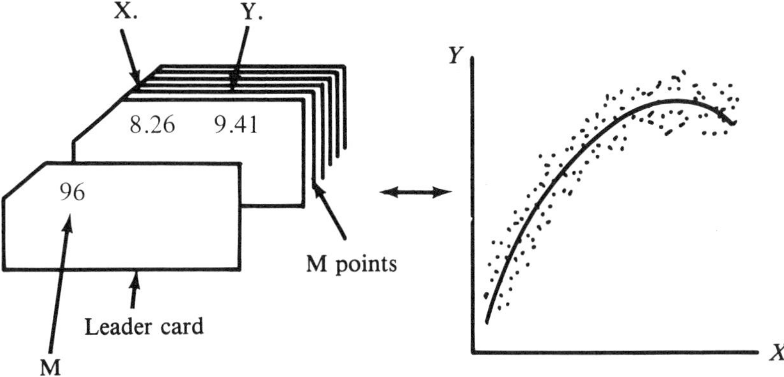

A leader card is added and declares the value of M (the number of data points). It appears from plotting these values that a second order polynomial of the form:

$$y = a_1 + a_2x + a_3x^2 \qquad \textbf{Eq. 15.6}$$

could be used to represent the data. It remains, however, to determine a_1, a_2, and a_3. By the method described in this section, it is possible to compute values of a_1, a_2, and a_3 that will best represent the given data. The strategy is as follows.

1. Establish what criterion is to be used in evaluating whether Eq. 15.6 effectively represents the data; that is, write an equation that expresses the *error* or deviation between the observed data values and the values as given by Eq. 15.6.
2. Having derived this error equation, use the methods of calculus to make the error a minimum; that is, take the first derivative of the error equation and set it equal to zero.

Step 1: Evaluation of Error

Consider the two typical data points shown in Figure 15.9.

Figure 15.9 Definition of error

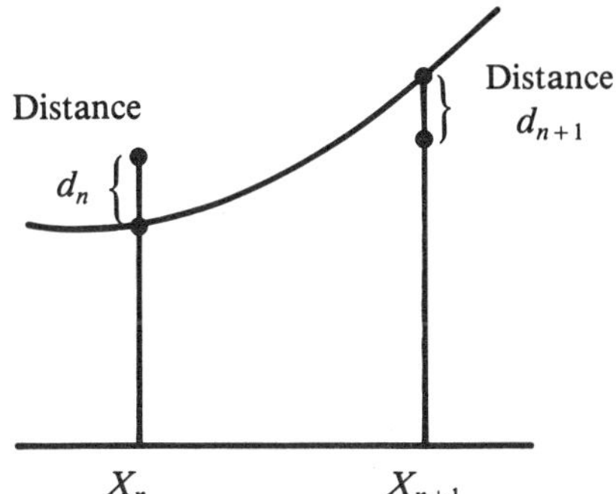

The nth data point is a small distance above the curve. This distance is actually that difference in two Y values:

$$d = \text{Distance} = Y_{\text{Observed}} - Y_{\text{Equation}} \qquad \textbf{Eq. 15.7}$$

where Y_{Observed} is the value of Y read from the nth data card and Y_{Equation} is obtained by substituting the value of X appearing on the nth data card into Eq. 15.6. At first glance, it appears that this distance could be used to represent the error. Note, however, that the distance as given by Eq. 15.7 will have a negative value for points that fall below the curve and a positive value for points that fall above the curve. This would mean that the average error for two points such as shown in Figure 15.9 would be small even though the individual distances are large. This difficulty could be circumvented by using the absolute value of these distances, but this creates problems when an attempt is made to take derivatives of the error equation.

A simpler solution is to define the error as the *square* of the distances. This eliminates the sign difficulty and results in the so-called "method of least squares" fit. The following steps define and proceed to minimize this value. Let S be the sum of the squares of the individual distance:

$$S = d_1^2 + d_2^2 + d_3^2 + \cdots + d_m^2$$

$$S = \sum_{i=1}^{m} [Y_{\text{Observed}} - Y_{\text{Equation}}]^2$$

$$S = \sum_{i=1}^{m} [Y_{(i)} - a_1 - a_2 X_{(i)} - a_3 X_{(i)}^2]^2$$

To minimize this function (obtain the best fit) take its partial derivatives with respect to a_1, a_2, and a_3

$$\frac{\partial S}{\partial a_1} = \frac{\partial S}{\partial a_2} = \frac{\partial S}{\partial a_3} = 0$$

and set them equal to zero.

Step 2: Minimize Error

$$\left.\begin{aligned} \frac{\partial S}{\partial a_1} &= -2\sum_{i=1}^{m} [Y_{(i)} - a_1 - a_2 X_{(i)} - a_3 X_{(i)}^2] = 0 \\ \frac{\partial S}{\partial a_2} &= -2\sum_{i=1}^{m} X_{(i)}[Y_{(i)} - a_1 - a_2 X_{(i)} - a_3 X_{(i)}^2] = 0 \\ \frac{\partial S}{\partial a_3} &= -2\sum_{i=1}^{m} X_{(i)}^2[Y_{(i)} - a_1 - a_2 X_{(i)} - a_3 X_{(i)}^2] = 0 \end{aligned}\right\} \qquad \textbf{Eq. 15.8}$$

The result is a set of three simultaneous equations written in terms of three unknown quantities (a_1, a_2, and a_3). Figure 15.10 shows these equations rearranged and set up to solve for the unknown a's. The 3-by-3 coefficient array is made up of various sums. For example, ΣX is the sum of all the X values appearing on the M data cards, and ΣX^2 is the sum of all the X values squared, and so on. The computer can evaluate these sums exceptionally well for the purpose of forming the two-dimensional coefficient array and the one-dimensional constant array. At this point, the value of the computer makes itself evident. Not only can it be used to accomplish the tedious task of obtaining the various sums needed to form the coefficient and constant matrices, but it can then be used to solve these simultaneous equations by the methods of the previous case study.

Figure 5.10 Simultaneous equations

$$\begin{aligned} Ma_1 &+ \Sigma X a_2 + \Sigma X^2 a_3 = \Sigma Y \\ \Sigma X a_1 &+ \Sigma X^2 a_2 + \Sigma X^3 a_3 = \Sigma XY \\ \Sigma X^2 a_1 &+ \Sigma X^3 a_2 + \Sigma X^4 a_3 = \Sigma X^2 Y \end{aligned}$$

OR

$$\begin{bmatrix} M & \Sigma X & \Sigma X^2 \\ \Sigma X & \Sigma X^2 & \Sigma X^3 \\ \Sigma X^2 & \Sigma X^3 & \Sigma X^4 \end{bmatrix} \begin{Bmatrix} a_1 \\ a_2 \\ a_3 \end{Bmatrix} \begin{Bmatrix} \Sigma Y \\ \Sigma XY \\ \Sigma X^2 Y \end{Bmatrix}$$

Coefficient matrix — Unknowns — Constants

Write statements that will determine ΣX; that is, write statements that will read the value of X from each data card and determine the sum of these values.

```
C.........................................................
C..     PURPOSE - DETERMINE ONE OF THE COEFFICIENTS     ..
C.........................................................
C
        SUMX = 0.0
        READ*, M
C
        DO 30 I = 1, M
C
            READ*, X, Y
            SUMX = SUMX + X
C
   30   CONTINUE
C
```

Next, write statements that will determine all elements in the coefficient matrix; that is, determine ΣX, ΣX^2, ΣX^3, and ΣX^4.

In the program segment to follow, each value of X is read from the data deck. X^2, X^3, and X^4 are then determined. A subscripted variable called SUMX is used to accumulate these terms:

SUMX (1) = ΣX
SUMX (2) = ΣX^2
SUMX (3) = ΣX^3
SUMX (4) = ΣX^4

```
C..........................................................
C..    PURPOSE - DETERMINE ALL THE COEFICIENTS           ..
C..........................................................
C
C              - - - - - IMPORTANT VARIABLES - - - - -
C
C     -- M          NUMBER OF DATA POINTS                 --
C     -- X,Y        INDIVIDUAL DATA POINTS                --
C     -- SUMX(1)    SUMMATION OF X    TERMS               --
```

```
C     -- SUMX(2)    SUMMATION OF X**2 TERMS                   --
C     -- SUMX(3)    SUMMATION OF X**3 TERMS                   --
C     -- SUMX(4)    SUMMATION OF X**4 TERMS                   --
C
         DIMENSION SUMX(4)
C
C                SET EACH ACCUMULATOR TO ZERO
C
         DO 10 I = 1, 4
C
            SUMX(I)  = 0
C
   10    CONTINUE
C
C                  HOW MANY DATA POINTS
C
         READ*,  M
C
C                   LOOP ENTRY POINT
C
         DO 40 COUNT = 1, M, 1
C
            READ*, X
C
            SUMX(1)  =  SUMX(1)  +  X
            SUMX(2)  =  SUMX(2)  +  X**2
            SUMX(3)  =  SUMX(3)  +  X**3
            SUMX(4)  =  SUMX(4)  +  X**4
C
   40    CONTINUE
C
C
         STOP
         END
```

Form a Coefficient Matrix

It now remains to use the sums just computed to form a two-dimensional coefficient matrix as originally shown in Figure 15.10. Each element of the coefficient matrix (which will be called *C*) equals one of the elements in the one-dimensional array SUMX.

$$\begin{bmatrix} C_{11} & C_{12} & C_{13} \\ C_{21} & C_{22} & C_{23} \\ C_{31} & C_{32} & C_{33} \end{bmatrix} \quad \begin{bmatrix} M & \Sigma X & \Sigma X^2 \\ \Sigma X & \Sigma X^2 & \Sigma X^3 \\ \Sigma X^2 & \Sigma X^3 & \Sigma X^4 \end{bmatrix}$$

You can determine which one by adding the two subscripts of *C* and subtracting 2.

```
C (I, J)          SUMX (K)
    \               /
     K = I + J - 2
```

The following statement defines the two-dimensional array C using this relationship. When I and J are both 1, a special condition exists. C(1,1) equals M. This is easily handled by an IF test.

```
C
      DO 80 I = 1, 3
C
         DO 80 J = 1, 3
C
            K = I + J - 2
C
            IF(K.NE.0) THEN
               C(I,J) = SUMX(K)
            ELSE
               C(1,1) = M
            ENDIF
C
 80   CONTINUE
```

Form a Right-Hand Constant

Finally to form the right-hand constants, statements similar to those used in forming the X sums are employed in the creation of the one-dimensional array CONST:

CONST (1) $= \Sigma Y$
CONST (2) $= \Sigma XY$
CONST (3) $= \Sigma X^2 Y$

In the final solution that follows, module 1 reads the data and forms the various sums. Module 2 uses these sums to define array C. Module 3 solves the simultaneous equations thus formed and prints out the solution values—the A values defining the equation that fits the data.

```
C...........................................................
C..   PURPOSE - FIND THE BEST SECOND ORDER POLYNOMIAL TO  ..
C..             FIT THE DATA                              ..
C...........................................................
C
C           - - - - - IMPORTANT VARIABLES - - - - -
C
C     -- CONST(1)   SUM OF THE Y TERMS                     --
C     -- CONST(2)   SUM OF THE XY TERMS                    --
C     -- CONST(3)   SUM OF THE X**2Y TERMS                 --
C     -- A          ARRAY OF SOLUTION VALUES               --
C
      DIMENSION SUMX(4), C(3,3), CONST(3), A(3)
C
C                       MODULE 1
C
C               SET ALL ACCUMULATORS TO ZERO
C
      DO 10 I = 1, 4
C
         SUMX(I) = 0.0
C
 10   CONTINUE
C
      DO 20 I = 1, 3
C
         CONST(I) = 0.0
C
 20   CONTINUE
C
C               HOW MANY DATA POINTS
C
      READ*, M
C
C               LOOP ENTRY POINT
C
      DO 50 COUNT = 1, M, 1
C
         READ*, X, Y
```

```
           SUMX(1)  = SUMX(1)  + X
           SUMX(2)  = SUMX(2)  + X**2
           SUMX(3)  = SUMX(3)  + X**3
           SUMX(4)  = SUMX(4)  + X**4
C
C                NOW DEFINE CONST ARRAY
C
           CONST(1)  = CONST(1)  + Y
           CONST(2)  = CONST(2)  + X*Y
           CONST(3)  = CONST(3)  + X**2*Y
C
   50   CONTINUE
C
C                        MODULE 2
C
C                DEFINE COEFFICIENT ARRAY
C
        DO 70 I = 1, 3
C
           DO 60 J = 1, 3
C
              K = I + J - 2
C
              IF(K.NE.0) THEN
C
                 C(I,J)  = M
C
              ELSE
C
                 C(1,1)  = M
C
              ENDIF
C
   60      CONTINUE
C
   70   CONTINUE
C
C
C                        MODULE 3
C
        STOP
        END
```

To simultaneous equation program to determine array of A values.

The program just completed will put the best second order polynomial through the data points given. However, it may be that the data represents a third or higher order polynomial. If that were so, a poor fit would have been achieved. Curve fitting is a trial-and-error procedure. If a second order curve does not represent the data very well, a higher order curve is tried.

It is natural then to review this case study to accommodate higher order polynomials. If the equations (coefficient and constant matrices) are examined for a fourth order curve, a pattern can be detected.

$$Y = a_1 + a_2x + a_3x^2 + a_4x^3 + a_5x^4$$

$$\begin{bmatrix} M & \Sigma X & \Sigma X^2 & \Sigma X^3 & \Sigma X^4 \\ \Sigma X & \Sigma X^2 & \Sigma X^3 & \Sigma X^4 & \Sigma X^5 \\ \Sigma X^2 & \Sigma X^3 & \Sigma X^4 & \Sigma X^5 & \Sigma X^6 \\ \Sigma X^3 & \Sigma X^4 & \Sigma X^5 & \Sigma X^6 & \Sigma X^7 \\ \Sigma X^4 & \Sigma X^5 & \Sigma X^6 & \Sigma X^7 & \Sigma X^8 \end{bmatrix} \begin{Bmatrix} a_1 \\ a_2 \\ a_3 \\ a_4 \\ a_5 \end{Bmatrix} = \begin{Bmatrix} \Sigma Y \\ \Sigma XY \\ \Sigma X^2Y \\ \Sigma X^3Y \\ \Sigma X^4Y \end{Bmatrix}$$

Observe the following:

1. If N is the order of the polynomial, there are N + 1 values of A and N + 1 simultaneous equations;
2. The maximum exponent of X in the summing terms is 2N. With this in mind, rewrite this case study allowing the reading of N (not to exceed 10) from the same leader card M is on, and form the coefficient and constant arrays.

Review Exercises

1. What is a "character constant"? Give an example.
★ 2. Describe how character information is stored.
3. What does the term "collating sequence" mean?
4. Describe how this collating sequence provides an easy way to accomplish an alphabetic sort.
★ 5. Explain why a character string consisting of four characters should only be compared with a character string of equal length in an `IF` test.
6. When a character string is very long, describe how to break the string up to account for the word size of the machine.
7. Describe one or more typical character operations performed while your program is being compiled.
8. Prepare a data deck consisting of 10 cards. On half the cards put the word `READ` starting in column 7. On the other half put the word `WRITE`. Write a program to determine which cards contain the command `READ`.
9. If an equation is defined by a series of Y values, explain how the area under this curve can be obtained with as little error as possible.
10.

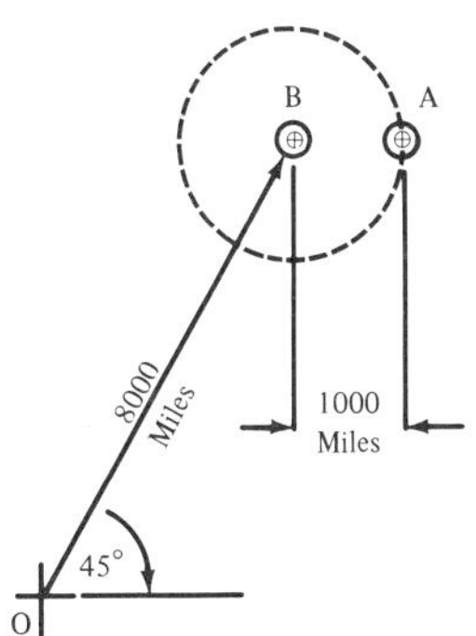

Planet A moves around planet B once every two hours. Planet B moves around center O once every hour. Simulate the motion of planet B at one-second intervals. Simulate the motion of planet A with respect to planet B. Add these two motions to determine the motion of planet A with respect to center O.

11. A train leaves point A traveling at 30 miles per hour but stops every 10 minutes to pick up passengers (one-minute stops). A train leaves point B traveling at 10 miles per hour (constant speed). Simulate the motion of both trains. Terminate the simulation when the trains meet.

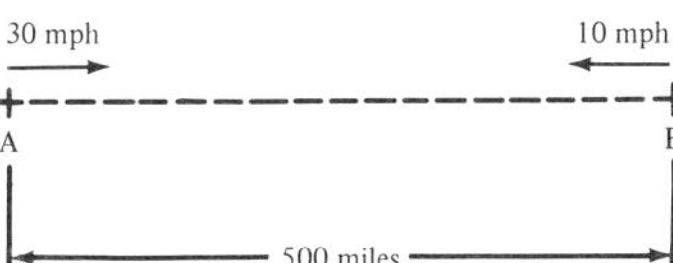

★ 12. Write a program that accomplishes a straight line curve fit for M data points. That is, determine the best slope m and best y intercept b.

$$y = mx + b \quad \text{or} \quad y = a_1 + a_2x$$

13.

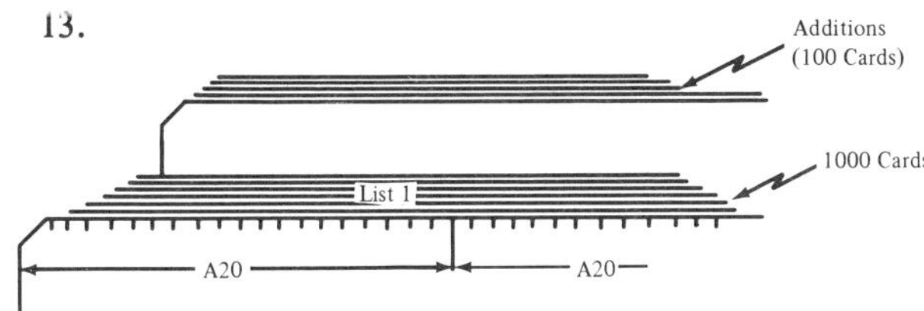

The mailing address of 1000 customers is recorded on data cards and consitutes a file called `LIST1`:

Columns	**Information**
1–20	Customer's Name
21–40	Customer's Street Address
41–60	Customer's Town Address
61–80	Customer's State Address

The next 100 cards represent similar information on customers that are to be added to the mailing list. Assume that neither `LIST1` nor its additions is sorted. Write a program to determine if the first name on the additions list appears anywhere in `LIST1`. If it does not, add this name to `LIST1`.

14. Repeat exercise 13 for all names on the cards that represent possible additions.
15. After the new `LIST1` is established, sort the list according to ZIP code (last five numbers in state address). Print the list.

Appendices

A. System Characteristics

	Classification	Word Length (bits)	Main Storage	Major Compilers	Real: Fraction	Real: Exponent	Real: Double	Internal Code
IBM								
SYSTEM 3	M	8	C,M	C,B,F	–	–	–	E
1130	M	16	C	F,R	–	–	–	E
360/40	SB	32	C	C,F,P	24	7	56	E
360/50	SB	32	C	C,F,P	24	7	56	E
370/series	GP	32	B,M	all	24	7	56	E
4300	GP	32	M	all	24	7	56	E
PDP								
11/45	M	16	C,M	C,B,F	24	8	56	A
11/60	M	16	M	C,B,F	24	8	56	A
11/70	M	16	C	C,B,F	24	8	56	A
CDC								
3000	M	24	C	C,F	36	11	–	B
6600	GP	60	C	all	48	11	–	B
CYB 170	GP	60	M,B	all	48	11	–	B
Univac								
1100	GP	36	C	all	27	8	60	A
90/70	GP	32	M	C,F,R	24	7		E

	Classification	Word Length (bits)	Main Storage	Major Compilers	Real: Fraction	Real: Exponent	Real: Double	Internal Code
DEC								
10	GP	36	C	C,B,F	27	8	54	A
20	GP	36	C	all	27	8	62	A
Burrows								
1700	M	8	M	C,B,F	–	–	–	–
2800	M	16	M	C,B,F	–	–	–	B
6700	GP	48	M	all	39	6	78	E
7700	GP	48	M	all	39	6	78	E
Xerox								
SIGMA 6	GP	32	C	all	24	7	56	E
Honeywell								
60	GP	32	M	C,F,R	24	7	–	E
6000	GP	36	C,M	all	27	8	57	E
NCR								
C 101	M	8	C	C,B,F	24	7	–	A
200	GP	64	C	all	56	7	–	A
Data General								
ECLIPSE 130	M	16	C,M	F,B,A	16	5	–	A

Keys to chart categories:

Classification
M = Mini-computer
SB = Small Business
GP = General Purpose

Main Storage
C = Magnetic Core
M = Magnetic Oxide Semiconductor
B = Bipolar Transistor

Major Compilers
C = COBOL
B = BASIC
F = FORTRAN
R = RPG
P = PL1
A = ALGOL

Internal Code
B = BCD
E = EBCDIC
A = ASCHII

My Computer

		Typical Value		
		16 bit	**36 bit**	**60 bit**
Maximum Size INTEGER	☐	6 digits	11 digits	18 digits
Precision of REAL Variables	☐	5 digits	9 digits	14 digits
Maximum Magnitude of REAL Variable	☐	$10^{\pm 38}$	$10^{\pm 127}$	$10^{\pm 308}$
Input Device Code	☐	READ (5,*) ← Device Code		
Output Device Code	☐	WRITE (2,*) ← Device Code		
Phone Number for Dial-up Service	________			
My Account Number	________			
My Password	________			
Programming Assistance Is Available in Room	________			

B. Use of the IBM 29 Card Punch

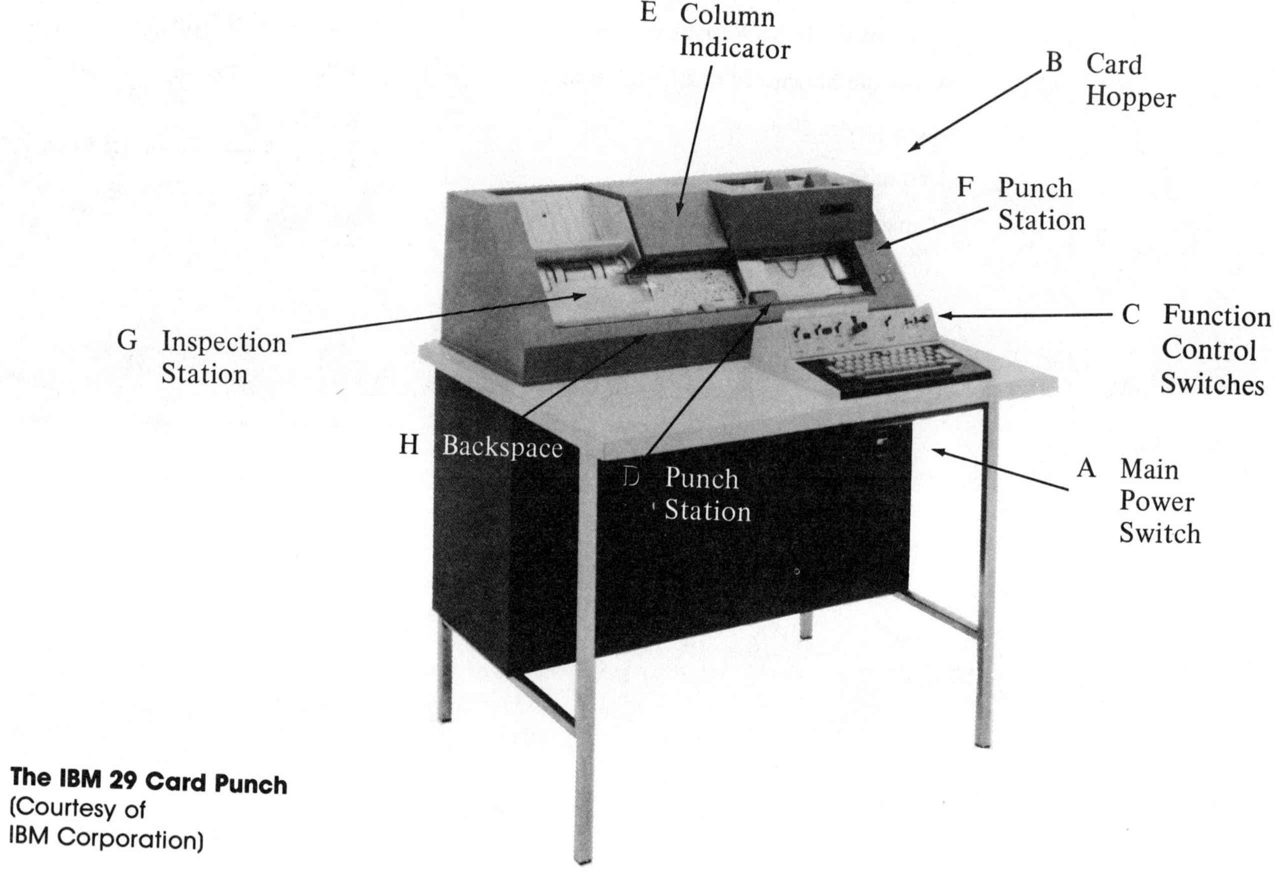

The IBM 29 Card Punch
(Courtesy of IBM Corporation)

Operating Instructions

1. Turn on Main Power Switch (A) and allow 30 seconds to warm up.
2. Load Card Hopper (B) with blank cards.
3. There is a group of four Function Control Switches (C) centered over the keyboard. Usually these should be placed in the up position.
4. On the right hand side of the keyboard there is a key marked FEED. Press this key twice. This will cause cards to leave the card hopper and be positioned at the Punch Station (D).
5. You may now start typing the FORTRAN statement on the input data just as if you were dealing with a typewriter. One noticeable difference is that the punch head obscures your view of which column you are punching. That information is displayed by the Column Indicator (E), which is visible through a small window located at the top center of the keypunch.
6. When you have completed punching information on the card, locate the RELease key on the keyboard (it's just above the FEED key). Pressing the RELease key causes the card to pass from the punch station to the Inspection Station (G).
7. Examine the card and see if any error in keypunching has been made. Assume you have typed a faulty character in column 59. (Each column on the card is numbered to help locate your errors.)
8. Pushing the DUPlicate button (top row center) will cause the information on the card at the inspection station to be duplicated on the blank card at the Punch Station. Using this feature, an error can be corrected without retyping the whole card. The idea is to duplicate all columns other than those with an error (column 59 for example). When the column with the error is reached, use the key board to make the correct entry. *Don't forget to throw away the faulty card.*
9. A Backspace Key (H) is located below the Inspection Station and it causes the card to backspace if necessary. If you inadvertently go by the column in which you intended to punch information, the backspace key can be used.

Correcting A Single Card

The procedures in steps 1–9 are used when there are many cards to be key-punched, i.e., when you first keypunch your program. To keypunch or correct a **single** card, it is more convenient to "**hand feed**" the cards involved.

1. Place the card to be corrected directly into the Inspection Station (G). There are slots at the top and bottom to permit the insertion of a card.
2. Place a blank card directly into the Punch Station (F).
3. Press the key marked REGister and start typing as described in step 4 of the operating instructions.

C1. Answers to Selected Problems

Chapter 1, page 23

1. Both of these
3. Central Processing Unit
5. Add, subtract, multiply, divide
8. Punched holes
11. Magnetic tape
15. No
16. Yes
18. 101
21. Convert instructions to machine language
25. Translated into machine language
28. FORmula TRANslation

Chapter 2, page 47

2. Waits until compiling complete
4. END statement
7. Yes
9. No
11. No
14. Data may appear anywhere
18. Integer
21. Instruction deck; data deck
25. Number of digits one memory location can hold; no
32. Should start in column 7
34. Series of statements that are repeated several times
36. Use column 6 to signal continuation card(s)

Chapter 3, page 75

1. a
4. c
7. a
10. e
11. c or d
13. a
15. b
17. c or d
19. a
21. c or d
25. b
28. a or d
30. c
32. b
35. e
38. c
40. b
44. b
46. Do not cause multiplication
48. Innermost
51. Use parenthesis

Chapter 4, page 95

1. You may select input/output device desired by using device code. Automatic "end of file" check.
5. Protection from overflow and to produce separation (blank columns between successive output fields.)
9. 9999
12. Use two output statements. One directing output to a magnetic tape device; the other to your console.
15. Just before the digit in column 8.
20.

```
PRINT*, '  Y-AXIS'
PRINT*, ' '
PRINT*, '6 X'
PRINT*, '  X'
PRINT*, '  X'
PRINT*, '5 X'
PRINT*, '  X'
PRINT*, '  X'
PRINT*, '4 X'
PRINT*, '  X'
PRINT*, '  X'
PRINT*, '3 X'
PRINT*, '  X'
PRINT*, '  X'
PRINT*, '2 X'
PRINT*, '  X'
PRINT*, '  X'
PRINT*, '1 X'
PRINT*, '  X'
PRINT*, '  X'
PRINT*, '  XXXXXXXXXXXXXXXXXXXXXXXXXXXXXXXXXXXXXXXXX'
PRINT*, '  0    1    2    3    4    5    6    7    8'
PRINT*, ' '
PRINT*, ' '
PRINT*, '                      X-AXIS'
STOP
END
```

Chapter 5, page 122

2. .AND. .OR.
5. When you must select one of many alternative blocks of code to execute.
7. To monitor the correct behavior of important variables in your program as the program executes.
10. Try to anticipate what could go wrong with your program. Use PRINT statements to keep a close check on the intermediate steps and calculations.
13. AUTHOR SUPPLIED PO . . .

```
C.....................................................
C DETERMINE IF POINT LIES INSIDE OR OUTSIDE THE CIRCLE
C.....................................................
C
C READ X AND Y LOCATION OF POINT AND RADIUS OF CIRCLE
C
  READ*, X, Y, R
C
C COMPUTE DISTANCE POINT LIES FROM CENTER OF CIRCLE
C
  DIST = (X**2 + Y**2)**(1. / 2.)
C
  IF (DIST.LT.R) PRINT *, ' POINTS IS WITHIN THE RADIUS'
  IF (DIST.EQ.R) PRINT *, ' POINTS IS ON THE RADIUS'
  IF (DIST.GT.R) PRINT *, ' POINTS IS OUTSIDE THE RADIUS'
C
  STOP
  END
```

14.

```
C.....................................................
C..      PROCESS 100 RECORDS. PRINT ALL WITHDRAWALS  ..
C.....................................................
C
         DO 20 I = 1, 100, 1
C
            READ *, AMOUNT
            IF ( AMOUNT.LT.0.0) PRINT *, I, AMOUNT
C
   20    CONTINUE
C
         STOP
         END
```

16.

```
C.........................................
C      DIVIDE LINE INTO FOUR EQUAL PARTS  ..
C.........................................
C
        READ*, X1, Y1, X4, Y4
C
        DELTX = (X4 - X1) / 3.0
        DELTY = (Y4 - Y1) / 3.0
C
C       COMPUTE POINT 2 LOCATION
C
        X2 = X1 + DELTX
        Y2 = Y1 + DELTY
C
C       COMPUTE POINT 3 LOCATION
C
        X3 = X1 + 2.0 * DELTX
        Y3 = Y1 + 2.0 * DELTY
C
        PRINT*, X2, Y2, X3, Y3
C
        DIST12=((X2-X1)**2+(Y2-Y1)**2)**.5
        DIST23=((X3-X2)**2+(Y3-Y2)**2)**.5
        DIST34=((X4-X3)**2+(Y4-Y3)**2)**.5
C
        PRINT*, DIST12, DIST23,DIST34
C
        STOP
        END
```

22.

```
C.................................................
C..     READ A VALUE OF X.  FIND OUT IF IT BELONGS  ..
C..     IN FRONT OR BACK HALF OF TABLE.             ..
C.................................................
C
C       READ THE X VALUE
        READ*, XNEW
C
C       DO A LOOP READ UNTIL MIDDLE OF TABLE IS REACHED
C
        DO 10 I = 1, 50
C
            READ*, X
C
  10    CONTINUE
C
        NOW CHECK XNEW AGAINST THIS MIDDLE VALUE
C
        IF(XNEW.LT.X) THEN
C
            PRINT*, 'NEW X VALUE BELONGS IN FRONT HALF
                                          OF TABLE'
        ELSE
            PRINT*, 'NEW X VALUE BELONGS IN BACK HALF
                                          OF TABLE'
        ENDIF
C
        STOP
        END
```

Chapter 6, page 155

2. Set up a loop construct that repeats as long as a specific condition remains "true."
6. Yes, consider the statement:

   DO 10 I = N, 20, 1

   If the value of N were 21 or greater, the loop would not be executed at all.
10. An integer variable or expression used in conjunction with the computed GO TO to determine which of the possible alternative branches should be selected.

16.

```
C......................................................
C.. HOW MANY TIMES DID BOX CARS COME UP IN 200 ROLLS? ..
C......................................................
C
      INTEGER COUNT, ROLL, TOTAL
C
      COUNT = 0
C
      DO 20 ROLL = 1, 200
C
          READ*, N1, N2
          TOTAL = N1 + N2
          IF(TOTAL.EQ.16) COUNT = COUNT + 1
C
  20  CONTINUE
C
      PRINT*, 'NUMBER OF TIMES =', COUNT
C
      STOP
      END
```

17.

```
C............................................
C..     EVALUATE TERMS IN ARC TANGENT EQUATION  ..
C............................................
C
        READ *, X
C
        TERM1 = X
        TERM2 = X ** 3 / 3.0
        TERM3 = X ** 5 / 5.0
        TERM4 = X ** 7 / 7.0
C
        SUM   = TERM1 + TERM2 + TERM3 + TERM4
C
        TERM5 = X ** 9 / 9.0
C
        PRINT*, 'SUM OF FIRST FOUR TERMS =', SUM
        PRINT*, 'VALUE OF FIRST TERM NEGLECTED=', TERM5
C
        STOP
        END
```

20.

```
C......................................
C..  READ AND PRINT TERMINAL LOCATIONS   ..
C......................................
C
      READ *, X1, Y1
      READ *, X2, Y2
      READ *, X3, Y3
      READ *, X4, Y4
C
      PRINT*, '                TERMINAL'
      PRINT*, '               COORDINATES'
      PRINT*, ' '
      PRINT*, '                    X                    Y'
      PRINT*, '    1      ',   X1, Y1
      PRINT*, '    2      ',   X2, Y2
      PRINT*, '    3      ',   X3, Y3
      PRINT*, '    4      ',   X4, Y4
C
C
C     ..................................................
C     .. COMPUTE DISTANCES ASSOCIATED WITH TERMINAL 1 ..
C     ..................................................
C
      DIST11 = 0.00
      DIST12 = ((X2 - X1)**2 + (Y2 - Y1)**2)**(1./2.)
      DIST13 = ((X3 - X1)**2 + (Y3 - Y1)**2)**(1./2.)
      DIST14 = ((X4 - X1)**2 + (Y4 - Y1)**2)**(1./2.)
C
      PRINT*, 'TERMINAL          1        2        3        4'
      PRINT*, '    1      ', DIST11, DIST12, DIST13, DIST14
C
C
C     ..................................................
C     .. COMPUTE DISTANCE ASSOCIATED WITH TERMINAL 2 ..
C     ..................................................
C
      DIST21 = DIST12
      DIST22 = 0.00
      DIST23 = ((X3 - X2)**2 + (Y3 - Y2)**2)**(1./2.)
      DIST24 = ((X4 - X2)**2 + (Y4 - Y2)**2)**(1./2.)
C
      PRINT*, '    2      ', DIST21, DIST22, DIST23, DIST24
C
      DIST31 = DIST13
      DIST32 = DIST23
      DIST33 = 0.00
      DIST34 = ((X4 - X3)**2 + (Y4 - Y3)**2)**(1./2.)
```

```
C
      PRINT*, '  3      ', DIST31, DIST32, DIST33, DIST34
C
      DIST41 = DIST14
      DIST42 = DIST24
      DIST43 = DIST34
      DIST44 = 0.00
      PRINT*, '  4      ',  DIST41, DIST42, DIST43, DIST44
C
      STOP
      END
```

Chapter 7, page 180

1. No, exponent may be real or integer when raising to a power
4. Radians
6. Real IF tests should be used with caution. If SQRT function (series approximation) results in 4.9999997, STOP will not be executed.
9. Set initial values to various memory locations.
14.

```
C..............................................
C..     DETERMINE THE TOTAL OF LIST 1 ELEMENTS   ..
C..............................................
C
        INTEGER SIZE1, SIZE2
        REAL SUM1, SUM2, X
C
        SUM1 = 0.0
        READ*, SIZE1
C
        DO 10 I = 1, SIZE1, 1
C
           READ*, X
           SUM1 = SUM1 + X
C
 10     CONTINUE
C
C..............................................
C..     DETERMINE THE TOTAL OF LIST 2 ELEMENTS   ..
C..............................................
C
        SUM2 = 0.0
        READ*, SIZE2
C
        DO 20 I = 1, SIZE2
C
           READ*, X
           SUM2 = SUM2 + X
C
 20     CONTINUE
C
        IF(SUM1.GT.SUM2) THEN
           PRINT*, 'LIST 1 IS LARGER. VALUE =', SUM1
        ELSE
           PRINT*, 'LIST 2 IS LARGER. VALUE =', SUM2
        ENDIF
C
        STOP
        END
```

18.

```
C..............................................
C..   READ MAGNITUDE AND INCLINATION OF TWO VECTORS ..
C..............................................
C
      REAL ANG1, MAG1, ANG2, MAG2, X1, Y1, X2, Y2
      REAL SUMX, SUMY, MAG, ANG
C
      READ*, ANG1, MAG1
      READ*, ANG2, MAG2
C
      X1 = MAG1*COS(ANG1/57.3)
      Y1 = MAG1*SIN(ANG1/57.3)
C
      X2 = MAG2*COS(ANG2/57.3)
      Y2 = MAG2*SIN(ANG2/57.3)
C
      PRINT*, 'VECTOR 1 X-COMPONENT = ', X1,
     *        'Y-COMPONENT = ', Y1
      PRINT*, 'VECTOR 2 X-COMPONENT = ', X2,
     *        'Y-COMPONENT = ', Y2
C
C..............................................
C..     ADD COMPONENTS - COMPUTE MAGNITUDE AND      ..
C..            INCLINATION OF RESULTANT.            ..
C..............................................
C
      SUMX = X1 + X2
      SUMY = Y1 + Y2
C
      PRINT*, 'TOTAL X-COMPONENT = ', SUMX
      PRINT*, 'TOTAL Y-COMPONENT = ', SUMY
C
      MAG = (SUMX**2 + SUMY**2)**0.5
      ANG = ATAN2(SUMY, SUMX)*57.3
C
      PRINT*, 'MAGNITUDE OF RESULTANT =', MAG
      PRINT*, 'ANGLE OF RESULTANT (DEGREES) =', ANG
C
      STOP
      END
```

21.

```
C..............................................
C..   DETERMINE MINIMUM AND MAXIMUM VALUE OF EQUATION ..
C..............................................
C
      REAL X, YMIN, YMAX
C
      X = 1.0
C
      YMIN=ALOG10(X+4.0)+ABS(X**3-64.0)
      YMAX=ALOG10(X+4.0)+ABS(X**3-64.0)
C
      DO WHILE (X.LE.10.0)
C
         Y=ALOG10(X+4.0)+ABS(X**3-64.0)
         IF(Y.LT.YMIM)YMIN = Y
         IF(Y.GT.YMAX)YMAX = Y
C
         X = X + 0.1
C
      ENDDO
C
      PRINT*, 'LARGEST VALUE =', YMAX
      PRINT*, 'SMALLEST VALUE =', YMIN
C
      STOP
      END
```

Chapter 8, page 212

3. Detailed, exact, effective, efficient.
7. Extra print statements.
11. The number of lines in one module should be restricted to a size that allows the reader to easily grasp the concept of what the module does. Making the module too large invites confusion.
14. Statement not written in proper form. Best detected during desk check.
18. Sequence, decision, loop.
22. Division by zero; trying to take the logarithm of a negative number; attempting to read when data deck is depleted. Many intermediate printouts.
24. Just as it looks when listed by the computer.

Chapter 9, page 266

1. Vector (one-dimensional array).
   Matrix (two-dimensional array)
   Three-dimensional arrays, etc.
4. READ*, (X(I),I=1,400)
6. Size of arrays must be specified as constants in DIMENSION statement.
9. Variable X appears in two type statements.

13.
```
C..............................................
C..    DETERMINE AVERAGE VALUE - DEAL WITH ONE  ..
C..             DIMENSIONAL ARRAYS              ..
C..............................................
C
      REAL X1(20), X2(20), X3(20), AVE1, AVE2, AVE3
      REAL DIFF1, DIFF2, DIFF3, SUM1, SUM2, SUM3
C
      DATA SUM1, SUM2, SUM3 /3*0.0/
C     ....READ THREE ARRAYS....
C
      READ*, (X1(I),I=1,20), (X2(I),I=1,20),
     1            (X3(I),I=1,20)
C
C     ****************************************
C     ** COMPUTE AVERAGE FOR THREE ARRAYS **
C     ****************************************
C
      DO 10 I = 1, 20,1
C
          SUM1 = SUM1 + X1(I)
          SUM2 = SUM2 + X2(I)
          SUM3 = SUM3 + X3(I)
C
   10 CONTINUE
C
      AVE1 = SUM1 / 20.0
      AVE2 = SUM2 / 20.0
      AVE3 = SUM3 / 20.0
C
C     ****************************************
C     ** FIND DIFFERENCE FOR EACH ELEMENT **
C     ****************************************
C
      DO 20 I = 1, 20 , 1
C
          DIFF1 = X1(I) - AVE1
          DIFF2 = X2(I) - AVE2
          DIFF3 = X3(I) - AVE3
C
          PRINT*, I, DIFF1, DIFF2, DIFF3
C
   20 CONTINUE
C
      STOP
      END
```

16.
```
C..............................................
C..  REVERSE THE ORDER OF ARRAY X GIVING ARRAY Y ..
C..............................................
C
      REAL X(100), Y(100)
      INTEGER I, K
C
      READ*, (X(I), I=1,100,1)
C
      DO 20 I = 1, 100,1
C
          K = 101 - I
C
          Y(I) = X(K)
C
   20 CONTINUE
C
      PRINT*, (Y(I),I=1,100,1)
C
      STOP
      END
```

20.
```
C..............................................
C..    REMOVE ELEMENT 50 FROM LIST OF X VALUES  ..
C..............................................
C
      REAL X(100)
C
      READ*, (X(I),I=1,100,1)
C
C     ****************************************
C     ** SET UP LOOP TO MOVE ELEMENTS 50 **
C     **      TO 99 UP ONE POSITION       **
C     ****************************************
C
      DO 10 I = 50, 99, 1
C
          X(I) = X(I+1)
C
   10 CONTINUE
C
      PRINT*, (X(I),I=1,99,1)
C
      STOP
      END
```

25.
```
C..............................................
C..  CHECK FOR DUPLICATE LISTING OF NUMBERS    ..
C..............................................
C
      INTEGER LIST1(300), LIST2(300), FLAG
      FLAG = 0
C
      READ*, (LIST1(I),I=1,300,1)
      READ*, (LIST2(I),I=1,300,1)
C
C     ***********************************************
C     ** CHECK TO SEE IF FIRST NUMBER IN LIST 1 **
C     **      APPEARS ANYWHERE IN LIST 2          **
C     ***********************************************
C
      DO 10 I = 1, 300, 1
C
        IF(LIST1(1).EQ.LIST2(I)) THEN
C
          PRINT*, 'ELEMENT 1 APPEARS IN POSITION ', I
          FLAG = 1
C
        ENDIF
C
   10 CONTINUE
C
      IF(FLAG.EQ.0) PRINT*, 'NO DUPLICATES DETECTED'
C
      STOP
      END
```

34.
```
C..................................................
C.. FORM SPECIAL MATRIX M - CALLED A UNIT MATRIX ..
C..................................................
C
      INTEGER M(10,10)
C
      DO 20 I = 1, 10, 1
C
          DO 10 J = 1, 10, 1
C
              IF(I.EQ.J) THEN
C
                  M(I,J) = 1
C
              ELSE
C
                  M(I,J) = 0
C
              ENDIF
C
   10     CONTINUE
C
   20 CONTINUE
C
      STOP
      END
```

Chapter 10, page 306

2. No
6. Read input values. Make CALLS, print desired results
8. It is not assigned a memory location of its own nor does it pick up the address of another variable. It is merely a place holder that shows where in a calculation this quantity appears.
10. When a subprogram must examine the values of an array defined (known) in the calling program, the address of the first element of the array is passed from the calling program to the using program. This address is called the **based address** of the array.

15.
```
C...............................................
C..     DETERMINE LOCATION OF LARGEST ELEMENT OF ..
C..                  ARRAY DATA                   ..
C...............................................
C
        FUNCTION LOCATN (DATA, SIZE)
C
        INTEGER SIZE
        REAL DATA(SIZE), BIG
C
        BIG = DATA(1)
        LOCATN = 1
C
        DO 10 I = 2, SIZE, 1
C
            IF(DATA(I).GT.BIG) THEN
C
                BIG = DATA(I)
                LOCATN = I
C
            ENDIF
C
 10     CONTINUE
C
        RETURN
        END
```

17.
```
C...............................................
C.EXAMPLE ARITHMETIC STATEMENT FUNCTION SUBPROGRAM.
C...............................................
C
        XPISTN(THETA) = 12.*(1.-COS(THETA))+24.-24.
     1            *SQRT(1.-(12.*SIN(THETA)/24.)**2)
C
```

19.
```
C...............................................
C..    COMPUTE FIRST TEN TERMS OF SINE FUNCTION  ..
C...............................................
C
        FUNCTION SIN2 (X)
C
        SIN2 = 0.0
        XSIGN = -1.0
C
        DO 20 I = 1, 19, 2
C
            DENOM = 1.0
C
            DO 10 K = 1, I
C
                DENOM = DENOM * FLOAT(K)
C
 10         CONTINUE
C
            XSIGN = XSIGN * (-1.0)
            TERM = XSIGN * X ** I / DENOM
            SIN2 = SIN2 + TERM
C
 20     CONTINUE
C
        RETURN
        END
```

21.
```
C...............................................
C..  DETERMINE AREA UNDER POLYNOMIAL OF POWER A  ..
C...............................................
C
        FUNCTION AREA(A, XINIT, XFINAL)
C
C
        DELTAX = (XFINAL - XINIT) / 100.
C
        AREA = 0.0
C
        DO 10 I = 1, 101, 1
C
            Y = X**A
            X = X + DELTX
            YPLUS = X**A
            AREA = AREA + ( Y + YPLUS ) / 2. * DELTAX
C
 10     CONTINUE
C
        RETURN
        END
```

26.
```
C...............................................
C..     LARGEST OR SMALLEST REATCH OF AN ARRAY   ..
C...............................................
C
        SUBROUTINE SEARCH(M, A, ELMT, LOC)
C
        DIMENSION A(100)
C
        ELMT = A(1)
        LOC  = 1
C
        IF(M.GT.0) THEN
C
C       ...........FIND LARGEST ELEMENT.........
C
            DO 10 I = 2, 100, 1
C
                IF(A(I).GT.ELMT)THEN
C
                    ELMT = A(I)
                    LOC = I
C
                ENDIF
C
 10         CONTINUE
C
        ELSE
C
C       ...........FIND SMALLEST ELEMENT...........
C
            DO 20 I = 2, 100,1
C
                IF(A(I).LT.ELMT)THEN
C
                    ELMT = A(I)
                    LOC  = I
C
                ENDIF
C
 20         CONTINUE
C
        ENDIF
C
        RETURN
        END
```

Chapter 11, page 339

3. Consumes twenty consecutive memory locations. The first 5 hold column 1 of the matrix. The last 5 hold column 4. It is in the 8th memory location.
5. This array is defined inside the subprogram only and is not shared with any other program (the array name does not appear in the argument list). Size of array must be defined by constants.
8. Place variables that are common to these subprograms in COMMON storage. These variables can then be eliminated from each argument list.
10. When it is necessary to pass information that is best represented by an equation. Area under a curve or root of an equation.

15.
```
C..................................................
C..FIND LARGEST FIRST ELEMENT - TAKE THAT ROW AND ..
C..        MOVE IT TO THE TOP OF ARRAY            ..
C..................................................
C
      SUBROUTINE CHANGE(A)
C
      DIMENSION A(14, 28)
C
      BIG = A(1, 1)
      LOCATN = 1
C
      DO 10 I = 2, 14
C
         IF (A(I, 1).GT.BIG) THEN
C
            BIG = A(I, 1)
            LOCATN = I
C
         ENDIF
C
   10 CONTINUE
C
      IF(LOCATN.EQ.1) RETURN
C
C     **********************************
C     ** SWAP ROW "LOCATN" WITH ROW 1 **
C     **********************************
C
      DO 20 I = 1, 28, 1
C
         TEMP = A(1,I)
         A(1,I) = A(LOCATN,I)
         A(LOCATN,I) = TEMP
C
   20 CONTINUE
C
      RETURN
      END
```

18.
```
C..................................................
C..DETERMINE IF ROOT TO LEFT OR RIGHT OF MIDPOINT ..
C..................................................
C
      SUBROUTINE ROOTS(Y, XLEFT, XRIGHT)
C
      EXTERNAL Y
C
      XMID = XLEFT + (XRIGHT - XLEFT) / 2.0
C
C     ....APPLY THIS VALUE TO THE EQUATION....
C
      YMID = Y(XMID)
C
      YLEFT = Y(XLEFT)
      YRIGHT = Y(XRIGHT)
C
C     IF TWO VALUES OF Y HAVE THE SAME SIGN, THE
C     PRODUCT OF THESE VALUES IS POSITIVE.
C
C          (PROBABLY NO ROOT IN THIS SPAN)
C
C     IF TWO VALUES OF Y HAVE OPPOSITE SIGNS THE
C     PRODUCT OF THESE VALUES IS NEGATIVE.
C
C            (ROOT DOES LIE IN THIS SPAN)
C
      PROD = YLEFT * YRIGHT
C
      IF(PROD.LT.0.0) THEN
C
         PRINT*, 'ROOT TO THE RIGHT OF MIDPOINT'
         RETURN
C
      ENDIF
C
      PROD = YMID * YRIGHT
C
      IF(PROD.LT.0.0) THEN
C
         PRINT*, 'ROOT TO THE RIGHT OF MIDPOINT'
         RETURN
C
      ENDIF
C
      PRINT*, 'ALL THREE Y VALUES OF SAME SIGN'
      PRINT*, '  NO ROOT EXPECTED IN SPAN'
C
      RETURN
      END
```

23.
```
C..................................................
C..SCALE EACH ROW OF A MATRIX - SCALE FACTOR GIVEN..
C..                BY VECTOR VALUE                ..
C..................................................
C
      SUBROUTINE SCALE (A, NROW, NCOL, VALUE)
C
      DIMENSION A(NROW,NCOL), VALUE(NROW)
C
      DO 20 I = 1, NROW
C
         FACTOR = VALUE(I)
C
         DO 10 J = 1, NCOL
C
            A(I,J) = A(I,J) * FACTOR
C
   10    CONTINUE
C
   20 CONTINUE
C
      RETURN
      END
```

Chapter 12, page 371

3. Since DSIN must be known to double precision accuracy, more terms are evaluated for this function.
6. Once a variable has been declared as a certain type, it must remain that type throughout the program.

11.
```
C..................................................
C.. COMPUTE 50 WEEKS PAY - USE DOUBLE PRECISION   ..
C..................................................
C
      DOUBLE PRECISION DAILY, SUM
C
      SUM = 0.0
C
      DO 20 I = 1, 50, 1
C
         DAILY = (2.0**(I-1)) / 100.
         SUM = SUM + DAILY
C
         PRINT*, DAILY, SUM
C
   20 CONTINUE
C
      STOP
      END
```

15.
```
C..................................................
C.. TRACK POSITION OF POINTS A AND B - USE COMPLEX..
C..                  VARIABLES                    ..
C..................................................
C
      COMPLEX A, B, RESULT
      REAL XAB, YAB, XBC, YBC, X, Y
      INTEGER TIME
C
      DATA THETA1, THETA2, DTHETA/60., 30., 6./
C
      TIME = 1
C
      DO WHILE (TIME.LE.60)
C
         XAB = 9.0 * COS(THETA1/57.3)
         YAB = 9.0 * SIN(THETA1/57.3)
         A = CMPLX(XAB, YAB)
         ----------------------------
         XBC = 6.0 * COS(THETA2/57.3)
         YBC = 6.0 * SIN(THETA2/57.3)
         B = CMPLX(XBC, YBC)
C
         RESULT = A + B
         X = REAL(RESULT)
         Y = AIMAG(RESULT)
         PRINT*, 'X = ', X, 'Y = ', Y
C
         THETA1 = THETA1 + DTHETA
         THETA2 = THETA2 + DTHETA
         TIME = TIME + 1
C
      ENDDO
C
      STOP
      END
```

16.
```
C.............................................
C. CHECK TRUE FALSE ANSWERS - USE LOGICAL VARIABLES .
C.............................................
C
      LOGICAL FEMALE(75), MALE(75)
      INTEGER GIRL, BOY
C
      READ (5,10) GIRL, (FEMALE(I),I=1,75,1)
   10 FORMAT(I5, 75L1)
C
   20 NUMBER = 0
C
      READ (5,10,END=60) BOY, (MALE(I),I=1,17,1)
C
      DO 40 I = 1, 75
C
          IF(MALE(I).EQ.FEMALE(I))NUMBER = NUMBER + 1
C
   40 CONTINUE
C
      IF(NUMBER.GE.70)PRINT*, BOY
C
      GO TO 20
C
   60 STOP
      END
```

Chapter 13, page 389

2. A group of subprograms that accomplish repetitive activities associated with a particular professional occupation such as accounting, civil engineering, aircraft controlling, trucking, etc.
4. Using an integer argument that is given a value 0, 1, 2, 3, . . . , which conveys if the solution has progressed properly or encountered some difficulties.
8. Make a copy of the arrays and feed these copies to the subroutine.

12.
```
C.........................................
C..     ESTABLISH SPECIAL TRIG SUBPROGRAM   ..
C.........................................
C
        SUBROUTINE TRIG( A, B, C, ANGA, ANGB)
C
        ANGA = ATAN2(A, B) * 57.3
        ANGB = 90.0 - ANGA
C
        C = SQRT(A**2 + B**2)
C
        RETURN
        END
```

17.
```
C.............................................
C..     DETERMINE ROOT BY HALF INTERVAL SEARCH  ..
C.............................................
C
        SUBROUTINE ROOTS(Y,XLEFT,XRIGHT,XROOT,MAIL)
C
        EXTERNAL Y
C
        DO 100 I = 1, 10, 1
C
            XMID = XLEFT + (XRIGHT - XLEFT) / 2.0
            YLEFT = Y(XLEFT)
            YMID  = Y(XMID)
            YRIGHT = Y(XRIGHT)
C
C       IF TWO VALUES OF Y HAVE THE SAME SIGN, THE
C       PRODUCT OF THESE VALUES IS POSITIVE.
C           (PROBABLY NO ROOT IN THIS SPAN)
C
C       IF TWO VALUES OF Y HAVE OPPOSITE SIGN, THE
C       PRODUCT OF THESE VALUES IS NEGATIVE.
C            (PROBABLE ROOT IN THIS SPAN)
C
            PROD = YLEFT * YMID
            IF(PROD.LT.0.0) THEN
                XRIGHT = XMID
                GO TO 100
            ENDIF
C
            PROD = YMID * YRIGHT
            IF(PROD.LT.0.0)THEN
                XLEFT = XMID
                GO TO 100
            ENDIF
C
C
C       IF THIS POINT IS REACHED ALL Y VALUES HAVE
C               THE SAME SIGN
C
            MAIL = 1
            RETURN
C
  100   CONTINUE
C
        MAIL = 0
        XROOT = XMID
C
        RETURN
        END
```

Chapter 14, page 411

2. a. Yes
   b. Yes
   c. XINIT
   d. No
   e. ____−20.76____14.2____4071.080
      ____203.770400000
4. −9999 to 99999*
   −.999999 to 9.999999
   −9999.9999 to 99999.999
   −999999 to 999999*
   Limited by exponent size only.
   *Size of integers is also restricted by processor.
8. Statements on the left. "1X" used to set carriage control character.
11. End parenthesis of FORMAT statement part of Hollerith field. FORMAT statement not terminated properly.

16.
```
C..............................................
C..     PRINT GRAPH AXIS USING FORMAT CONTROL   ..
C..............................................
C
    5   FORMAT(20X,1HX)
   10   FORMAT(19X,2H1X)
   20   FORMAT(19X,2H2X)
   30   FORMAT(19X,2H3X)
   40   FORMAT(20X,42(1HX))
   50   FORMAT(20X,1H0,5X,1H1,5X,1H2,5X,1H3,5X,
     1         1H4,5X,1H5,5X,1H6,5X,1H7)
C
        WRITE(2,30)
        WRITE(2,5)
        WRITE(2,5)
        WRITE(2,5)
        WRITE(2,20)
        WRITE(2,5)
        WRITE(2,5)
        WRITE(2,5)
        WRITE(2,10)
        WRITE(2,5)
        WRITE(2,5)
        WRITE(2,5)
        WRITE(2,40)
        WRITE(2,50)
C
        STOP
        END
```

19.

```
C.....................................................
C.. READ AND PRINT TERMINAL LOCATIONS - USING FORMAT ..
C.....................................................
C
      READ(5,10) X1, Y1
      READ(5,10) X2, Y2
      READ(5,10) X3, Y3
      READ(5,10) X4, Y4
   10 FORMAT(2F10.2)
C
      WRITE(2,20)
   20 FORMAT(1H1,23X,'TERMINAL',/22X,'COORDINATES',//)
      WRITE(2,30)
   30 FORMAT(26X,'X',12X,'Y')
C
      WRITE(2,40) X1, Y1
   40 FORMAT(4X,'1',5X,2F8.2)
      WRITE(2,50) X2, Y2
   50 FORMAT(4X,'2',5X,2F8.2)
      WRITE(2,60) X3, Y3
   60 FORMAT(4X,'3',5X,2F8.2)
      WRITE(2,70) X4, Y4
   70 FORMAT(4X,'4',2F8.2)
C
C     ................................................
C     .. COMPUTE DISTANCES ASSOCIATED WITH TERMINAL 1 ..
C     ................................................
C
      DIST11 = 0.00
      DIST12 = ((X2 - X1)**2 + (Y2 - Y1)**2)**(1./2.)
      DIST13 = ((X3 - X1)**2 + (Y3 - Y1)**2)**(1./2.)
      DIST14 = ((X4 - X1)**2 + (Y4 - Y1)**2)**(1./2.)
C
      WRITE(2,80)
   80 FORMAT(2X,'TERMINAL        1          2          3          4')
      WRITE(2,90) DIST11, DIST12, DIST13, DIST14
   90 FORMAT(4X,'1',4F8.2)
C
C     ................................................
C     .. COMPUTE DISTANCES ASSOCIATED WITH TERMINAL 2 ..
C     ................................................
C
      DIST21 = DIST12
      DIST22 = 0.00
      DIST23 = ((X3 - X2)**2 + (Y3 - Y2)**2)**(1./2.)
      DIST24 = ((X4 - X2)**2 + (Y4 - Y2)**2)**(1./2.)
C
      WRITE(2,100) DIST21, DIST22, DIST23, DIST24
  100 FORMAT(4X,'1',4F8.2)
C
      DIST31 = DIST13
      DIST32 = DIST23
      DIST33 = 0.00
      DIST34 = ((X4 - X3)**2 + (Y4 - Y3)**2)**(1./2.)
C
      WRITE(2,110) DIST31, DIST32, DIST33, DIST34
  110 FORMAT(4X,'3',4F8.2)
C
      DIST41 = DIST14
      DIST42 = DIST24
      DIST43 = DIST34
      DIST44 = 0.00
      WRITE(2,120) DIST42, DIST43, DIST44
  120 FORMAT(4X,'4',2F8.2)
C
      STOP
      END
```

Chapter 15, page 454

2. Character information is stored according to a number code where each character is represented by a two- or three-digit number.

5. The character string that is the longer of the two will always have a larger value.

12.

```
C................................................
C..DETERMINE COEFFICIENTS FOR BEST STRAIGHT LINE ..
C................................................
C
      DIMENSION SUMX(2), CONST(2)
C
      DATA SUMX(1),SUMX(2),CONST(1),CONST(2)/4*0.0/
C
      READ*, M
C
      DO 30 I = 1, M, 1
C
          READ*, X
          SUMX(1) = SUMX(1) + X
          SUMX(2) = SUMX(2) + X**2
          CONST(1) = CONST(1) + Y
          CONST(2) = CONST(2) + X*Y
C
   30 CONTINUE
C
      A1=(CONST(1)*SUMX(2)-CONST(2)*SUMX(1))
     1   /(FLOAT(M)*SUMX(2)-SUMX(1)**2)
      A2=(CONST(1)-FLOAT(M)*A1)/SUMX(1)
C
      PRINT*, 'A1=', A1, 'A2=', A2
C
      STOP
      END
```

C2. Answers to Quizzes

Quiz 1, page 11

1. Arithmetic, input/output, specification, and logic/control
2. Input/output: READ and PRINT;
   Arithmetic: +, −, *, and /;
   Control: IF, GO TO, STOP, DO, and DO WHILE;
   Specification: INTEGER, REAL, and CHARACTER
3. Language structure of individual statements is not difficult. Combining statements into a logical program is what is important.
4. Just as there is no fixed sequence in which chess pieces are moved, there is no fixed sequence of statements in writing a program.
5. For each student there are two records. The first gives six homework scores. The second gives the scores of three exams and the score achieved in the final exam.
6. 20%
7. 50%
8. Yes
9. No

Quiz 2, page 36

1. True.
2. Indicates the end of the instruction deck.
3. Permits transfer of control to this statement by a branching (control) statement. The numbers do not have to be in order.
4. Statements are executed sequentially. Use of a control statement can interrupt this order.
5. Column 7 to 72.
6. If a statement must continue to a second and third line, a nonblank character is placed in column 6 of these lines to signal that they are continuation lines.
7. A comment statement is used to provide English statements describing how the program works to help others read the program.
8. Placing a C in column 1.
9. The compiler generates the machine-language instructions to read three values and store them.
10. The computer inputs the next record from the input data file and loads the memory locations A, B, and C with the values found.

Quiz 3, page 46

1. Integer mathematics is faster.
2. Dividing one number by another (like the number 4 by the number 3 in the decimal system) produces a result with a repeating decimal. The computer cannot store all these digits.
3. Real numbers can have a small inaccuracy. This inaccuracy is usually quite small.
4. −19 (18,200) ($14.50) (14.50)
5. An algorithm defines in outline or schematic form how the problem is to be solved. The steps in a solution.
6. Use a table containing the names and a description of what each name stands for.
7. A graphic box diagram functionally defining (in English) the steps and the various paths in a program's solution.
8. The time it takes to track down faulty logic and make several rounds of corrections will far exceed the time to develop the program algorithm correctly.
9. Alphabetic information is permitted.
10. The string of characters starts and ends with a quotation mark.

Quiz 4, page 66

1. (b)
2. (c)
3. (e)
4. (a)
5. (d)
6. (b)
7. (c)
8. (a)
9. (a)
10. (a)
11. (c)
12. (c)
13. $x = H^2 - \frac{70}{H} + 5$
14. $x = H^2 - \frac{70}{H + 5}$
15. $x = \frac{H^2 - 70}{H + 5}$
16. $x = \frac{H^2 - 70}{H} + 5$

Quiz 5, page 72

1. Y=6.0*((X-3.1)**2.+(X**1.4/3.0))**0.5
   (X-3.1): Inner; (X**1.4/3.0): Inner; ((X-3.1)**2.+(X**1.4/3.0)): Outer
2. First: Subtraction X-3.1
   Second: Exponentiation X**1.4
   Third: Division $X^{1.4}$/3.0
3. Yes; real
4. No
5. X is not affected
   C changes—takes on the value of X+5.0.
6. The string of digits at each memory location is interpreted as a mantissa portion that is to be raised to an exponent portion of this word of memory.
7. The equal sign is a replacement operator.
   The variable on the left is to be replaced by the quantity (expression) on the right.
8. Fetch a copy of the contents of memory location N (the value 16). Subtract 2 from this value and store the result thus obtained (the value 14 in memory location N.
9. Yes
10. Explicit definition.

Quiz 7, page 86

1. No, to use the END= feature the form must be:

```
READ (5, *, END=70) A, B, C
```

2. The sequence of variable names (A, B, C in the preceding READ) specify what names the programmer is using to identify the memory locations loaded as a result of this READ operation.
3. By commas.
4. The type of a variable (either implicitly or explicitly defined) does not match the type read from the data file.
5. An identifying number used to distinguish which of several possible devices is to be used. Assigned by the computer center.
6. Mark placed at the end of a file to prevent reading beyond the end of the file.
7. An execution error results. Program terminates with a message such as END OF FILE ENCOUNTERED.
8. A false record positioned as the last record in a file containing some value (that is not appropriate to the problem statement) that is tested for to avoid an end-of-file error.
9. Slashes and commas allowed.
10. No, character information must begin and end with a quotation mark.

Quiz 8, page 93

1. Placement of information not highly restricted. Less chance of error.
2. Variable names do not belong as part of input record.
3. Yes, so that the number can be used in place of the asterisk in an input/output statement.
4. A FORMAT statement may be referenced by several READ/WRITE statements.
5. Placement of information so that the rightmost character is at the extreme right of the specified field.
6. Column 1 is used for special control features. Placing other than a blank in this column may produce unexpected spacing of output lines.
7. True.
8. One-to-one matching process.
9. True.
10. Use an F-code: F10.2, for example.

Quiz 9, page 118

1. The GO TO is too disruptive. It produces a radical interrupt in the otherwise smooth flow of the program.
2. An unconditional transfer causes a transfer without any decision involved (the GO TO statement). A conditional transfer statement uses a logical expression to determine which statement(s) are to be executed next.
3. $<$ .LT. = .EQ. $\leq$ .LE.
$>$ .GT. $\neq$ .NE. $\geq$ .GE.
4. a. Diamond
b. Parallelogram
5. The presence or absence of the word THEN.
6. No.
7. When more than two alternatives are present.
8. Only one statement should appear in a logical IF.

Quiz 10, page 136

1. Initial value, final value, incrementing value.
2. Use a negative incrementing value.
3. DO 20 COUNT=40,0,-2
4. Yes, but it cannot be an expression. Only the parameters can be expressions.
5. One.
6. Determine how many passes should be made through the loop.
7. It may not be changed.
8. To determine if the loop is behaving properly.
9. When the number of passes through the loop is not known ahead of time.
10. Yes, it shows their subordination.

Quiz 11, page 143

1. Making sure that the READ command is executed only as many times as there are records in the input file to support each READ request.
2. Fixed size. Variable size using header record. Variable size using trailer record.
3. A record placed at the head of a file telling the size of the file (how many records follow).
4. Initializing statement, indexing statement, and test statement.
5. To monitor the correct behavior of various key quantities of the program.
6. ( ) Show the START and END of a program.
7. The counter must be defined because the counter name appears in the expression portion of the indexing statement.
8. The counter keeps getting reset.

Quiz 12, page 165

1. a. X = +100. Initialization
X = X - 0.5 Indexing
IF (X.GE.-100.) Test
b. Yes
c. DO 40 X = +100. , -100., -0.5
2. The number to be represented has a string of digits that keeps repeating and repeating. It means that only a portion of the number can be stored in the assigned real memory location and the remaining portion is lost (producing a slight inaccuracy).
3. The error associated with that portion of some real numbers that is lost for the reasons explained in answer 2.
4. To add up a series of numbers, i.e., to determine their sum. Each time the indexing statement of a counter is executed, the value added or subtracted from the counter is a constant. For an accumulator the value added or subtracted is a variable.
5. A flag is used to tell at the end of a series of operations if a particular event occurred at some time during these operations. A flag might be used to signal that the end of a data file has been reached or to signal that the end has *not* been reached (there are more records in the file).

```
END = 0     (more records remaining)
END = 1     (data file depleted)
```

A flag might be used in the processing of the times taken by runners to run a mile at an athletic event. We might want to know if any runner was able to run a four-minute mile:

```
FAST = 0    (no four-minute-mile times)
FAST = 1    (at least one four-minute mile processed)
```

6.
```
C     HOT   - HIGH TEMPERATURE FLAG
C     TEMP  - TEMPERATURE READ FROM DATA FILE
C
      INTEGER HOT, I
      REAL TEMP
C
C     .....SET FLAG.....
C
      HOT = 0
C
      DO 30 I = 1, 30, 1
          READ*, TEMP
          IF(TEMP.GE.100.0) HOT = 1
   30 CONTINUE
C
      IF(HOT.EQ.1) THEN
          PRINT*,'TEMPERATURE 100 OR OVER DETECTED'
      ELSE
          PRINT*,'TEMPERATURES ALL BELOW 100'
      ENDIF
C
      STOP
      END
```

7.
```
C     HOT   - COUNTER OF NUMBER OF HOT DAYS
C     SUM   - ACCUMULATOR OF INDIVIDUAL TEMPERATURES
C
      INTEGER HOT, I
      REAL SUM, TEMP, AVE
C
      HOT = 0
      SUM = 0.0
C
      DO 30 I = 1, 30, 1
          READ*, TEMP
          SUM = SUM + TEMP
          IF(TEMP.GE.100.)HOT = HOT + 1
   30 CONTINUE
C
      AVE = SUM / 30.
      PRINT*, AVE, HOT
C
      STOP
      END
```

Quiz 13, page 174

1. Computers generally deal in binary notation. A number that is easy to represent in decimal may not be easy to represent in binary.
2. Flags and accumulators are software implemented.
3. Actions accomplished in the initialization portion of a program include the following:
   a. Declare the names and types of variables.
   b. Set counters and accumulators to their initial value.
   c. Set any flags to their initial state.
   d. Produce any special headings for the output.
   e. Process any leader records of input file.
4. The term "mixed mode" applies to any arithmetic operation that takes place while an arithmetic expression is being evaluated. As each operational symbol is reached, the operand to the left and to the right of the symbol is examined to determine the mode of the arithmetic operation to be used. The mode of the two operands should be the same and not mixed. The term mixed mode does not apply to the whole statement, just to the expression portion.
5. Operands.
6. `Y = 5 / X + 1`
7. `Y = ( 1 / 3 ) ** ( 1 / 2 )`
8. When the test data is presented to the program, the computed result will not be correct meaning that some expression is in error.
9. To cause an integer value to be treated as a real in an expression:

   `AVE=FLOAT(NYES)/FLOAT(NTOTAl)`
10. The first statement will be in error. The expression (1/3) is integer and will be evaluated as zero.
11.
```
C.............................................
C.    PURPOSE - CHECK THE HONESTY OF A ROULETTE   .
C.              WHEEL.                            .
C.............................................
C
C               ----IMPORTANT VARIABLES----
C     --NUMBER  WINNING NUMBER
C     --LOW     NUMBER OF TIMES A LOW NUMBER WINS
C     --HIGH    NUMBER OF TIMES A HIGH NUMBER WINS
C     --FLAG    FLAG TO DETERMINE IF 16 EVER A WINNER
C     --CARDS   CARD COUNTER
C     --PCNTLO  PERCENT OF LOW NUMBER WINS
C     --PCNTHI  PERCENT OF HIGH NUMBER WINS
C
      INTEGER HIGH,LOW,FLAG,I,CARDS,NUMBER
      REAL PCNTLO,PCNTHI
C
C           SET TWO COUNTERS TO ZERO
C
      HIGH = 0
      LOW = 0
C
C           SET FLAG TO INITIAL STATE
C
      FLAG = 0
C
C         ......PROCESSING LOOP........
C
      DO 40 CARDS = 1, 200, 1
C
        READ*,NUMBER
        IF(NUMBER.GE.1  .AND.  NUMBER.LE.12)LOW=LOW+1
        IF(NUMBER.GE.25) HIGH = HIGH + 1
C
C             ****SEE IF YOUR NUMBER (16) WON****
C
         IF(NUMBER.EQ.16) FLAG = 1
C
   40 CONTINUE
C
      PCNTLO = FLOAT(LOW) / 200. * 100.
      PCNTHI = FLOAT(HIGH) / 200. * 100.
C
      PRINT*,'HIGH=',HIGH, 'LOW=',LOW
C
C             ****DID YOUR NUMBER COME UP?****
C
      IF(FLAG.EQ.0)PRINT*,'YOUR NUMBER NEVER WON'
      IF(FLAG.EQ.1)PRINT*,'YOUR NUMBER DID WIN'
C
      STOP
      END
```

Quiz 14, page 205

1. It diverts your attention away from the *overall* strategy of solving the problem.
2. The algorithm should reach a solution (or close approximation) as quickly as possible.

3. Linear.
4. Syntax Scan; Logic Scan; Data Scan.
5. Processing Block; Decision Block; Loop Block.
6. GO TO statement.
7. Enter at the top. Exit from the bottom.
8. It makes the program easier to read.
9. No help to locate (isolate) errors in program.
10. Has the statement been written correctly in a grammatical sense (according to the rules of FORTRAN).
11.

```
C                  --OTHER VARIABLES--
C      -MODE      THE NUMBER 6, 7 OR 8 (WHICHEVER
C                 OCCURRED MOST FREQUENTLY
C      -NUMBER    THE NUMBER OF TIMES THIS MODE
C                 VALUE APPEARED
C
          INTEGER N1,N2,SUM,NO6S,NO6S,NO8S,MODE,I
C
          DATA NO6S,NO7S,NO8S / 3*0 /
C
          DO 20 I = 1, 1000, 1
C
              READ*, N1, N2
C
              SUM = N1 + N2
C
              IF(SUM.EQ.6) NO6S = NO6S + 1
              IF(SUM.EQ.7) NO7S = NO7S + 1
              IF(SUM.EQ.8) NO8S = NO8S + 1
C
   20     CONTINUE
C
C         **********************************************
C         *               ALL DICE ROLLED              *
C         **********************************************
C
   30     IF(NO6S.GT.NO7S) THEN
C
              NUMBER = NO6S
              MODE = 6
          ELSE
              NUMBER = NO7S
              MODE = 7
          ENDIF
C
C
          IF(NO8S.GT.NUMBER) THEN
              NUMBER = NO8S
              MODE = 8
          ENDIF
C
C
          PRINT*,'THE MODE OF THE SET IS ', MODE
          PRINT*,'THAT NUMBER OCCURS ',NUMBER,' TIMES'
C
          STOP
          END
```

Quiz 15, page 211

1. Focus is on details, not master strategy. Commitments are often made to permit the small modules to work, but are not best for whole program.
2. Tells the major subtasks needed for the completion of the project. Specifies what the major components or modules are needed.
3. As you move deeper, you provide more clarity to the solution. Gives more and more details as to how the solution is to be accomplished. The refinement process continues until you are sufficiently sure of how to write the necessary FORTRAN code for the module.
4. Top-down design provides strong management control of a project. Scope of subtasks better defined; functional definitions clearly stated; interrelationship of various modules clearly defined.
5. When the header statement declares the module type, anyone reading the program then knows what to expect as he or she reads the statements inside the module.
6. Linear only. Top to bottom.
7. The GO TO sets up a path that transfers control out the side of the module and then either forward or backward to some destination point. This alternate path is not desired.
8. The size of a module should be limited to about 60 lines. This is one page worth and represents the limit of information that can be handled at one time.
9. A program must be well written in a structured and well-documented fashion. This will make updates and expansions to the program less costly.
10.

```
C  NAME1 - NAME READ FROM HEADER RECORD
C  NAME2 - NAME READ FROM DETAIL RECORD
C  SSNO  - SOCIAL SECURITY NUMBER
C  SIZE  - NUMBER OF DETAIL RECORDS IN FILE
C  FOUND - FLAG TELLING IF NAME FOUND
C
   CHARACTER NAME1*20, NAME2*20
   INTEGER SSNO, SIZE, FOUND, I
C
C      ....READ SEARCH NAME AND FILE SIZE....
C              FROM HEADER RECORD
C  READ*, NAME1, SIZE
C
C      SET COUNTER AND FLAG TO CONTROL WHILE LOOP
C
   DATA I, FLAG / 0, 0 /
C
   DO WHILE (FLAG.EQ.0.AND.I.LE.SIZE)
C
      READ*NAME2, SSNO
      IF(NAME1.EQ.NAME2) FLAG = 1
      I = I + 1
C

   ENDDO
C
   IF(FLAG.EQ.0) THEN
      PRINT*,'SEARCH COMPLETE. NAME NOT FOUND'
      STOP
   ELSE
       PRINT*,'THE SOCIAL SECURITY NUMBER IS',SSNO
   ENDIF
```

Quiz 16, page 261

1. Arrays should be stored in the simplest form possible. One-dimensional is easier to deal with than two-dimensional.
2. 100.
3. READ(5,*)(GRADE(I),I=1,80)

   Implied DO INDEX
4. Yes.
5. Only one name following command READ, but 10F8.2 code in FORMAT implies ten values per record.
6. Size of array must be specified as *constants*.
7. Belongs to SPECIFICATION group. Supplies supportive information. Does not cause the execution of a hardware component.
8. DIMENSION A(120).
9. Yes, when M is equal to N.
10. Subscript exceeds value specified in DIMENSION statement.

11.
```
C.......................................
C.. PURPOSE - PROVIDE A LIST OF WINNERS    ..
C..           PROVIDE A LIST OF LOSERS     ..
C.......................................
C
C        --IMPORTANT VARIABLES--
C
C --NAME   ARRAY OF STOCK NAMES              --
C --BEGIN  PRICE AT START OF REPORT PERIOD   --
C --END    PRICE AT END OF REPORT PERIOD     --
C
      REAL BEGIN(200), END(200)
      CHARACTER NAME(200)*15
C
C     ....READ ALL INPUT RECORDS....
C
      READ*, (NAME(J),BEGIN(J),END(J),J=1,100,1)
C
      PRINT*,'        LIST OF WINNERS'
C
      DO 40 I = 1, 200, 1
         CHANGE = END(I) - BEGIN(I)
         IF(CHANGE.GT.BEGIN(I)*0.10)PRINT*, NAME(I)
 40   CONTINUE
C
      PRINT*,'        LIST OF LOSERS'
C
      DO 60 I = 1, 200, 1
         CHANGE = END(I) - BEGIN(I)
         IF(CHANGE.LT.0.0 .AND. ABS(CHANGE.GT.BEGIN
     +            (I)*0.10) PRINT*, NAME(I)
 60   CONTINUE
C
      STOP
      END
```

Quiz 17, page 295

1. Allows a large program to be divided into smaller, more manageable parts.
2. No, the STOP statement terminates execution and releases the central processing unit. The RETURN passes control back to the evoking program.
3. INPUT/OUTPUT is accomplished by the argument list.
4. Identifies the body of FORTRAN code defining the function. Identifies a memory location that receives the output of the function.
5. A short main program that sends test data to a subprogram to see if the subprogram is working properly.
6. The subroutine has both input and output arguments. The function subprogram has only input arguments.
7. Library functions, arithmetic statement functions, function subprogram, and subroutine subprogram.
8. You may create variable names without being concerned that the same name is used in any other program.
9. To evoke a SUBROUTINE subprogram.
10. The same as for naming a variable.
11.
```
C.......................................
C..   PURPOSE - DETERMINE THE MEDIAN OF      ..
C..             AN ARRAY OF SORTED NUMBERS ..
C.......................................
C
      FUNCTION MEDIAN(ARRAY, SIZE)
C
      INTEGER SIZE
      REAL ARRAY(100), TEST
C
C     ..VERIFY ARRAY SORTED CORRECTED..
C
      DO 20 I = 2, SIZE
         IF(ARRAY(I-1).GT.ARRAY(I)) THEN
            PRINT*,'ARRAY NOT SORTED CORRECTLY'
            RETURN
         ENDIF
 20   CONTINUE
C
C     ..IS SIZE AN ODD NUMBER?..
C
      TEST = SIZE/2*2-SIZE
C
      IF(TEST.NE.0) THEN
         MIDDLE=SIZE/2+1
         MEDIAN=ARRAY(MIDDLE)
      ELSE
C     ..SIZE IS AN EVEN NUMBER..
         MIDDLE=SIZE/2
         MEDIAN=(ARRAY(MIDDLE)+ARRAY(MIDDLE+1))/2.
      ENDIF
C
      RETURN
      END
```

Quiz 18, page 321

1. Where one DO loop lies wholly inside the range of another DO loop.
2. The index of the inner DO.
3. Where the range of the inner DO extends beyond the range of the outer DO. No.
4. Yes.
5. Where all elements of row 1 of the array are processed first, followed by all the elements in row 2, and so on.
6. READ*,(B(I,J),J=1,8),I=1,5)
7. Yes. In column order.
8. PRINT*,(C(1,J),J=1,12)
   PRINT*,(C(10,J),J=1,12)
9.
```
      DO 20 I = 1, 10
         PRINT*,C(I,1),'           ',C(I,12)
 20   CONTINUE
```
10. Subscript L.

Quiz 19, page 339

1. The "consistency of size" requirement does not apply to local or one-dimensional arrays.
2. It tells where in memory the array starts.
3. Two-dimensional arrays are stored consecutively (as one long string).
4. Column order.
5. You may specify the size of the array as a *variable* in the DIMENSION statement of the subprogram.
6. If several different names have been used to represent the same variable (memory location), an EQUIVALENCE statement can be used to equate these duplicate names. The statement can also be used to conserve the memory required by a program.
7. If several subprograms share memory, when one subprogram defines a variable in COMMON storage, all the other subprograms that have this variable in common may use this defined quantity and therefore need not pass the value as an argument.
8. COMMON storage can be used to conserve memory.
9. When many subprograms use different combinations of COMMON storage, it is desirable to set up several COMMON storage areas.
10. It warns the compiler that the name of an argument is not a variable or an array, but rather is the name of a subprogram.

Quiz 20, page 402

1. This applies to integer values only.
2. Mode of format codes in output statement is not correct. String of digits representing an integer value would be divided into a mantissa and exponent portion if F-code were followed.
3. Only digits up to and including two places after the decimal point will be transferred from memory location A to output.
4. 12345.678 (Decimal point need *not* be provided.)
5.

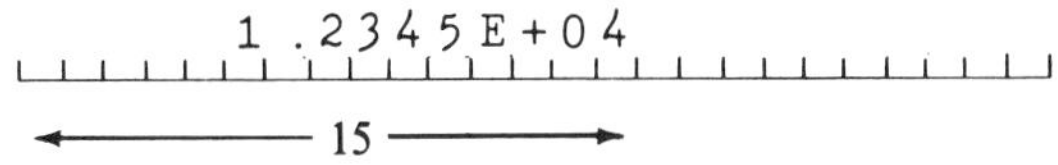

6. I = 617, J = 603, K = 5, and L = 9120.
7. Overflow and separation of output.
8. Causes specific format code to be repeated as many times as necessary.

   3I4,5F8.2

   ↑ Repeat code

Quiz 21, page 410

1. Five lines of output will be generated, each line containing a single real number.
2. Overflow Field width not sufficient.
3. A single line of input or a single line of output.
4. Carriage control. Tells where line is to be printed.
5. The L will not appear:

6.

```
      WRITE(2,10)
   10 FORMAT(1H1,100X,*PG.1*)
```

7. F16.3
8. Magnitude of value to be printed need not be known.
9. *-code H-code '-code
10. Output that presents the answers in a pleasant, easy-to-read fashion. Cuts down on misinterpreting output.
11.

```
   WRITE(2,1)
 1 FORMAT(1H1,1X,40(2H* ))
   WRITE(2,2)
 2 FORMAT(1X,'**                    CROSSTABULATION
  +                    **')
   WRITE(2,3)
 3 FORMAT(1X,'**  ETHNIC ORIGIN BY
  +  FAMILY INCOME   **')
   WRITE(2,4)
 4 FORMAT(1X,40(2H* ))
   WRITE(2,5)
 5 FORMAT(/,1X,5HRACE:,8X,7HINCOME:,/)
   WRITE(2,6)
 6 FORMAT(15X,'   0-4000',4X,'4001-6000',4X,'6001-8000',
  +4X,'8001-10000',4X,'OVER',5X'TOTAL')
   WRITE(2,7)
 7 FORMAT(2X,6(12H___________I))
   WRITE(2,8)
 8 FORMAT(2X,5HWHITE)
```

D. Non-Executable Statements

The following is a list of non-executable statements in the FORTRAN language.

BLOCK DATA
COMMON
COMPLEX
DATA
DIMENSION
DOUBLE PRECISION
END
ENTRY
EQUIVALENCE
EXTERNAL
FORMAT
FUNCTION
INTEGER
LOGICAL
NAMELIST
REAL
SUBROUTINE

E. Order of Specification Statements

Restrictions exist with respect to the placement of specification statements. These have been mentioned throughout the text. Adherence to the following order of these statements will satisfy all existing restrictions.

Type Statements
EXTERNAL Statement
DIMENSION Statement
COMMON Statement
EQUIVALENCE Statement
NAMELIST Statement
DATA Statement
Arithmetic Function Defining Statements
Executable Statements
FORMAT Statement
END Statement

F. Comparison of Full versus Subset Compilers

Features common to both the full subset compilers are defined by the FORTRAN-77 standards.

Assignment Statements
ARITHMETIC
LOGIC
CHARACTER

CONTROL Statements
Unconditional GO TO
Computed GO TO
Assigned GO TO
Arithmetic IF
Logical IF
IF-THEN-ELSE
ELSE IF

INPUT/OUTPUT Statements
READ, WRITE
Direct access I/O
End-of-file specifiers

Other
DIMENSION
COMMON
ASSIGN
EXTERNAL
STOP
PAUSE
FUNCTION
CALL
EQUIVALENCE
Named COMMON
CONTINUE
FORMAT
END
PROGRAM
SUBROUTINE
RETURN

Features that are available in the full and subset compilers as defined by the FORTRAN-77 standards.

	Subset Language	Full Language
Data Types		
INTEGER	Yes	Yes
REAL	Yes	Yes
DOUBLE PRECISION	No	Yes
COMPLEX	No	Yes
LOGICAL	No	Yes
CHARACTER	Yes	Yes
Arrays		
Maximum dimensions	3	7
Adjustable dimensions	Yes	Yes
Lower bound of subscript other than unity.	No	Yes
DO Statement		
Negative incrementation	Yes	Yes
Real or double precision variable	No	Yes
Parameters as expressions	No	Yes
Expressions		
Mixed mode arithmetic expressions	Yes	Yes
Relational and logical expressions	Yes	Yes
Generic functions	No	Yes
Character functions	No	Yes
Data Statement		
Allowed	Yes	Yes
Using implied DO	No	Yes

G. FORTRAN Library Functions

Trigonometric Functions

Generic Name	Function	Symbolic Form	Type of Argument	Type of Function	Definition
SIN	Trigonometric sine	SIN (X)	R	R	Sine of X
		DSIN (X)	D	D	
		CSIN (X)	C	C	X is in radians
COS	Trigonometric cosine	COS (X)	R	R	cosine of X
		DCOS (X)	D	D	
		CCOS (X)	C	C	X is in radians
TAN	Trigonometric	TAN (X)	R	R	tangent of X
		DTAN (X)	D	D	X is in radians
ASIN	Inverse sine function	ASIN (X)	R	R	$\sin^{-1}$ (X)
		DASIN (X)	D	D	value
ACOS	Inverse cosine function	ACOS (X)	R	R	$\cos^{-1}$ (X)
		DACOS (X)	D	D	value returned in radians
ATAN	Inverse tangent function	ATAN (X)	R	R	$\tan^{-1}$ (X)
		DATAN2(X,Y)	D	D	value returned in radians
SINH	Hyperbolic sine function	SINH (X)	R	R	sinh (X)
		DSINH (X)	D	D	
COSH	Hyperbolic cosine function	COSH (X)	R	R	cosh (X)
		DCOSH (X)	D	D	
TANH	Hyperbolic tangent function	TANH (X)	R	R	tanh (X)
		DTANH (X)	D	D	

Arithmetic Functions

Generic Name	Function	Symbolic Form	Type of Argument	Type of Function	Definition
SQRT	Square root	SQRT (X)	R	R	$X = x^{1/2}$
		DSQRT (X)	D	D	
		CSQRT (X)	C	C	X 0
EXP	Exponential	EXP (X)	R	R	e^x
		DEXP (X)	D	D	
		CEXP (X)	C	C	
ABS	Absolute value	IABS (M)	I	I	|X| Absolute value function.
		ABS (X)	R	R	
		DABS (X)	D	D	
		CABS (X)	C	D	
LOG 10	Common logarithm	ALOG10 (X)	R	R	$\log_{10}$ (X)
		DLOG10 (X)	D	D	
LOG	Natural logarithm	ALOG (X)	R	R	
		DLOG (X)	D	D	$\log_e$ (X)
		CLOG (X)	C	C	ln (X)
MAX	Largest element in argument list	AMAX0(I,J, ...)	I	R	Returns largest element in argument list of two or more elements
		AMAX1(X,Y,...)	R	R	
		MAX0(I,J,...)	I	I	
		MAX1(X,Y ...)	R	I	
		DMAX1(X,Y ...)	D	D	
MIN	Smallest element in argument list	AMIN0(I,J,...)	I	R	Returns smallest element in argument list of two or more elements
		AMIN1(X,Y,...)	R	R	
		MIN0(I,J,...)	I	I	
		MIN1(X,Y,...)	R	I	
		DMIN1(X,Y,...)	D	D	

Arithmetic Functions (continued)

MOD	Remainder from division of two arguments	MOD(I,J) AMOD (X,Y) DMOD (X,Y)	I R D	I R D	Modular arithmetic, remainder of division of X by Y.
INT	Truncation.	INT (X) AINT (X) DINT (X)	R R D	I R I	Drops the fractional part of X and returns the whole number portion.
ANINT	Nearest whole number	ANINT (X) DNINT (X)	R D	R D	Nearest whole number.
NINT	Nearest integer	NINT (X) IDINT (X)	R D	I I	Nearest integer number.

Other Functions

REAL — determines the real part of a complex argument.

AIMAG —determines the imaginary part of a complex argument.

CONJ — defines the conjugate of a complex function.

SIN — transfer of sign of first argument to second argument

ISIGN — same as above except integer arguments.

DSIGN — same as above except double precision arguments.

DIM produce positive difference between two real arguments.

IDIM — same as above except integer arguments.

FLOAT — converts integer argument to real

LEN — determines the length of a character string.

INDEX — determines the position of a substring "a_1" in a string "a_2".

ICHAR - value (position) of a character in the collating sequence.

CHAR — the character corresponding to the value (position) of the argument in the collating sequence.

ERF — computes an error function:

EQUATION HERE . . .

GAMMA —computes gamma function:

$u^{x-1}e^{-u}du$

Index